Acclaim for Mary Beth Norton's

IN THE DEVIL'S SNARE

A *Los Angeles Times* Best Book of the Year

A *Boston Globe* Best Book of the Year

A *Newsday* Best Book of the Year

Mary Beth Norton

IN THE DEVIL'S SNARE

Mary Beth Norton is Mary Donlon Alger Professor of American History at Cornell University. She is the author of *The British-Americans: The Loyalist Exiles in England, 1774–1789; Liberty's Daughters: The Revolutionary Experience of American Women, 1750–1800; Founding Mothers & Fathers: Gendered Power and the Forming of American Society,* which was a Pulitzer Prize finalist; and (with five others) *A People and a Nation* (6th ed., 2001). She has also served as the general editor of *The AHA Guide to Historical Literature* (3rd ed., 1995).

ALSO BY MARY BETH NORTON

Founding Mothers & Fathers:
Gendered Power and the Forming of American Society (1996)

Liberty's Daughters:
The Revolutionary Experience of American Women, 1750–1800 (1980)

The British-Americans: The Loyalist Exiles in England, 1774–1789 (1972)

———

(coauthor) *A People and a Nation* (sixth edition, 2001)

EDITOR

(with Ruth Alexander) *Major Problems in American Women's History*
(third edition, 2003)

The AHA Guide to Historical Literature (third edition, 1995)

(with Carol Groneman) *To Toil the Livelong Day:*
America's Women at Work, 1790–1980 (1987)

(with Carol Berkin) *Women of America: A History* (1979)

IN THE
DEVIL'S SNARE

The Salem Witchcraft Crisis of 1692

Mary Beth Norton

VINTAGE BOOKS

A DIVISION OF RANDOM HOUSE, INC.

NEW YORK

FIRST VINTAGE BOOKS EDITION, NOVEMBER 2003

Copyright © 2002 by Mary Beth Norton
Maps copyright © 2002 by David Lindroth, Inc.

All rights reserved under International and Pan-American Copyright
Conventions. Published in the United States by Vintage Books, a
division of Random House, Inc., New York, and simultaneously in
Canada by Random House of Canada Limited, Toronto. Originally
published in hardcover in the United States by Alfred A. Knopf,
a division of Random House, Inc., New York, in 2002.

Vintage and colophon are registered trademarks of Random House, Inc.

The Library of Congress has cataloged the Knopf edition as follows:
Norton, Mary Beth.
In the devil's snare : the Salem witchcraft crisis of 1692 /
by Mary Beth Norton. — 1st ed.
p. cm.
Includes bibliographical references and index.
1. Witchcraft—Massachusetts. 2. Massachusetts—History—Colonial
period, ca. 1600–1775. 3. Trials (Witchcraft)—Massachusetts—Salem.
4. Salem (Mass.)—History—Colonial period, ca. 1600–1775. I. Title.
BF1575 .N67 2002
133.4'3'097445—dc21
2001050500

Vintage ISBN: 0-375-70690-9

Book design by Robert C. Olsson

www.vintagebooks.com

Printed in the United States of America
20 19 18 17 16 15 14 13

*For the other Americanists and the other women
in the Cornell history department, and especially for
I. V. (Itsie) Hull*

Contents

IN THE DEVIL'S SNARE

Introduction

How long have you been in the snare of the devil?

—Justice of the Peace John Hathorne, 1692

S *ALEM.* The word alone evokes persistent images in the minds of twenty-first-century Americans: the misogynistic persecution of women, hysterical girls telling tales of being tormented by specters, falsely accused "witches" bravely refusing to confess, even—erroneously—women being burned at the stake. Few other events in colonial American history have so fascinated modern residents of the United States; few other incidents in the seventeenth-century Anglo-American colonies have been so intensively studied by historians. And yet much of the complicated Salem story remains untold. *In the Devil's Snare* is my narrative of that untold tale.

The basic facts can be briefly summarized. The witchcraft crisis began in mid-January 1691/2, O.S.,[1] when two little girls living in the household of the Reverend Samuel Parris of Salem Village (now Danvers), Massachusetts, began to suffer from fits that they and their elders soon attributed to witchcraft. In the months that followed, growing numbers of accusers claimed to be tortured by the apparitions of witches, and to see the ghosts of dead people charging the witches with killing them. Other accusers—most commonly neighbors of the suspects—came forward as well, to describe how they and their animals had been bewitched by the malefic acts of the accused. Around mid-September the crisis began to wane, and it limped to a close on November 5 with the filing of complaints against the last three witches to be formally charged. Legal proceedings extended from February 29, 1691/2 (the first official complaints), to late May 1693 (the final trials of suspects).

Those months encompassed legal action against at least 144 people (38 of

3

them male), most of whom were jailed for long periods; 54 confessions of witchcraft; the hangings of 14 women and 5 men; the pressing to death of another man by heavy stones; and the deaths in custody of 3 women and a man, along with several infants.[2] Throughout the crisis, the most active accusers were a group of young Salem Village and Andover women ranging in age from eleven to twenty, several of them servants (see appendix 3). Accordingly, as in no other event in American history until the rise of the women's rights movement in the nineteenth century, women took center stage at Salem: they were the major instigators and victims of a remarkable public spectacle.

Scholars have developed a variety of interpretations of the crisis. Some have detected natural causes for the girls' visions of ghostly specters: ergot poisoning or, most recently, an encephalitis epidemic.[3] One has argued that at least some of the accused really were practicing witchcraft and thus that some of the charges had merit. Several historians contend that the girls were faking their fits from the start, others that they were hysterical, angry, or delinquent adolescents.[4] The influential *Salem Possessed* (1974), by Paul Boyer and Stephen Nissenbaum, attributes the crisis to long-standing political, economic, and religious discord among the men of Salem Village, denying the significance of women's prominence as both accused and accuser.[5]

My narrative builds on the research and interpretations advanced in prior works on Salem; at the same time, it disagrees with many aspects of those interpretations. In addition to studying the trials, as have most other historians, I examine the broader crisis that produced the trials. Indeed, the search for documents to illuminate the origins and extent of that crisis has led me in directions I failed to anticipate when I first embarked on this project. Intrigued by the complex interrelationship of gender and politics in early America, I expected to base this volume largely on a feminist reinterpretation of familiar materials, primarily the court records published in the *Salem Witchcraft Papers* and other documents commonly consulted by Salem scholars. But I also wanted to learn how people in Essex County and New England in general (perhaps even in other colonies) reacted to the witchcraft allegations. Thus when I read published materials or visited archives, I cast my net widely, looking for correspondence and journals covering the entire period of the late 1680s through the early 1690s.[6]

What I found has led me to develop a new interpretation of the witchcraft crisis, one that places it firmly in the context of its very specific time and place: Essex County, Massachusetts, in the early 1690s. The county's residents were then near the front lines of an armed conflict that today is little known but which at the time commanded their lives and thoughts, as was demonstrated by the ubiquity of the subject in the letters and diaries I was reading. They called it the Second Indian War. Early American historians today term it King William's War. Whatever the name, after 1688 that struggle with the French and the Indians for control of New England's northeastern frontier dominated public policy and personal decisions alike. Historians have examined Salem Village itself, Massachusetts legal practice, and Puritan attitudes toward women, all of which provide essential background for comprehending the witchcraft crisis.[7] *In the Devil's Snare,* though, contends that the dramatic events of 1692 can be fully understood only by viewing them as intricately related to concurrent political and military affairs in northern New England.

Other scholars have touched on connections to the Second Indian War but did not explore them in detail. In the 1980s, I learned from Carol Karlsen's *The Devil in the Shape of a Woman* and an article by James Kences that some of the "afflicted girls" of Salem Village were refugees from the Maine frontier. When I started my research, I expected the accusers' familial origins to prove to be important for my analysis, but I had no idea that this book would become what it has: an exploration of the history of frontier warfare and its impact on the collective mentalité of an entire region. Yet the more I read the documents produced in New England in the last quarter of the seventeenth century, the more I realized that the evidence required such an approach. The histories of King William's War, King Philip's War (its equally brutal predecessor in the 1670s), and the Salem witchcraft crisis are intricately intertwined. *In the Devil's Snare* explicates those links through what has evolved into a dual narrative of war and witchcraft.[8]

This book primarily aims at presenting a comprehensive overview of the crisis as people in Essex County experienced it in 1692. Accordingly, for the most part it eschews applying modern-day terminology to the incidents it describes.[9] I have deliberately omitted attaching contemporary labels to the participants and their actions. Instead, *In the Devil's Snare* focuses on describing and analyzing the crisis in seventeenth-century terms—that is, on attempting to understand it as it was understood by those who lived through it, and to present *their* reactions to, questions about, and critiques of what happened during the seventeen months between January 1691/2 and May 1693. Precisely because the witchcraft crisis has become an iconic event in our collective past and has often been abstracted from its context by modern commentators, grasping the origins and significance of the episode in its own day is crucial to our understanding of its meaning.

A fundamental part of that understanding must rest on comprehending the worldview of late-seventeenth-century Puritan New Englanders, who lived in a pre-Enlightenment world that had not yet experienced the scientific revolution, with its emphasis on the careful study of physical phenomena through controlled experimentation and observation. In the world of 1692, many events lacked obvious explanations. Children suddenly sickened and died; animals suffered mysterious ailments; strange noises were heard or ghostly visions seen. Early New Englanders envisioned themselves as residing in what one historian has termed a "world of wonders," in which the universe of invisible spirits surrounding them was as real as the one they could see, touch, and feel. For them, visible and invisible realms coexisted and often intersected. With very few exceptions, they believed unhesitatingly in the existence of witches. When they encountered harmful events that otherwise seemed inexplicable, New Englanders often concluded that a malevolent witch had caused their troubles. And, as shall be seen, during the early 1690s residents of the Bay Colony were experiencing many setbacks that needed explanation.[10]

Behind most events in the crisis lay gossip. With one very short-lived exception, late-seventeenth-century New England had no locally produced newspapers or magazines, and so information spread primarily through talk among neighbors, friends, and relatives. (Letters, requiring scarce and expensive paper, were employed mainly for long-distance communication.) Occasionally the court records explicitly mention verbal exchanges, while at other times the existence of such must be inferred. But understanding the dynamics of the witchcraft crisis requires paying attention to the ways in which news was transmitted from person to person, farm to farm, town to town. The witchcraft accusations in Salem Village aroused curiosity throughout all of New England, especially in Essex County, and people must have constantly discussed the most recent fits and complaints of the afflicted, along with other news stemming from examinations and, later, trials. Gossip thus serves as a leitmotif in the pages that follow.[11]

Furthermore, basic to understanding the witchcraft crisis is recognizing the way in which it developed over time. As I shall argue subsequently, what eventually became a unique crisis did not begin as such. Instead, the initial fits and accusations, although unusual, did not lack precedent in either old or New England. But incidents in mid-April irrevocably altered the course of events, creating the singular episode now known simply as "Salem." Earlier historians have missed the far-reaching significance of that turning point because they have not organized their narratives in terms of a chronology of actual events. Instead, scholars have tended to discuss incidents involving particular accusers and suspected witches in a chronological context determined by the timing of court proceedings. Yet, as can be seen in appendix 1, prosecutions of suspects followed reported bewitchments at erratic and occasionally lengthy intervals. Employing what might be called a "legal chronology" serves as an effective means of organizing extraordinarily complex materials, but stands in the way of re-creating the burgeoning crisis as people lived through it.[12]

In the Devil's Snare traces the incidents of 1692 daily and weekly, showing which events stimulated increased numbers of complaints, demonstrating the impact of happenings outside courtrooms on occurrences inside them, and tracking the progress of specific accusations. (Distinguishing charges immediately accepted by the community from those that required further confirmation before official action was taken suggests that some stories—and some accusers—were regarded as more credible than others.) In addition, a chronological approach reveals the chaotic overlapping of incidents involving the various people accused of malefic practices. At the height of the crisis in late May, cascades of complaints not only continually introduced new names into the proceedings but also supplied additional accusations of individuals already jailed for several months. The minds of Essex County residents must have reeled from the shock as every day they learned of fresh spectral attacks launched by both old and new suspects, together and separately, against members of the core group of afflicted children and teenagers.

Traditional approaches to Salem witchcraft overlook or obscure these aspects of the crisis. Authors have not for the most part concerned themselves with depicting the developing day-to-day dynamics during 1692. Regardless of the specific interpretations they advance, most historians have adopted the same metanarrative, in which the examinations and trials of accused women constitute the chief focus. Accounts of legal proceedings fill their books. Scholars emphasize the common characteristics of many of the accused and largely ignore the background of the key accusers. Few pay much attention to accused men (even the six who were executed), to the important role played by the many confessors who validated the accusers' charges, or to the judges' possible motivations.[13] In general, stories about people from Salem Village examined early in the crisis have dominated most narratives; the numerous Andover confessors and people from other towns who were accused later have been largely ignored.[14]

This book abandons that standard metanarrative. Although courtroom proceedings are considered at length in the pages that follow, *In the Devil's Snare* moves out of the legal realm to examine the origins and impact of the witchcraft charges in Salem Village, Andover, Essex County, and Boston as well. It devotes a great deal of attention to the accusers, confessors, and judges; and it focuses, too, on the hitherto neglected men accused in 1692, including some who, for a variety of reasons, were jailed but never tried. And above all it poses a deceptively simple but rarely asked question: why was Salem so different from all previous witchcraft episodes in New England?[15]

Many historians have not even noted that 1692 *was* different, except perhaps in terms of the number of people accused. In part, that is because scholars have tended to write books that focus either on the Salem trials or on other colonial witchcraft episodes.[16] Thus contrasts have not been sharply and explicitly drawn. Then, too, the Salem crisis contained many elements common to earlier witchcraft incidents, thus obscuring the numerous anomalies. A large proportion of those accused at Salem were indeed the quarrelsome older women, some with dubious reputations, who fit the standard seventeenth-century stereotype of the witch. Most of them were accused of practicing maleficium—of harming their neighbors' health, property, children, or livestock—over a period of years, just as had been the case with other suspected New England witches for the previous half-century. Many others among the Salem accused were closely related to such stereotypical women; husbands, sisters, daughters, mothers, and sons of witches also had long been vulnerable to the same charges.[17]

Yet beyond those similarities lie many unique elements. Initially, the sheer numbers of accusers and accused alone cry out for explanation, because the next-largest New England witchcraft incident, in Hartford in the early 1660s, involved at most eleven formally accused malefactors.[18] In this regard the Salem outbreak rivaled the major seventeenth-century witch-hunts in England or Scotland, all but one of which it also postdated—another singular characteristic.[19] Likewise, the geographical reach of the accusations was remarkable; all prior episodes in the region involved only one or two adjacent towns, whereas the 1692 accused came from twenty-two different places, fifteen of those in Essex County. Although the crisis began in Salem Village and the trials took place in Salem Town, a plurality of the accused (more than forty) lived in Andover. Thus the term *Salem witchcraft crisis* is a misnomer; *Essex County witchcraft crisis* would be more accurate. [20]

Moreover, key accusers in previous witchcraft cases had most often been adult men; at Salem, the key accusers were women and girls under the age of twenty-five. And those accusers then charged witches not with committing maleficium, but rather with torturing and tempting them spectrally, complaints only rarely before heard in New England. Accusers most commonly lived near those they targeted; in 1692, by contrast, the Salem Village accusers had frequently never previously encountered the people they said had been tormenting them in spectral form.[21] Notably, a small but significant number of the accused also failed to fit the well-established patterns identifying likely

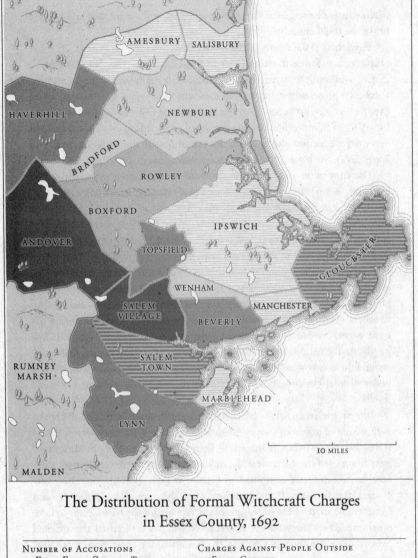

The Distribution of Formal Witchcraft Charges
in Essex County, 1692

NUMBER OF ACCUSATIONS
IN EACH ESSEX COUNTY TOWN

CHARGES AGAINST PEOPLE OUTSIDE
OF ESSEX COUNTY

1–2   7–10

3–4   11 and up

5–6

Billerica, 2
Boston, 1
Charlestown, 2
Malden, 2

Reading, 6
Rumney Marsh (Revere), 1
Wells, Me., 1
Woburn, 3

witches: some belonged to the church, and a few prominent men and women broke the mold entirely.[22]

Then there is the matter of the many convictions and executions. As other scholars have demonstrated, judges in Massachusetts (and, for that matter, in England and the other colonies) commonly expressed skepticism about witchcraft prosecutions and proved reluctant to convict—or subsequently to execute—accused witches. The special Court of Oyer and Terminer established to handle the first set of witchcraft prosecutions not only convicted every defendant but also oversaw the executions of almost all of them (see appendix 1). Such a result also requires explanation.[23]

The conviction and execution rates are rendered even more difficult to interpret because the young women who instigated the Salem witchcraft outbreak were precisely the sort of people commonly given short shrift by the high-status men who served as magistrates in the Massachusetts Bay Colony. Indeed, the lower-status men who sat on grand and petty juries also usually paid little attention to complaints registered by youthful females.[24] Why, then, would judges and jurors find these young women's extraordinary accusations credible? As daughters and servants who occupied the lower ranks of household hierarchies, their normal role was to be seen and not heard, to tend to others' needs, and to acquiesce in all tasks required of them. Yet during the crisis others tended to *them*, and magistrates and clergymen heeded *their* words. As the historian Jane Kamensky has observed, they turned their society and the courtroom "topsy-turvy," assuming roles denied to young women under normal circumstances.[25] What could have led to such a remarkable result?

One more element of the Salem crisis is equally notable: the relative speed with which opinions of the investigations and prosecutions reversed themselves. Usually, witchcraft suspicions lingered for years after the allegations were first raised in courtrooms. Even when defendants were acquitted, their neighbors commonly continued to believe in their guilt and initiated new charges against them. But within just a few short weeks in October 1692 a considerable share of the once-significant support for the trials seems to have evaporated. Few doubted the existence of witches or accused the afflicted persons of dissembling, but even so the validity of the convictions was called into question soon after the completion of the fourth session of the Court of Oyer and Terminer. Within five years, one judge and twelve jurors formally apologized for their roles in the affair, and within two decades the Massachusetts government also acknowledged its responsibility for what were by then viewed as unjust proceedings. The legislature at that time voted to compensate both survivors of the trials and the descendants of people who had been jailed or executed.[26]

To explain these anomalies it is necessary to abandon the intense focus on Salem Village common to most studies and to place the witchcraft crisis in the broader context of Essex County and northern New England. As the northeasternmost jurisdiction of the Bay Colony, Essex and its primary port, Salem Town, were deeply involved in the affairs of neighboring frontier settlements. In the 1660s and early 1670s, English outposts in coastal Maine and New Hampshire were at once prosperous, small, and isolated. Fishermen, farmers (especially raisers of livestock), fur traders, and sawmill operators resided quite peacefully alongside the Wabanaki peoples who farmed, hunted, and fished in the interior river valleys. But then King Philip's War (1675–1678) despoiled the northeastern frontier as well as southern New England, and just a decade later, late in the summer of 1688, another violent conflict erupted in Maine.

What the northern settlers called the First and Second Indian Wars dramatically changed their circumstances for the worse. Flourishing communities were wiped out and people and their property holdings destroyed. Families that had lived in Maine for two or three generations and had sunk deep roots in the soil were either killed or forced to abandon their homes, leaving behind houses, livestock, cultivated fields, and treasured possessions. The consequences were all the more devastating because they happened twice in quick succession: war broke out again just as refugees who had originally fled Maine in 1676 had successfully reestablished themselves and were once more expanding their settlements. In 1690, colonial forces suffered one defeat after another, and the frontier was again largely abandoned. It took decades before northern Maine was fully resettled, because although the second war ended in 1699, a third began just three years later.

The now-brittle pages of *York Deeds,* which contain depositions offered in the first decades of the eighteenth century, vividly convey a sense of the calamitous losses suffered by Maine families during the two wars. The elderly deponents laconically described a once-familiar world torn asunder by lethal conflict. Hannah Hazelton (York, 1728): "two of my Brothers . . . were both killed by the Indians as they were looking after their Cattle." Mary Cock (Boston, 1719): John Layton lived at Kennebec River for "many Years before the Indians drove him from thence as they did many Famalies at the East-ward at the same time." John Lane (Gloucester, 1734): Henry Donel "made Fish" on an island in Casco Bay for more than fifteen years "untill he was Pre-vented by the Indian War." Henry Libby (Scarborough, 1726): Joseph

Whinek "was killed & his Daughter with him by the Indians & was buried on his own Land." James Ross (Salem, 1734): he was born and raised in Falmouth "till drove from thence in the first Indian Warr & that he removed thither again between the First & Second Warr and lived there about Six Years untill he was taken [captive] in the Second Warr."[27]

The proximity of Essex County and Salem to Maine and New Hampshire necessarily involved their residents in both Indian wars. The county's towns served as temporary havens for many of the refugees during and after the first war and as permanent residences after the second. Essex County militiamen were frequently pressed into service on the Maine frontier; the county's vessels and sailors transported men and supplies to northeastern harbors, often bringing fleeing families back; its local military and political officials conveyed messages back and forth between Boston and the frontier, sometimes appending their own observations to the texts they forwarded in either direction.[28]

Not surprisingly, therefore, many people involved in the witchcraft crisis had intimate experience with the Indian wars (see appendix 2). Some of the accused, including two people who were executed, had lived in Maine, and some prominent accused men had regularly traded with or fought against the Indians. Judges, jurors, and witnesses alike had links to the northeast; among them were investors in frontier lands and leaders of militia units, all of whom had personal knowledge of northeastern affairs. Many of those involved in the crisis, it turns out, had known each other previously on the frontier. Most notably, as already mentioned briefly, a significant number of the key accusers and confessors came from Maine. Refugees from one or both wars, they— like many others who fled the frontier with them—sought shelter in Salem Village and nearby Essex County towns. Their families and lives shattered by the vicious frontier warfare, several of these young women were residing as servants in other people's households. For them, even more than for the long-time residents of Essex County, fears of Indian attack were ever-present, reviving terrifying memories of sudden raids that had killed relatives and friends and obliterated prosperous settlements.

In the Devil's Snare, then, contends that the witchcraft crisis of 1692 can be comprehended only in the context of nearly two decades of armed conflict between English settlers and the New England Indians in both southern and northern portions of the region. The ongoing frontier war, and the multiple fears it generated—in Maine and New Hampshire, in Essex County, and in Boston itself—thus supplies the answer to the question I posed earlier: why was Salem so different from all previous witchcraft episodes in New England?

A NOTE IN WHICH THE AUTHOR ADDRESSES THE NATURE OF PORTIONS OF HER ARGUMENT AND EXPLAINS THE REASON THEREFOR

At several points in this book I employ such phrases as "they must have thought," or "they could well have concluded," or "they must have discussed...." Although the overall evidence for my thesis is, I believe, convincing, for certain aspects of the argument I have only inferences, not the references to letters or diaries I would have preferred to cite. One reason for that lack of crucial pieces of evidence has been alluded to in this introduction: opinion swiftly and sharply turned against the trials. Based on my experience in searching for documents pertinent to the 1692 crisis, I believe that certain key pieces of evidence must subsequently have been destroyed, either by the participants themselves or by their descendants.

In support of that contention, I offer two examples. I posit herein the existence of extensive contemporary notes kept by adult observers of the "afflicted girls," especially the Reverend Samuel Parris.[29] Yet just one page of such a notebook survives today, and only because it seems to have been seized as evidence by an official immediately after it was composed. The other notes are no longer extant, and few of Parris's papers have survived at all. Nor, for that matter, have the papers of a majority of the judges apparently survived, despite the fact that they were among the most powerful and prominent men in the colony. Those papers that still exist reveal little about the trials.

Most significant, one of those judges, Waitstill Winthrop, corresponded regularly with his brother, Fitz-John Winthrop, in the 1680s and 1690s. But letters from 1692 and 1693 are mysteriously missing from the large Winthrop family collection in the Massachusetts Historical Society. Francis Bremer, editor of the Winthrop Papers, concurs with me that a descendant most likely purged the collection of "embarrassing" material before donating it to the MHS.[30]

I do not argue that Massachusetts officials engaged in a concerted conspiracy of silence, but rather that participants or their descendants decided individually, at different times and places, to remove traces of involvement in the trials from the written record.[31] I am convinced, for example, that Samuel Parris himself must have burned his notes, and that some officials almost certainly had a hand in the destruction of records that implicated them in dubious decisions. The eradication of the rest of the vanished material could have occurred at any time. But happen it did. The holes in the documentary record are too consistent and specific to be explained in any other way.[32]

CHAPTER ONE

Under an Evil Hand

Monday, January 25, 1691/2; York, Maine. About noon, in heavy snow, when (in the words of a contemporary historian) "the Inhabitants were in their unguarded Houses, here and there scattered, Quiet and Secure," about 150 Indians led by Madockawando, a sachem of the Penobscot band of the Wabanakis, took York completely by surprise. One by one they captured most of the town's garrisoned houses and split into small parties to burn houses and to kill livestock and people. Captain John Floyd, who with a small troop of militia rushed to the scene from Portsmouth, New Hampshire, found on his arrival that "the greatest part of the whole town was burned & robed," with nearly 50 killed and another 100 captured. Among the dead was the Reverend Shubael Dummer, who was, Floyd reported, "barbarously murthered stript naked Cut & mangled by these sons of Beliall." The Indians seemed to have known when and where to strike, and help had arrived much too late.[1]

From the neighboring town of Wells, the Reverend George Burroughs described "the Sorrowfull tideings" from York for the leaders of Massachusetts. "The beholding of the Pillours of Smoke, the rageing of the mercyless flames, the insultations of the heathen enemy, shooting, hacking, (not haveing regard to the earnest supplication of men, women, or Children, with sharpe cryes & bitter teares in most humble manner,) & dragging away others, (& none to help) is most affecting the heart." Burroughs concluded that "God is still manifesting his displeasure against this Land, he who formerly hath set to his hand to help us, doth even write bitter things against us."[2]

When he wrote that letter George Burroughs would not have known that about a week before the attack on York, two little girls living in the house of the Reverend Samuel Parris in Salem Village—a house Burroughs had once occupied—had begun to have strange fits. Nor, unless he had the occult powers eventually attributed to him, would he have known that as a result just three months later he too would personally experience "bitter things."

SALEM VILLAGE

In the winter of 1691–1692, Salem Village, a thinly populated rural precinct bordering the crowded, bustling seaport of Salem Town, simmered with contention, much of it revolving around the church. Its pastor, the Reverend Samuel Parris, had become the focal point for considerable discontent, which his actions in the coming months would magnify rather than dampen. Indeed, the strange behavior of the girls in his household beginning in mid-January would, as he later reflected, set off a "horrid calamity (which afterwards, plague-like, spread in many other places)."[3]

Land grants in the mid to late 1630s had initiated movement into the area that eventually became known as Salem Village, which was located north and west of the town center. Salem, the first permanent settlement in the Massachusetts Bay Colony, was founded in 1626 on a peninsula commanding a superb natural harbor, and the town quickly became the focal point of the area around Cape Ann. Immigrants flowed in during the 1630s, and furs and fish flowed out. The newcomers moved inland to found new towns and to settle in Salem's own hinterland, first referred to simply as "the Farms."[4]

As the decades passed, friction developed between the Town and the Farms. Residents of Salem Town wanted the tax revenues contributed by residents of the Farms; for their part, the Farmers, though usually outvoted by the more numerous Town dwellers, sought to avoid civic obligations in the distant Town. By the early 1670s the Farmers' fight for greater autonomy focused on their desire to build their own meetinghouse and to support their own minister. Like other residents of outlying areas of colonial New England settlements, they complained of the long weekly journey to the town center to attend church services, arguing that they should be able to establish their own parish. In October 1672 the Massachusetts General Court agreed to their request. For years thereafter, however, Salem Town still claimed the right to assess Farmers for ecclesiastical expenses, and the Farms, later Salem Village, did not become the independent town of Danvers until 1752.[5]

Ironically, the long-sought meetinghouse and minister—the subject of so much contention with Salem Town—also proved to be a major source of discord within Salem Village itself. Whether because strife in the Village came to focus on the church or because the Villagers made inappropriate choices of clergymen, each of the first four ministers who served the Village failed to earn consistent support from his parishioners. The first minister, James Bayley—a young Harvard graduate when hired in 1672—lasted the longest, until 1680. George Burroughs, who had fled Falmouth, Maine, in 1676, during the First Indian War, succeeded Bayley, but in early 1683 agreed to return to his former congregation. Deodat Lawson, an English immigrant, served in Salem Village only from 1684 to 1688; in the winter of 1688–1689 he ministered to troops on a campaign against the Indians in Maine, then settled in Boston. Finally, the Reverend Samuel Parris, whose ministry would prove the most controversial of them all, was hired in June 1689 and resigned approximately seven years later after a long and bitter struggle within the Village. Thus when one of the Andover men who confessed to witchcraft in the late summer of 1692 explained to the examining magistrates that the devil and his witches had targeted Salem Village for destruction "by reason of the peoples being divided & theire differing with their ministers," no one would have been surprised by his statement.[6]

Paul Boyer and Stephen Nissenbaum have argued persuasively that the Village was so contentious because of its anomalous status, neither wholly independent of nor wholly dependent on Salem Town. "Structural defects in its organization," they observe, "rendered the Village almost helpless in coping with whatever disputes might arise." The two hundred or so adult residents of Salem Village, in short, did not differ from settlers in other New England towns in being more cantankerous, but rather in not having any local means of resolving their quarrels. Deprived of formal decision-making bodies controlled by Villagers, they always had to appeal to outside authorities—to Salem Town, to the General Court, to synods of ministers, to arbitrators or mediators—to achieve solutions to their conflicts. Furthermore, persistent boundary disputes with neighboring towns kept tempers flaring on all sides.[7]

When some Villagers formally organized a church in November 1689, leading to Samuel Parris's ordination by neighboring clergy, they added fuel to the fire. Parris, born in England but raised largely in Barbados, attended Harvard for several years in the early 1670s but before completing his studies returned to Barbados to settle his deceased father's estate. After failing to establish himself as a merchant first in Barbados and later, in the 1680s, in Boston, he accepted the post as Salem Village pastor and sought ordination.[8]

Before his arrival, although successive Village ministers preached regularly to the congregation, the precinct had no "church" as Puritans understood it—a covenanted body of saints selected from the wider community. A clergyman could only be ordained by a church, and only an ordained clergyman could administer communion to its members or baptize babies. The organization of a church, with twenty-six original members in addition to Parris himself, created a formal, lasting division in the ranks of Villagers. Nothing more dramatically symbolized that division than the dismissal of nonmembers from the meetinghouse after the sermon on sacrament days, before the members took communion together. Adding to the exclusionary atmosphere was the church's decision in early 1690 to reject the so-called Halfway Covenant, which permitted the baptism of infants born to parents who had themselves been baptized but who had not formally joined a church. In Salem Village, the much-desired sacrament of infant baptism, already denied to those Villagers who did not belong to other nearby churches, would be limited to children who had at least one church-member parent. In his sermons, Parris likewise tended to stress the sharp distinctions between church members and other folk. Perhaps understandably, therefore, by late 1691 discontent with Parris's ministry permeated the nearly three-fourths of adult Villagers who had not joined the local church. That discontent took the form of refusing to contribute to his salary or to supply him with firewood, and of organizing for his removal. Parris responded primarily by sharpening his attacks on his opponents.[9]

Beginning in November 1691, Samuel Parris preached a sermon series on the first verse of Psalm 110: "Sit thou at my right hand, till I make thine enemies thy footstool." Emphasizing spiritual warfare between the saved and the damned, he told his congregation on January 3, 1691/2, that "the Church is separated from the world," and that "it is the main drift of the Devil to pull it all down." The devil, he asserted, was "the grand enemy of the Church," assisted by "Wicked & Reprobate men," presumably including his many detractors in Salem Village.[10] That was the last sacrament-day sermon Parris's nine-year-old daughter Betty and his somewhat older niece Abigail Williams heard before they began to behave strangely.[11]

"SADLY AFFLICTED"

A few days after January 15, Abigail Williams fell ill. Her cousin Betty may have sickened first or, more likely, soon thereafter.[12] In any event, Samuel Parris, his wife Elizabeth, and other observers quickly realized that this was no ordinary illness. The girls were "sadly Afflicted of they knew not what Distempers," wrote the Reverend John Hale of neighboring Beverly, the only independent eyewitness to these events who later described them in print. The children "were bitten and pinched by invisible agents; their arms, necks, and backs turned this way and that way, and returned back again, so as it was impossible for them to do of themselves, and beyond the power of any

Epileptick Fits, or natural Disease to effect." Further, "sometimes they were taken dumb, their mouths stopped, their throats choaked, their limbs wracked and tormented so as might move an heart of stone, to sympathize with them, with bowels of compassion for them."[13]

Parris, like any concerned parent or guardian under such circumstances, consulted physicians, "yet still they grew worse," Hale recalled. Finally, after what Parris described as a period of "several weeks," a doctor—believed to be William Griggs—concluded that the girls were "under an Evil Hand." The neighbors "quickly" accepted the diagnosis, according to Hale, deciding that the children were bewitched.[14]

William Griggs, an elderly, probably self-taught medical practitioner, was the only physician in Salem Village in 1692. He and his second wife, Rachel, lived in Rumney Marsh (Revere) during the 1660s, then spent more than a decade in Gloucester before moving to Salem Village sometime between 1685 and 1689. Although neither joined the Salem Village church, they almost certainly supported Samuel Parris. Rachel (though not her husband) had been a member of Boston's First Church, the same church Samuel Parris joined during his years in Boston; moreover, William Griggs Jr., the oldest son of his father's first marriage, also a First Church member after 1670, undoubtedly knew and associated with Parris while both resided in the town. Accordingly, it seems likely that Parris would have consulted William Griggs and trusted his judgment.[15]

Two years later, Samuel Parris reflected that the appearance of such afflictions "first in my family" was "a very sore rebuke, and humbling providence." That he also thought so in early 1692, and that Dr. Griggs had diagnosed witchcraft by mid-February, is suggested by the contents of Parris's two sacrament-day sermons on February 14. Continuing to preach on Psalm 110, verse 1, he spoke of how God was "sending forth destroyers" as a consequence of men's "slighting of Christ." He reminded his congregants—who certainly knew of the girls' fits—that Jesus "Governs his church, not only by his word & spirit, but by his Rod, & afflictions: therefore we are to beware of fainting when we are chastened, or despising the Rod." Undoubtedly reassuring himself as well as his listeners, Parris described the "eternal life" Christ promised to believers; "Satan would pluck them out of my hand," he intoned, "but . . . shall never be able to do it." He thus informed Villagers, and himself, that his faith would allow him to bear God's afflicting rod and that he understood that God "chastens us for our profit."[16]

During these weeks, Parris, following the standard religious advice in such cases, engaged in "Fasting and Prayer," not only by himself but also in conjunction with others. Hale described "two or three private Fasts at the

Ministers House, one of which was kept by sundry Neighbour Ministers" (surely including himself).[17] Unknown to the clergymen, however, Mary Sibley, a church member who lived near the parsonage and who therefore saw the children's sufferings in person, decided to try some traditional counter-magic rather than rely on the spiritual methods pursued by Parris and his col-leagues. She directed Parris's Indian slave couple, Tituba and John, in the making of a witchcake. Mixed from the children's urine and rye meal, baked in the ashes, it was then fed to the family dog. The ingestion of such a witch-cake, it was believed, would lead to the discovery of a witch's identity. And that indeed appeared to happen. Hale and other contemporaries concur that, after the countermagic was employed, "the Afflicted persons cryed out of the Indian Woman . . . that she did pinch, prick, and grievously torment them, and that they saw her here and there, where no body else could."[18]

Parris was horrified when he learned what had been done without his knowledge. Somewhat more than a month later, before communion on March 27, he admonished Goodwife Sibley in front of the church, charging that "by this means (it seems) the Devil hath been raised amongst us, and his rage is vehement and terrible, and when he shall be silenced, the Lord only knows." She—a church member!—had, he exclaimed, gone "to the Devil for help against the Devil," an action "accounted by godly Protestants . . . as dia-bolical." Abashed and repentant, Sister Sibley acknowledged "her error and grief for it"; the church accepted her apology.[19]

Still, Samuel Parris now confronted an even more pressing problem than before, for his daughter and niece had accused his female Indian slave of bewitching them. According to John Hale, after the witchcake incident and the initial accusation, Parris sought the best advice available to him, sum-moning "some Worthy Gentlemen of Salem, and some Neighbour Ministers [again surely including Hale himself] to consult together at his House." The men "enquired diligently into the Sufferings of the Afflicted," concluding along with Dr. Griggs that the fits were "preternatural," displaying "the hand of Satan." But they counseled Parris against taking hasty action; he should instead "sit still and wait upon the Providence of God . . . and to be much in prayer for the discovery of what was yet secret." And they took a further step, questioning Tituba herself. She admitted making the cake and said that "her Mistress in her own Country was a Witch" who had taught her some countermagic. But, she declared, "she herself was not a Witch."[20]

Who was Tituba, and what was "her own Country"? Many scholars have addressed those questions, some at great length. Every surviving piece of contemporary evidence identifies her as an Indian. Later tradition trans-formed her into an African or half-African slave, but the contemporary unanimity is convincing.[21] No late-seventeenth-century source describes her geographic origins, though a mid-eighteenth-century one does. Thomas Hutchinson, who in composing his history of the Bay Colony in the 1760s had access to documents that no longer exist, declared unhesitatingly that she was "brought into the Country from New Spain." More precision than that is probably impossible. Still, Hutchinson's statement might well mean that Tituba came from Florida or the Georgia Sea Islands, where most of the people termed "Spanish Indians" in early New England originated.[22]

Tituba, then, was almost certainly not born in New England, although her husband John might have been (nothing is known of his background). She was thus not of Wabanaki origin. Yet the surviving records consistently refer to her as "Tituba Indian," "the Indyen woman," "titibe an Indian Woman," or the like, implying that Villagers viewed her ethnicity as an inseparable part of her identity. Less than a month after the devastating raid on York and following more than three years of unrelenting frontier warfare, in other words, the first person identified as a witch in the Salem crisis of 1692 was someone known to all primarily as an Indian. The girls, asked who tormented them, thus named a woman with whom they were intimately acquainted, and who could be seen as representing the people who were then "tormenting" New England as a whole.[23]

According to Hale, just "a short time" after the "Worthy Gentlemen" questioned Tituba and advised Parris to await God's providence, "other persons who were of age to be witnesses, were molested by Satan, and in their fits cryed out upon Tituba and Goody O[sborne] and S[arah] G[ood] that they or Specters in their Shapes did grievously torment them." If the surviving documents accurately indicate the date of those others' initial fits, they took place on February 25. Hale's qualifying phrase "persons who were of age to be witnesses" revealed an important aspect of the crisis hitherto unremarked upon by the participants. In the 1690s, following legal doctrines laid down by Sir Matthew Hale about two decades earlier, English jurists had begun to hold that, as a general rule, children under fourteen were incapable of testifying under oath in court in capital felony cases, although exceptions could be made and adults could describe young children's behavior. The youth of Parris's daughter and niece made them possibly questionable witnesses, and so no legal steps were taken against Tituba or other possible witches until older sufferers emerged.[24]

The Salem Village residents who had their first recorded fits on February 25 and who attributed them to an apparition of Tituba were Ann Putnam and Elizabeth (Betty) Hubbard. Ann (often called Jr.), the twelve-year-old daughter of Thomas and Ann Carr Putnam, church members and staunch supporters of Samuel Parris, also failed to meet the standard age criterion for testimony in capital cases. Her father, generally known as Sergeant Thomas because of his post in the local militia, was a veteran of King Philip's War and the oldest male of the third generation of Putnams in Salem Village. Collectively, the Putnam family had prospered in the Village, its branches controlling substantial property by the 1690s. Yet subdivisions through inheritance had led to decreasing sizes of individual landholdings. The afflicted girl's mother, also Ann (usually called Ann Sr.), had been born in the northern Essex County town of Salisbury, the daughter of George Carr, a wealthy shipbuilder. Probably initially drawn to Salem Village because her older sister Mary was the wife of James Bayley, Ann Carr married Sergeant Thomas Putnam in 1678.[25]

Because Betty Hubbard was the first afflicted person older than fourteen, her torments could well have tipped the balance toward legal action. A seventeen-year-old indentured maidservant of Dr. William Griggs, she was also most likely an orphaned or impoverished great-niece of his wife, Rachel Hubbard Griggs. Betty had for a time lived in Boston as a servant of Isaac Griggs, a son of the doctor's first marriage. But when Isaac and his wife died in 1689, William paid his son's executor for the time remaining on Betty's contract. As a member of the household of the man who had originally diagnosed witchcraft, Betty—although not living as close to the parsonage as were the Putnams—would have been intimately familiar with the fits experienced by Abigail Williams and Betty Parris.[26]

Between February 25 and February 28, Betty and Ann Jr. identified not only Tituba but also Sarah Osborne and Sarah Good as their tormentors. They described being "most greviously tortor[ed]" by the apparitions of Osborne and Good by "pinching and pricking . . . dreadfully." Those who witnessed Betty's and Ann's agonies surely felt the same compassion for them as Hale and others had felt for the initial sufferers.[27]

The two additional women thus named as possible witches had both lived in Salem Village for years, although neither was born there. Sarah Warren Prince Osborne, aged about forty-nine in 1692, had moved to Salem Village from Watertown when she wed Robert Prince (whose sister married into the Putnam clan) in 1662. After her first husband's death, she scandalized Villagers by marrying Alexander Osborne, a young servant whose indenture she purchased. She and her second husband then became involved in a prolonged dispute (still unresolved in 1692) with the father and uncle of Sergeant Thomas Putnam, who were the executors of Robert Prince's estate. Prince had wanted to pass some land on to his two sons, who were Ann Jr.'s second cousins, while the Osbornes sought to acquire it for themselves. Sarah Solart

Poole Good, born in Wenham, was only thirty-eight years old, but she otherwise fit the classic stereotype of a witch. From a prosperous family, she had
become impoverished as a consequence of two unfortunate marriages and an
unfairly withheld inheritance. Known to be dissatisfied with her lot in life,
she had antagonized even those who tried to help her and had aroused suspicions that she was engaging in malefic practices, bewitching her neighbors
and their livestock.[28]

The first three accused witches, then, could be characterized thus: one
(Sarah Good) who had been previously suspected of witchcraft by her neighbors; one (Sarah Osborne) who was involved in a legal battle with the family
of an accuser; and one (Tituba) who was linked to the Indian war. Similar
patterns would appear again and again throughout the crisis.

The Afflicted Girls and Fortune-Telling

Readers of *In the Devil's Snare* who are familiar with the traditional story
of Salem witchcraft will have recognized that something has been missing
from my narrative: an account of the afflicted girls' fortune-telling circle in
the winter of 1691–1692. Usually, authors begin books on Salem with a tale
of bored children and teenagers experimenting together with occult practices, especially a venus glass, sometimes under the guidance of the slave
Tituba. As Bernard Rosenthal has definitively shown, however, no contemporary source links Tituba to fortune-telling by the afflicted.[29]

Furthermore, the contemporary evidence for group fortune-telling by
the young women who eventually were afflicted in Salem Village cannot
withstand scrutiny. Aside from a vague comment by Cotton Mather, the
entire interpretive superstructure rests on one passage from John Hale's
Modest Enquiry into the Nature of Witchcraft (1702). In 1692, he tells us, "I
knew one of the Afflicted persons, who (as I was credibly informed) did
try with an egg and a glass to find her future Husbands Calling; till there
came up a Coffin, that is, a Spectre in likeness of a Coffin. And she was
afterward followed with diabolical molestation to her death; and so dyed a
single person." Hale follows that story immediately with another tale, of a
woman he was "called to pray with, being under sore fits and vexations of
Satan," who had "tryed the same charm," and whom his prayers released
from "those bonds of Satan."[30]

Nothing in Hale's account links the two stories except for both women's experimenting with the same common form of fortune-telling, yet authors have conflated them to create group activity by the afflicted girls. Hale himself seems to have regarded them as separate incidents: the first he was only "credibly informed" about, the second he participated in; the first involved one of the youthful "Afflicted persons," the subject of the second could have been any woman of any age; the first occurred in 1692, the second is undated. Even if both incidents occurred in 1692, the second could easily refer to someone like the accused witch Sarah Cole (of Lynn) who claimed to be afflicted, and who confessed at her examination that years earlier, before her marriage, "she & some others toyed with a Venus glase & an Egg what trade their sweet harts should be of."[31]

Hale's *Modest Enquiry,* in short, provides evidence that *one* of the afflicted girls—someone who died single before 1697 (when Hale himself died, although his book was not published for another five years)—engaged in fortune-telling of a rather ordinary sort, probably although not necessarily prior to her affliction in 1692.[32] That Hale regarded this story as irrelevant to the development of the crisis, and that careful scholars today should regard it as equally irrelevant, is indicated by the fact that he failed to include it in his central narrative, which occupies pages 1–40 of his book. It appears instead much later, in the middle of a discussion of Satan's various relationships with human beings. Hale states that he intends it as a warning "to take heed of handling the Devils weapons," never identifying the tale in any way as a cause of the witchcraft crisis.

THE FIRST EXAMINATIONS

With four afflicted and three accused now among them, Villagers decided to take action. On February 29, Thomas Putnam, his brother Edward, and two men unrelated to any of the afflicted—Joseph Hutchinson and Thomas Preston—filed formal complaints with the Salem magistrates, John Hathorne and Jonathan Corwin, charging the three women with "Witchcraft, by them Committed and thereby much injury don" to the three children and Betty Hubbard. The accusations thus moved from the religious to the legal realm, and out of the three affected households into the wider community. That Hutchinson and Preston (both of whom later became skeptics) joined in the initial complaints reveals the extent of Villagers' concern over the condition of the tormented children in their midst. Ann Jr.'s complaints of new tortures that very night, and Betty Hubbard's early the following day, must have confirmed Villagers in their belief that legal steps had to be taken.[33]

Hathorne and Corwin were in their early fifties and related by marriage. Members of prosperous families that had settled in Salem early in the town's history, they both also had extensive links to the northern frontier. (Hathorne speculated in large tracts of Maine land, and Corwin owned valuable sawmills at Cape Porpoise, which he had acquired in 1676 by marrying the wealthy widow Elizabeth Sheafe Gibbs, who inherited them from her first husband.)[34] Experienced justices of the peace who had handled hundreds of cases previously, they soon made a crucial decision with immense consequences. Rather than following the customary procedure of conducting preliminary examinations in private, they would interrogate suspects in public. Moreover, in addition to preparing their own summaries of the evidence, they would ask that detailed transcripts be kept.

Nowhere did they record the rationale for these actions, but they were probably responding to intense community interest in the witchcraft accusations. Possibly Samuel Parris, Nicholas Noyes (of the Salem Town church), or other clergymen also urged them to adopt this course of action for the religious edification of local residents. Whatever their reasoning, the magistrates moved the first examinations from Nathaniel Ingersoll's tavern, the original location, to the meetinghouse, the largest building in the Village, so that many more people could attend. That first week in March, with the ground still frozen, there would have been little pressing work for farmers or their families, and the room was undoubtedly packed.[35]

John Hathorne conducted the first three examinations; he later seems to have run most of the others as well. These interrogations, like others he had undoubtedly orchestrated in the past, had a single purpose: to elicit a confession of guilt. In common with other seventeenth-century colonial magistrates, he assumed that the accused had committed the offenses in question. Indeed, that assumption was usually correct. People formally charged with crimes in early New England were convicted far more often than not. Even when a suspect won acquittal or conviction on a lesser offense, that outcome occurred not because the person was thought to be innocent of the serious crime, but rather because juries and judges often proved reluctant to condemn miscreants to death. Thus, earlier in the century people undeniably guilty of adultery (a capital offense in Massachusetts) were convicted instead of "lascivious conduct," and others thought to be witches were acquitted or jailed rather than hanged.[36]

Accordingly, when Sarah Good, the first to be questioned, stood before him in the crowded meetinghouse on March 1, Hathorne began with what to him was the central inquiry under traditional Bay Colony law.[37] The 1648 *Laws and Liberties of Massachusetts* had defined a witch as one who "hath or consulteth with a familiar spirit." (Such familiars, frequently in the shapes of animals, were believed to link witches to the devil and to suck nourishment from their bodies.) Even though the law referring to familiars had been superseded in the mid-1680s, Hathorne—simultaneously assuming and hoping to confirm her guilt—started by asking Goodwife Good, "What evil spirit have you familiarity with?" When she responded, "None," he inquired, "Have you made no contract with the devil?" Again, she answered with a negative. "Why doe you hurt these children?" he continued, trying to win an admission that if she had not personally hurt them, she had employed a "creature" to do so. Good persisted in her denials, and so Hathorne shifted tactics. Adopting a technique that would characterize all subsequent examinations and the trials, he "desired the children all of them to look upon her, and see, if this were the person that had hurt them." They did so, identified her, and "presently they were all tormented." Asked to explain the agonies of the afflicted, Sarah Good insisted that Sarah Osborne (not herself) was torment- ing them.

The official note-taker, Ezekiel Cheever, probably expressed the skepti- cism about her responses felt by many other listeners. "Her answers were in a very wicked, spitfull manner reflecting and retorting against the authority with base and abusive words and many lies shee was taken in," Cheever inscribed at the end of his transcript of the examination. Even her husband, William, publicly voiced doubts about Sarah. William told the magistrates he feared "that shee either was a witch or would be one very quickly." Pressed by Hathorne for specifics, he admitted he had none, but "her bad carriage to him" made him think that "shee is an enimy to all good." A day later he added that he thought he had seen "a wart or tett a little below her Right shoulder which he never saw before," thus suggesting the presence of the devil's mark on her body.

Next came Sarah Osborne.[38] Hathorne began with the same sequence of questions concerning familiarity with an evil spirit, contracting with the devil, and hurting the children, receiving similar denials. Then he explored her relationship to Sarah Good. Osborne indicated that she rarely saw her fellow defendant and hardly knew her. Undoubtedly hoping to spring a trap, Hathorne informed Osborne that Good had accused her of tormenting the children. "I doe not know [but] that the deveil goes about in my likeness to do any hurt," Osborne retorted, offering what would eventually turn out to be an important line of defense for accused witches. After Hathorne asked the afflicted to look at her, they readily identified her as one of their tormentors.

Then the interrogation took a different turn, based on remarks by Villagers in the audience. Someone reported that "shee said this morning that shee was more like to be bewitched than that she was a witch," a statement Hathorne asked her to explain. Osborne responded that once she was frightened in her sleep, "and either saw or dreamed that shee saw a thing like an indian all black which did pinch her in her neck and pulled her by the back part of her head to the dore of the house." That nightmare would have been hardly unusual for a woman in northern New England familiar with reports of scalping and the recent raid on York, and Hathorne did not explore it further. Instead, he pursued a point raised "by some in the meeting house": that "shee had said that shee would never be teid to that lying spirit any more." Wasn't that the devil to whom you referred? he pressed her. Osborne reluctantly admitted that "a voice" had told her not to attend meeting, but insisted she had resisted its message. Yet "her housband and others" declared that she had not been to church for over a year. Although she claimed she had been ill, Hathorne accused her of "yeild[ing] thus far to the devil as never to goe to meeting."

The transcripts of the examinations of Sarah Good and Sarah Osborne reveal dynamics that would continue inside various makeshift courtrooms for the duration of the crisis. Four distinct elements combined to create an unstable, often explosive mixture: the magistrates, assuming guilt; the accused, struggling to respond to the charges; the afflicted, demonstrating their torments; and the audience, actively involving themselves in the exchanges by offering information and commentaries. These early records disclose another aspect of the crisis as well: even the closest relatives of the accused sometimes questioned their innocence. William Good and Alexander Osborne were but the first of many to express doubts publicly about their spouses or other relations.

After the magistrates finished with Goody Osborne, they turned to Tituba. Undoubtedly Hathorne and Corwin had been among the "Worthy Gentlemen of Salem" who questioned Tituba previously at Parris's request, and to whom she had acknowledged some acquaintance with witchcraft but denied being a witch. Perhaps they anticipated similar responses. If so, they were to be surprised, because Tituba confessed to committing malefice— because, she later informed a critic of the trials, Parris beat her until she agreed to admit guilt.[39]

After starting by again denying that she was a witch, Tituba gradually made a series of shocking disclosures in response to Hathorne's persistent questioning.[40] The devil had appeared to her "and bid me serve him." Good and Osborne had hurt the children; she had seen them do so, along with the specters of two women and a man from Boston whom she could not identify. Sarah Good's familiar spirit was a yellow bird that "suck[ed] her between her fingers." Sarah Osborne had two familiars: "a thing with a head like a woman with 2 leggs and wings," and "a thing all over hairy" that "goeth upright like a man" and was two or three feet tall. Tituba herself had seen strange creatures. A hog, a "great black dogge," a red cat, and a black cat, all emissaries of the devil, had urged her to hurt the children. Finally, when they threatened to do worse to her, she had given in and attacked first Betty Parris and Abigail Williams, then Ann Putnam Jr. and Betty Hubbard. "I am very sorry for itt," though, she added, detailing her attempts to resist the pressures the devil and the witches had brought to bear on her to win her cooperation.

The four victims were, Samuel Parris later attested, "grievously distressed" at the outset of Tituba's examination but "immediately all quiet" during her confession. At the end of the examination, they again complained of tortures, assenting when Tituba identified Sarah Good as a guilty party. The day's session ended in disorder as Betty Hubbard experienced "an extreame fit" and Tituba was herself "very much afflicted," charging Good and Osborne with attacking her for confessing. Tituba claimed that the specters "blinded hir," also rendering her unable to speak freely.

Neither of the transcribers recorded the immediate reactions of the multitude in the meetinghouse to Tituba's revelations. But that her words deeply affected at least some of the hearers became evident that evening.[41] About an hour after nightfall, "a strange noyse not useually heard" frightened the Villagers William Allen and John Hughes. The two men saw "a strange and unuseall beast lyeing on the Grownd," which disappeared as they came closer, metamorphosing into "2 or 3 weemen" who flew swiftly away, "which weemen wee took to bee Sarah Good Sarah Osburne and Tittabe." Sarah Good's specter was seen as well at Dr. Griggs's house. There Betty Hubbard was watched over by Samuel Sibley (Mary Sibley's husband), among others. When Betty said that she saw Sarah Good's apparition on the table, "with all hear naked brast and bar footed bar lagded," Sibley was sufficiently convinced by her vision that, he later reported, "I Struck with my Staf wher She Said Sary good Stud." Betty then informed him that "you have heet har right acors the back you have a most killd hear."

That night, Sarah Good was jailed at the house of the constable, Joseph Herrick. In the morning, watchers (who quickly heard about the spectral appearance at Dr. Griggs's) told Herrick that she "was gon for some time from them both bare foot and bare legde," and Herrick's wife observed that Sarah's arm was "Blooddy from a little below the Elbow to the wrist," whereas the previous night her arms had been unmarked. So the reported blow on the back turned into a perceived one on the arm; and Villagers had convincing proof of Good's spectral rambling.

The magistrates had not completed interrogating the accused women. On March 2 and 3, they again questioned Tituba and Sarah Osborne, and on March 5, Tituba and Sarah Good. Of these six additional examinations (all of which seem to have taken place in jail), only one record survives, that of Tituba on March 2. Still, the others probably did not yield any significant revelations.[42] The second examination of Tituba certainly did, however, for Hathorne questioned the slave woman closely about her dealings with the devil. She indicated that she had enlisted in the devil's legion by signing his book with a mark "with red Bloud," and that the devil had showed her Good's and Osborne's marks in the same book. She also declared that Good had admitted signing the book, although Osborne would not confess. Further, the book contained nine signatures in all, "Some in Boston & some herein this Towne." She divulged the stunning news that the witches had held a meeting at Parris's own house, but "my master did nott See us, for they would not lett my Master See." Even though this testimony was not offered in public, its contents undoubtedly spread throughout the Village, as knowledgeable gossipers shared the additional information with others.[43]

Tituba's disclosures about the witch conspiracy continued to affect the impressionable William Allen and John Hughes, this time separately. On the evening of March 2, Allen was in bed when Sarah Good "vissabley appeared to him," sitting on his foot surrounded with "an unuseuall light," but she disappeared when he kicked her. As for Hughes, he was on his way home after dark from Samuel Sibley's (where the chief topic of conversation was undoubtedly Goody Good's spectral visit to Dr. Griggs's house the previous night) when he saw "a Great white dogg" that followed him before disappearing mysteriously. Later, in bed "in a classd Roome and the dore being fast," he saw "a Great light" and "a large Grey Catt att his beds foot." Accounts of such apparitions must have circulated around the Village in conjunction with Samuel Braybrook's report that while he was carrying Sarah Good to jail in Ipswich that same day she had leapt off her horse three times, and that Ann Putnam Jr. had "declared the same att her fathers house," thus demonstrating the accuracy of her spectral sight.[44]

The Reverend John Hale, for one, later recalled that he had found Tituba's confessions credible because of their consistency. Had she been lying, he thought, she would have contradicted herself. Moreover, she seemed "very penitent" for making a covenant with the devil, and she herself was afflicted by other witches for confessing. Finally, her confession "agreed exactly . . . with the accusation of the afflicted." Others most likely concurred with Hale's assessment. At the end of the first week of March 1691/2, therefore, the people of Salem Village and nearby towns had much to ponder and to discuss. Not least among their topics of conversation would have been new accusations. On March 3, Ann Jr. complained that Sarah Good's young daughter Dorcas "did immediatly almost choak me and tortored me most greviously." And three days later, during services on Sunday, March 6, she told "them that held me" that the specter of Elizabeth Bassett Proctor, the granddaughter of a woman accused of witchcraft in 1669, had choked, bitten, and pinched her three days earlier. She had seen Goody Proctor "amongst the wicthes" on March 3, Ann disclosed, but she did not recognize her until she saw her in church.[45]

TORMENTED YOUNG PEOPLE
AND NEIGHBORING WITCHES

The events of mid-January through early March 1691/2 in Salem Village were unusual but not unprecedented in either old or New England. Ever since the final decades of the sixteenth century, similar events had occurred: daughters—and sons—of pious families would experience mysterious afflictions; physicians would eventually diagnose witchcraft; specters would be seen and suspects named; and occasionally trials would be held. Most commonly, the suspects identified were (like Sarah Good) women widely thought to be witches or (like Sarah Osborne) women from families involved in disputes with those of the accusers. The trials did not always end in conviction, but families of the tormented youths rarely if ever questioned the legitimacy of their "preternatural" afflictions, although other observers sometimes did.

Seventeenth-century authors admitted the difficulty of distinguishing between the effects of disease and the devil's operations on the bodies of afflicted persons. The magistrates and judges in 1692 are known to have consulted a standard witchcraft reference work, the Reverend Richard Bernard's *Guide to Grand-Jury Men,* published in England in 1627. Bernard believed that both ministers and secular authorities had adopted an overly credulous approach to witchcraft accusations, and he urged caution in reaching the conclusion that such charges were valid. In particular, he warned that because certain illnesses could mimic diabolical tortures, it was necessary to seek "the judgement of some skilfull Physician to helpe to discerne, and to make a cleere difference betweene the one and the other." Nathaniel Crouch, a popular writer whose work was also reviewed by the magistrates in 1692, helpfully listed signs that would not appear in the case of "natural diseases." If the afflicted could reveal "secret things past or to come," that would occur only with "supernatural assistance." Or if the afflicted could "speake with strange Languages" or perform feats "far beyond human strength," those too constituted important evidence, along with an ability to talk without moving the lips. Other possible indications came from such physical signs as their bodies becoming "inflexible, neither to be bended backward nor forward with the greatest force," or "the Belly to be suddenly puft up, & to fall instantly flat again."[46]

From the late sixteenth century on, portrayals of young people's behavior "in their fits" both accorded with such signs of diabolical activity and bore a striking resemblance to descriptions of the Essex County afflicted in 1692. For example, in the mid-1590s several youths living in the household of Nicholas Starkie howled, "fell a tumbling, and after that became speachlesse sencelesse and as deade." Thirty years later, also in England, the daughters of Edward Fairfax "had many strange convulsions and risings in their bodies, and stiffness in their arms and hands, and whole bodies sometimes." In Hartford, Connecticut, in 1662 a young woman named Ann Cole experienced "extremely violent bodily motions . . . , even to the hazard of her life in the apprehensions of those that saw them." And Elizabeth Kelly, a child afflicted during the same outbreak, complained of a reputed witch that "she chokes me, she kneels on my belly, she will break my bowels, she pinches me," and on another occasion that she "torments me she pricks me with pins."[47]

A diagnosis of diabolic activity rather than disease—as occurred in the Starkie, Fairfax, and Hartford cases—did not answer every relevant question about such afflictions. Seventeenth-century authors emphasized that in all these cases the devil acted only with God's permission. "Devils doe much mischiefe, but even by these also doth God worke his will, and these doe nothing without the hand of his providence," observed the Reverend Mr. Bernard. "Neither Divels, nor Witches, nor wicked men, can doe any thing without the Lords leave." Thus the occurrence of such phenomena in a household should lead its members to examine their consciences and their behavior, to bear the afflictions patiently, and to engage in fasting and prayer to discern God's holy purpose behind their troubles. How had they offended God? Why was he testing their faith? What aspects of their lives needed reformation? Presumably the Reverend Samuel Parris and his clerical colleagues addressed those very issues during their meetings at the Salem Village parsonage in mid-February.[48]

A definitive verdict also required ascertaining the precise way in which

Satan was creating the torments. Had the devil entered the body and soul of his target, thereby causing possession? Was the devil torturing his victim's body but leaving the soul untouched, resulting in a different condition known as obsession? Or had the devil used one or more witches as intermediaries to effect the agonies? The Reverend Mr. Bernard sought the means to distinguish among the various diabolic manifestations. When, he declared, there was "not any suspicion at all of a Witch," or perhaps only "an idle, vaine, and foolish suspicion, without any good ground," then the devil probably acted directly. "Children . . . Young folkes . . . Women" were especially liable to obsession or possession by the devil, and in such cases only "the finger of God," summoned through prayer and fasting, could cast the devil out of the victim. Bernard warned his readers against assuming that witchcraft always lay behind afflictions. The devil acting directly, or even disease, could also have caused the problem.[49]

When the operations of witchcraft could reasonably be inferred, there still arose the question of identifying the witch. Bernard pointed out that although witches could be of either sex, they were more likely to be women than men. Ever since Eve, Satan had preferred to deal with women, who were "more credulous" and "more malicious" when displeased than men, "and so herein more fit instruments of the Divell." More talkative than men, women were also "lesse able to hide what they know from others" and consequently "more ready to bee teachers of Witchcraft to others," such as their children or servants. Finally, women, "proud in their rule," would busily command whomever they could. "And therefore," Bernard concluded, "the Divell laboureth most to make them Witches: because they, upon every light displeasure, will set him on worke, which is what he desireth." Above all, female or male, witches were *malicious spirits, impatient people, and full of revenge.*"[50]

Accordingly, in cases of affliction believed to result from witchcraft Bernard listed what he termed "probabilities, as may justly cause the suspected to be questioned." First came the propensity of the accused "to be much given to *cursing* and *imprecations*," especially for little or no cause. If after threats, "evill [came] to happen, and this not *once,* or *twice,* to one or two, but often, and to divers persons," then that was "a great presumption" of guilt. Another such presumption derived from "an implicit confession"—a statement by an accused that could be taken as an admission of culpability. Or perhaps the suspect had taken an inordinate interest in the afflicted person, repeatedly visiting despite being told to stay away. "The common report of neighbours of all sorts" too bore weight, particularly if the accused was "of kin to a convicted Witch," such as a child or grandchild, sibling, niece or nephew. Similar reasoning applied as well to accused servants or people "of familiar acquaintance" with a known witch. The testimony of another witch could also be important, "for who can better discover a Witch, then [*sic*] a Witch?" Finally, if the afflicted named suspects in their fits, "and also [told] where they have been, & what they have done here or there," or "seeme[d] to see" apparitions of the accused in their fits, "this is a great suspition."[51]

But Richard Bernard warned his readers not to jump to conclusions. He identified *presumptions* only, he stressed repeatedly. Each of the grounds for suspicion could have an innocent explanation as well as a diabolic one; for example, "rude and ill-mannered people," especially "some of the poorer sort," might not understand that they were not wanted at the house of an afflicted person. Likewise, "a common report" could rest "upon very weake grounds." More important, when the afflicted in their fits saw apparitions, that was, at base, "the devils testimony, who can lye, and that more often then speake truth." Such evidence alone would be insufficient in a capital case, for even when the devil told the truth, he did so with "lying intent," seeking "to insnare the bloud of the innocent." Certainly, Bernard asserted, Satan "can represent a common ordinary person, man or woman unregenerate (though no Witch) to the fantasie of vaine persons, to deceive them and others."[52]

At the end of the first quarter of the seventeenth century, Richard Bernard thus touched on many of the issues that later arose in cases of affliction in both old and New England. He intended to caution his readers against excessive credulity in dealing with witchcraft allegations, yet his advice could be, and was, taken in divergent ways. His reliance on doctors for the initial diagnosis of diabolic activity, for example, left little room for challenge if a physician rendered such a verdict and thus lent credibility to accusers, as Dr. Griggs did in Salem Village. Then, too, Bernard's "presumptions," especially those involving spectral visions, were difficult to interpret; indeed, any of the indicators he listed could be read either restrictively or expansively. A prime example lay in his treatment of the question that would eventually be of great significance in the 1692 crisis: Could Satan send the apparition of an innocent person to someone he afflicted? The apparition of *any* innocent person? Even Bernard's careful language on that matter, quoted above, implied through omission that a regenerate (church member) innocent could not be so represented by the devil, thereby suggesting that a specter of such a person could infallibly reveal guilt. In short, despite the existence of Bernard's lengthy treatise and other similar works, people wishing to investigate witchcraft accusations had to confront many questions for which the answers remained unclear.

Affliction stories aroused great interest among seventeenth-century clergymen and the general public, often finding their way into print. Accordingly, many published accounts of the agonies experienced by young people in the relatively recent past, and of the ways in which those torments had been handled by legal and clerical authorities, were available to the adult men and women who confronted the challenge posed by the "strange fits" of the suffering youths in Salem Village. Such narratives joined the works by authors such as Bernard in providing New Englanders with guides for handling the afflicted.

In the 1680s Increase and Cotton Mather, father and son clerics, both published compilations of witchcraft cases, most of them from New England. The books, which recounted tales of affliction and malefic bewitchment, constituted the Mathers' contribution to a contemporary, English debate over the existence and nature of witchcraft, a debate with no colonial counterpart. The Reverend Increase Mather's *An Essay for the Recording of Illustrious Providences* (1684) revealed to the world the story of Ann Cole and the Hartford outbreak of 1662, along with other cases such as that of John Stiles, a young Newbury boy who had fits in late 1679. Stiles, like the later Salem afflicted, complained of pinching and pricking sensations, experienced unusual bodily motions, and occasionally fell into swoons. The elder Mather also described the possession of Elizabeth Knapp, a sixteen-year-old servant of the Reverend Samuel Willard, in Groton, Massachusetts. Knapp had fits for about three months in the late fall and early winter of 1671–1672; she moved in peculiar ways, shrieked loudly, and was often struck dumb. Cotton Mather's *Memorable Providences, Relating to Witchcrafts and Possessions* (1689) added another tale of a tormented young person, whom he identified as a boy from Tocutt (Branford), Connecticut. He had found the account (possibly thirty years old) among the papers of one of his grandfathers, Mather indicated; it again described a youth troubled for months by fits that caused him to move and speak strangely.[53]

The stories of Elizabeth Knapp and the Tocutt boy are useful to examine in greater detail because of their differences from the later Essex County cases. Most important, neither led to a prosecution; they were both handled entirely by ministers. Indeed, the Tocutt boy never accused anyone of bewitching him, for his was a classic instance of possession by Satan. He, the son of a "godly Minister," carried on long conversations with the devil in his fits. Satan promised that "he should live deliciously, and have Ease, Comfort, and Money" if he would enter into a diabolic covenant. When the boy refused to succumb to such temptations, "the Devil took a corporal Possession of him," tormented him "extremely," and answered those who thereafter spoke to the boy, barking or hissing and sometimes voicing "horrible Blasphemies against the Name of Christ." Elizabeth Knapp's body (but not her soul, Samuel Willard decided) was likewise taken over by Satan, who attacked Willard as a liar and "a great black rogue." He announced to Willard and others, "I am a pretty black boy, this is my pretty girl; I have been here a great while." Unlike the Tocutt boy, the obsessed Knapp accused a neighbor woman of bewitching her and also admitted that she had signed the devil's covenant. Satan cut her finger with a knife and "then took a little sharpened stick, and dipped in the blood and put it into her hand, and guided it, and she wrote her name with his help," she recounted.[54]

The tormented young people of Tocutt and Groton in the 1660s and 1670s present an alternate model of seventeenth-century afflictions—of a road not followed in Salem Village. In both cases, the devil actually inhabited and spoke through the body of a possessed or obsessed person, which never happened in 1692. Furthermore, one of the young people did not accuse anyone of bewitching him. Although the other did, Samuel Willard, unlike Samuel Parris and his colleagues, did not immediately embrace the accusation. Instead, even though Elizabeth Knapp, whose eyes were "sealed up" in her fits, "knew her [the suspect witch's] very touch from any other, though no voice were uttered," Willard acted with careful deliberation, encouraging Knapp to pray with the suspect. Eventually, Knapp decided that "Satan had deluded her," and her complaints of bewitchment ceased, although the fits continued. Willard also took a skeptical approach to his servant's confession, remarking that he was not convinced she had actually agreed to a diabolic compact. Because her responses to his questions were contradictory, he regarded Elizabeth Knapp primarily as "an object of pity" and "a subject of hope" rather than as a soul lost forever to the devil.[55]

Samuel Willard in 1671 thus displayed a willingness to question the sorts of statements and behaviors that many Bay Colony magistrates and ministers failed to challenge twenty-one years later. His skepticism indicates that their later credulity need not be seen as the only possible contemporary response to the affliction of young people, and that some explanation of that credulity is required. As the introduction suggested, the impact of the ongoing conflict with the Wabanakis provides much of the necessary explanation, as will become evident in this book's later chapters.

In 1692 those wishing to combat the afflictions in Essex County were well aware of the Groton and Tocutt incidents, but they saw two other reports of afflictions published in the 1680s as constituting the most appropriate precedents for their actions. In Groton and Tocutt, ministers concluded that Satan was attacking his targets directly, without human intervention. Accordingly, the clergymen themselves dealt with the victims, and legal actions were never pursued (mere mortals, after all, could not arrest the devil and charge him with a crime). In Salem Village, by contrast, residents rapidly concluded that human agents—one or more witches, and not Satan's direct operations—had caused the afflictions. First Dr. William Griggs diagnosed bewitchment rather than a natural ailment, and then the sufferers named suspects who credibly fit known profiles of witches. When the case thereafter moved quickly into the hands of the magistrates, the relevant precedents became those involving legal rather than spiritual methods of combating afflictions.

Cotton Mather wrote about both earlier incidents. In 1688, he helped to treat the Goodwin children of Boston, the following year describing their torments at length in *Memorable Providences.* Later, when the first phase of the Salem proceedings ended, he included a substantial summary of the other case in *Wonders of the Invisible World,* his defense of the trials. As Mather pointed out (and John Hale concurred), a 1662 witchcraft prosecution in Bury St. Edmunds, England, described in a book printed two decades later, was "much considered by the Judges of *New England.*" Presided over by Sir Matthew Hale, who was widely known to be reluctant to convict witches without adequate evidence, the Bury St. Edmunds trial seemed to many the closest parallel to the Essex County episode. In the 1662 English case, Mather asserted, we "see the *Witchcrafts* here most exactly resemble the *Witchcraft* there; and we may learn what sort of Devils do trouble the World."[56]

The Bury St. Edmunds trial involved seven children and teenagers, six of them girls, from Lowestoft, Suffolk, who claimed to have been bewitched by two local widows, Rose Cullender and Amy Denny. None of the complainants, who came from four different families, testified at the trial; one was thought too young and the others too ill. Three attended the proceedings, but "fell into strange and violent fits, screeking out in a most sad manner, so that they could not in any wise give any Instructions in the Court who were the Cause of their Distemper." A learned doctor testified that "he was clearly of Opinion, that the persons were Bewitched." Parents and other relatives spoke for the young people, describing the tortures they had endured, including "feeling most extream pain in her Stomach, like the pricking of Pins"; experiencing convulsions, lameness, and "sometimes a soreness over their whole Bodies"; occasionally being unable to speak or hear; and vomiting up pins and nails. Furthermore, the afflicted complained of seeing the apparitions of Denny and Cullender, "to their great terrour and affrightment." Discerning the specters "sometimes in one place and sometimes in another," the girls would run to them, and "striking at them as if they were present," would be in turn "derid[ed] and threatn[ed]" by the apparitions. Once, one of the younger children "ran round about the House holding her Apron, crying *hush, hush,* as if there had been some Poultrey in the House," but the deponent (her aunt) "could perceive nothing."[57]

A notable aspect of the Bury St. Edmunds trial was its use of the same touch test employed by Samuel Willard in 1671. Judge Hale ordered Amy Denny to touch the hand of an eleven-year-old complainant as she lay "as one wholly senseless in a deep Sleep" on a table in the courtroom. At that "the Child without so much as seeing her, for her Eyes were closed all the while, suddenly leaped up . . . and with her Nails scratched her till Blood came" and had to be pulled away from Denny, still making "signs of Anger." Other tests were undertaken while the afflicted were "in the midst of their Fitts," with fists closed "in such manner, as that the strongest Man in the court could not force them open." Yet at Rose Cullender's "least touch . . . they would suddenly shriek out opening their hands, which accident could not happen by the touch of any other person."[58]

Not everyone, however, was convinced, and so one of the girls was taken aside, blindfolded, and touched by a randomly selected person. When *that* "produced the same effect" as the witch's touch, some leading barristers pronounced the bewitchment "a meer Imposture." But the girl's father explained that since—when his daughters came out of their fits—they turned out to have known everything that had happened in the interim, the apparently failed test should not be interpreted in that manner. Rather, it should be taken as "a confirmation that the Parties were really Bewitched" because "the Maid might be deceived by a suspicion that the Witch touched her when she did not." In the end, his argument (which even Cotton Mather found dubious) carried the day. The observers concluded, as did most of those in Essex County thirty years later, that "it is not possible that any should counterfeit such Distempers, . . . much less Children; and for so long time, and yet undiscovered by their Parents and Relations."[59]

During the three-day trial, neighbors offered maleficium tales to supplement the reports of afflictions. After the defendants had been given a chance to respond to the charges, Sir Matthew Hale instructed the jury that they had to answer two questions: Were the children bewitched? Had the prisoners done it? "That there were such Creatures as *Witches* he made no doubt at all," he informed the jurors, both because the scriptures said so and because "the wisdom of all Nations" (including the laws of England) declared witchcraft to be a crime. He then admonished them that *"to Condemn the Innocent, and to let the Guilty go free, were both an Abomination to the Lord."* The jury took just thirty minutes to convict the women. Soon thereafter, the afflictions ceased, and the next day the young people were able to affirm to the court the

truth of "what before hath been Deposed by their Friends and Relations."
Amy Denny and Rose Cullender were hanged three days later, still refusing
to confess.[60]

The introduction prepared by the anonymous editor of *A Tryal of Witches*
reveals one reason why the Bury St. Edmunds case took on such importance
in the thinking of people in Essex County in 1692. Sir Matthew Hale, he
declared, was a jurist notable for "his Integrity, Learning, and Law, . . . who
not only took a great deal of paines, and spent much time in this Tryal himself; but had the Assistance and Opinion of several other very Eminent and
Learned Persons." New Englanders revered Hale, who later became Lord
Chief Justice and who authored influential treatises on the law, not only for
his jurisprudence but also for his sincere piety. Although a member of the
Church of England, he was noted for his religiosity and for his close friendship with the well-known Puritan divine Richard Baxter. Therefore, New
Englanders, like the anonymous editor, could well conclude that *A Tryal of
Witches* was "the most perfect Narrative of any thing of this Nature hitherto
Extant" and turn to Hale's precedents for guidance at a time of crisis. Those
precedents allowed the admission of testimony about the spectral affliction of
children and teenagers, coupled such accounts with traditional stories of the
bewitchment of humans and livestock, and employed a touch test to help
determine guilt—all elements that were to play a major role in the Salem
convictions. New England magistrates might not be noted for their legal
learning (none were trained lawyers), but the great Sir Matthew Hale himself
seemed to legitimate their conduct of the trials.[61]

The other obvious precedent lay much closer to Salem in both time and
space. Four of the six children of the pious Boston mason John Goodwin
began suffering from fits during the summer of 1688. The Reverend Joshua
Moodey of Boston's Third Church described the children (aged five to thirteen, two boys and two girls) as "grievously tormented, crying out of head,
eyes, tongue, teeth breaking their neck, back, thighs, knees, legs, feet, toes
etc. & then they roar out, Oh my head, oh my neck." Their cries were "most
dolorous and affecting," Moodey recounted, but when the pain passed (usually in about an hour) they could "eat, drink, walk play, laugh as at other
times." In Cotton Mather's opinion as expressed in his narrative of the incidents in *Memorable Providences,* "the whole Temper and Carriage" of the
children rendered it unlikely that they would "Dissemble," and furthermore
"it was perfectly impossible for any Dissimulation of theirs to produce what
scores of spectators were amazed at."[62]

Investigation showed that the oldest of the four, Martha, had fallen ill
first, following an argument with the family's Irish laundress, whom Martha

had accused of stealing some linen. The woman's mother, Goody Glover, "an ignorant and scandalous old Woman" who had been described by her own husband as "undoubtedly a Witch" and who had already been accused of bewitching at least one woman to death, cursed the girl, who then started to have "strange Fits." After her siblings too were "tortured every where in a manner so very grievous, that it would have broken an heart of stone to have seen their Agonies," a prominent Boston doctor concluded that "nothing but an hellish Witchcraft could be the Original of these Maladies." In spite of the urgings of some that they employ countermagic, the pious parents determined "to oppose Devils with no other weapons but Prayers and Tears." A day of prayer at their house, held by several clergymen and devout laypeople, freed the youngest child from his fits, but the other children continued to be tormented, until the laundress and her mother were jailed. Thereafter they "had some present ease," until one of the children was verbally assaulted by a relative of the accused women, whereupon their fits resumed.[63]

When questioned, Goody Glover gave "blasphemous and horrible" responses, declared Mather; and she proved incapable of correctly reciting the Lord's Prayer no matter how many times it was repeated to her. At her trial before a court convened by the governor, Sir Edmund Andros, and headed by Joseph Dudley—and probably including three of the men who also served as judges in 1692—Glover claimed to speak only Gaelic, so she dealt with the judges through interpreters, even though "she understood the English very well," Mather insisted. A search of her house turned up "several small Images . . . made of Raggs, and stuff't with Goat's hair, and other such Ingredients." In court, Goody Glover confessed to witchcraft, demonstrating how she tortured the Goodwin children "by wetting of her Finger with her Spittle, and stroaking of those little Images." When she grasped an image, commonly termed a poppet (or puppet), one of the children "fell into sad Fits, before the whole Assembly." The judges, concerned about possible deception, repeated the experiment, but with the same result. Before convicting and sentencing Goody Glover to death, the court ordered a group of physicians to examine her to ensure she was not "craz'd." After the doctors pronounced her sane, she was executed on November 16, declaring ominously that "the Children should not be relieved by her Death, for others had a hand in it as well as she."[64]

Mather reported in *Memorable Providences* the accuracy of Goody Glover's prediction that the Goodwins would continue to experience spectral tortures. Yet although the children eventually named other suspected witches, no further arrests and executions occurred. The children occasionally saw specters, but only rarely could they identify specific individuals as causing their afflictions. Mather observed Martha Goodwin carefully, taking her into his own home and later reflecting that her "passions" taught him more about "Demoniacs" than did "all my Library." And others too had been instructed by her sufferings, because the Goodwin household had been "visited by all sorts of Persons" who witnessed the children's torments. To Mather, the lesson was clear: only the "Ignorant" would insist on "a Denial of Devils, or of Witches." His colleagues in other Boston and Charlestown churches concurred. In their jointly authored introduction to *Memorable Providences,* they commented that some people doubted "whether there are any such things as Witches," but that "no Age passes without some apparent Demonstration of it." Mather's book, they contended, provided "a further clear Confirmation, That, There is both a God, and a Devil, and Witchcraft: That, There is no out-ward Affliction, but what God may (and sometimes doth) permit Satan to trouble His people withal. That, The Malice of Satan and his Instruments, is very great against the Children of God."[65]

Taken together, the Boston and Bury St. Edmunds incidents provided the magistrates of 1692 with relevant valuable precedents and models, especially when supplemented with the learned writings of English and American jurists and clergymen. The behavior of the Salem Village afflicted, far from being unique, resembled various prior counterparts; other physicians, much more distinguished than Dr. William Griggs, had pronounced children bewitched on the basis of similar evidence. That Sir Matthew Hale, known to be cautious in his handling of witchcraft cases, had found spectral testimony credible was certainly reassuring. Goody Glover, confronted in the courtroom, had confessed her guilt and demonstrated dramatically and convincingly how she employed poppets to bewitch the Goodwin children. Faced with such overwhelming evidence, who—as Cotton Mather wrote— could possibly deny the existence of witches or their malicious intent?[66]

But at the end of the first week of March there remained the problem of properly identifying the witches responsible for the afflictions in Salem Village. Three had been named by one teenager and three children (who were too young to be wholly trustworthy witnesses), all of whom continued to suffer torments. One of those witches had confessed, naming the other two and also revealing the presence of additional, though still unidentified, witches in Boston and Salem Village. Two new suspects, Elizabeth Proctor and Dorcas Good, had been named but not questioned.

The examining magistrates, John Hathorne and Jonathan Corwin, did not yet have to consider whether the evidence they were developing would be sufficient for conviction at a trial. At the time, Massachusetts was being ruled by an ad hoc government established in April 1689 after the overthrow of the autocratic English governor, Sir Edmund Andros, in the colony's version of the Glorious Revolution. The Salem magistrates probably realized that no suspects would be tried until that interim government had been replaced by a formally reconstituted one, an event they knew would soon occur. In late January 1691/2, "almost at the same Time" as Bostonians learned of the raid on York, they heard that the Maine-born Sir William Phips had been appointed governor of the colony under a newly issued charter, and two weeks later a copy of the charter itself arrived, causing "much discourse," according to Samuel Sewall, a Boston merchant and magistrate. Although the ad hoc government had occasionally convicted men for capital offenses, it would have been foolhardy in the extreme to conduct a witchcraft trial knowing that its legitimacy would almost immediately be called into question. Consequently, until Phips arrived to organize the government under the new charter, there was little possibility of proceeding to a trial of anyone who had been, or might be, accused.[67]

Even so, Hathorne and Corwin confronted a daunting task. If Tituba's confession was credible (and certainly John Hale found it so), then they bore the responsibility of uncovering a witch conspiracy of unknown extent. Undoubtedly they sought advice on how to proceed from the best authorities available to them, certainly including Bernard's *Guide to Grand-Jury Men* and possibly William Perkins's *A Discourse of the Damned Art of Witchcraft . . .* (1608) and John Gaule's *Select Cases of Conscience Touching Witches and Witchcrafts* (1646). All three authors concurred on the essential points.

William Perkins, for example, stressed that a magistrate should not "proceede upon sleight causes . . . or upon sinister respects," but must have "speciall presumptions" before examining suspects in witchcraft cases. He listed the "certaine signes" that "at least probably, and conjecturally denote one to be a Witch," most of which accorded with those identified by Richard Bernard and discussed earlier in this section. "Notorious defamation," the accusation of a known witch, being a blood relation or "familiar friend" of a known witch, having cursed or quarreled with someone to whom "mischiefe" thereafter occurred: any one of these would constitute "a fit presumption" for a "strait examination." But Perkins also added another: "The devills marke" on the party in question would be suspicious, "for it is commonly thought, when the devill maketh his covenant with them, he alwaies leaveth his marke behinde him, whereby he knowes them for his owne." John Gaule agreed that such characteristics could lead to the "probable" identification of a witch, and he added more items to the list, such as the "lewd & naughty" life of a suspect.[68]

Magistrates questioning such a suspect had to be alert, the three men warned. "Faltering, faulty, unconstant and contrary Answers; upon judiciall and deliberate examination," asserted Gaule, were "more infallible" signs of culpability. Perkins too remarked that "if the partie examined be unconstant, or contrarie to himselfe in his deliberate answers, it argueth a guiltie mind and conscience which stoppeth the freedome of speech and utterance." Bernard, though, gave the fullest directions on how to proceed, indicating that magistrates should question a suspect only after having examined the afflicted (if possible), any knowledgeable relatives and neighbors, a physician, and the suspect's own family. Moreover, "a godly and learned Divine" should be recruited to prepare the suspect for "confession before Authority, when he or shee is examined." Then, during the interrogation of the suspect, the magistrates should pay attention to "his or her downe-cast lookes, feare, doubtfull answers, varying speeches, contradictions, cunning evasions, their lying, or defending of this or that speech and deede, or excusing the same. Also to observe, if any words fall from him or her, tending to some confession." If suspects refused to confess, advised Bernard, they should be confronted with the witnesses against them to see how they responded.[69]

Reading such instructions, Hathorne and Corwin could well have felt confident that they were proceeding in accordance with the most authoritative advice available, and that they were making good progress toward their goal. After all, Hathorne's questioning had elicited an explicit confession from Tituba and, it was thought, an implicit one from Sarah Good. Her identification of Sarah Osborne as the children's spectral tormentor, the authorities concluded, constituted exactly that implicit admission of guilt Richard Bernard advised magistrates to detect. "None here sees the witches but the afflicted & themselves," the summary of evidence prepared for Good's trial later observed, so Sarah Good "not being afflicted must consequently be a Witch."[70]

Yet, fatefully, the examining magistrates ignored one crucial piece of advice offered by Richard Bernard. The afflicted, the individual witnesses, and the suspects, he directed, should be questioned "apart, & not in the hearing one of another." Only after they had been carefully examined "alone" should they be brought together and the suspects be confronted in person by their accusers. Hathorne and Corwin, though, had already established the precedent of interrogating the accused in the presence of not only the afflicted but also the entire community. In the weeks and months to come, the impact of that procedure was to be both dramatic and wide-ranging.[71]

WILLIAM VAUGHAN (PORTSMOUTH) TO
MASSACHUSETTS GOVERNOR AND COUNCIL,
FEBRUARY 22, 1691/2:[72]

[Ransomed captives taken at York report that] the number of Indians Att York was noe lesse then two hundred able Fighting men, who have been long abroad & whose design was to meet with our men in the Woods haveing been (as they Say) advised by some of Sandy beach Captives that the Bostoners were provideing many Snow Shoes & Design'd a Considerable army out this winter to disrest them at Some of their head quarters which has made them very uneasy this winter & this Compa[ny] has been long out ranging the Woods to meet with ours or their tracts, which failing of they fell upon York[.] that the Indians Say at the fight at Macquait (where Capt Sherbon was Kill'd) if our men had Staid ashore one hour longer they would have left none alive. . . . That Mrs Dumer died in about 10 dayes after she was taken that 5 or 6 were kill'd in their march most children that were unable to travel & soe burthensome to them. That they have Sent 2 captives away to Canada to Satisfie the french with the truth of this Exploit, they formerly not beleiving the Indians report of what Service they doe against us. That the Enemy wants noe Amunition.

CHAPTER TWO

Gospel Women

MARCH 12, 1691/2–APRIL 19, 1692

I F THE FIRST five individuals accused in Salem Village—Tituba, Sarah Osborne, Sarah and Dorcas Good, and Elizabeth Proctor—fit standard profiles and so might have seemed logical suspects to local residents, those named next by the growing group of afflicted persons presented a sharp contrast. Everyone knew that women were more likely than men to be witches, but Martha Pennoyer Rich Corey and Rebecca Towne Nurse, the church members Ann Putnam Jr. named as her spectral torturers during the second week of March, appeared to be respectable matrons. Such iconoclastic accusations must have shocked the Village. That the charges were quickly taken seriously reveals how compelling and credible Villagers found the evident sufferings of the afflicted.

But once all seven females were complained against, it was perhaps not so surprising that in the following weeks the husbands of two and the church-member sister of a third joined them in the ranks of the accused. As was already indicated in the last chapter, experts concurred that people closely related to witches were themselves highly likely to become malefic practitioners. Thus Sarah Towne Cloyce (Rebecca Nurse's younger sister), Giles Corey, and John Proctor were all complained against by mid-April.

THE ACCUSATIONS OF MARTHA COREY AND REBECCA NURSE

At several unspecified times between March 7 and 12, Ann Putnam told her parents and other relatives that "goode Corie did often appear to her and tortor her by pinching and other wayes." Her repeated charges led her uncle, Edward Putnam, a deacon of the Salem Village church, and Ezekiel

Cheever, also a church member, to decide to call on Goody Corey because she was "in church covenant with us" and they "thought it our duty to goe to her and see what shee would say" in response to Ann's complaints. Martha, who had joined the Village church in April 1690, lived with her second husband, Giles, in an outlying area of the Village still known as Salem Farms. The prosperous but quarrelsome Giles, about eighty years old in 1692, had married Martha (who was considerably younger) as his third wife in 1685.[1]

On the morning of Saturday, March 12, Cheever and Edward Putnam went to Thomas Putnam's house to announce their intention to visit Goodwife Corey later in the day. They directed Ann to "take good notice" of the clothing Martha Corey's purported specter was wearing at her next appearance, so they could see whether or not the girl had correctly identified the apparition that troubled her. In the early afternoon, after returning expectantly to the Putnam household, they learned from Ann that in the interim the specter "came and blinded her but told her that her name was Corie and that shee should see her no more before it was night because she should not tell us what cloathes shee had on."

Probably troubled by the little girl's report, Cheever and Putnam nevertheless proceeded as planned. When they arrived at their destination around midafternoon, they found Martha Corey alone. "As soone as we came in," they later recounted, "in a smiling manner shee sayeth I know what you are come for you are come to talke with me about being a witch but I am none I cannot helpe peoples talking of me." Edward replied that they had come not because of gossip but because Ann had specifically named her. "But does shee tell you what cloathes I have on?" Martha asked, "with very great eagernes" repeating the inquiry when the men—undoubtedly stunned into silence—did not answer immediately. Finally they revealed to Goody Corey what Edward's niece had said about having been blinded by her apparition. "Shee made but litle answer to this," the men recalled, "but seemed to smile at it as if shee had showed us a pretty trick."

Discussions of identifying specters through their clothing must have arisen from Village gossip following Tituba's confession eleven days earlier. Responding to John Hathorne's queries, she had described the clothes worn by the specters she saw: the man (perhaps the devil) who had appeared to ask her to serve him was tall and white-haired, wearing either "black" or "Searge" clothing, and one of the two Boston women was dressed in "a black Silk hood with a White Silk hood under itt, with top knotts," while the other had "a Searge Coat with a White Cap."[2] No one recorded the ensuing gossip, but it surely focused on how descriptions of clothing could help to reveal the identities of otherwise unknown specters. Martha Corey appeared well aware that people were speculating she might be a witch and that clothes could form a part of the identification. She seemingly hoped to use that potential weapon to her advantage instead of falling victim to it.

The three conversed at some length about the little girl's complaints and witchcraft in general.[3] Putnam and Cheever expressed their concern about "how greatly the name of God and religion and thee church was dishonured" by Martha's being accused, but Corey appeared more interested in stopping the pervasive gossip. Her visitors surely could not think her guilty of witchcraft, she insisted, because "shee had made a profession of christ and rejoyced to go and hear the word of god and the like." Putnam and Cheever responded that "witches had crept into the churches" and that "an out ward profession" was insufficient proof of innocence, but Goody Corey, they reported, "made her profession a cloake to cover all." When Martha indicated that "shee did not thinke that there were any witches," they pronounced themselves "fully satisfied" that Tituba, Good, and Osborne were guilty as charged. Martha then derided the three as "idle sloathfull persons," so that "if they were [witches] wee could not blame the devill of making witches of them." Despite her skepticism about the three suspects, she exclaimed that "the devill was come down amongst us in great rage and that God had forsaken the earth." Perhaps she referred to the Indian war, or perhaps she was contending that Satan had afflicted Ann directly, without the intervention of witches.

Martha Corey probably ended the encounter with her fellow church members believing that she had made at least some progress in refuting the charge that she was a witch. She had forcefully reminded her visitors of her standing as a professed Christian and a member of the Salem Village church, had differentiated herself from the "idle sloathfull" folk already accused, and had exposed what she undoubtedly did think was a "pretty trick"—Ann's explanation for her inability to describe Corey's clothing accurately. But if Martha interpreted the results of the conversation in that way, Edward Putnam and Ezekiel Cheever came away from it feeling very differently. Upon returning to Thomas Putnam's they learned that, as the specter had earlier predicted, it had not afflicted Ann in their absence. To them, the "pretty trick" was obvious: the blinding of Ann had prevented the girl from definitively identifying Martha Corey as her tormentor. That the apparition indeed later returned after dark (making an accurate description of her clothing impossible) only confirmed them in that opinion.

What stimulated Village gossip about Martha Corey being a witch is not revealed in surviving records, but Ann surely did not originate the charge. Quite possibly the very church membership of which Martha was so proud led to her accusation. Three years before her marriage to Henry Rich about 1680, Martha had borne a bastard mulatto son, who lived in the Corey household. Her acceptance into the church, given her personal background and the exclusivity of church membership in Salem Village, must have set tongues to wagging. On at least one other occasion in seventeenth-century New England, the admission to church membership of a woman with a checkered sexual past fomented an uproar among her neighbors. The same could well have happened in the case of Martha Corey, causing speculation about the validity of her reputed adherence to Christianity.[4]

Sunday, March 13, brought Ann new miseries, but not from Martha Corey's specter. Instead, the little girl complained of being afflicted by an apparition she could not positively identify: "I did not know what hir name was then," Ann later deposed, "tho I knew whare she used to sitt in our Meeting house." A witness elaborated: "she saw the apperishtion of apale fast [*sic*] woman that Sat in her granmothers seat." Soon, most likely within twenty-four hours, Ann knew the woman's name: Rebecca Towne Nurse, the seventy-year-old wife of Francis Nurse, a substantial Village yeoman. Goody Nurse belonged to the Salem Town church, although she often attended services in the Village.[5]

Many of Goodwife Nurse's Towne relatives lived in neighboring Topsfield; her natal family had a long-standing dispute with various Putnams over the boundaries of their respective lands and towns. It is not difficult to imagine that Ann had heard about many confrontations between the two extended families, and that Rebecca Nurse's name came easily to her lips once it was suggested to her. But precisely how that occurred became a subject of contention. Nurse's son-in-law John Tarbell later inquired at the Putnam house about how Ann learned the unidentified specter's name. "Who was it that told her that it was goody nurs?" he asked. Tarbell recorded the response: the Putnams' nineteen-year-old maidservant, Mercy Lewis, replied, "it was goody putnam that said it was goody nurse: goody putnam said it was mercy lewes that told her: thus they turned it upone one an other saying it was you & it was you that told her." Regardless of the exact origin, the new apparition now had a name.[6]

On Monday, Martha Corey called at Thomas Putnam's, having been asked to do so—by whom is not recorded.[7] Edward Putnam witnessed the consequences. As soon as Goody Corey entered the house, Ann "fell in to grevious feets of Choking blinding feat and hands twisted in a most grevious maner and told martha Cory to her face that she did it, and emediately hur tonge was dran out of her: mouth and her teeth fasned upon it in a most grevious maner." When at last Ann regained control of her tongue and could speak, she told Martha that "ther is a yellow burd a sucking betwen your fore finger and midel finger I see it." She moved toward the visitor to see the bird more clearly, but Edward saw Corey put her finger on the place Ann had identified "and semed to give a hard rub," at which point Ann could see nothing and was again blinded. To anyone who had heard Tituba's testimony about Sarah Good's spectral yellow bird sucking her in the same spot, the implication was obvious: the two women shared the same animal familiar. The girl furthermore described how Goody Corey's specter had "put her hands upon" Bathshua Pope's face during Sabbath services the previous day, and as Ann demonstrated what she meant "emediately her hands were fasned to her eyes that they Cold not be pulled from them except they should have ben broaken off."

For Martha, worse was yet to come. Ann reported that she saw "a speet at the fier with a man apon it and Goodey Corey you be a turnning of it." At that, Mercy Lewis "toock a stick and struck at" the spectral torture scene, which (Ann reported) first vanished, then quickly reappeared. When Mercy declared that she would strike again, Ann warned her, "do not if you love your self," but Mercy ignored the admonition. She then "Cryed out with a grevious pane in her arme" and Ann disclosed that she had seen Martha Corey's specter hit Lewis "with an Iron rood." The two "gru so bad with panes," Edward recounted, that "we desired goodey Cory to be gone." This time Martha Corey could not have misinterpreted the meaning of the encounter.

The apparition Ann Putnam Jr. described at the hearth would have resonated deeply with anyone who learned of it. Readers of Cotton Mather's *Memorable Providences* would surely recall that in 1688 the eleven-year-old John Goodwin had complained of being "roasted on an invisible Spit, run into his Mouth, and out at his Foot, he lying, and rolling, and groaning." Martha Corey's turning a spectral spit clearly connected her to the tortures experienced by the Goodwin children. But there was also another obvious link: redeemed captives of the Wabanakis had returned with tales of English settlers being "roasted" to death by slow fires. Such stories would carry particular meaning for those who lived, or had lived, on the northeastern frontier, and who had not only heard the tales but could realistically believe themselves in imminent danger of meeting just such a fate.[8]

FRIDAY, AUGUST 11, 1676; FALMOUTH, CASCO BAY, MAINE.
The little girl called Mercy was about three years old, living with her parents and perhaps a young sibling or two, surrounded by her father's

extended family. Her grandfather George Lewis had brought his wife and three children to Maine from England in the mid-1640s; four more children—including her father, Philip—were born in America. On Wednesday, August 9, some Wabanakis had killed a cow belonging to Captain Anthony Brackett. An Indian named Simon, who had been hanging around Captain Brackett's farm for several weeks, said he would find the culprits. Early on Friday morning, Simon returned with the men responsible for the killing. They invaded Brackett's house, took his weapons, and asked him "whether he had rather serve the *Indians*, or be *slain by them*." Faced with that choice, Brackett surrendered, along with his wife and children. But his brother-in-law tried to resist and was killed.[9]

The Indians moved through the area called Back Cove, striking one farm after another on the mainland north of the peninsula on which the town of Falmouth was situated. At Robert Corbin's, they surprised him and his brother-in-law Benjamin Atwell while they were haying in the fields, killing them and capturing their wives and several children. They next slew James Ross and his wife, taking some of their children captive. Two men traveling by canoe managed to warn the town, but the losses of people killed and captured mounted as the day wore on. Mercy's parents escaped with her to an island in the bay, along with their minister George Burroughs and others, but her father's extended family was hard hit. The dead Benjamin Atwell and James Ross were her uncles by marriage, the captured Alice Atwell and the dead Ann Ross her father's sisters. Her paternal grandparents were among those slain. Many of her cousins were killed or captured, including all but one of the children of another of her father's sisters, Mary Lewis Skilling. One more uncle—her father's brother John—and his wife died later in the war.

Altogether, wrote a survivor five days later, eleven men died and twenty-three women and children were killed or captured at Casco on August 11. "We that are alive are forced upon Mr. Andrews his Island to secure our own and the lives of our families we have but little provision and are so few in number that we are not able to bury the dead till more strength come to us," he told his mother-in-law in Boston, pleading for assistance of any sort.[10] The help the refugees received permitted them to leave. Mercy and her parents probably moved temporarily to Salem Town, where her uncle-by-marriage Thomas Skilling died a few months later, possibly from a wound suffered in the attack. By 1683, they had returned to rebuild their lives in Casco Bay. She was then ten years old.[11]

CHART I

The Lewis Family in Two Wars

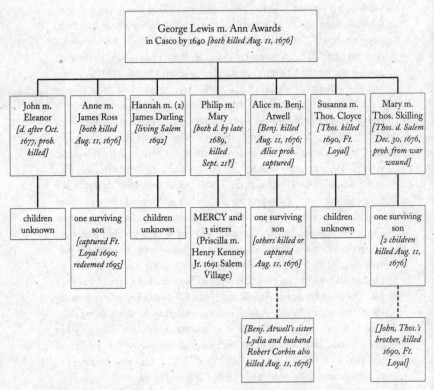

George Lewis m. Ann Awards
in Casco by 1640 [both killed Aug. 11, 1676]

John m. Eleanor [d. after Oct. 1677, prob. killed]	Anne m. James Ross [both killed Aug. 11, 1676]	Hannah m. (2) James Darling [living Salem 1692]	Philip m. Mary [both d. by late 1689, killed Sept. 21?]	Alice m. Benj. Atwell [Benj. killed Aug. 11, 1676; Alice prob. captured]	Susanna m. Thos. Cloyce [Thos. killed 1690, Ft. Loyal]	Mary m. Thos. Skilling [Thos. d. Salem Dec. 30, 1676, prob. from war wound]
children unknown	one surviving son [captured Ft. Loyal 1690; redeemed 1695]	children unknown	MERCY and 3 sisters (Priscilla m. Henry Kenney Jr. 1691 Salem Village)	one surviving son [others killed or captured Aug. 11, 1676]	children unknown	one surviving son [2 children killed Aug. 11, 1676]
				[Benj. Atwell's sister Lydia and husband Robert Corbin also killed Aug. 11, 1676]		[John, Thos.'s brother, killed 1690, Ft. Loyal]

Source: Primarily *GDMNH*, augmented by information from *York Deeds* and *MHGR*

Martha Corey's departure that Monday did not end Mercy Lewis's torments. Mercy told those present that "she saw shadows like women but Cold not disarn [w]ho they were." She too began to have fits: "she was Choked and blinded her neck twicted her teeth and mouth shut," Edward Putnam reported, noting that it took two or three men to hold her down. Later that evening, Mercy was "drawn toward the fier by unseen hands as she sat in a Chare," even though two men were holding on to it. Edward himself stepped between the chair and the fire "and lifted with my stringht together with the other two and all little enuf to prevent her from going in to the fier with her feat formost." Not until eleven o'clock that night did Mercy's fits cease.

Eventually, Mercy dated the start of her own bewitchment from Martha Corey's arrival at Thomas Putnam's on March 14.[12]

That Monday, Abigail Williams, too, declared that Goody Corey was afflicting her, hauling her "to & fro" and pinching her. She also reiterated Ann's earlier accusation of Elizabeth Proctor. The next day, Abigail named Rebecca Nurse, and Betty Hubbard joined the chorus against Martha Corey. By the sixteenth of March, in short, four suffering accusers had become five, and five accused witches seven. Moreover, the afflicted—with the exception of the most recent recruit, Mercy Lewis, who had not yet named anyone—concurred on the identity of those who were causing their torments. Residents of the Village must have been stunned by the extent of the devil's assault on them.[13]

The repeated fits thoroughly disrupted daily household routines. Older girls and teenagers performed essential domestic labor as assistants to the female heads of their families—in these cases, a mother, a mistress, and aunts. Now their labor was either unreliable or unavailable. The maidservant Mercy Lewis had previously been "atending" the child Ann, but now she too was numbered among the afflicted. A maidservant who was being inexorably drawn into the fireplace or a niece who was being sporadically hauled "to & fro" could not make her customary contribution to the necessary work of the family. Moreover, curious and concerned neighbors—like the two anonymous men who held Mercy Lewis's chair away from the fire on the evening of March 14—stopped by in large numbers to witness the extraordinary events and to assist in caring for the sufferers. The neighbors' constant presence would likewise have proved a bar to the resumption of quotidian life.[14]

Within a short period of time, the young women became the focal points around which all other members of the households revolved. That alone was extraordinary. Usually, girls—whether daughters, nieces, or servants—resided at or near the bottom of the familial hierarchy, with brothers, mothers, and ultimately fathers ranked above them. Subordinates in seventeenth-century society commonly served their superiors, and so too had the "afflicted girls" of Salem Village. But now others, including both male and female neighbors and familial superiors, were serving *them.* Most notably, the male heads of their households and other adult men of their families gave them hours of concentrated attention, probably for the first time in their lives. Notes taken at the time by Edward Putnam later provided the court with a detailed description of his niece Ann's and Mercy Lewis's behavior in the presence of Martha Corey on March 14. Similarly, for months the Reverend Samuel Parris carefully observed the actions of his niece Abigail Williams, keeping precise track of her fits and accusations.[15]

Thus the Putnam, Parris, and Griggs households were turned upside down during that third week of March 1691/2. Girls having fits, adult men scrutinizing their every move, a myriad of bystanders at all hours of the day and night, and little or no assistance available: no wonder, then, that Ann Carr Putnam reported that by Friday, March 18, she was "wearied out in helping to tend my poor afflected Child and Maid." When she lay down in the middle of that afternoon "to take a little Rest," Ann Sr. was quickly "all-most prest and Choaked to death," and, she later recalled, "had it not been for the mircy of a gratious God and the help of those that ware with me: I could not have lived many moments." Those who were present—presumably, her neighbors—witnessed Ann Sr.'s torments at the hands of what she now recognized as Martha Corey's specter. Goody Corey, she recounted, "fell upon me . . . with dreadfull tortors and hellish temtations," bringing her "a little Red book in hir hand and a black pen urging me vehemently to writ in her book." Not only did Martha Corey then return "severall times" later that day, but the apparition also reappeared on Saturday the nineteenth, as did that of Rebecca Nurse, "and they both did tortor: me agrate many times . . . because I would not yeald to their Hellish temtations."[16]

Goody Putnam thereby became the first to follow Tituba in describing the devil's book—an object that, in many guises, was eventually to appear in numerous statements by both accusers and confessors. The afflicted later referred repeatedly to being tempted to write their names in Satan's book, while confessors typically described actually having done so. More than two decades earlier Elizabeth Knapp had been the first New Englander to indicate that the diabolic covenant was embodied in a book rather than merely a piece of paper. Samuel Willard's account of her afflictions, widely available in published form after 1684 in Increase Mather's *Remarkable Providences,* almost certainly influenced the statements offered eight years later during the witchcraft outbreak. The historian Jane Kamensky has cogently argued that the obsession with books (especially small, easily concealed ones) evident in the Salem records resulted from an explosion in the availability of such volumes after the mid-1680s. After decades in which the sole Bay Colony press published nothing but sermons and official documents, not only were several printers in Massachusetts and the middle colonies now producing almanacs and primers, but increasing numbers of booksellers were also importing books on such topics as astrology and fortune-telling. Because all sorts of occult practices were linked to the devil, clergymen and magistrates could readily envision the dangers potentially lurking in the pages of those volumes. Such concerns induced them to ask the leading questions of many confessors that elicited concurring responses, although Ann Sr.'s vision of the "little Red book" appears to have been her own.[17]

Just as the addition of Betty Hubbard to the ranks of the original sufferers helped to instigate the first formal complaints, so Ann Carr Putnam's torments convinced Village men to take further legal action. Ann Jr. had been accusing Goody Corey for well over a week, Abigail Williams for five days, and Betty Hubbard for three, without any complaint being filed. But on Saturday, March 19, the day after Goody Putnam initially complained of Corey's specter, Edward Putnam and Henry Kenney (a relative by marriage of Mercy Lewis) complained to Hathorne and Corwin against Martha Corey "for suspition of haveing Comitted sundry acts of Witchcraft and thereby donne much hurt and injury unto the Bodys" of the two Ann Putnams, Lewis, Williams, and Hubbard. The justices issued a warrant ordering that Goody Corey be brought in for questioning on Monday, March 21.[18]

That same Saturday there arrived in Salem Village its former pastor, the Reverend Deodat Lawson. Lawson, who was living in Boston in 1692, later recalled that reports of the "Very Sore and Grievous Affliction[s]" in his one-time parish had deeply concerned him. Accordingly, he "frequently consulted with them and fervently (by Divine Assistance) prayed for them," then decided to go to the village to see for himself the "very amazing, and deplorable" condition of the afflicted.[19]

Lawson took lodgings at Nathaniel Ingersoll's inn, centrally located between the meetinghouse and the parsonage. The first afflicted person he encountered was Mary Walcott—daughter of Jonathan Walcott, captain of the local militia—who was not yet numbered among the formal complainants. The seventeen-year-old came to Ingersoll's to speak to Lawson, presumably to welcome him back to the Village. Claiming to have been bitten by a specter during their conversation, she showed him the bite marks on her wrist. Following that unsettling experience, Lawson called on his successor, Samuel Parris. In his presence Abigail Williams had what he described as a "grievous fit." The girl, Lawson recounted, "was at first hurryed with Violence to and fro in the room," evading another visitor's attempts to hold on to her and "sometimes makeing as if she would fly, stretching up her arms as high as she could, and crying, 'Whish, Whish, Whish!' several times." Abigail saw Goody Nurse's specter in the room, revealing that Nurse was asking her to sign the devil's book. She also ran near the fire, beginning "to throw Fire Brands, about the house," while others present informed Lawson that in other fits she, like Mercy Lewis, "had attempted to go into the Fire."[20]

Lawson, Parris, and any others present at the parsonage during Abigail's fit must have been struck by the congruence of her behavior and that of one of the Lowestoft afflicted in 1662 and of the Goodwin children in Boston in 1688. The Lowestoft girl had run around the house saying "hush, hush," and the Goodwins had waved their arms "like the Wings of a Bird" and had appeared to move "with an incredible Swiftness through the air." Moreover, like Mercy Lewis and Abigail Williams, Martha Goodwin too had earlier been inexorably drawn toward the fire with so much "violence," Cotton Mather wrote, that one or two people could hardly prevent her from throwing herself in. Later commentators, most notably Thomas Hutchinson, would interpret such similarities as providing evidence of fraud, but in 1692, as Hutchinson later observed, the "conformity" of the behavior of the Goodwin and Lowestoft afflicted "was urged in confirmation of the truth of both; the Old England demons and the New being so much alike." One does not have to accept Hutchinson's conclusion to recognize that Mercy's and Abigail's behavior showed their familiarity with the earlier bewitchment stories. Consciously or unconsciously, the Salem Village afflicted had incorporated the previously recorded behaviors into their own repertoires.[21]

The next day, the Reverend Mr. Lawson presided at Sabbath services attended by Martha Corey and the currently afflicted persons. His recollections of the day added two more names to those sufferers already identified: Bathshua Pope and Sarah Vibber (or Bibber). Mistress Pope, the Village woman said by Ann Jr. to have been attacked by Goody Corey's specter in church the previous week, was probably in her late thirties, but little is known about her other than the high status indicated by her title. Though afflicted, she is not listed as a sufferer in any surviving legal complaint. Sarah Vibber, approximately thirty-six, must have been considerably poorer. She and her husband, John, who was most likely an immigrant from the Channel Islands, did not own land of their own but instead lived in other people's houses in the neighboring town of Wenham.[22]

Through her father's family Mary Walcott, afflicted during her talk with Lawson on Saturday, was the great-niece of Nathaniel Ingersoll. Her mother, Mary Sibley Walcott, the sister-in-law of the woman who instigated the making of the witchcake, had died in 1683; her stepmother after 1685 was Thomas Putnam's sister, Deliverance. Thus she and Ann Jr. were stepcousins. Mary's oldest brother, John, had served as a militia sergeant in the war on the Maine frontier in 1689 and subsequently led a small contingent of Village volunteers northeastward in May 1690, but her family's roots in Maine went deeper than that. Another great-uncle (Nathaniel's older brother), George Ingersoll, lived at Casco Bay for many years and would have known members of Mercy Lewis's natal family well. He relocated to Salem late in 1675, returned to Casco in the 1680s, but then moved his family back to Salem after September 1689 and was still living there in 1692. Although Mary had not herself lived in Maine, she must have heard many stories of the frontier and the Indian war from her brother and her Ingersoll relatives.[23]

On Sunday, March 20, Lawson declared, the "several Sore Fits" the afflicted suffered during the morning service "did something interrupt me in my First Prayer; being so unusual." Following the singing of the first psalm, Abigail Williams boldly demanded, "Now stand up, and Name your Text," commenting after the clergyman did so that "It is a long Text." Mistress Pope, too, interjected her opinions into the service, remarking aloud with respect to the sermon, "Now there is enough of that." During that sermon, Abigail cried out that she saw Goody Corey sitting "on the Beam suckling her Yellow bird betwixt her fingers"—thus indicating that she was well acquainted with the details of Ann Jr.'s vision of Martha six days earlier—and Ann herself remarked that she saw a yellow bird sitting on Lawson's hat as it hung beside the pulpit, but, he noted with relief, "those that were by, restrained her from speaking loud about it." Matters evidently went more smoothly during the afternoon service, although Abigail again took the lead, declaring contemptuously, "I know no Doctrine you had, If you did name one, I have forgot it."[24]

The disruptions Lawson described (with what must have been considerable understatement) were indeed "unusual," to put it mildly. Normally the congregations in Puritan meetinghouses sat quietly and respectfully, often taking notes on the sermons for later study and contemplation. Only during periods of religious ferment, such as the Antinomian crisis of 1636–1637 or Quaker missionizing in the 1660s, had New England clergymen ever been so directly challenged in their pulpits. The afflicted people's behavior on Sunday, March 20, mimicked their actions during the examinations held in the same meetinghouse almost three weeks earlier. Then their antics nominally supported authority (for the magistrates relied on them to help reveal the guilt of the accused), but on both occasions they in reality turned gender and age hierarchies upside down. Women, especially young women, were not expected to speak unbidden in either court or church—indeed, in the latter, they were often not expected to speak at all. By their intrusions into the normal ordering of Sunday services as well as by their disruptions in the makeshift courtroom, they signaled that reversals in Village life during the witchcraft crisis would not remain confined to individual households, but would extend to public spaces as well.[25]

The afflicted people were active that Sunday, but the witches' specters were not. Ann Carr Putnam later attested that she "had agrat deal of Respitt between my fitts" on March 20. And although the apparition of Rebecca Nurse made initial appearances to Betty Hubbard and Mary Walcott, both declared that Nurse's specter did not hurt them. The witches, then, seemingly observed that Sabbath, awaiting Martha Corey's examination the following day.[26]

Interpreting the Afflicted Girls' Depositions

The chronology in the preceding section (and that which will follow in the rest of this book) was developed in part by assuming the accuracy of dates specified in depositions offered by the afflicted girls weeks or months after the events in question. For example, Betty Hubbard swore on August 4 that the specter of Martha Corey had afflicted her on March 15. An obvious question arises: how could Betty have recalled the date with such specificity? The inquiry becomes even more pressing if one contemplates four separate depositions submitted by Abigail Williams on May 31. On the "14.20.21.&23 dayes" of March and the "12.13.& 14 dayes" of April, she attested, Martha Corey's specter afflicted her. On the "15.16.19.20.21.23.31 dayes" of March, April 13, and the "4th & 29" of May, she was attacked by Rebecca Nurse's specter. And on the "14.21.& 29" days of March and the "2.&.13" days of April, she was tortured by the apparition of Elizabeth Proctor, whereas "divers times" in April but especially on the "4.6.11.13 dayes" John Proctor was her tormentor.[27]

Since it is extraordinarily unlikely that a child like Abigail could remember such details and differentiate them so precisely, one possibility is that she was making it all up on the spot. Yet sometimes other evidence confirms the dates she and others gave; for instance, Deodat Lawson's narrative indicates that Abigail complained of Goody Corey on March 20, just as her May deposition asserted. Moreover, the afflicted girls' adult relatives often submitted depositions supporting their statements and the details of timing therein.[28]

Therefore another explanation is needed. I have concluded that exact dates in retrospective depositions (not all of which contain such information) reflect the existence of now-lost notes taken by adult observers of the afflicted, and that accordingly such dates can be trusted for the purposes of creating a chronology of the crisis. In earlier instances of affliction, adults, especially clergymen, took careful notes on the behavior of tormented young people. Such records formed the basis of Samuel Willard's detailed account of Elizabeth Knapp and Cotton Mather's narrative of the Goodwin children. Samuel Parris (and the senior Putnams, along with perhaps a few others) must have similarly recorded the details of the behavior of the young people in their households. Indeed, one page of Parris's notes survives; covering April 4 through April 12, it is included in the evidence against John Proctor. For April 12 in particular, the notes give a minute-by-minute account of events as Abigail Williams, Mary Walcott, and John Indian had fits in which they accused the Proctors' specters of afflicting them.[29]

Not all of the afflicted girls' statements can be trusted in the matter of timing, however. For example, at the examination of Dorcas Hoar on May 2, Abigail Williams exclaimed that "this is the woman that she saw first before Tituba Indian or any else," a declaration unsupported by other evidence (and, tellingly, never included in a sworn deposition). Likewise, on June 30 Ann Jr. swore that she had been afflicted since early March by the specter of Sarah Wilds. Again, that allegation is not reflected in documents created in March. Still other statements, especially those made by afflicted teenagers from households without supportive adults (for example, servants who accused their masters), lack specificity altogether: "severall times sence the later end of June," "Sometime in July," and so forth. But the very vagueness of such declarations, made in the near-certain absence of any written record, helps to underscore the likely accuracy of precise dates found in other documents.[30]

THE EXAMINATION OF MARTHA COREY

At noon on Monday, March 21, everyone once again returned to the Salem Village meetinghouse. The building was "Thronged with Spectators," Deodat Lawson remarked, "many hundred" in all. Among the crowd were "most" of the afflicted females. Proceedings began with "a very pertinent and pathetic Prayer" offered by the Reverend Nicholas Noyes, pastor of the Salem Town church. Martha Corey too asked to pray, "sundry times," but John Hathorne told her, "We do not send for you to go to prayer." The magistrates enlisted Samuel Parris to take notes, presumably because Ezekiel Cheever, the scribe at the first examinations, would participate in the hearing by reporting on his encounter with Goody Corey nine days earlier.[31]

"You are now in the hands of Authority," Hathorne began portentously.[32] "Tell me now why you hurt these persons." Goodwife Corey responded with an assertion of innocence: "I never had to do with Witchcraft since I was born. I am a Gospell Woman." Asked her reaction to the complaints of the afflicted, she replied obliquely, "The Lord open the eyes of the Magistrates & Ministers: the Lord show his power to discover the guilty."

The examining magistrate quickly focused on her conversation with Edward Putnam and Ezekiel Cheever, who interjected a warning "not [to] begin with a lye." Why had she asked "if the child told what cloths you wore"? Hathorne wanted to know. Goody Corey proved unable to supply a satisfactory answer. First she said that Cheever, not she, had introduced the subject, then that her husband had informed her that "the children told what cloaths the other wore." But Cheever retorted that she spoke "falsly" and Giles denied having discussed the subject with her. Hathorne berated her: "You dare thus to lye in all this assembly You are now before Authority. I expect the truth . . . Speak now & tell who told you." Finally, Martha admitted to having learned about gossip on the subject. "I had heard speech that the children said I troubled them & I thought that they might come to examine," she ventured, but identified no one source of information. Hathorne, dissatisfied, continued to press for further details, until Abigail Williams altered the course of the examination by exclaiming, "There is a black man whispering in her ear," an observation immediately joined by Mary Walcott.

Thus appeared for the first time at an examination a figure that would become nearly ubiquitous in subsequent Salem records, the spectral "black man," who was either the devil or his emissary. Historians have tended to equate this "black man" with the man wearing black or serge clothing described by Tituba in her confession, but only one of the other thirty-five people who saw the "black man" mentioned his clothes.[33] More likely than a reference to wearing apparel is that the adjective alluded to the specter's dark or swarthy complexion—indeed, that the specter the witnesses envisioned resembled an Indian. On numerous occasions seventeenth-century colonists employed the word "black" to mean "Indian," as when in fall 1689 a militia troop in Maine was described as comprising "Both White & Blacke" soldiers, or when a witness in the Hartford witchcraft cases of 1662 testified that he had seen an accused woman in the woods with "two black creatures like two Indians but taller." Recall, too, Sarah Osborne's earlier nightmarish encounter with "a thing like an indian all black" she described during her examination on March 1. Cotton Mather made the connection explicit. Recording in *Wonders of the Invisible World* that confessing witches called

Satan "the *Black Man*," he added, "they generally say he resembles an *Indian*."[34]

The association among Indians, black men, and the devil would have been unremarkable to anyone in the Salem Village meetinghouse. English settlers everywhere on the continent had long regarded North America's indigenous residents as devil worshippers and had viewed their shamans as witches. Puritan New Englanders, believing themselves a people chosen by God to bring his word to a previously heathen land, were particularly inclined to see themselves as antagonists of the "devilish" Indians. In March 1692, people beset by an actual Wabanaki menace immediately to the north and east would have regarded as shocking but unexceptional a concurrent spectral attack featuring an instigator of a local witch conspiracy who looked like a Wabanaki. As John McWilliams has observed, the male Indian's "spectral presence in Salem village and to the north was a sure sign of the devil's impending war against New England." Abigail Williams's words linked invisible and visible worlds, implying the existence of an alliance between Satan and the Wabanakis. Thus the frequent references to the "black man" by confessors and the afflicted establish a crucial connection between the witchcraft crisis and the Indian wars.[35]

Abigail's observation of the "black man" led Hathorne to ask what the man had said.[36] After Corey responded that she had heard nothing, all the afflicted suffered "Extream agony." The magistrate began urging Corey to confess, while she insisted that "we must not beleive distracted persons." A witness (whose written testimony has not survived) then reported that Corey had remarked that "the girl" and "the Devil could not stand before" her. Corey denied having said as much, but "3 or 4 Sober witnesses confirm'd it." "What can I do many rise up against me?" Martha cried. Hathorne had only one answer: "Why confess." Goody Corey replied that she would indeed confess if she was guilty, but she was not.

Hathorne then moved on to the details of the children's testimony: with what instrument had she struck Mercy Lewis during the spectral roasting scene? what bird were they describing? and did she think the children bewitched? "They may [be] for ought I know," Martha responded. "I have no hand in it." She knew nothing of a bird or of how Mercy had been hurt. Why did she try to prevent her husband Giles from attending the examinations on March 1? Hathorne inquired. A member of the audience answered for her: "she would not have them help to find out witches." The magistrate accused her of regarding the afflictions as "a laughing matter." After she rejected his characterization, Parris recorded in the transcript, "Severall prove it." Desperate, Martha wailed, "Ye are all against me & I cannot help it."

The focus then shifted from question-and-answer to action-and-response as the torments of the afflicted began to take over the examination. "When she bit her lip severall of the afflicted were bitten," Parris noted, and "when her hands were at liberty the afflicted persons were pincht." The Reverend Mr. Noyes observed aloud, "she practiseth Witchcraft in the congregation there is no need of images." According to Deodat Lawson, the afflicted "produced the Marks [of the bites and pinches] before the Magistrates, Ministers, and others." When Martha Corey leaned against the minister's seat, "being the Barr at which she stood," the afflictions intensified. Bathshua Pope, complaining "of grievous torment in her Bowels as if they were torn out," hit Goody Corey on the head with her shoe. If Martha Corey shuffled her feet, the afflicted "stamped fearfully," and, Lawson noted, they "asked her why she did not go to the company of witches which were before the Meeting house mustering? Did she not hear the Drum beat?" The afflicted declared that "23 or 24" witches were "in Armes" outside the building.[37]

In the midst of what must have been utter chaos, Hathorne pressed even harder: "Did you not say you would open our eyes why do you not?" "Were you to serve the Devil ten years tell how many?" "What book is that you would have these children write in?" Martha's primary response to such questions, recorded Parris, was laughter. Surely she was hysterical rather than scornful. The examination ended with Hathorne questioning Corey about the nature of the Trinity, and finally with a "triall" in which "her hands being eased by them that held them on purpose," the afflicted "immediately" suffered fits "& the standers by said she was squeezing her fingers." "Do not you see these children & women are rational & sober as their neighbours when your hands are fastened?" Hathorne thundered. When the marshal quickly observed, "she hath bit her lip," the afflicted fell into "an uproar." Hathorne again demanded that Goody Corey confess to having hurt them. When she would not, he halted the proceedings, ordering her jailed in Salem Town. "After she was in Custody," Lawson reported, her specter no longer appeared to torture the afflicted.[38]

Justice Hathorne clearly found the examination of Martha Corey frustrating, for it was far less successful than his first set of interrogations. The accused resolutely refused to admit her guilt despite being confronted with the testimony of numerous witnesses and with what seemed to be incontrovertible evidence of her practice of witchcraft in front of everyone. Hathorne's failure to elicit a confession led to events in the meetinghouse-courtroom being controlled by the antics of the afflicted. Although the session began as a legal examination he was orchestrating, it ended in turmoil when one of the afflicted hit Goody Corey on the head with a shoe and they all stamped their feet noisily in unison. Thus the magistrates' failure to follow Richard Bernard's advice about conducting examinations of accused and accuser separately and in private had significant consequences that left them struggling to maintain a proper decorum.

The report of two dozen armed witches "mustering" to a "Drum beat" outside the meetinghouse summoned up images of invisible malevolent militias rising to do battle against God's people in concert with the spectral Indian seen advising Martha Corey. Salem Village, its residents would have concluded by late that afternoon, surely lay in the front lines of a battle to the death against the forces of evil in both the visible and invisible worlds.

"A WOMAN OF YOUR PROFESSION"

Early the next morning (March 22), the apparition of Rebecca Nurse—wearing, reasonably enough for that time of day, "hir shift" and perhaps her nightcap—came once again to Ann Carr Putnam, also bringing "a litle Red book" for Ann to sign and, Ann disclosed, threatening "to tare my soule out of my body" if Ann would not comply with her request for a signature. For nearly two hours Goody Putnam carried on a heated conversation with Goody Nurse's specter, during which they argued over "severall places of scripture" Ann cited. Although the argument ended, the tortures continued most of the day.[39]

That same Tuesday, a small delegation called on Rebecca Nurse at her home.[40] Daniel Andrew, his brother- and sister-in-law Israel and Elizabeth Hathorne Porter, and Peter Cloyce (a member of the Salem Village church and Rebecca's brother-in-law) had been asked to speak to Goody Nurse, "to tell her that several of the Aflicted persons mentioned her." They found her ill, but nevertheless she "blest god," because she had "more of his presents in this sickens then sometime shee have had." The group later reported that "of her owne Acord" Rebecca started to discuss the spectral afflictions, especially those in the Parris household, remarking how she "was greved for them though shee had not been to see them." She was concerned for her own health, she explained, because she had occasionally had fits in the past, and "people said it was Awfull to: behold." Even though she had not visited the afflicted, "she pittied them with: all her harte: and went to god for them."

Goody Nurse then remarked that she thought that some of the accused "wear as Innocent as shee was"; after "much to this purpos" the visitors finally told her "we heard that shee was spoken of allsoe." She "sate still awhille being as it wear Amazed," they reported, and said "if it be soe the will of the

Lord be done." Asserting her innocence, she mused, "what sine hath god found out in me unrepented of that he should Lay such an Affliction upon me In my old Age." The visitors concluded their account with the observation that—unlike Martha Corey in similar circumstances—"we could not decern that shee knewe what we came for before we tould her."

The next day, Deodat Lawson called "on purpose" to see the "very sober and pious" Ann Carr Putnam. He found her lying in bed recovering from a fit, and at her and her husband's request he prayed with her. But she soon had another fit, eventually starting "to Converse personally" with Goody Nurse. "Are you not ashamed, a Woman of your Profession, to afflict a poor Creature so?" Ann asked. Lawson recorded that she first "seemed to dispute with the Apparition about a particular Text of Scripture," then appeared to be seeking a text that would force the specter to depart. Finally, she blurted out, "It is the third Chapter of the Revelations." Reluctant to employ a Biblical text as a charm, Lawson at first hesitated to read the passage, but then he decided "I might do it this once for an Experiment." Sure enough, before he had finished reading the first verse, the fit ended. Thomas and "the Spectators" then informed Lawson that "she had often been so relieved by reading Texts that she named."[41]

Sometime that same March 23, Deacon Edward Putnam and his cousin Jonathan Putnam filed a formal complaint against Rebecca Nurse for having afflicted Ann Carr Putnam, her daughter, and Abigail Williams. They also complained separately against Dorcas Good, the four- or five-year-old daughter of the jailed Sarah Good. Ann Jr. had first named Dorcas as her afflicter nearly three weeks earlier, but no action was taken against the little girl at that time. Now, though, another complainant had recently been added: two days before, Mary Walcott declared that Dorcas had "com to me and bit me and pinch me." The affliction of a teenager once more led adults to take legal steps that a child's lone accusation did not elicit. Dorcas and Goody Nurse were both arrested and held at Ingersoll's inn until their examinations.[42]

On Thursday, March 24, at 10 a.m. Villagers again gathered in large numbers at the meetinghouse to listen to the interrogation of accused witches, and their pastor again took notes.[43] The Reverend John Hale began the proceedings with a prayer. Instead of starting with questions to the examinee, as he previously had, John Hathorne immediately turned to the younger Ann Putnam and to Abigail Williams to ask if Rebecca Nurse had tormented them. Before the multitude, Ann Jr. had "a grievous fit," and both children confirmed their accusations of the old woman. Henry Kenney broke in with the unsolicited comment that since Nurse had entered the meetinghouse "he was seizd twise with an amaz'd condition." Hathorne next confronted Goody Nurse with Ann Carr Putnam, "who accuseth you by credible information," and with a formal statement by Edward Putnam about her spectral attacks on Ann Jr. Rebecca Nurse insisted, "I am innocent & clear," adding that she had been ill and unable to leave her house for over a week.

But then Goody Putnam cried out, "Did you not bring the Black man with you, did you not bid me tempt God & dye?" Nurse, saying, "Oh Lord help me," spread her hands, at which "the afflicted were greviously vexed," recorded Samuel Parris in the official transcript. Hathorne called Goody Nurse's attention to the seeming consequences of her movements, and Mary Walcott and Betty Hubbard "both openly accused her of hurting them." The age of the afflicted again entered into Hathorne's thinking: "here are these 2 grown persons now accuse you," he told Goody Nurse. How do you respond? How can you "stand with dry eyes" while witnessing such torments? Under pressure, Rebecca continued to assert her innocence.

The afflicted, though, declared that Nurse was surrounded by spectral birds and that "the Black Man" was whispering to her during the examination, so "she could not hear what the Magistrates said unto her." Hathorne ruminated, "What uncertainty there may be in apparitions I know not, yet this with me strikes hard upon you that you are at this very present charged with familiar spirits." Calling for "an upright answer," he inquired, "have you any familiarity with these spirits?" Goody Nurse replied, "none but with God alone," and Hathorne changed the topic. Referring to "an odd discourse" about her illness "in the mouths of many," he asked about wounds; she said she had none. Neither had she "been led aside by temptations" to witchcraft, nor had she had "visible appearances more than what is common in nature." How "sad" it was, the magistrate then observed, that two church members like herself and Goody Corey had been accused of such an offense. At that Bathshua Pope cried, "a sad thing sure enough," and (Parris noted) "many more fell into lamentable fits."

Perhaps it was at that moment that Ann Carr Putnam endured "a grievous fit . . . to the very great Impairing of her strength, and wasting of her spirits, insomuch as she could hardly move hand, or foot." Her husband asked permission to carry her out of the meetinghouse and, she later remembered, as soon as she emerged from the building "it pleased Allmighty God for his free grace and mircy sake to deliver me out of the paws of thos Roaring lions: and jaws of those tareing bears." For the next two months she suffered no more fits. The meetinghouse itself had thus become Satan's territory; only by leaving it could she obtain relief from her suffering.

Hathorne pressed on, asking Rebecca Nurse for an opinion of the sufferers' torments: were they "voluntary or involuntary"? The old woman tried to evade the question, and might not have even understood it clearly (or so Parris thought), though she finally admitted, "I do not think these suffer against their wills." But she also added—perhaps contradictorily—that she did think them "bewicht." Those answers would seem to have given the magistrate an opening to push her further on characterizing the afflictions, but Parris recorded no follow-up questions. (He did, however, note at the end of the transcript that he had omitted "many things" because of "g[r]eat noyses by the afflicted & many speakers.") Instead, Hathorne asked Goody Nurse to explain why her movements were mimicked by the afflicted, who thereby seemingly endured "violent fits of torture." Receiving no satisfactory answer, he directed Parris to read "what he had in characters taken from Mr. Tho: Putmans wife in her fitts," inquiring, "What do you think of this?" "I cannot help it," Rebecca Nurse replied, "the Devil may appear in my shape." With that, the examination came to a close, and she was sent to jail in Salem Town.

There is no extant record of Dorcas Good's examination, which followed Goody Nurse's, but Deodat Lawson reported that the magistrates and clergymen present "Unanimously" informed him "that when this Child did but cast its eye upon the afflicted persons, they were tormented, and they held her Head, and yet so many as her eye could fix upon were afflicted." Moreover, the tortured Villagers complained that she had bitten them, "and produced marks of a small set of teeth." Later in the week, Hathorne and Corwin (accompanied by Lawson and the Reverend John Higginson of Salem Town) went to the jailer's house to question Dorcas further in a calmer atmosphere. She told them that her mother had given her "a little Snake" that sucked on the lowest joint of her forefinger, and there "they Observed a deep Red Spot," a sign of regular contact with her animal familiar. She too was ordered jailed.[44]

Villagers who attended the public examinations of Rebecca Nurse and Dorcas Good subsequently told Deodat Lawson that "the whole assembly was struck with consternation, and they were afraid, that those that sate next to them, were under the influence of Witchcraft." So pervasive was the devil's influence in Salem Village that its residents felt sure of no one. When church members like Martha Corey and Rebecca Nurse and a little child like Dorcas Good could fall into the devil's snare, who was safe from his wiles? Giles Corey surely cemented those fears when he came forward that same March 24 with new evidence against his wife. He deposed that the previous Saturday, after the formal complaint had been filed against Martha, he had strangely been prevented from praying in his usual manner. And he reported that "my wife hath ben wont to sitt up after I went to bed, & I have perceived her to kneel down to the harth, as if she were at prayer, but heard nothing." Perhaps, he implied, she prayed not to God, but to Satan, and her diabolic influence had stopped his own attempt to communicate with the divinity. Information about his testimony must have spread quickly through the Village.[45]

The court records preserve only brief snatches of the many Village conversations during the next few days. On the morning after Goody Nurse's examination, two yeomen encountered each other near a neighbor's house. One "askt how the folks did at the village"; the other replied, "he heard they were very bad last night but he had heard nothing this morning." Three days later at Nathaniel Ingersoll's, two young men (and possibly more) were "discoursing concerning the examyning of sewerall persons suspected for wiches," with Goody Ingersoll and "some of the afflicted persons." One of the men remarked that "I hard that goody procter was to be examyned to morrow to which goody Ingarsoll replyed she did not beleve it for she heard nothing of it." Joan Ingersoll's gossip network was better informed than the young man's; although both Ann Jr. and Abigail Williams had accused Elizabeth Proctor, no formal complaint had yet been issued against her.[46]

As residents talked, Satan's reach was expanding beyond Village boundaries. In Salem Town on March 25, Betty Parris—sent by her father to the home of a friend, Stephen Sewall, in hopes that a change of scene might ease her torments—again saw "the great Black Man," who promised her that if she would serve him, "she should have whatsoever she desired, and go to a Golden City." Stephen's wife assured the girl that "it was the Divel, and he was a Lyar from the Beginning, and bid her tell him so, if he came again." Betty, dutiful once more, reported to her hostess that she did just that. And in nearby Ipswich members of the Fuller family became convinced on March 23 or 24 that Rachel Hatfield Clinton, an impoverished and embittered neighbor they had long thought was a witch, had instigated the sudden collapse of a servant girl. After Rachel walked past a Fuller household en route to confront various other family members about "what Lies . . . we raisd of hur," the girl fell down as though "Ded," remaining without "any Apperance of Life" for more than three hours. Convinced that Rachel's malefice had caused the strange occurrence, on March 29 they complained formally against her "on grounded Suspision of witchcraft." She too was ordered held for further legal proceedings.[47]

TWO SERMONS AND A DIABOLIC SACRAMENT

On Thursday, March 24, a regular lecture day in Salem Village, Samuel Parris ceded his pulpit to his predecessor, Deodat Lawson. A few months later, Lawson published an expanded version of his sermon, "Christ's Fidelity the only Shield against Satans Malignity," in an edition dedicated to the examining magistrates and the ministers of the Salem Town church, Nicholas Noyes and John Higginson. A group of other clergymen, including Increase and Cotton Mather and Samuel Willard, signed a preface recommending the "Weighty, profitable, and Seasonable Truths" contained in the sermon. Thus Lawson's words can be taken as representing the views of many other ministers at this early stage of the crisis.[48]

Lawson began the printed text as he most likely began the sermon, with a brief address aimed specifically at the Village congregation. God had singled them out "by giving liberty to Satan, to range and rage amongst you," he declared. Most "astonishing" was the involvement of people they had believed to be "real members of His Mystical body" but who now had been represented as Satan's "Instruments . . . against their Friends and Neighbors." He prayed that the community would be delivered from "the pernicious consequences of Satan's malicious Operations." In particular, he commended Samuel Parris to their "Spiritual sympathy"; the pastor needed their assistance, given the "awful circumstances" in his own household.[49]

The sermon itself focused on Satan as "the Fountain of malice." Because the devil was an angel, though a fallen one, he had powers far beyond those of any "meer mortal," and he employed those powers to attack humans' souls and bodies. He targeted people's minds, creating "strange and frightful Representations to the Fancy, or Imagination, and by violent Tortures of the body, often threatning to extinguish life." Members of the congregation had around them "sundry Examples" of Satan's "Lower Operations," Lawson pointed out. "And whosoever, hath carefully observed these things, must needs be Convinced, that the Motions of the Persons Afflicted . . . are the meer effects of Diabolical Malice and Operations, and that it cannot rationally be imagined, to proceed from any other cause whatsoever." Lawson did not doubt that during that fourth week of March he had witnessed the devil's handiwork, and he believed that no one else should doubt it either.[50]

The devil, both "indefatigable" and "implacable," would use whatever means he could to advance his aims, Lawson went on to assert. Satan's extraordinary powers allowed him to attack people either directly or "by imploying some of mankind or other creatures." To conceal his aims, he tended to use the latter method when dealing with human beings, contracting with witches "that they shall be the Instruments by whom he may more secretly Affect, and Afflict the Bodies and Minds of others." If he could recruit church members into his ranks, so much the better: they "may the more readily pervert others to Consenting unto his subjection." Once people submitted to the devil, he could then—as he had in the Village—"use their Bodies and Minds, Shapes and Representations, to Affright and Afflict others."[51]

Satan especially targeted God's own "Covenant People," Lawson declared, but they could rest assured that he could go no farther in attacking them than God permitted. The Lord was "lengthening the Chain of the Roaring Lyon . . . so that the Devil is come down in great wrath," but he did so "to Serve his own most Holy Designs, in the World." The minister then explicated what he saw as those "Holy Designs" in the present case. God was speaking to Villagers "with an unusual and amazing loudness," calling on them to ask themselves, "What meaneth the Heat of this great Anger?" The Lord insisted on "True and unfeigned Reformation" of the "Provoking Evils" into which his people had fallen. In an extraordinary passage, Lawson then addressed any in his audience who might "by Covenant explicite or implicite" have agreed to serve the devil. "All Mankind is now . . . set against you," he proclaimed, and so too are God and Christ. "You are utterly undone forever, ... Doomed to those Endless, Easeless, and Remediless Torments" unless God chose to be merciful. Such a fate awaited witches even if they somehow managed to "Evade, the Condemnation of mans Judgment, and escape a violent death by the Hand of Justice."[52]

Hearing their former pastor speak such remarkable words must have reinforced the fears Villagers had felt during the examinations earlier in the day. Who among them—which of their longtime neighbors or acquaintances, even their relatives—had secretly allied themselves with Satan? Whom could they trust? And could they halt the spread of the afflictions?

Lawson suggested answers for the last question at least, although he offered no assistance with the first two. Villagers, regenerate and unregenerate alike, needed to change their behavior. Possibly God had dispatched "this Fire of his Holy displeasure, to put out some Fires of Contention, that have been amongst you." Perhaps they had given Satan a crucial opening by employing countermagic against the afflictions and by engaging in other occult practices. Anyone who tried such experiments, he warned, was "in great Danger to become a prey unto Satans malice, being . . . seduced by his subtilty into an intire subjection to his Infernal powers." Lawson also cautioned his audience against "Rash Censuring of others," aiming his advice explicitly at the families of the afflicted and the accused. If the innocent come under suspicion, he observed, the cause was "GODS pleasure supreamly permitting, and Satans Malice subordinately troubling," not "Ill will, or disrespect" on the part of one party or the other. "Reflecting on the Malice or Envy of your Neighbours" would only "have uncomfortable and pernicious influence, upon the Affairs of the place, . . . bringing in Confusion and every evil work."[53]

The cleric exhorted different groups of his listeners to "special Dutyes" at this time of crisis.[54] Villagers generally should show "Compassion towards, those poor afflicted persons, that are by Divine Permission, under the Direful Influences of Satan's malice." The magistrates should see themselves as "Father[s]" to the afflicted, doing "all that in you Lyes, to Check and Rebuke Satan." The afflicted should take comfort in being "the visible Covenant People of GOD" and have faith that Christ would triumph in the end. And all should defend themselves against the devil's operations by every possible means. God had turned "this poor Village" into "the Rendezvous of Devils, where they Muster their infernal forces appearing to the afflicted, as coming Armed, to carry on their malicious designs." Thus Villagers had to "ARM; ARM; ARM" and enlist as "faithful Souldiers under the Captain of our Salvation, that by the Shield of FAITH, ye and we All may Resist the Fiery Darts of the Wicked." Lawson, the one-time chaplain to colonial troops in Maine, and his audience both could well have linked those metaphorical "Fiery Darts" to Wabanaki arrows.

Lawson concluded his sermon by alluding to God's "Unsearchable" providence and people's inability to comprehend his aims in visiting such afflictions on them. "Yet may we say in the midst of the terrible things which he doth in righteousness; He alone is the GOD of our Salvation." Accordingly, Villagers needed to "Repent of every Sin, that hath been Committed; and Labour to practice, every Duty which hath been Neglected." Then the Lord would deliver "his Poor Sheep and Lambs, out of the Jaws, and Paws, of the Roaring Lyon."

If their former pastor's message to them thus ended on a hopeful note, in that sincere repentance could possibly alleviate their current troubles, residents of Salem Village received no such assurance from their current minister three days later. Samuel Parris marked Sunday, March 27, a regular sacrament day, with a discourse on John 6:70: "Have I not chosen you twelve, & one of you is a Devil." On learning the text for the day, Sarah Towne Cloyce strode out of the meetinghouse. According to a witness, she "flung the doore after her violently, to the amazement of the Congregation." Sarah Cloyce's behavior that Sabbath seems to have called her to the attention of the afflicted.

Eight days later, she joined her older sister Rebecca Nurse in the ranks of the accused.[55]

Parris's uncompromising March 27 sermon was, he noted, "Occasioned by dreadfull Witchcraft broke out here," with two church members being "vehemently suspected for shee-Witches."[56] The church contained devils as well as saints, and Christ knew who, and how many. Indeed, "we are either Saints, or Devils, the scripture gives us no medium." (Where he thought that Manichean view placed those in his audience who did not belong to the church, he did not reveal.) In any event, "none are worse than those that have been good, & are naught: & might be good, but will be naught." Parris directed his listeners to be "deeply humbled" by the presence of witches in their midst. Urging them to pray "that God would not suffer Devils in the guise of Saints to associate with us," he also advised them to ask the Lord to ensure that no "true Saint" would ever be falsely accused. As a preface to the day's celebration of communion, he warned any devils among them against partaking of the Lord's Supper. If any did so, they would "incurr the hottest of Gods wrath." No one, he asserted, could "maintain communion with Christ, & yet keep up fellowship with Devils."

In the course of his sermon, Parris directly addressed the defenses offered by the two women whose examinations he had witnessed and recorded. Speaking to Martha Corey's contention that she could not be a witch because she was a "Gospel Woman," the minister argued that since devils could be found in churches, "Let none then build their hopes of Salvation meerly upon this, that they are Church-members." And in response to Rebecca Nurse's observation that "the Devil may appear in my shape," he admitted that although Satan would undoubtedly "if he could" misrepresent "the best Saints" in that way, "it is not easy to imagine that his power is of such extent, to the hazard of the Church." Thus Parris utilized the common belief in God's authority over Satan—a point Lawson had stressed—to maintain that it was unlikely that the Almighty would allow the devil to display deceptive apparitions of saints to the afflicted. In adopting that line of argument, he accepted the implications of Richard Bernard's statement earlier in the century that the unregenerate (but not, by inference, the regenerate) could be falsely represented in spectral form.

In spite of differences in the tone of their sermons, Lawson and Parris concurred on essentials. The devil was abroad in Salem Village. Church members could be found among the witches. The afflicted were innocent victims of Satan's wrath, deserving the pity and sympathy of others. God governed all these events; by permitting the devil such latitude, he intended to convey a message to Villagers—and perhaps, by implication, to other New Englanders as well. They should search their hearts and seek genuine repentance for their sins in order to relieve their troubles.

To facilitate such reflections, Salem, both Town and Village, observed a public fast for the afflicted on Thursday, March 31.[57] What happened in the visible world that day was not recorded; the texts of the sermons preached (and who preached them) are unknown. But Abigail Williams described the activities in the invisible world, revealing that the witches celebrated a sacrament with "Red Bread and Red Drink" in the pasture next to her uncle's house. In a fit the next day, Mercy Lewis recounted that the witches at the sacrament "would have had her eat some: but she would not." Instead, she had turned away her head, insisting, "That is not the Bread of Life, that is not the Water of Life; Christ gives the Bread of Life, I will have none of it!"

Mercy also reported seeing "a White man" accompanied by "a great Multitude in White glittering Robes" in her fit, where she thought herself in "a Glorious Place." Demonstrating that she, like Ann Carr Putnam, was well acquainted with the Bible, she indicated that the "Multitude" had sung Revelation 5:9 and Psalms 110 and 149. The first verse of Psalm 110 was that upon which Parris had preached frequently in the preceding months, so the text would have been familiar to her. Both the sixth verse of that psalm and the seventh verse of Psalm 149 referred to God's judgments against the heathen, mentioning his "two-edged sword" and the "dead bodies" that would fall in his wake "in the day of his wrath." Revelation 5:9 contained "a new song" revealing how the lamb that had been slain "hast redeemed us to God by thy blood." Surely not by chance did Mercy choose texts so appropriate to the experience of her own family and so expressive of her desire for revenge against the heathen Wabanakis who had killed them.

THE PROCTORS, THEIR MAID, AND SARAH CLOYCE

Following the reports of the diabolic sacrament near Parris's house, people began to see gatherings of recognizable specters in a variety of settings. In early April, a young man named Stephen Bittford was spending the night at the house of James Darling, Mercy Lewis's uncle by marriage. He later deposed that at midnight, "being parfittly awake," he saw standing in the room near him both Rebecca Nurse and Elizabeth Proctor, "whom I very well knew." He then experienced a "very grate paine" in his neck, producing stiffness that lasted for several days. About the same time or perhaps a few days later, Benjamin Gould, a yeoman in his mid-twenties from Salem Town, saw in his room the apparitions of Rebecca Nurse, Elizabeth and John Proctor, Martha and Giles Corey, Sarah Cloyce, and Rachel Griggs, the doctor's wife. Gould's naming of Goody Griggs had no discernible impact—no one else ever seems to have seen her among the witches, and the accusation was never acted upon—but John and Elizabeth Proctor's names kept resurfacing, not just in these but also in other contexts.[58]

For example, Abigail Williams repeatedly cited Goody Proctor as one of her afflicters in late March and early April, charging that Proctor's specter, together with that of Rebecca Nurse, "almost pulled out" her bowels on several occasions. Mercy Lewis identified Elizabeth as one of her tormentors on March 26, and Betty Hubbard named her the first week of April. Any of these, or perhaps Mary Walcott, could have been the afflicted person who at Nathaniel Ingersoll's on March 28 reacted to the gossip about a likely accusation of Elizabeth Proctor by making "sport" of seeing her apparition, thus eliciting a sharp rebuke from Goody Ingersoll. Then on April 4, Abigail complained of John Proctor as well, saying to his specter, "are you come to, you can pinch as well as your wife." She repeated her accusation of John two days later and, Samuel Parris noted, "the like I hear at Tho. Putmans house."[59]

John Proctor, about sixty years old in 1692, married his third wife Elizabeth in 1674. John had immigrated with his parents from England to Ipswich, where he still owned part of the family property. Elizabeth, born in Lynn, was the sister of the militia captain William Bassett. Tavern owners in Salem Farms on the Ipswich Road, the Proctors attended church services in Salem Town rather than the Village. The family was both prosperous and large (six children from his first two marriages, five from the third). Elizabeth ran the tavern while John and his oldest son, Benjamin, managed the farm.[60]

Elizabeth Bassett Proctor, as was indicated in chapter 1, seems to have been singled out initially because her grandmother was thought to have been a witch, but the accusation of her husband most likely stemmed from a different source: his attitude toward the Proctors' maidservant, Mary Warren. That Warren suffered torments in March emerged from a conversation between John Proctor and Samuel Sibley early in the morning of March 25. John informed Samuel that he was en route to the Village "to fetch home his jade he left her there last night." He would "thresh the Devil out of her," he told Sibley, remarking that the afflicted persons "should rather be had to the Whipping post," for "if they were let alone so we should all be Devils & witches quickly." Indeed, he revealed, "when she was first taken with fits he kept her close to the Wheel & threatened to thresh her, & then she had no more fits till the next day he was gone forth," when in his absence she again fell into fits.[61]

Since Samuel Sibley was Mary Walcott's uncle (and his wife had suggested the making of the witchcake), he surely repeated the story of John Proctor's skepticism about the afflictions many times during the next few days in a variety of Village settings. He and those to whom he spoke would have been shocked, their suspicions aroused, by Proctor's callous attitude toward the tortured young people in their midst. As John Hathorne had implied during the examination of Rebecca Nurse, a lack of sufficient concern for the afflicted could indicate complicity in their torments.

Two brief passages in Mary Warren's later testimony underscore John Proctor's adamant opposition to the role she played early in the crisis. On one occasion "her Master threttned her to burn her out of her fitt," she recalled, possibly by thrusting "hot tongs downe her throat." Another time, she recounted, while she was in the midst of a fit he told her, "if ye are Afflicted I wish ye were more Afflicted." When she asked why, he responded, "because you goe to bring out Innocent persons." Samuel Sibley and Mary Warren were undoubtedly not the only people to whom John Proctor expressed such opinions about the falsity of her accusations, and word of his attitude would have spread quickly through the Village.[62]

The absence of Warren's name from the legal record before March 25, despite the fact that she had been previously afflicted, raises an important issue already touched on briefly in another context: the crucial role of adult men in legitimizing the complaints of the afflicted persons. Sergeant Thomas Putnam, Jonathan Walcott, and Samuel Parris all believed in the validity of the fits suffered by the children and young women in their households. Accordingly, they (and in the Putnam case, other male relatives) took notes on the behavior of the afflicted and pressed forward with formal legal complaints against suspected witches. But John Proctor had little sympathy for, or patience with, Mary Warren. Without support from her master, she could not press charges against anyone, and so information about her early sufferings emerged retrospectively for other reasons. The afflicted persons—and others, like Benjamin Gould—proffered initial accusations, but those charges were pursued only if they made sense to a number of adult male gatekeepers. The heads of the households in which afflicted young people resided composed the first such gatekeeping level; the next comprised the examining magistrates, and the third the judges and jurors.[63]

John Proctor did not believe Mary Warren. Therefore any accusation she made while living in his household went nowhere. Gould's vision of Goody Rachel Griggs among the specters likewise failed to meet the initial test, one applied by men who associated with Griggs's husband. Gould's was but the first of many accusations proposed but not pursued to the point of formal complaint.

Charges not followed up, afflictions not recorded—the existence of such phenomena leads to another important question: what made an accusation credible to male gatekeepers? That question had a variety of possible answers, some of which have already been suggested: a long-standing reputation as a witch or a relationship to a suspected witch, hostility between the families in question, explicit lack of sympathy for the afflicted. There would be others, too, some of which (as shall be seen in subsequent chapters) had direct links to the war against the Wabanakis.

Whenever Mary Warren's sufferings began, and whomever she accused, early in April her torments eased. Probably on Sunday, April 3, Warren put up a "note for thanks in publick" at the meetinghouse in gratitude for her improved condition, despite John Proctor's stated opposition to such "Bills for publick prayer." According to Edward Putnam, the other afflicted people then insisted that "she had signed the book; and that was the reason she was better." Mary Warren's role in the crisis was about to change: starting as one of the afflicted, she would become a confessed witch—but not before her master and mistress had first faced formal charges.[64]

On April 4, Jonathan Walcott and his uncle Nathaniel Ingersoll appeared before Hathorne and Corwin to file formal complaints against Elizabeth Proctor and Sarah Cloyce on behalf of themselves and "Severall of theyr Neighbours." The two women, the complainants stated, had done "great hurt & damage" to Mary Walcott, Ann Putnam Jr., Mercy Lewis, Abigail Williams, and a new sufferer, John Indian. The justices, departing from their usual practice of responding quickly to such complaints, delayed issuing a warrant until Friday, April 8. The likely reason for that delay emerged from the details of their directions to the constable: he was to bring the accused to "the publike Meeting house in the Towne" on Monday, April 11. For the first time during the crisis, an examination would take place in the Town, not the Village, and Hathorne would not be the chief examiner. Some of the colony's council would attend the proceedings, which would be conducted by Thomas Danforth, the deputy governor. Undoubtedly, making such arrangements took some time.[65]

Sarah Towne Cloyce, formally charged alongside Goody Proctor on April 4 and examined with her a week later, was approximately twenty years younger than her sister Rebecca Nurse. Born in Salem about 1641, she first wed Edmund Bridges Jr. of Topsfield. In the early 1680s, as an impoverished widow with five children, she married the widower Peter Cloyce. Both joined the Salem Village church, he as an original member in 1689, she the following year. Her second husband had been born in Watertown, but he and several of his brothers moved to Maine, where they lived until fleeing to Essex County during King Philip's War. Peter remained in Salem Village thereafter, but his brother Thomas returned to Falmouth, where he was killed in 1690. Thomas Cloyce's wife Susanna was the sister of Philip Lewis, Mercy's father. In other words, Sarah Cloyce and Mercy Lewis were closely related by marriage; Sarah was the sister-in-law of Mercy's paternal aunt.[66]

Probably for that reason, Mercy Lewis did not take an active role in accusing Sarah Cloyce, although she did participate in the prosecution of Rebecca Nurse and a third Towne sister, Mary Easty, who was accused later in April. Testimony about Sarah Cloyce having afflicted Mercy came not from her but from Ann Jr. Indeed, on the one occasion Mercy evidently named Sarah Cloyce, she quickly recanted. Ephraim Sheldon attested on April 10 that he had earlier witnessed one of Lewis's fits at Ingersoll's tavern. "I heard her cry out of Goodwife Cloyce and when she came to herselfe she was asked who she saw. she answered she saw no body they demanded of her whether or noe she did not see Goodwife Nurse or Goodwife Cloyce or Goodwife Gory [sic]. she answered she saw no body."[67]

According to Samuel Sewall, one of those present, "a very great Assembly" attended the examination of the accused witches in the Salem Town meetinghouse on the morning of April 11. Hathorne, Corwin, Danforth, and Sewall were joined as presiding magistrates by Isaac Addington (the colony's secretary) and two other councilors. Once again, Samuel Parris took notes. Nicholas Noyes opened the proceedings with a prayer, and John Higginson closed them similarly. In his diary, Sewall observed only that " 'twas awfull to see how the afflicted persons were agitated."[68]

Thomas Danforth began with John Indian, inquiring, "who hurt you?"[69] John accused both Sarah Cloyce and Elizabeth Proctor of repeatedly choking him and urging him to sign their books. Goody Cloyce eventually broke in with a question: "when did I hurt thee?" "A great many times," John replied. "Oh! you are a grievous liar," retorted Sarah. But John persisted, stating that she had most recently tortured him "yesterday at meeting."

Danforth next turned to Mary Walcott, who claimed that Goody Cloyce had also tormented her, sometimes accompanied by Rebecca Nurse, Martha Corey, and "a great many I do not know." After Walcott fell into a fit, Danforth addressed Abigail Williams, asking her about the witches' sacrament she had witnessed near her uncle's house. This time she gave more details: about forty witches attended, and the "deacons" were Sarah Cloyce and Sarah

Good. She had actually spoken to Goody Cloyce, asking her, "Is this a time to receive the Sacrament, you ran-away on the Lords-Day, and scorned to receive it in the Meeting-House, and, Is this a time to receive it?" Abigail also disclosed that another witch meeting had occurred in the interim near Ingersoll's tavern. Since Nathaniel was a deacon, the witches seemed to be flaunting their contempt for the Village's religious leadership. Goodwives Cloyce, Nurse, Corey, and Good had all participated in the latter meeting, Abigail announced. At that, Sarah Cloyce asked for some water and, Parris recorded, she "sat down as one seized with a dying fainting fit." Several afflicted persons then had fits, and some exclaimed, "Oh! her spirit is gone to prison to her sister Nurse."

The deputy governor then directed his attention to Elizabeth Proctor.[70] Admonishing both her and the afflicted to tell the truth, "as you will answer for it before God another day," he questioned Walcott, Lewis, Putnam Jr., and Williams about whether Proctor had hurt them; all were struck dumb and could not respond. But John Indian assured Danforth that "this is the woman that came in her shift and choked me." When Ann Jr. was once again able to speak, she declared that Proctor's specter "saith she hath made her maid [Mary Warren] set her hand to it." Abigail then chimed in, asking the accused, "Did not you tell me, that your maid had written?" Goody Proctor denied everything. "I take God in heaven to be my witness, that I know nothing of it, no more than the child unborn."

After Abigail and Ann Jr. both had fits, the examination descended into chaos. The girls claimed to see Elizabeth Proctor's apparition on the beam in the meetinghouse, then accused John Proctor, there to support his wife, of committing witchcraft as well. "Immediately, many, if not all of the bewitched, had grievous fits," noted Parris. Some of the afflicted shouted that Goodman Proctor was "going to take up Mrs. Pope's feet.—And her feet were immediately taken up," Parris interjected. John Proctor declared his innocence, but Abigail accused him of attacking Bathshua Pope, who quickly "fell into a fit."

Danforth instructed Goodman Proctor, "The children could see what you was going to do before the woman was hurt. I would advise you to repentance, for the devil is bringing you out." Abigail predicted that Proctor would hurt Goody Vibber, then Mary Walcott, then others. All had fits. Meanwhile, Parris remarked, Betty Hubbard "was in a trance during the whole examination." And the minister, continuing his close observation of his afflicted niece, added at the end of his transcript a description of how she touched Goody Proctor's hood "very lightly" during her examination "with open and extended fingers" after trying to strike her with a fist. "Immediately," Parris recorded, "Abigail cried out, her fingers, her fingers, burned, and Ann Putman took on most greviously, of her head, and sunk down."

The councilors next formally convened to consider the results of the examination Danforth had just conducted. After Parris read over his notes, Abigail and Ann Jr. accused John Proctor of having afflicted Bathshua Pope, among others. Mercy and Mary also formally charged him with hurting them. The council ordered John and Elizabeth Proctor and Sarah Cloyce to be held in custody, and the next day it directed that they, Rebecca Nurse, Martha Corey, and Dorcas Good all be sent to prison in Boston.[71]

Although the jailing of suspected witches had previously eased the sufferings of the afflicted at least temporarily, this time that did not happen. Indeed, the next day at the Salem Village parsonage John Indian, Mary Walcott, and Abigail Williams all complained of being tortured by both John Proctor and Sarah Cloyce. Parris, who was trying to write a report on their behavior for the authorities, found himself unable to focus on that task because "so great were the interruptions" from the fits his niece and slave experienced in his presence. John Indian "cryed out of Goody Cloyse, O you old Witch, & fell immediately into a violent fit that 3 men & the Marshall could not without exceeding difficulty hold him," Parris commented. Mary, "who was knitting & well composed," identified his attackers as Cloyce and the Proctors. Meanwhile, Abigail, in a fit, declared that she saw John Proctor's specter sitting in the marshal's lap. Parris had to send John and Abigail out of the room "that I might have liberty to write this without disturbance." He ended with a final observation: "Just now as soon as I had made an end of reading this to the Marshall Mary W[torn] immediately cryed O yonder is Good: Proctor & his wife & Goody Nurse & Goody Korey & G[torn] Cloyse & Goods child & then said O Goodm: Proctor is going to choke me & Immediately she was choakt."[72]

By the middle of April, then, according to the afflicted, the witches were no longer exclusively acting alone; they were cooperating in groups of two or more to torture their targets. They had even met twice in large numbers at central locations in the Village. Each time new reports of such malefic activity reached the ears of New Englanders, the perception of a spectral attack on the region was reinforced.

For example, the two-month-old baby daughter of John Putnam Jr. (a cousin of Sergeant Thomas) was seized with "strange and violent fitts" like those of the bewitched. John's mother declared that "she feared there was an evell hand upon it," and although the family called in the doctor immediately, the baby girl died "a cruell and violent death being enuf to peirs astony hart."

John subsequently attributed his daughter's death on April 15 to his having "Reported sum thing which I had hard consarning the mother of Rebekah Nurs: Mary Estick and Sarah Cloyes"—in other words, to his gossiping about a witchcraft accusation once made against Joanna Towne.[73]

Not surprisingly, consequences also followed elsewhere. In Malden, Mistress Mary Swayne Marshall, sister of a militia major, declared that on April 8 the specter of Elizabeth Colson of Reading, the teenage granddaughter of a woman long believed to be a witch, had knocked her down, "Strikeing of me deafe and Dumm Tortering my body in most parts; Chokenig [*sic*] of me quite dead for Some time." Colson, she declared, had bruised her head, wrung her neck, and even dislocated her shoulder. And much farther away, in Stamford, Connecticut, a maidservant named Kate Branch (who was described as being of French origin) began having fits resembling those suffered by the Salem Village afflicted. Although the case record does not date the onset of her torments precisely, they seem to have begun during the first full week of April, after people in coastal southern New England would have had time to learn of the examinations of Martha Corey and Rebecca Nurse ten days to two weeks earlier.[74]

Kate's master, Daniel Wescott, who accepted the truthfulness of her complaints and acted as her ally and supporter throughout the proceedings, later described her symptoms in a statement presented to the magistrates. She had felt "a pinching & pricking at her breast," and she had sobbed uncontrollably, falling down "on the flooer with her hands Claspt." She said she saw a cat that spoke to her and promised her "fine things" but also threatened to kill her. Her master recounted that "some times for severall dayes togather she'd be almost wholly dumb at other times singing Laughing, Eating, Rideing." After two weeks of fits she saw an apparition of a witch in the middle of the night, "a woman . . . having on a silk hood, & a blew apron." Eventually, she identified a particular tormentor, Elizabeth Clawson, describing her clothing. Her master called on Goody Clawson "& saw the woman named Exactly atired as she was described per the person afflictted." Thus a test that could not be carried out with Martha Corey in Salem Village was successfully applied to Elizabeth Clawson in Stamford. Kate named another witch as well, Mercy Holbridge Disborough, and on April 25 her master filed formal charges against the two women on her behalf.[75]

The Connecticut accusations are notable for the contrast they provide to the contemporaneous Salem Village outbreak. Southern Connecticut remained almost untouched by the war to the north; the region suffered few significant losses of men, houses, livestock, or crops. Although Kate Branch's fits mimicked those of the Village afflicted, no one else ever followed her lead in the Stamford area. Moreover, the only people she named as witches fell into the most common categories: women with longtime local reputations for malefice and their relatives. The authorities, too, moved slowly and cautiously against those Kate accused. Still, at least one magistrate found Kate's accusations entirely credible. Jonathan Selleck of Stamford penned what seems to be the only surviving personal letter from a 1692 justice of the peace who examined an afflicted person. Writing to his brother-in-law, Selleck matter-of-factly described Kate Branch's fits and spectral conversations, showing no inclination to question the validity of her visions. Deeming her a "poore gail," Selleck complained of delays in pursuing her accusations by other magistrates who had not had direct contact with her. "I feare that all the persons: the gail names are nought [guilty]: & I desyr the lord to make discovery of them," he commented. Justice Selleck, like his Essex counterparts, did not doubt the reality of agonies he personally witnessed. But the atmosphere in which those torments occurred differed greatly from that in Essex County, and so the consequences were equally different.[76]

Historians have not recognized the connections between Kate Branch's afflictions in Stamford and those in Salem Village, because trials in the Connecticut cases (as shall be seen later in this book) postdated the cases heard by the Salem Court of Oyer and Terminer. Scholars have, in fact, classified the Stamford cases as "not-Salem."[77] Yet Kate's fits closely resembled those she would have learned about in news from Massachusetts, and their timing was too exact to be coincidental. Of course, the absence of a Connecticut crisis comparable to that in Essex County does not by itself prove that the looming presence of the war on the northeastern frontier was *the* crucial factor in creating the contrast between the two regions. Yet at the same time it is highly suggestive that a teenage maidservant could experience severe and prolonged fits in 1692 in southern New England and not set off a regionwide panic like that which occurred simultaneously two hundred miles north in Massachusetts.

THE THIRD CONFESSION

In the memoir of the witchcraft crisis he wrote in 1697, John Hale recalled that its beginning was "very small, and looked on at first as an ordinary case which had fallen out before at several times in other places, and would be quickly over." Hale referred primarily to the first afflictions in Samuel Parris's household, but his observation could have been applied almost as accurately to all the occurrences in Salem Village through April 17. Until then, even though church members and their spouses now numbered among the accused, the outbreak still had a precedent: the rash of witchcraft accusations in Hartford and environs in 1662.[78]

But circumstances changed dramatically on April 19 with the examinations of two people officially complained against the day before. For reasons explored in this section and the next two chapters, the two—the elderly Bridget Oliver Bishop of Salem Town and the teenager Abigail Hobbs, daughter of William Hobbs of Topsfield—established new patterns that would endure throughout the remainder of the crisis. Because both suspects lived outside the Village, the accusations themselves signaled that a new phase of the witchcraft episode was beginning. Even more significant, the fourteen-year-old Abigail joined Tituba and Dorcas Good in confessing to witchcraft, and the substance of her revelations brought immense consequences.

Over the previous year and a half, Abigail Hobbs had displayed a notably cavalier attitude toward the devil, thus supplying wagging tongues with more than enough information to ensure that her name would quickly surface as a suspect in 1692. For example, when chided by others for her "wicked cariges and disobedience to hir father and Mother" or for her "rude" and "unseemly" behavior, she had replied that she was not "a fraid of any thing" because of a compact with Satan. Abigail spoke freely to several people about having "Sold her selfe boddy & Soull to the old boy" and about having "seen the divell and . . . made a covenant or bargin with him." Another teenager reported that Abigail, shortly before she was formally accused of being a witch—asked why she was not "ashamed" of her poor conduct—told her to "hold my tonge . . . & bid me look there was old nick . . . sate over the bedsted." Such playfulness extended to religion as well. Once, while she and her stepmother Deliverance were visiting a youthful neighbor, she remarked that "my mother is not baptized. but said I will baptize hir and immediatly took watter and sprinckeled in hir mothers face and said she did baptized [*sic*] her in the name of the ffather Son and Holy Ghost."[79]

Thus it was perhaps not surprising that on April 13, two days after the examination in Salem Town, the younger Ann Putnam complained of tortures at the hands of the specter of Abigail Hobbs, her irreverent approximate contemporary in age. The same apparition next attacked Mary Walcott, then Mercy Lewis. Less than a week after the first recorded accusation against her, Abigail Hobbs was questioned at the Salem Village meetinghouse.[80]

Hathorne began his interrogation of the teenager on Tuesday, April 19, with the same injunction to speak the truth he had given others.[81] "Are you guilty, or not?" he asked her. Abigail admitted, "I have seen sights & been scared. I have been very wicked. I hope I shall be better: if God will keep me." When the magistrate asked her to explain the "sights," she revealed that she had indeed seen the devil, but only once, "at the Eastward at Casko-bay." In response to the magistrate's further questions, she indicated that they had met one day in the woods three or four years earlier. Satan had promised her "fine things" if she would make a covenant with him, and she had done so, but, she added, "I hope God will forgive me." A cat and "things like men" had asked her to sign their books; she had done that as well, promising to serve the devil for two years (or perhaps four; her subsequent answers were inconsistent).

Hathorne then explored the details of her covenant with Satan. "Are you not bid to hurt folks?" he inquired. Abigail replied that yes, she had hurt Mercy and Ann Jr. by pinching them, with the devil as an intermediary. He "has my consent, & goes & hurts them . . . in my shape," she explained. With what witches did she associate? Hathorne asked, and Abigail admitted knowing Sarah Good in the invisible world. "The Devil told me" Goodwife Good was a witch, she disclosed. Questioned about the "great meetings" of witches, Abigail denied having attended any, although she acknowledged having heard about "great hurt done here in the village."

Abigail next contradicted the earlier statement that she had met the devil only once years earlier by describing a conversation with him "about a fortnight agoe." Satan, she said, at that time appeared to her "like a black man with an hat." She admitted speaking to animal familiars, but under close questioning from the magistrate denied that they sucked her body. Confronted with further detailed inquiries about exactly how the animal familiars spoke to her, Abigail suddenly and conveniently could no longer hear. The afflicted then declared that "they saw Sarah Good & Sarah Osborn run their fingers into the examinants ears; by & by, she this examinant was blind with her eyes quite open." Eventually Abigail exclaimed, "Sarah Good saith I shall not speak," and so Hathorne and Corwin directed that she be removed to prison.

At the end of his transcript Parris commented that none of the bewitched people was tormented during Abigail's confession, and that after she finished, Mercy, Ann Jr., and Abigail Williams "said openly in Court, they were very sorry for the condition this poor Abigail Hobbs was in: which compassion they expressed over & over again." The afflicted were probably as surprised by Abigail's statement as was everyone else, and their reaction reflected their confusion.

John Hathorne finally had extracted the second major confession he had sought for the six weeks since Tituba first appeared before him to confess her dealings with Satan. A teenager had acknowledged contracting with the devil and consenting that he appear in her shape to torment several of the afflicted.

During her confession, no one had been tortured, which seemed to validate her revelations. Significantly, Abigail Hobbs had met the devil—in the shape of a "black man"—on the Maine frontier about four years earlier, or just a few months before the Wabanakis renewed their attacks on the English settlements. Furthermore, she encountered Satan in the woods (the Indians' domain) near her residence in Falmouth, one of the Indians' chief targets in both the first and second wars. Those who heard her confession readily grasped the connection between Satan and the Wabanakis.[82]

Abigail Hobbs's statement on April 19 set off a chain of events that within thirty-six hours explicitly linked the witches' and the Wabanakis' assaults against New England. As a result, witchcraft complaints exploded, expanding both geographically and numerically. During the next seven weeks, fifty-four people were formally accused of being witches, a sharp increase from the ten who had been complained against in the seven weeks prior to April 17. The nature of the witchcraft episode had changed dramatically and irrevocably. To understand why, it is now necessary to begin this tale anew, in another time and place: a small settlement on the New Hampshire frontier during the early summer of 1689.

CHAPTER THREE

Pannick at the Eastward

SEPTEMBER 1675–JANUARY 1691/2

Thursday, June 27, 1689; Cocheco (Dover), New Hampshire. The seventy-four-year-old Major Richard Waldron, a magistrate and militia officer, had dealt with native peoples for almost five decades, and so he surely felt little alarm when about thirty members of the Pennacook and Saco bands of the Wabanaki people arrived unexpectedly at his trading post during the last week of June 1689. Scattered outbreaks of violence between Indians and settlers had marred the preceding nine months, but the "Company of young men" led by the sachem Kankamagus (also called Hawkins) informed the major that "a great number of Indians were not far from them with considerable quantities of beaver, who would trade with him the next day." Waldron undoubtedly welcomed that news, for he had a reputation as a sharp dealer, perhaps even a cheat, in his commerce with the Indians.[1]

Others, though, already knew that he should be on the alert for trouble. Five days earlier, two Pennacooks had appeared at the home of a militia major in Chelmsford, Massachusetts, warning him that "damage will undoubtedly be done within a few days at puscataqua & that Major Walden in particular is Threatned." The officer forwarded the information through proper channels, sending a messenger to Thomas Danforth, president of the province of Maine. On the morning of June 27, Danforth passed on the warning, urging that Waldron be given "speedy" notice of the threat. But by the time his message arrived at its destination, it was too late.[2]

That same day at Cocheco the visiting Pennacooks and Sacos were treated cordially; therefore, when some of the women, complaining of the "dull weather," sought shelter for the night in the settlement's garrisoned houses, they were allowed to sleep by the fires. After midnight, the women rose and opened the doors to the men outside, informing them of how many people lay in each chamber, and the men divided appropriately. Major Waldron, sleeping in an inside room, jumped out of bed when the men entered and— one of the attackers later recalled—"drove them out with his sword through two or three doors." But a raider stunned Waldron by hitting him on the head with a hatchet. They then "hauled him out, and set [him] up upon a long table in his hall and bid him judge Indians again." After they stabbed him numerous times, they "bid him order his book of accounts to be brought and cross out all the Indian debts." The Wabanakis tortured Waldron until he died, burning his garrison and several other Cocheco houses as a final gesture of contempt and defiance. Twenty-three residents of the settlement died that day; twenty-nine were captured.[3]

THE FIRST INDIAN WAR

The Wabanakis targeted Major Richard Waldron in 1689 not only because of his notoriously duplicitous trading practices, but also because he had twice betrayed them during what everyone in the region called "the First Indian War"—that is, the conflict today most commonly referred to as King Philip's War (1675–1678). Indeed, more than a decade after the 1689 Cocheco raid, the Wabanakis still kept alive the memory of Waldron's perfidy in the mid-1670s. The Reverend John Williams, captured in 1704 at Deerfield, Massachusetts, recorded that some Jesuits he encountered in New France "justified the Indians in what they did against us, rehearsing some things done by Major Walden above thirty years ago, and how justly God retaliated them in the last war."[4]

King Philip's War, which began in Rhode Island and Plymouth Colony in June 1675, ended in southern New England soon after Philip's death on August 12, 1676, but continued in the north until spring 1678. Historians generally agree that in the south the war's origins lay in conflicts over land and Christian missionizing, as Nipmucks and Narragansetts joined King Philip's (Metacom's) Wampanoags in a prolonged struggle to maintain their cultural autonomy in the face of increasing Anglo-American encroachment.[5]

In northern New England, though, the sources of conflict in the mid-1670s are more obscure.[6] In the sparsely settled region located beyond the Merrimack River—roughly the northern boundary of Massachusetts— Anglo-American villages lived in uneasy juxtaposition with similarly sized (even somewhat larger) villages of Wabanaki peoples. From Pemaquid in the north to the Piscataqua River in the south, English settlers had established fur-trading posts and fishing stations, along with farming communities of

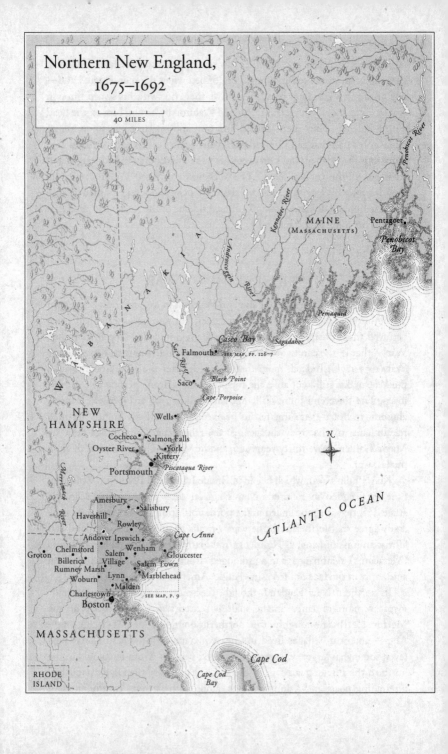

Northern New England,
1675–1692

|———| 40 MILES

Penobscot River

MAINE
(MASSACHUSETTS)

Pentagoet

Penobscot
Bay

Kennebec River

Androscoggin River

River

Pemaquid

Casco Bay
Sagadahoc

Saco River
Falmouth
SEE MAP, PP. 126–7

Saco
Black Point
Cape Porpoise

NEW
HAMPSHIRE
Wells

Cocheco
Salmon Falls
Oyster River
York
Kittery
Portsmouth
Piscataqua River

N

Merrimack River

Amesbury
Salisbury
Haverhill
Rowley
Andover Ipswich
Cape Anne
Groton
Chelmsford
Wenham
Billerica
Salem
Gloucester
Rumney Marsh
Village
Woburn
Salem Town
Lynn
Marblehead
Charlestown
SEE MAP, P. 9
Boston

ATLANTIC OCEAN

Malden

MASSACHUSETTS

RHODE
ISLAND

Cape Cod

Cape Cod
Bay

varying sizes. Most of the coastal English settlements lay between Casco Bay and Kittery, which was located on the northeastern shore of the Piscataqua, but one large trading and farming community had grown up further north, near the mouth of the Kennebec River. Dotting the coastline southward from Falmouth, on Casco Bay, to the Piscataqua were the towns of Black Point (Scarborough), Saco, Wells, and York. On the Piscataqua's south shore in New Hampshire lay Portsmouth (or Strawberry Bank), the major northern port. Inland, up the river, were such communities as Cocheco, Oyster River (now Durham, New Hampshire), and Salmon Falls (now Berwick, Maine), the sites of large numbers of sawmills.[7]

Although the region was inhabited only by about 3,600 English people, its scattered settlements flourished before the mid-1670s. Exports of peltry, fish, and timber from the "eastward"—that is, Maine and New Hampshire—fueled the Massachusetts economy, providing the colony's major source of income. In 1675, about 440 fishing boats operated off the coast between Boston and the Kennebec, employing perhaps a thousand men, and at least fifty sawmills each produced up to a thousand feet a day of white pine boards. The timber industry also supplied shipbuilders in the colonies and the home country with valuable masts and spars. One Bostonian pronounced "the Eastwards . . . the best Land in New England," with "Good harbours" well-situated for fishing, and predicted that the settlers there "may Soone outdoe this people." In large part because of such profitable potential, Massachusetts fought first to seize control of the region (originally governed by other proprietors) and then, after the mid-1660s, to maintain its dominance there. Northeasterners, many of whom were not Puritans, chafed at the authority of "the Bostoners" but simultaneously recognized the value of the protection that subordination to the Bay Colony afforded them.[8]

The Wabanakis in the region were most commonly identified by the name of the river valleys in which their villages were located: Sacos, Androscoggins, Kennebecs, Penobscots, and so forth. Such villages consisted of multiple groups of family bands organized around older men and their wives, children, and other relatives. The villages were simultaneously intertwined and autonomous; no single Wabanaki chief sachem ruled the whole, but sachems of the different villages were related to one another by blood or marriage, and they often cooperated in both peace and war. By the final quarter of the seventeenth century, the Wabanakis had become heavily reliant on the manufactured items they obtained by trading furs to the Europeans, French as well as English, who had moved into their territory. Vital as that commerce was to both peoples—for the settlers in the region needed the income they earned by selling furs in Europe as much as the Indians needed guns and knives—the fur trade nevertheless was a source of constant friction, for each side regularly suspected the other of cheating.[9]

The presence of French settlers and Catholic priests in the region north-east of Penobscot Bay complicated such commercial relationships, for English and French traders competed for the same pelts and moose hides. From the mid-1620s on, l'Acadie (as the French called the area) or Nova Scotia (as the English referred to it) changed hands repeatedly as the two nations struggled for preeminence along the northeast coast. After the 1650s Acadians—by the 1670s a mixed group of French, Scots, and Wabanakis—traded primarily with "les Bastonnais," despite the fact that under the Treaty of Breda in 1667 France had once again regained control of the region. From the New Englanders' perspective, the greatest threat to their well-being was posed by Jean Vincent d'Abbadie, Baron de Castine, whose headquarters at Pentagoet on Penobscot Bay (now Castine) was located dangerously close to their northernmost outpost at Pemaquid. Castine married the daughter of Madockawando, chief sachem of the Penobscots, and was an adopted Wabanaki, which made him all the more dangerous.[10]

Yet in all likelihood war would not have erupted in the region had it not been for the armed struggle between Indians and Anglo-Americans in south-ern New England. The Wabanakis, who would have preferred to remain neutral in King Philip's War, found themselves pulled inexorably into the conflict by the demands of the opposing forces. On the one hand, the English distrusted their Wabanaki neighbors, making peaceful relationships nearly impossible to sustain during the southern war; on the other, the Wampa-noags, Nipmucks, and Narragansetts sought assistance and shelter from their fellow Algonquians in the north, especially after the death of King Philip. In consequence, fighting began in the vicinity of Casco Bay in September 1675, lasting until what one contemporary termed a "patched up" peace was nego-tiated in the same place in April 1678.[11]

Trouble had actually started during the summer of 1675, when some sailors abused the wife of Squando, a Saco sachem, leading to the drowning of her young child. In July, Sylvanus Davis, one of the Kennebec traders, learning of the outbreak of war to the south, asked nearby Wabanakis to surrender their weapons to prove their commitment to peace. Some complied, but others resisted, on the grounds that they needed their guns for hunting. Both inci-dents angered the Indians. On September 9, a small band of Wabanakis attacked a farm outside of Falmouth. The next day Lieutenant George Inger-soll (Mary Walcott's great-uncle) investigated the "great smoke" he had seen from the town, thereafter reporting to Andrew Alger that he and his men had found a house in ruins, with six people killed and three missing. The elderly

Thomas Wakely and his wife were dead, "neer halfe burnt," lying "halfe in, & halfe out of the house." Their adult son had been shot and "his head dashed in peices"; their daughter-in-law, "bigg with Child," had been scalped; and two of their grandchildren had "their heads dashed in peices, & laid by one another with their bellys to the ground, & an Oake plank laid upon their backs."[12]

New Englanders were well acquainted with death, but not this sort of death. Women dying in or shortly after childbirth, babies failing to survive the first year of life, adults falling victim to fatal accidents or mysterious illnesses: all were familiar (if not always easily explicable) occurrences. Yet Ingersoll's vivid description revealed that he and his small militia contingent had found the carnage at the Wakely farmstead truly horrifying. English settlers in northern New England had never experienced the like before. For their part, southern New Englanders would not have seen any similar sights for nearly four decades prior to 1675—not since 1637, when the Pequot War ended. Scenes resembling those Ingersoll depicted in such graphic detail would become all too common in the months and years that followed, but familiarity did not foster indifference. As later observations quoted throughout this book will demonstrate, New Englanders like George Ingersoll never grew accustomed to the violent death that seemed to emerge without warning from the forests, then to disappear quickly and unobtrusively whence it had come.

Lieutenant Ingersoll responded to the Wakelys' deaths by requesting reinforcements, fearing that "a company of Indians" was still in the area. And his suspicions proved all too correct. In subsequent weeks, small bands of Wabanakis raided garrison houses and farms in Saco, Black Point, Salmon Falls, and elsewhere. (Andrew Alger and one of Ingersoll's own sons were both among the more than fifty settlers killed.) By late October, a militia officer reported that "it is hardly imaginable the pannick fear that is upon our upland plantations & [people in] scattered places [are] deserting their habitations." Not all the English settlers thought the Indians' aggression unprovoked. Thomas Gardner, who ran the trading post at Pemaquid, told John Leverett, the governor of Massachusetts, that he attributed the assaults in part to "our owne Acttings." Because "these Indianes Amongst us live most by Hunting," he reminded Leverett, they needed their guns for subsistence. How then could the English legitimately have asked them to surrender their firearms? To clinch his point, Gardner observed that "these Indianes in these parts did never Apeare dissatisfied untill their Armes wear Taken Away," warning that the Wabanakis would now probably turn to the French for aid.[13]

The autumn hit-and-run raids and the colonists' attempts to retaliate ended with the early onset of especially heavy snowfalls that year. Over the next few months, the Massachusetts government dispatched to Maine companies of "country soldiers" to augment the inadequate regional militia forces. The troops, however, proved a mixed blessing to local residents and stimulated great controversy, especially in Black Point. There taxpayers later complained bitterly that they had not asked for the soldiers and had derived little benefit from their presence, yet they had nevertheless been required to pay the soldiers' expenses. Even more galling, they explained, was the fact that the local commander, Joshua Scottow, who had moved to Maine from Boston a few years earlier, had used the men for his own personal gain, employing them to pave his yard, move his barn, and build a palisade for his property.[14]

Perhaps the soldiers stationed in Maine did serve to deter attacks, for the Wabanakis did not resume their campaign when good weather returned. (Or possibly they merely needed to tend their own crops and complete their usual spring fishing.) Governor Leverett reported in mid-June 1676 that "the Eastern parts have been & are quiet," with Indians "coming in, professing they desire to bee at peace." Even some "that have been active & had taken prisoners are come in, brought in theire captives & delivered them up freely," he revealed, expressing his hope that such actions represented "reall" sentiments. Even so, he added, the authorities would "keepe a strict eye upon them."[15]

Leverett's caution appeared more than justified when the Wabanakis dashed expectations of renewed peaceful relations by launching a major assault on Falmouth on August 11. As was seen in chapter 2, thirty-four residents of the town, including many of Mercy Lewis's relatives, either died or were captured that day. Although initially the survivors assumed that they would soon be able to return to their homes, later fighting in the region rendered that impossible, and Falmouth was abandoned for five years. Falmouth's minister George Burroughs did not return until 1683, after a four-year stay in Salisbury and a difficult two years as pastor of the contentious parish at Salem Village.[16]

A few days after the assault on Falmouth, other Wabanakis raided the trading post at the mouth of the Kennebec. Frightened settlers abandoned settlements all along the coast north of Black Point. Thomas Gardner and other residents of Pemaquid, for instance, sought to escape from "the barborous heathen" by fleeing to Monhegan Island, whence they wrote to Boston to request a ship to carry away their many "distresed ffamilies." Gardner, well acquainted with the Wabanakis, listed three sources for the renewed conflict. The "cheefest" was the influence of hostile natives "from the westwards" (by which he meant the southern Algonquians), but also important had been the Wabanakis' lack of gunpowder the previous winter, which had caused many deaths, they "haveing nothing to kill food." A final contributing factor was "the perfidious & unjust dealing of som English . . . who have Stollen Eight or Nine persones from the Indianes." Gardner was referring to an incident in November 1675, when a Boston vessel under the command of William Waldron (a son of the major, armed with a formal commission from his father) had sailed to Acadia, nominally to trade but "principaly to take Indians." Through subterfuge and force they had captured several groups of Wabanaki people, including a "Sagamore & his squaw," then sailed to the Azores to sell them into slavery. Even though some of the perpetrators were subsequently arrested and tried in Boston, irrevocable damage was thereby done to Indian relations in the northeast.[17]

Whether Kankamagus and his June 1689 retinue knew of Richard Waldron's indirect involvement in these kidnappings fourteen years earlier is unknown, but he and his people were very well aware of the direct role the old trader had played in other reprehensible acts during the mid-1670s.

The first occurred in September 1676. Throughout the summer, as Governor Leverett remarked in June, Wabanakis and other Algonquians had gathered at Cocheco and other posts to demonstrate their peaceful intentions. The Pennacooks, who lived in the Piscataqua region, remained neutral during the first year of the war, and in early July 1676 Waldron confirmed that neutrality by negotiating a treaty not only with them but also with the Sacos and other Wabanaki villagers living as far north as Casco Bay. In the treaty, both sides promised to keep the peace; the Indians agreed not to assist or shelter combatants from the southern war. Major Waldron and his associates later admitted that they could not "Charge those that had made the Pease with any breach of Articles Save only that of entertaining our Southern Enemies."[18]

Nevertheless, in early September Waldron hastened to comply with orders he received from Boston to capture all the Indians at his trading post, an unknown number of whom had trickled in from the south, both before and after King Philip's death. The recent arrival of 130 soldiers from Massachusetts under the leadership of Captain William Hathorne (younger brother of the later Salem magistrate) allowed him to accomplish that feat by pretending to enlist the able-bodied men in the colonial forces. On September 6, as he informed his superiors,

> I drew up the Indians at Cocheco upon the open Ground before my house under the Notion of takeing them out into the Service, such of them as I saw meet, upon assembled I made them eate & Drink, & then surrounded them with the Army & calling the chiefe Sagamores into the Center I told them what must bee don, only that the Innocent should not be damnified, they surrendered their Armes 20 in Number. we have taken 80 fighting Men & 20 old men, & 250 women & children[,] 350 in all.

When he dispatched the prisoners to Boston by ship, as the authorities had directed, Waldron advised the colony's leaders to make distinctions among the captives, who included some Indians who "before the Pease had been very Active Against us but since have lived quietly & Attended Order." According to the Reverend William Hubbard, a contemporary chronicler of the war, seven or eight of the captives were executed in Boston and another two hundred or so sold into slavery elsewhere. The rest, including the Pennacook sachem Wannalancet, were eventually freed to return home—and to remember how Richard Waldron had betrayed them and their families, for most of those sold, like most of those captured, must have been women and children.[19]

Frontier dwellers accurately predicted the consequences of Waldron's deceit, anticipating "Suddain Spoyle" that would leave them "in a More danger[ous] Condision" than before. That was precisely what happened. While Captain Hathorne and his men sought (largely futilely) to engage the Indians in battle elsewhere, the Wabanakis attacked Wells, then the small settlement at Cape Neddick, and finally, in October, the Black Point fort itself. Joshua Scottow had gone to Boston to defend himself against charges of misappropriating the soldiers' labor the preceding winter. In his absence, the inhabitants of the fort mounted only a feeble defense before slipping away by sea while their resident magistrate, Henry Jocelyn, negotiated with besieging Indians in the forest outside the fort. When Jocelyn returned to find the post deserted except for his own family, he had no choice but to capitulate. Brian Pendleton, the magistrate in Saco, reported that after soldiers stationed there learned of the loss of Black Point, "thay weare as mad to make away as ever I saw any men." The fishermen, too, hurried to leave, "supposinge it noe boote to stay here against such a multitude of enemyes." All the towns northeast of York and Wells then disintegrated, their residents dispersing primarily into various locations in Essex County. A lack of detailed records makes it impossible to trace the specific destinations of most of the refugees. Most likely, they relocated to towns where they already had friends or relatives.[20]

In the wake of these disasters, a November attempt to negotiate another treaty and arrange for the return of captives failed, and so in February 1676/7 Richard Waldron sailed northeast along the coast with militiamen from Maine and Salem (the latter under the command of Lieutenant Thomas Fiske) to attack the Wabanaki homeland and rescue captives by force or, failing that, to try once more to reach an agreement to end the fighting. After a series of frustrating meetings in different locations, Waldron managed to ransom three settlers. But fearing that the Indians intended to ambush him during one of their negotiating sessions, he again acted treacherously and struck first—under a flag of truce. One of the Wabanaki sachems was killed in the fighting; another, a "Notorious Rogue," Waldron executed the next day. In the melee the colonists also captured Madockawando's sister.[21]

Some months later, in early July 1677, a group of Wabanaki sachems excoriated Waldron's perfidious actions in a message to the "governor of Boston" carried by a released female captive. "This is to let you to understand how major walldin served us," they declared; "is that your fashing to com & m[a]ke pese & then kill us we are afraid you will do so agen Major Waldin do ly we were not minded to kill no body. . . . Major Waldin have bin the cause of killing all that have bin kiled this sommer."[22]

The year 1677, indeed, lacked the long hiatus in fighting that had marked 1676. In mid-April, for example, Waldron recounted to his superiors recent losses on both shores of the Piscataqua. In the space of six days, two men had been killed at Wells and seven adults and children at Kittery, along with two men in New Hampshire. Seven captives had been taken but some were rescued or freed almost immediately. The Indians, he declared, "run Sculking about in Small parties like Wolves"; "wee have had parties of men after them . . . can't Certainly say they have kil'd any of them." Attempting to reestablish a presence on the coast, Massachusetts reoccupied the Black Point fort and sent a small company to the mouth of the Kennebec. The Indians then again attacked Black Point twice. In May, they were repulsed and their leader killed, but during another clash in June they inflicted heavy casualties on colonial forces.[23]

After the second Black Point battle, Governor Edmund Andros of New York decided to intervene by dispatching soldiers to Pemaquid. Bay Colony leaders distrusted Andros's motives (in part because they suspected that Albany merchants had been supplying the Wabanakis with guns and ammunition) but could hardly object openly to his assistance, which was desperately needed. Resources were stretched so thin that "the Eastern Deputies" in the General Court asked their colleagues in June to order all refugees to return to Maine, and requested that "those that remaine may be comanded not to depart without licence from authoritie upon their perrill." Furthermore, they urged that "those young men that are out of Imployment & not capeable of provideing for themselves may be Impressed into the service of the country." Rumors that Castine had promised to aid the Indian alliance increased the anxieties of colonial officials.[24]

The war entered a unique phase when in June and July the Wabanakis targeted fishing craft as well as farms and trading posts. The Indians managed to take more than twenty ships, most of them from Salem, but in mid-July members of one crew overpowered their captors and sailed their ship into Marblehead harbor, where their arrival precipitated one of the most brutal episodes of the war. Filled with the families of captive fishermen and bulging with refugees, Marblehead gave the Indians an "angry" and "clamorous" greeting. A crowd at the docks asked the sailors "why we kept them alive and why we had not killed them." Although informed that the fishermen hoped to receive some payment for the captives to offset their losses of gear and clothing, the Marbleheaders remained dissatisfied. Surrounding the men and their prisoners, a group of women "drove us by force from them," James Roules later attested,

> and laid violent hands upon the captives, some stoning us in the mean-
> time, because we would protect them, others seizing them by the hair, got
> full possession of them, nor was there any way left by which we could res-
> cue them. Then with stones, billets of wood, and what else they might,
> they made an end of these Indians. We were kept at such distance that we
> could not see them till they were dead, and then we found them with their
> heads off and gone, and their flesh in a manner pulled from their bones.

He had recognized none of the women, Roules declared. But members of the mob had complained that if the Indians had been turned over to authorities in Boston, they would have been freed. The female rioters insisted that "if there had been forty of the best Indians in the country here, they would have killed them all, though they should be hanged for it." No one could stop the murderers, Roules indicated, "until they had finished their bloody purpose."[25]

Roules's claim that he did not know any of the rioters is striking. The Marblehead fisherman might have lied to protect longtime acquaintances, or perhaps (as he said) the "tumultation these women made" had so confused him that he could not identify any individuals. But it is also possible, even likely, that James Roules really did *not* know them, and that instead of being local residents the turbulent women were among the many refugees who had flocked into Essex County from Maine the previous year. Under those circumstances—if they were indeed widows and bereaved mothers from the frontier—their vicious treatment of the Wabanakis exemplified their fury at the destruction of their homes and families.[26]

Both sides, then, felt enraged in July 1677. Superficially, there appeared little hope of reconciliation. Yet that month a group of Kennebec sachems took the first tentative steps toward ending the bloodshed. Insisting that "we are owners of the country & it is wide and full of engons & we can drive you out," they nevertheless indicated that "our desire is to be quiet." Although they complained to Bay Colony authorities that the Kennebecs had been "all way for peace" while "you allways broke the peace," they asked to resume normal relations, proposed a prisoner exchange, and declared, "we can fight as well as others but we are willing to live pesabel." We would like to trade with you, they said, "as we have done for many years we pray you send us such things as we name powder cloth tobacko liker corn bread."[27]

Massachusetts responded positively to the overture, as did Andros's men at Pemaquid. On July 17, Anthony Brockholst, the commander there, reached agreement with the Kennebec sagamores, including Moxis. Both sides concurred in ceasing all hostile acts and releasing all captives. The Wabanakis agreed to return the fishing vessels they had taken and to subject themselves to English law. If people on either side caused injury to those on the other in the future, the combatants decided that aggrieved parties should apply for relief to the appropriate authorities (settlers to the sachems, Indians to the magistrates) instead of seeking revenge directly. In August, first Squando (who initially rejected the treaty) and then Madockawando accepted the same terms in further negotiations conducted at Pemaquid in the presence of Joshua Scottow. Yet despite the evidently successful agreement, sporadic violence continued for months, in part because Massachusetts officially refused to acknowledge the validity of a treaty signed by Andros's representative, and in part because Wabanaki sachems disagreed among themselves over the benefits or drawbacks of a peace accord. A final treaty, with broader provisions than the first, was eventually signed at Casco in April 1678.[28]

THE SECOND INDIAN WAR BEGINS

Hostilities between the Anglo-Americans and the Wabanakis erupted again just ten and a half years later. In the interim, former residents returned to

Maine's frontier and new settlers flocked in. By 1688, not only was the region between Wells and Falmouth fully resettled, but new towns were also being established to the northeast of Casco Bay. As the size of the population and the area of settlement expanded, the colonists increasingly ignored elements of the Casco accord the Indians regarded as vital: a requirement that settlers pay a "yearly Tribute of Corn," that they respect the Wabanakis' fishing rights on the Saco River, and that they not open new lands to settlement unless those lands had first been properly purchased. If the underlying friction that helped to instigate the First Indian War stemmed from the fur trade, that which underlay the second came rather from conflicts over growing numbers of land grants issued by Bay Colony authorities without regard to Indian claims to the soil.[29]

Although rumors of possible Indian plots against resettled frontier communities emerged in early 1682 and again two years later, reports of "surly" Indians actually threatening the residents of Maine appeared only in January 1687/8 and thereafter. On August 6, 1688, several Sacos fired on settlers' cattle ravaging their cornfields, initiating a confrontation that ended with "verey threatning words to the English of Shooting them." The first deaths of settlers, though, occurred in western Massachusetts, when in mid-August Indian raiders from French Canada slew some members of English families living in the upper Connecticut Valley.[30]

Taken together, the two evidently unconnected and widely separated incidents in August 1688 set off a panic in Massachusetts and on the Maine frontier. Wild rumors about 200—or 700, or 2,000—local Indians gathering at Pennacook with French officers and French Indians to "consult about a war with the English" flashed through the countryside. Gossipers were assured that "all the Youngmen were for fighting against the English, but the Elder men did oppose them," that "they have erected A Fort of four Acres of Ground," even that "credible persons" had intimated that "some of our owne Gentlemen" had a "hand in this evil designe" because "it is not for the Kings Interest" that New Englanders control the colony. That last insinuation would bubble to the surface again and again during the next nine months, for Bay Colony residents deeply resented the fact that their original charter had been abrogated in 1684 and their colony subsequently incorporated into the larger Dominion of New England. In particular, they intensely distrusted Sir Edmund Andros, the autocratic former governor of New York named to head the dominion by King James II.[31]

Andros, who had had considerable experience in dealing with Native Americans in New York and who had intervened in Maine affairs in 1677, was absent as fear increasingly gripped northern New England. He and some of the members of the Dominion's governing council had gone to New York at the end of July; other councilors were away from Boston. In their absence, the remaining council members—evidently Joseph Dudley, William Stoughton, John Usher, and Samuel Shrimpton[32]—ordered military supplies sent to the frontier and directed local militia commanders "to take and destroy all [Indians engaging] in acts of hostility and to seize all suspected persons," even those who offered no resistance. Captain Benjamin Blackman of Saco responded by ordering the arrest of twenty Wabanakis. Although the group included Hope Hood (an Androscoggin leader) and "the Donys" (father and son sachems of the Kennebunks), most of the captives were women and children.[33]

What happened next might best be termed a tragedy of errors. Having seized the Indians, Maine's military and political leaders did not know what to do with them. First the small group of prisoners was shipped north to Falmouth. There Edward Tyng, the local magistrate, decided that the captives should instead be transported south to Boston. In early September, small groups of Wabanakis, mystified by these moves, inquired at several different houses in Maine "why Capt Blackman tooke the Indians att Saco & sent them away"; at one, asking if Governor Andros had issued the order for the arrest, they were told perceptively that since Andros was in New York, the whole affair was likely "onely Blackmans folly." No matter: fearing for the safety of their kinfolk, the Wabanakis captured sixteen English settlers from scattered locations along the coast to hold as hostages for the return of their people. Faced with a quickly escalating crisis, the councilors in Boston decided to dispatch the captive Indians north to Falmouth once more, authorizing their associate William Stoughton to negotiate a general prisoner exchange. For reasons that remain obscure, Stoughton failed to make contact with the Wabanakis, and on September 19 he sailed back to Boston, leaving the captives in Falmouth under Tyng's control and still on shipboard. That very day the first blood was shed. On an isolated point of land in Casco Bay a small party of Indians holding some of the English prisoners encountered an equally small group of settlers. They skirmished, and in the aftermath of the fight "the youngmen" among the Wabanakis killed four of their captives. "Egeremett the Sachem Seemed to be troubled att" that action, one of the surviving English prisoners later observed. Edgeremet, a Kennebec sagamore, had good reason to be concerned. A war that would last until 1699, and which would devastate both Indian and Anglo-American communities of Maine and New Hampshire, had begun.[34]

When Sir Edmund Andros at last returned to Boston from New York in mid-October, he found "a Pannick feare" prevailing throughout northern

New England. By then, two troops of militia had been raised to serve under Edward Tyng's command in Falmouth; the Casco Bay village of North Yarmouth had been attacked and temporarily abandoned; more settlers and militiamen had been killed; and Tyng had shipped all but one of the Indian captives *back* to Boston yet again.[35] Andros, who had visited the eastern settlements in the late spring, had plundered Castine's outpost at Pentagoet, and had left that region "in great Peace" in May, was astonished and infuriated by the chaos precipitated in his absence. He reported acidly to London that he had made the councilors "Sencible of the Unadvised Seizeing of Indians & their Raiseing & Sending fforces without Authority." After criticizing his subordinates' actions in no uncertain terms, he set about trying to repair the damage he believed they had caused.[36]

As a first step, the governor ordered the much-traveled prisoners freed, they "being Charged with noe particuler Cryme." Expecting—or at least hoping for—reciprocity on the part of the Wabanakis, he issued a proclamation calling on them "to Release all Christian Captives" and requesting that the Casco Bay settlers' murderers be turned over to Massachusetts authorities. He also ordered the outfitting of several vessels that could be used to protect Maine's valuable fishing outposts.[37]

Andros's efforts came to naught, as the Wabanakis responded to the proclamation by attacking additional settlements northeast of Casco Bay. The governor then led a 600-man army in a winter campaign against the enemy, and, although he never encountered the Wabanakis directly, he subsequently boasted that his efforts had "reduced [them] to great Extremityes" by destroying their food supplies. But Andros's opponents later offered a very different interpretation of his actions. His winter campaign had been overly costly and "ineffectuall." What precipitated the war was not Blackman's seizure of the Wabanakis but instead Andros's raid on Pentagoet, which had invited retaliation by the Indian allies of the French. Andros had then compounded the problem by not hurrying back to Boston when informed of the outbreak of hostilities. His opponents "particularly Objected" to the release of the Indian prisoners, "some of them knowne Enemies to the English, . . . without any Exchange of our English Captives then in the Enemies hands."[38]

Many New Englanders, indeed, expressed outrage at the governor's order freeing the Wabanakis captured at Saco. Sylvanus Davis, who had relocated from the Kennebec to Falmouth when Maine was resettled, complained that the men had been "Cruell mordrous Rogs in the first Indian war"; it was, he emphasized, *very straing that a govnor shoold bee soe Carless of his majestys subjects & Intrest.* He and others hinted darkly that Sir Edmund Andros, from the Isle of Jersey and "of a French extract, so in the French interests," had had "Sinister designs . . . as to our Troubles with the Indians"; perhaps, Davis wrote, Andros had planned his winter campaign "to impovrish this country."[39]

Throughout the winter of 1688–1689, after the Wabanakis' release, New Englanders told each other tales of Andros's supposed complicity with their enemies in the war. Most of these stories were reputed to have originated with individual natives: "Solomon thomas Indian . . . [said that] when the fight shoold bee att East ward the governor woold sit in his Wigwam and say o brave Indians"; "John James Indian of his owne volontary mind say[d] that the govornor was a Rouge and had hired indians to kill the English"; another Wabanaki declared that "the Governor had more love for them the Indians, then for his Majesties Subjects the English."[40] The anti-Andros tales did not end with such rumors; two former soldiers, for example, deposed that during the winter at his Pemaquid fort Andros had given powder and shot to the sister of Madockawando and the wife of Moxis. One added that the men in the fort afterwards "did very much Question among themselves wheither Sr Edm: Andros did not Intend the Destruction of the English Armie, and brought them theither to be a sacrifice to their heathen Adversaries."[41]

Were the two soldiers telling the truth? Probably. Andros could have been making a friendly gesture toward the sachems he still hoped to conciliate. As events early in King Philip's War had shown, northern Indians now depended on guns for hunting, and without gunpowder and bullets they could not kill the game that provided much of their food during the winter. As a result of Andros's destruction of their stores, the Penobscots found themselves in dire straits for lack of food by late in the season. A timely gift of bullets and gunpowder, Andros could well have concluded, might work to his long-term advantage by easing tensions and paving the way for renewed negotiations. In practical terms, it might also prevent the Wabanakis from raiding English settlements in search of food.[42]

Were the rumors of Andros's treachery true? Surely not—but that New Englanders found them compelling, and that they were so pervasive, is revealing. The gossip disclosed an exceptional level of distrust of the colony's leadership. In the spring, such fears contributed significantly to the movement that turned Andros out of office during the Massachusetts phase of the Glorious Revolution. Boston's merchants and political leaders acted against Andros on April 18, 1689, even before they received definite word that James II, Andros's patron, had been replaced on the throne by William of Orange and his wife Mary (James's Protestant daughter). A traveler from the

West Indies had recently brought fragmentary information implying that such a change had occurred, but the Bostonians would not have official notice of the alteration in the English monarchy until late May. Yet they nonetheless ousted Governor Andros a month after his return from Maine. According to one of the governor's partisans, his overthrow resulted from "many foolish and nonsensicall storys" that he was "confederated with" the French and Indians, and that "the Indian war was but a sham, for hee design'd noe evil to the Indians, but the destruction of the Country." Those tales had "misera-bly distracted" New Englanders, he wrote, making them believe that Sir Edmund was their "great Enemy."[43]

The uprising against Andros by prominent Bostonians had disastrous consequences for Maine residents.[44] As news that the governor had been deposed and arrested spread to the northern posts, the militiamen pressed to serve in Andros's forts and garrisons deserted in droves. Not that they needed to: as one of its first acts, the new "Council for Safety of the People and Con-servation of the Peace" ordered Edward Tyng and the other Maine magis-trates to reduce the size of frontier garrisons immediately and to dismiss the officers in charge, who, along with Andros, were suspected of communicating with "the french & eastern Indians in order to the destruction of New England."[45]

Chaos ensued. One beleaguered commander still at his post reported that the Wabanakis were saying that the Massachusetts authorities "doe intend to Slight and Disowne these Esterne parts." If true, he observed, that news would cause people to "leave theire habitations and Stocks and Desartt the Country." Frontier communities that had previously complained of the cost of supporting Andros's garrisons—and of the constant militia service to which they were subjected—now wondered how they would be defended if the Indians chose to act. The residents of Saco did not have long to wait for an answer. Just three days after the toppling of Andros's regime, eight or ten Wabanakis, "sundry of them well known" in the town, launched a surprise attack. They burned two houses and wounded five or six people. The next day they moved on to nearby Cape Porpoise, burning a house and killing one man. On April 25 the leaders of Wells informed "the Superior Power now in being in Boston" that inhabitants of the two communities had been forced to flee to a garrisoned island, "where they remaine in a deplorable case, and are subject to starving, or murder, or both if speedy succor be not afforded."[46]

That "Superior Power" consisted initially of such Dominion councilors as Wait Winthrop and Bartholomew Gedney, and the man they quickly desig-nated as governor: the elderly Simon Bradstreet, the last elected to the post before the charter was abrogated in 1684. Eventually, the councilors reasserted the validity of the old charter, held elections under it in the spring of 1690, and operated the government on an ad hoc basis (with Bradstreet continuing as governor) until the new charter issued by William and Mary was implemented in May 1692. Bradstreet and the council, in other words, had to confront the war on the Maine–New Hampshire frontier at the same time they were attempting to consolidate their authority over the Bay Colony itself.[47]

And there was much to confront, especially after the June 27 assault on Cocheco and the killing of Richard Waldron. The councilors' first instinct was to leave New Hampshire residents to their own devices. Responding to desperate pleas for help from the Portsmouth magistrates in the wake of the Cocheco raid, Bradstreet advised them to "put yourselves into such a way . . . as may accommodate the present emergency in the best manner you may," explaining that Massachusetts could not at that time "impress men, or levy money" to assist them. But then the Wabanakis in quick succession attacked Black Point, Sagadahoc, Saco, and Oyster River. In early August, the Indians turned their attention to the stronghold at Pemaquid. On August 3, after a two-day battle, the town and fort surrendered to a combined force of three or four hundred Penobscots and Frenchmen. There the sachems Madockawando and Moxis asserted confidently to the fort's commander that "Sir Edmund Andros was a great rogue and had almost starved them all last winter, but now he be a prisoner, and they no care for the New England people[.] They [will] have all their own Countrey by and by."[48]

The threat to their valuable province of Maine led the self-proclaimed rulers of Massachusetts to respond to the looming disaster by dispatching a flurry of orders raising troops, placing a bounty of £8 on every scalp of a "ffighting man," and promising militiamen any plunder they might acquire in the course of their service. Yet few men volunteered, and those pressed into the forces seemed inadequate to the task in both quantity and quality.[49] From the Maine frontier came nothing but discouraging news: of settlers leaving by the score, "soe that wee Grow weaker & weker every day"; of village after village "in a miserable shattered Condition"; of people "brought so Exceeding Low that they are Just Redy to desert." Indeed, after a second attack on their settlement, the residents of North Yarmouth and the soldiers garrisoned there decided to abandon the town. Such desperate circumstances led the pious magistrate and militia leader Robert Pike, of Salisbury, one of the northernmost towns of Massachusetts proper, to wonder aloud whether "we may be a peopl saved of the Lord tho a peopl that distroy our selvs."[50]

In mid-September, the beleaguered frontier residents finally got a break when a Dutch ship sailed into Casco Bay from Pemaquid with a timely warn-

ing to Sylvanus Davis, now in command of Fort Loyal, built in 1680 to protect Falmouth. The Wabanakis were massing to the north, "Resolved to use
theire uttermost Indevor to Destroy Casco: perteculerly & all the Engles In
Jenerall." Davis immediately wrote to Boston for help, and over the next few
days he and others peppered the Massachusetts Council with more detailed
information. Some of the most authoritative came from Richard Waldron's
adult daughter, acquired in a prisoner exchange on September 17:

> the Indians tell the woman that . . . they resolve forth with to Set upon
> this towne, which they reckon as their owne alreadie & then to their
> design in taking and ruining the whole province, they deride and scoff at
> us after a strange manner, they say they are much encouraged by some
> Gentlemen in Boston for the mannaging the warr against us which makes
> them go on with undaunted courage.

For once, the governor and council reacted effectively. After persuading Benjamin Church, an experienced Indian fighter from King Philip's War, to take
command of troops raised in Plymouth and Boston, they quickly dispatched
both men and provisions to Falmouth on board several vessels, including the
colony's sloop *Mary*, captained by John Alden.[51]

The ships and troops arrived on Friday afternoon, September 20, just in
time to save the town. Church realized that an attack was imminent, so he
landed his men after nightfall, having previously kept them concealed below
decks. Thus, when the Wabanakis assaulted Falmouth the next morning by
crossing Anthony Brackett's farm in order to reach the peninsula on which
the town center was located, they encountered unexpected resistance from
the Massachusetts soldiers as well as from local militiamen. Sylvanus Davis
reported "a fierce fight" lasting about six hours, in which the New Englanders
"forced them to Retreate & Judge many of them to bee slaine . . . there was
Grate firings on Both sides." The English lost eleven soldiers killed and ten
wounded, some of whom died later. How many townspeople were among the
casualties is uncertain. But the Reverend George Burroughs again survived
an attack on Falmouth; on September 22 Church declared himself "well Satisfied with" Burroughs, who had been "present with us yesterday in the
fight."[52]

For Burroughs and others like him who had also lived in Falmouth thirteen years earlier, the assault must have stimulated bitter memories, for during the First Indian War, too, the Wabanakis had attacked the town by first
raiding the farm of Anthony Brackett. Yet in the aftermath of the victory of
September 21, 1689, the dangers must have seemed happily in the past. In his

memoirs, Church recalled that "the poor inhabitants wonderfully rejoiced that the Almighty had favoured them so much." The Falmouth residents jubilantly observed to Church that "it was the first time that ever the eastward Indians had been put to flight."[53]

And "fly" the Wabanakis did. The Reverend Cotton Mather commented in his history of the war that they "Retired into the howling Desarts"—which he also termed "their inaccessible Swamps"—"where there was no Coming at them." Church and the militia commanders attached to his command (Major Jeremiah Swayne, Captain William Bassett, Captain Simon Willard, and others) repeatedly sent out scouting parties, but except for one brief encounter a few days after the Falmouth attack, Church reported, they could not "make Discovery of Any Boddy of the enemy only soom few sculkin Roges." Eventually, the Massachusetts government ordered most of the army disbanded, leaving only a limited number of soldiers stationed in Maine and New Hampshire over the winter.[54]

The Bay Colony proclaimed a day of thanksgiving for December 19, 1689. "The God of Heaven," it announced, did "mitigate His many Frowns upon us in the Summer past, with a mixture of some very signal Favours." Consequently, "our Indian Enemies have had a Check put upon their Designs of Blood and Spoil," and "we have such hopes of our God's adding yet more perfection to our Deliverances." As Massachusetts officials had done in the past and as they would do in the future, they thus attributed both their defeats and their victories to God's will. As his chosen people, they could do no else.[55]

One sour note remained. After all, the Indians who held Waldron's daughter had told her that "they are much encouraged by some Gentlemen in Boston for the mannaging the warr." To whom did they refer? If regarded as credible, the remark could be taken in two quite distinct ways. For the leaders of the Glorious Revolution in Massachusetts, it surely meant Andros and his aides, still held under guard in Boston but nevertheless able to communicate easily and openly with the outside world. To partisans of the former governor, however, it meant the greedy Boston merchants and their political allies. In the defense of his conduct submitted to authorities in London after his return, Sir Edmund Andros charged that soon after he was overthrown the Wabanakis were "supplyed with Amunicon and Provision out of a Vessell sent from Boston by some of the Cheife Conspirators before the Insurrection to Trade with them," which "Encouraged and Enabled [them] to renew and pursue the Warr."[56]

To residents of the frontier, of course, what mattered was not *who* was trading arms and ammunition to the French and the Indians, but simply the allegations that such trade was commonplace. For the people of Maine and New Hampshire, mercantile profits or possible diplomatic advantages paled in comparison to the threat to their families and communities posed by armed Wabanakis. No wonder, then, that the swirling rumors charging that *someone* was engaging in commerce with the enemy always found ready listeners on the northeastern frontier.[57]

THE DISASTERS OF 1690

Monday, February 24, 1689/90; Boston. Samuel Sewall and his wife hosted a dinner party for twenty, including Governor Simon Bradstreet and his wife, William Stoughton, Cotton Mather of the Second (North) Church, the merchant Thomas Brattle, and the two pastors of Sewall's Third (South) Church, Samuel Willard and Joshua Moodey. What should have been a pleasant and festive occasion, though, turned to "bitterness," Sewall noted in his diary, when the post arrived from Albany with the "amazing news" of "the Massacre at Schenectady by the French." He filled in the details at the actual date of the event, February 8–9: "Schenectady, a village 20 miles above Albany, destroy'd by the French. 60 Men, Women and Children murder'd. Women with Child rip'd up, Children had their Brains dash'd out. Were surprise'd about 11 or 12 aclock Satterday night, being divided, and secure." Governor Bradstreet, reading the dispatches at Sewall's before and after dinner, must have been struck by the irony of a phrase he had drafted just eleven days before the attack: "This Winter season forbids the stirring of our Indian enemies," he had confidently informed the ministry in London.[58]

Sewall's brief diary entry encapsulated most of the key points about the raid: the French and Indians had attacked about midnight, in the middle of winter when such an onslaught was least expected; the village had been unguarded, in part because of internal dissension; and the raiders had shown little mercy to their victims, regardless of age or sex. By early March, one new and terrifying piece of information emerged from the maelstrom of reports. French and Indian prisoners captured and interrogated by those who chased the raiders revealed that their party had not been alone in undertaking a wilderness march in winter. They had departed from Montreal, but believed that another large group had left Quebec, headed for New England.[59]

Tuesday, March 18, 1689/90; Salmon Falls. The Schenectady prisoners' information proved to be horrifyingly accurate. Early on March 18, "between break of the day & sunrise—when most were a bed & no watch kept neither in fort nor house," a force of about sixty "Half Indianized French, and Half

Frenchified Indians," led by a French officer and Hope Hood of the Androscoggins, attacked the village of Salmon Falls. The next day, two Portsmouth
magistrates described "the dreadfull destruction" to the council. The fort and
more than twenty houses had been burned, many cattle killed, and eighty to
a hundred people killed or captured, of whom "between twenty & Thirty
[were] able men." Pursuing militia from Portsmouth, York, and Cocheco had
eventually caught up with and skirmished with the raiders, but did not know
what casualties they had inflicted.[60]

Again a captive taken after the battle provided important information.
The French soldier indicated that they had intended to strike a "more east-
erly" site, before being dissuaded by Hope Hood, whom they had encountered in the woods and who had "pilotted [them] to fall upon Salmon falls."
When asked their original destination, he replied that they "came forth . . .
principly against Monsuir Tyng & the place where he lived." Denied a victory
at Falmouth the preceding September by Benjamin Church's timely arrival,
the force of French and Indians had once more targeted Fort Loyal.[61]

Before news of the Salmon Falls raid arrived in Boston, Bay Colony leaders had already decided to take the initiative in the war for the first time. Acting on a proposal submitted in January by a group of merchants including
Bartholomew Gedney and Captain John Alden, they committed themselves
in mid-March to launching an expedition against the French at Port Royal,
Acadia. The plan involved joint public-private financing, with merchant subscribers and volunteer soldiers alike profiting from shares of any resulting
plunder. On March 20, Governor Bradstreet explained to the ministry in
London that in "the general opinion of the whole Countrey" the Indian war
could not be ended, "nor will their Majesties subjects here ever live in Peace;
but by the dislodging and removal of those ill neighbours the ffrench." Success in this endeavor, he predicted, could spur New England to attack
Canada itself. To general acclaim, the council chose the Maine-born baronet
Sir William Phips as commander in chief. At the same time the Port Royal
expedition was being planned, councilors also reacted positively to requests
from Albany for assistance in attacking Quebec or Montreal. In late March
Bradstreet proposed an intercolonial meeting to discuss such a scheme.[62]

The immediate difficulties faced by the northeastern settlements came a
distant second to grandiose strategies, for the Bay Colony's leaders quickly
concluded that the settlers' "own carelessness and want of vigilance" had
caused both the Schenectady and Salmon Falls tragedies. "We find that
hardly any Garrison has been taken except by Surprize," observed Samuel

Sewall, writing for the council. Such reasoning clearly implied that the victims of the raids bore primary responsibility for their own terrible fates, and therefore that Massachusetts could not be blamed for any losses. If frontier residents would merely stay on their guard, they could defend themselves easily enough. Fitz-John Winthrop of Connecticut (brother of Wait Winthrop, the Massachusetts councilor) fully concurred with that conclusion. When settlers displayed "unpardonable negligence" and failed to take appropriate steps to preserve their own safety, "such a people are miserable and canot be saved," he observed in response to reports of the assault on Schenectady.[63]

So, after ordering 120 additional men from the Essex County militia sent northeastward, the council devoted its main energies to completing the arrangements for Phips's Port Royal expedition, which sailed from Boston on April 20. The next day, Samuel Sewall and William Stoughton set off for Manhattan, where on May 1 they promised that Massachusetts would contribute men and matériel to a combined colonial attack on Montreal. And on April 24, the council dispatched John Hathorne and Jonathan Corwin to Maine and New Hampshire to investigate "the State and Condition of the Inhabitants there." It directed them to ascertain how many soldiers were stationed at the various outposts, to advise the residents on how best to defend themselves, and to recommend the return to Massachusetts of any provincial soldiers "uncapeable of Service or of more than absolute necessity to be continued."[64]

Hathorne and Corwin acted quickly. Just six days later, they wrote from York to summarize their findings. Many garrisons had no soldiers at all; others, Black Point and Saco among them, had six or fewer. Most of the troops were stationed at York, Wells, and Kittery (a total of about a hundred under two different commanders) or Falmouth, which housed sixty men under Captain Simon Willard. Then they issued recommendations to the leaders of the beleaguered province. Echoing parts of their instructions word for word, they advised constant scouting, attacks on Wabanaki fishing places, and withdrawal into a few garrisons that could be easily defended. They also exhorted the frontiersmen to take "due Care" that "you may not be supprized by the enemy and Sudenly destroyed as other places have benn."[65]

When the Essex magistrates returned to the Bay Colony, they must likewise have presented proposals to the governor and council for the future disposition of the troops then stationed on the frontier. No extant record reveals what advice they offered their superiors, nor is there a surviving account of the council's deliberations. But the councilors concluded that Willard's men were no longer needed in Falmouth. If Hathorne and Corwin had strongly advocated maintaining a garrison there, it is hard to imagine the council having made that decision. On Thursday, May 15, responding to orders from Boston, Captain Willard marched his sixty soldiers out of Fort Loyal.[66]

About daybreak on Friday, May 16, a combined force of four or five hundred Wabanakis and French soldiers fell on Falmouth. This time, no Benjamin Church sailed into the harbor to save the town.

Tuesday, May 20, 1690; Falmouth, as described by Captain Sylvanus Davis:

> about 3 Clok after noone wee ware taken. They fought us 5 days & 4 nights in which time thay kild & woonded the Greatest parte of our men Burned all the howses & att last wee ware forst to have a perly with: them in order for a surender . . . wee Demand if thare was any french amongst them & if thay wold Give us quarter thay Answred thay ware french men & that thay woold Give us Good quarter . . . & that wee shoold have liberty to march to the next English towne. . . . but as soone as thay had us in theire Coustady thay Broke theire Articcuels sufred our wiming & Children & our men to bee mad Captiffs in the Hands of the Heathen to bee Cruelley murdred & Destroyed many of them & espetishal our wonded men, only the french kept my self & 3 or 4 more & Carried us over Land for Canada.

The attackers, Davis said, were led by Madockawando and "thoes Indians that wee had in hould that Sir Androus ordred to bee clered," accompanied by Castine himself.[67]

The loss of Falmouth and about two hundred people stunned New Englanders, leading to the immediate abandonment of the small settlements southwest of Casco Bay. "Nothing now remains Eastward of Welles," reported Major Charles Frost and others from Portsmouth on May 22, noting that two ships sent to Casco to investigate had observed burning buildings everywhere along the coast. Three or four hundred refugees, "most women & Children," had arrived in Portsmouth that week; "Wells will desert if not forthwith reinforced." That threat elicited a council order to send 120 more militiamen to Wells and York, but the outlook appeared gloomy. One discouraged New Englander wrote, "We are precipitated into such distress & danger, as we have never seen before. . . . God is now come forth against us with an ax, a French ax, accompanied with Indian Hatchetts, & our very roote is like to receive the Stroake thereof." Multiplying their woes, Thomas Danforth, president of the province, reportedly told Maine residents in response to their "earnest addresses [to Boston] . . . for Succour" that "the Lord Jesus Christ was King of the Earth as well as the heavens, and if he [Jesus] did not help them he [Danforth] could not."[68]

Yet other news, as Samuel Sewall commented in his diary, partly "abates our sorrow for the loss of Casco": on May 22 word arrived from Sir William Phips that his attack on Port Royal had been successful. A great deal of plunder had been taken, and those who invested in the enterprise, including Sewall himself, seemed likely to profit handsomely. Heartened by the victory, the council proceeded with its larger plan of launching a naval expedition against Quebec, also to be led by Phips, in coordination with the overland assault on Montreal. The major burden of the Montreal campaign was to be borne by New York and Connecticut. Although Massachusetts contributed some money, the colony reneged on its initial commitment of troops because of its need for men elsewhere.[69]

As men and supplies were being gathered in Boston and Albany for the projected attacks on the French strongholds on the St. Lawrence River, the war in the northeast continued. Even more than before, reports reaching Boston and London revealed that northern New England's resources were being stretched to the breaking point. For example, on July 4 a militia troop led by Captain John Floyd set out from Exeter to destroy some Pennacook cornfields near the Piscataqua River. "Perceiving their Motion," the Wabanakis attacked Exeter in the men's absence, taking a garrison and scattering its defenders. On July 6 Floyd's men and the same group of Wabanakis engaged in a "Bloody Action," from which Floyd eventually had to retreat to Portsmouth after taking heavy casualties. The Indians, as they had at Falmouth, seemed to have an uncanny knowledge of where colonial troops were or, more precisely, where they were *not*.[70]

Although one writer described Essex County as "moste of itt in Armes goeing to releive those parts," the more common response from those called up was reluctance and complaint. As demands for men mounted, local leaders balked. So many were being pressed into provincial service, contended Nathaniel Saltonstall of Haverhill and others, that their own towns were being left undefended.[71] That less than one quarter of the 3,000 men needed for the Quebec expedition volunteered—despite the promise of plunder— added to the difficulty. Samuel Sewall recorded in his diary in late July that two militia majors had told the council "that if so many be press'd for Canada as the Order mentions, the fronteers will draw in." And the problem extended beyond manpower: when Captain John Alden, acting on the council's orders, went to Marblehead to confiscate the town's cannon for the campaign against Quebec, he was opposed "in a tumultuous and riotous manner" by men who claimed that "it was unreasonable, that the Gunes should be tacken away from the Towne since they laye open to their Enemie."[72]

On August 9, 1690, the Phips fleet finally sailed for Quebec, where it failed miserably in October. Contrary winds, smallpox raging through the ranks, and poor tactical decisions together crippled the effort; all that Phips accomplished was to ransom some prisoners, including Sylvanus Davis. The remaining ships began to limp back into Boston in mid-November. Long before that, the Albany expedition, commanded by Fitz-John Winthrop, had also collapsed. An anticipated large contingent of Iroquois warriors never materialized; there were insufficient numbers of canoes to transport the men up Lake Champlain; and smallpox and mysterious fevers decimated the troops. Winthrop abandoned the march in mid-August, when his men had gone just 100 miles beyond Albany. Like other New Englanders, Winthrop attributed his failure to "Providence," whereas Governor Jacob Leisler of New York blamed the commander himself. He ordered Winthrop's arrest but freed him after Connecticut protested vigorously.[73]

In contrast to the disappointing news from Canada, that from the northeastern frontier finally improved in the fall of 1690. Hope Hood, one of the Anglo-Americans' bitterest enemies, was accidentally killed by some of his own allies. Further, an expedition led by Benjamin Church against the Wabanakis' headquarters captured the wives and families of Kankamagus and the Androscoggin sachem Worombe, in addition to destroying the Indians' winter food stores.[74] In November a returned captive reported that the Wabanakis were "very poor and low," because they had suffered "considerable" losses, including Hope Hood and other men "of principal Note." They were, he revealed, "weary of the Warr, and have this several months been meditating how to mediate, and bring about a peace with the English." Perhaps unsurprisingly, then, several sachems, including the men whose families had been captured, came to Wells seeking a truce. Since the colonists too were encountering great difficulty sustaining the war effort after their Canadian disasters, they welcomed the opportunity to negotiate. On November 29 Captain John Alden arranged a cease fire (until May 1) and an exchange of captives with Worombe, Kankamagus, Edgeremet, and three other sachems. That the two sides distrusted each other intensely became obvious in a notation on the document: "Signed & sealed Interchangeabley upon the Water in Canoes at Sackatehock when the wind blew hard."[75]

New Englanders, most notably Governor Simon Bradstreet, pondered the meaning of the terrible defeats and the potential peace. "The awfull Frowne of God" had caused the failure of the Quebec campaign, Bradstreet proclaimed, though some would blame those in charge of the expedition. God's providence "appearing against us . . . [was] to be specially remarked," he observed, citing the contrary winds and bad weather that delayed the invasion fleet, coupled with the retreat of the overland army that allowed men from Montreal to reinforce Quebec just before Phips arrived. These events "plainly" revealed "the finger of God therein, and shall our ffather Spit in our Face, and we not be ashamed?" Bradstreet inquired. Bay Colony residents had to humble themselves before God, seek out the cause of these disasters, "and reforme those sins that have provoked so great Anger to smoke against the prayers of his people." Yet the truce held out some hope. "The Success of this, as all other our Affayres is with God, who we hope in all these darke dispensations of his providence, will at length cause light to breake forth upon us on whome alone is our dependance and Expectations."[76]

A WAR OF ATTRITION

The "halfe peace" (as the Indians called it) held until May, despite the continuing distrust on both sides. At least in part, the successful truce undoubtedly stemmed from the inability of either side to mount much of an offensive. Certainly Massachusetts was afflicted by "misery," wrote one Cambridge resident in March, a result not only of the losses of men and money in the Quebec debacle but also of their longer-term consequences. To pay the public's debts to the soldiers and suppliers of the expedition, the General Court voted to issue paper money that could be used for tax payments. Even with that infusion of currency, the heavy taxation "much Impoverished" everyone. On top of that, the returning soldiers had brought "small pox, & feaver" back with them, and many noncombatants also died. For example, in mid-February a Portsmouth resident reported that thirty-four local residents had already died from the disease, and another forty were ill. Surveying this scene, a Bostonian commented, "wee shall need noe Enimie to distroy us for wee shall doe Itt fast Enough of our selves."[77]

The Massachusetts authorities prepared carefully for the scheduled resumption of peace talks at Wells on May 1, naming an experienced team of negotiators: Thomas Danforth, William Stoughton, Bartholomew Gedney, Robert Pike, and two local militia leaders. But on the appointed day the sachems failed to appear. Instead, one man claimed to represent Edgeremet and two to represent Worombe. Other Indians attended only "in private capacity." Those Wabanakis present assured the skeptical colonists that the others were hunting but would appear within twenty days; they turned over two young captives and insisted that "all the Sagamores are desirous to have a constant and Everlasting peace made with the English." After some debate, the Massachusetts representatives agreed to continue the truce for the stated period. Before the team departed to return to Boston, Old Dony, the once-imprisoned Kennebunk leader, "made a very passionate speech . . . the design whereof was to expresse the joy of the Indians at what was done."[78]

But when the allotted time ended, no one appeared. The colonists feared the worst, and with reason. On June 13, shortly after the arrival of a militia troop from Essex County, the Kennebec sachem Moxis and perhaps two hundred Indians attacked Wells. The timely intervention saved the town; the assault was repelled; and Robert Pike, for one, breathed a sigh of relief: "the lord is gracious and . . . his mercy indures forever," he penned immediately upon learning the good news.[79]

What had happened? Old Dony and the others who went to Wells on May 1 might have represented a "peace party" among the Wabanakis, and they could well have been later overruled by the sachems, who were perhaps not quite so desirous of peace as had been alleged. Or what the Wabanakis told the leaders of Wells in a formal parley during the battle could have been accurate. They attacked first, the Indians declared, for three reasons. Castine had captured three Englishmen, and they expected the settlers to retaliate against them; they had lost four men, whom they thought the settlers had killed; and the English "gave them noe satisfaction for the two captivs which they brought into Wells at our last treaty with them." All three revealed the Wabanakis' deep-seated suspicions of the Anglo-Americans' motives and behavior. Any action by an ally could result in assumptions of Wabanaki responsibility. Unexpected deaths meant English killers. Unreciprocated goodwill equaled bad faith. The arguments added up to a rationale for the resumption of a destructive war everyone would probably have preferred to halt.[80]

In the weeks and months following the June raid on Wells, the Wabanakis altered their tactics—an adjustment probably dictated by limited resources. Rather than continuing to mount large-scale assaults, the Indians turned to small hit-and-run raids targeting farmers and livestock. Northern New England's leaders quickly understood what was happening; as early as June 17 the Portsmouth magistrates concluded that the Wabanakis "are resolved to starve us, by allarming us every where, & keeping us from attending our corn & by Killing our cattell." Two days later a Kittery magistrate warned that the "enymie" was "constantly killinge and destroyinge both fatt and lean cattell and it is taken for granted without some speedy help coms that they will not leave a beast alive in the whole province."[81]

Yet when an opportunity presented itself the Wabanakis could still come together on short notice. During the summer, Massachusetts dispatched yet another expedition to the eastward to locate and attack the Indians. Following long delays caused by inadequate personnel, the soldiers finally sailed from the Piscataqua on August 1. After futilely searching for signs of the enemy from Saco to Casco Bay, they were reembarking on their sloops when the Wabanakis struck. They "Appered in grete Nombers and violently Assaulted us Indeaoringe to sorrownd us beefore wee could Recover the slopes Killed & wounded sundery," reported the expedition's leaders, Daniel King and John March. "Wee Cannot Imagin there Number to be lese then Three Hondred & parte of them ffrench." Once again, the enemy had materialized, seemingly from nowhere, at a moment when the English were most vulnerable. And once more the Bay Colony's leaders contemplated "an awfull frowne of Providence, under which we have cause to be humbled."[82]

After a summer of constant raids that forced the settlers to stay in garrisons—so that the residents of Wells, for example, were able to grow only as much corn as would sustain them for half a year—the fall of 1691 brought the prospect of worsening conditions. The leaders of Wells, among them George Burroughs (who had moved there from Falmouth prior to the fall of Fort Loyal), told Massachusetts authorities in late September that "our Stockes both of Cattle & Swine are much diminished" and that the Wabanakis had been "a sore scourge to us . . [. by] dayly lying in wait to take any that goe forth." Indeed, just a few days earlier a seventeen-year-old had been captured when he ventured no farther than a "gunn shott" from a garrison "to fetch a little wood in his armes." Two months later the commander of the troops stationed at Wells revealed that "they have allready Killed So many Cattle for the Souldires, that they have hardly left where with to Sustain their one [own] family's this winter & that many famylyes have hardly bread to eat."[83]

On October 30, citing the "growing Distresses of the Country," the governor and council for the first time requested assistance from Plymouth, Rhode Island, and Connecticut. The enemy, they declared, was "flusht with Success," and they needed to raise "a considerable fforce." Till now, "the vast charge" of defense had rested solely on the Bay Colony, the other governments being "providentially more remote from the present Seat" of the war. But the "Common Cause" and the "Comon Enemy" should bring them together, Massachusetts' leaders argued. Nothing came of their plea. Although Connecticut tried to recruit some volunteers, none were willing to serve, and both Plymouth and Rhode Island refused to help. Fortunately for the Bay Colony, the Indians too seemed to lack resources for warfare that winter, and after late October they ceased their raids. The frontier towns, Cotton Mather later observed, "a little Remit[ted] their Tired Vigilance" that winter.[84]

Then, on January 25, 1691/2, the Wabanakis destroyed York in a surprise attack, shortly after Samuel Parris's daughter and niece began having fits.

CHAPTER FOUR

The Dreadfull Apparition
of a Minister

APRIL 19–MAY 9, 1692

W HEN ABIGAIL HOBBS confessed in mid-April that the devil had
recruited her as a witch in Maine in 1688, northern New England
was still reeling from the shock of the devastating attack on York.
The war and Abigail's earlier residence at Casco Bay appear to have had
little to do with the initial accusation that she was a witch; those charges
stemmed rather from widespread gossip about her recent irreverent behavior
in Topsfield, which was recounted in chapter 2. Yet the remarkable consequences that quickly followed her confession resulted from the linkage she
created between the specters' assaults in Essex County and the Wabanakis'
attacks on the northeastern frontier.

In the days after the April 11 examinations of Sarah Cloyce and the Proctors, Abigail Williams had continued to be tortured by witches already
jailed—Rebecca Nurse, both Proctors, Martha Corey. But first Ann Putnam Jr. and then Mercy Lewis named new suspects: not only Abigail Hobbs
but also Giles Corey, who joined in tormenting them. In response to the
renewed spectral activity, Ezekiel Cheever and John Putnam Jr.—the latter
perhaps spurred into action by the death of his baby three days before—filed
a complaint on Monday, April 18, against Abigail Hobbs, Giles Corey, Mary
Warren, and Bridget Bishop.[1]

Bridget Oliver Bishop, the only one of the four not previously connected
publicly to the crisis, lived in Salem Town. A woman in her early fifties with a
bad reputation, she had been tried and acquitted on witchcraft charges twelve
years earlier. The evidence eventually presented in her case revealed that for
decades her neighbors had suspected her of engaging in malefic practices. Yet

Goody Bishop, as she stated at her examination (without contradiction from any of the many people in attendance), knew none of the suffering accusers personally, nor had she ever been in the Village meetinghouse before. The complaints against her, then, had a very different source from the preceding ones, which revolved around intra-Village relationships. Nothing reveals which of the afflicted named her first, or when that event occurred. Despite the formal charge registered with John Hathorne and Jonathan Corwin, the most important accusers of Bridget Bishop lived outside Salem Village.[2]

Abigail Hobbs's confession, and the gossip it and its similar successors aroused, had a dramatic impact on Bridget Bishop and others whom their Essex County neighbors had long suspected of malefic acts. If the devil was actively seeking new recruits for his war in the invisible and visible worlds, people concluded, his agents would most likely be the witches already resident in their midst.

In his later testimony during the prosecution of Dorcas Hoar of Beverly, John Hale inadvertently revealed the dynamic process involved in the cases of Bishop, Hoar, and numerous others. "When discourses arose about witchcrafts at the village," Hale attested, "then I heard discourses revived of Goody Hoars fortune telling." All the talk of witches in Salem Village in the first months of 1692, in short, stimulated the memories, and the mouths, of Hale's neighbors. The resulting gossip in Beverly (or, in the case of Bridget Bishop, Salem Town) soon made its way to Salem Village, passed by eager talkers from farm to farm, tavern to inn.[3]

In the weeks and months to come, after learning from such a chain of gossip that the residents of Beverly or Andover or other towns in the region believed that certain neighbors were possible allies of Satan, the core group of young Village accusers—Ann Putnam Jr., Mercy Lewis, Abigail Williams, Betty Hubbard, Mary Walcott, and (after April 24) a new addition, Susannah Sheldon—incorporated charges against those suspects into their complaints of spectral torturers. By corroborating accusations that originated elsewhere, the Village afflicted simultaneously validated the opinions of their fellow Essex County residents and reconfirmed their own position at the vortex of the crisis. Their affirmation of others' charges encouraged the expression of even more accusations, thereby renewing and repeating what became seemingly endless cycles of suspicion, gossip, and complaints, leading to more suspicion, more gossip, and additional complaints.

Although the intervening conversations cannot be traced, occasionally it is possible to identify the origins of some of the tales that instigated accusations. For instance, the story that must have inspired Ann Jr.'s spectral vision in early May of the "gray-head" man she called "old father pharoah," Thomas

Farrar Sr., of Lynn, resulted from his behavior one night in the spring of 1690. Thoroughly drunk, Goodman Farrar stumbled into a neighbor's house, insisted it was his, and prepared for bed despite the alarmed protestations of his hostess. He then announced that he would "goe to prayer" and "spake about the fallen Angels" before dozing off. Testimony in Farrar's prosecution for drunkenness six months later showed that gossip about his mumbled prayer had spread far and wide. In the supercharged atmosphere of late spring 1692, this two-year-old story was transformed into the charge that Goodman Farrar had been overheard praying to Satan. Who changed it or how the mutation occurred is unknown. But Ann, like the other afflicted young people, turned snatches of gossip into formal accusations, and rumor-mongering in various Essex County towns thus became witchcraft charges in the Village.[4]

The talk about local witches, fortune-tellers, and the like spread all the more widely and intensely through the region because Abigail Hobbs's confession on April 19 caused Essex County residents to connect their fears of neighbors long suspected of malefic acts with their newer concerns about the consequences of the Second Indian War, a pattern that soon manifested itself in several different towns.

FOUR SUSPECTS AND ANOTHER CONFESSION

Giles Corey, who seems to have been the first person questioned on April 19, appeared among the accused primarily for the same reason that men usually did: his relationship with a female witch. Giles's testimony against his wife, offered during and after her examination, had not sufficiently differentiated himself from her, and consequently he ended up facing witchcraft charges.[5]

After Hathorne sternly enjoined Corey to tell the truth, he asked the afflicted, "Which of you have seen this Man hurt you?" Walcott, Putnam Jr., Lewis, and Williams answered in the affirmative, while Hubbard could not speak. Benjamin Gould stated cautiously that he had seen Giles's specter and had then been hurt, but "cannot affirm that it was he." Sarah Vibber, taking an active role in this interrogation (perhaps because Giles had termed her husband a "Damned Devilish Rogue"), repeatedly interpolated questions and comments of her own.

The interrogation focused largely on statements Giles had made about his wife: the charge, offered after her examination, that she had stopped him from praying, and a claim (reported by several witnesses) "that he knew enough against his Wife, that would do her Business." Hathorne unsuccessfully asked for further explanations of both remarks. And "did you not say, when you went to the Ferry with your Wife, you would not go over to Boston now, for you should come yourself next Week?" Hathorne inquired. Giles responded that he meant he could not afford to travel all the way to the Boston prison with her, but Hathorne's question implied quite another interpretation: had Giles not thereby accurately predicted his own arrest and imprisonment for witchcraft? In an experiment such as that employed with Martha, one of Giles's hands was loosed, and (Samuel Parris recorded) "several were afflicted. He held his Head on one Side, and then the Heads of several of the Afflicted were held on one Side. He drew in his Cheeks, and the Cheeks of some of the Afflicted were suckt in." The mimickry was yet another indication of guilt, so John Hathorne ordered Corey sent to jail.

After Abigail Hobbs offered her startling confession as described at the end of chapter 2, the third examinee of the day was the Proctors' servant, Mary Warren.[6] "As soon as she was coming towards the Bar the afflicted fell into fits," Parris noted. Warren proclaimed her innocence, but Hubbard "testifyed against her" before having "a violent fit." (Presumably, Betty read a short statement she submitted in evidence, describing how Mary pressured her to sign the devil's book while saying, "if you Sat your hand to the book you Shall be well for i did So and i am well.") Justice Hathorne observed, "You were a little while ago an Afflicted person, now you are an Afflicter," and inquired, "How comes this to pass?" Mary replied that she regarded her situation as "a great Mercy of God." The magistrate, astonished, responded, "What[,] do you take it to be a great mercy to afflict others?" Betty then revealed that "a little while after this Mary was well, she . . . said that the afflicted persons did but dissemble," a statement that caused all the complainants—including John Indian and Bathshua Pope, neither previously tormented that day—to be "grievously afflicted." When Hathorne informed Warren about Abigail Hobbs's confession, the examinee herself had a fit. "Some of the afflicted cryed out," Parris commented, "that she was going to confess, but Goody Korey, & Procter, & his wife came in, in their apparition, & struck her down, & said she should tell nothing."

From then on, Mary was rendered incapable of sustained speech. At first "she did neither see, nor hear, nor speak." She eventually tried to talk, but Parris recorded that she repeatedly fell into fits after uttering such phrases as "Oh! I am sorry for it," "Oh Lord help me," "I will tell, I will tell," and "they did, they did." After some time the magistrates gave up on Warren, ordering her to be taken out of the meetinghouse.

Bridget Bishop was then brought in, and again "all fell into fits."[7] Goody Bishop, "turning her head & eyes about," announced that "I am clear." But Mary Walcott insisted that her brother Jonathan had recently struck at

Bishop's specter with a sword, tearing her clothes, and, Parris noted, "upon some search in the Court, a rent that seems to answere what was alledged was found." Hathorne confronted her with an accusation drawn from gossip: "they say you bewitcht your first husband to death." Bishop, "verie angrie," denied that charge, shaking her head and by that motion seemingly causing more torments.

The accused and the magistrate next engaged in a dialogue about what constituted witchcraft. If she had not signed the book, had she dealt with "familiar Spirits"? If not, how could her apparition hurt the afflicted? Hathorne observed that "you seem to act witchcraft before us, by the motion of your body." When Bishop responded, "I know not what a Witch is," Hathorne pounced. "How do you know then that you are not a witch?" Bewildered by the question, Bishop continued to assert her innocence. "I am not come here to say I am a witch to take away my life," she exclaimed, indicating that she thought the consequence of confession would be conviction and execution. "Have you not heard that some have confessed?" inquired the examiner. No, replied Goody Bishop, but two men insisted that they had informed her of the confessions. "You are taken now in a flat lye," asserted Hathorne, but Bishop denied having heard what the men said. As he frequently did, Parris ended the transcript with a note. After the examination, he observed, when a bystander asked the accused "if she were not troubled to see the afflicted persons so tormented, the said Byshop answered no." In Parris's eyes, Bridget Bishop, like John Proctor and Rebecca Nurse, apparently condemned herself by indifference to the sufferings of the afflicted.

The magistrates then returned to Mary Warren, who, brought back to the meetinghouse, was "immediately taken with fits." Under questioning, she denied having signed the devil's book, once more had fits, and was sent out again. After "a considerable space of time," she was returned to the makeshift courtroom, but still could not speak. And so Hathorne and Corwin ended the public part of the examination. Later, "in private, before magistrates and Ministers," Warren faced more questions. How far had she yielded? What had she been told to do, to be well? Again, however, she appeared unable to talk. At last, Parris noted, "her lips were bit so that she could not speak. so she was sent away."[8]

Over the next two days, out of the public eye, the magistrates and ministers examined Mary Warren further at Salem prison.[9] She was then better able to talk and, despite being interrupted by frequent fits, she offered further details of the Proctors' witchcraft and her involvement in it. Elizabeth Proctor, she declared, had "puld me out of the Bed, and told mee that Shee was a witch, and had put her hand to the Book." Her master had brought her a book to sign, but she had merely touched it with a wet finger, which never-theless left a black mark. The examiners sternly instructed her "that it was he[r] own Vollantary act . . . she was told the devil could have done nothing: if she had not yeilded and that she for eas to her body: not for any good of her sould: [*sic*] had done it." The maidservant was then "much grieved and cryed out," insisting that she had touched the book only because her master and mistress had threatened to harm her if she did not comply with their request.

Asked whether she had seen the apparitions of others since she had been jailed, Mary named Sarah Good and Giles Corey. She had not disclosed the "wholle truth" earlier, she explained, "becaus she was thretned to be torn in peices: if she did," but now she was prepared to tell all. Had she tormented the afflicted? the examiner inquired. No, she answered, "but when she heard: they were aflicted in her shape: she began to fear it was the devil" who did so. Still, she denied having consented to Satan's employing her specter to afflict others. After Mary admitted that she had touched the devil's book twice, Nicholas Noyes "asked her whether she did not suspect it to be the devils book before she toucht it the second time: she said she feare it was no good book: being asked what she ment by no good book: she said a book to deceiv."

When Abigail Hobbs was examined in prison on April 20, she again revealed the devil's interest in recruiting witch-allies in Maine. Abigail declared that prior to her initial examination she had been visited by the apparition of Judah White, "a Jersey maid that lived with Joseph Ingerson [Ingersoll] at Cascoe, but now lives at Boston," with whom she was "very well formerly acquainted." The maidservant, she indicated, had been wearing "fine Cloaths," thus suggesting that she had successfully completed a diabolic pact. Moreover, the specter of her one-time friend had been accompanied by that of Sarah Good—a sure sign she had enlisted in Satan's ranks. Together the two apparitions urged Abigail not to confess and disclosed that Sarah Osborne was also a witch. Abigail then obeyed the devil's order to torture Ann Jr., Mercy, and Abigail Williams by sticking "thorns" into "images . . . in wood like them." After Satan informed her she had been successful, her tar-gets "Cryed out they were hurt by Abigail Hobbs." Finally, Abigail acknowl-edged something she had previously denied: she had participated in the "great meeting in Mr. Parris's Pasture," where she "did Eat of the Red Bread and drink of the Red wine."[10]

By the close of these examinations, then, four more suspected witches had joined the nine already in prison, and two of them had acknowledged their complicity with Satan. Even more important, Abigail Hobbs's confessions pointed everyone's attention toward events in Falmouth and on the Maine frontier, with striking results.

Abigail Hobbs in Casco Bay

Abigail Hobbs's confession on April 19 and her later testimony revealed that she had lived in Falmouth in 1688, probably longer. But with whom, and under what circumstances? Some have hypothesized that she was a servant in Maine, but she would have been very young (aged just ten or eleven that year) to have gone so far from home to work. Moreover, during her confessions she twice referred to "our house" in Falmouth; had she been a servant, she would have said, "my master's house."[11] Her use of the possessive pronoun "our" thus suggests she was living with her family or at least with relatives. Even though I have found no definitive proof of the Hobbs clan's presence in Falmouth during the mid-1680s, I believe that William Hobbs, Abigail's father, moved his household there between 1683 and 1689.

One genealogist has concluded that Abigail's father was a son of Morris Hobbs of Hampton, New Hampshire. In 1660, William seems to have been living in Lynn, but in April 1668 a William Hobbs joined a group of men from Wells in petitioning Massachusetts about a controversial political matter (one of the other signers was Peter Cloyce, the eventual second husband of Sarah Towne Bridges). If William Hobbs was from Hampton, or if he was the Wells petitioner of the same name, the northeastern frontier would have been familiar territory to him.[12]

Although Hobbs and a partner purchased land in Topsfield in 1660, his name first appears as a resident in November 1668, and so he could have signed the Wells petition the preceding spring. He and his wife, Avis, whose birth surname is unknown, called their first recorded daughter (born in Topsfield in 1670) "Avis" and their first recorded son "William." Given common naming patterns in seventeenth-century families (in which oldest sons and daughters were usually named for their parents), the couple probably married shortly before coming to Topsfield. Their wedding is not noted anywhere in Essex County; accordingly, it might have occurred in Maine or New Hampshire, where many documents were lost during the two Indian wars. Hobbs failed to prosper in Topsfield: his property holdings were small, and he never held even the lowest elective office. After having children regularly from 1670 to 1682, William and Avis Hobbs disappear from the Topsfield church records, until he was assessed for the minister's salary in late 1689. I therefore think that when Falmouth was resettled in the mid-1680s William took the opportunity to move to Maine.[13]

The family probably rented property at Casco from approximately 1683 until after the Wabanaki assault in September 1689. By the time of the witchcraft crisis in 1692, Hobbs had been married to a new wife, Deliverance, for at least eighteen months. That no surviving document records Avis Hobbs's death or William's remarriage suggests again that those events occurred in another jurisdiction, perhaps in Maine, where so many records were lost. In addition, that Deliverance had never been baptized implies that she grew up where that rite was not available to her parents— for example, the Maine frontier, which had few ordained ministers. Most of the Hobbs children could also have died during the family's residence in Maine, since only Abigail and one of her brothers can subsequently be traced in the extensive published records of Essex County. It is unlikely, however, that Avis Hobbs or her children were killed by the Indians; no deaths of women or children were described in the aftermath of the September 1689 attack on Falmouth, nor were there many prior to that date either.[14]

If these speculations are correct, Abigail Hobbs lived in Falmouth with her family for about six years, from age six or seven to age twelve. Even if she did not reside there with her family or for that many years, she had to have known Mercy Lewis in the small frontier community. Moreover, if Abigail's father was the son of Morris Hobbs, Abigail and Mercy were related by marriage: the mothers-in-law, respectively, of their aunts (Mary Hobbs Cass and Mary Lewis Skilling Lewis) were the sisters Martha and Hannah Philbrick. Unremarkably, therefore, the accusation of Abigail Hobbs initially emerged from the extended Putnam household, where Mercy Lewis had undoubtedly avidly discussed the irreverent behavior of her former Falmouth acquaintance and possible distant relative.[15]

"A WHEEL WITHIN A WHEEL"

On April 21, Thomas Putnam addressed a letter to Hathorne and Corwin. Offering "humble and hearty thanks" for the "great care and pains" the magistrates had so far taken on behalf of the afflicted, he ventured to tell them "of what we conceive you have not heard, which are high and dreadfull: of a wheel within a wheel, at which our ears do tingle." His news, he declared, showed "the tremendous works of divine providence" the Village was experiencing "not only every day but every hour."[16]

Putnam's missive enclosed the report of a vision that had appeared to his daughter the previous evening. Ann saw "the Apperishtion of a Minister at which she was greviously affrighted and cried out oh dreadfull: dreadfull here is a minister com." The specter tortured Ann while she carried on a dialogue with him, resolutely refusing to write in his book "tho he tore me al to peaces." "It was a dreadfull thing," she told him, "that he which was a Minister that should teach children to feare God should com to perswad poor creatures to give their souls to the divill." After repeatedly refusing to tell her who he was, the specter finally revealed his identity:

> presently he told me that his name was George Burroughs and that he had had three wives: and that he had bewitched the Two first of them of death: and that he kiled Mist. Lawson because she was so unwilling to goe from the village and also killed Mr Lawsons child because he went to the eastward with Sir Edmon and preached soe: to the souldiers and that he had bewicthed a grate many souldiers to death at the eastword, when Sir Edmon was their. and that he had made Abigail Hobbs a wicth and: severall wicthes more . . . and he also tould me that he was above wicth for he was a cunjurer.[17]

Thus there emerged for the first time during the witchcraft crisis the name of George Burroughs, who was to be convicted of witchcraft and hanged in August. Burroughs, in many ways the key figure in the entire affair, linked Salem Village and Falmouth, Essex County and Maine, the Wabanakis and the witches. When Cotton Mather wrote *The Wonders of the Invisible World* in the fall of 1692 to defend the trials, "Government" (that is, Governor Sir William Phips) ordered him to include "some Account" of the prosecution of Burroughs in his book, making it the one case Mather described that he himself did not select for consideration. When (also in the fall of 1692) Increase Mather penned *Cases of Conscience* to question some of the verdicts, he revealed that Burroughs's was the only trial he attended, and that, despite his general criticisms of the proceedings, "had I been one of his Judges, I could not have acquitted him." The minister's importance was therefore clearly understood in 1692, but Burroughs has hitherto received remarkably little attention from historians of the witchcraft crisis.[18]

Abigail Hobbs's confession of April 19, coupled with Ann Jr.'s spectral encounter with George Burroughs on the evening of April 20, transformed the 1692 witchcraft crisis from a serious but not wholly unprecedented set of incidents into the extraordinary event that played out over the next six months.[19] Immediately after Abigail confirmed the devil's presence in Falmouth and Ann Jr. revealed that Burroughs, his minion, had worked in concert

CHART 2

Cumulative Total of New Formal Witchcraft Complaints, February–June 1692

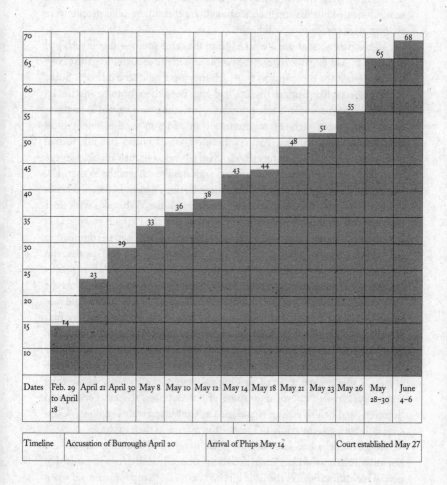

Dates	Feb. 29 to April 18	April 21	April 30	May 8	May 10	May 12	May 14	May 18	May 21	May 23	May 26	May 28–30	June 4–6
	14	23	29	33	36	38	43	44	48	51	55	65	68

Timeline	Accusation of Burroughs April 20	Arrival of Phips May 14	Court established May 27

with the Wabanakis by bewitching Sir Edmund Andros's troops, the number of accusations skyrocketed. Before the end of April, fifteen new complaints were filed—thus more than doubling the number of accused witches in just ten days. Between Monday, May 2, and Monday, June 6 (after which came a nearly month-long hiatus in accusations), another thirty-nine people were charged with committing witchcraft.

All the new accusations stemmed from the same source—the ties Abigail and Ann Jr. had drawn between the visible and invisible assaults against New England—but the mechanisms by which they were produced differed. Some of the suspects, like Bridget Bishop, had long been thought to be witches by their fellow townspeople. Such individuals, including men known as fortune-tellers and practitioners of countermagic in addition to the stereotypical quarrelsome older women, had commonly aroused gossip but not formal complaints. Others did not fit such standard patterns but instead, like George Burroughs, were suspected of complicity with the French and the Wabanakis. The connection forged by Abigail Hobbs and Ann Putnam Jr. coupled Essex County residents' concerns about the conflict with the Wabanakis with their ongoing anxiety about bewitchment. Believing that their region was engaged in warfare with spectral as well as real attackers, they hastened to complain to the authorities about anyone they thought was linked to the devil in any way.

Satan's most obvious allies consisted both of suspected local malefic practitioners and of people with frontier ties. The coalition between Satan and the Wabanakis identified by afflicted accusers and confessors gave Essex residents' current situation cosmic significance and made them sensitive to any hint of collusion between their fellow colonists and visible or invisible enemies. Like Cotton Mather, many concluded that "the Prodigious War, made by the Spirits of the Invisible World upon the People of New-England, in the year, 1692, . . . might have some of its Original among the Indians, whose chief Sagamores are well known unto some of our Captives, to have been horrid Sorcerers, and hellish conjurers and such as Conversed with Dæmons." Consequently they sought avidly to identify the traitors in their midst.[20]

Abigail Hobbs had known George Burroughs in Falmouth, but she did not initially name the clergyman as Satan's cohort. Instead, Ann Jr. made that crucial identification. Yet the little girl had been less than four years old when Burroughs left Salem Village in 1683, and she had no direct personal knowledge of him. At the same time, her statement showed that people around her who knew a great deal about the minister had discussed him at considerable length in her hearing. Those people were her parents and, most notably, Mercy Lewis, who had known him well in Falmouth and for whom the tales of Burroughs's bewitchments "at the eastward" had a particular resonance.

Indeed, the emphasis in Ann's vision on events in Maine, especially those related to the Indian war during Sir Edmund Andros's campaign in late 1688 and early 1689, strongly suggests Mercy Lewis's influence on the impressionable younger girl.

In the late morning of April 21, on the road near Nathaniel Ingersoll's tavern, Abigail Williams too saw Burroughs's apparition. Benjamin Hutchinson, Ingersoll's adoptive son, later attested that in his presence Parris's niece "said that there. was a lettell black menester that Lived at Casko bay he told me so and said that he had kild 3 wifes two for himself and one for mr Losen and that he had made nine Weches in this plase and said that he Could hold out the hevest gun that Is in Casko bay with one hand which no man Can Case hold out with both hands." Hutchinson struck with a pitchfork at the place where Abigail saw the specter, and Abigail informed him that he had torn Burroughs's coat. About noon, inside the tavern, Abigail again saw Burroughs's apparition, but claimed it was quickly replaced by that of a gray cat. Hutchinson thrust his rapier at the spot she pointed out. After falling into a fit, Abigail announced that Benjamin had killed the cat, but that "immedetly Sary good come and carrid hur away."[21]

Like Ann's, Abigail's vision connected Burroughs to Casco, and to the deaths of his previous wives and of Deodat Lawson's spouse. But it also differed from hers, in that it hearkened back to Tituba's revelation of the existence of nine witches, attributing all of them to Burroughs's making. It furthermore included a rudimentary physical description lacking from Ann's: Burroughs was "lettell" and "black"—the latter a term that suggested both a swarthy complexion and a tie to the "black" Wabanakis. And it repeated a piece of gossip about Burroughs's unusual strength, a topic that would recur in the coming months. Abigail too had heard talk about Burroughs from her elders, but talk that diverged from that heard by Ann Jr. Most notably, in the Parris household, unlike the one that contained Mercy Lewis, the bewitching of Andros's soldiers seemingly played no part in discussions of the clergyman and his possible diabolical activities.

George Burroughs, the subject of all these conversations, was thirty-nine years old the spring of 1692. Born in Virginia, he was the son of Nathaniel Burroughs, a well-to-do English merchant who moved to Maryland, then soon returned to England. George's mother, Rebecca, remained in America until the mid-1670s, when she left to rejoin her husband. She raised her son in Roxbury, Massachusetts, where she joined the church in 1657. George attended Harvard as a member of the class of 1670; his contemporaries there included Samuel Sewall (1671) and James Bayley (1669). By early 1673, he had married Hannah Fisher of Dedham. The first of his eventual nine surviving children by three wives was baptized at Roxbury in February 1673/4, and he joined that church a few months later. Soon thereafter he moved his small family to Casco, where to encourage him to stay as the settlement's clergyman he was granted 200 acres of valuable land crossing Cleeves' Neck, the peninsula lying between the Casco River and Back Cove that housed the main settlement. Yet neither then nor later was Burroughs formally ordained; he accordingly could preach to his congregations but could not baptize children or administer communion.[22]

Life at Casco Bay would not have been easy even before the beginning of King Philip's War in the north in September 1675, but subsequently conditions worsened considerably. Families fought over the possession of crucial supplies of gunpowder; the town's residents (including Philip Lewis and his brothers-in-law Thomas Cloyce and Thomas Skilling) complained of the "timorousnes and cowardize" of their militia lieutenant, George Ingersoll; and in December, Governor John Leverett of Massachusetts pronounced the entire province of Maine "much wasted," with "houses corn & cattle most destroyed," and "many ffamilys . . . distressed." By April 1676 the colony's leaders were admitting to English authorities that the settlements north of the Piscataqua, "by reason of their Remote Liveing one from another, . . . could not be preserved, but are mostly destroyed—many of the people being Slaine, and the rest retired to places of better Security."[23]

One such place of security was Falmouth—at least until the attack of August 11, 1676. Then it too was largely abandoned, with many of its residents, Burroughs and his family among them, fleeing south to Essex County. He settled temporarily in Salisbury, which was the birthplace and childhood home of Ann Carr, who probably knew him there prior to her 1678 marriage to Thomas Putnam. He witnessed, and must have taken sides in, an acrimonious dispute between Salisbury's minister, the elderly John Wheelwright, and Major Robert Pike, who disagreed vehemently with each other about a variety of matters. In 1676 their quarrel escalated, with Pike accusing Wheelwright of defamation, then trying to oust the clergyman from his pastorate; and with Wheelwright subsequently excommunicating Pike one Sabbath in early 1677 while he and his militiamen were absent responding to an alarm. The town thereupon promptly split into two factions. The Carrs sided with Pike (whose daughter had married Ann's brother), whereas Burroughs, who served briefly as Wheelwright's assistant, occupied the town pulpit for a time after the minister's death in November 1679, and later associated with Wheelwright's sons in Maine, in all likelihood supported the aged clergyman. In September 1677, a commission appointed by the Massachusetts General Court rebuked everyone involved in the affair: Pike had been "too litigious," Wheelwright had acted with "too much precipitancy," and the townsmen who tried to eject Wheelwright from his post had engaged in "evill practice."[24]

If Burroughs ever had thoughts of succeeding Wheelwright as the leader of the Salisbury congregation, the affray (and perhaps his role in it) would have rendered that unlikely, if not altogether impossible. Accordingly, George Burroughs had to look elsewhere; and so too at the same time did Salem Village, following the less-than-amicable departure of James Bayley, its first minister. In April 1680 Villagers voted to seek a new pastor for their church, with the proviso that they hear candidates preach before committing themselves to anyone. After a tryout period of unknown duration, the Village and Burroughs reached an initial agreement in November, which was reconfirmed by both sides approximately a year later. For the first nine months of his stay in his new parish, while a parsonage was being constructed, Burroughs, his wife, and their two children lived in the house of John Putnam Sr. and his wife, Rebecca. The Putnams later testified at the minister's trial that "all the time that said Burros did live att our house he was a very sharp man to his wife, notwithstanding our observation shee was a very good and dutifull wife to him." The cleric's mistreatment of his wives—like his strength—was to become a recurring theme of the discussions about him.[25]

In September 1681, Hannah Burroughs died, perhaps from complications following the birth of her fourth (and third surviving) child. Since the minister's salary for his first year had not yet been completely paid (he received it two months later), John Putnam paid for the two gallons of canary wine Burroughs ordered from a Salem Town tavern for Hannah's funeral. The following year, now ensconced in the same parsonage that would later house Samuel Parris, Burroughs married a young widow, Sarah Ruck Hathorne, whose first husband was Captain William Hathorne, the man whose troops had made possible Richard Waldron's capture of the two hundred Wabanakis at Cocheco in September 1676. The minister's second wife, eventually the mother of four of his children, was thus the sister-in-law of the examining magistrate, John Hathorne. Even more than the members of the Putnam and Parris households (whose talk of Burroughs's spousal abuse led Ann Jr. and Abigail Williams to accuse him of bewitching two wives to death), Hathorne would have been aware of the persistent tales of mistreatment, some of which involved his younger brother's widow. Reports of George's "unkindness" to Sarah or times he "fell out with" her would certainly have reached Hathorne's ears long before Burroughs was charged with being a witch. Indeed, the magistrates questioned the minister about at least one such story during his examination.[26]

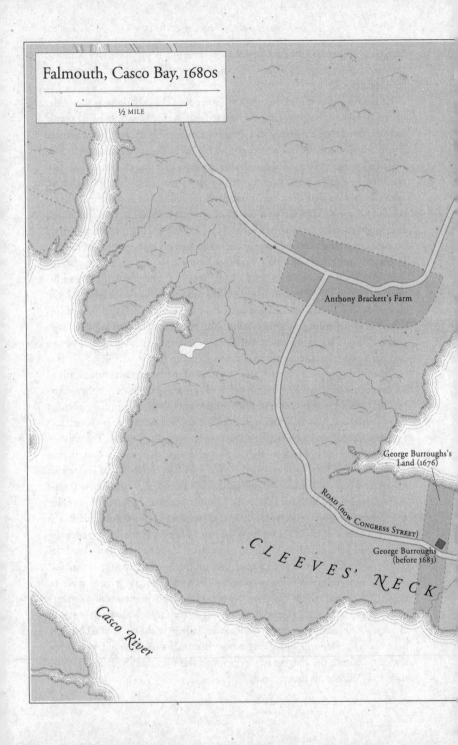

Falmouth, Casco Bay, 1680s

½ MILE

Anthony Brackett's Farm

George Burroughs's
Land (1676)

ROAD (now CONGRESS STREET)

George Burroughs
(before 1683)

C L E E V E S'   N E C K

Casco River

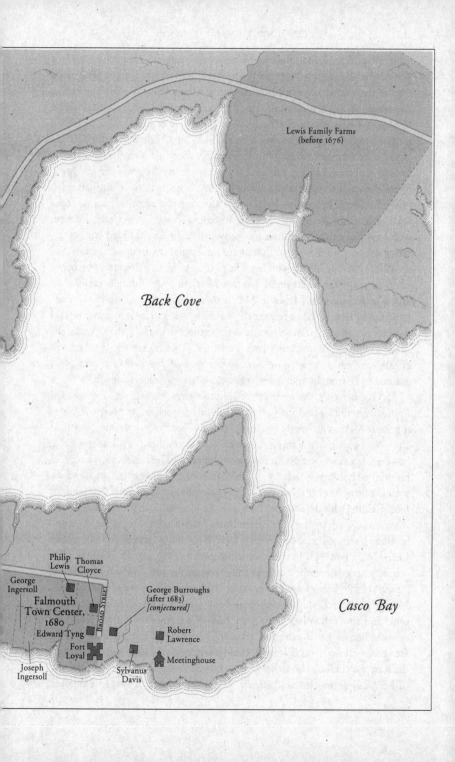

Lewis Family Farms
(before 1676)

Back Cove

Casco Bay

Philip Thomas
Lewis Cloyce

George
Ingersoll

George Burroughs
(after 1683)
[conjectured]

Falmouth
Town Center,
1680

Edward Tyng

Robert
Lawrence

Fort
Loyal

Joseph
Ingersoll

Meetinghouse

Sylvanus
Davis

BROAD STREET

By mid-April 1682, Burroughs was enmeshed in controversy with a parishioner who accused him of paying more attention to "pulpit preaching" than to the spiritual care of his flock. Perhaps that feeling was widespread; in any event, his salary was not paid on time, and in early March 1683 he left the Village, moving his family back to Falmouth. The clergyman, however, returned to Salem Village to settle accounts in late April. He and other Villagers were surprised when John Putnam Sr. then had him arrested for the unpaid debt from his wife's funeral and other outstanding liabilities, because it was clear to everyone that Burroughs had no assets to seize until after his salary had been fully paid. In the end, although the minister had to come back once more for a court hearing in Salem Town in late June, Putnam withdrew the suit after Burroughs proved that he had ordered part of his salary arrears paid directly to Putnam to satisfy his remaining obligations.[27]

While George Burroughs lived in Salem Village, Falmouth was being resettled under the direction of Thomas Danforth, who formally established a new government in Maine in March 1680. Danforth supervised the construction of Fort Loyal to protect the rebuilt town, and in September he laid out new house lots, primarily to the west and north of the fort, "to make the Town compact," as residents later explained. To advance the resettlement efforts, the town took possession of portions of the property previously granted to Burroughs and other large landowners on Cleeves' Neck.[28]

In October 1683, the minister, offered 100 acres "further off" in exchange for the centrally located 170 that had been taken, declined to accept, informing the town that he "freely" surrendered the property, "not desiring any land any where else, nor any thing else in consideration thereof." (The town did, however, later give him about 100 acres of marsh.) The remaining 30 acres of his original holding, which lay approximately half a mile west of the new fort, were confirmed to him. Later that year, he exchanged 7 acres of that land for John Skilling's house and lot, conveniently located near the meetinghouse, which was sited to the east of the fort. John Skilling's by-then-deceased brother Thomas had been Mercy Lewis's uncle by marriage; and Philip Lewis's own house lot in the resettled community lay near Joseph Ingersoll's property approximately a quarter mile west of the fort. As will be recalled, Abigail Hobbs knew Joseph Ingersoll's maidservant "very well." Accordingly, Mercy Lewis and Abigail Hobbs probably lived in close proximity to each other in Falmouth village during the mid-1680s. Another quarter mile west of their homes lay Burroughs's remaining 23 acres. Since he undoubtedly farmed or cut wood on that land, the clergyman would have regularly passed the Lewis and Hobbs households as he moved between his house (to the east of Fort Loyal) and his land on the west side of town. Thus, in Falmouth

George Burroughs, Mercy Lewis, and Abigail Hobbs must have encountered each other frequently, perhaps on a daily basis.[29]

Life in Falmouth during the mid-1680s was difficult, for wholly rebuilding a previously abandoned community took considerable effort. The residents had few resources to spare, so Burroughs's problems collecting his salary persisted. Moreover, local politics were acrimonious, especially during the regime of Sir Edmund Andros. Rejecting the legitimacy of all New England land titles that did not mention the Crown as the ultimate owner of the property, Andros insisted that settlers reregister and revalidate their deeds, in the process paying new fees. Many Maine residents resisted this requirement, which would have enriched Andros and his subordinates. In Falmouth, the opposition to the land policy was led by Robert Lawrence, whose family had deep roots in the area. By contrast, Edward Tyng, Sylvanus Davis, and Joshua Scottow, all of whom arrived in Maine during or after King Philip's War, tried to win others' compliance with the new procedures. Lawrence and Davis engaged in a long series of squabbles, legal and otherwise, with Davis arguing that Lawrence's land titles were faulty because they did not derive from the "Right Saggamore," and Lawrence countering that Davis had baldly announced that "it was free for any man to take a patent for anothers land notwithstanding hee had Improved it never soe much." The conspicuous absence of the signature of George Burroughs from a May 24, 1689, Falmouth petition against Tyng, Davis, and their ally Lieutenant Thaddeus Clark implies that he took the side of those three men in the heated dispute.[30]

Whether because of a lack of funds or because once again (as in Salisbury and Salem Village) a deeply divided community produced a congregation difficult to handle, by 1686 George Burroughs had begun negotiating with Black Point (Scarborough) about possibly relocating there. On March 30 of that year he was even described as "Minister of Bla[ck] Poynt." In November, Joshua Scottow, the settlement's leading resident, donated ten acres to be given to a minister, and Burroughs accepted that land, planting some crops on it to confirm his title. In February 1686/7 Scarborough provided for "Coting & haling of the ministers wod for one yeare." Yet Burroughs did not completely sever his ties to Falmouth, although in 1688 he sold the remaining twenty-three acres of his original grant. Evidently, he continued to preach in both places. As was pointed out in chapter 3, he was in Falmouth during the September 1689 attack, being commended for his conduct by Benjamin Church. At that time the commander also observed that Burroughs "had thoughts of removeing" because "his present maintainance from this Town by reason of thier poverty, is not enough for his livelihood." So, Church commented, "I shall Encourage him to Stay promissing him an allowance from the publique Treasury for what Servis he shall do for the Army."[31]

As already noted, the apparition of George Burroughs explained to Ann Jr. on April 20, 1692, that he killed Deodat Lawson's child because Lawson "went to the eastward with Sir Edmon and preached soe: to the souldiers." Church's observation about trying to assist the impoverished minister by hiring him as an army chaplain suggests why Burroughs might have been angered by Lawson's employment with Andros: perhaps he had wanted the job himself. It is easy to speculate that Burroughs could have expressed his jealousy or frustration about Lawson's chaplaincy in the hearing of Mercy Lewis, the chief source of Ann Jr.'s information about Burroughs's years in Maine. That is especially likely because Mercy actually lived for a time in George Burroughs's household. Exactly when she did so is not clear, but she probably moved in with the clergyman and his family following her father's death, which occurred some time after April 1689. He could well have been killed by the Wabanakis during the September 21 assault on the town.[32]

Burroughs's specter also told Ann Jr. that "he had bewicthed a grate many souldiers to death at the eastword, when Sir Edmon was their." Unlike the murder of Lawson's child, which might have had a personal motive, the malevolent killing of soldiers in Maine during Andros's campaign could have had only one purpose: assisting the devil-worshipping Indians in their war against God's people. That George Burroughs had indeed spectrally allied himself to Satan and the Wabanakis might well have appeared likely to any-one who contemplated his uncanny ability to survive the attacks on Falmouth in August 1676 and September 1689, followed by his remarkably prescient decision to leave the Casco Bay region sometime in the winter of 1689–1690, mere months before both Falmouth and Black Point fell to the Wabanakis in May 1690. When nearly all the defenders of Fort Loyal were killed by the French and Indians, George Burroughs was no longer there. He had moved south to the relative safety of Wells, where he replaced another clergyman who had decided to seek an even more secure post still farther from the front lines of the war.

Before Burroughs left Casco, however, his wife Sarah died, and he sent her body back to Salem for burial. In Wells, he met and married a third wife, Mary; together they had a daughter, his last child. That Salem Villagers gos-siped about the circumstances of Sarah's death, and that George's remarriage followed it fairly quickly, became evident in another of Ann Jr.'s spectral visions, this one occurring on May 5. Sarah's apparition, the little girl revealed, "tould me that Mr Burrough and that wife which he hath now kiled hir in the vessell as she was coming to se hir friends because they would have one another." In short, some people at least seem to have thought that Sarah Ruck Hathorne Burroughs was still alive when she boarded the ship that brought her body to Salem, and that Mary Burroughs as well as her husband had something to do with her predecessor's death.[33]

George Burroughs, as befitted his position as one of the two remaining ministers in Maine—the other was Shubael Dummer, in York—became one of the leading residents of Wells, a member of the select group of men who regularly wrote to the Massachusetts governor and council to report on conditions in their beleaguered community and province. In July 1691, for example, he signed a joint letter seeking assistance that described Wells as "the front of all the Estern part of the Contrey Remoatly Scituated; for Strength weak; and the Enemie beating upon us." When the Wabanakis attacked Wells the previous month, the men reported, they had killed or taken "upward of an hundred head of cattell beside Sheep and horeses," and their corn too was "in great hazard" of being lost. To prevent further losses of men and resources, the leaders of Wells asked the authorities in Boston to adopt a policy that "the Inhabitants of this province may not Quit theire places with out liberty first obtayned from Leguel Authority." Two months later, Burroughs and the others reported that the Indians "still distress us, by holding us off from our improvements, Keeping us in close Garrison." The "heathen," they wrote, were "a sore scourge to us." The last letter Burroughs addressed to Boston, on January 27, 1691/2, described the destruction of York two days earlier. Writing of their "low condition, & eminent danger," the leaders of Wells observed that "the course of God's most sweet & rich promises, & gracious providences may justly be interrupted by the sins of his People." They prayed, "The Lord set his eyes upon us for good, & build us, not pull us downe, & plant us, & not pluck us up."[34]

Wells as a community would not be "plucked up," but George Burroughs soon would be. In the days, weeks, and months following the revelations of April 19 and 20, he became the indispensable man, named over and over again as the leader of the devil's sacrament and other witch meetings. That the "lettell black menester" would be regarded as "the Head & Ringleader of all the Supposed Witches in the Land" (to adopt a phrase coined by his descendants more than fifty years later) was entirely appropriate. It was both especially "dreadfull" and especially suitable that a clergyman lead the witches. Who better than a man of authority, with intricate knowledge of the Bible and of Satan's ways, to bring more recruits into the devil's legions? Who better than a man who had lived both on the Maine frontier and in Salem

Village to unite the visible and invisible devil worshippers who were together assaulting New England? And who more likely to initiate his accusation than Mercy Lewis, a young woman who knew him well, and most of whose family had been killed in the attacks he so remarkably escaped unscathed?[35]

NINE ACCUSATIONS AND ANOTHER IMPORTANT CONFESSOR

Ann Putnam Jr.'s vision of a malevolent George Burroughs on the evening of Wednesday, April 20, set off a rash of spectral sightings over the next few weeks. The first came just a few hours later, "Att or about midnight" that very night, when Mercy Lewis too encountered an apparition. In her case it was a "very gray headed man," who introduced himself as George Jacobs (Sr.) of Salem Village. He had had "two wives," he revealed, and he beat Mercy with a stick while ordering her to write in his book, which she resolutely refused to do. The next day at about four in the afternoon, following Parris's weekly Thursday lecture, Abigail Williams and Mary Walcott saw more visions in the great room at Ingersoll's tavern. Abigail and Mary charged that the specter of Deliverance Hobbs "bitt mary walcot by the foot" and that Deliverance and her husband William "goe both of them a long the table." Benjamin Hutchinson struck at the apparitions with his rapier, leading the girls to exclaim that he had "stabed goody hobs one the side."[36]

Mary and Abigail went on to insist that "the roome was full of them." Hutchinson and Eleazar Putnam (a cousin of Sergeant Thomas) both thrust their rapiers repeatedly at the specters. Finally the girls announced that the men had "killed a greet black woman of Stonintown and an Indian that come with her for the flore is all covered with blod." A third apparition "they knew not" also lay dead. The witches and their Indian allies had not been vanquished, however: Williams and Walcott looked outside "& said they saw a greet company of them one a hill."[37]

Those two were not alone in seeing witches as infesting Salem Village on April 21, for that same day Thomas Putnam and John Buxton filed complaints against nine people from Topsfield, Salem Village, and Salem Town "for high Suspition of Sundry acts of Witchcraft" aimed at Ann Jr., Mercy, Mary, and unnamed additional Villagers. Hathorne and Corwin duly ordered all nine arrested and brought in for examinations the next day, Friday, April 22. For the first time in the 1692 crisis, a large group was accused simultaneously. A pattern that would become commonplace thus emerged in the immediate aftermath of the initial identification of George Burroughs as the leader of the witches.[38]

The subjects of the formal complaints on April 21 were a varied lot, ranging from Mary Black, a slave belonging to Lieutenant Nathaniel Putnam of the Village, to Mistress Mary English, whose husband Philip was a wealthy merchant in Salem Town. Most, though, resided in Topsfield, which suggests that Abigail Hobbs's confession had drawn people's attention to malefic activity in that town. The Topsfield contingent comprised Abigail Hobbs's father and stepmother; Sarah Averill Wilds, who had a long-standing reputation as a witch; Mary Towne Easty, the sister of Rebecca Nurse and Sarah Cloyce; and Nehemiah Abbott Jr., who seems to have resembled a male apparition described by some of the afflicted. With the exception of Sarah Wilds, whom surviving records identify as first named by Deliverance Hobbs on April 17, no one complained against on April 21 can be linked to an accusation recorded in Salem Village at an earlier date.[39]

A huge crowd attended the examinations in the Salem Village meeting-house on April 22—"much people, and many in the windows," remarked Parris in his notes on one of the interrogations. So many spectators attended, in fact, that the accusers had difficulty obtaining "a clear view" of the suspects, and at least one man had to be taken outside so they could "view him in the light" as they attempted to identify him. It is impossible to reconstruct the precise order in which the suspects were questioned, because the records of three of those examined on April 22 have not survived. Still, it appears that the first to be interrogated was Deliverance Hobbs, the stepmother of the confessed teenage witch.[40]

Hathorne and Corwin began with an experiment involving the suspect's identity. Parris observed that "the Magistrates had privately ordered who should be brought in, & not suffered her name to be mentioned." They then asked Mercy Lewis and another whom Parris did not identify, "Do you know her?" The two were "struck dumb," but Ann Jr. offered the correct answer: "it was Goody Hobbs, & she hath hurt her much." This unusual episode deserves comment, since it constituted one of the few recorded instances in which the magistrates tried to test the accusers. That Hathorne and Corwin ventured it with Deliverance Hobbs suggests that they thought the Village afflicted would not know the Topsfield woman by sight.[41]

Williams and Walcott, who said they had seen Deliverance's specter the day before at Ingersoll's tavern, did not speak up to identify her. Instead, Ann Jr., who could not initially put a name to Rebecca Nurse, a Village resident she must have seen regularly at Parris's services, *did* recognize Deliverance Hobbs of Topsfield on April 22. So how did Ann Jr. know her? The obvious answer to that question is that Mercy Lewis, although herself "struck dumb" when asked the identity of the suspect, was the source of the little girl's information. Mercy had almost certainly known the entire Hobbs family in Falmouth in the 1680s and was perhaps their distant relative. Although William Hobbs's Topsfield property lay near some of that claimed by Thomas Putnam, the two men (and their respective wives) had no documented feud or prior association. The only person in Ann Jr.'s life with probable knowledge of the "mystery" suspect's identity was the Putnams' maidservant.[42]

After Ann Jr. successfully named Deliverance Hobbs, both John Indian and Mary Walcott accused the examinee of tormenting them.[43] Hathorne next posed a series of questions—starting with "Why do you hurt these persons?"—that elicited staunch denials from Goody Hobbs. So he adopted another tack, inquiring about *her* reported affliction by Sarah Wilds on April 17. In response, she described seeing apparitions of "a great many birds cats & dogs" and also admitted seeing "the shapes of severall persons." Asked to name them, she mentioned only two: Goody Wilds and Mercy Lewis. The former, she said, had "tore me almost to peices," but she denied that Lewis's specter had done her any harm. Deliverance's identification of Lewis's apparitional form simultaneously threatened to convert Mercy from afflicted to afflicter (as had already happened with Mary Warren) and suggested that Deliverance and Mercy had indeed known each other previously. Pressed to produce the names of specters she could identify, the Topsfield woman, who undoubtedly had few acquaintances in the Village, chose a reputed witch from her own town and a local maidservant with whom she had probably been acquainted in Maine.

The examination then proceeded without reference to the naming of Mercy Lewis. The justice asked Goody Hobbs if she had signed the devil's book, and if not, how could she explain her transformation from tormented to tormentor? The two little girls shouted that they saw her apparition "upon the Beam," and John Indian and others had fits. Under what must have been extraordinary pressure, Deliverance began to give way. Instead of denying complicity in Satan's deeds, she first indicated that she could not speak. Then, in reply to the repeated question, "Have you signed to any book?" she stammered reluctantly, "It is very lately then." Pushed to give an exact date, she revealed she had signed "the night before the last" (April 20), and Parris noted that—as had happened before—the sufferings of the afflicted ceased when she began to confess.

In response to the insistent interrogation, Deliverance accused Sarah Wilds both of bringing the devil's book to her and of joining with Sarah Osborne to supply her with "images" of those they wished her to torment. Yet, aside from an afflicted child named first by the magistrate in a leading question, Goody Hobbs could not identify any of her victims. Asked if Osborne and Wilds were accompanied by a man, she joined others in describing "a tall black man, with an high-croun'd hat." The justices assayed another test after the examination, enlisting a group of women to search Deliverance's body for evidence that her specter had been struck by Benjamin Hutchinson's rapier the day before. She admitted having a "very sore" place caused by a "Prick" on her right side, which the searchers confirmed. Parris also remarked upon an injury to her left eye, "which agrees with what the afflicted farther said that Benjamin Hutchinson after wards toucht her eye with the same Rapier." Following her confession and the apparent physical corroboration of Walcott's and Williams's vision the previous day, Hathorne and Corwin ordered her jailed.

When Deliverance declared that Goody Wilds "tore me almost to peices," she adopted a phrase introduced by Ann Jr. on April 20 in describing her spectral encounter with George Burroughs and reiterated by Mary Warren on April 21.[44] Such references to "tearing to pieces," which would become nearly as ubiquitous in subsequent months as sightings of the "black man," were exceedingly rare in the previous history of afflicted accusers and confessors in old and New England. In the past, tormented young people had tended to describe Satan's beguiling promises of fine clothing, wealth, and "ease" from "burdensome" labor or had simply complained of current tortures, rather than emphasizing Satan's warnings of greater suffering to come. The threat of dissection, although not wholly unique, assumed a greater prominence in 1692 than in comparable episodes in other times and places.[45]

The warning therefore appeared to have a particular resonance for the late-seventeenth-century residents of Essex County, and the context of the Second Indian War could well provide the explanation for its salience. Returning captives and witnesses to wartime atrocities told tales of how companions and family members had been brutally slain, scalped, and occasionally cut to shreds. That was the fate, for example, of Robert Rogers, one of the Salmon Falls prisoners, who tried but failed to escape his Wabanaki captors. He was stripped naked, tied to a stake, and partially burned. Then the Indians pulled the fire away from him and "Danc'd about him, and at every Turn, they did with their knives cut collops of his Flesh, from his Naked Limbs, and throw them with his Blood into his Face. When he was Dead, they set his Body down upon the Glowing coals, and left him tyed with his Back to the Stake." Horror stories such as these spread rapidly through northern New England's gossip networks. The fear of Indians that pervaded the region thus included not just apprehensions of death or captivity but also of torture and dismemberment. In light of the perceived alliance between Satan and the Wabanakis, such suffused dread could easily have been vocalized in what became the commonplace description of the devil's threats to "tear [the afflicted] to pieces" if they did not comply with his demands. Indeed, in recounting a series of dissection narratives, Cotton Mather explictly termed the Wabanakis "Devils," thus linking the Indians to Satan precisely in this context.[46]

After Deliverance Hobbs was taken away, the magistrates questioned the woman she said had recruited her into the devil's legion: Sarah Averill Wilds. Sarah, who had been born in England and migrated as a child with her parents to Ipswich, became the second wife of John Wilds, a well-off Topsfield resident, in 1663. A member of the Topsfield church, she was about sixty-five years old in 1692. The magistrates' perfunctory examination showed that Deliverance's confession had convinced them of Goody Wilds's guilt, and their order to hold her for trial seemed even more predetermined than the others issued that day. "Here is a clear evidence," Hathorne proclaimed, "that [you have] been not only a Tormenter [but that] you have caused one to sig[n the] book, the night before last." The sufferers had fits, cried out that they saw Wilds's apparition on the beam in the meetinghouse, and "con[firmed] that the accused hurt th[em]." In addition, Parris reported, "she was charged by some [with] hurting John Herricks mo[ther]." Testimony taken later revealed the origin of that charge, which was obviously being much discussed by local gossipers. Sarah's purported victim had been the deceased Mary Gould Reddington, sister of John Wilds's first wife, Priscilla Gould. Nearly two decades earlier Mary had complained to many people (including John Hale) that Sarah Wilds "assaulted [her] by witchcraft . . . bewitched her & afflicted her many times greiviously."[47]

Another examinee that day was more fortunate. Ann Jr. identified Nehemiah Abbott Jr., a Topsfield weaver in his late twenties, after a naming test like that employed with Goody Hobbs. Ann then declared that she saw his specter "upon the beam." Just such a vision of Deliverance had preceded *her* confession, Hathorne informed Abbott, "and if you would find mercy of God, you must confess." Abbott nevertheless proclaimed his innocence "in all respects." Hathorne admonished the afflicted, "charge him not unless it be he," and doubts seemed to arise in their minds. "This is the man say some, and some say it is very like him," Parris recorded in his transcript. Ann reiterated her identification, but Walcott retreated: "He is like him, I cannot say he is he." Lewis then insisted, "it is not the man." With Ann now asking, "be you the man?" and an impasse apparently developing, the magistrates decided that Abbott should be sent out of the room while they questioned "several others." When he returned following the additional examinations, the afflicted (Parris noted) "in the presence of the magistrates and many others discoursed quietly with him, one and all acquitting him, but yet said he was like that man, but he had not the wen they saw in his apparition." The justices then dismissed Nehemiah, who thus became the one person known to have been freed permanently in 1692 after formal questioning. Mercy's decisive role in creating the outcome by declaring Ann Jr.'s initial identification faulty revealed that she had effectively assumed the leadership of the primary group of accusers.[48]

One of those interrogated in Abbott's absence was Mary Easty, the third Towne sister to be accused. Williams, Walcott, Hubbard, Lewis, and Putnam Jr. all charged her with afflicting them on the spot, while John Indian cried that he "saw her with Goody Hobbs." In the face of her accusers, who alternately could not speak, mimicked her movements, and suffered from fits, Mary Easty proclaimed her innocence. Then what had caused these torments? Hathorne pressed her. "It is an evil spirit, but wither it be witchcraft I do not know," Easty replied. Hathorne, pronouncing it "marvailous" that she should not think them bewitched "when severall confess that they have been guilty of bewitching them," ordered that she join her sisters in jail.[49]

As was already indicated, the examination records for three of those interrogated on April 22 are apparently no longer extant. Mistress Mary Hollingsworth English of Salem Town was the heir of the wealthy merchant William Hollingsworth and his wife Eleanor. Probably because her husband Philip English, who will be discussed later in this chapter, was a French-speaking native of the Isle of Jersey, and her deceased mother had once been defamed as a witch, even Mary English's high status did not prevent her from being charged with witchcraft. Still, what event triggered her accusation is unknown.[50]

In the other two cases, however, those of Sarah and Edward Bishop of Salem Village, enough evidence survives to suggest the origins of the charges. Like Mary English, Sarah Wilds Bishop, daughter of John Wilds by his first wife and stepdaughter of Sarah Averill Wilds, was closely related to a suspected witch. In addition, she had previously been accused of bewitching a neighbor—a woman, Christian Trask, whose death in mid-1690 had been ruled a suicide, but which was sufficiently strange to arouse suspicions that it involved "some extraordinary work of the devill." Sarah's husband Edward was evidently targeted because of his skeptical attitude toward the accusers, just as John Proctor had been. According to Robert Calef, a later critic of the trials, Edward Bishop attended the Salem Town examinations on April 11, and while at the inn in the town subdued a "very unruly" John Indian so that he became "very orderly." When John had a fit while the Villagers were returning home, Bishop struck him, commenting that he was certain "he could cure them all" by the same means. As soon as Bishop left the group, Calef recorded, he was accused of being a witch.[51]

Even with eight new suspects in jail and nine examinations completed, the magistrates did not end their day on April 22 after closing the public session in the meetinghouse.[52] As they had done with other recent confessors, they headed for the Salem prison to take an additional statement from Deliverance Hobbs without masses of spectators present. "She continued in the free acknowledging herself to be a Covenant Witch," their record of her second confession began. Thereafter emerged a series of remarkable details. Whereas that morning Deliverance had spoken briefly and haltingly, naming no one but Sarah Wilds, Mercy Lewis, and Sarah Osborne, and offering few specifics about her malefic activity, late in the day she was primed with information that, the court clerk Stephen Sewall later commented, "fully agrees with what the afflicted persons relate." In the interim, of course, Deliverance had been jailed in the company of her stepdaughter Abigail, Mary Warren, and other arrestees, who were far better informed than she about what had been said heretofore by the afflicted and by earlier confessors.

The previous morning, Deliverance revealed, Sarah Wilds had invited her to a witch meeting "in the Pasture by Mr Parris's House." Additional attendees included the Proctors, the Coreys, and Goodwives Nurse, Good, Osborne, and Bishop. "Mr Burroughs was the Preacher," presiding at a devil's sacrament, where Goody Wilds and Goody Nurse distributed "Red Bread, and Red Wine Like Blood." The clergyman, who was accompanied by "a Man in a long crowned white Hat," had "prest them to bewitch all in the Village, telling them they should do it gradually and not all att once, assureing them they should prevail." Deliverance claimed that she had not participated in the sacrament, which led the others to threaten her with new tortures. And "she saw when Abigail Williams ran out to speak with them," but she was "strucke blind" so could not see to whom the little girl had spoken. As she finished her statement, her stepdaughter was brought in and fell into a "dreadful fitt." Deliverance then disclosed that Giles Corey and "the Gentlewoman of Boston" were "striving to break her Daughters Neck."

Several aspects of this confession require extended analysis. Goody Hobbs had conflated Tituba's two Boston women of unspecified rank and a high-status man into one "gentlewoman" from the larger town, thus introducing into the Salem crisis a mysterious figure whose possible identity later became the subject of speculation. Second, despite Stephen Sewall's positive assessment, the confession did *not* "fully agree" with Abigail Williams's statement. As was discussed in chapter 2, the devil's sacrament the little girl described— during which she had conversed with the "deacon" Sarah Cloyce—occurred in Parris's pasture on March 31. Deliverance Hobbs said the one she attended took place on the morning of April 21. That the significant time discrepancy was apparently overlooked in the preparation of the case against the accused demonstrated how fully the authorities were invested in believing the truth of what they heard from afflicted and confessors alike. Moreover, Abigail Williams and Deliverance Hobbs identified different "deacons" at the diabolic sacrament, and Hobbs explicitly declined to identify Goody Cloyce as a witch. Instead, because she was "strucke blind," she could not see Abigail's conversational partner. Like Mercy Lewis, that other former Falmouth resident, Deliverance and Abigail Hobbs never testified against the woman who was now married to Peter Cloyce, a man whose brother Thomas they would have known in Casco.[53]

Finally and most important, Goody Hobbs's confession on April 22 established a template for many others that followed. She was the first to see her former pastor George Burroughs as the celebrant of the diabolic sacrament, thereby linking Ann Jr.'s vision of him as the witches' leader with Williams's and Lewis's earlier descriptions of satanic communions. Burroughs, who could not administer the sacrament in the visible world because he had not been ordained, freely did so in the invisible world under the aegis of the devil. Further, Deliverance named participants in the event with great specificity, as others would in later confessions. Yet her list had certain unique and significant characteristics. The only people formally accused prior to April 21 whom she omitted were Rachel Clinton (who was unknown to people in Salem Village and was never accused by anyone there) and Sarah Cloyce—along with, counterintuitively, the four confessors who preceded her. That pattern, in which confessors did not identify other confessors as participants in malefic gatherings, persisted until late July, when some Andover confessors finally began to name each other as Satan's allies.

How much time passed before Essex County residents learned the contents of Goody Hobbs's detailed confession is not clear. But even without knowing what she had said, the multitudes who attended the April 22 examinations had much to contemplate and discuss thereafter. They had witnessed extraordinary torments and physical effects among the afflicted and had heard another confession of guilt. And they had watched a diverse group of people be jailed for complicity in the devil's plot against them, thus suggesting its widening scope and import.

ANOTHER ACCUSER FROM MAINE
AND HER FIRST TARGET

After the flurry of activity on April 22, there followed a full week of relative calm, marked by no formal legal proceedings and a smaller number of spectral sightings. Villagers' attention must have shifted from the existing group of young accusers to another teenage resident who that week endured afflictions for the first time. A refugee from Maine like Mercy Lewis, she too would have known George Burroughs in her former home. Not by coincidence did she begin having a series of strange spectral encounters just four days after the minister was first identified as the leader of the witches, nor was it surprising that her initial tormentor was the apparition of the French-speaking merchant Philip English.

In the Salem Town meetinghouse on Sunday, April 24, Susannah Sheldon was "afflicted in a very sad manner" when a spectral Philip English "step[ped] over his pew and pinshed her."[54] En route home to the Village after services, she again met Mr. English, accompanied by "a black man with a hy crouned hatt on his head and a book in hish [*sic*] hand." English explained to her "that black man were her god and if shee would touch that boock hee would not pinsh her no more nor no bodie else should." The following day, English's specter reappeared to underscore the point: "if shee would not toutch the book hee would kill her."

For the next week, Susannah continued to see frightening apparitions. Two women and a man "brought their books and bid her touct them." She asked the specters for their names, and one volunteered that she was "old good man buck lyes wife and the other woman was her daughter mary." Goody Buckley also revealed that she had been a witch for ten years. "Then shee opened her brest and the black man gav her two litle things like yong cats and she pit them to her brest and suckled them." On successive days, Susannah saw the apparitions of Bridget Bishop, Mary English, and the Coreys in various combinations, usually accompanied by the black man wearing a tall hat. Goody Bishop admitted having been a witch for twenty years (a fact confirmed by the black man), and the Coreys choked and hit Susannah to prevent her from eating. She saw Martha Corey put a hairless "thing like a blake pig . . . to her brest and gave it suck . . . then she gave it to the blak man then went to praier to the blak man." Bridget Bishop had "a streked snake . . . [in] her bosom mrs. English had a yelo bird in her bosom." And Goody Bishop "told mee that she had kiled foar women two of them wear the fosters wifes and john trasks wife and did not name the other."

SUNDAY, OCTOBER 10, 1675; BLACK POINT.

"When the Indeans came first it was on a Lords day in the morning," Eleanor Barge recalled some months later, describing how the Wabanakis killed two men near Richard Foxwell's garrison house. Early the following day the Indians "went to dunstone & fell upon Left. Alger, & the Dunston people, . . . which made the wime[n] that lived at blew poynt much afrayd, & the most part of the wimine & the children [including herself] fled away to bla[ck] poynt." There she personally asked Captain Joshua Scottow to send some men to help the people at Dunstan, including Lieutenant Arthur Alger and his brother Andrew. But Captain Scottow replied, "there should not a man goe of[f] the Necke, for sayd Mr Scottow, they had warening enough & lyberty Enough [to have escaped] they & Arther Alger too . . . if they perish they perish." Some of those who had taken refuge at Scottow's garrison volunteered to aid the people under attack at Dunstan, but Scottow stopped them by declaring that "we hade brought our wifes & Children there & if we were killed whoe should Maintain them." Goody Barge recounted Scottow's explicit threat: "if the men goe away, I will turne away the wimine & children after." One of the would-be volunteers sharply rebuked Scottow, calling it "a verry unhumain thing that men should be in distres and we should not see to [have?] them Releved."⁵⁵

Among the alarmed people in the Black Point garrison that day were William Sheldon, his wife Rebecca, and their little daughter Susannah, who would then have been under two years old. Rebecca Scadlock Sheldon must have been particularly terrified by the news of the attack on Dunstan, for her sister Anne was married to Arthur Alger. She and her husband were surely dissatisfied not only with Captain Scottow's refusal to aid the outlying settlement but also with his decision instead to dispatch a messenger to Saco to the "Contry soldiers" stationed there. Nine men responded to the call for assistance, but before they arrived at Dunstan a small company of militia from Salmon Falls under Captain John Wincoll appeared on the scene to engage the Indians. On October 13, first Wincoll's men and then those from Saco came under fierce fire from the Wabanakis. Pinned down on the shoreline at a place called Saco Sands and in sight of, but across the water from, the Black Point garrison, Wincoll sent two men to Scottow with a desperate request for aid.⁵⁶

Contemporary accounts of Joshua Scottow's response to this second call for succor differ dramatically. One of those trapped on the Saco Sands later testified that Scottow "would not send any helpe to us," even though he had more than forty men currently in his garrison, whereas Richard Foxwell's equidistant post, with only seven men, sent five to assist them. In contrast, a group of witnesses who were at Black Point at the time attested that Scottow did all he could to save the endangered troops, supplying residents with guns and ammunition, and insisting to reluctant volunteers that "wee could not answer to god, men, nor our owne conscience unless wee used the utmost of our endeavour to relieve those men." Yet it was impossible to reach the beleaguered militiamen quickly, they reported, "because of the suff [surf] of the sea, the wind blowing ffresh upon the shore." The commander of the twenty men eventually sent from Black Point to Saco Sands subsequently explained that "they having two rivers to passe and the tide, being about three parts in they Could not come to their timely releife."[57]

Such descriptions of the difficulty of traveling rapidly from Black Point to reach the imperiled men on October 13 have the ring of truth. Yet all nine of the Saco men died on the beach that day, along with several of Wincoll's militia, and in consequence Joshua Scottow's name was indelibly blackened. The men in the Black Point garrison, who by several contemporary accounts were reluctant to jeopardize their own safety in an attempt to save the soldiers, soon began to assure everyone that they would have gone to help the men on the Saco Sands had Scottow not stopped them from doing so.[58]

Reports of Scottow's cowardice and selfishness spread widely through northern New England's gossip networks, expanding to include accounts that he refused aid to others as well. And when Massachusetts stationed soldiers at Black Point during the late fall and winter of 1675–1676, as was pointed out in chapter 3, Scottow was charged with using those men for his own personal gain. William Sheldon, whose fortified house served as a garrison, joined other residents in sustained criticism of Scottow's conduct. Sheldon also had personal reasons to detest Scottow, for Andrew Alger died in the assault on Dunstan on October 11, and Arthur Alger was fatally wounded at the same time. Brought with other injured men to Black Point after the battle, Arthur died at William Sheldon's garrison on October 14, 1675. The young Susannah must have witnessed both her uncle Arthur's death agonies and her aunt's and mother's consequent grief.[59]

Major Richard Waldron later informed Scottow that because of the nasty and pervasive gossip about his cowardice, "it is very difficult to gett men to serve you, Such an odium is on your name here, that men openly professe, they had rather be hanged then Serve under your command."

The "rumors and reproaches" climaxed in several cases in which Joshua Scottow and those who censured his conduct clashed in court—once before Justice William Stoughton in Maine and twice in front of the Suffolk County court in Boston. Captain Scottow emerged victorious from these legal battles, much to the disgust of the frontier dwellers.[60]

As noted in chapter 3, Black Point surrendered to the Wabanakis while Joshua Scottow was defending his conduct in Boston in October 1676, and the region was not resettled until 1680 and thereafter. When the Sheldons and other former residents returned to Black Point in the early 1680s, so did Scottow. Susannah must have grown up hearing her parents denigrate the high-status neighbor they would have regarded as at least partially responsible for her uncle's death. After Captain Scottow became George Burroughs's patron in the mid-1680s, seeking to lure him from Falmouth to Black Point, Burroughs too probably became the subject of negative comments in the Sheldon household. At the very least, the minister's association with the hated Scottow would not have worked in his favor with the Sheldons and other long-term residents of the area; that could even explain why they failed to construct a house for him.[61]

In the early fall of 1688, shortly after the Second Indian War began, William Sheldon relocated his family to Salem Village. His oldest son Godfrey, 24, who volunteered for militia service in Maine after the fall of Fort Loyal in Casco, was killed by the Indians in early July 1690. William himself died (probably from gangrene or tetanus) in Salem Village at the age of 68 in December 1691, two weeks after he fell and cut his knee. Accordingly, in late April 1692, when she saw the spectral vision of Philip English coming toward her in the Salem Town meetinghouse, Susannah was living in Salem Village with her recently widowed mother, Rebecca; her older brother, Ephraim; and her four sisters (two older and two younger than she).[62]

The target of Susannah Sheldon's first accusation, Philip English, was one of the wealthiest merchants in New England. Born Philippe L'Anglois on the Channel Isle of Jersey in 1651, he immigrated to North America as a young man. By far the most prominent member of the small Jerseyan community in Essex County, English had long engaged in commerce with Spain, the Caribbean, and his home island. Like other northern New England merchants, he traded salt fish for manufactured goods from Europe and produce from the tropics. Accordingly, ships owned or employed by him would have sailed frequently along the coast of Maine, north to French Acadia, and beyond to the Newfoundland Banks. As a native French speaker whose business placed him potentially in regular contact with the French (and their Wabanaki allies), English undoubtedly aroused the suspicions of his Anglo-American neighbors after the Second Indian War began in 1688. Despite—or perhaps because of—his prominence and wealth, his origins and mercantile pursuits made him a marked man in the climate of fear pervading Essex County in 1692.[63]

A prime indication of the extent of that fear had surfaced during late May 1690, about two weeks after the fall of Fort Loyal. Rumors flew through the countryside that Isaac Morrill, a "jarzy man or French man" long resident in Essex County, had been seen carrying a concealed gun and reconnoitering "Pikes Garason" at Salisbury. Other stories claimed that he and another Jerseyan named George Mousher had been attempting to persuade local slaves to "goe for canada and Joyne with the french against the English and So come downe with the french and Indians upon the backside of the cuntry and distroy all the English and Save none but only the Negro and Indian Servants and . . . the french would come with vessells and lay at the harbours that none Should escape." Morrill was reported to have dispatched four French spies to "veiw all our garrisons & our strength," and to have himself "veiwed all the garrisons Eastward & westward so far as new Yorke." It was even said that "some Easterne garrisons were watched by women."[64]

Although the scare involving Morrill and Mousher seems to have dissipated without incident, the generalized fear of the French did not vanish. In late December 1691, the Massachusetts Bay General Court issued an order revealing the continuing concern of the colony's leaders about potential internal enemies. Even though New England's Protestants had welcomed refugee Huguenots after the revocation of the Edict of Nantes in 1686, the General Court observed that some recent arrivals had been "of a contrary Religion and Interest." The presence of "such a mixt Company amongst us, especially in and about the Sea Ports and Frontier Towns," endangered the "Publick Safety" in "a time of War." Accordingly, it ruled that after January 31, 1691/2, no French person could "take up their Residence, or be in" port or frontier towns without permission from the authorities, nor could they set up shops or engage in any trade. Philip English had long since established himself in Salem Town, so whether the order applied to him might have been contested, but as a practical matter it singled him out for special attention.[65]

In addition, English violated local norms defining appropriate conduct in business. As the administrator of the estate of his mother-in-law, Eleanor Hollingsworth, he aggressively asserted claims to two tracts of land that Richard Hollingsworth (Mary English's grandfather) had decades earlier informally designated for his younger son, Richard, but for which he had never drafted legal conveyances. Neighbors' testimony in the two cases, both filed in the fall of 1690, revealed that they all regarded the land as rightfully belonging first to Richard Hollingsworth Jr. and then later to his widow. Yet English contended that since Richard Sr. had died "withoute Alienating the Same from his Heire at Law" (that is, his older son, William, Mary's father), the land should fall to Philip, as Mary's husband, "by Linniall Desent." In the early- and mid-seventeenth-century colonies, many transactions were conducted orally, and men were expected to respect those agreements, even though written records were lacking. English's lawsuits therefore must have scandalized such witnesses as William Beale of Marblehead. Beale had been present when Richard Sr. agreed with Thomas Farrar to break up and fence four acres of land for Richard Jr. That land had been held by the younger Hollingsworth "without Contradicktion by any man as I know of," Beale assured the court. Not surprisingly, English lost both cases as local juries upheld customary claims rather than the letter of the law, but he appealed at least one of them to the Court of Assistants, where the outcome is unknown.[66]

William Beale eventually swore that he believed Philip English bewitched him because of that testimony. English had come to him in spring 1690 "in A fauneing & flattering manner" to offer money in return for supporting him in the case, Beale recalled in August 1692. He, though, had not only indicated that he would appear on the other side, but had also recruited Goodman Farrar as an additional witness against English. As he was discussing the Hollingsworth land title with Farrar, Beale remembered, "my nose gushed out bleedeinge in A most extraordinary manner." And there was more maleficium to come. Explaining how he had seen English's "plaine shape" in his bedroom in late March 1691, and how he had struggled on that occasion "not to thinke that hee was a wich," Beale revealed that his prayer to "Our omnipotent Jehovah for his blessing & protecktion" had caused the apparition to vanish. Shortly before that spectral vision, one of his sons died from "A stoping in his throate" and soon afterwards another expired suddenly, in a way his nurses had "admired & wondred" at. Although Beale did not make his reasoning explicit, the implication was obvious: the witch Philip English had caused his sons' deaths in retaliation for William's opposition to his land claims.[67]

Beale's testimony against Philip English resembled many other tales of witchcraft recited by witnesses in the 1692–1693 Salem trials. In all of them, a colonist imputed to a suspect injuries that occurred after the witch was angered in some way, usually (but not always) because the witness had refused to comply with a request. But had Susannah Sheldon not encountered Philip English's apparition in the Salem Town meetinghouse on April 24 and renewed her accusation several times thereafter, Beale would probably never have publicly voiced his suspicions of the wealthy Mr. English. Only in the context of the war against the French and the Wabanakis did Philip English become a plausible candidate for the designation "witch." Under normal circumstances, his claims to his wife's uncle's land would have aroused resentment, even anger—but not witchcraft accusations.

In most cases of maleficium brought to light during the 1692 crisis, similar dynamics were at work, but they involved people, especially women who, like Bridget Bishop, had long-standing reputations for witchcraft. Unlike the accusation of English, they did not originate with an afflicted person from Salem Village. As was indicated at the beginning of this chapter, by late April the names of many suspected witches had surfaced in Essex County's gossip networks. Wagging tongues conveyed the tales orally from other towns to Salem Village, where the afflicted then turned them into formal charges.

SOME "USUAL SUSPECTS"

On Saturday, April 30, Jonathan Walcott and Sergeant Thomas Putnam filed formal witchcraft charges against Philip English and George Burroughs, along with the teenage Sarah Morrell of Beverly and the widows Lydia Dustin of Reading, Susannah Martin of Amesbury, and Dorcas Hoar of Beverly. The authorities could not immediately proceed against the men, because Burroughs was living miles away in Wells, and English had fled to Boston, where he hid in the home of a friend until located and arrested at the end of May. Little is known about Morrell, although she might have been related to Isaac Morrill, the "jarzy man" suspected of conspiring against the colony in 1690. The records of the case against Lydia Dustin have not survived, but Robert Calef later reported that she had been thought to be a witch for "20 or 30 Years" and that it was said of her, "if there were a Witch in the World she was one." In that respect, she resembled Dorcas Hoar and Susannah Martin, the other older women accused with her.[68]

Susannah North Martin, in 1692 a sixty-seven-year-old widow, had been suspected of malefic practices by her neighbors in Amesbury and Salisbury for more than three decades. William Brown told the court that his wife, Elizabeth, had years earlier accused Martin of pricking her repeatedly with spectral "nayls & pinns." After formally complaining against Martin, Goody Brown began suffering from "a strang kind of distemper & frensy uncapibl of any rasional action," a condition that had persisted for decades, and two doctors diagnosed bewitchment. Robert Pike, who recorded William Brown's deposition, personally attested to the accuracy of Brown's characterization of his wife's circumstances. Many similar depositions detailing Martin's witchcraft were eventually considered at her trial.[69]

Thus when Susannah Martin appeared for her examination at the Salem Village meetinghouse on Monday, May 2, her reputation surely preceded her.[70] "Many had fits" as soon as she entered the room, Parris recorded. Abigail Williams identified the examinee as Goody Martin, some were struck dumb, and Ann Jr. threw a glove at her. Martin "laught," calling the behavior "folly." Is "the hurt of these persons" folly? a shocked Hathorne inquired. After Lewis, Walcott, and the newest member of the group, Susannah Sheldon, accused her of afflicting them, the magistrate asked Goody Martin for her reaction to the charges. First denying practicing witchcraft or consenting to the tortures, she contended (as had Sarah Osborne) that the devil "can appear in any ones shape." Next Martin went on the attack, declaring that she did not think her accusers were bewitched, that "they may lye for ought I know," and indeed that the afflicted might be "dealing in the black art."

Martin thus proposed publicly for the first time a line of attack to which the accusers were indeed vulnerable: the charge that they themselves were witches, or at least that they consorted too closely with the devil. The ready communication of the afflicted with the invisible world certainly suggested the possibility that they might have joined the ranks of Satan's allies, and the accusers' awareness of that fact probably accounted for their repeated insistence that they had responded negatively to the witches' importunities to sign their books and enlist in the devil's legions. Above all else, the afflicted Villagers had to distinguish themselves from Satan's allies, interpreting the invisible world for their fellow colonists but simultaneously maintaining a firm distance from it.

Accordingly, they (including John Indian and Betty Hubbard) quickly suffered new torments following Martin's attempt to turn the tables. Some cried out that Martin's specter was "upon the beam" and others that "the black man" was whispering in her ear, both visions that had come to be regarded as indicating a person's guilt. Moreover, the afflicted added a new behavior to their repertoire: first Abigail, then others "could not come near her." John Indian, for example, "was flung down in his approach to her." Asked for an explanation, Martin ventured, "It may be the Devil bears me more malice than an other," but Hathorne had a different interpretation: "God evidently discovers [reveals] you." To emphasize the point he added, "all the congregation think so."

The afflicted also reacted by having fits when Dorcas Hoar was brought in for her examination that same day. Several accused the Beverly widow of having attacked them spectrally on April 24 or 25; in addition, Hubbard and Walcott asserted that her apparition had admitted choking "her own husband." They thus showed themselves to be well acquainted with a story that must have made the rounds after William Hoar died "very sudingly" the previous winter. The coroner's jury appointed to investigate the death asked that the corpse be stripped. Jurors later reported that Goody Hoar then "brake out in a very greate pashtion," wringing her hands and stamping her feet on the floor. You "wiked wretches," she cried, "what doe you think I have murdered my husband?"[71]

After Dorcas denied having any part in her husband's death, Sheldon made the surprising and unusual allegation that Dorcas Hoar "came in with two cats, & brought me the book, . . . & told me your name was Goody Bukly," thus transforming the accusation of the Village resident Sarah Buckley she had offered a few days earlier into a complaint against Goody Hoar.[72] Hathorne vigorously pursued the reinterpreted vision, pressing Hoar about "those cats that suckt your breast" and inquiring about her association with Goody Buckley. "I never knew her," Dorcas asserted, but Goodman William Buckley, a Village shoemaker, "testifyed that she had been at the house often." Goody Hoar hastily explained, "I know you but not the woman," although "many by-standers" accused her of distorting the truth.

Meanwhile, most of the afflicted (including Sarah Vibber, "free from fits hitherto" that day) asserted that "a black man" was speaking to Goody Hoar, directing her not to confess. "They say the Devil is whispering in your ear," Hathorne informed her. "I cannot help it if they do se it," Hoar responded. After Susannah Sheldon and others repeated the claim about the spectral conversation, Dorcas retorted sharply, "There is some body will rub your ears shortly." The afflicted "immediately" complained of being "rubbed," Parris observed, and the magistrate proclaimed it "unusual impudence to threaten before Authority." As was the case with Goody Martin, several afflicted persons who "were carried towards her" could not approach Goody Hoar at all. Asked to explain, she declared, "I do them no wrong, they may come if they will." But Parris remarked at the end of his notes that "the afflicted were much distressed" throughout the examination.

The women first identified as witches by Katherine Branch in Stamford, Connecticut, during that last week of April fit the same pattern as Dustin, Hoar, and Martin. Evidence gathered in the Connecticut cases showed that the maidservant's initial charges targeted women who had long been gossiped about as possible practitioners of maleficium. Elizabeth Clawson, who was engaged in a long-running feud with Katherine's master, Daniel Wescott, was thought to have caused the deaths of some livestock and at least one baby. Neighbors believed that Mercy Disborough too had bewitched the children and livestock of her enemies. Over the next few months the Connecticut magistrates continued to investigate Katherine's allegations, but in the absence of other afflicted complainants they moved cautiously and with the traditional careful deliberation.[73]

A CONFEDERATE OF THE DEVIL

On April 30, a "perticuler Order from the Governor & Council" called for the arrest of George Burroughs of Wells, "he being Suspected for a confederacy with the devil in opressing of Sundry about Salem." That directive from Major Elisha Hutchinson in Portsmouth to the marshal of Maine and New Hampshire revealed that Hathorne and Corwin consulted their fellow magistrates before moving against the minister. The decision to act on the reported spectral visions of the clergyman had thus been reached at the highest level of the colony's government. Only Burroughs among the 1692 accused received such treatment, which once more underscores his significance in the minds of his judges and accusers alike.[74]

The marshal quickly carried out his orders. By May 2, he had brought Burroughs to Portsmouth, and two days later he turned his prisoner over to the "Authority" to be held at the tavern of Thomas Beadle in Salem Town until he could be questioned. Even before the clergyman physically returned to Essex County, his specter again began appearing to the afflicted. First he came to Walcott, who "formerly well knew" him and described him as "biting pinching and almost choking me urging me to writ in his book." Then Hubbard, who had not seen or known the minister before, declared that on the night of May 3 the specter of "a little black beard man" wearing "blackish aparill" and identifying himself as "borrous" offered her a book with "lines . . . read as blod." Thereafter the apparition came to her "every day & night very often" until his examination on May 9. Echoing his earlier words to Ann Jr., he informed Betty that "he was above a wizard; for he was a conjurar." He urged Betty to run away and to sign his book, threatening to kill her and "tortoring me very much by biting and pinching squesing my body and runing pins into me."[75]

On Thursday, May 5, George Burroughs returned to speak spectrally with Ann Jr. After "greviously" tormenting her and futilely pressing her to write in his book, he predicted to her that "his Two first wives would appeare to me presently and tell me a grat many lyes but I should not beleve them." Sure enough, the little girl recounted, she was "immediatly . . . gratly affrighted" by the sight of "Two women in winding sheats and napkins about their heads." The women's specters, "very red and angury," told Burroughs's apparition that "he had been a cruell man to them, and that their blood did crie for vengance against him." After they prophesied that "he should be cast into hell," his specter vanished. They then turned to Ann and explained that Burroughs had murdered both of them—the first in the Salem Village parsonage, the second (with the assistance of his current wife) on shipboard as she was returning from Maine to her family in the Village. "They both charged me that I should tell these things to the Magestraits before Mr Burroughs face," Ann declared, disclosing that the specters had foretold their possible reappearance at that time if the clergyman did not admit his misdeeds.[76]

That same day a Salem resident, Elizar Keyser, saw what he believed to be a "diabolicall apperition" after he encountered George Burroughs in the makeshift prison at Thomas Beadle's. Keyser first met Captain Daniel King, a frontier militia leader, who insisted that the minister was "a Child of god, a Choice Child of god, and that God would Clear up his Inocency." King urged Keyser to visit Burroughs's chamber to speak with him, presumably so that he too would become convinced of the clergyman's innocence. But Keyser demurred, initially claiming that "it did not belong to such as I was to discourse [with] him he being a Learned man," then reluctantly admitting the real reason for his reticence: "my Opinion or feare was, that he was, the Cheife of all the persons accused for witchcraft or the Ring Leader of them all." And if that was true, then "his Master meening the divell had told him before now, what I said of him"—Keyser, in short, had already told others that he believed Burroughs was the witches' leader. Because King seemed to be "in a passion," though, Keyser complied with his wishes and met with Burroughs, who "did steadfastly fix [his] eys upon mee." That night, Keyser saw "very strange things appear in the Chimney . . . [and] quaver with a strainge Motion," followed by a light "aboute the bigness of my hand . . . which quivered & shaked" and was seen by his maidservant as well. He had no doubt that he had experienced a supernatural phenomenon.[77]

Two days later Mercy Lewis, Burroughs's former maidservant, joined others in conversing with the clergyman's specter. On the evening of May 7, she recounted, the apparition brought her "a new fashon book" and told her she could write in it, "for that was a book that was in his studdy when I lived with them." Not recognizing the book, she refused. Burroughs then boasted that "he could raise the divell" and admitted bewitching "Mr. Sheppards daughter" (Ann Jr.'s second cousin). When Mercy asked how he could bewitch someone in the Village while being held in Salem Town, he revealed that "the divell was his sarvant and he sent him in his shapp to doe it." Burroughs also confessed that he had recruited Abigail Hobbs and "severall more" into Satan's forces, and he repeatedly tortured Mercy, "as if he would have racked [her] all to peaces," telling her that he would kill her unless she signed his book.[78]

About the same time, Susannah Sheldon too encountered the apparition of her one-time pastor. Confirming his identity, he helpfully explained that he was "borros which had preached at the vilage," simultaneously threatening to starve or choke her to death or "tear [her] to peesses" if she would not sign his book. On the night of May 8, he appeared to ask if she were planning to testify against him the next day; when she said yes, he menacingly declared "hee would kil [her] beefoar morning." Earlier that same day, he had also appeared to Mary Walcott, to whom he revealed more details of Hannah Burroughs's death. "He would have kiled his first wife and child: when his wife was in travil but he had not power," the spectral cleric revealed to Walcott. So instead "he keept hir in the kithin tell he gave hir hir deaths wound." Walcott, like Ann Jr., saw the specters of Burroughs's first two wives "in their winding sheets," crying for vengeance against him.[79]

Even on the very day of his examination Burroughs did not cease his spectral activity. He pinched Goody Vibber's arm as she was en route to the Village for the examination; never having met him before, she could not identify his apparition until she saw him in person later. Meanwhile, he appeared to Susannah at Ingersoll's tavern to confess that he had not only killed his two wives but also "two of his own children" and "three children at the eastward." As for Mercy, that morning he tried bribery in addition to threats: he "caried me up to an exceeding high mountain and shewed me all the kingdoms of the earth and tould me that he would give them all to me if I would writ in his book," Mercy revealed. Once again, though, she resolutely refused: "I tould him they ware non of his to give and I would not writ if he throde me down on 100 pitchforks."[80]

Those who attended the examination of George Burroughs in Salem Village on Monday, May 9, magistrates and people alike, would have been well aware of all his spectral appearances during the preceding ten days; indeed, he was specifically questioned about most of them during the interrogation. Joining Hathorne and Corwin in presiding over the session were the councilors William Stoughton and Samuel Sewall, who could well have been selected because of their prior acquaintance with George Burroughs. Sewall knew the minister at Harvard, and at least once (in November 1685) he had hosted him at dinner. Stoughton would have met him when he went to Falmouth in September 1688 to try to negotiate a hostage exchange with the Wabanakis, if he had not known him before.[81]

A detailed transcript of the examination either was not kept or does not survive, but an existing summary shows that the first part of the interrogation was conducted "in private none of the *Bewitched* being present." In that initial phase, Burroughs was asked about reputed failures to take communion and to have his children baptized, both of which he admitted. He was also questioned about reports that his Falmouth house was "haunted" and that he had forbidden his second wife to communicate with her father without his approval, both of which he denied. All these tales would have reached the magistrates through gossip networks. The very existence and accessibility of such stories demonstrated that Burroughs's various activities had long fascinated the residents of northern New England.[82]

Then Burroughs was brought into the presence of the afflicted, and "many (if not all of the Bewitched) were greivously tortured," notes the summary. Not surprisingly, the minister's former congregants, Susannah and Mercy, took the lead, with Susannah first testifying about her vision of his wives "in their winding sheets" accusing him of murder. She also referred to "the soldiers," but what exactly she said has been lost; presumably, she repeated Ann Jr.'s charge that he had bewitched some of Andros's forces in 1688–1689. When Mercy's statement about her spectral encounter with him was about to be read, "he lookt upon her & she fell into a dreadful & tedious fit." The same then happened to both Mary and Betty when their statements were introduced. Next, Ann Jr. and Susannah attested that he had asked them to write in his book. Called upon to respond to these charges, Burroughs characterized them as "an amazing & humbling Providence, but he understood nothing of it." He also observed wonderingly that "when they begin to name my name, they cannot name it."

After Ann Jr. and Susannah both declared that "his 2 wives & 2 Children did accuse him," the afflicted were "so tortured" that the judges ordered some of them removed. Sarah Vibber, still present, attested that "he had hurt her, tho she had not seen him personally before as she knew." The magistrates then reviewed other evidence against him. They ordered Elizar Keyser's statement read, along with the confessions of Abigail and Deliverance Hobbs, and they took additional testimony from men who had known George Burroughs in Casco. Most of these new depositions pertained to demonstrations of the clergyman's unusual strength. Finally, John Putnam Sr. testified about Burroughs's relationship with his first wife in the early 1680s, when the couple had lived in his house.

The content of the examination showed that the presiding magistrates prepared for it with great care. They had already gathered significant evidence against George Burroughs, not only gossipy reports and prior statements of the afflicted (both of which had been employed in earlier examinations, although to a lesser extent) but also formal witness testimony offered at the examination itself—a unique occurrence. A good part of that testimony, moreover, pertained to events in Maine years earlier. Some statements (the record is unclear) could have been offered in the form of depositions, but at least two men from the northeastern frontier testified in person on May 9. Everything the magistrates did, in short, singled George Burroughs out for special attention.

So too did the actions of the bewitched. George Burroughs's first spectral confession to Ann Jr. on April 20 established two important patterns and his second appearance to her on May 5 added another. As has been shown, the afflicted began to see his shape repeatedly and with increasing frequency as his examination date approached. His numerous appearances signaled his importance and demonstrated both his ubiquity and his power. In addition, his specter and eventually others started to confess to the afflicted not only that they were witches but also that they had committed other crimes, most commonly murder. Before April 20, specters had appeared to the afflicted people and had tormented them to try to enlist them in Satan's ranks, but they had not confessed to other offenses. After Burroughs's apparition confessed to Ann Jr., so too did many others admit guilt to her and the other afflicted persons.

And the spectral visions of Ann Jr. on May 5 originated still another new and important aspect of the crisis. As has been indicated, she saw not only George Burroughs but also the ghosts of his two former wives, who accused him of killing them and directed her to inform the magistrates about his crime. They thus became the first of many dead people whose spirits rose from their graves (often in their winding sheets, as in Ann Jr.'s vision) to charge suspected witches with murder. In his *Essay for the Recording of Illustrious Providences* in 1684, Increase Mather had revealed that the ghosts of the dead could sometimes appear to the living in an attempt to right terrible wrongs, especially murders "not discoverable in any other way." The people who received such visions, declared the elder Mather, had a special responsibility to carry the messages of the dead to the ears of the living.[83]

Accordingly, the core group of young female accusers took on new roles in the crisis after April 20, especially following May 9. As was seen in chapter 1, English legal experts concurred that a confession of guilt was the best proof of a witch's identity. Yet the magistrates had for the most part failed to persuade the accused to confess. Only a few of the examinees so far—Tituba,

Dorcas Good, Mary Warren, Abigail and Deliverance Hobbs—had formally admitted their guilt, while many more, including George Burroughs himself, insisted on their innocence in the face of what appeared to be overwhelming evidence to the contrary. The contest with Satan in the visible world had reached an impasse. In the invisible world, however, specters proved far more accommodating. Burroughs's apparition freely admitted killing his first two wives to Ann Jr., Mercy, Susannah, and Mary, among others. His confession had then been validated by the ghosts of his dead wives, who revealed to Ann Jr. and others (including Mary) not only the fact of the murders but also the details of how they had been carried out. The clergyman also acknowledged working in concert with the Indians by bewitching Sir Edmund Andros's troops. Thus in the invisible world the afflicted, in effect, assumed the role of magistrates. They listened to the testimony of spectral witnesses (the murder victims) and extracted the confessions that Hathorne and Corwin could not.

And that, even more than the continuing reorientation of the afflicted girls' households around their needs, constituted a role reversal of major proportions. The magistrates had by now come to rely almost wholly on the core group of accusers (Lewis, Putnam Jr., Walcott, Hubbard, Williams, Sheldon) for evidence of witchcraft during the examinations. Time and again Hathorne had done his best to interrogate suspects carefully in order to expose the contradictions and falsehoods in their stories that would reveal their involvement with the devil. Yet he rarely succeeded. Instead of being uncovered by the magistrates' questioning, even before May 9 witches were being revealed by the fits, visions, and mimicking movements of the afflicted Villagers. In the weeks and months after the examination of George Burroughs, the process moved even farther along the same path, as spectral confessions to the bewitched and appearances of the dead turned into witchfinding, and as the magistrates ceased all attempts to conduct meaningful examinations of the accused. Moreover, on May 14 Governor William Phips finally arrived to implement the new charter. A new phase of the crisis began, involving not only examinations but also trials.

NATHANIEL SALTONSTALL (HAVERHILL) TO [MASSACHUSETTS GOVERNOR AND COUNCIL], APRIL 30, 1692:[84]

Capt Daniel Lad came to my lodging & . . . informed [me] that Joseph Ayers a Beaver Hunter belonging to this Towne, who had been from home about 6 weekes upon this or some other designe, hunting, was return'd, & before severall 6 or 7 persons, he being himself present, did declare & affirm, that in his rang[e] he was at Quabaug, & there divers times did see Indians at that place, & mett 3 men there, whome he called Indian Traders, who had frequent Correspond[ence] with the Indians; & traded with them Amunition, & brought in Beaver from them often times. . . .

I charg'd Daniel Lad with this report as a falshood; He then told me, He had it as abovementioned, & That he did purposely acquaint me with it, as a matter grevious to him, so that farther enquirie might be made, & our own people not suffered to supply the enimie with materialls for the destruction of this Country, & keeping the Warr on foot.

If this report be true, There is no hopes of an end of this vicious Warr, as it now lies upon the Outward frontier Townes, & may, before it is over, peirce our verey bowells.

CHAPTER FIVE

Many Offenders in Custody

APRIL 30–MAY 31, 1692

T HROUGHOUT LATE APRIL and early May, the specters of those already in jail continued to appear regularly to the afflicted. For instance, on Saturday evening, April 30, Sarah Vibber saw Sarah Good standing near her bed. The apparition, she said, "Looked upon my child 4 years old and presently upon it the child was stracke into a great fit." Just two days later, Goody Vibber accused Good of attacking her "by presing my breath almost out of my body" and of again tormenting the child, which "cried out and twisted so dreadfully by reson of the torture . . . that it gott out of its fathers Armes." So too on May 2 and 3, Rebecca Nurse's apparition came to torture Mary Walcott. On her second visit Goody Nurse's specter readily admitted having had "a hand in" the deaths of several people, including Benjamin Holton and Rebecca Sheppard of the Village.[1]

Despite such repeated appearances, the most important developments during May pertained not to existing complaints but to new ones.[2] The month saw a dramatic increase in the number of suspects in jail, as the pace of accusations quickened following the identification of George Burroughs as the witches' leader. The arrival of Governor William Phips in midmonth generated further waves of complaints. As Massachusetts officials finally began to prepare for conducting trials, more charges flooded in to the Essex County magistrates. Although the names of "usual suspects" resembling Bridget Bishop and Dorcas Hoar appeared among the newly accused, the afflicted persons also began to target prominent men and women, who might best be termed "unusual suspects." Such accusations have not received much attention from scholars, in part because they have appeared so incongruous and in part because they have not fit easily within common categories of analysis.

For example, some of these people, although arrested and jailed, were never tried for witchcraft, and so legal historians (who study trials) have ignored them. Many were men, and so feminist historians (who have focused on accused women) have also overlooked them. Further, the names of some were recorded only by the later critics of the trials. If from the outset male gatekeepers found accusations wholly lacking in credibility, those initially named were never formally charged with malefic practices. Because legal proceedings against almost all such people were attenuated for one reason or another—some who were arrested, for instance, broke out of jail before they could be tried—surviving court records contain little information about them. Thus researchers must look elsewhere for insight into their accusations.[3]

Historians have frequently characterized the complaints against wealthy and prominent figures as examples of "overreaching" by the afflicted late in the crisis. Many accounts then interpret such charges as helping to discredit the core group of young accusers, contending that the iconoclastic complaints were a key factor in bringing the crisis to a close. As Bernard Rosenthal has pointed out, however, such arguments are mistaken. The relevant accusations actually began to emerge in mid- to late May, soon after the examination of Burroughs, and they continued to be offered regularly, if sporadically, thereafter. What linked them all—and what nearly all historians have failed to recognize—was the relationship of their targets to the Indian wars on the Maine frontier. Scattered among other accusations of more stereotypical "witches," and lacking the extensive documentation of prosecutions more vigorously pursued, these crucial allegations of complicity with Satan have never received the attention they deserve. Several will be discussed at length in this chapter in the appropriate chronological context.[4]

TWO MALE WITCHES AND TWO MORE CONFESSORS

At the end of April, the specter of John Willard, a Village resident who had earlier helped to "tend" the child Ann Putnam, began to appear to his former charge, to whom he revealed his culpability for a horrid crime. After tormenting her for several days in a row, Ann Jr. declared, Willard not only "sett upon me most dreadfully" but also indicated that "he had whiped my little sister sarah to death and he would whip me to death if I would not writ in his book." Subsequently, Ann saw the infant Sarah's apparition. The baby, who died at approximately six weeks of age in December 1689, appeared to her "crieing out for vengance against John Willard," along with the specter of "John Wilknes first wife," who declared that Willard had caused her death as well. (John Wilkins, whose young wife Lydia died in January 1688/9, was a cousin of Willard's wife, Margaret.)[5]

Facing these disturbing charges and the prospect of examination and jail, Willard sought assistance from his wife's grandfather, the eighty-one-year-old Bray Wilkins. After Ann Jr. named him, Willard "came to my house greatly troubled," Wilkins later recalled, "desiring me with some other Neighbours to pray for him." Wilkins explained to his grandson-in-law that he was on his way out of the house on business, but would comply with his request "if I could come home before night." Unfortunately, his return was delayed, and so Wilkins did not act on his promise. No noticeable consequences ensued immediately, but on May 4 Wilkins encountered Willard in Boston at a dinner at a relative's house attended by "many friends," including the Reverend Deodat Lawson and his second wife. During the dinner, Wilkins reported, Willard "lookt after such a sort upon me as I never before discerned in any," and almost immediately Wilkins was "taken in a strange condition," finding himself in utter "misery," unable to urinate and feeling pain "like a man on a Rack." Lawson and the other dinner guests were "all amazed," but Wilkins believed he knew the cause of his sudden illness: "I was afraid that Willard had done me wrong."[6]

Wilkins's suspicions could only have been confirmed in the days that followed. While he remained in Boston, a woman thought to be "skilfull" in medical matters called to help him. Well aware of the events in Salem Village, she inquired "whither none of those evil persons had done me damage," then expressed her fear that witchcraft was creating his mysterious ailment. Three or four days later Bray Wilkins chose to return home, even though he was afraid the journey would endanger his life. There he learned that his seventeen-year-old grandson Daniel, who had earlier declared that "it were wel If the sayd Willard were hanged," had also fallen ill. An unnamed physician (later described as "the french Doctor") declared the sickness "preter natural" and would not prescribe any remedies. On May 9, Susannah Sheldon reported a vision of four dead people, who "turned As Red As blood" when they accused John Willard of murdering them. The next day, she saw Willard's apparition suckling "two black piggs on his breasts" while Elizabeth Colson of Reading (first accused a month earlier by Mary Marshall) "suckled As it Appeared A yellow bird." Susannah asked Willard how long he had been a witch. After he replied "twenty years," she said that the specters "kneelled to Prayer to the Black man with a loung Crouned hat" before vanishing.[7]

That same May 10, without a formally recorded complaint, John Hathorne and Jonathan Corwin issued a warrant for John Willard's arrest on a charge of witchcraft. Anticipating such an order, Willard had already fled the Village and could not be located. That day, also without a recorded complaint, the magistrates additionally ordered the arrest of a seventeen-year-old

Villager, Margaret Jacobs, and her grandfather, George Jacobs Sr., the old man whose specter had tormented Mercy Lewis on the night of April 20.[8]

Those additional arrests stemmed from a confession the magistrates elicited in the late afternoon or early evening of May 9, after the examination of George Burroughs. Sarah Churchwell, George Jacobs's maidservant, confessed to having signed the devil's book. Her statement, no longer extant, implicated her elderly, crippled master, who walked with the aid of two canes, and it must have named his granddaughter as well. Mercy Lewis later claimed that at Sarah's examination she "perswaded her to confess" and that consequently on the night of the ninth Jacobs had tortured her "most cruelly" by beating her with his canes. In a later confession, Sarah indicated that, like Mary Warren, she had once been afflicted. When she was "unable to doe her service as formerly," her angry master called her "bitch witch & ill names." Although Sarah did not say so, George Jacobs Sr. (like John Proctor under similar circumstances) had probably beaten her severely.[9]

In all likelihood, Sarah Churchwell's experience paralleled Mary Warren's. As an afflicted maidservant with a skeptical master, she was never formally listed as tormented. When her condition improved, the other accusers would have insisted that she had surrendered to the devil, signing his book in order to escape from torture. The day after Sarah's confession, Abigail Williams thus declared that George Jacobs Sr.'s specter had disclosed to her having recruited six people—his maidservant Sarah Churchwell, his granddaughter Margaret, her parents, and Philip and Mary English—into the ranks of the witches.[10]

FRIDAY, SEPTEMBER 17, 1675; SACO.

Warned of an impending attack, John Bonython and his family abandoned his imposing house on the north side of the Saco River to take refuge with Major William Phillips in his fortified garrison on the opposite bank. They left just in time. The next morning, Richard Waldron later reported, "the Indians rifled and burnt Severall houses," including Bonython's. The party of about forty Wabanakis then crossed the river and moved half a mile upstream to set fire to Phillips's valuable grist- and sawmills, planning "thereby to draw them out of the house, and soe to Surprise both them & itt." But Major Phillips, forewarned, instead prepared to defend his garrison house, now filled with about fifty people: fifteen men and thirty-five women and children. Among them were Bonython's daughter and son-in-law Eleanor and Arthur Churchwell and his granddaughter, Sarah, who was then about eight years old.[11]

The Wabanakis surrounded the house and, "Creeping deckt with ffearns and boughs," began to shoot at any movement they saw inside. They wounded several men, including Major Phillips himself, but otherwise made little progress in their aim of capturing the garrison. Major Waldron vividly described the Indians' plan to burn the house and how it was thwarted purely by chance:

> they gott a pair of old truck wheels and ffitted them up with boards & Slabbs ffor a barricadoe to Safeguard the Drivers thereby Endeavouring to burn the house haveing prepared combustible matter as birch rinds pitchwood Turpentine & powder . . . before they came at the house there was a little wett ground into which the Wheels sunk & that obstructed their driveing itt fforward they Endeavouring to gett it out of the dirt again by turning a little on one Side thereby layeing themSelves open to them in the house which oportunity they Improved & made them quitt their work and ffly.

Despite the failure of their attempt to burn the settlers out of the garrison, the Wabanakis continued to shoot at it all night, then finally marched away the next morning, Sunday, September 19. Although everyone in the house survived, their fortuitous escape from a terrible death must have been one of the major reasons they, including William Phillips and his family, quickly sought havens elsewhere. The Bonythons and the Churchwells moved to Marblehead, where John died in February 1676/7. Whether the Churchwells returned to Saco in the 1680s is unknown, as is the fate of Sarah's mother; Arthur survived until 1710. Sarah probably ended up in Salem Village because she was related by marriage to the Ingersoll family and thus to Mary Walcott.[12]

Wartime losses had accordingly transformed the granddaughter of one of the wealthiest and most distinguished men in Maine into an unmarried maidservant in a backwater village. She had good reason to resent her fate and to blame both the Wabanakis and inept colonial leaders for her unenviable existence.

On May 10, 1692, although the constable could not find John Willard, he brought in Margaret Jacobs and her grandfather. That same day the magistrates examined George Jacobs Sr., apparently at Thomas Beadle's tavern in Salem Town. "Here are them that accuse you of acts of witchcraft," the justices began, referring to Abigail Williams and Sarah Churchwell. The latter charged that Jacobs had afflicted her at Ingersoll's inn the previous night. She also acquiesced in the examiner's statement that "when you wrote in the book you was showed your masters name." Jacobs insisted on his innocence, and when asked to explain the reported actions of his specter he contended, like Susannah Martin, that "the Devill can go in any shape." Sarah took an active part in her master's interrogation, calling on him to confess, telling him he had led "a wicked life," and revealing that he did not conduct family prayers. When asked why, he responded that he could not read, an answer the magistrates deemed unacceptable. Directed to say the Lord's Prayer, "he mist in severall parts of it, and could not repeat it right after Many Trialls," which was seen as a nearly certain sign of guilt. Yet the old man still resolutely denied being a witch, or having persuaded his son George Jr. and granddaughter Margaret to sign Satan's book.[13]

The next day, also at Beadle's tavern, Margaret Jacobs confessed that "she was a witch or that she had Set her hand to the Devil's booke." Months later, she explained that at her examination the sight of the afflicted falling down "did very much startle and affright me," and that when she exclaimed that she "knew nothing, in the least measure, how or who afflicted them," the magistrates told her, "without doubt I did, or else they would not fall down at me." The justices also warned her, she revealed, that "if I would not confess, I should be put down into the dungeon and would be hanged, but if I would confess I should have my life." Accordingly, her "own vile wicked heart" had led her to try to save her life not only by confessing but also by identifying both George Burroughs and her grandfather as fellow witches.[14]

Margaret's recollection of what Hathorne and Corwin told her at her May 11 examination marks the earliest explicit record of what eventually became one of the magistrates' most controversial tactics: preserving the lives of confessors so that they could testify against others, while simultaneously prosecuting people who refused to admit their guilt. That the justices adopted this procedure about three weeks after Deliverance Hobbs became the first to name many names indicates that they quickly realized how important such confessions could prove to be in building cases against the suspects.

While Margaret was admitting her guilt on May 11, a man named Joseph Flint went to inform George Jacobs Sr., who was being held in another room at the tavern, about what his granddaughter was saying. Flint later described the old man's reaction to that news. "She was charged not to confess," Jacobs exclaimed, then hastily explained that he meant "if she were Innocent and yet Confest she would be accessary to her owne death." But both Flint and the magistrates interpreted the outburst as an indication of guilt, and it led

Hathorne and Corwin to interrogate Jacobs again immediately. At that second examination, Ann Jr. and Abigail Williams "had each of them a pin stuck in their hands, and they said it was this old Jacobs," Parris noted. Ann also claimed that Jacobs's specter told her he had been a witch for forty years, and that he promised "she should be as well as his Grand daughter" if she would write in his book. The magistrates asked for Jacobs's reactions to the testimony of Lewis and Williams that he had afflicted them on April 20 and May 10, respectively. Those statements were "false," he declared; "I know not of it, any more than the child that was born to night."[15]

Parris's observation that pins were found stuck into the hands of two of the afflicted during George Jacobs Sr.'s second examination constitutes the first point in the trial records that such manifestations can be precisely dated. Physical effects of the apparitions had been noted before, but teeth marks or even bleeding from a pinch differed from actual pins. Some historians have cited such incidents as evidence of fraud on the part of the core group of accusers. As Rosenthal has remarked, if a specter did not jab the pins into the girls' bodies, then either the girls themselves or a confederate had to have done so. Yet the afflicted, if sufficiently mentally disturbed, could have stuck themselves with pins (or injured themselves in other ways) without conscious or rational intent, so the appearance of pins in their bodies does not necessarily prove consistently fraudulent behavior on their part. Still, it does indicate that some complainants may have been deliberately faking on some occasions.[16]

With George Jacobs Sr., his granddaughter, and Sarah Churchwell safely in custody and the constable out searching for John Willard—whose apparition nevertheless reemerged that same May 11 to torment both Lewis and Hubbard—Hathorne and Corwin decided the next day to return to the Salem Town jail to reexamine earlier confessors. The magistrates thereby learned many new details about the spectral conspiracy they believed was confronting New England.[17]

THE SECOND CONFESSIONS OF
ABIGAIL HOBBS AND MARY WARREN

The renewed questioning of Abigail Hobbs on Thursday, May 12, focused solely on George Burroughs and malefic activities in Casco.[18] Did the minister bring you poppets of his wives, his children, or "the Eastward Souldres" to "stick pinns into"? the justices inquired. Abigail said no, but admitted that Burroughs had directed her to afflict various residents of Falmouth, although she remained vague about the identity of most of her victims. Some "lived att the fort side of the River about half a mile from the fort, toward Capt. Bracketts," she disclosed, and more resided "Just by the Other toward James Andrews's." Her targets were, Abigail declared, "both Boys and Girls," who "dyed" from the afflictions. Burroughs "in Bodily person" had brought her the necessary small images, along with pins to stick into them. And "when he appeared to tempt mee to set my hand to the Book, he then appeared in person, and I felt his hand att the Same time," Abigail indicated. She admitted being acquainted with Sarah Burroughs, but denied knowledge of "any poppits pricked to kill her."

The teenager identified by name only one of her purported victims: Mary Lawrence. In response to leading questions, Abigail said that she had stuck "thorns" into "the middle of [Mary's] body" because Mary had spoken badly of her. But the initiative to harm Mary had not been hers alone. Burroughs had brought her Mary Lawrence's image "in his own person Bodily . . . Abroad a little way of[f] from our house . . . Before this Indian Warr." When the justices asked why Burroughs had targeted Mary, Abigail informed them that he told her "He was angry with that family." As was pointed out in chapter 4, Mary's father, Robert Lawrence, led the opposition to Sylvanus Davis and Edward Tyng, and Burroughs in all likelihood was aligned with the latter two men in Falmouth during the 1680s. The resulting antagonisms must have been fierce indeed for a girl as young as Abigail Hobbs to be aware of them.

Hathorne and Corwin surely found Abigail's second confession less useful than they had hoped. She now acknowledged that Burroughs had asked her to afflict other residents of Casco through the use of poppets and pins, and also that she had herself killed some people by malefice. She even admitted having been a witch "these Six years," for she had signed not one but two covenants with the devil (the first for two years, the second for four). But at the same time she denied any knowledge of the most serious charges advanced by Putnam Jr., Lewis, and Williams, taken collectively: that Burroughs had killed his second wife and that he had bewitched Andros's troops during the winter of 1688–1689. Instead, she revealed only that the clergyman had taken revenge on the daughter of one of his political opponents and had asked her to afflict unnamed, unknown numbers of "Boys and Girls." Moreover, when the magistrates asked if she had seen "severall Witches at the Eastward," she responded unhelpfully, "Yes, But I dont know who they were."[19]

From the magistrates' perspective, then, their examination of Mary Warren that same day must have proved more satisfactory. Although she added little to their case against the clergyman, she had much to say about others who had previously been accused, and she revealed the identity of two more witches, for whom they immediately issued arrest warrants.

The justices began interrogating Mary Warren essentially where they had stopped on April 21, posing questions about John Proctor's bringing her the devil's book.[20] Had she realized what she was doing when she touched it? they asked. "I did nott know itt then but I know itt now," she admitted. She also confessed having employed thorns and poppets to afflict Putnam's daughter and Parris's niece. Pressed to reveal more, she indicated that the apparitions of two Salem Town women, Alice Parker and Ann Pudeator, had brought her poppets of Lewis and Walcott, respectively, and that she had stuck pins in both. Furthermore, the specters had been in a talkative mood: "Goody parker told me she had bin a Witch these 12 years & more; & pudeator told me that she had done damage." She listed Goodwives Nurse, Cloyce, and Bridget Bishop as witches, along with Dorcas Good and Giles Corey. She also revealed that Goody Corey "att my masters house in person" had predicted that "I should be condemned for a Witch as well as she hir-self, . . . & she said that the children would cry out & bring out all." But Warren denied knowing how long John and Elizabeth Proctor had been witches; "they never told me."

The clergymen John Higginson of Salem Town and John Hale of Beverly arrived near the end of the examination, just in time to witness the "dreadfull fitts" Warren suffered upon again hearing the names of Alice Parker and Ann Pudeator. The women's specters then seemed to vie with each other by con-fessing to a series of murders, most of them involving deaths at sea. (For example, Parker's apparition, reported Warren, said she had "cast away" Cap-tain Thomas Westgate's vessel.) The admissions included Pudeator's state-ment that she had killed her husband "by giving him something whereby he fell sick and dyed" about a decade earlier. Goody Parker disclosed that she had bewitched Mary's sister, striking her dumb, and Goody Pudeator's apparition revealed that she and Burroughs had tried to hinder the current prosecution by bewitching the magistrates' horses. Finally, Burroughs's specter informed Mary that "he killed his wife off of Cape Ann." (Mary War-ren, unlike Abigail Hobbs, thus demonstrated her familiarity with the gossip about Sarah Burroughs's death.)

In ordering the immediate arrest of Alice Parker and Ann Pudeator, Hathorne and Corwin charged them with afflicting Warren that very day during her examination. Both women lived in Salem Town, as did (evidently) Warren's own family. Alice, about whom little is known, was married to John Parker, a mariner; her neighbors had suspected her of witchcraft for at least eight years. Ann Pudeator had lived in Falmouth in the 1650s and 1660s with her first husband, Thomas Greenslade, but they moved to Salem before the First Indian War. (Two of her adult children remained behind in Casco.) After Thomas's death she married Jacob Pudeator, a Jerseyan blacksmith who was probably twenty years her junior, and whose first wife she had nursed in a final illness in 1676. Jacob died in August 1682, and so she had been widowed for nearly a decade. Ann had long been suspected of practicing maleficium and perhaps of killing both her second husband and his first wife.[21]

The record of Goody Pudeator's examination on May 12 does not survive, but that of Alice Parker does.[22] The magistrates confronted the sailor's wife with Warren's charge that her apparition had admitted destroying Captain Westgate's ship and crew. Goody Parker denied any part in the loss of the vessel and rejected the claim that she had bewitched Mary's sister. Mary, who was "grievously afflicted" throughout Parker's interrogation, described the reason for that allegation: after her father had failed to fulfill a promise to mow some grass for Goody Parker, she had come to their house, "and told him he had better he had done it." Soon thereafter, Warren reported, "Her Sister fell ill and shortly after Her Mother was taken ill, and dyed." Mary thereby implied that the angry witch had attacked them both. Warren also affirmed that Parker's specter told her about attending "the Bloody Sacrament in Mr Parris's Pasture" along with about thirty other witches. And Mary, like the afflicted at the examinations of Susannah Martin and Dorcas Hoar ten days earlier, was unable to approach Parker, "but fel backward immediately into a dreadful fitt."

Warren was not Goody Parker's only accuser that day. Margaret Jacobs attested that she had seen Alice's specter "in the North feild" the previous Friday night (May 6). Marshal George Herrick, who had arrested her, "affirmed to her face" that she had announced to him that "there were threscore Witches of the Company," and Alice was unable to explain how she had produced that figure. One of the ministers of her church, Nicholas Noyes, testified about a previous conversation with her "in a Time of sicknes" about "her witchcrafts whether she were not Guilty." All in all, by the end of the examination Hathorne and Corwin appeared to have good reason to think that Parker was a witch.

After they finished the examinations on May 12, the magistrates ordered a group of seven prisoners (including Mary English and Bridget Bishop) moved to Boston, to join some already incarcerated there. Tituba, Sarah and Dorcas Good, Sarah Osborne, John and Elizabeth Proctor, Rebecca Nurse, Sarah Cloyce, George Burroughs, and Susannah Martin had all been sent to the larger facility following their interrogations; Osborne, ill when arrested, had recently died in Boston. Hathorne and Corwin probably regarded the

Salem Town jail as already overcrowded, so they directed that Jacobs, Parker, and Pudeator be held in Boston as well. They also might have had little confidence in the ability of the Essex County jailer to prevent a determined prisoner from fleeing from custody. Less than a year earlier they had tried a case involving a successful escapee who had taken advantage of doors carelessly left open. A fellow prisoner testified that a jailer should be "a responsabel Man and fathful," but that William Downton was "nather." He explained: "the counti has a good preson and tou dores and tou lockes to each Dor[,] a preson yeard and a lock to the gat[e] but the gat[e] stands al wa[y]s open," as did "the nor[th] dor." Presumably the presence of so many accused witches had led to improved security, but Hathorne and Corwin surely wished to take no chances with the suspects.[23]

On either May 12 or 13, Mary Warren also accused another person of witchcraft: the thirty-seven-year-old Abigail Soames, who had been living at the home of Samuel Gaskill, a prominent Quaker in Salem Town.[24] A single woman from Gloucester, Abigail was recuperating from smallpox and, according to Goody Gaskill, had "kept her Bed for most part these thirteen months," except for occasionally going out "in the Night." When Soames was questioned at Thomas Beadle's on Friday, May 13, under the watchful eye of the Reverend Mr. Noyes, Warren suffered especially "dreadful" fits. Soames's apparition, commented an anonymous scribe, "bitt her so dreadfully that the Like was never seen on any of the aflicted." Asked to explain Warren's torments, Soames replied that "the Enemy hurt her" (thus suggesting that perhaps Satan was attacking Warren directly) and attempted to number herself among the afflicted. Insisting that she was "Distracted many atime," she declared that "I thought I have seen many a Body hurt mee, and might have accused many as well as she doth," particularly certain residents of Gloucester.

The examination of Abigail Soames is significant because it marked the first time that the magistrates employed the version of a touch test that would eventually become commonplace. "Soams being Commanded while Warren was in a dreadful fit, to take Warren by the hand, the said Warren immediately recovered," recorded the scribe. "This Experiment was tryed three times over and the Issue the same." Conversely, however, Warren could not touch Soames. "Altho she Assayed severall times to do it with great Earnestness she was not able, But fell down into a dreadful fit." Asked why she could not approach Soames, Warren revealed that "she saw the apparition of Somes come from her Body, and would meet her, and thrust her with Vialunce back again." The scribe remarked that whenever Soames looked at Warren she "struck her into another most dreadful and horible fit," and so "she practised her Witchcrafts several times before the Court."

After the examination had concluded, both Mary Warren and Margaret Jacobs saw the apparition of George Burroughs. The spectral clergyman bit Warren, "which bite was seen by many," the scribe recorded, and Burroughs predicted to Jacobs "that her Grandfather would be hanged," which made her weep. Also present were two other apparitions. The spectral gathering certainly seemed to indicate that the examinee, Abigail Soames, had actively participated in the witch conspiracy.

Five months later, Thomas Brattle, a prominent critic of the trials, recorded the explanation for the efficacy of the touch test developed by "the Salem Justices, at least some of them." The afflicted, having been first struck down by "venemous and malignant particles, that were ejected from the eye" of the suspected witch, were cured because the witch's touch allowed the particles to "return to the body whence they came, and so leave the afflicted persons pure and whole." Although Brattle thought that reasoning dubious, the magistrates clearly found it persuasive for many crucial months.[25]

On May 14, Hathorne and Corwin, acting on a new complaint filed by Thomas Putnam and Nathaniel Ingersoll, ordered the arrest of eight more people for afflicting the core group of sufferers and unnamed others. Those listed on the warrant included all persons already identified as witches but not yet taken into custody, along with several new suspects. Three of the group fled to avoid arrest, but the other five were apprehended and brought to Salem Village in preparation for questioning on Tuesday, May 17, at Ingersoll's inn.[26]

Those examinations, though, were postponed a day because of a long-anticipated but nonetheless unexpected event: the arrival of the new governor. On the evening of Saturday, May 14, Sir William Phips sailed into Boston harbor on the *Nonesuch,* an English frigate. "Candles are lighted before He gets into Townhouse," Samuel Sewall recorded in his diary. "Eight companies [of militia] wait on Him to his house, and then on Mr. [Increase] Mather to his. Made no volleys because 'twas Satterday night." When they learned of Phips's arrival, Hathorne and Corwin traveled to Boston to participate in the welcoming ceremonies and to be sworn in as councilors.[27]

CONTINUED PROCEEDINGS UNDER NEW AUSPICES

Sir William Phips, whom Cotton Mather described in his diary as "one of my own Flock, and one of my dearest Friends," was closely aligned with both

Mathers, father and son. Increase Mather, dispatched to London in spring 1688 by the leaders of Massachusetts Bay, achieved remarkable success as lobbyist and emissary over the next three years. Although criticized in some quarters for his inability to resurrect the old charter (an outcome many New Englanders would have preferred), Mather exercised great influence not only on the drafting of the charter of 1691 but also on the appointment of the governor and councilors who would implement it. London officials were barraged with sharp criticism of the "Bostoners" after Andros's overthrow in April 1689, yet Mather managed to win a charter that retained some of the colony's traditional autonomy. Even more significant, perhaps, as his proud son Cotton observed, "all the *Councellors* of the Province, are of my own Father's Nomination." The elder Mather thus ensured that at the outset of the new regime all the important decisions would continue to be made by essentially the same men who had been running the colony for years.[28]

And their leader would be Sir William Phips, a native of Maine and a hero of the Second Indian War for his capture of Port Royal in Acadia in 1690, in spite of his failed excursion against Quebec later that same year. The son of an Indian trader and gunsmith, Phips had been born near the mouth of the Kennebec River in 1651 at a family homestead destroyed in August 1676, during the First Indian War. He grew up well acquainted with the local Wabanakis and their ways, and while governor in the 1690s accounted himself an expert on Indian affairs. Apprenticed to a shipbuilder in his youth, Phips had little formal education. Although he learned to read as an adult, he could barely sign his own name. While working as a shipwright in Boston in the early 1670s, he met and married a young widow, Mary Spencer Hull, whose father lived for a time in Saco as a partner of Brian Pendleton. Between his wife's siblings and his own numerous siblings and half siblings, William Phips had many close relatives familiar with affairs in Maine. Some of them had lived at Casco or Black Point and knew George Burroughs.[29]

In 1687, Phips, by then a ship captain obsessed with treasure seeking, located the valuable wreck of a Spanish galleon on a reef off the coast of Hispaniola. After Phips returned to England with a cargo of gold and silver worth more than £200,000, King James II knighted him as a reward for his service to the crown and nation. Over the next few years Phips lived alternately in London and Boston, while in England assisting Increase Mather in his dealings with colonial officials, and while in New England participating sporadically in the war effort. From March 1691 until his appointment as governor the following November, he remained in London, simultaneously defending his conduct during 1690, proposing a new expedition against

Canada, advancing various schemes involving trade and development in Maine, and promoting his candidacy for governor.

When he arrived on May 14, Sir William Phips must have been shocked to discover that jails in Boston and Salem were bulging with thirty-eight people awaiting trial for witchcraft. (Initial word of the crisis reached London long after his departure.) He later wrote, indeed, that he found "this Province miserably harassed with a most Horrible witchcraft or Possession of Devills which had broke in upon severall Townes" and filled with "the loud cries and clamours of the friends of the afflicted people" demanding that he take action against the suspects. "The generality of the people," he asserted, "represented the matter to me as reall witchcraft and gave very strange instances of the same."[30]

Amid the festivities celebrating the onset of a new regime, he therefore had to move swiftly to establish appropriate legal machinery to organize the necessary grand jury sessions and trials. On Monday, May 16, his commission as governor of Massachusetts (and head of New England's militia) was formally read, and he and the other office-holders present were sworn in. The council included several men who had participated in questioning the suspected witches—Samuel Sewall and Bartholomew Gedney in addition to Corwin and Hathorne—as had the new lieutenant governor, William Stoughton. Another councilor, Robert Pike of Salisbury, did not attend the ceremony because he was busy recording depositions in the case of Susannah Martin. These experienced men, Phips later indicated, advised him as he decided how to handle the unexpected crisis.[31]

The first council meeting on May 24 appears to have been largely ceremonial, but three days later the council took an important substantive step. "Upon Consideration, That there are many Criminal Offenders now in Costody some whereof have lyen long, and many inconveniences attending the thronging of the Goals, at this hot Season of the year, There being no Judicatories or Courts of Justice yet Established," read the official minutes, "Ordered, That a Special Commission of Oyer and Terminer be made out." A few days earlier, the governor had summoned an assembly to meet on June 8, but that assembly might well take weeks or months to reestablish a full court system. Royal governors could convene special courts if necessary; Phips therefore employed the common colonial device of a Court of Oyer and Terminer ("to hear and determine" in French legal terminology) to handle the witchcraft prosecutions. Nine judges (who will be discussed in the next chapter) were named to the court. Stephen Sewall, Samuel's brother and the man who had sheltered Betty Parris in March, was appointed court clerk, and Thomas Newton—an English lawyer practicing in Boston who had a year earlier prosecuted the Leisler rebels at a Court of Oyer and Terminer in New York—was named as attorney general.[32]

Several days later, Sir William Phips dictated letters to London reporting on his reception in Boston and his first two weeks as governor of the colony. Surely overemphasizing considerably, although for obvious reasons, he remarked that "the harts of the People here are very much Transported with joy & their mouths Filled with expressions of Thankfullnesse to their Majesties" for the new charter government. Phips described the public reading of his commission and the charter, the convening of the council, the swearing-in ceremonies, and his call for elections to the assembly. He did *not* mention his establishment of a Court of Oyer and Terminer, or the reason for it. Instead he wrote to the Earl of Nottingham, the secretary of state, "the small t[ime] since my arrivall admitts of noething more that is Matter [to] acquaint your Lordship with." To William Blathwayt, the secretary for plantations, he said essentially the same thing: "I have but little to say at present, for the short time Since my Landing could not produce much." Phips might possibly have seen the setting up of a special court to deal with unresolved criminal cases as so routine as to require no comment on his part. Yet that those thirty-eight "Offenders now in Costody" were charged with witchcraft was certainly unusual. Most likely, Phips's councilors advised him to write nothing official about the evolving crisis for the time being, and to wait instead until more of the outcome could be known.[33]

While the governor was organizing his administration in Boston, the specters, especially those of John Willard and Sarah Buckley, appeared repeatedly in Salem Village. The first of many subsequent episodes of witch-finding by members of the core group of accusers occurred on the evening of May 14. In yet another indication of her leadership role, Mercy Lewis was taken to Wills Hill, the home of the Wilkins family, to see "the afflected parsons there." Mercy, asked whether she saw any apparitions, declared that Willard was attacking both Bray Wilkins and his grandson Daniel, a vision reconfirmed by Ann Jr. the next night. Ann furthermore disclosed that Willard's specter told her that he wanted to kill Daniel, "but he had not power enufe yet to kill him: but he would goe to Mr Burroughs and git power to kill daniel wilknes." Then on Monday, May 16, Mercy and Mary Walcott informed a group of onlookers that Willard and Buckley were "upon his Throat & upone [Daniel's] brest and presed him & [choked] him." After Daniel died that same night, a coroner's jury officially concluded that "to the best of our judgments we cannot but apprehend but that he dyed an unnatural death by sume cruell hands of witchcraft or diabolicall act as is evident to us both by what we have seen and heard consarning his death." When he noted the teenage Daniel's decease, Parris recorded beside his name "bewitched to death."[34]

The next day Marshal George Herrick wrote to Hathorne and Corwin in Boston to inform them that the elusive fugitive John Willard had finally been captured in Nashaway (Groton), and that "he No sooner arrived butt the afflicted persons made such an out crye that I was forced to pinion him."[35] On May 18, the magistrates themselves returned to Salem Village to conduct the interrogation. "That you were fled from Authority . . . is an acknowledgment of guilt," intoned Hathorne, "but yet notwithstanding we require you to confess the truth in this matter." Willard admitted being "affrighted" and thinking that "by my withdrawing it might be better," but proclaimed his innocence. The magistrates confronted him with testimony involving not only the current afflictions but also the "dreadfull murders" with which he had been charged, reading to him statements by Lewis, Putnam Jr., and Sheldon. Six sufferers accused Willard of afflicting them then and there. Other witnesses against Willard also intervened. Benjamin Wilkins, Bray's youngest son, testified that despite protestations of "natural affections" for his wife and her family, Willard "abused his wife much & broke sticks about her in beating of her." Another man remarked that Willard had been "very cruel to poor creatures." And when Willard suggested that "my wife might be called," a third man stepped forward to attest that Willard "with his own mouth told him of beating his wife."

The justices next employed physical tests. Susannah attempted to approach Willard, "but fell down immediately." When they asked her why she could not come near the accused, she explained that "the black man stood between us." Willard then took her hand, with no discernible effect on her torments. But when Warren "in a great fit" was carried to him, he "clasping his hand upon her arm," she recovered, just as she had five days earlier at the examination of Abigail Soames. Willard, quick to recognize a contradiction, asked "why . . . was it not before so with Susannah Sheldon?" The "standers by" responded, "because . . . you did not clasp your hand before," thus revealing both their intense scrutiny of Willard and their belief in the reliability of touch tests.

At the close of the examination, the magistrates asked Willard to recite the Lord's Prayer. And that he proved unable to do. Parris reported that "he stumbled at the threshhold," then that he "mist" several other phrases on later attempts. Willard "laught" nervously, commenting, "it is a strange thing, I can say it at another time. I think I am bewitcht as well as they," and finally declaring, "it is these wicked ones that do so overcome me." Hathorne kept pressing Willard to confess, pointing out to him, "there is also the jury of inquest for murder that will bear hard against you." But Willard refused. "If it was the last time I was to speak I am innocent," he insisted.

On that busy May 18, the magistrates questioned and ordered held one more suspect in addition to Willard and the other five men and women whose examinations had originally been scheduled for the day before. The record of the interrogation of Dr. Roger Toothaker of Billerica and Beverly has not survived, but a deposition drawn up two days later revealed why he must have become a suspect. Toothaker, the only male medical practitioner to be accused of witchcraft in seventeenth-century New England, had practiced countermagic. A year earlier, Roger had boasted that "his Daughter had kild a witch" through a method he had taught her—filling an "Earthen pott" with an afflicted person's urine and placing it "stopt . . . very Close" in "a hott oven" overnight. At about the same time, Toothaker had also diagnosed two "strangly sick" children, one from Salem and one from Beverly, as being "under an Evill hand." The second of those afflicted youngsters, an unnamed child of Philip White of Beverly, was the niece or nephew of Sir William Phips.[36]

Hathorne and Corwin took another step that day as well: ordering Mary Towne Easty freed from custody.[37] (Perhaps their colleagues on the new council had urged them to release people about whose guilt they were less than certain.) Goody Easty, unlike her sisters, had not been named by any confessors, nor had any of the afflicted reported being tormented by her specter since her examination almost a month earlier. A few fragmentary references suggest that all but one of the core group had retracted accusations of Mary Easty.

The exception was Mercy Lewis, who within twenty-four hours after Easty's discharge began suffering "very Dreadfull" fits at the home of Constable John Putnam Jr., her master's cousin. Late in the evening of May 19, Putnam and Marshal George Herrick concluded that Mercy "could not continue long in this world without A mittigation of thoes Torments." About dawn they left her to go into town to file a new formal complaint and to ask Hathorne to issue a second warrant for the arrest of Goody Easty.

Throughout the day on May 20, other afflicted teenagers and children, singly and in pairs, came to view the tormented maidservant, as did many other Villagers. First Walcott, then Putnam Jr. and Williams, and finally Hubbard all attested that they saw Easty's specter torturing Mercy. Lewis herself was "speachless" and "in a dase" most of the day, but according to Walcott, Easty's apparition "put a chane aboute her nick and choaked her."

According to Ann Jr. and Abigail, the specters of John Willard and Mary Witheridge joined Easty's in attacking the victim. Edward Putnam later described Mercy's condition: "for all most the space of two days and a night she was choked allmost to death in so much we thought sumtimes she had banded her mouth and teath shut and all this very often untell shuch [*sic*] time as we under stood mary easty was laid in Irons." On May 23, the magistrates again examined the reimprisoned Goody Easty. The record of that interrogation is no longer extant, but most of the afflicted seem to have once again complained against her. Essentially single-handedly, Mercy Lewis had prevented Easty from being freed, a development that underscores her leadership of the sufferers.

During these two weeks immediately following Governor Phips's arrival, with trials apparently imminent, the pace of accusations accelerated and the number of complaints multiplied. Various male Putnams, Ingersolls, Walcotts, and their allies filed formal charges against three people on May 21, four on May 23, four on May 26, and nine on May 28. Moreover, the specters of those already imprisoned repeatedly reappeared to torment the afflicted. On May 23, Sir William Phips directed "that Irons should be put upon those in Prison" to quiet the "renewed" outcries against spectral tortures committed by the suspects being held for trial. In short, jail alone was not enough—chains were now required to restrain the witches' fury. Robert Calef, the trials' later critic, wrote acidly that Phips's order constituted "the first thing he exerted his power in." Even if not precisely accurate, that observation correctly captured the sense of urgency with which the governor approached the witchcraft crisis.[38]

Another eighteen-year-old, Elizabeth Booth, also joined the ranks of the afflicted in late May. The daughter of a twice-widowed mother who lived in the Village, she accused Daniel Andrew (a well-to-do relative of the Jacobs clan) and John and Elizabeth Proctor of tormenting her. In addition she complained against the Proctors' fifteen-year-old daughter Sarah and Goody Proctor's sister, Mary Bassett DeRich (whose husband was a Jerseyan). More sufferers then joined the chorus against Sarah Proctor, and a few days later against Sarah's older brothers, William and Benjamin. Susannah Sheldon continued to focus primarily on her initial target, Philip English. On May 22 English "brougt his book and drod his knife and said if I would not touch it he would cut my throt," she declared. The specter of a dead man appeared to accuse English of having "murdered him and drounded him in the se[a]." The apparition directed Susannah to "tell master hatheren and told me that I should not rest tel I had told it." In response, English threatened to "cut [her] leges of[f]" and insisted that "he would go kill the govenner," who was "the gretes innemy he had." If he were captured, the still-fugitive English proclaimed, he would "kil 10 folck in boston before next six day."[39]

All in all, living through the last two weeks of May must have left people in Essex County, especially the examining magistrates, feeling overwhelmed by the rapidly expanding crisis. Each day brought new reports of bewitchments caused by both new and existing suspects. Thus, to take random examples, on Sunday, May 15, Mary Walcott complained of being afflicted by Willard and Buckley; and Susannah Sheldon, by Elizabeth Proctor and two others. Two days later, Vibber, Walcott, and Lewis all accused Willard, while Sheldon named a large group of seven tormentors, including Willard, the Englishes, and the Proctors. On Friday, May 20, while various afflicted persons declared that Mary Easty was tormenting both Mercy Lewis and themselves, Elizabeth Booth was accusing the Proctors and their daughter Sarah; Sheldon, too, experienced tortures at the hands of four specters. And so it went, day after day, with even more bewitchments on the days when suspects were examined, May 18 and 23. At the four examinations on the 18th for which some evidence still exists, for instance, nine different complainants endured a total of nineteen separate afflictions. People who attended those interrogations, and who heard the daily gossip about the torments suffered seemingly everywhere in the Village, would have sensed a menacing invisible world all around them.[40]

Therefore it is hardly surprising that Essex County residents like Joseph Bayley experienced strange phenomena they attributed to witchcraft. On May 25, Bayley was riding with his wife on the road to Boston when at his first sight of John Proctor's house he felt "a very hard blow strook on my brest which caused great pain in my Stomoc & amasement in my head." At the Proctor homestead, he saw John and Elizabeth watching him from inside; then, after a period of speechlessness, he felt another painful blow, which made him alight from his horse. While standing in the road, he thought he saw a woman turn herself into a cow. Finally, upon his return home to Newbury, "I was pinched and nipt by sumthing invisible for sumtime." More serious were the torments experienced by James Holton four days later. Holton's family, fearing the worst, called in Walcott and Hubbard as witch-finders. The young Villagers reported seeing the specters of the Proctors and their children "a presing of him with there hands one his stomack." After the teenagers were themselves "dreadfully" afflicted by the Proctors' apparitions, Holton reported that he "had ease of my pains."[41]

Those formally accused on May 21 and 23, including Sarah and Benjamin

Proctor and their aunts Mary DeRich and Sarah Hood Bassett, were probably questioned on Tuesday, May 24. Again, the examination records have not survived, but an eyewitness account of that day, probably written about five years later, offers a unique perspective on proceedings in the Salem Village meetinghouse. Captain Nathaniel Cary of Charlestown, a wealthy mariner and merchant, accompanied his wife Elizabeth to Salem Village after they learned disturbing rumors that she had been named as a witch. "By advice," Cary recalled, they went to the Village on May 24 "to see if the afflicted did know her."

From a "convenient place" in the meetinghouse, Cary watched as Hathorne and Corwin conducted the interrogations. "The Prisoner was placed about 7 or 8 foot from the Justices, and the Accusers between the Justices and them," Cary recorded. Suspects were ordered to look directly at the magistrates, "with an Officer appointed to hold each hand, least they should therewith afflict them." If the accused glanced at the afflicted, "they would either fall into their Fits, or cry out of being hurt by them." After the examinees had been questioned, they were asked to say the Lord's Prayer "as a tryal of their guilt." Cary also witnessed and described the touch test: one of the afflicted would try but fail to approach a prisoner voluntarily, would suffer a fit, and be carried to the accused to be touched. Next, he recounted, "the Justices would say, they are well, before I could discern any alteration."[42]

Cary knew John Hale, and at the end of the day asked him to arrange a private meeting between his wife and her principal accuser, Abigail Williams. Instead of the parsonage, as originally planned, the encounter occurred at Ingersoll's inn, where John Indian served the Carys. "To him we gave some Cyder," Cary remembered, and "he shewed several Scars, that seemed as if they had been long there, and shewed them as done by Witchcraft." All the accusers, not just Abigail, entered the room, and "began to tumble down like Swine, and then three Women were called in to attend them." The afflicted named Elizabeth Cary as their tormentor; the magistrates, who were in a room nearby, ordered her to appear before them. When Elizabeth, forced to stand "with her Arms stretched out," and denied the chance to lean on her husband or to take his hand, complained of feeling faint, Justice Hathorne retorted that "she had strength enough to torment those persons, and she should have strength enough to stand." John Indian, brought into the room, suffered from a fit, which the girls attributed to Mistress Cary's witchcraft. While Nathaniel watched, the magistrates used the touch test to cure John. Captain Cary, protesting against the "cruel proceedings, . . . uttered a hasty Speech (That God would take vengeance on them, and desired that

God would deliver us out of the hands of unmerciful men)." The judges initially directed that Elizabeth Cary be held in Boston, but Nathaniel was able to have his wife moved to Cambridge, which was closer to their home, although he could not prevent her being chained.

The Carys had hoped to preempt a formal accusation of Elizabeth by confronting Abigail Williams privately prior to the filing of an official complaint. Only a man accustomed to deference from younger, poorer, and female colonists—perhaps even from justices of the peace—would have tried such a ploy. But the tactic backfired. John Hale either could not arrange such a meeting or connived at the tests of Elizabeth Cary that followed. Captain Cary's account highlights the magistrates' belief in the validity of touch tests and the recitation of the Lord's Prayer, demonstrating as well that by late May the questioning of suspects had become perfunctory. At least from the vantage point of the accused and their allies, the actions of the afflicted appeared to determine a suspect's fate. The examining magistrates were assuming the guilt of everyone brought before them, regardless of sex or status.

At the same time, though, some accusations totally lacked credibility and so were rejected by male gatekeepers. In a particularly notable case, a woman who fit the description of the mysterious "gentlewoman of Boston" was named as a witch, most likely first by her afflicted maidservant but then later by others. Never formally charged, she later became a prime example of selective prosecution cited by critics of the trials.

AN AFFLICTED FORMER CAPTIVE
AND HER MISTRESS

Some time during the last two weeks of May, the maidservant Mercy Short, a redeemed captive of the Indians, went to the Boston jail on an errand for her mistress, the widow Margaret Webb Sheafe Thacher, who was the mother-in-law of the magistrate Jonathan Corwin. Although the nature of that errand is nowhere recorded, Mercy was probably carrying gifts, perhaps food or blankets, to the imprisoned Mistress Mary English, who as the wife of a wealthy Salem merchant involved in trade with Maine would have been well known to Mistress Thacher, who was both the daughter and the widow of men of comparable standing and with similar business interests. At the jail, Mercy Short had a fateful encounter with Sarah Good, who asked her for "a little Tobacco." Instead of complying with the request, Mercy threw "an Handful of Shavings at her," exclaiming, "That's Tobacco good enough for you"! In the words of Cotton Mather, who later counseled Mercy Short and who detailed her subsequent afflictions, "that Wretched woman bestowed some ill words upon her, and poor Mercy was taken with just such, or perhaps much worse, Fits as those which held the Bewitched people then Tormented by Invisible Furies in the County of Essex."[43]

Inferring an Identity

The story of Mercy Short's visit to the jail and the rest of this section both make a key inference: that Short, the afflicted girl about whom Cotton Mather wrote at great length, was the maidservant of Mistress Margaret Thacher. On what evidence does this inference rest?

Five crucial pieces of data combine to make the identification likely. First, on May 31 the prosecutor Thomas Newton named "Mrs Thatchers maid" as a potential witness in the upcoming witchcraft trials. Other than Judah White, identified by Abigail Hobbs as a witch and therefore more likely a suspect than a witness, Mercy Short is the only Boston maidservant known to have had any link to the trials before the fall of 1692. Second, Mather recorded that Mercy Short lived with her mistress "near half a mile" from his North Church. Margaret Sheafe Thacher's longtime residence in the block bounded by Washington, Devonshire, and State Streets, and Dock Square, was almost exactly that distance from Old North, and her house was also located very near the Boston jail.[44]

Third, Mistress Thacher was herself accused of witchcraft in 1692, for reasons no historian has ever been able to explain. But being the master or mistress of an afflicted servant could lead one to be suspected—recall, for example, the accusation of Goody Griggs after the bewitchment of Betty Hubbard, of George Jacobs Sr. after the affliction of Sarah Churchwell, or of Elizabeth Proctor after the bewitching of Mary Warren. Indeed, Mercy Short herself probably accused her mistress, mimicking Warren and Churchwell. Fourth, the pious Margaret Thacher owned property in New Hampshire, making her a likely mistress for a returned captive. And fifth, the probable friendship of Margaret Thacher and Mary English would explain another point scholars have never even addressed: why did Mercy Short's mistress dispatch her to the Boston jail that day? Mercy worked for a high-status woman (otherwise Mather would have referred to her as Mercy's "dame," not her "mistress"). What errand would a high-status woman have asked her servant to perform in such an unlikely location, other than aiding an acquaintance in need?[45]

None of these points by itself would be sufficient to draw the conclusion I do. Taken together, though, they suggest a strong probability, in large part because this identification explains much that is otherwise inexplicable. If "Mrs Thatchers maid" was not Mercy Short, who was she? Why would a Boston woman of Margaret Thacher's prominence and relationship to one of the examining magistrates be accused of witchcraft in 1692, if not through some other direct tie to the events in Essex County? Mercy Short, if a maidservant in a frontier-linked household apparently afflicted by Sarah Good, would provide that missing connection.[46]

Mercy, the daughter of Clement and Faith Short of Salmon Falls, had been captured by the Wabanakis in the raid that destroyed that town on March 18, 1689/90. She was subsequently redeemed by Sir William Phips in Quebec eight months later, returning to Boston with his fleet. Her parents and three of her siblings died in the attack, while she and six or seven other brothers and sisters were carried off into Canada by their Indian captors. On that long, difficult trek through the forests in the late winter of 1690, she witnessed the torture and death of Robert Rogers, which was recounted in chapter 4. Indeed, that very description probably came from Mercy herself to Cotton Mather, who included it in his published account of the war. The Wabanakis made Rogers's death by fire and dismemberment an explicit object lesson for Mercy and the other captives. After they "bound him to the Stake," they "brought the rest of the Prisoners, with their Arms tied to each other, so setting them round the Fire," Mather recorded. The New Englanders thus, Mather wrote, had "their Friends made a Sacrafice of Devils before their Eyes," but they could not even shed a tear, "lest it should, upon that provocation, be next their own Turn, to be so Barbarously Sacrificed."[47]

Mercy would also have witnessed the violent deaths on that march of other Salmon Falls captives who refused to do their new masters' bidding—of a five-year-old boy killed by a hatchet blow to the head, whose "Breathless Body" was "chopt . . . to pieces before the rest of the Company"; and of a teenage girl whose master beheaded and scalped her, then showed the scalp to the other captives, telling them "they should all be Served so" if they did not behave. Again, Mercy herself probably served as Mather's source for these vivid and disturbing depictions of scenes she would have recalled with horror. That Sarah Good's curse led to her being tormented by "Invisible Furies" is thus hardly surprising.[48]

Mercy Short's probable Boston mistress, Margaret Thacher, was the daughter of Henry Webb and the widow of Jacob Sheafe, wealthy merchants who both died in 1660. Webb and Sheafe had business interests in Maine and New Hampshire, and Mistress Thacher retained control of some of their property, most notably land and a mill in Cocheco, not far from Mercy's home in Salmon Falls. (She also had extensive holdings in Boston, including the home in which she lived and acreage abutting Phips's house.) Several years after her first husband's death, she married the Reverend Thomas Thacher, who relocated to Boston from Weymouth after his first wife died in 1664. From 1669 until his death in 1678 Thacher served as the founding minister of the Third Church, also known as Old South, established by dissidents from the First Church. (The split occurred when the First Church recruited as its pastor the Reverend John Davenport, a prominent opponent of the Halfway Covenant.) A number of men with links to Maine and the witchcraft crisis were members of the Third Church, among them Samuel Sewall, Joshua Scottow, Edward Tyng, John Alden, and Thomas Brattle, along with another whose name has not yet been introduced into this narrative, but who will appear later, Hezekiah Usher Jr.[49]

The one surviving letter in Margaret Thacher's handwriting, addressed to her daughter Elizabeth Corwin in 1686, reveals a woman of little formal education but great piety. Most of the letter consists of religious reflections; for example, she wrote that she hoped "we may bee com trees of Riteousnes the planten of the Lord that he may onli be glorious and glorified in us." Sending her "afectinat love" to Jonathan Corwin and her grandchildren, she added with respect to the "three lelest on[e]s" that she was "humbeli beging the Lord allmiti to bles them and make them pillors in his howes and polished stons in his biulding." Mistress Thacher was, in short, just the sort of person who four years later could well have taken into her home an orphaned former captive of the Maine Indians.[50]

Mather described Mercy Short in that late spring of 1692 as having endured "a world of misery, . . . for diverse weeks together, and such as could not possibly bee inflicted upon her without the Immediate efficiency of some Agent, or Rational or Malicious." Eventually, she was delivered from her torments by "the multiply'd prayers of His people," and she thereafter remained free from fits until the winter of 1692–1693. But then the afflictions returned while she was attending services at Mather's North Church. The fits were so terrible that instead of returning home to her mistress she was given refuge by a "kind Neighbour," who offered her housing while Mather tended to her spiritual needs and recorded her visions. Although the discussion that follows, then, is based on Mercy's agonized statements months after May 1692, there is no reason to believe that her initial fits differed significantly from the later ones, except in that Cotton Mather recorded the latter but not the former.[51]

Mercy described the devil as "A Short and a Black Man" who was "not of a Negro, but of a Tawney, or an Indian colour; hee wore an high-crowned Hat, with strait Hair; and one Cloven-Foot." A number of specters came with him to torture her; these resembled "most exactly . . . several people in the Countrey, some of whose Names were either formerly known, or now by their companions told unto her." The apparitions "assisted, or obeyed, their Devillish Master" in carrying out "hideous Assaults" on their victim. The book the devil offered her to sign was filled not only with signatures but also "with the explicit (short) Covenants of such as had listed themselves in the Service of Satan, and the Design of Witchcraft; all written in Red characters." After trying and failing to persuade the maidservant merely to touch the book, the specters tormented her by sticking her with pins, sitting on her, or preventing her from eating. "But Burning seem'd the cruellest of all her Tortures," Mather observed. "They would Flash upon her the Flames of a Fire. . . . The Agonies of One Roasting a Faggot at the Stake were not more Exquisite, than what Shee underwent." Although Mather described Mercy as "in a Captivity to Spectres," the resemblance of her current torments and those she had witnessed or endured as a captive of the Wabanakis seems to have escaped him.[52]

Mercy's visions, though, explicitly linked her present invisible captors with her former visible ones. She informed Mather that the specters would leave her in chains (just as Sarah Good must have been chained in the Boston jail when they met) while attending their witch meetings, but afterwards "the whole Crew, besides her daily Troublers, look'd in upon her, to see how the work was carried on." And when they did so, she saw "French Canadiens and Indian Sagamores among them, diverse of whom shee knew, and particularly Nam'd em." Moreover, they showed her a book of Catholic devotions that they consulted at their gatherings.[53]

Mercy's fits also involved conversations with or about an older woman, who could well have been Margaret Thacher, and toward whom she showed considerable ambivalence. "Must the Younger Women, do yee say, hearken to the Elder?" she once asked. "They must bee another Sort of Elder Women than You then! they must not be Elder Witches, I am sure." Expressing sentiments in which the young women afflicted in Salem Village would surely have concurred, she exclaimed, "Pray, do you for once Hearken to mee," before adding, "What a dreadful Sight are You! An Old Woman, an Old Servant of the Divell! . . . Tis an horrible Thing!" But at the same time she called the specters "Wicked Wretches" for "show[ing] mee the Shape of that good Woman," who "never did me any Hurt." Despite that inoffensiveness, she told them, "you would fain have mee cry out of her." That Mercy did indeed name names in her fits, presumably including that of her mistress, is evident from Mather's discreet observations on the subject. The apparitions, he revealed, "wore the shape of several, who are doubtless Innocent as to the Crime of Witchcraft," as well as others who were probably "as Dangerous and as Damnable Witches as ever were in the World." But he would not identify any of these people publicly, for "had we not studiously suppressed all Clamours and Rumours that might have touched the Reputacion of people exhibited in this Witchcraft, there might have ensued most uncomfortable Uproars."[54]

Uproars as such—that is, formal witchcraft complaints pursued in court—there might not have been, but gossip in Boston about Mercy Short and her visions there definitely was. Mather alluded briefly to stories told about her "by Rash People in the coffee-houses or elsewhere." And that coffee-house talk eventually led to repeated witchcraft accusations directed against Mistress Margaret Thacher. Thomas Brattle, her fellow member of the Third Church, referred to those charges in his later critique of the trials. "It is well known," Brattle wrote, "how much she is, and has been, complained of," yet the judges had never issued a warrant for her arrest. "This occasions much discourse and many hot words, and is a very great scandal and stumbling block to many good people," he observed. "Certainly distributive Justice should have its course, without respect to persons; and altho' the said Mrs. Thatcher be mother in law to Mr. Corwin, . . . yet if Justice and conscience do oblige them to apprehend others on the account of the afflicted their complaints, I cannot see how, without injustice and violence to conscience, Mrs. Thatcher can escape."[55]

Thomas Brattle drafted his commentary on the trials in early October, after Mistress Thacher had been repeatedly accused but never formally charged. Months earlier, it was not yet clear that nothing would come of the complaints against her. Rather, on May 24 status (though admittedly not as high a rank as Mistress Thacher's) and a prominent husband did not prevent the magistrates from ordering Mistress Elizabeth Cary jailed. Moreover, included among the thirteen people formally accused on May 26 or 28 were three more high-status folk with links to the frontier: Mistress Mary Bradbury (wife of Thomas Bradbury, a Salisbury magistrate and militia leader), who was not arrested for another month; Captain John Floyd, commander of the colonial troops stationed in Portsmouth; and—most important—John Alden, frequent master of the colony's sloop *Mary* and a wealthy merchant from one of the founding families of the former Plymouth Colony.[56]

SOME USUAL AND UNUSUAL SUSPECTS

The examinations of most of the people complained against during the previous week occurred at the Salem Village meetinghouse on Tuesday, May 31, where Bartholomew Gedney joined Hathorne and Corwin in investigating these latest witchcraft allegations. In addition to the two high-status men, the suspects interrogated included several relatives of those already jailed and women from six different towns, all of whom had long-standing reputations for maleficium. Philip English, who had finally been captured in Boston on May 30 after hiding at the home of an acquaintance for more than a month, was questioned on the 31st as well, although no record of his examination survives.[57]

Prominent among those accused in late May were two sisters, Mary Allen Toothaker of Billerica and Martha Allen Carrier of Andover. Martha Carrier, later termed by Cotton Mather the "Queen of Hell," eventually became a key figure in the crisis, but Mary Toothaker, probably targeted primarily because of suspicions of her already-jailed husband Roger, aroused less concern. (Indeed, she may not have been arrested until late July, since the existing records in her case date from that period.)[58]

Daughters of a large and prosperous family that settled in Andover before 1662, neither Mary nor Martha married well. Roger Toothaker, though a doctor, had only a small amount of inherited property, and Thomas Carrier, Martha's husband, was a young Welshman who fathered her first child before their marriage. Both couples lived at first in Billerica. Although Mary and Roger remained there, the Carriers moved back to Andover, probably during the late summer or early fall of 1690. Unfortunately, they appear to have carried New England's then-raging smallpox epidemic to the town—or at least the selectmen thought they did—and town officials ordered the family quarantined lest through "wicked carelessness" they spread the disease further. But that step came too late. Ultimately, the town's vital records attributed ten deaths to the devastating illness; the deceased included four of Martha Carrier's own relatives. Statements by the afflicted and her neighbors showed that gossip laid three additional deaths to her charge as well, and that people in both Billerica and Andover had suspected her of malefic activity for some time.[59]

As had by then become commonplace, the interrogation of Martha

Carrier, in front of "spectators Magistrates & others," revolved around the statements and actions of the afflicted.[60] Williams, Hubbard, Walcott, and Warren complained of spectral torments; Putnam Jr. indicated that she had been stuck with a pin; Sheldon saw "the black man"; and Lewis's "violent fit" was cured by a touch test. Goody Carrier denied seeing any "black man," though some of the afflicted said he was "wispering" in her ear. "You see you look upon them & they fall down," observed Hathorne. "It is false the Devil is a liar," Carrier retorted, and she boldly scolded the magistrate: "it is a shamefull thing that you should mind these folks that are out of their wits."

The afflicted, exhibiting "the most intollerable out-cries & agonies," alleged that she had "killed 13 at Andover," claiming they saw "13 Ghosts" in the room. Finally, Samuel Parris recorded, "the Tortures of the afflicted was so great that there was no enduring of it, so that she was ordered away & to be bound hand & foot with all expedition." As soon as that aim was effected, the afflicted had "strange & sodain ease." And Parris added one more point that underscored the ongoing shift in power from the justices to the suffering teenagers: "Mary Walcot told the Magistrates that this woman told her she had been a witch this 40 yeares." Evidently at the examination itself, Walcott had elicited a confession that Hathorne, Corwin, and Gedney had been powerless to obtain. The role of the afflicted in communicating with the invisible world had assumed such centrality in the legal proceedings that it was even encroaching on the magistrates' function within the public space of the courtroom.

The other two "usual suspects" formally accused on May 28 and examined on May 31 were Wilmot Reed (or Redd) and Elizabeth Jackson Howe. At the examination of Goody Reed, the wife of a Marblehead fisherman, Lewis, Walcott, and Williams seemed especially tormented, and Elizabeth Booth made her first recorded appearance among those afflicted during an interrogation. Hubbard accused Reed of bringing her the book to sign. Employing a phrase commonly used by the Wabanakis to describe killings, she declared that Reed had threatened to "knock her in the head, if she would not write." She and three others were cured by a touch test. Asked "what she thought these Persons ailed," Reed responded only that they were "in a sad condition."[61]

Elizabeth Howe defended herself more vigorously, probably because she had had longer and more extensive experience responding to witchcraft allegations.[62] In her early to mid-fifties in 1692, Goody Howe lived with her blind husband James and their children on the family property in Topsfield near the boundary of Ipswich. Testimony offered at her trial (which will be discussed in chapter 7) revealed that she had been suspected of witchcraft for about a decade, and that the accusations had been sufficiently serious to cause the rejection of her application for membership in the Ipswich church. At Howe's examination, Lewis and Walcott "quickly" fell into fits, and Ann Jr. "said she had hurt her three times," displaying a pin stuck into her hand. Hathorne pressed the examinee: "Those that have confessed, they tell us they used images & pins, now tell us what you have used." Goody Howe disavowed guilt, exclaiming, "You would have me confess that which I know not." A touch test eased the fits of both Susannah Sheldon and John Indian, but they and others could not approach Howe on their own—they had to be carried. "What do you say to these things, they cannot come to you?" the magistrate inquired. Goody Howe could offer no explanation, and Hathorne had the last word: "That is strange that you should do these things & not be able to tell how."

No comparable examination records survive for the two prominent men complained against on May 28, but their roles in the war in Maine unquestionably instigated the accusations. John Floyd and John Alden joined George Burroughs in the ranks of suspected witches because of the belief that they, too, were in league with the Wabanakis, the French, and the devil.

Captain John Floyd (or Flood), aged fifty-six in 1692, was possibly born in Scituate. As an adult, he lived in Lynn, then Malden, and after about 1681 in Rumney Marsh (later Chelsea, now Revere), the original home of his wife, daughter of the wealthiest man in that town. Floyd fought in both Indian wars, the first as a lieutenant. His conduct as a militia captain in the second aroused considerable criticism from both inside and outside the ranks. In early April 1689, for example, men under his command at Saco River mutinied, deserting their post and marching toward Boston, evidently in the hope of winning redress of their grievances. When he was accused in late May 1692, Captain Floyd had been home in Rumney Marsh on leave for about a month. The accusation stopped him from returning to his post. Thus the complainants (listed as "Mary Walcott, Abigail Williams & the rest") could well have believed they had prevented him from resuming his assistance, spectral and otherwise, to New England's enemies.[63]

Two incidents in Floyd's career as a militia officer during the war appear particularly relevant to the later charge that he was a witch. In late May 1690, the governor and council dispatched Floyd and his company to defend the Piscataqua region against the attack that seemed likely after the fall of Fort Loyal earlier that month. About two weeks later, they ordered him to command sixty of the men newly raised for frontier defense, establishing a base at Portsmouth. In early July, as will be recalled from chapter 3, Captain Floyd and his men were stationed in Exeter, but left the town undefended while they sallied forth to destroy some Indian cornfields. Not only did the Wabanakis attack the town in his absence, they also assaulted Floyd and his men on their return from the sortie. During a deadly encounter at Wheelwright's Pond, several officers and many men were killed. "Captain Floyd maintained the Fight . . . several Hours, until so many of his Tired and Wounded men Drew off, that it was time for him to Draw off also," Cotton Mather later wrote, his choice of words downplaying the seriousness of what had happened. Floyd's men, suffering significant casualties, had deserted him in the field of battle.[64]

Others then abandoned his company a few weeks later. When the captain caught up with one of the absconders in September and asked him, "whi he ded sarve me so," the deserter replied (in Floyd's words), "he woold sarve me woors before he had dun with me for sayd he I care nott for you nor for none and sayd that he hopt that he shoold wash his hands In my blood." Floyd's futile persistence on the battlefield, Mather observed, drew harsh criticism from "some that would not have continued at it so long as he." Among those who died under John Floyd's command appear to have been four men from Salem Village, including, significantly, Susannah Sheldon's older brother, Godfrey.[65]

The second occasion involved the attack on York in January 1691/2. As was indicated in chapter 1, Floyd and his men arrived from Portsmouth too late to do more than describe the extent of the disaster. One New England diarist undoubtedly expressed an opinion shared by many when he wrote scornfully that Floyd's troops "lay in pay at pascataq[ua], when this ruine befell York, & went After the mischiefe was don, to bury the dead." Once again, New Englanders thought that Floyd had neglected his duty. He had effectively defended neither Exeter nor York, yet his men had nevertheless suffered terrible losses and they seemingly had no respect for his leadership. His dereliction appeared to have caused numerous deaths of fighting men and civilians. Many men and women were accused of witchcraft in 1692 for far less serious offenses than John Floyd's.[66]

The actions of the other "unusual suspect" questioned on May 31 aroused just as much suspicion. Captain John Alden, son of John and Priscilla Alden, had had a long and distinguished career as a merchant and ship captain. A member of Boston's First Church, then the Third, he was in his mid-sixties when accused in 1692. In an account of his examination he prepared about five years later at the request of Robert Calef, Alden described confronting the "jugling tricks" of the "Wenches" in Salem Village. He recounted how one accuser, probably Ann Putnam Jr., had shouted out a remarkable charge: "There stands Aldin, a bold fellow with his Hat on before the Judges, he sells

Powder and Shot to the Indians and French, and lies with the Indian Squaes, and has Indian Papooses." Neither Alden nor subsequent historians have said much about the specifics of these allegations, but upon investigation they turn out to have been well grounded in fact and widely circulated gossip.[67]

Under both Sir Edmund Andros and the subsequent interim government, Captain John Alden commanded the colony's sloop *Mary* as it pursued various official errands, most of them along the coast of northern New England and Acadia. Alden's wife, Elizabeth, the daughter of William Phillips, had inherited a share in her father's valuable sawmills along the Saco River; accordingly, Alden had familial, professional, and public-service reasons alike for frequent trips into what became largely enemy territory after the autumn of 1688. Not surprisingly, rumors swirled around his multiple activities on the northeastern coastal frontier.[68]

In their influential *Salem Possessed*, Paul Boyer and Stephen Nissenbaum term Nathaniel Cary and John Alden "distant and essentially symbolic figures" to the young accusers in Salem Village. Cary may well have fit that description, but for three of the afflicted (Mercy Lewis, Susannah Sheldon, and Sarah Churchwell) and two of the confessors (Abigail and Deliverance Hobbs) Captain Alden was neither "distant" nor "symbolic." Instead, he would have been a regular if sporadic presence in their lives in Maine. Alden, usually but not always at the helm of the *Mary*, made at least sixteen round-trips from Boston to various harbors along the northeastern coast between October 1688 and April 1692, carrying soldiers and supplies to the beleaguered frontier forts and communities. In the late summer and early fall of 1689, for example, he sailed frequently among Boston, Portsmouth, and Falmouth, ferrying the men and matériel that successfully repelled the Wabanaki attack on Falmouth in mid-September. In summer 1690, he was assigned to gather guns for the Quebec expedition, an unpopular task that aroused the Marblehead mob action described in chapter 3. And after the capture of Port Royal, he sailed often to that destination, located deep in enemy territory.[69]

On some of those voyages Captain Alden met with the enemy in an official capacity, arranging the release of captives or, in one case, at Sagadahoc in November 1690, negotiating the temporary truce that lasted until May 1691. At other times, however, his contacts with the French or the Wabanakis appeared less benign. During the winter of 1688–1689, for instance, at the direction of Sir Edmund Andros, Alden carried provisions to Castine at Pentagoet. A soldier later testified that he had accompanied Alden on this mission to assist a man regarded as "an enemy to the Interest of the Kings subjects & an aider & abetter of our enemies the Indians." So much food was delivered to Castine, he complained, that "we suffered so as that for two dayes, we that were souldiers had no food allowed us although there was enough before" the delivery.[70]

Alden's independent activities also lent themselves to sinister interpretations. For example, in July 1689 he visited Edward Randolph, a subordinate of Andros then being held in the Boston jail, to converse about what he had recently learned from Castine at Pentagoet; that conversation was surely overheard and gossiped about in the town. Randolph told an English correspondent that Alden "says Casteen told him that Moxas was lately returned from Canada with Supplyes," that several warships had arrived at Quebec, and that England and France were now at war. Knowledgeable Bostonians might well have asked themselves why Captain Alden had not only met with Castine, but had then conveyed to the distrusted Andros's imprisoned assistant the substance of the conversation. Or again, in November 1690, Alden asked for the use of the *Mary* to redeem captives in Acadia and to carry supplies to Port Royal, declaring that he wanted "to inquire into the State of the people there being subjected to the obedience of the Crown of England." The General Court agreed to the plan, if Alden tried to return within four to six weeks and bore the expenses himself, and if—intriguingly—he did not "carry with him any amunition more then for the Necessary use of the vessell." Alden's similar voyage in March 1690/1 elicited like conditions, with a precise statement of how much gunpowder he could take ("one Barrel and halfe") and with the specific injunction "You are not to Trade any Armes or Amunition." The provisos implied that officials in Boston suspected that Alden was trading with the Indians or the French under the guise of sailing to Port Royal on colony business.[71]

And it was not only the Boston authorities who entertained such suspicions. In August 1691, John Alden arrived in Salem with orders for colonial militiamen assigned to the ketch *Endeavour* to convoy his vessel (the ketch *Ann*) to Port Royal. Bartholomew Gedney, a longtime friend and business associate of Alden's, later informed his superiors in Boston that the men at first refused to sail to Port Royal until they had been paid for their past two months' service, and that when they had received that compensation, they still would not serve under Alden's command. Their captain, Benjamin Allen, recounted their reasoning: "they Generally said that said Oldin was Reported to bee an Old Indian trader & was going to trade with the frenche & therefore many of them did then Reply they would be hanged before they would goe with him said Oldin." A Bay Colony official, pronouncing the men's actions to be "mutiny," directed Hathorne and Corwin to arrest the perpetrators, in order to, in Gedney's words, "salve the honor of the Government: &

prevent the hurt of such Examples." In their response to the charges, the men insisted that Benjamin Allen too "alwayes spoke against goeing to all the Company," presenting the voyage to them as a voluntary one and asking for a show of hands from those willing to go. They explained, "Butt was observed that neither he nor any one else did [hold up their hands]; It being left to your Petitioners voate wee did not hold ourselves obliged to goe."[72]

Whether the men were prosecuted for their refusal to serve under John Alden is unknown. But retrospectively their decision proved wise, for he and those who sailed with him to Port Royal on that voyage in September 1691 were captured by the French under Castine, who also recaptured the town. Among those taken prisoner were John Alden Jr., Edward Tyng (formerly of Falmouth, who had been designated to command Port Royal under English rule), and John Nelson, one of Boston's leading merchants. Castine dispatched Nelson, a valuable captive, to Quebec, sending Captain Alden back to Boston to collect £200 to ransom his ship, his son, Tyng, and various other English prisoners.[73]

When John Alden returned to Boston on that mission in October, he brought with him a number of Englishmen, including a ransomed captive who lost no time telling his dramatic story—a tale with significant negative implications for Captain Alden's reputation.[74] Mark Emerson, once a member of the garrison at Sagadahoc, had been held prisoner first by the Wabanakis, then by the French, for nearly two and a half years. In a formal statement presented to the authorities, he described his travels with the Indians, then his sale to some French people living at a place called Quithmaquig on the St. John's River, in Acadia. "The Last winter & spring," he recalled, "both French & Indians were forced to eate their Doggs, & some of their Captives, for haveing noe Powder nor shott could not kill a Fowle, though they swam in great Numbers before their Doors." Those dire circumstances had changed for the better, though, when Captain John Alden sailed up the river in the *Mary* in March 1690/1, on the very voyage during which the Massachusetts government had enjoined him not to trade arms or ammunition. He "brought them all supplys, as Powder & shott, Rum, Tobbaccoe, and Bread, with other Necessaries, or they had all perished," Emerson explained.

And he went further. "The Indians have a saying," he revealed, "that Mr Alden is a good Man, & loves Indians very well for Beaver, & hath been with them often, since the Warr to their Great Relief." Emerson disclosed that he had asked the captain to ransom him in March, but that Alden had refused to pay the "little" that was asked for him, saying "he came to Trade, & not to redeem Captives." Emerson was then ransomed in October through the generosity of John Nelson, who passed through Quithmaquig on his way to prison in Quebec.

The Bostonian who forwarded Mark Emerson's statement added information of his own. Captain Alden was said to have carried "16 Barrles of Powder with Lead & other Thinges, Convenient for Trade to assist our Enemies to Kill our Friends" on his ill-fated September voyage, he reported. And he also revealed how the governor and council of Massachusetts had reacted to the former captive's revelations. Mark Emerson "will swear itt, when called to, but our Authority [the governor and council], will not hear him against Mr Alden, tho' severall others prof[es]s to swear the same."

Emerson thus supplied New England's gossipers with the evidence they needed to support the already widespread belief that John Alden was an "Old Indian trader & was going to trade with the frenche." The Salem seagoing militiamen who thought as much in July 1691 had been absolutely correct in their assessment of their potential captain's current intentions and past activities. Ann Putnam Jr.'s charge in Salem Village on May 31, 1692, would therefore have come as no surprise to any of her listeners, much less to Alden himself or to the examining magistrates, who had heard Emerson's charges at least semiofficially months earlier.

Emerson surely told the truth. How many veteran sailors from Alden's numerous voyages "to the eastward" had sat afterwards in Boston or Salem taverns and told their fellows about calling not just at Falmouth, Port Royal, or other English-controlled harbors, but also at French outposts or native villages? According to the man who transcribed Emerson's narrative "from his owne Mouth," other witnesses were prepared to "swear the same." Mark Emerson had no reason to like Alden (whose failure to ransom him in March 1690/1 had kept him in captivity for several additional months), but the former soldier also had no reason to lie either about the difficult straits in which he and his captors had found themselves in the early spring of 1690/1, or about John Alden's fortuitous appearance with supplies. Likewise, the Wabanakis' reputed saying, Alden "loves Indians very well for Beaver," appears an appropriate judgment for an "Old Indian trader." The Wabanakis, according to Emerson, did not suggest that Alden traitorously favored them or the French, but rather indicated that a quest for profitable pelts motivated him above all else.

Then, too, it was doubtless true that "Authority" (the ultimate male gatekeepers) did not wish to consider bringing charges of trading with the enemy against John Alden, a member of the colony's elite and a friend, fellow congregant, and business associate of many of them. He supplied the colony with valuable, even essential services, and if he chose to make some profit (or simply to recoup unreimbursed expenses) from certain clandestine stops on voyages undertaken chiefly at the colony's behest, such acquaintances as Bartholomew Gedney seemed prepared to look the other way. They might even have invested in his enterprises. One could certainly speculate, on the basis of Emerson's recollection that the Wabanakis reported that Alden "hath been with them often, since the Warr," that Captain John Alden was one of the merchant captains who sailed to Maine shortly after Andros's overthrow in April 1689 to sell vital ammunition and supplies to the Wabanakis.[75]

One of the most compelling indications that the leaders of the Bay Colony were prepared to disregard what they learned from Mark Emerson in the fall of 1691—or at least an indication of their total dependence on Captain Alden's sailing skills, contacts, and knowledge of the Maine coast—was their decision in March 1691/2 to employ the captain once more to sail east on colony business. In dispatching Alden and the militia captain James Converse to Maine, the governor and council told them to parlay with the Wabanakis and to redeem as many of the captives taken at York in January as possible, in addition to retrieving Edward Tyng and Alden's son. The mission was partially successful, for a number of the captives were released to the Anglo-Americans, but Tyng died en route as a prisoner to France and John Alden Jr. had already been sent to Quebec.[76]

By the time Captain Alden returned from that voyage, probably in late April, the witchcraft crisis had exploded in Essex County. The connection to Maine, initially established a week or so earlier, made Alden vulnerable to charges of witchcraft for his by then well-known involvement in trading with the French and Indians. But the precipitating factor that caused the authorities to finally move against Alden, who, according to one document, had been "complained of a long time," seems to have been news conveyed to Boston by Elisha Hutchinson on May 19. Two recent escapees from the Indians near Pentagoet had just arrived at Portsmouth, he revealed. They reported that "Castene had been at the port whence they came. . . . Exspecting to find goods there which he Sayd Capt Alden owes him & promist to leave there, but finding none threatens what he will do when he meets him againe." The information that their greatest French enemy, Castine, had been "promist" goods by John Alden appears to have been the last straw. Nine days later, John Alden was formally accused of being in league with the devil.[77]

Thus in the heated atmosphere of May 1692 the Salem Village afflicted accomplished what a returned Indian captive had not achieved seven months earlier: causing the arrest of a member of the colony's elite. Susannah Sheldon, Mercy Lewis, and Mary Walcott—all with significant ties to Maine—

were among John Alden's most active accusers. Surely they saw Alden's collusion with the Wabanakis, devil-worshippers who had devastated their families, as an indication of his fidelity to Satan. In contrast to many of their accusations, in which they parroted the concerns of other Essex County residents about malefic activities by distrusted neighbors, in charging John Alden (and John Floyd, as well) with witchcraft these afflicted young women spoke for themselves and for many other refugees from the northeastern frontier. That the magistrates listened to them, whereas they had listened neither to Mark Emerson nor to many earlier complaints from Maine about illegal trading, discloses that the justices too saw the crisis facing New England as resulting from an alliance of their enemies in the visible and invisible worlds and further underscores the extent of the power now being wielded by the youthful female accusers.

Nowhere was that made clearer than by Bartholomew Gedney's reaction to the complaint against his former business associate. Alden, confronted with the standard charges that he pinched the tormented young people and struck them down with his glance, "appealed to all that ever knew him, if they ever suspected him to be such a person, and challenged any one, that could bring in any thing upon their own knowledge, that might give suspicion of his being such an one." The Salem magistrate replied, "he had known Aldin many Years, and had been at Sea with him, and always look'd upon him to be an honest Man, but now he did see cause to alter his judgment." Gedney in fact "bid Aldin confess, and give glory to God." Alden responded that "he hoped he should give glory to God, and hoped he should never gratifie the Devil . . . [and] hoped God would clear up his Innocency." After several of the afflicted had been cured by the touch test, the captain told Justice Gedney "that he could assure him that there was a lying Spirit in them, for I can assure you that there is not a word of truth in all these say of me." That such assurances, which once would have carried a great deal of weight with his longtime acquaintance, did Alden no good speaks volumes about the mindset of the examining magistrates. He was committed to the marshal, and sent to jail in Boston.[78]

After observing the examinations on May 31, the new attorney general, Thomas Newton, informed the colony's secretary, Isaac Addington, that he had "beheld strange things scarce credible but to the spectators." Indeed, he added, "I must say according to the present appearance of things," John Alden and Philip English "are as deeply concerned as the rest, for the afflicted spare no person of what quality soever neither conceale their Crimes tho' never soe hainous." In short, even someone previously unfamiliar with the proceedings found the evidence of the tormented young people convincing, although it was directed against high-status men. Indeed, that they targeted such men, not attempting to "spare" them or "conceal" their offenses, seemed a mark in the young female accusers' favor, an indication of the truth of their charges.[79]

Newton's and Gedney's approving reactions to what they saw as plausible charges against men of their own rank reveal the inadequacy of historians' standard interpretation of such accusations as inexplicable and overwrought. Because many of the high-status people identified by the accusers were, like Mistress Margaret Thacher, protected from formal charges by their friends and relatives, most of their names remain unknown today, as does an indication of precisely when they were accused. But in all likelihood many such names first emerged, like those of English, Thacher, Floyd, and Alden, during the four to six weeks after the initial accusation of the Reverend George Burroughs on April 20. The people in question were variously described at the time as "some . . . [with] great estates in *Boston*" or as "Gentlemen of the Councell Justices of the peace Ministers and severall of their wives."[80]

Where names and the timing of specific accusations are known, as is the case with two justices and several clergymen or their spouses, they will be considered later in this book. But extant documents fail to list any member of the Massachusetts Council among the accused, in spite of the statement in the letter just quoted. That, of course, is hardly surprising: if any charge was likely to be disbelieved and suppressed by the male gatekeepers, it was one naming a man (or men) who served with them on the colony's primary governing body. And yet, given the logic of these accusations, such a charge was perhaps the most obvious of all. In the context of the government's near-total failure to prevent the devastation of flourishing northeastern frontier communities during the war, witchcraft accusations directed at those viewed as responsible—of wealthy council members, their allies and relatives—could easily be pursued by those whose families and livelihoods had been destroyed.

MAJOR ELISHA HUTCHINSON (PORTSMOUTH) TO ISAAC ADDINGTON (BOSTON), MAY 19, 1692:[81]

here is Just now two men, that were taken on Monday sevennight by a Small open Sloope . . . & ware caryed in to a place a little East of Penobscot. . . . Say there Captain that toke them, tels them, the ffrench General or Comander that was at the takeing of Casco fforte, was com in to that place from St Johns, (they saw him, he came in a Small biscan Shalop) Enformes he was bound to Castene to See what Strength he could raise to Joyne him & his fforces to com against Pescataque, one of these men Say the Captain Tould him the ffrench & Indians difer about the way of their coming, the ffrench are for coming by water, the Indians for coming by land, the other Saith that the Captain tould him they intended to com by Land: And Saith there is a ship of Thirty or 36 guns with three hundred men & two Small Vesels arived from ffrance at St Johns & is going to Port royal. . . . Say that Castene had been at the port whence they came the morning before they came there Exspecting to find goods there which he Sayd Captain Alden owes him & promist to leave there, but finding none threatens what he will do when he meets him againe.

CHAPTER SIX

Endeavors of the Judges

WITH THE ESTABLISHMENT of the Court of Oyer and Terminer on May 27, the witchcraft crisis moved into a new phase. Hitherto John Hathorne and Jonathan Corwin had handled most of the examinations, with occasional assists from Bartholomew Gedney, Samuel Sewall, and Thomas Danforth. Now grand and petty juries composed of Essex County men and a large panel of distinguished judges would assess the validity of the evidence the justices of the peace had gathered, and would determine the ultimate fate of the many people accused, arrested, and jailed. The court would begin its first session on June 2, but that could not happen without considerable preliminary work. Jurors had to be summoned, witnesses and confessors reinterviewed, and depositions collected. The primary responsibility for many of those tasks still fell on Hathorne and Corwin, as the men most familiar with the evidence unearthed so far. Thomas Newton, the prosecutor, also had to decide whom to try first and how to present his case most effectively to the grand and petty juries. The court had no predetermined schedule, so much would depend on the success of the first prosecutions.

PREPARING FOR THE TRIALS

In late May, while they continued interrogating new suspects in Salem Village, Hathorne and Corwin also began preparing for the first formal proceedings against those who had been accused much earlier. On May 23, by "order of the Governor & Councill," they took sworn statements from Abigail Williams, and from Samuel Parris, Thomas Putnam, and Ezekiel Cheever against the first three accused witches: Tituba, Sarah Good, and Sarah

Osborne (the latter even though she had died about two weeks previously). They also recorded several testimonies about the recent afflictions attributed to Mary Easty. Eight days later, on May 31, Abigail offered further detailed depositions against Elizabeth and John Proctor, Martha Corey, and Rebecca Nurse. That same Tuesday, Ann Carr Putnam swore to the truth of her earlier statements concerning the tortures visited upon her by the apparitions of Goody Corey and Goody Nurse between the 18th and 23rd of March. She also attested that at the very time she was listening to the magistrates reread her testimony, "I was again re-assaulted & tortured by my before mentioned Tormentor Rebekah Nurse." Her daughter, present in the room, swore that she had seen not only Goody Nurse's specter but also those of Martha Corey and Sarah Cloyce attacking her mother.[1]

For his part, Thomas Newton sent directions to Boston to transport eight of the prisoners to Salem Town, although he observed that "I fear we shall not this weeke try all that we have sent for, by reason the tryalls will be tedious, & the afflicted persons cannot readily give their testimonyes, being struck dumb & senceless for a season at the name of the accused." He also ordered that Tituba and "Mrs Thatchers maid" (most likely Mercy Short) "be transferred as Evidences but desire they may not come amongst the prisoners but rather by themselves." And he asked that the records of Bridget Oliver Bishop's trial for witchcraft before the Court of Assistants in February 1679/80 be dispatched to Salem as well.[2]

The next day, June 1, Hathorne and Corwin once more examined most of the confessors being held in the Salem Town prison, attempting to put them on record again before they might be called to testify in a court proceeding. Questioning Abigail and Deliverance Hobbs, Mary Warren, and Sarah Churchwell brought the magistrates confirmation of continued spectral activity, especially by George Burroughs. Abigail confessed to having seen Burroughs, Bridget Bishop, Good, Osborne, and Giles Corey "at the generall meeting of the Witches in the feild near Mr Parrisse's house." She also charged that two or three nights previously Burroughs's specter "came & sat at the window & told her he would terribly afflict her for saying so much against him." Her stepmother accused the minister of recently having "almost shooke her to pieces" because she would not sign his book. Mary Warren's contribution to their joint statement revealed that about two weeks earlier a large group of apparitions headed by Burroughs, who "had a trumpett & sounded itt," had invited her to "a feast at Mr parrisses." Goody Nurse and Goody Proctor told her they were "Deacons" and "would have had her eat some of their sweet bread & wine," but she had refused and as a consequence they "dreadfully afflicted her at that tyme." The magistrates noted at the bottom of the page that while they were taking these sworn statements Nurse's apparition came to afflict all three deponents and that "Mr English then run a pin into Maryes hand as she attested."[3]

Hathorne and Corwin recorded another, separate statement from Warren that Wednesday. In it, she focused on Bridget Bishop, whose specter, she claimed, had appeared repeatedly to torment her and to ask her to sign the book. Even though Goody Bishop could not torture Mary directly, "being in Chanies" in prison, she had brought another apparition with her to do so, "which now she knowes to be Mrs Cary." (Presumably, these torments had occurred before Mistress Elizabeth Cary was herself jailed and chained on May 24.) The magistrates transcribed Sarah Churchwell's second confession, also dated June 1, on the other side of the same piece of paper. In addition to her master, Sarah accused Ann Pudeator and Bridget Bishop. Goody Bishop, she said, had admitted killing "John Trask's Child." And Sarah herself admitted having used "Images" brought by Goody Pudeator to torture Mercy Lewis, Ann Putnam Jr., and Betty Hubbard. Pudeator had assured her that "the persons whose likeness they were, would be afflected," so she had taken thorns and "stuck them in the Images." (Some time later, regretting this confession, Sarah declared that she had "undon hur self" because she was threatened with being thrown into the "dungin" with "mr Borows" if she did not confess.)[4]

On that same June 1, Ann Carr Putnam, who had been free from torments between late March and the previous day, again suffered greatly at the hands of the apparition of Rebecca Nurse. The specter "tould me that now she was come out of prison she had power to afflet me," Ann declared. Goody Nurse's apparition, back in Salem Village with Nurse herself, threatened to murder her and acknowledged killing several Villagers, among them "young John Putnams Child." Ann Sr. also saw a frightening vision of "six children in winding sheets" who revealed themselves to be the offspring of her sister Sarah Carr Baker, alleging that they had been killed by Rebecca Nurse, Mistress Elizabeth Cary, and "an old deaf woman att Boston [Margaret Thacher?]." They directed Ann to transmit their accusation to the magistrates, "or elce they would tare me to peaces for their blood did crie for vengance." Ann further was visited by the specter of "my own sister Bayley and three of hir children in winding sheets," who informed her that Rebecca Nurse had murdered them as well.[5]

All the activity in the invisible world during the last few days of May and the first day of June was clearly linked to the imminent convening of the Court of Oyer and Terminer. On May 30, William Stoughton and Samuel Sewall issued a call for jurors—eighteen "honest and lawfull men" for the grand jury, and forty more "Eligbel alike" for juries of trials, the larger number of the latter allowing both for the possibility of multiple juries and for potential challenges to jurors by defendants. How many of the forty men summoned on May 30 actually served on trial juries in June or later is not clear, but twelve of the men who heard cases in the Court of Oyer and Terminer can be identified. They came from Wenham, Topsfield, Ipswich, Boxford, and Beverly; most had prior experience as jurors in the county, and some had been town officeholders. The foreman, Captain Thomas Fiske, a sixty-year-old Wenham selectman, had fought in King Philip's War under the command of Richard Waldron. John Ruck of Salem Town, the wealthy father of George Burroughs's second wife, served as foreman of the grand jury for at least the first court session in early June.[6]

Precisely which members of the Court of Oyer and Terminer were present at the first or later trials is unknown, since the official records of the sessions are no longer extant. The council's order setting up the court on May 27 named nine judges, all of whom were also councilors: William Stoughton, John Hathorne, Jonathan Corwin, Samuel Sewall, Bartholomew Gedney, John Richards, Nathaniel Saltonstall, Waitstill Winthrop, and Peter Sergeant. Five of these men would constitute a quorum, as long as one of the five was Stoughton, Gedney, or Richards. Collectively, the justices had many years of political and judicial experience. Several, indeed, had served as judges on the Court of Assistants during previous witchcraft trials.[7]

William Stoughton, the lieutenant governor and chief judge, who was about sixty-one in 1692, had graduated from Harvard with the class of 1650. Originally planning to enter the ministry, he studied at Oxford and preached in Sussex, but returned to Massachusetts in 1662, thereafter entering public life. First elected an assistant in 1671, he retained his positions as councilor and judge under various regimes until the deposing of Andros in April 1689. Even though he then lost his position on the council because he was regarded as too closely aligned with the ousted governor, the interim council selected him as one of its two emissaries to New York in spring 1690 to plan the joint expedition against Montreal. His friendship with the Mathers earned him the lieutenant governor's post under the new charter.[8]

Greatly respected for his knowledge of both theology and law, Stoughton could be rigid and imperious, traits that he exhibited during the Salem trials and which he had also displayed in earlier court appearances. A sense of how he conducted himself during legal proceedings can be gained from a petition submitted by Falmouth's Robert Lawrence to Governor Andros, probably in 1687. Stoughton had presided over a court session in Maine that was scheduled to adjudicate one aspect of the long-standing dispute between Lawrence and Sylvanus Davis. But instead of hearing that case, Stoughton called Lawrence to task for defaming Davis's ally Edward Tyng, a council member, as a "Hipocriticall Rogue." Lawrence admitted employing the phrase, but defended himself by arguing that at the time of the slander Tyng had not yet become a councilor, and so "I thought I stood upon as Good Ground as mr Ting." Moreover, Tyng had "afterwards . . . past by & forgotten" the offending words. But, Lawrence reported, "Mr Stoughton tould mee Capt Ting had noe power to pass by such an affront with divers other words in setting out the hainousnesse off so great A Crime as hee termed it not suffering mee to speake for my selfe & as I saw being resolved to Condem me I was forced to be silent." After denying Lawrence an attorney, Stoughton fined him a substantial amount. That picture of a man certain of his judgments and unwilling to entertain any opposition is confirmed by every fragment of surviving evidence about the chief justice's conduct during the witchcraft trials.[9]

While not so learned as Stoughton, two other judges had also graduated from Harvard: Nathaniel Saltonstall (class of 1659), and, as already indicated, Samuel Sewall (class of 1671). Saltonstall, of Haverhill, was the grandson of one of the Bay Colony's first leaders. A militia officer for Essex County first chosen in 1666, a justice of the peace after 1669, and an assistant from 1679 until 1686 as well as a member of the interim council after April 1689, Saltonstall had had a great deal of experience in military and judicial affairs at both local and colony-wide levels. Sewall, a man of more modest origins, embarked upon a career in the ministry after college, but his marriage in early 1676 pulled him instead into the orbit of his new father-in-law, the wealthy merchant and mintmaster John Hull. Thereafter Sewall engaged in commerce, also serving as a militia officer and eventually as an assistant during the last three years of the old charter and its resurrection in 1690–1691. A third judge, Wait Winthrop, attended Harvard for two years but did not graduate. Wait and his brother, the colonial military leader Fitz-John— grandsons of John Winthrop, the longtime governor of Massachusetts, and sons of John Jr., governor of Connecticut—have accurately been termed "men of ordinary talent, lacking their grandfather's driving moral purpose and their father's breadth and creative intelligence." Both Wait and his brother sat on the council under Andros, but Wait nevertheless took an active role in Andros's overthrow, thereafter serving as a councilor under the interim government.[10]

The other judges were, like Sewall, wealthy merchants. John Richards, a member of the Mathers' Second Church, was a major in the militia first elected an assistant in 1680. Peter Sergeant, like Sewall a well-to-do member of the Third Church, helped to oust Andros in April 1689. And Bartholomew

Gedney, the Salem magistrate who occasionally joined Hathorne and Corwin in questioning suspected witches, owned a wharf and a shipyard in Salem Town. A prominent speculator in Maine lands, he possessed valuable mills at North Yarmouth (in the northern reaches of Casco Bay). He had served as an assistant in the 1680s, under both the old charter and the Dominion of New England, and he was an experienced justice of the peace.[11]

The judges of the Court of Oyer and Terminer were no strangers to each other. Not only had many of them served together as councilors or militia officers, they were also linked by an intricate web of marital relationships. As has already been noted, Corwin's sister had been married to Hathorne's now-deceased brother. One of Wait Winthrop's sisters was married to Corwin's brother; another of his sisters wed the widower John Richards during the trials. George Corwin, the nephew of both Wait Winthrop and Jonathan Corwin, served as sheriff of Essex County in 1692; his wife Lydia was Gedney's daughter. Only Stoughton (a bachelor), Sergeant, and Sewall stood outside this tightly related circle, but the latter two were connected to Winthrop in another way, through their common membership in the Third Church. Moreover, Sewall's diary entries demonstrate that Stoughton was among his closest associates in the 1680s; that he also socialized frequently in Boston with Richards, Winthrop, and Sergeant; and that when in Salem he would call on both Gedney and Hathorne.[12]

Sir William Phips later described these men collectively as "persons of the best prudence and figure that could then be pitched upon," declaring that he had depended on them for "a right method of proceeding in cases of witchcraft." According to John Hale, the justices "showed a conscientious endeavour to do the thing that was right," and, despite their past experience in witchcraft cases, they systematically "consulted the Presidents [precedents] of former times and precepts laid down by Learned Writers about Witchcraft." Hale noted specifically that the judges had familiarized themselves with two important treatises—Richard Bernard's *Guide to Grand-Jury Men* and Joseph Keble's chapter on "Conjuration" in his book on the common law—along with the more general works on witchcraft discussed in chapter 1.[13]

What law, exactly, was the court applying? When the old charter was revoked in 1684, with it died the 1648 *Laws and Liberties*, which criminalized conjuring with "a familiar spirit." In 1688, during the Dominion of New England, the trial of Goody Glover was presumably conducted under prevailing English law, a witchcraft statute passed by Parliament in 1604. Between April 1689 and May 1692, Massachusetts courts might possibly have reverted to enforcing the 1648 statutes, but under the charter of 1691 another legal code would have to be adopted. In mid-June, the first session of the new assembly

voted to continue all laws then in force until its second session in the fall; at
that time—after the Court of Oyer and Terminer had been dissolved—it formally adopted the 1604 English law almost word for word (with a significant
exception that will be considered later). In all likelihood, then, the judges of
the Court of Oyer and Terminer thought of themselves as applying existing
English law. As shall be seen below, indictments in 1692 frequently employed
the exact language of the 1604 statute. Thus the judges would have been particularly interested in the information contained in the volumes by Bernard
and Keble, as well as the ubiquitous, all-purpose legal reference, Michael
Dalton's *The Countrey Justice*, which went through multiple editions during
the seventeenth century after its first publication in 1618.[14]

The English statute, entitled "An Acte against Conjuration Witchcrafte
and dealinge with evill and wicked Spirits," defined as a capital offense occult
practices that employed "any Witchcrafte Inchantment Charme or Sorcerie,
wherebie any person shalbe killed destroyed wasted consumed pined or lamed
in his or her body, or any parte thereof." Anyone who used similar charms or
sorcery to locate hidden treasures or lost items, to hurt livestock or other
property, or to try but fail to injure a victim, would be liable for a jail term of
a year and a stint in the pillory. A second such offense would make this lesser
crime capital. Benefit of clergy was not allowed in these cases, but a widow
could still receive her dower and children their inheritance.[15]

Joseph Keble's *An Assistance to Justices of the Peace*, published in London in
1683, constituted the most up-to-date law book available to the judges.
Keble's discussion of witchcraft incorporated wholesale Michael Dalton's language in *The Countrey Justice*, and Dalton's analysis in turn rested on material
he had compiled from Richard Bernard and another book published early in
the century, Thomas Potts's *The Wonderfull Discoverie of Witches in the Countie of Lancaster* (1613). Dalton dealt not only with the subject already discussed
in chapter 1—"presumptions" that could properly lead to the interrogation of
a suspected witch—but also with the much more difficult conundrum of how
to find adequate *legal* proof of a suspect's guilt. Keble reprinted Dalton's summary of the magistrate's dilemma in such cases: "Now against these Witches
being the most cruel, revengeful, and bloudy of all the rest, the Justices of the
Peace may not alwayes expect direct evidence, seeing all their works are the
works of darkness, and no witnesses present with them to accuse them." And
so Keble/Dalton offered "certain observations" (based primarily on conclusions drawn from Bernard and Potts) to assist in the "better discovery" and
conviction of such malefactors.[16]

Keble/Dalton first addressed the issue of familiar spirits, commonly in the shape of animals, which sucked a teat on the witch's body. "And besides their sucking, the Devil leaveth other marks upon their body," Keble observed—perhaps blue or red spots or other anomalies, which were "insensible, and being pricked will not bleed." Devil's marks would often be found "in their secretest parts, and therefore require diligent and careful search," but when located would prove that a person had indeed made "a league with the Devil." A witch's property should be searched for "Pictures of Clay or Wax," charms or potions, or books about witchcraft. Also important would be "the Testimony of other Witches, confessing their own Witchcrafts, and witnessing against the suspected, . . . that they have been at their meetings; that they have told them what harm they have done, &c." So too, "the examination and Confession of the children (able & fit to answer), or Servants of the Witch," concerning the witch's malefic activities, would carry great weight. But best of all would be "their owne voluntary Confession . . . of the hurt they have done, or of the giving of their souls to the Devil, and of the Spirits which they have."[17]

Reading such directives, the judges would have recognized that Hathorne and Corwin had made an excellent start on compiling evidence necessary for conviction. Several people had admitted their guilt, identifying other witches who also attended the specters' malefic meetings. Some children and servants had, under questioning, implicated their parents or employers. The existence and use of images (poppets) had also been described. Yet a nagging problem loomed: many suspects did not confess directly to the magistrates. Instead, their specters had admitted guilt to the afflicted Villagers. How should such spectral confessions be assessed? And could the torments the accusers said they had suffered at the hands of apparitions be accepted as evidence of witchcraft? Reassuringly, the great Sir Matthew Hale had answered yes to that last question in the Lowestoft case in 1662, and he had also employed a touch test to indicate guilt. But legal counsel alone could not address all the issues the court would have to consider.

When the newly appointed justices Samuel Sewall, Wait Winthrop, and Peter Sergeant attended Sabbath services on May 29, they accordingly surely looked to their pastor, Samuel Willard, for further guidance on these difficult matters. Willard, a member of the same Harvard class as Nathaniel Saltonstall, succeeded Thomas Thacher as the minister of Old South after Thacher's death in 1678. The following year, he married his second wife, Eunice, the daughter of Edward Tyng, the magistrate and wealthy landowner with whom George Burroughs was aligned in Casco. In the 1660s, as previously noted, Willard served as minister at Groton, and in that capacity he had observed and reflected upon the diabolic possession of his servant, Elizabeth Knapp. Consequently, the Reverend Mr. Willard appeared remarkably well positioned to speak authoritatively on the 1692 witchcraft crisis: not only was he a learned and respected preacher who had had past experience with an afflicted girl, but he also had at least secondhand knowledge of George Burroughs, believed to be the witches' leader.[18]

His expectant congregation would not have been disappointed, because on the afternoon of Sunday, May 29, Samuel Willard began a sermon cycle based on the text 1 Peter 5:8–9: "Be sober, be vigilant, because your adversary the devil, as a roaring lion, walketh about seeking whom he may devour: whom resist steadfast in the faith."[19] In that sermon, which Sewall carefully recorded in his notebook, Willard asserted that "there is a Devil," indeed "innumerable" devils, although the word was "used in the singular nu[m]ber." Proof of the existence of devils came from the scriptures, from the fact that "diabolical operations" have been "evident to such who are intelligent," and from "the Confession of those who have been in covenant with the Devil." Satanic "evil angels" were "individual, rational or intellectual beings" whom God had banished from heaven to live in this world. Willard instructed his listeners that "they are invisible substances they do oft assume shapes which they do present to us."

Only through "Errour or folly" would people deny that devils existed, the clergyman insisted. Skeptics gave Satan "great advantage against men," for "none are more led captive by the Devil then such who believe there are no such beings." The "innumerable company of Devils" strove to "turn the world up side down," but people should take heart from the fact that "God overules & enlarges or Stratons their Power as he pleases." Satan, Willard warned, "is allwayes setting himself to do man harm," because he envies God and hates Christ's gift of salvation to humanity. In pursuit of his goals, the devil even "employes men to mischief one another. There are witches to tempt others to the same diabolical art & to afflict others."

Willard ended his sermon with a disquisition on "the woful condition of all unregenerat men," who were uniformly "under the Power of the Devil." Perhaps he selected the text from 1 Peter, which related so directly to current events, as a means of reaching this conventional conclusion in a way that would have had an unusually powerful effect on his congregation. But for Sewall, Winthrop, and Sergeant, their pastor's words could well have had quite a different primary resonance. He had assured them in the strongest possible terms that devils existed, that they commonly employed witches to "mischief" their targets, and that devils, although usually invisible, "do oft assume shapes which they do present to us." If the judges contemplated those statements carefully over the next few days (as the faithful were supposed to do while rereading their sermon notes), they would have approached their judicial responsibilities with confidence in the righteousness of the enterprise.

The same must also have been true of John Richards, their colleague on the bench, who a few days later received a thoughtful letter dated May 31 from *his* pastor, Cotton Mather, about the "noble service" to which God had called him: "the service of encountering the wicked spirits of our air, and of detecting and confounding of their confederates."[20] Predicting that "our good God will prosper you in that undertaking," Mather informed Richards that the congregation of the Second Church had been "fasting and praying before him for your direction." In such cases, God "doth usually answer with the most favorable assistances," the clergyman assured his congregant, citing a comparable instance where a fast had brought "a remarkable smile of God upon the endeavors of the judges to discover and extirpate the authors of that execrable witchcraft."

Mather began the substance of his missive with the central issue, advising Richards not to "lay more stress upon pure specter testimony than it will bear." When he was certain or had "good, plain, legal evidence that the demons which molest our poor neighbours do indeed represent such and such people to the sufferers," that constituted a "presumption," but not yet sufficient proof that the suspects were witches. The judges should not proceed upon "the bare supposal of a poor creature's being represented by a specter," for they would thereby be granting too much "credit" to "diabolical representations." That admonition seemed clear and straightforward enough, but Mather undercut his argument by contending that God would "ordinarily" quickly vindicate an innocent person whom an apparition falsely represented. Mather pointed out the "dreadfully real" impact of the witchcraft: "our dear neighbors are most really tormented, really murdered, and really acquainted with hidden things, which are afterwards proved plainly to have been realities." The witches responsible for such effects were just as guilty as a man who killed his neighbor by stabbing him in his heart. But how to prove who had employed devils "in this work of darkness"?

Like Dalton and Keble, Cotton Mather indicated that a "credible confession" was the best evidence of guilt (and he assured Richards that a man of his "sagacity" would have no difficulty distinguishing reliable from unreliable confessions). Obtaining such confessions could be difficult, however, Mather admitted. Even though God might "thunder-strike their souls" and cause witches to confess unexpectedly, the magistrates should not rely solely on that providence. "Cross and swift questions" might work, or interrogating witches in a way that would expose and thereby forfeit their dependence on the devils for answers. Revealing their inability to recite the Lord's Prayer properly could be helpful because subsequently asking witches to explain that failure could well cause them to confess. But even without confessions all was not lost. Witches' own words—if they demonstrated "such a knowledge of woeful circumstances attending the afflicted people, as could not be had without some diabolical communion"—could prove guilt. So, too, wounds given to specters and found on the bodies of suspects provided "very palpable" evidence. Poppets, if located, constituted more proof, and beyond that: "I am thinking that some witches make their own bodies to be their puppets." Thus if their movements caused "the same thing, presently, and hurtfully, and more violently done by an unseen hand unto the bodies of the sufferers," then that too exposed the malefice of witches. Finally, witch marks, if identified as "magical" by expert physicians, were worth considering.[21]

Although Cotton Mather cautioned Judge Richards against relying too heavily on "pure specter testimony," his summary of acceptable evidence encompassed certain spectral phenomena—for example, a witch's seemingly innocuous movements injuring the afflicted, or wounds appearing on the body of a suspect after an apparition had been struck with a weapon. Then, too, while remarking that an inability to repeat the exact words of the Lord's Prayer alone should not be regarded as conclusive, Mather thought that interrogating suspects about such a failure could reveal guilt. In his willingness to employ searches for witch's marks, the minister furthermore validated traditional means of identifying witches. His position on the latter test accorded with the advice the judges received from reading Joseph Keble's treatise, but Mather went beyond Keble (and Dalton) in endorsing a reliance on physical manifestations with spectral origins. In the absence of the best evidence, confession, the clergyman clearly hoped to identify "palpable" proof of invisible phenomena. In general, the justices would follow Keble's prescriptions, but they would also adopt Mather's expansive definition of the admissible proofs of witchcraft.

THE TRIAL AND EXECUTION OF BRIDGET BISHOP

After calling the Court of Oyer and Terminer into session at the Salem Town courthouse on Thursday, June 2, Chief Judge William Stoughton administered the oath of office to Thomas Newton and Stephen Sewall. And then the proceedings began with a meeting of the "Grand Enquest" (the grand jury). Probably because the evidence against Bridget Bishop seemed the most compelling, Newton decided to start with her. Witnesses were also summoned to testify against Rebecca Nurse and John Willard; a group of men examined the bodies of Willard and John Proctor, unsuccessfully searching for witch marks; and a women's jury was convened to similarly examine several female suspects.[22]

The women's jury, led by a Salem Town chirurgeon and apothecary, Dr. John Barton, issued two reports on June 2. After inspecting the bodies of Bridget Bishop, Rebecca Nurse, and Elizabeth Proctor "by dilligent search," the jurors initially explained that they found "apreternathurall Excresence of flesh between the pudendum and Anus much like to Tetts & not usuall in women . . . & that they were in all the three women neer the same place." By contrast, they saw nothing unusual on the bodies of Alice Parker, Susannah Martin, or Sarah Good, whom they also searched. Several hours later, a reexamination revealed that the strange teatlike "piece[s] of flesh" on the first three women had disappeared, being replaced by "dry skin," and also that Susannah Martin's breast, which in the morning "appeared to us very full," was now "all lancke & pendant." The jurors' findings implied that in the interim the four women had all been sucked by their animal familiars.[23]

While the women's and men's juries were looking closely at the suspects' bodies, the grand jury was hearing testimony from witnesses who told stories about Bridget Bishop's bewitchments in years past.[24] The afflicted Villagers and their adult male supporters (Thomas Putnam, Nathaniel Ingersoll, Samuel Parris) must also have testified before the grand jury, describing the torments the girls suffered on the day of Bishop's examination, because the five surviving indictments all refer to April 19. Drawing on the words of the English witchcraft law, the jury charged that Goody Bishop had during her interrogation "Tortured Afflicted Pined, Consumed, wasted: & tormented" Mercy Lewis, Abigail Williams, Betty Hubbard, Ann Putnam Jr., and Mary Walcott.

The precedent thereby established was to be followed throughout the trials. Although testimony on a variety of topics would be accepted as evidence against suspects, the indictments, which consistently invoked the phrasing of the 1604 statute, commonly pertained to spectral torments visited upon the afflicted in the presence of witnesses, which usually meant during examinations. Undoubtedly Thomas Newton, experienced lawyer that he was, chose this method of proceeding because the indictments thus appeared to satisfy the legal requirement for at least two witnesses to the same act of witchcraft. Although some historians have questioned the validity of the form of these indictments, they resembled others issued by English courts about the same time.

After the grand jury had issued the indictments, a trial (petty) jury convened to hear the case against Goody Bishop.[25] Cotton Mather, who did not attend the proceedings but who had access to documents no longer extant, described the trial in *Wonders of the Invisible World.* "There was little occation to prove the *Witchcraft*," he wrote, "it being evident and notorious to all beholders." The problem was "to fix the *Witchcraft* on the Prisoner at the Bar."

First, he indicated, the bewitched people testified that "the *Shape* of the Prisoner did oftentimes very grivously Pinch them, Choak them, Bite them, and Afflict them, urging them to write their Names in a *Book,* which the said Spectre called, *Ours.*" One of the afflicted further attested that Bishop's specter had transported her to the side of a river and threatened to drown her if she would not sign the book, while others affirmed that Bishop's apparition had bragged of killing "sundry Persons, then by her named." Susannah Sheldon revealed having that very day witnessed a confrontation between Bishop's specter and the *"Ghosts"* of a pair of twins, who told her "to hir face that she had murthered them in setting them into fits wher of they dyed." As to the truth of this charge, Mather observed, "there was in the Matter of Fact but too much suspicion."

Various witnesses then described the torments of the afflicted at Bishop's April 19 examination, recounting how they were "struck down" if she looked at them and how they "painfully" mimicked the movements of her body. "Many of the like Accidents now fell out, while she was at the Bar," Mather reported. One man recounted the incident in which Jonathan Walcott's sword thrust at Bishop's apparition had seemingly torn her coat. And then the confessor Deliverance Hobbs attested that Goody Bishop had tried to persuade her to deny her confession and to that end had "whipped her with Iron Rods." She also placed Bishop at "a General Meeting of the Witches, in a Field at *Salem-*Village," revealing that Bishop "partook of a Diabolical Sacrament in Bread and Wine then administred."

To make it "unquestionable" that Bridget Bishop had committed the acts charged in the indictments, Mather wrote, "there were produced many Evidences of OTHER *Witchcrafts,* by her perpetrated." Ten witnesses attested at the trial to Goody Bishop's past malefic practices. Some of the tales dated back to the late 1670s; they involved disappearing money, strange accidents, spectral appearances by Bridget Bishop in her own or animal shapes (especially to men at night when they were in bed), the unexplained sickness of livestock, and the mysterious deaths or chronic illnesses of children after acrimonious encounters with her. A man and his son also testified that in 1685, while working to "take downe the Cellar wall of The owld house she formerly Lived in," they had discovered "Severall popitts made up of Raggs And hoggs Brusells with headles pins in Them with the points out ward." (Mather remarked that Bishop could not give a "reasonable or tolerable" explanation of the poppets.)[26]

After all the witnesses had testified, the jury of women reported finding "a preternatural Teat" on Bridget Bishop's body. She was then given a chance to defend herself (no criminal defendant was allowed an attorney under English law at the time) but, Mather insisted without going into detail, was caught in *"gross Lying"* seven times during her statement. Chief Justice Stoughton then turned the case over to the jury, instructing them thus about the law: "they were not to mind whether the bodies of the said afflicted were really pined and consumed, as was expressed in the inditement; but whether the said afflicted did not suffer from the accused such afflictions as naturally *tended* to their being pined and consumed, wasted, etc. This, (said he,) is a pining and consuming in the sense of the law." How long the jury deliberated is unknown, but Bridget Bishop was convicted and sentenced to hang.[27]

Reconstructing the Trials

Because the official records of the Court of Oyer and Terminer have been lost, it has been thought impossible to know how the witch trials themselves were conducted. As has been seen in this book, surviving transcripts of preliminary examinations reveal much about the early phases of the crisis. Many historians, though, have equated examinations, or the investigation of what the participants called "presumptions," with the later search for sufficient legal proof of guilt, which was another task entirely. Piecing together existing fragments of information can allow at least a partial reconstruction of the actual trials. Cotton Mather and Thomas Brattle—supporter and critic of the proceedings, respectively—concur, for example, on the standard sequence of events in the courtroom. First the afflicted were questioned (and frequently suffered from fits, just as they had during the examinations). Then confessors were brought in, and next, witnesses to past acts of maleficium by the defendant were permitted to tell their stories. The results of searches for witch's marks would be presented, and finally the accused folk would offer whatever defense they could. Further details also emerge from the accounts of people (notably Deodat Lawson) who attended and later wrote about specific trials.[28]

But what, precisely, was said to grand and petty juries by all those witnesses? When the foreman of the grand jury or Stephen Sewall, clerk of the court, wrote on the surviving documents "sworn before the grand inquest" or "jurat in curia" [sworn in court], the answer is obvious. The response to that question is much less clear when the document at issue has no notation or only one. What does such an absence mean? Does no notation indicate that this statement was never presented to either jury? Does one mean that it was heard by one body, but not the other?

Interpretation is both assisted and complicated by Stephen Sewall's "Memorandum" on a document in the case of Rebecca Nurse: "There were in this tryall as well as other Tryalls of the Same Nature Severall Evidences viva voce which were not written & so I can give no Copies of them Some for & Some against the parties Some of the Confessions did also mention this & other persons in their Severall declarations." In short, even if all the written records survive for a particular case (which itself is nearly impossible to determine), some testimony was probably presented orally and its contents cannot now be recovered.[29]

But to say that any narrative of the trials constructed today is therefore necessarily incomplete is not to say that the exercise is meaningless. In analyzing the legal material for this book, I have reached the following conclusions, which are reflected in all the trial narratives herein.

First, most of the informal narratives prepared by the complainants or their adult supporters, although they may have been read to the accused at examinations, were *not* later introduced into evidence in court. Very few such narratives have notations indicating they were presented to either grand or petty juries. Notably, for example, Susannah Sheldon's many lurid visions seem not to have been recast as depositions, which could well indicate prosecutorial skepticism about the validity of her testimony. Second, formal statements sworn at the grand jury could also have been presented "viva voce" to the petty jury, even though Sewall did not consistently write "jurat in curia" on all of the records. Third, and conversely, evidence labeled as "sworn in court" but carrying no notation by the grand-jury foreman was probably not considered by that body. Since the petty jury sometimes heard cases a month or two after the grand jury (see appendix 1), the prosecutor had time to recruit additional witnesses to fill in gaps in his case. Most documents in this category contain maleficium stories.

Fourth, confessors probably appeared in most cases, testifying orally rather than in writing. I have assumed that such people repeated to the petty jury the contents of previously recorded confessions. Fifth, sworn testimony by adult supporters of the afflicted children and teenagers probably carried great weight in the trials, for many of their statements are recorded as "jurat in curia." Sixth, since criminal defendants were never allowed to swear to their innocence (for fear they would lie and endanger their immortal souls), exculpatory evidence was probably also not presented under oath and thus would not have been designated as "sworn." That, coupled with Sewall's comment about oral testimony for defendants, has led me to assume that any pro-defense statements found today in the surviving documents were in fact considered by the petty jury.

During the June 2 court session, probably after Goody Bishop was convicted and taken away, Ann Carr Putnam publicly described under oath yet another remarkable vision. Several people had appeared "in winding sheets" at her bedside to accuse John Willard, Martha Corey, and/or William Hobbs of killing them and to threaten to "tare Me to peices" if "I did not Goe & tell mr Hathorne." Subsequently, Willard's apparition admitted to her having caused thirteen deaths, one of them that of his wife's relative, Lydia Wilkins. Six of those he admitted killing were children, including the Putnams' baby, Sarah. (Ann's spectral vision thus reconfirmed accusations first broached by her daughter in late April.) But even though the grand jury the next day took additional testimony and issued indictments against both Rebecca Nurse and John Willard, the Court of Oyer and Terminer adjourned its first session on June 3 without conducting another trial. Perhaps Thomas Newton had decided that he needed more time to collect evidence in these and other pending cases.[30]

Following Bridget Bishop's conviction, the number of reported bewitchments and accusations declined significantly, and people in Salem Village must have breathed a collective sigh of relief. Yet the afflictions did not stop completely. The very day Bishop was found guilty, a Village woman named Joanna Childin reported seeing the ghosts of two people who accused Rebecca Nurse and Sarah Good of killing them. The next day, Sarah Vibber described how John Proctor's apparition came to her "urging me to drink: drink Red as blood." On Saturday, June 4, several witnesses attested that Job Tookey, a sailor who had served in King Philip's War and had once been stationed at Black Point, boastfully told them that "he had Learneing and could Raise the divell when he pleased." Moreover, Tookey (who had probably encountered George Burroughs in Maine) asserted that "he would take mr Burrows his part." When he was questioned three days later by the Salem magistrates, Tookey declared that "I knew not then what I said"; perhaps he was claiming to have been drunk. After being charged with a number of murders by Elizabeth Booth and three other afflicted persons (each describing visions of ghosts accusing Tookey and "cryeing out for vengeance"), he was sent to jail.[31]

Then, on June 8, Booth saw eight apparitions of dead people accusing the Proctors, John Willard, or Martha Corey of having caused their deaths. Unlike most ghosts, who simply made charges, these explained to Elizabeth why they had been killed. The deaths stemmed either from neighborly exchanges gone wrong or, in three cases, from people's failure to follow Elizabeth Proctor's advice on medical matters. For example, the specter of Booth's stepfather, Michael Shaflin, charged that Goody Proctor killed him because she had not been consulted soon enough during Shaflin's fatal illness, nor had the family subsequently followed her advice. Other disagreements caused by "som diferance in a rekninge," by failures to supply or pay for certain items, or to mend a broken spinning wheel rounded out the list. That such minor, commonplace disputes and differences of opinion could end up being interpreted as motives for murder—at least when one of the parties was a suspected witch—reveals a great deal about the mindset of people in Essex County in early June 1692. Residents saw the potential for malefice everywhere, and petty quarrels now appeared serious enough to describe formally to the august Court of Oyer and Terminer.[32]

Bridget Oliver Bishop, the first convicted witch, provides an excellent example of this altered climate of opinion, for (with one undated exception) the maleficium tales told at her trial all originated between 1678 and 1686. No one from Salem Town had voiced a recent complaint against her. The same group of negative stories had been circulating for at least six years, but the authorities did not regard them as sufficiently compelling to bring her to trial for a second time until the afflicted Villagers translated long-standing Town gossip into complaints of spectral tortures. Then, in the context of fears of a combined assault from the visible and invisible worlds, and with witches and Indians coordinating their attacks on New England, the accusations took on a new and convincing urgency.

The conjunction of two events could have heightened Essex County concerns. On Friday, June 10, Bridget Bishop was hanged on Gallows Hill in Salem, without, remarked Robert Calef, "the least Confession of any thing relating to Witchcraft." The judges probably did not attend the execution, but at least one of the afflicted accusers, Sarah Vibber, was there.[33]

On Saturday, June 11, a large band of Wabanakis (led by Madockawando, Moxis, Edgeremet, Worombe, and others), accompanied by some French officers and men, attacked Wells, which was but lightly defended. Settlers took refuge in the garrison; some men were on board sloops in the harbor. The enemy assaulted both the ships and the garrison, but could take neither, despite a two-day-long battle that continued into Sunday night. Eventually, they burned the town and killed all the livestock they could find, while terming the garrison's defenders cowards for refusing to come out to fight. Cotton Mather later wrote that in their frustration the Wabanakis "fell to Threatning and Raging, like so many Defeated Devils." They took a captive from the town "out of Gun-Shot," torturing him "after a manner very Diabolical" in the sight of the horrified people in the garrison. "They Stripped him, they Scalped him alive, and after a Castration . . . they Slit him with Knives, between his Fingers and his Toes; They made cruel Gashes in the most Fleshy parts of his body, and stuck the Gashes with Firebrands, which were afterwards found Sticking in the wounds." Thus, concluded Mather, "they Butchered One poor Englishman, with all the Fury that they would have spent upon them all."[34]

Did anyone view the attack as revenge for Goody Bishop's execution? It would have been easy for New Englanders to reach such a conclusion, but no such reasoning is recorded in surviving documents.

QUESTIONS AND CAVEATS BEGIN

Following the hanging of Bridget Bishop, afflictions in Salem Village ceased almost entirely for two full weeks. Between June 10 and June 24, specters tortured only three victims, and no new suspects were jailed. Of those three sufferers, just one—Susannah Sheldon—was included in the core group. The first victim was Jonathan Putnam, Sergeant Thomas's younger cousin. When his sudden illness appeared attributable to witchcraft, the family called in Mercy Lewis, who the previous month had identified the apparitions tormenting members of the Wilkins clan. This time, she named Rebecca Nurse and Martha Carrier as those responsible for Jonathan's condition. Three days later, Jemima Rea, the eleven-year-old daughter of a King Philip's War veteran, likewise accused Rebecca Nurse—along with her sister Sarah Cloyce and a third woman—of causing her "strange fitts." Finally, on Tuesday, June 21, Sheldon charged the specters of Lydia Dustin and Sarah Good with conducting a concerted campaign against her. The two apparitions had not only tormented her but had repeatedly tied her hands with cord, witnesses revealed, and objects had been mysteriously and frequently transported out of the house in which she was staying temporarily. (As was becoming commonplace, Sheldon's afflictions had physical manifestations. That continued into the following week, when she once again accused Goody Good of having bound her hands so tightly she could not easily be freed.)[35]

Although such events must have aroused much talk in the Village, the fact that their number and frequency were so reduced, and that the main group of accusers (with the notable exception of Sheldon) now appeared relatively free of torments, might have suggested to some that the height of the crisis had passed. Perhaps the death of Goody Bishop had served the purpose of freeing the afflicted from at least some of their sufferings, just as the conviction and execution of the Lowestoft witches in England had cured the children who complained against them. Indeed, Cotton Mather later wrote in *Wonders of the Invisible World*, a Salem Town woman who had angered Bridget Bishop a decade earlier, and who subsequently became "Froward, Crazed . . . [and] unreasonable," had begun to recover with the arrest of Bishop and Alice Parker. She then regained her sanity entirely after the two women were executed.[36]

And perhaps the slight easing of tensions, the halt in what had been an unrelenting daily round of new bewitchments, formal accusations, and examinations, allowed some of the residents of Essex County and Boston to contemplate at slightly greater distance the bewildering events that had surrounded them for the past five months. Whether for that or some other cause, the weeks just prior to the second session of the Court of Oyer and Terminer witnessed the development of the first tentative criticisms of the proceedings.

Few surviving documents reveal any challenges to the magistrates prior to the execution of Bridget Bishop. Four suspected witches did attack Mary Warren's credibility about two weeks after her May 12 confession, charging that she had earlier repeated "Severall times" in the Salem Town jail that "hir Head was [so] Distempered that Shee Could not tell what Shee Said" when she was afflicted. "I thought I saw the Apparission of A hundred persons," Mary had revealed, but when she recovered "Shee Could not Say that Shee saw any of [those] Apparissons at the time Aforesaid." Therefore, she had exclaimed, "the Majestrates Might as well Examine Keysars Daughter that has Bin Distracted Many Yeares . . . as well as any of the Afflicted persons." But the joint statement would have been seen as self-interested (even though those who signed it had not been accused by her at the time), and nothing indicates that the judges took it seriously.[37]

After Goody Bishop's hanging, however, and despite the fact that she had long been regarded as a witch, concerns about the witchcraft prosecutions began to surface, albeit in limited and sporadic ways. Such concerns took three forms: caveats voiced by the colony's clergymen, both singly and collectively; a petition campaign that was decisively squelched by the arrest of its chief instigator; and a concerted effort by members of the Nurse family to prevent Rebecca's conviction in the wake of her indictment for witchcraft.

Probably at its meeting of June 13, the Massachusetts council decided to ask "several ministers" for their opinions "upon the present witchcraft in Salem village." Why the council requested that advice was not recorded, but that it did so suggests that questions had already been raised about the nature of the proceedings. The council meeting was attended by Governor Phips and four of the judges—Stoughton, Winthrop, Sewall, and Sergeant—and so the appeal for the clergy's guidance came from a near quorum of the Court of Oyer and Terminer.[38]

On June 15, the clergymen responded with a lengthy document, the "Return of Several Ministers," which conveyed an ambiguous message. Perhaps, like one of their number, Cotton Mather, they did not necessarily concur with "the *Principles*, that some of the Judges had espoused," but at the same time acknowledged "their exemplary *Pietie*, and the *Agony* of Soul with which they sought the Direction of Heaven" and therefore "could not but speak honourably of their *Persons*, on all Occasions." And the most important "principle" a magistrate "espoused" with which the clergy disagreed was that advanced by the revered chief judge, William Stoughton: that specters could not represent the shapes of innocent people. Accordingly, the ministers couched their response in careful language, on the one hand supporting the justices' overall efforts but on the other raising some specific questions, especially about the interpretation of spectral evidence.[39]

Acknowledging the "deplorable" condition of "our poor neighbours, that are now suffering by molestations from the invisible world," they thanked "our honourable rulers" for their attempts "to defeat the abominable witchcrafts which have been committed in the country."[40] But, they warned, in pursuing prosecutions the judges should exercise "a very critical and exquisite caution," for fear of being misled by "things received only upon the devil's authority." Too much "credulity" could lead to "a long train of miserable consequences, and Satan [could] get an advantage over us." In particular, when people "formerly of an unblemished reputation" had been accused, the ministers recommended that "all proceedings thereabout be managed with an exceeding tenderness towards those that may be complained of."

For specific advice on detecting witchcraft and on identifying and convicting those responsible, the clergymen referred the judges to "such judicious writers as [William] Perkins and [Richard] Bernard," thus reconfirming contemporary observations (discussed in chapter 1) about the impact in 1692 of the writings of these two men in particular. Following Bernard, they counseled the magistrates against too much "noice, company and openness" during initial examinations. Moreover, only tests of undoubted "lawfulness" should be employed to uncover witches. Like Perkins and Bernard, they drew a distinction between "presumptions" that could lead to an inquiry and the proof necessary for conviction. Evidence for either presumptions or convictions "ought certainly to be more considerable than barely the accused person's being represented by a spectre unto the afflicted," they pointed out, "inasmuch as it is an undoubted and a notorious thing, that a demon may, by God's permission, appear, even to ill purposes, in the shape of an innocent, yea, and a virtuous man." The ministers also expressed doubt whether "alterations made in the sufferers, by a look or touch of the accused, [are] an infallible evidence of guilt"; such changes instead could result from "the devil's legerdemain." Perhaps giving "remarkable affronts" to the devils by "our disbelieving those testimonies whose whole force and strength is from them alone" might even put a stop to the current "dreadful calamity," they averred.

But after having called into question several of the tactics the magistrates were employing in their dealings with suspects, the clergymen retreated in their last paragraph when they returned to the praise of the magistrates with which they began. "Nevertheless," they concluded, "we cannot but humbly recommend unto the government, the speedy and vigourous prosecutions of such as have rendered themselves obnoxious, according to the directions given in the laws of God, and the wholesome statutes of the English nation, for the detection of witchcrafts."

In addition to summarizing what the "several ministers" said, it is also important to point out what they did *not* say. They did not contest the validity of the sufferings of the afflicted young people, nor did they challenge the belief that those torments originated in the invisible world. They did not dispute the reality of the girls' spectral visions, but instead asked whether those visions ("the devil's authority") could be trusted unhesitatingly. While urging "exceeding tenderness" toward accused people with good reputations, they said nothing about those persons who have been termed herein "usual suspects"—women (and a few men) who had long been thought to be witches.

The justices in fact might well have interpreted much of the ministers' statement, not simply its final paragraph, as an endorsement of their efforts. The clergymen had told them that they were doing good work in combating the "abominable witchcrafts" afflicting Essex County. If asked, the judges would surely have denied placing too much emphasis on "barely the accused person's being represented by a spectre unto the afflicted" in the one trial they had already conducted. As Cotton Mather's narrative showed, spectral evidence and touch tests constituted only part of the case against Bridget

Bishop—confessions and testimony about past maleficium also played a major role in her conviction. In addition, since Goody Bishop could hardly have been seen as someone "formerly of an unblemished reputation," the justices might even have thought that most of the clergy's recommendations did not apply to their treatment of her. Robert Calef thus with some reason later charged that the "Return of Several Ministers" gave "as great or greater Encouragement to proceed in those dark methods, than cautions against them."[41]

Yet still the document might have raised some doubts in the mind of a careful reader, especially one who had perused Cotton Mather's May 31 letter to John Richards. Even though Mather later claimed not only that he agreed with the joint statement's contents, "but it was *I* who drew it up," the clergymen disputed some of the positions he had taken just two weeks earlier. He had essentially endorsed using as evidence "alterations made in the sufferers, by a look or touch of the accused," when he mused that the witches "make their own bodies to be their puppets." Further, his position on whether the devil could represent an innocent person as a spectral shape was not as clearcut as the group's: he had indicated that such a thing would happen, but rarely and under special circumstances, whereas the group statement said nothing about incidence. Then, too, that key question was not one on which Richard Bernard or William Perkins offered the judges much guidance. As will be recalled from chapter 1, Bernard had indicated that the devil might mischievously represent an "unregenerate" innocent person as a specter, but he had said nothing about whether a guiltless regenerate church member could be so represented. Perkins had not discussed the issue at all.[42]

Surely Samuel Willard too participated in drafting the "Return of Several Ministers." And his sermons on the text of 1 Peter 5:8 on June 12 and 19— bracketing the drafting of that statement—reflected greater skepticism about the witchcraft prosecutions than had the one he delivered on May 29. That Sunday, of course, he almost certainly did not know that John Alden, a member of his congregation, had been formally accused the day before in Salem Village. The homilies he delivered in mid-June, after Captain Alden had been jailed, thus had a different tone from that of his first treatment of the subject. On June 12, he stressed Satan's "Subtilty," instructing his listeners (who included Judge Sewall), "dont believe the Devil" and warning that "if it were possible he would deceive the very Elect." Emphasizing that Satan exhibited "peculiar rage" against the "children of God," he explained that the devil "emproves every opportunity against them." Their adversary's "malice," Willard declared, was exerted with greatest force "where the Gospel comes. Here he raises all his Powers & dos his utmost to oppose."[43]

The June 19 sermon applied such general statements to a specific instance, that of John Alden, who, though unnamed, was clearly the topic of Willard's discourse (which also probably addressed the complaints against Mistress Margaret Thacher, the widow of his predecessor). The clergyman exclaimed about how Satan defamed good folk as a part of his campaign against God's people. Inveighing against the "raising of scandelus reports," he asserted that "thos that cary up & downe such reports are the devills brokers." And then he broached the crucial question: "wether the devill cane represent the person of a good man doing a bad action." Responding unambiguously to his own inquiry and directly challenging the position adopted by Justice Stoughton, Willard asserted that "the devil may reprisent an inosent, nay a godly person, doing a bad ackt." Terming such an event an "extraordinary dispensation of providence," he told his congregation that "it calls us to selfe examination, selfe abasing," especially those "nextly concerned." The Bible made it clear that "the devill cane do this upon divine permission & will do it with out he be prevented by god." Satan could accordingly take on "the Image of any man in the world," Willard insisted, without "the consent of the party in thus reprisenting it." The devil, moreover, did not need to employ witches to attack his victims. No one thinking "rationally," he contended, could reject the conclusion that Satan "cane perswade the person aflicted that it is done by the person thus reprisented." Willard closed his sermon by reassuring the congregation that God was "just & ritious still," despite such "darke" and "unacountable" occurrences, and he urged his listeners "not to be daunted" by the devil's recent assaults.[44]

At about the same time, another Boston minister also stepped forward to question the use of spectral evidence in the trials. The Reverend William Milborne, a former resident of Bermuda who ministered to the town of Saco, Maine, between 1685 and 1688, must have known George Burroughs well during the latter's part-time sojourn in nearby Black Point during those same years. Milborne, pastor of the First Baptist Church in Boston, worked with Wait Winthrop and other members of the court and council for the over-throw of Andros in April 1689, but that past association did not soften his criticism of his former allies in June 1692. Instead of raising his objections in the context of a sermon, Milborne drafted two petitions, one of which sur-vives. He planned to present both to the new Massachusetts assembly, which convened on June 8.[45]

Like the ministers' joint statement, Milborne's petition focused primarily on the "several persons of good fame and of unspotted reputation" who had been committed to jail during the current crisis. Unquestionably, George Burroughs would have been included in such a category, along with John

Alden, John Floyd, Rebecca Nurse, and a few others. "Bare specter testimonie" supported charges against "many whereof we cannot but in Charity Judge to be Innocent," the petition alleged, expressing the opinion that "if said specter testimonie pass for evidence [we] have great grounds to fear that the Innocent will be condemned." In such circumstances, no one could be wholly exempt from "the like accusation," Milborne asserted. The petition concluded with a request that the assembly members "by your votes" provide that "no more credence be given thereto than the word of God alloweth."[46]

The document, which reputedly garnered "several" signatures besides Milborne's own, prematurely came to the attention of the governor and council, which on June 25 summoned Milborne to appear before them to explain his connection to such "Seditious and Scandalous Papers or writings" containing "very high Reflections upon the Administrations of Publick Justice within this their Majesties Province." After Milborne admitted that he had written the papers and signed one of them, he was ordered to post £200 bond for his good behavior or to be jailed. Presumably, he chose the former course of action, and he seems to have been effectively silenced thereafter.[47]

In addition to the general complaints about the prosecution of people with good reputations that emerged in mid- to late June, the fate of one such person in particular sparked a major campaign. After June 3, with Rebecca Nurse facing four indictments for witchcraft, her family used the nearly month-long hiatus in court proceedings to gather evidence. In early May, they had drafted and circulated a statement attesting to her good character, but its thirty-nine signatures had not prevented her indictment. So now they chose another tack: questioning the credibility of the accusers.[48]

Goody Nurse had been indicted for bewitching four people during her March 24 examination "and divers other dayes & times as well before as after": Ann Putnam Jr., Mary Walcott, Betty Hubbard, and Abigail Williams. Of this group, the Nurses attacked the last two. James Kettle declared that Betty had told him "severall untruthes" on a Sunday in late May. Joseph Hutchinson Sr. recounted an undated conversation with Abigail Williams about her interactions with the devil. Parris's niece described in detail two different books, both "rede as blode," which "the blacke man" ("the devell") had repeatedly brought to her. "I asked her if shee was not afraid to see the devell," Hutchinson reported. "Shee said at the first shee was and did goe from him but now shee was not a fraid but Could talke with him as well as shee Could with mee."[49]

Although Hutchinson did not make his meaning explicit, he implied that Abigail's easy ability to converse with Satan hinted at an alliance with him—or at least that her conduct raised doubts about her veracity. Once more a key question had been raised about the standing of an afflicted accuser that could be extended to them all: Were they entirely innocent? Could their ready communication with Satan and the witches reveal their complicity with the evil angels? Could they really be believed when they insisted they had never signed the devil's book?

The other attacks on the accusers' character were more blunt and direct. Former employers of Mercy Lewis, in a statement that is unfortunately badly torn, seem to have accused her of "stand[ing] stifly" to "untruth[s]" while she lived with them in Beverly two and a half years earlier. Robert Moulton described how Susannah Sheldon "Controdict[ed]" herself when she told conflicting stories about crossing a stone wall: first she said "the witches halled her Upone her bely through the yeard like a snacke [snake] and halled her over the stone walle," but next she declared simply that "she Came over the stone wall her selfe." Sheldon had also claimed "that she Rid Upone apoole to boston and she said the divel Caryed the poole." Such a statement, like Abigail's, implied that she was more likely to be a witch than bewitched. Most vulnerable, though, was Sarah Vibber. The Nurses collected four separate statements from her current and former neighbors describing her as an "unruly turbulent" person who was "double tongued" and could "fall into fitts as often as she plesed." As the second court session approached, the family had thus armed itself with ammunition to deploy against some of Goody Nurse's accusers.[50]

The Nurse Family Campaign

No one has previously connected the undated attacks on the accusers to each other or to the Nurse family, yet they were almost certainly solicited by the Nurses in June, after Rebecca's indictment but before her trial. Most of the statements have discernible links to the Nurses. Joseph Hutchinson Sr., an ally of Francis Nurse and an opponent of Samuel Parris, signed the petition on behalf of Goody Nurse circulated by Francis in early May. Samuel Nurse, the eldest son of the family, witnessed Robert Moulton's statement against Susannah Sheldon. And that the Nurses targeted Sarah Vibber for special attention became evident at Rebecca's trial, when a statement by Sarah Nurse, discussed later in this chapter, revealed that she had been carefully scrutinizing Goody Vibber.[51]

The depositions summarized above without clear ties to the Nurse family are those questioning the truthfulness of Mercy Lewis and Betty Hubbard. Yet viewing them as a part of the campaign seems justified because *only* the Nurses, among all the families of the accused, took documented steps to attack the credibility of the core group of accusers. (Some other families also produced petitions signed by supporters.) The Nurses, moreover, acted far more aggressively on behalf of Rebecca than other families acted for suspects from their households. Only they, for example, are known to have asked Stephen Sewall for copies of court records after a trial.[52]

THE SECOND SESSION OF THE COURT OF OYER AND TERMINER

When the court reconvened on Tuesday, June 28, the prosecutor Thomas Newton continued to focus his (and its) attention primarily on "usual suspects" who resembled Bridget Bishop. Over the next five days, the grand jury took testimony in eight cases and the petty jury or juries held five trials. Of the nine suspects who came before the court that week, six—Sarah Good, Susannah Martin, Elizabeth Howe, Sarah Wilds, Martha Carrier, and Dorcas Hoar—had long been regarded as witches. As for the other three, two (Elizabeth and John Proctor) were related to a reputed witch (Elizabeth's grandmother Ann Burt), and even Rebecca Nurse faced two allegations of maleficium, although both were of relatively recent origin.[53]

Newton started with Sarah Good, the embittered, destitute Villager who had been one of the first three accused witches. He prepared carefully for the grand-jury hearing and the trial; the surviving documents include a paper headed "Titabes Confession & Examinacon against her selfe & Sarah Good abstracted," which covers not only that subject but also lists witnesses and summarizes relevant information about Good from four more confessions. To the grand jury, Newton presented several different types of testimony: reports of past incidents of maleficium attributed to Sarah Good, sworn statements by the afflicted, and evidence of recent bewitchments and spectral activity involving the defendant. During the grand-jury session, Mary Warren had fits, which Susannah Sheldon attributed to Sarah Good's specter. Susannah also declared that she had seen Good's apparition use "invisible hands" to take a "sauser" from a table in the jury room and place it out of doors. Samuel Parris's deposition could well have been particularly persuasive. The Salem Village pastor reaffirmed in person the truth of what he, Thomas Putnam, and Ezekiel Cheever had sworn before Hathorne and Corwin on May 23. Parris not only described the sufferings of his daughter Betty and niece Abigail, along with Ann Putnam Jr. and Betty Hubbard, during the examination of the first three accused witches on March 1, but he also affirmed that when Tituba began to confess and was herself thereafter tortured she "openly charged" Good and Sarah Osborne "as the persons that afflicted her the aforesaid Indian." The grand jury then issued three indictments against Sarah Good, for afflicting Betty Hubbard and Ann Putnam Jr. on March 1 (and before and after), and for attacking Sarah Vibber on May 2 (and before and after).[54]

Sarah Good's trial began that Tuesday and seems to have continued into the next day. First the afflicted, then confessors, then witnesses to maleficium would have been called to testify. The jury heard Putnam Jr. and Walcott swear that they had been tortured by Good's apparition and that they had also seen her specter assault others. Goody Vibber described her own affliction and that of her child, indicating as well that she had seen Good's specter tormenting both Mercy Lewis and John Indian during the April 11 examinations in Salem Town. An afflicted person, probably Vibber, claimed to have been stabbed "in the breast" during the court session by a knife held by Good's apparition. After court officials found part of a knife blade on her, a young man identified the blade as one he had broken and thrown away the day before. Robert Calef, reporting this incident, noted that the young man was "dismist" and the witness merely "bidden by the Court not to tell lyes" before being allowed to resume her testimony. To Calef and modern observers alike, the story illustrates the court's unwillingness to question its basic assumptions about the truthfulness of the complainants; to the judges, it probably constituted a minor distraction.[55]

Deliverance Hobbs, her stepdaughter Abigail, and Mary Warren undoubtedly repeated the parts of their confessions that pertained to Goody Good: Deliverance, that she saw Good at the witch meeting in Parris's pasture presided over by George Burroughs; Abigail, that she knew that Good was a witch and had been prevented by Good from confessing fully on April 19; and Mary, that Good had asked her to sign her book. The most detailed statement, though, would have been Tituba's. She charged Good with hurting the children (especially Ann Jr.), with having forced her to torment them as well, and with taking her riding on a pole. Additionally, Tituba declared that she had seen Good's name in the devil's book. Newton could also have pointed out to the petty jury that Sarah's young daughter Dorcas had confessed, disclosing her mother's involvement with witchcraft, and that Sarah Good's statement implicating Sarah Osborne in the torturing of the children revealed her own culpability. Good's charge constituted an implicit confession of guilt, Newton believed, since she was not afflicted yet knew about such spectral activity, for "none here sees the witches but the afflicted and themselves."[56]

Finally, Sarah Good's neighbors told their stories of maleficium and of recent spectral manifestations. Samuel and Mary Abbey, with whom the Goods had once lived, attested that she had behaved "very crossely & Mallitiously, to them & their Children" ever since they expelled the "Turbulant" woman and her family from their household two and a half years earlier. Goody Good subsequently employed witchcraft to kill their livestock, the Abbeys charged. The son and grandson of Zechariah Herrick described problems with cattle that had followed Herrick's refusal to allow the Goods to live in his house. Samuel Sibley and Marshal Joseph Herrick both repeated tales about Good's spectral movements shortly after her examination, and witnesses attested to Susannah Sheldon's strange experiences with tightly bound hands. Whether Newton referred to the report of the jury of women that found nothing preternatural on the defendant's body on June 2 is uncertain. Also not clear is what Sarah Good argued in her own defense. Perhaps she contended, as she did informally on March 2, that too much of the evidence against her depended on the word of an Indian, and questioned whether the prosecutor had actually found the required two witnesses to each of her purported acts of witchcraft. But whatever she said, it was in vain, and she was convicted.[57]

On Wednesday, June 29, the court turned its attention to Susannah Martin, the elderly Amesbury widow initially complained against two months earlier. Newton seems to have presented only a brief case to the grand jury, including just two of the many depositions describing her past malefic activities. But on the basis of sworn testimony from several accusers and Samuel Parris, the grand jury issued indictments against her for afflicting Mercy Lewis and Mary Walcott before, during, and after her May 2 examination.[58]

Cotton Mather chose to include an account of Goody Martin's trial in *Wonders of the Invisible World.* When the bewitched testified, Mather observed that "there was an extraordinary Endeavour by *Witchcrafts,* with Cruel and frequent Fits, to hinder the poor Sufferers from giving in their Complaints." The judges, he indicated, accordingly displayed "much Patience" in eliciting their testimony. To buttress those agonizingly extracted statements, the court also heard from adults who had witnessed earlier torments. Thomas Putnam, his brother Edward, and Nathaniel Ingersoll described under oath the events at Martin's May 2 examination and asserted that "we have seen the marks of sev- erall bittes and pinchs which [the afflicted] said susannah martin did hirt them with." Since no confessors had named Martin, the justices proceeded to hear the extensive maleficium evidence against her, much of it gathered the previous month by Robert Pike. Six witnesses who had deposed before Pike in Salisbury journeyed to Salem to reaffirm their testimony in person, and others appeared at the trial for the first time. For the most part, these men and women told familiar tales of mysterious appearances by Martin's specter, usu- ally at night and sometimes in animal shapes; of her muttered threats and their subsequent losses of livestock; and of a variety of negative consequences that resulted whenever they angered her.[59]

Yet Joseph Ring's story differed dramatically from the rest. Ring, a twenty-seven-year-old Salisbury resident and war veteran, described several diabolic encounters with the specter of Thomas Hardy, who carried him to "mery meeting[s]" also attended by Susannah Martin's specter. Ring owed Hardy, a man who lived on Great Island (in the middle of the Piscataqua River), a gambling debt incurred just before they left with a militia troop to try to relieve the besieged Fort Loyal at Casco Bay in May 1690. After the militia failed to save the fort's occupants from their terrible fate, Ring was repeatedly haunted by visions of Hardy, along with "a company of several other creaturs" of "hidious shapes" who made "dreadfull noyse" as they rode together on horseback along Essex County roads. Hardy "threatned to tear him in peeces," Ring told the court; and on occasion the spectral militia "did fors him away with them into unknown places where he saw meettings and festings and dancing and many strange sights." Hardy, remarked Mather, had trapped Ring in "a snare of Devillism," as demons carried him "from one *Witch-meeting* to another, for near two years together." The court and Mather focused on Goody Martin's reported presence at "several of those hellish Randezouzes," but she hovered on the periphery of Ring's account. Far more important for him were the recurrent frightening encounters with Hardy's "company" of apparitions, who, with their threat to "tear him to peeces," revealed their alliance with the same Wabanakis who had destroyed Fort Loyal. Ring's obsession with the threat the French and Indians posed to northern New England and to him personally thus manifested itself in demonic visions of the invisible world.[60]

Because it supported his case, Thomas Newton probably also introduced into evidence the report of the jury of women from June 2, which implied that Goody Martin had been sucked that day by an animal familiar. Finally, she was given a chance to defend herself. Mather reported that "her chief Plea was, *That she had led a most virtuous and holy Life*," a characterization he rejected out of hand. Instead, he pronounced her "one of the most impudent, scurrilous, wicked Creatures in the World." She was, of course, convicted.[61]

The judges then took up a case in which the outcome would have appeared considerably less certain: that of Goodwife Rebecca Nurse. Not only had her family busily collected relevant evidence both for her and against her accusers, but Rebecca herself took a significant step on her own behalf. The day before, she had petitioned the court, challenging the findings of the women's jury that examined her body earlier in the month. One of those women, she asserted, indeed the one "known to be, the Moaste Antient Skillfull prudent person of them all as to Any such Concerned," had disagreed with the others, declaring that everything she saw on Nurse's body arose from "A naturall Cause." Rebecca informed the judges that she had explained to the jurors the source of the apparent irregularity, "decending partly from an overture of Nature and difficult Exigences that hath Befallen me In the times of my Travells [childbirths]." She asked that a new women's jury be convened to reexamine her body, suggesting the names of some she deemed "Moast Grand wise and Skillfull" to participate on it. "Being Conscious of My owne Innocency," she concluded, "I Humbley Begg that I may have Liberty to Manifest it to the wourld partly by the Meanes Abovesaid." A statement from her daughters, Rebecca Preston and Mary Tarbell, probably accompanied the petition. They expressed their willingness to testify that their mother had been "trobled with an Infirmity of body for many years," which the women's jury had misinterpreted. But the court apparently did not comply with this request.[62]

The proceedings began with testimony by the afflicted and their adult supporters. Ann Jr. swore to her own torments and the sufferings she had watched Nurse's apparition inflict on others. Parris, Ingersoll, and Ann's father described under oath the events of Nurse's examination on March 24. Adults also attested to seeing on Ann's body the marks "of bite and Chane" and to finding "pins thrust into her flesh," tortures she attributed to Goody Nurse. Other witnesses probably repeated in court what they said to the grand jury on June 2: Walcott, that Nurse's specter had confessed to several murders; Abigail Williams, that she had seen the defendant's apparition "at a sacrament sitting next to [the man] with an high crowned hat, at the upper end of the Table"; Ann Sr., that Nurse's specter had tormented her repeatedly in mid-March.[63]

Some of the testimony pertained to recent troubles attributed to Goodwife Nurse. Parris and John Putnam Sr. recounted Mercy Lewis's witchfinding at Jonathan Putnam's on June 18; John Putnam Jr. and his wife Hannah described the heartrending death of their baby from "strange and violent fitts" on April 15. Deliverance Hobbs and Mary Warren would have repeated their accounts of seeing Nurse at witch meetings led by George Burroughs, revealing that she had been one of the "deacons" who distributed the bread and wine. And the widow Sarah Holton told the one classic story of malefice presented at Rebecca Nurse's trial. Sarah recalled that, following a confrontation with Goody Nurse three years earlier ("because our piggs gott into hir field"), her husband Benjamin had experienced "strange and violent fitts acting much like to our poor bewicthed parsons." After months of "languishing," he had died "a cruel death," but "the Doctor that was with him could not find what his distemper was."[64]

In contrast to earlier defendants, Rebecca Nurse must have offered more than a pro forma defense. In addition to the petition signed by thirty-nine people who declared that in all the years they had known her "we never had Any: cause or grounds to suspect her of Any such thing as she is now Acused of" and the statements impeaching the witnesses, the Nurses presented a document signed by John Putnam Sr. and his wife Rebecca, revealing their belief that their daughter Rebecca Sheppard and son-in-law John Fuller (both said by ghosts to have been killed by Goody Nurse) had died from "a malignant fever" rather than witchcraft. Nathaniel Putnam Sr., another of Sergeant Thomas Putnam's uncles, joined the petitioners in confirming Rebecca Nurse's good character. And at the trial itself new negative information emerged about one of the complainants. Sarah Nurse, Rebecca's adult daughter, declared that during the proceedings she saw Goody Vibber "pull pins out of her Close and held them betwene h[er] fingers and Claspt her hands round her knese and then she Cryed out and said goody Nurs prict her."[65]

The Nurses might also have contended that a specter could appear in the shape of an innocent person. The "Return of Several Ministers" and Samuel Willard's June 19 sermon, with their insistence that the devil could indeed create apparitions representing guiltless parties, had surely aroused considerable comment among the knowledgeable. Accordingly, it was probably during Nurse's trial (where that point was most relevant) that, Robert Calef later reported, "one of the Accusers cried out publickly of Mr. *Willard* Minister in *Boston,* as afflicting of her." Willard's sermon would have attracted the accusers' attention, given the threat it posed to the credibility of their charges.

But the judges, several of whom were members of Willard's congregation, would not entertain the accusation. "She was sent out of the Court," Calef recorded, "and it was told about she was mistaken in the person." As was true of Mistress Margaret Thacher, Samuel Willard's prominence protected him from the serious consequences of a witchcraft charge.[66]

The petty jury, returning after deliberations of unknown length, initially announced a verdict of not guilty. According to Calef, the accusers "made a hideous out-cry" when they heard the outcome, and the judges also appeared "strangely surprized." One "exprest himself not satisfied," another "said they would have her indicted anew." Then Stoughton took the matter in hand. Insisting that he "would not Impose upon the Jury," he nevertheless asked if the jurors had sufficiently considered something Goody Nurse "let slip" during her trial. When Deliverance and Abigail Hobbs came into court to testify against her, Rebecca had exclaimed, "What, do these persons give in Evidence against me now, they used to come among us." The chief judge deemed those words an implicit confession of guilt. The jurors went out to reconsider, but they could not agree on a verdict. Thomas Fiske, the foreman, asked that Goody Nurse be permitted to explain her meaning, so the jury returned to the courtroom to request clarification. But Rebecca remained silent, being (as she later indicated) "something hard of hearing, and full of grief," and so, declared Fiske, "these words were to me a principal Evidence against her." She was accordingly convicted. Until it was too late, the jury did not hear Goody Nurse's explanation that she "intended no otherways, than as they were Prisoners with us, and therefore did then, and yet do judge them not legal Evidence against their fellow Prisoners."[67]

Even after the verdict, the Nurse family did not abandon their campaign to save Rebecca. Her relatives asked Fiske for an explanation of the jury's change of heart; they elicited her own written statement of why she had not answered the crucial question; and they obtained copies of relevant court documents from Stephen Sewall. They probably presented all these materials to Governor William Phips with their request for a reprieve, which he initially granted. But, recorded Calef, "the Accusers renewed their dismal outcries against her," and "some *Salem* Gentlemen" [Hathorne? Corwin? Gedney?] then persuaded him to rescind it.[68]

Robert Calef pronounced the original verdict "remarkable," but that was so only in the context of 1692. Earlier New England juries would surely have reached the same conclusion on the basis of similar evidence. The conviction of Rebecca Nurse, not her initial acquittal, constituted the truly "remarkable" event in June 1692. In ordinary times, her status as a church member and her generally good reputation would have protected her from (for instance) anything more than sporadic gossip about her mother or quiet repetitions of Sarah Holton's suspicions about the cause of her husband Benjamin's death. Not only would Goody Nurse not have been convicted in previous decades, she most likely would never even have faced formal witchcraft charges. Moreover, in the unlikely event of a trial, she undoubtedly would have found the judges her allies, not her antagonists, for historically juries had been more eager than judges to convict suspects.[69]

What differed in 1692 was not simply William Stoughton's influential insistence that a specter could not represent an innocent person, and his consequent outspoken belief in the guilt of anyone who was so represented. Calef described two other justices as also dissatisfied with the initial verdict, and further emphasized that "some *Salem* Gentlemen" (not Stoughton, who was from Dorchester) had persuaded the governor to annul his reprieve. Goody Nurse's conviction constitutes one of the most persuasive pieces of evidence that the Massachusetts authorities in general believed unhesitatingly in the truth of the witchcraft allegations. These men, members of the council as well as judges of the Court of Oyer and Terminer, were by midsummer heavily invested in the belief that Satan lay behind the troubles then besetting their colony. And with good reason: if the devil was active in the land, how could they—mere mortals outwitted by the evil angel's many stratagems and wiles—be responsible for their failure to defend Maine and its residents adequately? Unable to defeat Satan in the forests and garrisons of the northeastern frontier, they could nevertheless attempt to do so in the Salem courtroom.

After the difficulties presented by the prosecution of Rebecca Nurse, Thomas Newton and the justices and jurors were probably relieved to turn to the case of Elizabeth Jackson Howe of Topsfield, who had been formally accused and examined in late May. On Thursday, June 30, both the grand and petty juries heard testimony against Goody Howe, much of which involved charges of maleficium. Just as in the case of Bridget Bishop, the Salem Village afflicted played a relatively minor role in Howe's accusation and later in her trial. The two indictments charged Elizabeth Howe with afflicting Mercy Lewis and Mary Walcott, but the "sundrey other Acts of witchcraft" also encompassed within their wording constituted the bulk of the evidence against her.[70]

In *Wonders of the Invisible World*, Cotton Mather revealed that the judges employed a touch test during this trial, observing that in the "greatest Swoon" of the afflicted, "they distinguished her *Touch* from other Peoples, being thereby raised out of them." He also indicated that the "present Sufferers" had seen "Ghosts" that accused Howe of killing them. Even so, the most compelling testimony came from Howe's neighbors, detailing fears of her that went back more than a decade. The most serious charge accused Elizabeth Howe of having bewitched and murdered the young daughter of Samuel and Ruth Perley in the early 1680s. That allegation, which was widely known and discussed in many households, obstructed Goody Howe's application to join the Ipswich church and seems to have set off a wave of gossip that generated stories involving bewitched horses and beer. At the same time, however, a number of statements submitted to the court attested to Elizabeth Howe's good character; several witnesses declared that she forgave those who accused her of being a witch. The judges and jurors were not convinced; she too was found guilty.[71]

A similar case—the prosecution of a "usual suspect" in which the afflicted Villagers were only peripherally involved—was considered by the grand jury that same Thursday, then tried two days later on Saturday, July 2. Sarah Averill Wilds, another Topsfield resident, was apparently first publicly named as a witch in Abigail Hobbs's April 19 confession. Still, in front of the grand jury on June 30 both Ann Jr. and Mary Walcott swore that Goody Wilds's specter had initially afflicted them weeks before that, in early March (Ann) or early April (Mary). This time, the girls' adult supporters failed to confirm the alleged chronology. In a carefully worded statement, Thomas Putnam and Nathaniel Ingersoll swore only to the events at Sarah Wilds's April 22 examination, remarking in addition simply that they had "often" heard Mary, Ann Jr., Mercy Lewis, and Abigail Williams say "that one gooddy wilds of Topsfield did tortor them." Clearly, whatever notes the adults had made during the girls' fits did not support dating accusations of Wilds before April 19, and the adults, while still allied with the accusers, wanted to avoid taking a false oath. Mary (but not, apparently, Ann Jr.) testified at Goody Wilds's trial, perhaps because Thomas Newton feared that the younger girl had lied. Walcott's testimony might have seemed more plausible because she indicated that she had not initially been able to identify the specter she saw early in April as that of Goody Wilds.[72]

The sole surviving indictment of Sarah Wilds, for bewitching Mercy Lewis on, before, and after April 22, added "and Sundery orther Acts of Witchcraft" to embrace all the instances of maleficium recounted by Wilds's neighbors. As was indicated in chapter 4, suspicions of Wilds evidently dated from allegations spread nearly two decades earlier by Mary Reddington, the sister of John Wilds's first wife. John Hale, whom Goody Reddington consulted at the time, told the court that her story made him wonder whether Sarah had bewitched one of her stepsons. John Wilds recalled that he had

confronted Mary's husband years earlier "& told him I would arest him for
his wifes defaming of my wife but the said Reddinton desired me not to doe
it for it would but waste his Estate & that his wife would [be] done with it
in tyme." So John Wilds had not filed suit against his brother-in-law, and
tales had continued to circulate about his second wife Sarah ever since, primarily involving bewitched loads of hay and dead cattle. The jury, finding the
combination of spectral and malefic evidence convincing, rendered a guilty
verdict.[73]

The trial of Goody Wilds was the last held during the court's second session, but the grand jury heard several additional cases. On June 30, it took
testimony from witnesses against Elizabeth and John Proctor, then on July 1
it considered evidence against Martha Carrier and the next day heard from
witnesses against Dorcas Hoar. It issued two indictments against Goody
Proctor and two against her husband. On July 1 the jury indicted Carrier for
two spectral attacks, and on July 2 it also issued two true bills against Hoar.
Then the court adjourned until early August.[74]

The other justices probably returned to Boston immediately, but the three
Salem magistrates had more work to do. On that same July 2, at Thomas
Beadle's inn, they conducted two examinations, questioning Mistress Mary
Bradbury and Ann Pudeator. The seventy-seven-year-old Mistress Bradbury, originally accused on May 26, was not arrested until June 29, presumably because her husband Thomas was one of the most prominent residents
of Salisbury and an Essex County militia captain. The record of her examination has not survived, but during it Walcott, Putnam Jr., Hubbard, Vibber,
and Warren all suffered the usual torments. Ann may have instigated this
accusation, or at least been particularly fervent in pursuing it. Salisbury was
her mother's birthplace, and she later claimed to have seen a vision of her
uncle, John Carr, "in a winding sheet," informing her "that mis Bradbery had
murthered him and that his blood did Crie for venjance against her."[75]

The magistrates began their second interrogation of Ann Pudeator by
confronting her with Sarah Churchwell's claim in her June 1 confession that
Pudeator had brought her the devil's book. After Pudeator denied ever having seen Churchwell before, the magistrates moved on to another accuser,
Lieutenant Jeremiah Neal, who charged Pudeator with having killed his wife
after "often" threatening her. The afflicted had fits, with Warren being cured
when Pudeator took her wrist. Walcott insisted she had seen the examinee in
the spectral company of the recently convicted Goody Nurse. Pudeator was
then returned to jail, and Mistress Bradbury joined her.[76]

The Salem magistrates also had to deal with a new complaint. On Friday,

July 1, Thomas Putnam and his cousin John Jr. filed formal charges against Mistress Margaret Hawkes of Salem Town (formerly of Barbados) and her slave Candy for afflicting Walcott, Warren, and Putnam Jr. The record of Mistress Hawkes's interrogation on July 4 is no longer extant, but Candy's revealed that she, like other maidservants, accused her mistress of making her a witch. Asked how she effected her tortures, Candy showed the examiners two poppets, at the sight of which Warren and Deliverance and Abigail Hobbs were "greatly affrighted and fell into violent fits." All of them, Hathorne noted, "said that the black man and Mrs. Hawkes and the negro stood by the poppets or rags and pinched them, and then they were afflicted." The magistrates, accompanied by Nicholas Noyes, conducted several experiments on Candy's poppets. When part of one was burned, the afflicted complained of being burned; when the other poppet was put into water, two of the sufferers "almost choaked" and a third ran toward the river, apparently trying to drown herself. The evidence of witchcraft must have seemed clear to all who beheld the phenomena.[77]

That the brief surge of skepticism a few weeks earlier had dissipated in the wake of the court's second session is confirmed by a July 11 letter from Jacob Melijn, a Dutch merchant resident in Boston, to a friend in New York. "Throughout the countryside," Melijn wrote, "the excessive gullibility of the magistrates has caused that which the tormented or possessed people bring in against someone together with other trivial circumstances to be taken as substantially true and convincing testimony against the accused." Skeptical about the young accusers (but not about Satan's wiles), Melijn "fear[ed] too much is believed," warning of a conspiracy by "the devils and their devilish artificers, whose work it is whenever possible to seduce god's elect." Deeming the crisis "another punishment of God" visited upon New England, he described the afflicted as possibly "possessed by the Devil" (and thus potentially Satan's agents rather than people tormented by him). He told his correspondent that he had asked "Mr. Mather" (probably Increase) "for something interesting and worth reading" on the subject, but had not received anything yet. Thus he sought from his friend "a pamphlet that points out and refutes in a godly way these superstitions and mistakes." Melijn spelled out his own opinion: "it goes against the Rule of God's word, that a person can broker a contract with the Devil, the hellish enemy as it is called, and extend his chains so that they bring about at will the deaths of other innocent people, old and young, babies and the unborn, and overthrow the whole rule of God's divine providence."[78]

On July 12, William Stoughton signed a death warrant for the five women convicted by the court at its second session. Exactly a week later, on Tuesday the 19th, they were all hanged on Salem's Gallows Hill. At the execution, Calef later wrote, the Reverend Mr. Noyes urged Sarah Good to confess, telling her "she was a Witch, and she knew she was a Witch." But Good, cursing him as she once had cursed Mercy Short, called him a "lyer," insisting "I am no more a Witch than you are a Wizard, and if you take away my Life, God will give you Blood to drink."[79]

The next day, a group of John Alden's acquaintances observed a fast at his house in Boston "upon his account." Samuel Willard prayed, as did James Allen (minister of the First Church) and Joshua Scottow. Samuel Sewall read a sermon, and Cotton Mather sang "the first part" of Psalm 103, presumably the verses that praised God's many blessings, emphasized his forgiveness of sins, and declared that he "redeemeth thy life from destruction." The point was not to proclaim Alden's innocence but rather to decline to judge him guilty and instead to implore God to help him to "Learn the *Lessons*" of the "hard . . . school" to which God had allowed the devil to consign him.[80]

By mid-July, the Court of Oyer and Terminer was slowly and carefully working its way through the accumulated backlog of witchcraft cases. New complaints kept trickling in, but the executions of six convicted witches appeared to have had the desired effect, for the number of reported afflictions had been greatly reduced. The judges could reasonably have expected matters to continue in the same vein over the next few months, although they might equally have anticipated difficult decisions in the future. (Newton, after all, had chosen to prosecute first those defendants who seemed most likely to be easily convicted, primarily "usual suspects.") Yet soon the crisis took a very different turn, one that first would cause it to expand swiftly, then ultimately to collapse with nearly equivalent speed.

FRANCIS HOOKE AND CHARLES FROST (KITTERY) TO SIR WILLIAM PHIPS, JUNE 30, 1692[81]

We would not have been soe bould as to have troubled your excelency with those rude lines, but that we are constrayned to it by the late and continuall out crys of that small handfull of people yett remayning in this poore country; whos constant fears ar such as they they are in continuall expectation of being destroyed and cannot beleeve any thinge less consideringe our circumstances exept your excellency out of pure care & pitty will be pleased for to take some speedy measures to strengthen our hands agaynst the comon enemy which we expect dayly to be upon us agayne a discovery of which we have almost every day, soe as that we dare not adventure from our houses about our family concerns, but with the hazard of our lives, . . . [We] doe tak it for granted that the Indions are not farr from us; besids all we are informed that the french & Indions are sertaynly gathering into a head for to com this way on us & how soon we cannot say: all these things have put such fears on our people in each towne that they are redy to take winge.

CHAPTER SEVEN

Burroughs Their Ringleader

JULY 15–SEPTEMBER 8, 1692

E VEN THOUGH THE PACE of witchcraft accusations appeared to have slowed in mid-July, events in an Essex County port town demonstrated that the climate of fear producing those complaints had not vanished, thereby presaging the continuation of the crisis. With the memory of the assault on Wells a month earlier fresh in their minds, the people of Gloucester endured a demonic attack.

It began when the family of Ebenezer Babson heard noises around their house "almost every Night." They saw men running away and discerned voices discussing a possible assault. After moving to a nearby fortified house for safety, the Babsons and their neighbors heard men "Stamping and running, not far from the Garrison" night after night. Once Ebenezer thought he saw two Frenchmen, "one of them having a Bright Gun upon his Back, and both running at a great pace towards him"; at other times, he and others believed they spotted Indians. For more than two weeks, Gloucester militiamen had regular encounters with shadowy figures who melted away into the swamps and forests when shot at. On July 18, a troop of sixty men arrived from Ipswich to help them combat "these inexplicable Alarms," but after another week had passed the Gloucester folk concluded that the attackers were spectral rather than real. The local minister, John Emerson, maintained that "the Devil and his Agents were the cause of all the Molestation," a viewpoint with which Cotton Mather tended to concur. The "Ambushments against the Good People of Glocester," he observed, could well have been caused by "Dæmons, in the Shape of Armed Indians and Frenchmen." These incidents thus would constitute "a Prodigious piece of the Strange Descent from the Invisible World, then made upon other parts of the Country." Like

Joseph Ring of Salisbury, the residents of Gloucester found themselves surrounded by malevolent forces impossible to combat.[1]

As the invisible world was assaulting Gloucester, its manifestations also continued to appear elsewhere. One evening in mid-July in Salem Town, for example, a man thought he saw the apparition of Ann Pudeator as he walked along the street. "In a moment of time she pasid by me as swifte as if a burd flue by me," he indicated; the specter then disappeared into Pudeator's house. In Andover, Joseph Ballard, whose wife Elizabeth had been sick for several months, decided that her illness might have been caused by witchcraft. Taking a course of action followed previously by members of the Wilkins and Putnam families in similar situations, he recruited two of the afflicted Salem Villagers as witch-finders, probably returning home with them on July 14. No contemporary source clearly identifies these young women, but they most likely were Mercy Lewis and Betty Hubbard, both of whom had earlier engaged in successful witch-finding, and who are recorded as having viewed Elizabeth Ballard and having named her spectral attackers at an unspecified time. The two youthful Villagers initiated what would be the final, dramatic phase of the witchcraft crisis.[2]

THE CRISIS BROADENS

Although the surviving evidence is incomplete, the witch-finders appear to have named as Elizabeth Ballard's afflicters a seventy-two-year-old widow, Ann Foster, her forty-year-old daughter, Mary Lacey Sr., and her eighteen-year-old granddaughter, Mary Lacey Jr. When the widow Foster was examined in Salem Village over a three-day period (July 15, 16, and 18), she readily confessed her involvement with witchcraft, explaining that Martha Allen Carrier had recruited her into the diabolic ranks six years earlier. The devil had come to her several times in the shape of a bird, she disclosed, all the while promising her "prosperity," but Goody Carrier had warned that "if she would not be awitch the divill should tare her in peices and Cary her away." Foster acknowledged bewitching a hog and using poppets to kill or injure several children at Martha's request. She also admitted accompanying Carrier to a witch meeting in Salem Village about two months before. "Ther [I] did see mr Burroughs the minister who spake to them all," Ann recounted, further indicating that "she hard some of the witches say that their was three hundred & five in the whole Country, & that they would ruin that place the Vilige."[3]

After giving Foster time to reflect on this confession, the magistrates visited her at the Salem prison, where she reconfirmed her statement in the presence of John Hale. Responding to Hale's additional inquiries, she offered homely details of the spectral gathering. She had "carried Bread and Cheese in her pocket" to the Village, where she and the other Andover participants "sat down together under a tree and eat their food" before the meeting started. Goody Foster also expressed her belief that Burroughs and Carrier were planning to kill her. Because she had confessed and exposed them, she explained, their specters had appeared to her armed with "a sharp pointed iron like a spindle, but four square, and threatned to stab her to death with it." A month later, when Hale called again at the prison, Foster reiterated the same fear.[4]

On Wednesday, July 20, in a confession no longer extant, Mary Lacey Sr. admitted to four Essex County magistrates—Hathorne, Corwin, Gedney, and John Higginson, son of the Salem Town minister—that she too had attended the Salem Village witch meeting, traveling on a pole with her mother and Goody Carrier.[5] The following day, she described seeing Elizabeth Howe and Rebecca Nurse (both hanged two days earlier) and Mistress Mary Bradbury being "Baptised by the old Serpent at newburry falls" about two years previously. She also conceded that she had afflicted both Elizabeth Ballard and Timothy Swan, another Andover resident then suffering from a mysterious illness. And she disclosed that Martha Carrier's sons Richard (age eighteen) and Andrew (age sixteen) were numbered among the local witches.

Of the three related women, the most voluble confessor proved to be Mary Lacey Jr., who offered the magistrates considerable detail about local diabolic activities. The teenager acknowledged that she had afflicted Goody Ballard and Goodman Swan, and that she rode on a pole to the Village witch meeting, where she recognized George Burroughs and saw Satan as "a black man" with "a high crowned hat." The devil, she indicated, had exhorted them all to "make more witches if we can & says if we will not make other persons sett there hand to the Book he will tear us in peaces." She agreed with her mother that Andrew and Richard Carrier were involved in bewitching others. Richard, she disclosed, had attended the Village meetings with her. Because Andrew Carrier had been beaten by his master, he and his brother were currently afflicting his master's child.

"Why would they hurt the Village people?" the magistrates asked Mary. "The Divill would sett up his Kingdome their & we should have happy days," the girl replied, going on to describe the devil's sacrament at the Village. (She had some difficulty with the color of the bread, at first calling it "brownish," but later adding, probably in response to an unrecorded leading question, that some of it "look't of a Reddish Color.") The justices took the opportunity of having a willing witness to inquire about a number of matters that concerned them, some specific and some general. How many people had Martha Carrier bewitched to death? Mary readily named seven—men, women, children. How had Goody Carrier killed them? "She Stabbed them to the hart with pinns needles & knitting needles," both "on there bodye[s]" and through the use of poppets, the confessor explained. "Doe you hear the Divel hurts in the Shap of any person without there consents?" the magistrates asked, responding to the concerns expressed the previous month by Samuel Willard and other clergymen. "No," Mary replied, obligingly. "When any person Striks with a Sword or Staf at a Spirit or Spector will that hurt the body?" "Yes," came the answer, equally obliging, and with it the further information that both her mother and her grandmother had been injured in that manner in the Village in recent months.

The magistrates, not surprisingly, expressed particular interest in George Burroughs and Martha Carrier. "Goody Carrier told me the Divell Said to her she should be a Queen in hell," Mary revealed. And who would be king? the justices inquired. "The Minister," the teenager replied. "What kind of Man Is Mr Burroughs?" Why, "a pretty little man and he has Come to Us Somtimes In his Spiritt in the Shape of a Catt & I think somtimes In his proper Shape."

Mary Warren, present and afflicted during the examination, took the confessor's hand without being hurt after she finished. "Mary Lacey did Ernestly ask Mary Warren Forgiveness for afflicting of her and both fell a weeping Together," recorded the note-taker, describing what he must have thought an affecting scene. The magistrates then brought in Goody Lacey, whose daughter urged her to "repent and Cal upon God," and finally Ann Foster, whom they accused of not being sufficiently forthcoming in her confessions thus far. She quickly supplied more useful information, confirming several of the deaths that her granddaughter had attributed to Martha Carrier. She further disclosed that Mary Allen Toothaker and her daughter, Martha Emerson, had attended the malefic gathering in Salem Village, where the Laceys and Foster had all signed the devil's book, using a pen and red ink "like blood." After Warren, in a fit, "Cried out Upon Richard Carrier," the magistrates issued a warrant to arrest him and his brother.[6]

When they interrogated the Carriers on July 21 and 22, the justices at first found them uncooperative.[7] Even though the Laceys, mother and daughter, confronted the young men, accusing them of assisting in the torture of Timothy Swan because of "Mrs. Bradberys account or quarrel She had with him," and urging them to confess, Richard in particular was "Verry Obstinate." But after the afflicted were "Grevously tormented," the magistrates ordered Richard and Andrew carried into another room and bound "feet & hands." When Richard returned "a Little while after," he proved far more forthcoming. Readily describing Satan as a black man with a high-crowned hat, he admitted signing the devil's "little Red" book by making a red mark in it and watching his brother do likewise (with their mother looking on). He had given Satan permission to afflict both Goody Ballard and Goodman Swan in his shape, and twice he had attended witch meetings in Samuel Parris's pasture. "I heard Sarah Good talk of a minister or two," Richard revealed; "one of them was he that had ben at the Estward & preached once at the Village, his name Is Burroughs and he Is a little man." Among the others at the meeting were his uncle Roger Toothaker, who had died in prison in June, his aunt Mary, and his cousin Martha.

Asked to name additional attendees, Richard Carrier replied with a much longer list of participants than Goody Foster, her daughter or granddaughter, or his brother Andrew could supply. As someone who had undoubtedly visited his mother in jail during the nearly two months she had been imprisoned, he knew the names of other suspects, some of whom he had surely encountered in person. And so he identified many witches for the magistrates, including some who had been executed (Nurse, Howe, Bishop, Wilds) and some awaiting trial (Willard, the Proctors, the Coreys, Bradbury). He acknowledged having afflicted three people in Salem Village: Williams, Walcott, and Parris's wife, Elizabeth. When Satan baptized him at Newbury Falls, the others with him included Nurse, Howe, and Bradbury. Goody Nurse had "handed the bread about" at the devil's sacrament, where he drank the wine but did not eat. "The Divel told them they Should over Come & Prevail" when they signed his book, Richard declared. "The Ingagement was to afflict persons & over Come the Kingdome of Christ, & set up the Divels Kingdome & we were to have hapy Days."

Just a day later, John Proctor and other (unnamed) imprisoned suspects wrote from the Salem jail to a group of Boston clergymen, charging that Richard and Andrew Carrier had been tortured to make them confess. The petitioners informed Increase Mather, Samuel Willard, James Allen, John Bailey (Allen's assistant), and Joshua Moodey that the young men had been "tyed . . . Neck and Heels till the Blood was ready to come out of their Noses," and that Proctor's son William had earlier received the same treatment. Such actions, they charged, resembled "Popish Cruelties." The judges, accusers, and jury had "Condemned us already before our Tryals, being so much incensed and engaged against us by the Devil." They begged the ministers to attend their upcoming trials, "hoping thereby you may be the means of saving the shedding our Innocent Bloods."[8]

How the five recipients of this missive responded is unknown. Samuel Willard had continued to preach his sermon cycle on 1 Peter 5:8 during July, but without the explicit references to the witchcraft crisis evident in his sermon of June 19. Instead, he phrased the later homilies generally, presenting his message in purely spiritual terms. Possibly the mid-June sermon aroused so much controversy he thereafter deliberately toned down his words and his actions, or perhaps he feared that another witchcraft accusation directed at him would not so immediately be rejected by the judges. If anyone took positive steps, it might well have been the Reverend Joshua Moodey. Himself a former resident of New Hampshire who had once been unlawfully imprisoned, and with a wife rumored to have been named as a witch in June, Moodey was probably the most likely of the group to sympathize with the prisoners' plight. Indeed, he reportedly soon intervened in another case, as shall be seen shortly.[9]

The jailed petitioners also asked the ministers to endorse their "Humble Petition" to Governor William Phips. In that separate document, which no longer survives, they evidently asked to be tried in Boston, or alternatively "to have these Magistrates changed, and others in their rooms." Knowing that Sir William had initially reprieved Rebecca Nurse (although he subsequently rescinded that action), they perhaps thought he would react positively to their complaints of mistreatment and their request for a change of venue or at least for different judges. But Governor Phips failed either to alter the composition of the court or to move the trials.[10]

The extent of the governor's support for the trials has not been fully appreciated, because historians, misled by Phips's subsequent attempts to distance himself from the proceedings, have erroneously believed that he spent most of the summer of 1692 in Maine. Yet surviving council minutes prove that Phips met regularly throughout June and July with the judges of the Court of Oyer and Terminer. Not every judge attended every council meeting, but Stoughton, Sewall, Winthrop, Richards, and Sergeant usually participated, and occasionally Gedney, Corwin, and Hathorne showed up as well. Therefore, Sir William must have been well informed about the progress of the witchcraft trials. For instance, at the July 4 council meeting (attended by Phips, Stoughton, Sewall, Winthrop, and Sergeant) the governor undoubtedly received a full report on the just-concluded second session of the court, and at the July 25 or 26 council meeting the same men, plus Richards, certainly discussed the prisoners' July 23 petition. The futility of that plea for help becomes evident when one realizes that the men passing judgment on it were the judges and their council colleagues.[11]

To conclude that the governor and his councilors did *not* discuss the trials at such sessions would be to believe in a highly improbable, if not wholly impossible, absence of communication on a subject of pressing importance to everyone. That Phips, initially sympathetic to the request for a reprieve for Rebecca Nurse, wilted under pressure from the "Salem gentlemen," and that he took no action in response to the Proctor petition, suggests his heavy reliance on his advisory council and his support for the Court of Oyer and Terminer's conduct of the witchcraft prosecutions. The governor further demonstrated his complicity in the trials by perpetuating the same official silence about the crisis he had initiated in May. On July 21, Sir William Phips wrote to London without mentioning the trials or the unprecedented group execution of five women for witchcraft just two days before.[12]

John Proctor and his fellow prisoners were not the only alleged witches who reacted to the outcome of the court's second session by seeking changes in their circumstances. Nathaniel Cary, whose wife Elizabeth had been jailed since late May, attended the trials in Salem, "to see how things were there managed." When he saw that "Spectre-Evidence was there received, together with Idle, if not malicious Stories, against Peoples Lives," he determined to take action. Enlisting others to help, he first petitioned William Stoughton to move his wife's trial to their own Middlesex County. When that effort failed, he organized her successful escape on July 30, probably by bribing the Cambridge jailer. She traveled first to Rhode Island, where she eventually realized she was not safe from pursuit, and so she moved on to New York. In October her husband joined her, and that colony's new governor, Benjamin Fletcher, was reportedly "very courteous" to them both.[13]

Philip and Mary English too fled from confinement at about the same time. Unlike Mistress Cary, they had not been jailed in chains but instead had been allowed to post bail and to have some freedom of movement in Boston as long as they stayed in the prison each night. The oral history handed down in their family implicated Samuel Willard and especially Joshua Moodey in their escape. One of their descendants reported that after inviting the Englishes to attend services at Old South, Moodey had preached on Matthew 10:23, "If they persecute you in one city, flee to another." Later, he reputedly called on the couple in the Boston prison to ensure that they had grasped his meaning, informing them that he had "persuaded several worthy Persons in Boston, to make Provision for their Conveyance out of the Colony." They took the opportunity thus offered, and—leaving two young daughters behind in Boston to board with friends—the Englishes ended up in New York, where, like the Carys, they were said to have been received warmly by the governor and other wealthy residents of the city.[14]

While Elizabeth Cary and Philip and Mary English were deciding to travel south, Sir William Phips was at last preparing to sail to the northeast. In his letter to London of July 21, he explained that he planned "landing Some Forces behind them [the Wabanakis], and [to] attaque them at the Same time by land." His primary goal was to construct a new fort at Pemaquid in an attempt to reestablish a permanent Anglo-American presence on the northern Maine coast. In late July and early August, Phips delegated parts of his authority to Winthrop and Stoughton, making arrangements for civil and military governance in his absence. He also named a replacement for Thomas Newton, who resigned his post as attorney general after the completion of the court's second session. The new prosecutor for the witchcraft trials (who would serve for the duration of the Court of Oyer and Terminer and under its successor body as well) was Anthony Checkley, another trained English lawyer, who had lived in Boston for nearly three decades.[15]

At the end of the month in Salem, Gedney, Hathorne, Corwin, and Higginson pursued the leads given them by the Foster-Laceys and the Carriers, ordering the arrest of Martha Emerson of Haverhill and her mother, Mary Toothaker of Billerica. They also issued warrants for three other women charged with afflicting Elizabeth Ballard and Timothy Swan, most notably Mary Tyler Post Bridges of Andover. Goody Bridges confessed, as did, at least partially and initially, Martha Emerson. She conceded, as her father, Roger Toothaker, had claimed months earlier, that she had kept "a womans urin: in a glass" as a form of countermagic. Martha also identified her aunt and namesake, Martha Carrier, as a fellow witch. Yet Martha Emerson "after ward" (it is not clear how soon) recanted this statement, declaring that "what she had said was in hopes to have favour: & now she could not Deny god: that had keept her from that sin: & after said though he slay me I will trust in him."[16]

Questioned on July 30, Martha's mother, Mary Allen Toothaker, offered a more complete confession that highlighted some of the complex links between the witchcraft crisis and the Second Indian War.[17] "This May last," she told the four Essex magistrates, "she was under great Discontentedness & troubled with feare about the Indians, & used often to dream of fighting with them." After acknowledging that she had afflicted Swan and unnamed others, Goody Toothaker revealed that "the Devil appeared to her in the shape of a Tawny man and promised to keep her from the Indians and she should have happy dayes with her sone," who had been wounded in the war. Asked if she had signed the devil's book, she answered that "he brought something which she [took] to be a piece of burch bark and she made a mark with her finger by rubbing off the whit Scurff. And he promised if she would serve him she should be safe from the Indians." Was she supposed to serve Satan? the magistrates asked. Yes, she replied; she was "to praise him with her whole heart, and twas to that appearance she prayed at all tymes for he said he was able to delyver her from the Indians And it was the feare of the Indians that put her upon it."

Thus the devil, himself appearing in the shape of an Indian and bringing her (appropriately) a piece of birch bark for her "signature," won Goody Toothaker's allegiance by promising to protect her from the Wabanakis. Her covenant with the "tawny" Satan superficially appears paradoxical, but if the evil angel himself commanded the Indians, his visible-world counterparts and allies, the agreement made perfect sense. Certainly it did to her.

Twice, Goody Toothaker declared, she attended spectral assemblies in Salem Village, along with her sister, her nephews Richard and Andrew Carrier, the Foster-Laceys, Mary Bridges, Elizabeth Howe, and others. There, she heard "the Beating of a drum" and "the sound of a trumpet," both necessary for the mustering of a malevolent witch militia to assault New England. "There was a minister a litle man whose name is Burroughs that preached at the Village meeting of witches," where "they did talk of 305 witches in the country," Mary revealed, confirming the numbers originally supplied by Ann Foster two weeks earlier. "Their discourse was about the pulling down the Kingdom of Christ and setting up the Kingdom of satan." After "several afflicted persons" indicated that they saw "the black man" with her, she agreed that he was present at the examination. The magistrates also inquired about the "woman that stirred them up to afflict Swan [Mary Bradbury]" and about Martha Emerson's involvement in witchcraft. Goody Toothaker agreed that an (unidentified) older woman was "most busie about [Swan] and encouraged the rest to afflict him," but she resisted implicating her daughter. "She never knew her daughter to be in this condition before this summer," Mary insisted, noting that Martha had once attended a gathering at the Village with her, but that she had not seen her sign the book there, although "a great many did."

Because Mary Toothaker confessed to being a witch on July 30, she was in jail in Salem two days later on August 1, when a small party of Indians attacked her neighborhood in Billerica. All the occupants of two households near hers were killed. Had she been home, she too would probably have died.

Upon hearing the news, she undoubtedly concluded that Satan had fulfilled his promise to "delyver her from the Indians." Perhaps that was why she never retracted her confession.[18]

THE COURT'S THIRD SESSION (1)

In early August, Cotton Mather exclaimed to a relative, "Our good God is working of miracles." After the execution of five witches who "impudently" proclaimed their innocence, he exulted, "our God miraculously sent in five Andover witches, who made a most ample, surprising, amazing confession of all their villainies, and declared the five newly executed to have been of their company." Even more important, all had concurred on "Burroughs being their ringleader." Since "other confessors . . . come in daily," they could now look forward to "a prospect of a hopeful issue" of "this prodigious matter."[19]

Whether the judges and jurors of the Court of Oyer and Terminer shared Mather's optimism during that first week of August is unknown. He could speak theoretically, but they had to deal with the realities of grand-jury sessions and trials. During the court's third session, which convened on Tuesday, August 2, and lasted four days, the grand jury issued indictments in four cases (two of which were also tried) and the petty jury or juries adjudicated six. The exact dates of four of the trials—those of John Willard, George Jacobs Sr., and John and Elizabeth Proctor—went unrecorded. Martha Carrier (who had been indicted on July 1) faced the judges on August 2 and 3, at the beginning of the session, and George Burroughs did so on August 5, at its end; the other cases fell in the middle. The grand jury heard testimony against Burroughs on August 3; against Mary Easty that day and the next; and against Jacobs and Martha Corey on the fourth. It indicted Goody Easty for bewitching Mercy Lewis and Betty Hubbard on May 23 during her second examination, and indicted Goody Corey for attacking the same two sufferers on March 21, during her examination. Both women then had to wait until September for their trials.[20]

Cotton Mather's account of Martha Carrier's prosecution, in which he memorably referred to her as "this Rampant Hag," revealed that it followed the standard pattern. The bewitched orally described being tormented by her specter, and their adult supporters attested to the sufferings at Carrier's examination on May 31. Indeed, Thomas Putnam and his cousin John Jr. swore that "had not the Honored Majestrats commanded hir to be bound [at that time] we ware redy to think she would quickly have kiled sum of them." Hubbard and Walcott, those Carrier had been indicted for afflicting, both formally testified that she had tortured not only them but also Mercy Lewis,

Abigail Williams, and Ann Putnam Jr. An Andover twelve-year-old, Phoebe Chandler, described recent torments she had endured, which she attributed to Martha Carrier and her son Richard. The very phenomena evident at Carrier's examination, Mather reported, "were also now seen upon her Tryal," and her alleged indifference to the sufferings of the afflicted also became an issue. In the courtroom, a witness recalled a relevant conversation with Goody Carrier the previous spring. Informed that her specter had been seen outside Ingersoll's inn by a "maide" whose neck was "twisted . . . almost round," she had replied callously, "it is no matter if hir nicke had ben quite of[f] if she sayd I was thiere."[21]

Although neighbors and her nephew, Allen Toothaker, told tales of her malefice, statements by the Andover confessors seemed to carry the most weight at Carrier's trial. Mather noted that Ann Foster and the two Laceys testified that they had attended witch meetings with her, one a diabolic sacrament and a second "Bodily," not spectral. Although her sons Richard and Andrew had both implicated her, Mather indicated, "this Evidence was not produced . . . , inasmuch as there was other Evidence enough to proceed upon." In the courtroom, Susannah Sheldon once again "had her hands Unaccountably ty'd together," a feat which she said Martha Carrier's specter had effected. How, or even whether, Martha Carrier tried to defend herself against such a varied onslaught is not recorded, and she must have been easily convicted.[22]

John Willard had been indicted in early June for bewitching four of the afflicted (Lewis, Putnam Jr., Williams, and Hubbard) at his May 18 examination. Significantly, however, the grand jury at the same time declined to charge him with the concurrent affliction of Sheldon, whose excessive antics and disturbing visions could well have called her credibility into question. Yet Ann Jr. was found believable despite her youth: she testified to both the grand and petty juries about her visions of Willard from late April through mid-May. Ann Carr Putnam probably reaffirmed her sworn statement of June 2 about the many ghosts who claimed that Willard had killed them. The clerk's notations reveal that once again Samuel Parris, Thomas Putnam, and Nathaniel Ingersoll supported the young accusers in court. And Sarah Vibber swore to seeing Willard's apparition torment Lewis and Walcott on May 17 as well as to her own sufferings at his hands.[23]

A significant proportion of the testimony pertained to Willard's spectral attacks on his Wilkins relatives, especially his wife's deceased second cousin, Daniel, and her ailing grandfather, Bray. The coroner's jury, Parris, and Daniel's relatives all concluded that the young man had died as a result of Willard's malefice, and evidence to that effect was presented in court.

Daniel's father, for example, described how Ann Jr., Mercy, and Mary Walcott had seen Willard's apparition assaulting Daniel. Other Wilkins family members, including Bray himself, also attested to the torments Willard had visited upon the older man. And there was more: witnesses described Willard's physical abuse of his wife and the "strange" events (including "hideous noyse") that appeared to follow when she voiced complaints about his treatment of her. They in addition attributed recent sufferings to his malefice. Rebecca Wilkins (Daniel's sister) attested that the previous week "shee se John wilard seting in the Corner and hee said that hee wold afflick me that night and forthwith hee did afflick me"; Samuel Wilkins (cousin of Rebecca and Daniel) described a series of mysterious occurrences a month earlier that culminated in Willard's appearance one night in his bedroom accompanied by other specters, warning that "they would cary me away before morning."[24]

Confessors too contributed to Willard's conviction. Richard Carrier, who on July 22 had named Willard as a participant in a Salem Village witch meeting and had accurately described him as "a black hared Man of a Midle Statture," must have repeated that story in court. A list of witnesses prepared for the trial indicated that Margaret Jacobs and Sarah Churchwell appeared to describe how he "diswaded [them] from confession," though whether spectrally or in person is not clear. Whatever defense Willard offered was not recorded.[25]

Also indicted earlier (on June 30) but tried at this session of the court were John and Elizabeth Proctor. Elizabeth was charged with tormenting Lewis and Walcott on April 11 during her examination, and John with afflicting Lewis at that same time. (The grand jury declined to indict him for afflicting Walcott, however; they must have found that evidence inadequate.) John was also indicted for torturing Warren on March 26, but no account of that spectral assault has survived. In general, the same witnesses appeared against both Proctors. The afflicted and their adult supporters repeated the usual stories of torment, and the witch-finding episode at James Holton's house in late May was described at some length. The teenager Elizabeth Booth took an especially active role against her neighbors the Proctors, swearing to having been tortured by their apparitions and probably attesting orally to her detailed statement (sworn before the grand jury) listing the ghosts that had appeared to her on June 8 to accuse both Proctors of killing them.[26]

Confessors who had named the Proctors—Deliverance and Abigail Hobbs, Richard Carrier, and especially Mary Warren—would have recounted in court their stories of the couple's attendance at witch meetings. Warren, guided by Checkley, most likely reiterated that John Proctor had brought her the devil's book to sign and that his wife had given her poppets representing the afflicted. She surely described the occasion on which Elizabeth Proctor had called herself a "deacon" at a diabolic sacrament. In addition to such testimony, new allegations emerged at the trial. Elizabeth's teenage nephew John DeRich (whose mother Mary had also been accused of witchcraft) charged that his aunt, uncle, and three of his cousins "did all afflict this deponent and do continually every day" and that they "would have him . . . to sett his hand to a Booke."[27]

Against such an array of accusations the Proctors probably offered a defense centered on two petitions signed by acquaintances and on the arguments made in John Proctor's earlier plea for help to the Boston clergymen.[28] One of the petitions, with twenty signatures from both men and women, stated simply that the subscribers "never heard or understood that [the Proctors] were ever suspected to be guilty of the crime now charged apon them" and that they had led a "christian life in their famely and were ever ready to helpe such as stood in need."

The second, more elaborate, directly addressed the crucial question of whether God permitted Satan "to personate, Dissemble, & therby abuse Inocants." The thirty-one male signers indicated that they thought such an outcome might "be A Method within the Seveerer But Just Transaction of the Infinite Majestie of God." Admitting that they could not "Go into Gods pavillions Cloathed with Cloudes of Darknesse Round About," so they could not know why God had allowed this terrible judgment to happen to the Proctors, they nevertheless asserted that "as to what we have ever seen, or heard of them—upon our Consciences we Judge them Innocent of the crime objected." The court disregarded such contentions and convicted both Proctors, but Elizabeth pleaded that she was pregnant, which led to her being temporarily reprieved.

The case of George Jacobs Sr. was considered by the grand jury on August 4 and probably by the petty jury that same day. The grand jury issued a true bill against him for afflicting Walcott on May 11, but rejected a companion indictment for bewitching Lewis. Hubbard, Walcott, Putnam Jr., and the confessors Warren and Churchwell all swore at the trial that Jacobs's specter had tormented them and that they had seen him attack others as well. John DeRich described how Jacobs's apparition had "Knockt me downe with his stafe" and had tried to drown him because "I would not Sett mi hand to his boocke." Sarah Vibber's testimony must have caused a sensation; she attested under oath that "she Saw him this George Jacobs at the Gallows when Goody Olliver [Bishop] was executed & the black man help him up." Jacobs's own granddaughter Margaret, another confessor, accused him of being a witch, testimony supported by Joseph Flint's recollection of his May 11 conversation with the old man about Margaret's confession. Finally, the marshal, George Herrick, and a men's jury reported on examinations of George Jacobs's body. They had located what seemed to be witch's teats, because he could not feel any sensation when they inserted pins through the suspect spots. Again, the jury rendered a guilty verdict.[29]

THE COURT'S THIRD SESSION (2): THE TRIAL OF GEORGE BURROUGHS

The grand jury considered the case of George Burroughs on Wednesday, August 3. For the purpose of obtaining indictments, Anthony Checkley appears to have focused almost exclusively on the same evidence that had been presented by Thomas Newton at the clergyman's May 9 examination, along with a few additions.[30] Ann Jr. recalled her visions of Burroughs on April 20 and May 5, repeating what his specter had confessed about his actions in Maine and the deaths of his wives and Deodat Lawson's family. She then reported that that very morning she had seen the ghosts of "Mis Lawson and hir daughter Ann," who had "tould me that Mr Burroughs murthered them." Earlier today, too, she had seen the ghost of "goodman fullers first wife," who explained that the minister had killed her "because there was sum differance between hir husband and him." Several adults from both inside and outside the Putnam family attested that they witnessed one or more of these visions, and that Ann had described to them "what she said she saw and hard from the Apperishtion of Mr. George Burroghs and from thos which acc[used him] for murthering of them."

Hubbard, Walcott, and Vibber testified again about their sightings of the clergyman's apparition before his May 9 examination. Mercy Lewis repeated her tales of Burroughs insisting that she sign his "new fashon book" and his offering her "all the kingdoms of the earth" if she would only do so, confiding as well that "he tould me I should not see his Two wifes if he could help it because I should not witnes against him." And Mercy was clearly eager to "witness against" her former employer. When, at the same grand-jury hearing, Elizar Keyser described the strange lights that had materialized in his chimney on May 5 after his encounter with the imprisoned Burroughs at Beadle's tavern, Mercy jumped in, interjecting, "Mr Borroughs: told her: that he made lights: in Mr Keyzers chimny."

Perhaps the most important new testimony came from Mary Warren, who depicted for the grand jury a spectral encounter with the minister the previous month. After choking her "almost to death," she revealed, Burroughs's apparition "sound[ed] a Trumpett and Immediatly I saw severall com to him as namely Capt Allding Mis Cary and gooddy pudeator." (Thus two high-status witches, one still in jail and one now at large, had readily responded to Burroughs's signal, making it absolutely clear that he was their leader.) All the specters "urged me to goe along with them to their sacremental meeting and mr Burroughs brought to me bread to eat and wine to drink which I refuseing he did most greviously torment me," Mary added. After hearing such accounts and two pieces of evidence about Burroughs in Maine, the grand jury issued four indictments, charging him having afflicted Betty Hubbard, Mercy Lewis, Ann Putnam Jr., and Mary Walcott on the day of his examination and "Divers other Dayes and times, as well before as after." His victims had been "Tortured afflicted Pined Consumed wasted and Tormented," the grand jury declared, and he had also committed "Sundrey other Acts of Witchcraft."[31]

Two days later, on Friday, August 5, the judges took up what everyone recognized was *the* crucial case in the witchcraft crisis. A "vast concourse of people," including Increase Mather, Deodat Lawson, John Hale, and perhaps Governor William Phips himself, traveled to Salem to attend the trial of the man who (as Cotton Mather put it) "had the promise of being a King in Satan's Kingdom, now going to be Erected." The first official part of the proceedings the spectators would have witnessed was Burroughs's vigorous exercise of the right to reject jurors seated in his case. He used "his liberty in challenging many," Lawson recalled twelve years later.[32]

Cotton Mather took particular care in following the governor's orders to chronicle Burroughs's trial in *Wonders of the Invisible World.* His summary of the evidence was both comprehensive and accurate (judging by the surviving documents), and his narrative supplies details of the proceedings available nowhere else. Because he knew the book would be read by people who had attended the trial, his description of the events in the courtroom is probably generally reliable. Yet Mather's investment in supporting the verdict colored every aspect of his account, and so it must be read with an understanding of how his bias affected the story he crafted for his audience.

Recognizing that some of his readers would be skeptical about the guilt of a clergyman, and furthermore that proving Burroughs's culpability was essential to defending the trials, Mather laced his treatment of the case with references to appropriate legal and religious authorities. He also emphasized the compelling nature and overwhelming quantity of the testimony presented against the minister. Summing up the evidence at the outset of his narrative, Mather enumerated five or six bewitched people, eight confessors, and nine witnesses to the minister's "extraordinary Lifting, and such feats of Strength, as could not be done without a Diabolical Assistance." In toto, "about thirty Testimonies were brought in against him," Mather revealed, "nor were these judg'd the half of what might have been considered for his Conviction." Even so, they were sufficient "to fix the Character of a Witch upon him according to the Rules of Reasoning, by the Judicious *Gaule,* in that Case directed."[33]

As was customary, the trial began with statements by "the Parties Bewitched." By pointing out that such accounts "have a room among the *Suspicions* or *Presumptions,* brought in against one Indicted for Witchcraft," Mather indicated his familiarity with the legal arguments made by William Perkins and Richard Bernard that were discussed earlier in this book. In his summary of the oral evidence, Mather focused in particular on the testimonies that Putnam Jr., Lewis, and Warren had given to both grand and petty juries. Perhaps, too, Walcott played an important role. She was especially likely to complain of being bitten, a theme Mather stressed in his account of the trial. After the sufferers "cry'd out of *G.B.* Biting them," he claimed, "the print of the Teeth would be seen on the flesh of the Complainers, and *just* such a Set of Teeth as *G.B.'s* would then appear upon them, which could be distinguished from those of some other mens." Eliciting such testimony "cost the Court a wonderful deal of Trouble," Mather observed, because the sufferers "would for a long time be taken with Fits, that made them uncapable of saying anything." He recorded that William Stoughton asked Burroughs "who he thought hindred these Witnesses from giving their *Testimonies*?" When the defendant answered that perhaps it was the devil, Stoughton reportedly "cast him into very great Confusion" by inquiring, *"How comes the Devil so loathe to have any Testimony born against you?"*[34]

Mather also described the murdered people who appeared spectrally to the bewitched to accuse Burroughs, focusing in particular on "the Apparitions of two Women, who said, that they were *G.B.'s* two wives, and that he had been the Death of them." Burroughs, Mather indicated, "had been infamous for the Barbarous usage of his two late Wifes, all the Country over." Possibly such infamy made it less shocking when at the trial one of the bewitched "was cast into Horror at the Ghost of *B's* two Deceased Wives then appearing before him, and crying for *Vengeance* against him." At that, several others among the afflicted, who had been out of the room, were called in and "concurred in their Horror of the Apparition, which they affirmed that he had before him." The clergyman, "much appalled," denied he saw anything; and, Mather hastened to add (though unconvincingly), this vision in any event played no role in his conviction.[35]

Deodat Lawson, not surprisingly, concentrated in his account of Burroughs's trial on similar sightings of the ghosts of his own first wife and daughter, who, Lawson noted, had died more than three years before. The afflicted "did affirm, that, when the very ghosts looked on the prisoner at the bar, they looked red, as if the blood would fly out of their faces with indignation at him," Lawson recalled. The former military chaplain and Village cleric vividly depicted the scene: "several afflicted being before the prisoner at the bar, on a sudden they fixed all their eyes together on a certain place of the floor before the prisoner, neither moving their eyes nor bodies for some few minutes, nor answering to any question which was asked them." Once the group trance had ended, "some being removed out of sight and hearing, they were all, one after another, asked what they saw; and they did all agree that they saw those ghosts." Lawson, like Mather, thus disclosed that the justices had taken steps to test the visions of the afflicted by examining them separately, although the method chosen did not exclude the possibility of pre-arranged collusion.[36]

After the bewitched came the confessors. Mather stressed the significance of such testimony in the minds of "Judicious Writers," who "have assigned it a great place in the Conviction of *Witches, when Persons are Impeached by other notorious Witches, to be as ill as themselves.*" He revealed that these witnesses "confessed their own having been horrible *Witches*," adding that since their confessions they too had been "terribly Tortured by the Devils and other Witches" as a consequence. Such people attested that Burroughs had attended the witch meetings; that he had supplied them with poppets and thorns to afflict others; and that "he exhorted them with the rest of the Crew, to Bewitch all *Salem Village.*" Lawson added that the confessors described "some hundreds of the society of witches, considerable companies of whom were affirmed to muster in arms by beat of drum." Burroughs summoned them to the meetings "from all quarters . . . with the sound of a diabolical trumpet," and "did administer the sacrament of Satan to them, encouraging them to go on in their way, and they should certainly prevail." Although Mather and Lawson did not name or otherwise identify the confessors who testified against George Burroughs, the group of eight in all likelihood comprised Abigail and Deliverance Hobbs, Ann Foster and her granddaughter, Richard Carrier, Mary Toothaker, Mary Warren, and Margaret Jacobs.[37]

John Hale reported that subsequently he spoke "seriously" to one of the female confessors who had described the minister's exhortations at the Village witch meeting. "You are one that bring this man to Death, if you have charged any thing upon him that is not true, recal it before it be too late, while he is alive," Hale told her. She responded, Hale recalled, that "she had nothing to charge her self with, upon that account." Hale's own possible doubts were thus assuaged, at least for the moment.[38]

Cotton Mather reminded his readers that the witches of Lancashire had been convicted in 1612 on no other testimony than that supplied by confessors and the bewitched. But in the case of George Burroughs, much more evidence was adduced, he observed, especially documentation of his "Preternatural Strength," which was characteristic of some witches and could therefore be used to expose them. Although the minister was "very Puny," he had frequently performed acts "beyond the strength of a Giant." For example, he had held out a heavy seven-foot gun with one hand, "like a Pistol, at Armsend." He had also carried "whole Barrels fill'd with *Malasses* or *Cider*" from canoe to shore with no difficulty. To Increase Mather, at least, such tales appeared to prove Burroughs's guilt. Several persons swore at the trial, the senior Mather wrote soon afterwards, that "they saw him do such things as no man that has not a Devil to be his familiar could perform," and he accordingly declared that he too would have voted to convict his fellow cleric.[39]

These convincing stories were told at Burroughs's trial by acquaintances from Casco Bay who had known him there in the mid- to late 1680s. They—including Captain Simon Willard, the brother of Samuel Willard—primarily repeated gossip they had heard from others or even boastful statements made by the clergyman himself. For example, Captain Willard swore that in September 1689 Robert Lawrence commended Burroughs for his strength, "saying that we none of us could doe what he could doe." Lawrence then described how the cleric could hold out a heavy gun with one hand. Burroughs had concurred, showing the others how he picked up the gun, "but: I saw him not hold it out then," Willard conceded. The captain also reported that he had himself tried to hold the "very hevie" gun but could not do so for long even with both hands. Another story stemmed solely from one of Burroughs's boasts. Samuel Webber attested that when he lived at Falmouth in the mid-1680s he had "heard much of the great strength" of the minister, and so he raised the subject with Burroughs one time when the clergyman came to his house. "He then told mee that he had put his fingers into the Bung of a Barrell of Malasses and lifted it up, and carryed it Round him and sett it downe againe," Webber recounted. Burroughs's obvious pride in his unusual strength thus came back to haunt him at his trial.[40]

Not until after the minister's execution did a witness come forward who claimed to have actually *seen* Burroughs perform such feats. On September 15, Thomas Greenslade (the son of Ann Pudeator by her first marriage, perhaps seeking to win a reprieve for his mother, who had by then been convicted of witchcraft) swore that during the early fall of 1688 at Joshua Scottow's house in Black Point he had seen Burroughs both hold out a six-foot-long gun by "putting the forefinger of his right hand into the Muzle of said gunn" and carry a "full barrell of Malasses with but two fingers of one of his hands in the bung." Mather explained Greenslade's belated appearance in the Salem courtroom not by a possible desire to save his mother's life, but rather by arguing that the witness had been "over-perswaded by some Persons to be out of the way upon *G.B.'s* Tryal." Who those reputed silent allies of the clergyman might have been is unknown, but if they existed they presumably came from Maine, as did both Greenslade and Burroughs.[41]

The final set of prosecution witnesses testified about Burroughs's "Domestick Affairs," proving him to be "a very ill Man" of the poor character "which had been already fastned on him," Mather remarked. He summarized a group of testimonies about the clergyman's "harsh Dealings" with his first wife in Salem Village and his second there and in Falmouth. The witnesses ranged from John Putnam Sr. and his wife Rebecca to former neighbors and a servant from Casco. Hannah Burroughs and her husband had fought over his request that she "give him a written covenant under her hand and Seall that shee would never reveall his secrits," the Putnams disclosed. For her part, Sarah Ruck Hathorne Burroughs had reputedly been "affrighted" of her husband and told a neighbor she was afraid to write to tell her father how George was mistreating her. Witnesses described the widespread "common report" of strange happenings in and around the Burroughs home in Casco, such as the possible apparition of "something like a white calfe." The clergyman had also claimed that he knew what his wife was thinking and saying about him in his absence. Once, after "Chiding" Sarah for her comments about him to her brother while the siblings were riding home together alone from strawberrying, Burroughs insisted that *"My God makes known your Thoughts unto me."* Such stories certainly implied that George Burroughs was a witch, hinting at both knowledge gained through occult means and secrets that had to remain deeply hidden.[42]

All in all, Mather concluded, "never was a Prisoner more eminent" for the signs of guilt at his initial interrogation and later trial than George Burroughs. Legal experts (in this case John Gaule, although Mather did not identify him specifically) had alerted examiners to take special notice of *"faltring, faulty, unconstant, and contrary Answers"* when a suspect was questioned, and Burroughs had produced nothing but *"Tergiversations, Contradictions, and Falshoods"* in his responses. His attempts to defend himself, at least as reported by Mather, were disastrous. For example, his inability to explain the strawberrying incident suggested to the court that "by the assistance of the *Black Man,* he might put on his *Invisibility,* and in that *Fascinating Mist,* gratifie his own Jealous Humour, to hear what they said of him." Or again, when he was offering a rejoinder to the tales about the gun, he declared "that *an* Indian *was there, and held it out at the same time."* None of the witnesses, Mather indicated, "ever saw any such *Indian;* but they supposed the *Black Man,* (as the Witches call the Devil; and they generally say he resembles an *Indian*) might give him that Assistance."[43]

The clergyman also "gave in a Paper to the Jury" with a prepared argument.[44] Burroughs had previously acknowledged that witches existed and that "the present Sufferings of the Country are the effects of *horrible Witchcrafts,*" Mather reported. Yet at his trial he advanced quite a different contention, claiming that *"there neither are, nor ever were Witches, that having made a Compact with the Devil, can send a Devil to Torment other people at a distance."* The judges, indicated Mather, recognized the source of this assertion "as soon as they heard it" as a passage "Transcribed out of *Ady"*—that is, Thomas Ady's *A Candle in the Dark* (1656), republished in 1661 as *A Perfect Discovery of Witches,* which contended that contemporary English witchcraft beliefs had no scriptural basis and thus that they should be discarded.

That the court, or at least one member of it (perhaps William Stoughton?), was sufficiently familiar with the contents of Ady's volume to immediately identify a single passage drawn from a densely argued book suggests that the justices had indeed carefully studied the witchcraft literature prior to the trials. In fact, the judges knew that literature better than Burroughs did. Questioned about his "paper," the minister insisted that "he had taken none of it out of any Book." Instead, he revealed that "a Gentleman gave him the Discourse in a Manuscript from whence he Transcribed it." Thus an unidentified high-status supporter, possibly Captain Daniel King of Salem (who had previously spoken up for the clergyman), had supplied Burroughs with an argument copied from Ady's book, but he had not told the minister its origin. Burroughs's use of the passage then backfired as the court deemed his answer an "Evasion" and another one of his lies.

Although the minister had a few allies, he evidently was not able to supply the court with the same sorts of petitions as those that backed the Proctors or Rebecca Nurse. After his arrest, the residents of Wells did petition the Massachusetts government, but not on Burroughs's behalf: complaining of their "destressed Condition . . . with referanc to their Spirrituall Concerns," they merely requested "a minester to be Chaplin to the soldiers, and also minester of the Towne," not mentioning the reason why they now lacked a resident pastor. And George Burroughs himself seems to have ultimately resigned himself to his fate. According to John Hale, even though Burroughs "denied all" and said he was convicted by "false Witnesses," he in the end "justified the Judges and Jury in condemning of him; because there were so many positive witnesses against him."[45]

THE WONDERS OF THE INVISIBLE WORLD

The day before George Burroughs's trial, Cotton Mather delivered his major sermon on the witchcraft crisis, "A Discourse on the Wonders of the Invisible World," which he a few months later included in his longer eponymous volume.[46] Insisting that only those "under the Influence of the *Devil*" would deny the evil angel's existence, the younger Mather explained that "there is a sort of Arbitrary, even Military *Government,* among the *Devils.*" Likening these devils to "vast Regiments of cruel and bloody *French Dragoons,* with an *Intendant* over them, overrunning a pillaged Neighbourhood," he also linked the *"Sooty Devils"* to the *"Swarthy Indians"* whose *"Powawes,* used all their Sorceries to molest the first Planters here" and who since "have watered our Soil with the Blood of many Hundreds of our Inhabitants." And now, Mather proclaimed, "the *Devil* in *Great Wrath*" has made a "prodigious *descent*" on "our poor *New-England.*" Presenting himself usually as "a small *Black man,*" he "has decoy'd a fearful knot of proud, froward, ignorant, envious and malicious creatures, to list themselves in his horrid Service, by entring their Names in a *Book* by him tendred unto them."

After describing the sufferings of the afflicted and the claims of the confessors, Mather addressed what he termed "a most agitated Controversie among us": whether "many *innocent,* yea, and some *vertuous* persons" had been abused by the devil, who had possibly assumed their shapes to afflict others. The *"multitude* and *quality* of Persons accused of an interest in this *Witchcraft*" by the apparitions had raised doubts in the minds of "very many good and wise Men," he explained, creating a *"Snarled"* and *"dismal"* question for the judges. Quite rightly, the justices had thus far employed "the *Spectral Evidences*" to lead them to further inquiries about suspects, and they had then "by the wonderful Providence of God, been so strengthened with *other evidences,* that some of the *Witch Gang* have been fairly Executed." But what was to be done with those accused people "against whom the *evidence* is chiefly founded in the *dark world*"? Mather had posed a key question, but he offered no direct answer. Instead, he suggested that New Englanders pray for guidance for the judges, and that they reform the behavior which had brought God's wrath down upon them.

Cotton Mather thus conceded that some of the spectral identifications might be questionable, but he expressed no doubt about the validity of the confessions. Consequently, he probably watched in fascinated horror as more and more people acknowledged their involvement with Satan in the weeks that followed.

During the third session of the Court of Oyer and Terminer, afflictions,

CHART 3

Cumulative Total of New Complaints, Examinations,
and Confessions, July–September 1692

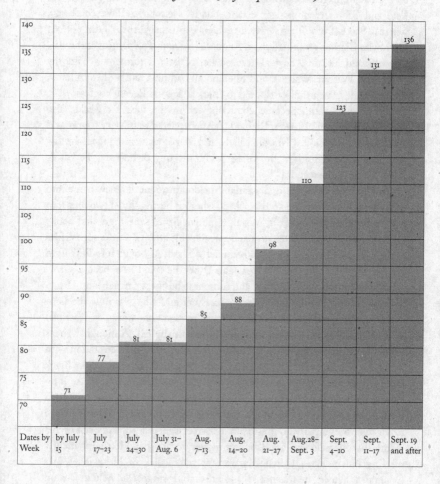

Note: Includes only incidents in which dates are known.

accusations, and examinations continued unabated. Mary Post (the twenty-eight-year-old daughter of the confessor Mary Tyler Post Bridges), Margaret Scott of Rowley, and Mary Johnson Clarke of Haverhill were all interrogated by the Salem magistrates while the trials were being conducted. Records for Post and Scott are no longer extant, but it is clear that Post confessed, whereas Scott (from other surviving evidence a "usual suspect") did not. At Goodwife Clarke's examination on August 4 in Salem Town, most of the Village afflicted had fits. Several accused her of having tormented Timothy Swan, and Warren, Walcott, and Sheldon all had pins removed from hand, arm, or neck, which they attributed to Clarke's agency. Recent confessors, in a pattern that would become commonplace in the next six weeks, also appeared at the examination. Richard Carrier declared that Mary Clarke was among those baptized at Newbury Falls, and Mary Post insisted that "she saw this mary Clarke Spirit at the village witch meeting & that she did eat & drink There as the rest did."[47]

At Clarke's examination, Susannah Sheldon introduced a new name into the proceedings when she accused "Mr. Usher" of having thrust two pins into her hand. Hezekiah Usher Jr. was a prominent Boston merchant and bookseller whose accusation later attracted considerable attention from such critics of the trials as Thomas Brattle and Samuel Willard. Although it is difficult to discern why Sheldon accused Hezekiah Usher, he could have been a surrogate for his untouchable brother and sometime business partner John Usher, who had been Sir Edmund Andros's treasurer and who was now the lieutenant governor of New Hampshire. Eleven years later he was to be described as "universally hated" in the province he nominally led. Although Usher's actions as lieutenant governor after 1692 contributed to the detestation with which he was regarded by 1703, a girl like Susannah growing up in Black Point would surely have been familiar with the opprobrium attached to John Usher's name because of his work for the hated Andros. Hezekiah himself, a member of the Third Church, was notorious for the acrimony of his marriage to the widow of a Harvard president. The marriage, indeed, had been such a failure that his wife and her daughter by her first husband left permanently for England in 1687. Although a warrant was issued for Hezekiah Usher (when is not clear), he was not sent to prison but was instead held in Boston under house arrest.[48]

Unlike Usher, the ordinary Andover men, women, and children accused in great numbers in August were immediately questioned and then jailed. Almost all of them confessed. The spiraling circle of accusations leading to confessions leading to more accusations and more confessions began on Wednesday and Thursday, August 10 and 11, when Sarah Carrier, 8, and

Thomas Carrier Jr., 10, joined their older brothers in confessing to being witches and accusing their mother of recruiting them into Satan's ranks. Sarah admitted having been a witch for two years, identified her aunt Mary Toothaker and her cousin Martha Emerson as witches also, and revealed that the previous Saturday (August 6) she had afflicted Ann Putnam Jr. and ten-year-old Sarah Phelps of Andover, in concert with a twenty-two-year-old neighbor, Betty Johnson. Sarah denied having attended a witch meeting at the Village, but her brother indicated that he had gone to one in Andover at John Chandler's on August 9. "Their were 10 in Company with him," including Betty Johnson, he disclosed, and they had "rid upon 2 Poles." His mother, he confessed, had ordered him to afflict three victims.[49]

Betty Johnson (the niece of Mary Johnson Clarke and granddaughter of the Reverend Francis Dane of Andover), who was also interrogated on August 10 and 11, offered further details. She too had been recruited and baptized by Martha Carrier and had subsequently afflicted Phelps, Walcott, and Putnam, as well as others from Andover, including both Timothy Swan and Elizabeth Ballard. Unlike the younger Carriers, she had gone to a Village witch meeting—a "Mock Sacrement" with a "short" minister, George Burroughs. The witches there agreed "to afflict folk: & to pull downe the kingdom of Christ & to sett up the devils kingdom." Among the more than seventy other witches at this meeting were Mary Toothaker and her daughter, Goody Carrier, and Captain John Floyd. Indeed, she indicated that the specters of those four witches were attending her examination, "threaten[ing] to tere her to peices" for confessing. Bringing out three poppets, two made of "rags or stripes of clothe" and the other of "birch Rhine," she helpfully demonstrated how she had employed them to torture her many victims. She also showed the magistrates (and a group of women) where her familiar sucked her. Betty listed not only two earlier confessors as fellow witches, but also someone new: Daniel Eames of Boxford.[50]

That Thursday, the magistrates also questioned another of Betty Johnson's aunts, the forty-year-old Abigail Dane Faulkner (Abigail's sister, Elizabeth Dane Johnson, was Betty's mother). Goody Faulkner refused to confess though urged to do so by her niece, and even though four young people were all tormented in her presence, then "Helped up out of their fitts" by her touch. When she was seen squeezing a cloth, the afflicted declared that "Daniell Eames & Capt Floyd was upon that cloth when it was upon the table." Goody Faulkner ventured a defense—"she said she had looked on some of these afflicted: when they came to Andover & hurt them not"—but it went nowhere: "she was told it was before she had begun to afflict them." Daniel Eames, 28, interrogated two days later, was equally unwilling to con-

fess, despite apparently inflicting tortures on three sufferers and being implicated by three confessors. He insisted that when Mary Toothaker came to
him in a dream he had resisted her enticement "to signe to Sattan." At his
examination the confessor Mary Post declined to name him as a witch,
instead listing Margaret Scott and Rebecca Nurse as among the members of
"her company." By including them, she, like Betty Johnson (who had named
Burroughs and Floyd), revealed her knowledge of events beyond the borders
of Andover.[51]

On Friday, August 19, after a quiescent week during which only two afflictions had been recorded and two new complaints filed, the four men and one
woman convicted at the third session of the court were hanged together in
Salem.[52] Just as people thronged the trial of George Burroughs, so many
seem to have attended his execution, Thomas Brattle probably among them.
Brattle wrote that "in the opinion of many unprejudiced, considerate and
considerable spectatours, some of the condemned went out of the world not
only with as great protestations, but also with as good shews of innocency, as
men could do." Singling out John Proctor and John Willard for special praise
for their "whole management of themselves," Brattle recounted how the convicted "forgave their accusers" and "spake without reflection on Jury and
Judges" while praying "earnestly for pardon for all other sins." All in all, he
observed, they "seemed to be very sincere, upright, and sensible of their circumstances on all accounts."

Robert Calef focused his account on Burroughs, who, he said, "made a
Speech for the clearing of his Innocency, with such Solemn and Serious
Expressions, as were to the Admiration of all Present." Burroughs concluded
by perfectly reciting the Lord's Prayer, which "drew Tears from many" and
raised fears that "the Spectators would hinder the Execution." But, Calef
recorded, as soon as Burroughs was "turned off" [hanged], Cotton Mather
exhorted the crowd from horseback, reminding them that Burroughs was "no
ordained Minister," and pointing out that "the Devil has often been transformed into an Angel of Light." This "did somewhat appease the People,"
Calef commented, and so the executions continued.

After the death of George Burroughs, two stories circulated about events
that had occurred the day before his execution. Margaret Jacobs, it was said,
went to him, acknowledging that she had lied when she accused him and her
grandfather. She begged Burroughs to forgive her, and he not only complied,
but then prayed "with and for her." The other tale was less benign. Several
women who later confessed to being witches revealed that on the night of
August 18 "there was a great meeting of the witches Nigh Sarjent Chandlers"
where the minister "exhorted" them. They participated in a sacrament, and

after they had finished Burroughs doffed his hat, "tooke leave & bid them Stand to their faith, & not own any thing." When one man said he "hoped he should see him again," Burroughs had replied that he "thout not." Despite that reported response, Burroughs's death did not remove him from his position as the reputed leader of the witches, for confessors continued to name him in the coming weeks.[53]

And afflictions continued as well, in Salem Village as well as in Andover. For example, shortly after the August executions the wife of the Villager Benjamin Hutchinson suffered severe torments. "She being in such excessive mesiry she said she beleved that she had an evell hand upon hir," Hutchinson later reported. Therefore he consulted Mary Walcott, "one of our next neighbors," asking her to "come and look to se if she could se any body upon hir." Walcott immediately identified the jailed Villagers Sarah Buckley and her daughter Mary Witheridge as Goody Hutchinson's tormentors, and she just as quickly was tortured herself, while Benjamin's wife improved. Hutchinson then went to the sheriff to request that he "take sume course with thos women that they might not have souch power to torment." George Corwin ordered Buckley and Witheridge to be chained, after which—Benjamin declared—Goody Hutchinson became "tolorable well."[54]

Also following the executions, the Salem magistrates questioned Rebecca Blake Eames of Boxford, Daniel Eames's fifty-one-year-old mother. They elicited a confession from her, but they must have found its lack of detail unsatisfactory, except for its admission that her son, too, was a witch. In sharp contrast were the confessions they obtained on August 25 and subsequently, after a group of three young female residents of Andover began complaining of torments that echoed those of the Salem Village afflicted. The fits appear to have begun on Saturday, August 20, and in the flood of confessions that resulted the magistrates must have thought they were finally uncovering the full extent of the conspiracy against New England.[55]

The first to be afflicted seems to have been sixteen-year-old Martha Sprague (occasionally referred to as "alias Tyler" because of her widowed mother's remarriage to Moses Tyler), quickly followed by Rose Foster, who was thirteen, and a few days later by Abigail Martin, age nineteen. Rose Foster was Rebecca Eames's granddaughter, and because Moses Tyler's first wife had been one of Rebecca's sisters, Rose and Martha were step-first-cousins, once removed. The girls were both, therefore, related to Rebecca and Daniel Eames—Rose by blood, Martha by marriage.[56]

Although the formal complaints have not survived, the first people these Andover girls complained against were also their relatives: three daughters and a stepdaughter of Mary Tyler Post Bridges. Both Goody Bridges and

Mary Post, a daughter by her first marriage, had already confessed to witchcraft. In all likelihood, Moses Tyler (who was simultaneously Martha's stepfather, Rose's great-uncle, and Mary Tyler Bridges's brother) filed the charges on August 23 or 24 with Dudley Bradstreet, an Andover justice of the peace. The four accused young women were then arrested by Ephraim Foster, Rose's father, who was the current Andover constable. Such familial links among accuser and accused, nonexistent in Salem Village, would be perpetuated in the coming weeks by many Andover confessors, who tended to identify relatives as their accomplices in witchcraft, just as relatives were their companions in daily life.

The Salem justices questioned Hannah Post (26), Sarah Bridges (17), Mary Bridges Jr. (13), and Susannah Post (31), probably in that order, on Thursday, August 25. After some initial resistance, all of them confessed to being witches, naming each other and their sister/half sister/stepsister Mary Post as their associates, but resisting implicating their mother. They described signing the devil's book in blood, being baptized, and attending Andover meetings involving two hundred or more witches, who convened at John Chandler's garrison house. Mary Warren, Richard Carrier, Mary Post, and probably other afflicted and confessing persons attended and participated in the interrogations. The sisters who confessed earlier also interjected observations into the later examinations. For example, Susannah Post at first refused to acknowledge having tortured Martha and Rose, but after her half sister Mary Bridges accused her of "afflict[ing] by sticking Pins into Cloaths," Susannah conceded that she had done so. Mary and Sarah Bridges, the two youngest girls, proved the most cooperative. Mary informed the judges that she had "bin in this Snare" since the spring, having been recruited by the devil's false promises of "fine Cloathes," and that, in addition to that in Andover, she had attended a Village witch meeting, carried on a pole "over the tops of the trees" by "the black man." Collectively, the sisters confirmed that nine people already in custody were witches.[57] They also named three new ones, none of whom proved willing to confess, despite being confronted by a large group of sufferers that comprised three Village and two Andover afflicted persons, and five Andover confessors.[58]

Also on August 25, Moses Tyler filed charges against other people his great-niece and stepdaughter accused of having "woefully afflicted & Abused" them. On this occasion he was joined by Samuel Martin, whose daughter Abigail too had begun to complain of torments. William Barker Sr. (46), his niece Mary Barker (13), and Goody Mary Osgood Marston (27) were arrested by Ephraim Foster and questioned in Salem Town on Monday, August 29. Mary Marston and Mary Barker concurred that the devil, a black man, had persuaded them to sign his book and to afflict Rose, Martha, and Abigail. Both also acknowledged having been at a Village witch meeting, but they offered few other details about their malefic activities or their accomplices.[59]

William Barker Sr. was much more forthcoming. In two confessions that day, he admitted having been "in the snare of the devil" for three years. Satan, he explained, had promised to "pay all his debts" and allow him to live "comfortably," which he found very attractive because "he had a great family, the world went hard with him." After signing the devil's book, he had attended a witch meeting and sacrament in Salem Village with about one hundred others, "upon a green peece of ground neare the ministers house." George Burroughs, "a ringleader in that meeting," had summoned the witches there with a trumpet that could be heard "many myles off." Some of the witches had "Rapiers by their side," Barker disclosed, thereby continuing the military theme suggested by Burroughs's use of a trumpet. Satan chose to attack the Village first "by reason of the peoples being divided & theire differing with their ministers," but the witches planned "to fall next upon Salem and soe goe through the countrey." Once they had established the devil's kingdom, "all persones should be equall" and there would be "neither punishment nor shame for sin" and "no day of resurection or of judgement." Some unnamed leaders of the conspiracy had told him that there were "about 307 witches in the country" (surely close enough to the number supplied by Ann Foster and Mary Toothaker to be regarded as accurate by the justices). And he added a new piece of information as well, one revealing that residents of Essex County knew about the concurrent witchcraft cases to the south: "In the spring of the yeare the witches came from Connecticut to afflict at Salem Village but now they have left it off."[60]

William Barker Sr. declared flatly that the sisters Elizabeth Dane Johnson and Abigail Dane Faulkner "have been my Enticers to this great abomination," thus leading the justices to issue a warrant that same August 29 for the immediate arrest of Elizabeth Johnson, her eleven-year-old daughter, and her fourteen-year-old son. On Tuesday, August 30, the magistrates reexamined Abigail Faulkner in prison. This time she confessed, explaining that "she did look with an evil eye on the afflicted persons & did consent that they should be afflicted: becaus they were the caus of bringing her kindred out: and shee did wish them ill." The next day, Goody Faulkner's sister and nephew both joined her in acknowledging guilt. Their admissions echoed those of their neighbors: the devil had baptized them; they had attended meetings at Chandler's and the Village (with George Burroughs, said Elizabeth); they had afflicted Martha, Rose, Abigail, and others in Andover.

Although Satan came to them in the form of a white bird and a black cat, he "mostly apears . . . like a black man."[61]

The Johnsons did not name any new witches (Elizabeth claimed, "I do not know any but them that are brought out"), but another person examined that Wednesday did. William Barker Jr., 14, admitted that, like his father, he had been baptized by Satan, had signed his book, and had tormented Martha Sprague. And he identified other afflicters: Samuel Wardwell, his wife, and his daughter and stepdaughter. Members of the Wardwell clan were consequently arrested and interrogated that very day. All of them confessed. Samuel, a forty-nine-year-old carpenter from New Hampshire, conceded that he had been "discontented" and had "foolishly" become involved with fortune-telling and the black man; his stepdaughter Sarah Hawkes, 21, and wife Sarah, 41, described attending a Village witch meeting with three other Andover residents; his daughter Mercy, 18, acknowledged having been baptized and signing the devil's book with "a red Mark Upon a peace of Paper wher she saw no other names." During Sarah Wardwell's examination (and probably during the others too), Mary Warren, the three most active Andover afflicted, and three Andover confessors endured the usual torments. In these and in many other examinations, then, the earlier confessors regularly joined the Village and Andover afflicted in accusing new examinees. For their part, the magistrates no longer seemed to distinguish among the different groups of sufferers. The justices appear to have accounted all the testimony equally credible. Their conflation of the afflicted and the confessors once again raised questions about the possible alliance of the accusers with the devil and his witches.[62]

William Barker Jr.'s confession also led the magistrates to the widow Mary Ayer Parker. Her wealthy husband, Nathan, an original settler of Andover, had died in 1685. She too was related to Moses Tyler and thus to Martha Sprague and Rose Foster, for one of her daughters had married Moses' brother. At her examination on September 2, confessors from both Salem Village and Andover had fits and required her touch to release them from their sufferings. Accused of having previously tortured Martha Sprague, Timothy Swan, and Sarah Phelps, Mary responded, "I know nothing of it," claiming to have been a victim of mistaken identity, for "there is another woman of the same name in Andover." But her step-great-niece Martha insisted, "this is the very woman," and Mary's defense fell on deaf ears. After William Barker Jr. "to her face" identified her as "one of his company," and Mary Warren endured a fit that left her with "blood runeing out of her mouth," Goody Parker was held for trial.[63]

Between mid-July and the first two days of September, the witchcraft crisis was largely confined to Andover. People from only a few other towns (neighboring Rowley and Boxford, Haverhill, and Billerica) were accused in those six weeks. But starting on September 3, it must have seemed likely that the crisis would explode throughout all of northeastern Essex County, as accusations surfaced nearly simultaneously in Gloucester, Reading, and Marblehead. Little is known about many of these cases, for few complaints or examinations have survived. Yet a significant number involved accused or accusers with ties to the Maine frontier. Perhaps not coincidentally, Lieutenant Governor John Usher feared an imminent attack by the French and Indians at that very moment. On September 5, he successfully requested a loan of seven barrels of gunpowder from the Massachusetts government to assist in preparing his province of New Hampshire to counter the expected invasion.[64]

At that precise juncture, the recently widowed Mary Swayne Marshall, sister of Major Jeremiah Swayne, a frontier militia leader, complained against three female afflicters from Reading. Nicholas Frost of Kittery, the son of another militia major, Charles Frost, himself became the subject of an accusation. And when on September 3 Ebenezer Babson of Gloucester—the man whose family served as the focal point of the spectral assault on the town in July—filed two witchcraft charges on behalf of his widowed mother, one of the accused was Elizabeth Dicer, a former resident of Saco who later described herself as "of Piscataqua."[65]

For this flurry of defendants questioned on Monday, September 5, four examination records are still extant: those of Margaret Prince of Gloucester and the three Reading residents accused by Mary Marshall. Betty Hubbard, who had relatives in Gloucester, accused Prince of having killed a woman there; she, Mary Warren, and two young women of the Booth family were afflicted at Prince's examination, where the suspect resolutely insisted on her innocence. So too did two of the Reading women, but the third, Mary Taylor (a forty-year-old mother of five), though at first proclaiming her innocence, eventually broke down under the pressure. As always, the afflicted and previous confessors collapsed at her glance. Simon Willard recorded that "Tayler was told she had a dangerous eye: that struck folk down which give ground to think she was a witch." But she did not admit guilt until after Samuel Wardwell and Major Swayne both chimed in, accusing her of involvement in the death of Wardwell's brother-in-law. She conceded first that "she had in a passion wished bad wishes" against Mary Marshall after Marshall accused her, then that she had signed the devil's "birch Rhine" and had associated with the jailed Lydia Dustin. But she insisted that she had not been baptized by the devil, nor had she bewitched Wardwell's relative.[66]

Attention shifted back to Andover two days later, where a formal touch test was staged with a large group of suspects. Although no one knew it at the time, this extraordinary event (probably precisely because of its remarkable nature) put an end to the most active phase of accusations and examinations during the witchcraft crisis. A few new formal charges were filed thereafter (the last came in early November, with witch-finding by the indefatigable Betty Hubbard), but after the touch test in Andover on September 7 and follow-up activities involving a group of children a week later, the Andover magistrates stopped issuing arrest warrants. Reported afflictions did not cease so abruptly, yet once the chain of Andover examinations and confessions was broken, the witchcraft crisis essentially disintegrated. And so the small but growing numbers of accusations in places like Gloucester, Reading, and Marblehead remained just that—a few scattered charges—rather than starting yet another phase of a burgeoning crisis.[67]

The circumstances of the Andover touch test are known only through an account drafted later by several of the women. Mistress Mary Osgood, Mary Tyler (whose husband was the brother of Moses Tyler and Mary Tyler Bridges), Hannah Tyler (Mary's daughter), Deliverance Dane (sister-in-law of Elizabeth Johnson and Abigail Faulkner), and Abigail Barker (sister-in-law of William Sr.) recounted that they and others, having been accused by the afflicted persons, were summoned to the Andover meetinghouse. After a prayer, they were all blindfolded, and their hands placed on the tormented accusers. "Then they said they were well, and that we were guilty of afflicting them," the women indicated. "We knowing ourselves altogether innocent of the crime, we were all exceedingly astonished and amazed, and consternated and affrighted even out of our reason," the women recalled. In those circumstances "some gentlemen" (presumably, the Salem magistrates) told them that "we were witches, and they knew it, and we knew it, which made us think that it was so." Because "our understandings, our reason, our faculties, [were] almost gone, we were not capable of judging our condition." Besides, the justices had used "hard measures" (which they did not identify) against them. All these factors "rendered us incapable of making our defense," and consequently we "said any thing and every thing which they desired, and most of what we said, was but, in effect, a consenting to what they said."[68]

One member of this group, Mary Tyler, later described to Increase Mather the specific reasons for her confession. En route from Andover to Salem after the touch test, she declared, her brother-in-law John Bridges (husband of Mary Tyler Post Bridges) rode with her. "All along the way . . . her brother[-in-law] kept telling her that she must needs be a witch, since the afflicted accused her, and at her touch were raised out of their fits, and urging her to confess herself a witch." On the road, she rejected his pleas, but when they had arrived in Salem Town she was taken to a room, where John Bridges and the Reverend John Emerson combined to insist that "she certainly was a witch, and that she saw the Devil before her eyes at that time (and, accordingly, the said Emerson would attempt with his hand to beat him away from her eyes)." As a result, she recalled, "she wished herself in any dungeon, rather than be so treated." Goodman Bridges asserted that "God would not suffer so many good men to be in such an error about it, and that she would be hanged if she did not confess." Finally, she "became so terrified in her mind that she owned, at length, almost any thing they propounded to her."[69]

After these events in early to mid-September, Robert Calef later wrote, Dudley Bradstreet, the Andover justice of the peace who had issued arrest warrants for thirty to forty of his fellow townspeople, declined to continue ordering the apprehension of more suspects. Consequently, Calef reported, Bradstreet was himself said to have bewitched nine people to death, and he was forced to flee for his own safety, along with his brother John, another local magistrate. Calef then attributed the end of the Andover accusations (as opposed to the last arrests there, which occurred sooner) to "a worthy Gentleman of Boston," who filed a £1,000 suit against the Andover afflicted for defamation, demanding legal proof of the validity of their allegations of witchcraft against him. "From thence forward," Calef declared, "the Accusations at Andover generally ceased."[70]

Why and how did Andover become such a focal point for the crisis? Before Joseph Ballard called in the two Salem Village witch-finders in mid-July, Andover had only one accused witch, the "usual suspect" Martha Carrier. But the witch-finding by the afflicted girls set off a chain of examinations and confessions that, in the end, produced by far the largest number of recorded accusations in 1692. Like Salem Village, Andover had been touched by the Indian wars, and the families of many of those prominent in the accounts of the witchcraft crisis produced men who served in either the first or second conflict. Andover itself was attacked on April 8, 1676, and the accused witch Mary Parker lost a son in battle the following year. Andover militiamen, like those from Salem Village, were repeatedly called upon for frontier service after 1688. The people of the town thus had good reason to fear the Indians in 1692, and so the links posited herein between the second war and the witchcraft crisis apply to Andover no less than they did elsewhere in Essex County.[71]

But at the same time, they seemingly apply no more to Andover than to other places. Just as Salem Village's divisiveness and inability to resolve its conflicts internally made it a likely progenitor of the witchcraft crisis, so

Andover's opposite mentalité led its residents to perpetuate the crisis, once the chain of confessions began. In the Village, long-standing feuds and disagreements had familiarized townspeople with continual dissent and discord, with people who refused to do as they were asked (in this case, confess to witchcraft after being accused), and, most notably, with unresolvable conflicts because of the lack of meaningful local authority. Residents of Andover, a separate jurisdiction with its own government, were accustomed to resolving their disputes within town boundaries, and like other New Englanders they placed a heavy value on consensus, on the need for individuals to concur with the majority opinion when pressed to do so by others. The accounts of the confessing Andover women emphasize their reluctant surrender to peers and superiors—"gentlemen," clergy, relatives—all of whom urged them to acknowledge their guilt, insisting that so many "good men" could not have erred in their judgment. Two of the confessors, for instance, later explained that they had been "press'd, and urg'd, and affrighted" until they said "anything that was desired." Later, a group of their neighbors attested that the women had been "unreasonably" pushed by "their relations and others" to admit the truth of "that evidence that was so much credited and improved against people." In the end, then, the women (and some men) gave in to the larger group, as seventeenth-century New Englanders were expected to do.[72]

Another, related dynamic also lay behind the Andover confessions. A careful reading of the surviving records reveals the crucial significance of confessions by children and youths (below the age of twenty-five) both in confirming earlier identifications of witches and in creating new ones. When Richard, Andrew, Sarah, and Thomas Carrier Jr. all confessed and implicated their mother, that seemed to verify testimony against her by other witnesses. The same was later true of William Barker Jr. and the children of Abigail Faulkner, Mary Bridges, and Mary Tyler. Furthermore, as the preceding narrative has suggested, young people seemed especially likely to identify as witches not only "them that are [already] brought out" (as Elizabeth Johnson Sr. put it on September 1) but also to mention others for the first time. Thus Betty Johnson, the Post-Bridges sisters, and William Barker Jr. all supplied the names of new suspected witches. These unmarried Andover young people, like their parents and unlike the afflicted girls of Salem Village (who gloried in saying "no," if only to the devil), obediently did as they were told. Directed by the magistrates to confess, they readily did so. Their mothers, aunts, fathers, and uncles sometimes initially resisted the demands for confession, but they did not. Dutifully, they acknowledged their culpability and that of others. Ironically, precisely because they behaved like ideal New England children, they—in company with the afflicted, who went to the opposite extreme—helped to cause the executions of several Andover residents.

ADDRESS OF 259 INHABITANTS OF NEW HAMPSHIRE TO KING WILLIAM AND QUEEN MARY, AUGUST 10, 1692[73]

Wee humbly presume to lay before your Majesties our present deplorable Condition, vizt, That wee are but foure poore towns dayly Exposed to annoyance from French and Indian Enemies, who have already made such incursions upon us that many have bin destroyed, and the rest reduced to such Extream poverty and want, that wee are no longer able to subsist of our selves, much less to support a distinct and seperate Government. Our present standing being by the assistance of our Neighbours of the Massachusetts who are at a Charge of keeping a constant number of Soldiers among us for our Defence, and without the Continuance thereof, Wee shall be Exposed to ruine, or necessitated to quit the Province to the enemy to save our own lives.

CHAPTER EIGHT

All Sorts of Objections

A S THE MAGISTRATES in Andover and Salem handled the flooding cascade of confessions following the adjournment of the third session of the Court of Oyer and Terminer, criticism of the use of spectral evidence in the trials surfaced once again. This time, the caveats came not from an outsider like William Milborne but instead from a member of the council itself. Four days after the conviction of George Burroughs, Robert Pike, the militia leader and Salisbury justice of the peace who had collected much of the maleficium evidence against Susannah Martin, wrote to his fellow councilor, Jonathan Corwin, expressing his concern about the "doubtfulness and unsafety of admitting spectre testimony against the life of any that are of blameless conversation, and plead innocent."[1]

In a thoughtful letter and an enclosed essay, Pike spelled out his reasons for believing that "diabolical visions, apparitions, or representations" were "more commonly false and delusive than real, and cannot be known when they are real and when feigned, but by the Devil's report; and then [can]not be believed, because he is the father of lies." Pike posited three possible explanations for the spectral visions of the afflicted: first, their eyes might be "abused" and their senses "deluded," so that they thought they saw something they really did not; second, they might see the devil himself "in the shape and likeness of a person or thing"; and third, "sometimes persons or things themselves do really appear." Still, all that could truly be said by a witness in such a case was that "I did see the shape or likeness of such a person, if my senses or eyesight were not deluded," because anything more would rely on Satan's evidence. Pike acknowledged that some resolved this dilemma by insisting that "the Devil do not or cannot appear in the shape of a godly person, to do hurt." But he pointed out that others rejected that position, leaving the issue uncertain, although it was "the very hinge upon which that weighty case depends." For his part, Pike aligned himself with those who believed that Satan could and did assume the shape of innocent parties.

To the experienced Salisbury magistrate, the chief difficulty lay in the unreliability of any testimony about specters. He did not doubt that the afflicted and the confessors saw what they said they saw, although he acknowledged that some people think "they do but counterfeit." (Pike's remark constitutes the first time such a contention was committed to writing in 1692, even though he himself did not advance it.) Interpreting their visions caused the problem. Ultimately, Pike asserted, it did not matter whether the accusers were faking. "If they counterfeit, the wickedness is the greater in them, and the less in the Devil: but if they be compelled to it by the Devil, against their wills, then the sin is the Devil's," he told his fellow councilor. In either case, when the question of guilt turned on that evidence alone "the lives of innocent persons are alike in danger by them, which is the solemn consideration that do disquiet the country."

In the essay he sent with his letter, Robert Pike addressed some of the legal issues involved in obtaining convictions, attempting to define what witness testimony would be sufficient to prove the guilt of a suspected witch.[2] He concluded that assessing legal adequacy was so difficult that it would be better "for the present, to let a guilty person live till further discovery, than to put an innocent person to death." Moreover, he enumerated the various activities and claims of the Village afflicted (for instance, that they knew who was tormenting others as well as themselves, and that they saw the ghosts of the dead), pointing out that "whatsoever is done by them that is supernatural, is either divine or diabolical." Emphatically, he insisted that "none of these actions of theirs have any warrant in God's word." Thus, for example, the afflicted were acting in an "utterly unlawful" way when they conversed with ghosts. The devil, not God, was torturing them; and just as surely the devil was creating their visions. Although the Salisbury councilor did not say so explicitly, he implied that in their involvement with the supernatural and the diabolical, the afflicted themselves might be verging on, or actually engaging in, witchcraft.

The "last and greatest question," Pike asserted, was a simple one: how could they know that the devil was not acting without any human involvement at all? Satan, he insisted, "is always the doer, but whether abetted in it by anybody is uncertain." And how would one determine whether a witch was involved? Was the devil "a competent witness" who could be relied on to reveal his accomplices? As for other potential witnesses, the afflicted could only convey knowledge that came from the devil. The confessors, indeed, could testify against themselves, but when they named another witch who denied culpability, their information too came from the devil and had to be judged untrustworthy.

He concluded with three arguments he must have regarded as clinching his case. Why would someone, he asked, plead innocence and simultaneously act witchcraft "in the sight of all men, when they know their lives lie at stake by doing it[?] Self-interest teaches every one better." Second, why would the devil accuse his own witches? "They are a considerable part of his kingdom, which would fall, if divided against itself." Finally, Pike admitted that sometimes God through his providence would reveal hidden things. But he had just proved that in this case the knowledge came from Satan, not from God. Here, "where the Devil is accuser and witness," what reliance could possibly be placed on any of it?

How many other people agreed with Robert Pike is not clear. But such sentiments as his were certainly beginning to circulate in Massachusetts by mid-August. Another member of the council, John Foster, took those ideas seriously enough to ask Cotton Mather for his current opinion about "the horrible witchcrafts among us." On August 17, Mather responded by reiterating his previous positions: that spectral evidence alone was inadequate for conviction and that the devil could appear in the shape of an innocent person, but nevertheless that "a very great use is to be made of the spectral impressions upon the sufferers." Such visions, Mather wrote, "justly introduce, and determine, an inquiry into the circumstances of the person accused, and they strengthen other presumptions." In the trials thus far, God's "encouraging presence" had been evident with the "excellent judges," for "scarce any, if at all any, have been tried before them, against whom God has not strangely sent in other, and more human and most convincing, testimonies." Mather thus continued to insist, as surely did the judges as well, that no one had been convicted solely on the basis of spectral evidence, and that the visions of the afflicted served primarily to initiate "presumptions" that then produced the more extensive investigations that unearthed the legal proof essential to affirm guilt. He did retreat from one of his earlier positions, however, conceding that perhaps Satan could "impose upon some harmless people" through tests of "look or touch" as well as through the appearance of apparitions. Whatever Foster and the other councilors decided, Mather concluded, they should above all endeavor to "strengthen the hands of our honorable judges in the great work before them."[3]

The examining magistrates—Hathorne, Gedney, Corwin, Higginson—responded to the concerns of such councilors as Pike and Foster (and undoubtedly other critics as well) by posing leading questions to willing confessors about some of the aspects of the proceedings that were clearly arousing negative comment. For example, on August 25 Sarah Bridges was asked "what She thought of the afflicted whether they Ware witches," as Pike had implied in his letter to Corwin. She replied, "no they were Honest persons that helped to bring out the witches." The examination records did not always record the inquiries, but their content can readily be deduced from confessors' reported statements. On August 29, William Barker Sr.'s interrogation probably proceeded thus, with posited questions in brackets: "[What do the witches say about the afflicted people?] The witches are much disturbed with the afflicted persones because they are descovered by them, [What do they say about the judges?] They curse the Judges Because their Society is brought under, [Are the afflicted people themselves guilty of witchcraft?] They wold have the afflicted persones counted as witches but he thinks the afflicted persones are Innocent & that they doe god good service [Has any innocent person been accused?] And that he has not known or heard of one innocent persone taken up & put in prisone."[4]

The rising chorus of criticism caused Mather to decide to undertake a systematic defense of the trials, one that through publication would reach many more people than he had hitherto spoken to or corresponded with. By September 2, he had completed a partial draft of his book, which he sent to Lieutenant Governor William Stoughton. Expressing the hope that he could "help very much to flatten that fury which we now so much turn upon one another," Mather requested permission to publish accounts of some of the trials, "which being inserted in this treatise will much vindicate the country, as well as the judges and juries." He also asked Stoughton to correct any errors in the draft, especially with respect to "the jealousies among us, of innocent people being accused." And, finally, he expressed the hope that Stoughton, or perhaps "the judges jointly," would endorse his project "in a line or two" that he could include in the book. Whether the chief judge altered any of Mather's original language is not known, but he apparently directed Stephen Sewall to provide the minister with the necessary court documents, and he also expressed his official approbation of *The Wonders of the Invisible World* when it appeared later in the fall.[5]

On September 5, Governor Phips, recently returned from Maine (where since August 11 he had been supervising the construction of Fort William Henry at Pemaquid), presided over the first meeting of the council in more than a month. The next day, the Court of Oyer and Terminer reconvened in Salem for its fourth session. A new set of petty jurors was impaneled for these trials, perhaps because George Burroughs had challenged so many men at his.[6]

THE FINAL SESSION OF THE COURT
OF OYER AND TERMINER

What turned out to be the last session of the court—although the judges could not have known it at the time—stretched over two weeks. Between Tuesday, September 6, and Saturday, September 17, with a two-day break on Sunday and Monday the 11th and 12th, the grand jury heard fifteen cases and the petty jury or juries tried fourteen defendants. For the first time, confessors were among those who faced trial. Yet in most ways these proceedings resembled all the others. Everyone charged was indicted for at least one offense, and everyone tried was convicted.[7]

The first to face the trial jury was Dorcas Hoar, the "usual suspect" from Beverly who had been indicted on July 2. Four afflicted people, supported by adult Putnam men, attested to the agonies they and others had experienced at Hoar's examination on May 2 and thereafter. All the depositions elided the issue of whether any torments had predated that event, as had also been true in the prosecution of Sarah Wilds. Most of the testimony came from Hoar's Beverly neighbors. They described her fortune-telling activities (she seems to have specialized in accurately predicting that apparently healthy children "would not live Long"), her anger when crossed, and a young man's belief that Hoar, Wilds, and other witches had formed a "Confederacy" to attack him two years earlier. One of the most persuasive witnesses for the prosecution was surely John Hale, who reported his discussions with Dorcas about her fortune-telling over a period of years, and his own now-dead daughter's suspicions (which he had attempted to assuage) that Goody Hoar was bewitching her. His testimony revealed that Dorcas Hoar had continued to tell fortunes long after she had assured him that she had "renounce[d], or reject[ed] all such practices."[8]

Two other women who had been indicted previously were also tried during that first week of the court session. On Thursday, September 8, Martha Corey (jailed since late March, indicted in August) finally faced the judges. Perhaps the most important testimony came from Edward Putnam and Ezekiel Cheever, who together recounted their conversation with her on March 12 and vividly depicted the sufferings of the afflicted at her examination. Putnam also testified alone, describing the torments endured by Ann Jr. and Mercy Lewis when Corey called at Thomas Putnam's household. Ann Carr Putnam probably repeated orally the testimony she had already given against Rebecca Nurse, in which she attested to her sufferings at the hands of the specters of Nurse and Corey on March 18. The other key witnesses would have been the confessors who had listed Goody Corey as a participant in various malefic activities, especially the meetings led by George Burroughs (Mary Warren, Deliverance Hobbs, and Richard Carrier). The extant documents contain no reports of traditional maleficium, so it is not clear whether any such evidence emerged orally at the trial.[9]

The next day, Mary Towne Easty too had to defend herself against what must have been the difficult-to-refute testimony of adults who described sufferings of young people—in her case, those of Mercy Lewis on May 20, as well as of all the afflicted at her second examination on May 23. The depictions of Lewis's agonies were particularly heartrending, as eight men (including Mercy's uncle, James Darling) recalled in detail the maidservant's "sad condition the greatest part of the day being in such tortors as no toungue can express" and her repeated pleas to God either to save her from death or to offer her soul salvation. Two witnesses also told maleficium stories about Goody Easty. The defendant did the best she could to exonerate herself, imploring the judges to intervene on her behalf and to "councell" her on her case. She submitted statements from jailers in both Ipswich and Boston declaring that she had behaved herself in a "Sobor and civell" manner while in custody. She also called as character witnesses her children, her pastor, and various members of the Topsfield church. And, drawing on the arguments then being advanced by critics of the trials about the overreliance on spectral evidence, she requested that "the Testimony of witches, or such as are afflicted, as is supposed, by witches" might not be regarded as definitive "without legal evidence concurring" against someone like herself, who had "for many yeares Lived under the unblemished reputation of Christianity."[10]

The other cases heard that week involved grand-jury proceedings as well as trials. On Wednesday, September 7, the grand jury formally charged Alice Parker with bewitching Warren and Walcott, and she seems to have been tried later that same day. Remarkably, the indictments were based not (as was usual) on afflictions during her examination, but rather on tortures her specter had recently visited upon her victims. According to mutually supportive depositions offered to both inquest and petty juries by five of the sufferers, Parker's apparition had attacked them all, along with two others, the previous night. As the first to accuse Goody Parker, Mary Warren not surprisingly contributed the most detailed account, alleging that Parker "brought: me a poppit: & a needle: & thretned: to stab: me if I would not stick the needle into the Poppit: & she did run: the needle a little way into me." Warren also repeated the charges she had first advanced on May 12, claiming that Parker's specter had confessed to causing four deaths at sea as well as to bewitching Mary's own mother and sister. Finally, several of Goody Parker's neighbors recounted maleficium tales dating back to 1684.[11]

On September 7 the grand jury in addition considered the case against Ann Greenslade Pudeator (also originally accused by Mary Warren on May 12). The widow Pudeator was then tried on Saturday, September 10. Only one indictment survives, charging her with afflicting Warren during her second examination on July 2. Four of the afflicted and two confessors testified to either the grand or petty jury or both that they and the others had been afflicted by Goody Pudeator then and at other times, and that they "verily" believed she was a witch. Warren again took the lead, swearing that Pudeator's specter had confessed to killing her husband and his first wife, along with the wife of John Best. Best himself (seconded by his son, John Jr.) supported that allegation, attesting that he "did often hear my wife saye that Ann pudeater would not Lett her alone untill she had killd her By her often pinching & Bruseing of her Till her Earms & other parts of her Body Looked Black . . . & [she] stood in the Belefe of itt as Long as she Lived." After her conviction and condemnation, Ann Pudeator petitioned the judges, complaining that the Bests' testimony was "altogether false & untrue," as was that of the two confessors, and futilely asking that "my life may not be taken away by such false Evidence and wittnesses as these be."[12]

The other case wholly resolved during the first week of the September court session was that of Mistress Mary Bradbury. As has been seen, Mistress Bradbury had been identified by confessors as one of the main instigators of the tormenting of Timothy Swan. At the grand-jury proceeding on Friday the 9th, five witnesses described how her specter tortured them during her July 2 examination. Both Mary Walcott and Ann Putnam Jr. revealed that they had seen the ghost of John Carr (Ann's uncle) accusing Mistress Bradbury of killing him, attesting as well that they had seen her apparition afflicting Swan. The grand jury indicted her for bewitching Swan on July 26 and Sarah Vibber on July 2.[13]

At the trial later that same day, the petty jury considered the evidence already heard by the grand jury as well as additional testimony.[14] The confessors who named Mary Bradbury would have been brought in to repeat their identifications—both Mary Laceys and Richard Carrier, certainly, and perhaps Mary Toothaker. One witness declared that he thought Mistress Bradbury had bewitched a ship on which he sailed to the West Indies about eleven years earlier, and Richard Carr (Ann Jr.'s uncle) swore that he, his father, and another observer (who also testified) believed that years earlier they had seen Bradbury turn herself into a spectral "blue boar" that then attacked their horses. Richard's brother, James, attested that in the early 1670s he had become strangely ill for nine months after a courtship visit to the young widow Rebecca Wheelwright Maverick. Rebecca had "most curtuously" invited him to "com oftener" to her house, James recalled, thus suggesting that he was a preferred suitor. When he called next, James told the jury, the defendant's son William was also there, but Rebecca Maverick "did so corsely treat the said william Bradbery that he went away semeing to be angury." James then became sick, and, as everyone in the courtroom knew, during his extended illness Rebecca married William Bradbury.

James Carr did not have to spell out for the jury the inference he drew from that chain of events: Mistress Bradbury, wanting her son to obtain the widow Maverick for himself, had bewitched his rival James so that William would have a clear field. James drove home his point by informing the jury that a doctor had pronounced him "behaged" because medications did not appear to improve his condition. After James identified Mistress Bradbury as a suspect, the doctor had exclaimed that "he did beleve that mis Bradbery was a grat deall worse then goody [Susannah] mertin." Not until after James successfully struck a spectral cat that appeared in his bedroom one night did his health improve. "I beleve in my hart," he concluded, "that mis Bradbery the prisoner att the bar has often afflected me by acts of wicthcraft."

To counter such evidence of afflictions and maleficium Mistress Bradbury offered a sworn statement from her current pastor attesting to her good character and to her "works of charity & mercy to the sick & poor." Robert Pike, who prepared that deposition, added his own affirmation that he had known Mary "upward of fifty years" and fully concurred with the clergyman's judgment. Pike's son John, a minister, joined in the same positive assessment of her character. One hundred fifteen Salisbury townspeople submitted a petition on her behalf. Mistress Bradbury herself addressed the judges directly, insisting that "I am wholly inocent of any such wickedness . . . I am the servant of Jesus Christ & Have given my self up to him as my only lord & saviour." The devil's works, she declared, were "horid & detestible"; she had tried to live her life "according to the rules of [God's] holy word." But, like all the other defenses accused witches offered to the Court of Oyer and Terminer, hers fell on deaf ears.[15]

Although the petty jury's work that week ended with the trial of Mary Bradbury, the grand jury considered three more cases: those of Giles Corey, Abigail Hobbs, and Rebecca Jacobs, the daughter-in-law of the executed witch George Jacobs Sr. Ann Putnam Jr. and Mercy Lewis both swore to having been afflicted by Corey's specter in mid-April; other afflicted witnesses attested that he had tortured them at unspecified times. A Village maidservant, seconded by Walcott, revealed that she had seen Giles's apparition sitting in his regular seat in the meetinghouse during a lecture on the day before Bridget Bishop's execution (June 9). John DeRich described appearances of his specter on August 20 and September 5, indicating that Corey wanted to borrow "some platers" from him to use for "afeast." Since no indictments survive in this case, it is not clear what true bills the grand jury issued, but there must have been at least one.[16]

Rebecca Jacobs and Abigail Hobbs had both confessed to being witches, the latter having done so repeatedly in a variety of settings. The grand jury thus probably found it easy to indict Hobbs for bewitching Mercy Lewis during her April examination, and for in 1688 "in Cascoe Bay in the Province of Mayne in New England Wickedly and Felloniously" covenanting with "the Evill Spirritt the Devill." The teenager was then tried and convicted the following week, based on her own confession, testimony by the afflicted, and statements she had earlier made to acquaintances about her dealings with the devil. But Rebecca Jacobs's case posed greater difficulty. The defendant's mother, Rebecca Fox, petitioned the court, describing her daughter as "a Woman broken & distracted in her mind" for more than twelve years. She asked the judges to pay "due regard" to Rebecca's insanity (to which she and others were prepared to swear) "that so there may not be stresse laid on the Confession of a Distracted Woman to the Prejudice of her life." And the grand jury did take that plea into account. Although they charged Rebecca Jacobs with afflicting Betty Hubbard during her examination, they refused to indict her for covenanting with the devil.[17]

On Sunday, September 11, during the court's brief hiatus, the Reverend Samuel Parris used both his morning and afternoon sermons to reflect on "the condemnation of 6 Witches at a Court at Salem," one of them being Martha Corey, a member of his own church. His text, Revelation 17:14, spoke of a "War with the Lamb" but predicted God's ultimate triumph. "In our dayes," Parris asserted, "How industrious & vigorous is the Bloody French Monarch, & his Confederates against Christ & his Interest." In this very land "& some neighbouring Places," he asked his listeners rhetorically, "how many, what Multitudes, of Witches & Wizards had the Devil instigated with utmost violence to attempt the overthrow of Religion?" The two sermons abounded in martial terminology, as Parris discussed Satan's "Army," wartime "Captive[s]," and "good Souldiers of Christ." In keeping with the theme, he insisted, "Here are no Newters. Every one is on one side or the other." Parris's depiction of the witches' assaults in terms that summoned up images of attacks by the Indians and French must have sent shivers of fear through his audience—fear for their lives and for their souls. Parris warned the congregation of internal as well as external enemies. Previously, witches had been found only in "Barbarous Desarts" (Cotton Mather employed a similar phrase to describe the Maine forests, and Parris probably meant the same), but now they were common in "the Civilest & Religious Parts." His remark about "so many of this Damned brood" of witches having been found "in a Village of 14 Houses in the North" (surely Falmouth, home to George Burroughs and Deliverance and Abigail Hobbs) only underscored the danger of the combined threats from the visible and invisible worlds.[18]

That Sabbath, the Village congregation voted "in public by a general consent" to excommunicate Goody Martha Corey. The following Wednesday, Parris, Nathaniel Putnam, and the two church deacons visited her in prison to inform her of the church's action. They found her "very obdurate, justifying herself and condemning all that had done any thing to her just discovery or condemnation." Her "imperiousness" would not permit them to have more than "a little discourse" with her, and she "was willing to decline" their prayer. So they pronounced "the dreadful sentence of excommunication," and left.[19]

Some time between Monday, September 12, and Friday, September 16, several more accused witches escaped from custody in Boston. Edward and Sarah Bishop and John Alden broke out of jail, and Hezekiah Usher fled from house arrest to Rhode Island. Alden and Usher probably waited to learn the fate of Mistress Bradbury, another high-status defendant, before they took such a drastic step. Her conviction would have convinced them that, despite their prominence, they too had no chance of success in the Court of Oyer and Terminer. A letter describing their escape also remarked on the deaths of two Groton men at the hands of the Wabanakis and repeated a recent message from the northeastern frontier reporting that "our scouts" had located "about 80 or 100 Indians . . . in the night siting at thaire fires hammering of slugs for their gunns." The scouts had come so close "they could see the Indians and heare them talke." Samuel Parris was thus not the only Massachusetts resident who linked witches and the war in a single document in mid-September 1692.[20]

The court began its second week of proceedings on Tuesday, September 13, with a grand-jury session on the case of the Andover confessor Ann Foster, continuing the next day with her daughter Mary Lacey Sr. Since both women had confessed, that they would be indicted was obvious. Foster was formally charged with bewitching Hubbard and Walcott, Lacey with afflicting Hubbard and Lewis. Another confessor considered at the same time was Samuel Wardwell, who had actively participated in others' examinations, urging them to confess. But he recanted, telling the grand jury on September 13 that his written confession "was: taken: from his mouth and that he had said it: but: he said he belyed: himselfe: he also said it was alone one: he: knew he should dye for it: whether he owned it or no." The grand jury indicted Wardwell for bewitching Martha Sprague and for making a covenant with the devil. Clearly, the jury believed his initial confession, not his recantation.[21]

All three of these confessors were tried and convicted later in the week. No information survives about the Foster and Lacey trials; presumably, the women's own confessions and the testimony of other confessors (primarily Andrew and Richard Carrier and Mary Toothaker) condemned them. According to Robert Calef, Samuel Wardwell's confession and spectral evidence were marshaled against him at his trial. If a later remark by Cotton Mather is accurate, his confession included an otherwise unrecorded report that "at their Cheef Witch-meetings, there had been present some French canadians, and some Indian Sagamores to concert the methods of ruining New England." Such a statement would surely have added to the credibility of the confession in the minds of the jurors and further confirmed for them the existence of a conspiracy of visible and invisible worlds.[22]

One other confessor also faced the judges that week: Abigail Dane Faulkner. As was previously noted, after refusing to confess on August 11, she had changed her story at the end of the month, admitting that she attended the witch meeting at Chandler's garrison and that she consented to the devil's torturing people for her. Both Village and Andover afflicted joined in describing their torments at her hands for the grand and petty juries. The grand jury indicted her for bewitching Sarah Phelps and Martha Sprague, and at her trial such confessors as Mary Barker and William Barker Sr. would have appeared against her. After she was convicted and sentenced to death, she pleaded pregnancy and was reprieved.[23]

The remaining cases that came before the Court of Oyer and Terminer at its final session involved people who had not confessed. The grand jury indicted Sarah Buckley and her daughter Mary Witheridge for tortures inflicted on several sufferers at their May 18 examinations, but they were not tried until January, at which point they were acquitted. Those defendants whose cases advanced past the indictment stage in September were not as fortunate. Wilmot Reed, Margaret Scott, and Mary Parker were all indicted and convicted during the second week of September. Parker could well have been found guilty solely on the testimony of the confessors William Barker Jr. and Mercy Wardwell, and on the words of those who said she had afflicted them, for no other documents survive in her case. The prosecutions of Reed and Scott are also sparsely documented, perhaps suggesting the haste with which the evidence against them was compiled. Four afflicted Villagers testified against Goody Reed; so did witnesses to a heated exchange between Reed and a Mistress Syms in Marblehead five years earlier, which people believed had resulted in Reed's bewitching Syms. Goody Scott's neighbors in

Rowley, the evidence showed, had long thought her a witch. The afflicted people of Andover and Salem Village appear to have played only a limited role in her conviction.[24]

When the court adjourned on Saturday, September 17—until, it was thought, the first week of November—one piece of legal business remained unfinished. Giles Corey, indicted on the 9th, had when called up for his trial pleaded "not guilty," but then refused to respond to the next ritual question: would he be tried by God and his country (that is, by a jury)? The traditional English punishment for such a failure to agree to a trial was called the *peine forte et dure,* which directed placing heavy stones on a defendant's prone body until he either entered a plea or died. Samuel Sewall recorded in his diary that "much pains was used with him two days, one after another, by the Court [including Sewall himself?] and Capt. Gardner of Nantucket who had been of his acquaintance: but all in vain." On Sunday evening, then, everyone concerned understood that unless Corey changed his mind (or the magistrates relaxed their insistence that he formally agree to be tried) he would suffer a terrible death the next day.[25]

That night in Salem Village, Ann Putnam Jr. suffered "grievously," her father soon reported to Judge Sewall. The witches assaulting her threatened that "she should be Pressed to Death, before Giles Cory." But in the midst of "a little Respite" from her agonies, she saw an apparition in a "Winding Sheet." The ghost told her that Corey "had Murdered him, by Pressing him to Death with his Feet; but that the Devil there appeared unto him, and Covenented with him, and promised him, He should not be Hanged." Now, the ghost revealed, God had "Hardened" Corey's heart so that he would not listen to the court and would die in the same way he had once killed another. Putnam informed Sewall that everyone in town had forgotten Giles Corey's having beaten and kicked a servant to death in 1675 (before Ann was born), but that his daughter's vision now caused people to "Remember [it] very well." To Cotton Mather, who later included the story in *Wonders of the Invisible World,* the tale constituted yet another confirmation of God's providential intervention in human affairs and the validity of the spectral visions seen in the Village. To a modern reader, Ann's experience seems rather an indication of the persistence of gossip. Putnam, after all, remarked in his letter that several of the jurors who had acquitted Corey were "yet alive." They certainly had not forgotten the case, and they would have talked, at the time and more recently. And Ann had long since proved herself to be a remarkable collector of gossip.[26]

"About noon, at Salem, Giles Corey was press'd to death for standing Mute," Sewall wrote on Monday, September 19. Robert Calef later revealed that Giles's "Tongue being prest out of his Mouth, the Sheriff with his Cane forced it in again, when he was dying." Historians have long speculated about the reasons for Corey's dramatic act of defiance, but Calef's initial explanation has as much validity as any: understanding that the jury had "cleared none upon Tryal," and "knowing there would be the same Witnesses against him," Giles Corey "rather chose to undergo what Death they would put him to."[27]

Most of those condemned at the fourth session of the court were scheduled to hang on Thursday, September 22. At nearly the last minute, Dorcas Hoar confessed. John Hale, Nicholas Noyes, and two other ministers—with the endorsement of Bartholomew Gedney—wrote hastily to Boston on September 21 to ask that Goody Hoar be reprieved for a month. She had acknowledged "the heynous crime of witchcraft" and having signed the devil's book. Dorcas, they indicated, also "gives account of some other persons that shee hath known to be guilty of the same crime." Being in "grat distress of Conscience," she "earnestly craves a little longer time of life to realize & perfect her repentance for the salvation of her soule," the clergymen explained. Governor William Phips had again sailed for Pemaquid on the 16th, so Lieutenant Governor Stoughton responded to the petition, granting the requested reprieve and thus saving Dorcas Hoar from the gallows.[28]

Even though several confessors were among those convicted in September, only Samuel Wardwell, who had recanted, was included in the September 22 death warrant. The other seven people hanged that day were Martha Corey, Mary Easty, Alice Parker, Mary Parker, Ann Pudeator, Margaret Scott, and Wilmot Reed. Robert Calef has left the only account of the execution. When the cart carrying the group to the gallows "was for some time at a sett," he wrote, the afflicted and other observers commented that "the Devil hindered it." Goody Corey died after "an Eminent Prayer upon the Ladder," and Mary Easty's "last farewell" to her family drew "Tears from the Eyes of almost all present." Calef, relaying eyewitness reports, termed Easty "as Serious, Religious, Distinct, and Affectionate as could well be exprest." Nicholas Noyes, though, remained unmoved by the scene. "What a sad thing it is to see Eight Firebrands of Hell hanging there," he exclaimed.[29]

THE DISSOLUTION OF THE COURT

Even before the executions, the critical voices first heard loudly in August continued to clamor for attention. On September 20, Cotton Mather described himself to Stephen Sewall as "continually b[eset?] with all sorts of Objections, and Objectors against the [torn] work now doing at Salem."

Consequently, he explained, he more than ever felt the urgent need to complete his book on witchcraft. Thus he dispatched "my most *importunate request*" for the trial records of perhaps as many as a dozen "principal witches" so that he could include summaries in the book. Please, he implored the court clerk, also send a letter in which you "intimate over again, what you have sometimes told me, of the awe which is upon the hearts of your juries, with [respect?] unto the validity of the spectral evidences," and include "your observations about the confessors and [torn] the credibility of what they assert." Mather underscored the importance of the request by pointing out that Governor Phips himself had directed him to ask Sewall for this information. "There are some of his circumstances with reference to this affayr, which I need not mention, that call for the Expediting of your Kindness," the clergyman added cryptically. Two days later, he followed up the letter by discussing the publication project in person with Stoughton, Hathorne, Stephen Sewall, and the Reverend John Higginson at the home of the court clerk's brother, Judge Sewall.[30]

To what "circumstances" involving the governor was Cotton Mather discreetly referring in his letter? Sir William Phips's biographers point out that both the governor and his wife, Mary Spencer Phips, met some of the criteria that identified witches in 1692. Phips had consulted a fortune-teller, and had taken the resulting predictions very seriously; he was a successful treasure hunter, thus possibly implying access to occult knowledge; he and his wife both had extensive links to Maine and even to George Burroughs. One of their household servants (captured by Phips at Port Royal in 1690) was the daughter of Castine and the granddaughter of Madockawando. Moreover, Lady Mary Phips was related through her sister to a woman accused of witchcraft in the late 1650s, in an incident sufficiently well known that John Hale included it in the book on witchcraft he wrote in 1697. Lady Phips does indeed seem to have been named as a witch in 1692. Two critics of the trials claimed as much a decade later, and a pamphlet published in England in 1694 disclosed the possible precipitating factor. While Sir William was away (that is, either during the month after the first week of August, or between September 16 and 29), his wife apparently signed an order for the release of one of the accused female witches, which the jailer then obeyed. The pamphleteer wrote that he mistrusted the tale until he saw the "Discharge under the Keepers hand attested a true Copy." For this act, the anonymous writer revealed, the jailer lost his job, "as he himself told me."[31]

Sir William Phips could therefore have felt compelled to support the prosecutions to the greatest extent possible in order to protect himself and his wife from possible accusations. That, indeed, is the argument advanced by

Phips's biographers. In the absence of definitive evidence, it is impossible to determine the governor's motivations with any certainty. But surviving documents make two things clear. First, contrary to many scholars' assumptions, Phips was well informed about the trials and firmly supported them while they lasted. He also strongly encouraged Cotton Mather to defend them in print. But second, once public opinion turned sharply against the trials—a shift that had occurred by the second week in October—Phips quickly and successfully sought to disentangle himself from the proceedings.

The governor might even have sensed a new climate of opinion immediately upon his return from Pemaquid on September 29 after a brief absence of thirteen days. In the interim, of course, eight executions had taken place. In the unseemly rush to convict defendants during the final court session, people had been found guilty on the basis of evidence that failed to meet the standards set forth even by such defenders of the trials as Cotton Mather. Whereas previously Mather had contended that spectral testimony had been used to supply "presumptions" that led to investigations which then uncovered maleficium complaints, he could not argue the same with respect to the prosecutions of Martha Corey or Mary Parker. In addition, Mary Easty and Mary Bradbury (the latter condemned, but reprieved "from the intercession of some friends," revealed Thomas Brattle) had presented strongly worded testimonials to their good character. Easty herself movingly petitioned Phips, the judges, and "the Reverend ministers" before her death, asking not for her own life but rather that "no more Innocentt blood may be shed." She knew the judges "would not be gulty of Innocent blood for the world," she wrote, but knowing herself to be innocent, "I know you are in the wrong way." She asked that the accusers be questioned "strictly" and kept separated for "some time," and that more of the confessors might be tried, "I being confident there is severall of them has belyed themselves and others." How many people other than the addressees knew the contents of Easty's petition is uncertain. But she touched on the very issues that outspoken critics were raising, and some of the "Reverend ministers" of Boston were indeed reflecting on the trials.[32]

Increase Mather, hitherto publicly silent on the subject, and Samuel Willard, sporadically vocal earlier in the summer, both prepared their own publications for the press that fall. Mather, deliberately linking himself to the Englishman John Gaule, who had urged caution in witchcraft prosecutions in his 1646 *Select Cases of Conscience touching Witches and Witchcrafts*, gave his work a similar title: *Cases of Conscience Concerning Evil Spirits Personating Men*. Willard's title, *Some Miscellany Observations on our present Debates respecting Witchcrafts, in a Dialogue Between S. and B. By P. E. and J. A.*, presented the nominally anonymous author as a supporter of Philip English and John Alden. The incorrect publication information on the first page, "Philadelphia, Printed by William Bradford, for Hezekiah Usher, 1692," summoned up the name of another fugitive member of Willard's Third Church. Willard's authorship of this pamphlet was well known to contemporaries; when Jacob Melijn sent a copy of it, along with *Cases of Conscience* and *Wonders of the Invisible World*, to a New York friend in late October, he identified it as "a dialogue by Mr. Willard."[33]

Historians have debated the relative influence of these two publications and have argued about whether they helped to effect the dissolution of the court. The works may have seen print too late to have influenced the governor's decision in that form, but on the other hand both reflected the thinking of prominent and influential Bostonians in late September and early October 1692. In addition, they seem to have circulated in manuscript prior to their publication, as did the preface that Willard drafted for *Cases of Conscience*. Also available in manuscript during the same period was a lengthy "letter" to an unnamed clergyman written on October 8 by Thomas Brattle, the wealthy merchant who belonged to Willard's Third Church. All three works can thus be used to expose the nature of the discussions that led to the end of the primary phase of the trials.[34]

Although Increase Mather and Samuel Willard presented their positions in varying formats and adopted different argumentative styles, both focused on similar issues: Could the devil appear in the shape of an innocent person? Were touch tests reliable? What evidence would be required to convict a witch? What uses, if any, could be made of confessions and of the spectral visions of the afflicted people? And just as the ministers concurred on the key questions, so too they largely concurred on the answers. Starting from the premises that devils and witches existed and that Satan could afflict humans with or without the assistance of witches, Willard and the senior Mather insisted that the images of innocents *could* be represented to others by the devil, that touch tests constituted "the Devil's testimony," and that the afflicted people's evidence had a "Diabolical" rather than an "Authentick" origin. Indeed, the afflicted might be possessed or obsessed rather than bewitched, which rendered their testimony even more doubtful. The only way to convict a witch, Mather wrote, was by "a free and Voluntary Confession of the Crime made by the Person Suspected and Accused After Examination," or "if two credible Persons shall affirm upon Oath that they have seen the Party accused speaking such words, or doing things which none but such as have Familiarity with the Devil ever did or can do." Confessions that named other witches were, however, unreliable. So Willard asserted, "If people have by their own account given themselves up to the Devil, the Father of Lies, . . . what Credit is to be given to the Testimony of such against the Lives of others?"[35]

Despite their criticism of the ideas and methods used to convict the witches in the trials, Willard and Mather nevertheless declined to find fault with the judges and jurors who had applied touch tests and accepted spectral testimony as reliable. (The men in question, after all, were members of their congregations, their friends and associates.) Willard dealt with the issue by wholly ignoring it. For his part, Mather insisted that if an innocent person were condemned—not that any *had* been, he added quickly—Satan's "deluding and Imposing on the Imaginations of men" caused the injustice, and "the Witnesses, Juries, and Judges were all to be excused from blame."[36]

In an unpaginated afterword to his tract, inserted at the last minute to gloss over differences with his son's nearly simultaneous production of *Wonders of the Invisible World,* Increase went even further, terming the "Worthy Persons" who had been involved with the trials "wise and good men" who had "acted with all Fidelity according to their Light." They deserved New Englanders' "Pitty and Prayers" rather than "Censures." Moreover, he pointed out, "the Judges affirm that they have not Convicted any one meerly on the account of what *Spectres* have said, or of what has been Represented to the Eyes or Imaginations of sick bewitched persons." He then appended his own approbation of the conviction of George Burroughs at the only proceeding he had attended in person. As was indicated previously, in Increase Mather's opinion the descriptions of Burroughs's unusual strength met his test for convincing proof: witnesses had seen him "do such things as no man that has not a Devil to be his Familiar could perform."

Thomas Brattle began his manuscript in a similar vein, claiming that he did not intend to "cast dirt on authority, or any way offer reproach to it," but he quickly shifted to a hard-hitting critical analysis.[37] His prose was less restrained and more impassioned than that of his clerical contemporaries, his critique more wide-ranging than theirs. Brattle, who later became a fellow of the Royal Society, took a more secular, scientifically oriented approach to the problem of witchcraft than did the ministers, while still not questioning the existence of Satan or his human allies. He too rejected touch tests and charged that afflicted and confessors alike consorted dangerously with the devil. But he also raised other troubling questions, and he named names. If they believed everything the accusers said, why had the judges never ordered the arrest of Mistress Margaret Thacher? Why had they allowed Hezekiah Usher to remain in "a private house" rather than jailing him? Why had they not vigorously pursued the high-status fugitives Elizabeth Cary, Philip and

Mary English, John Alden? Already, he claimed, the husbands of some of the Andover confessors realized that they had erred when they pressed their wives to confess, and they deeply regretted their "rashnesse and uncharitablenesse" in doing so. To the list of distinguished judges and councilors supporting the trials he counterposed a list of equally distinguished (but publicly silent) critics: the former governor Simon Bradstreet, the former deputy governor Thomas Danforth, the one-time judge of the Court of Oyer and Terminer Nathaniel Saltonstall, and several Boston justices of the peace.

Brattle singled out his own pastor, Samuel Willard, for special praise. As the minister to three of the judges, Brattle declared, Willard had been "very solicitous and industrious in this matter," and if his "notions and proposals" had only been adopted at the outset of the troubles, "they would never have grown unto that heigth which now they have." What Willard's strategy for dealing with the crisis would have been, Brattle did not reveal, but he gave some possible clues in his lengthy discussion of the way the young Willard had handled his obsessed maidservant Elizabeth Knapp two decades before. "I often think of the Groton woman," Brattle wrote, asserting that there was as much reason to arrest and jail those she accused then as there was to arrest and jail others now. Yet Knapp had later admitted "that all was mere fancy and delusion of the Devill's." That nothing came of her false charges, Brattle implied but did not say, stemmed from Willard's dealing with her afflictions in a spiritual rather than legal manner and from his skepticism about the statements she made in her fits. Perhaps, then, Willard made a similar proposal about treating the Salem Village afflicted early in the crisis.[38]

In addition to forcefully critiquing the trials, Thomas Brattle's letter inadvertently revealed the extent of continuing support for the proceedings in Salem. A rising chorus of voices had been raised against the court, but Brattle also referred repeatedly (if briefly) to the court's multitude of advocates he and his allies were opposing. "The great cry of many of our neighbours" insisted on the truthfulness of the confessions, he acknowledged. Those skeptical of witch-finding by the afflicted had not been able to influence the credulous, he admitted. Unfortunately, Brattle wrote, Samuel Willard "has as yet mett with little but unkindness, abuse, and reproach from many men," and the judges have been "apt to speak very hardly" of their critics. The dissension depicted in such statements accords well with Governor Phips's characterization of the atmosphere in Boston in early October as a "strange ferment of dissatisfaction," replete with "Passion" and with the possibility of "kindling an inextinguishable flame" or with Cotton Mather's description of *"Animosity"* and *"Paroxysms"* of rage "Embroiling" the town.[39]

The primary public advocate of the trials, other than the judges themselves, was of course the younger Mather, who developed his ideas most fully in *Wonders of the Invisible World*, which was printed in mid-October but carried a date of 1693 because Governor Phips had ordered a halt to publications on the trials. Increase Mather declared at the close of *Cases of Conscience* that it was "strange" for people to think he and his son disagreed, for "I perused and approved of that Book before it was Printed," yet readers then and now have recognized the different emphases of the contemporaneous works by father and son—a divergence of opinion that Increase publicly denied, yet could not wholly obscure. Where the senior Mather's treatment of the trials suggests caution and doubt, his son's exudes certainty and confidence that the court had not erred in the past, and would not err in the future.[40]

Describing 1692 as "this extraordinary Time of the *Devils coming down in great Wrath upon us,*" Cotton Mather informed his readers that he had set himself the task of exposing "the whole PLOT of the Devil, against *New-England.*" That there was such a plot should astonish no one, he explained, for New Englanders had settled in "those, which were once the *Devil's* Territories," and Satan had in the past also attempted to expel them, although his current efforts were "more Difficult, more Surprizing" than ever. And so "an Army of *Devils*" had "horribly" attacked "the *First-born* of our *English* Settlements" and had subsequently assaulted other places as well. No one could doubt the existence of the "terrible Plague," he contended, especially because of all the confessions that concurred in their *"main strokes."* Indeed, if the devils could somehow force "Scores of Innocent People [to] Unite, in *Confessions* of a Crime," then that result was so "prodigious" that "it threatens no less than a sort of a Dissolution upon the World" and "all the Rules of Understanding Humane Affayrs are at an end." Acknowledging that some guiltless persons might have been accused, Mather expressed the hope and expectation that such defendants would ultimately be cleared, but insisted simultaneously that God might well have allowed the devil to represent the shapes of people who had committed lesser offenses than witchcraft "for their perpetual Humiliation."[41]

Yes, Mather admitted, the Salem justices of the peace had adopted some "disputed Methods" in their fight against the witches, but "none but what have had great Precedents in other parts of the World" (and he summarized long passages from Richard Bernard, John Gaule, and William Perkins to prove the point). He defended the use of such spectral evidence as the ghostly accusations and confessions, for those sightings provided "a sufficient occasion for Magistrates to make a particular Enquiry" even though such reports "may be defective enough in point of Conviction." Mather then proceeded to establish the context for his treatment of selected Salem prosecutions by describing the Bury St. Edmunds trial presided over by Sir Matthew Hale in 1662; he also cited another precedent, the witch trials at Mora, Sweden, in 1669–1670, during which "Hundreds of their Children" taken to a "Diabolical Rendezvouz" at night had afterwards confessed to writing their names in the devil's book in blood, to eating and drinking with him, and to attempting to kill a minister and other people.[42]

In what he clearly regarded as the most important part of the book, Mather, drawing on the materials supplied him by Stephen Sewall, wrote at length about the five prosecutions he chose as exemplars: George Burroughs, Bridget Bishop, Susannah Martin, Elizabeth Howe, and Martha Carrier (in that order). With the exception of Burroughs, whom he was directed to include, all were "usual suspects"; all except Martin had been named by confessors; and every one of them had been accused of maleficium by numerous witnesses. These particular prosecutions, Mather had obviously concluded, best supported his defense of the trials. Just as obviously, he avoided writing about more controversial and questionable convictions (such as those of Martha Corey or Rebecca Nurse), nor did he address the specifics of any of the confessions he cited in general terms. The discussion of the trials closed with a statement dated October 11 and signed by William Stoughton and Samuel Sewall, confirming that the clergyman had accurately reported *"Matters of Fact and Evidence"* and the "Methods of Conviction" employed in the Salem proceedings.[43]

In early to mid-October, then, Sir William Phips faced a major dilemma. Hitherto a supporter of the trials, he now found himself trapped in a heated debate involving a leader of the Second Church on one side and the chief pastor of the Third on the other, with the other minister of Old North (Increase Mather) wedged somewhere uncomfortably in the middle; and between the judges of his special court, on the one hand, and their former colleague Nathaniel Saltonstall and other distinguished present and past leaders of the colony (Simon Bradstreet, Thomas Danforth, Robert Pike), on the other, along with the articulate critic Thomas Brattle.[44]

It was in exactly this context that the governor wrote the first letter to England in which he acknowledged the existence of the witchcraft crisis.[45] On October 12, he addressed four separate missives to colonial officials. Two described his activities at Pemaquid and advocated "the Conquest of Cannada"; a third complained that too many men among Massachusetts' leaders still clung to "that Idoll the old Charter"; and the fourth simultaneously informed London officials of the crisis and distanced himself from it. Phips briefly described the complaints of the afflicted, explained that he had established the Court of Oyer and Terminer with his lieutenant governor as the chief judge, revealed that more than twenty people (including some confessors) had been convicted of witchcraft, and parroted the standard line that the judges "began their proceedings with the accusations of the afflicted and then went upon other humane evidences to strengthen that."

Next, to be blunt, he lied. "I was almost the whole time of the proceeding abroad in the service of Their Majesties in the Eastern part of the Country," Phips falsely claimed (as shown herein, he had in fact been in Boston during most of the court sessions). "As soon as I came from fighting against their Majesties Enemyes and understood what danger some of their innocent subjects might be exposed to . . . I did before any application was made unto me about it put a stop to the proceedings of the Court." Elsewhere in the letter, Phips more precisely described his directives, which had not in fact halted all legal activity in the witchcraft trials. He had ordered that no new arrests should be made, except in cases of "unavoydable necessity"; and he had decided to "shelter from any Proceedings against them" anyone about whom the "least suspition" of innocence could be entertained. He concluded by indicating that he would await the monarchs' further orders before taking further steps.

The governor's interim solution probably satisfied no one and clearly did little to stifle the debate then roiling the colony's political and religious elite. Supporters of the trials must have decried the partial halt to the proceedings, while opponents would have been upset that arrests and prosecutions would continue during the many months it would take to receive definitive answers from London.

Yet even before at last writing to London, Phips had taken additional steps to resolve his dilemma by looking elsewhere in America for advice. On October 5, he dispatched a series of questions about witchcraft to the clergymen of New York, but their reply, dated October 11, would not have arrived until after he sent his letters of October 12. The eight inquiries addressed topics ranging from the general—Are there witches? What constitutes witchcraft?—to the specific: Can a specter represent an innocent person? Does the sighting of an apparition supply proof sufficient for conviction? Can the evidence of an apparently blameless life offset a spectral accusation? Could people tortured by the devil remain in relatively good health? In response, four Dutch and French ministers from New York concurred that witches existed, that witchcraft required "an alliance with the Devil," and that Satan could "assume the shape of a good man, and present this shape before the eyes of the afflicted, as the source of the afflictions which they suffer." God could "thrust a sinful, though faithful and pious man into such calamitous experience in order to try his piety and virtue," and therefore employing spectral evidence to convict anyone would be "the greatest imprudence." The devil might in fact be attacking the afflicted and the supposed afflicter at the same time, trying to bring the latter "into bad repute and danger of his life." Thus far the New Yorkers had aligned themselves largely with the trials' critics. But then they gave some credence to the other side, declaring that an apparently good life could indeed conceal "devilish practices," and that the afflicted could have been tormented for months with "no wasting of the body, and no weakening of their spirits." Satan could even have made his victims stronger, they contended.[46]

A fifth New York cleric, a minister of the Church of England who served as chaplain to English troops stationed in the town, replied separately to the same questions. He essentially agreed with the others but placed greater emphasis than they on the devil's many deceptions. "The minds of men, especially of the ignorant or depraved, can easily be and frequently are deceived by the Devil," John Miller wrote. Accordingly, spectral visions could not be trusted, nor did people's previous lives (good or bad) convey reliable information about whether or not they were witches. He also asserted that afflicted people such as those in Massachusetts were probably not "maliciously enchanted by any sorcerer, but deluded by the Devil to promote the misery and ruin of the human race," thus raising once again the likelihood that Satan had acted directly, without any human intermediaries.[47]

At about the same time he was reading these statements from New York, Sir William Phips would have learned that Samuel Wardwell was not the only Andover confessor to disavow his self-incriminating statements. On October 18, twenty-six men from that town petitioned the governor and council on behalf of their wives and other relatives, pointing out that some of the penitents now said that "they have wronged themselves and the truth in their confessions." Further, Increase Mather could well have informed his friend the governor about the contents of his and Thomas Brattle's conversations with a group of Andover women in the Salem jail on October 19, during which many of them retracted both their confessions and their accusations of others. Abigail Barker, for example, "bewail'd and lamented her accusing of others, whom she never knew any evill by in her life time; and said that she was told by her examiners that she *did* know of their being witches and *must* confesse it; that she did know of their being baptised, &c.: and must confesse it; by the renewed urgings and chargings of whom at last she gave way, and owned such things as were utterly false, which now she was in great horrour and anguish of soul for her complying with."[48]

Phips could also have heard about the contents of a statement approved on October 17 by a group of Connecticut ministers, who directly addressed the issue of what evidence would be adequate to convict a witch. The colony of Connecticut had also established a Court of Oyer and Terminer to handle several witchcraft trials, including those of Elizabeth Clawson and Mercy Disborough. As will be recalled from chapter 2, the two women had been originally accused by the afflicted servant Katherine Branch back in April. Their intertwined trials began on September 14, but the court adjourned five days later after the jury failed to reach a unanimous verdict in either case. Before the court reconvened, the justices asked a group of clerics for their advice on the matter. In their formal response, the Connecticut ministers rejected any evidence of witch's marks unless confirmed by "some able physitians," suggested that maleficium stories provided "very slender and uncertain grounds" for conviction, and declared themselves unable to determine whether Kate's fits had been caused by "counterfeiting," hysteria, the devil, or witchcraft. Most significant, however, they pronounced the evidence of "the appearance of their spectres to her to be very uncertain and failable from the easy deception of her senses & subtile devices of the devil." Therefore, they indicated, they did not "think her a sufficient witness."[49]

Even though Governor Phips was not a particularly skillful politician, he must have realized that the best way to quiet the political and theological firestorm raging during the third week of October would be to dissolve the court permanently rather than merely suspend some of its proceedings, as he had done by October 12. In addition, now that prominent Bostonians were challenging the court, he and his wife were no longer so vulnerable to possible accusations. Yet political and personal reasons could not by themselves provide adequate justifications for halting the trials before the Court of Oyer and Terminer. Which arguments carried the most weight with him is not wholly clear. In his reports to England, Phips stressed his growing realization that apparitions could appear in the form of innocents, despite Stoughton's insistence to the contrary. Perhaps he also concluded that spectral evidence had played a greater role in leading to convictions than the judges, or Cotton Mather, had previously admitted. Many of those similar confessions Mather found so convincing, after all, involved reports of spectral witch meetings and baptisms, and either the Andover men's petition or Increase Mather or both had informed him of the multiple withdrawals of such confessions. The Connecticut clergy's emphasis on Satan's "subtile devices" could have carried great weight with him.

Because such a notion had a known advocate on the council, it is also possible that Miller's stress on the devil's ability to afflict the sufferers without the assistance of witches provided the clinching argument. The councilor Robert Pike, it will be recalled, had forcefully advanced that very contention in his letter to Jonathan Corwin in early August. For the first time since mid-June, too, the elderly Pike traveled from Salisbury to Boston to attend council meetings. He was there on October 14 and 22, along with a majority of the judges. Pike, a sharp critic of the legal proceedings who had a history of outspokenness, would not have allowed the matter to drop.[50]

The surviving minutes fail to record that the court's future was a subject of discussion at these meetings or during those which followed on October 25 and 26. Yet Samuel Sewall noted in his diary on the 28th that William Stoughton had raised the issue in council meetings "several times before" that day. Surely the topic engaged the councilors' attention both inside and outside their official gatherings. On October 26, Sewall recorded the results of what appear to have been many formal and informal conversations. A bill calling for a fast and a "Convocation of Ministers" to consult about the witchcraft crisis had passed in the assembly by a vote of 33 to 29. Even though the governor and council did not concur, "the season and manner of doing it, is such, that the Court of Oyer and Terminer count themselves thereby dismissed." Two days later, Sewall remarked that Stoughton had once more "desired to have the advise of the Governour and Council as to the sitting of the Court of Oyer and Terminer next week; [he] said should move it no more; great silence, as if should say do not go." On Saturday the 29th, Phips finally declared flatly that the court "must fall."[51]

Just over two weeks later a teenager named Mary Herrick, who had been afflicted for about two months, came to John Hale and his fellow clergyman, Joseph Gerrish of Wenham, to offer a remarkable statement. For several days she had been afflicted by two apparitions, one of Mistress Hale, the other of the dead Mary Easty. Although John Hale's wife tormented her "by pinching, pricking and Choaking," Goody Easty's specter had appeared for a very different reason. Easty announced that "she Came to tell her She had been put to Death wrongfully and was Innocent of Witchcraft." Easty, indeed, "Came to Vindicate her Cause and she Cryed Vengeance, Vengeance." The apparition directed Herrick to go to the two clergymen with an account of her vision. "Then she would rise no more, nor should Mrs. Hayle Afflict her any more," Goody Easty promised. Herrick also disclosed that Easty had first appeared to her the night before her execution on September 22. "I am going upon the Ladder to be hanged for a Witch, but I am innocent," the specter declared, adding, "and before a 12 Month be past you shall believe it." Herrick indicated that she had at the time doubted the truth of her vision, and so she had not reported it; "but now she believeth it is all a delusion of the Devil." That one of the afflicted herself would so soon come to question the origins of her suffering and reject the guilt of such an active spectral tormentor as

Mary Easty reveals above all else the rapidly changing climate of opinion in the colony.[52]

THE FINAL TRIALS

One of the most controversial tasks in which the Massachusetts legislature engaged during the fall of 1692 was setting up the colony's new judicial system. The substance of the disagreements is not recorded, but not until November 25, after at least seven full days of debate stretching over nearly a month, did the assembly members reach consensus. At the top of the new system sat the Superior Court of Judicature, which thus acquired the responsibility for dealing with the many suspected witches who were either still jailed or had recently been released on bond to await their trials. On December 7, the council selected the new judges. William Stoughton continued as chief justice. The veterans John Richards, Wait Winthrop, and Samuel Sewall were also chosen, along with one new member: Thomas Danforth, a prominent critic of the Court of Oyer and Terminer.[53]

By contrast, the passage of a new witchcraft law seems to have aroused little controversy; the bill was introduced on December 12 and adopted two days later. As was indicated in chapter 6, it essentially mirrored then-current English law. But it omitted the provision of the 1604 English statute that preserved dower and inheritance for the heirs of executed witches, and that omission caused the Privy Council to disallow the statute three years later. Historians have concluded, undoubtedly correctly, that the altered language was intended primarily to protect the Essex County sheriff, George Corwin, who had already seized all or part of the estates of several of those who had been hanged.[54]

As the judges of the new court contemplated their responsibilities in an atmosphere of skepticism about the trials in which most of them had participated under different auspices, they could well have looked south to Connecticut for divergent precedents. Since Wait Winthrop corresponded regularly with John Alleyn, one of the Connecticut judges, he would have learned that when that colony's Court of Oyer and Terminer reconvened on October 28 to deal with the suspended prosecutions of Elizabeth Clawson and Mercy Disborough, Clawson had been acquitted and Disborough convicted. Yet the latter was found guilty only after one member of the original jury had been replaced, a procedure the colony's Court of Assistants thought so irregular that they soon reprieved her death sentence. The assistants further insisted that the evidence presented in court against Disborough had not sufficiently satisfied the criteria for conviction set forth by William Perkins,

Richard Bernard, and Increase Mather. The "miserable toyl they are in in the Bay" served as "warning enof" that inadequate proof would "make hanging work apace," the Connecticut magistrates wrote. Any reader of those words would have understood their implicit rebuke of the Massachusetts judges. The language suggesting that questionable verdicts had been reached must have stung someone like Samuel Sewall, coming as it did from peers and colleagues.[55]

The Massachusetts legislature took its final action of the fall session on December 16, when—"Upon Consideration of many persons now in Custody within the County of Essex, charged as Capital Offenders"—it authorized a meeting of the new Superior Court in the form of "a Court of Assize and General Gaol Delivery" on January 3, 1692/3. On December 23, the court issued a new call for men to serve on the necessary grand and petty juries. Some of the judges, Governor Phips reported in late February to the secretary of state in London, "were convinced and acknowledged that their former proceedings were too violent and not grounded upon a right foundation," and so in the 1693 trials they adopted "another method."

In particular, persuaded by Increase Mather and others that Satan could appear in the shape of an innocent person, and that "the look and touch of the suspected persons was not sufficient proofe against them," the justices did not place "the same stress" on such evidence as they had before. Phips observed that of the fifty-two people tried in two court sessions in January and February, only three were convicted. Although he did not say so, at least nine of the defendants (including Philip and Mary English) were not even indicted. Among those tried and acquitted were Richard Carrier, Mary Lacey the younger, Mary Toothaker, and Mary Marston.[56]

The three suspects convicted, even under the stricter new rules of procedure, were Sarah Wardwell, Betty Johnson, and Mary Post. All three had confessed. On September 1, Sarah Wardwell (Samuel's widow) had admitted covenanting with the devil six years earlier, attending Village witch meetings, and afflicting Martha Sprague. Betty, described as "but simplish at the best" by her grandfather, the Reverend Francis Dane, had on August 11 given a full confession in which she described witch meetings and devilish baptisms and named other witches. And Mary Post, one of the unmarried daughters of Mary Tyler Post Bridges, had accused ten others of witchcraft in addition to acknowledging her own complicity with the devil. The three were all indicted twice: for covenanting with Satan and for afflicting others—Timothy Swan (Post), Ann Putnam Jr. (Johnson), and Martha Sprague (Wardwell). Yet, as Anthony Checkley informed the governor, all three condemned women were "under the same circumstances" as "some of the cleared." Mary Post's sister

Hannah and her stepsister Sarah Bridges, for example, had also confessed and named others as witches. Why had they been acquitted and she convicted? Following his attorney general's logic, Phips issued reprieves for the three women.[57]

By several accounts, Lieutenant Governor Stoughton was outraged at Phips's action. He had already signed a death warrant encompassing the three and five more convicted earlier; Phips reprieved the others as well, "untill their Majesties' pleasure be signified and declared." Stoughton, "filled with passionate anger," left the bench in disgust at a court session in Charlestown in early February. "Who it was that obstructed the Execution of Justice, or hindred those good proceedings they had made, he knew not," Stoughton reportedly declared, "but thereby the Kingdom of Satan was advanc'd, &c and the Lord have mercy on this Country." Thomas Danforth took over as chief judge for the rest of that session, although Stoughton returned to preside over the final set of trials in late April and early May.[58]

Only a few people remained to be tried by then. Captain John Alden, who had returned from New York by December 22 and had posted bond on December 31, appeared before the court on April 25 and was freed without further proceedings. Most of the remaining defendants were Andover confessors, many of them young people who presumably had been released from prison on bail over the winter. Every one of them was acquitted, including Mary Bridges Jr., William Barker Jr., Susannah Post, and two young daughters of Mary Tyler. Among the last to be freed was Tituba, who had languished in jail longer than anyone else. On May 9, a grand jury in Ipswich declined to indict her, writing "ignoramus" on a document charging that "Tittapa an Indian Woman Servant to mr Samuel Parris of Salem village" had "Wickedly & felloniously . . . Signed the Devills Booke" and "become A detestable Witch." Reportedly, Parris refused to pay the costs of her imprisonment, and she was sold to an unidentified person who supplied the necessary funds.[59]

Indeed, even after acquittals, prisoners in general could not be released until their fees were paid. Accordingly, some remained in jail for weeks or months after they were cleared of all charges. Thus, for example, Lydia Dustin, acquitted in early February, was still imprisoned when she died in mid-March. Such a delay too was the fate of Mary Watkins, a maidservant from Milton who had accused her dame (a Goody Swift) of being a witch and a child-murderer. Called up for examination in May 1693, Mary admitted that "they were falsce reports and that she had ronged" her dame. According to Robert Calef, she then "accused herself of being a Witch," but the grand jurors so distrusted her confession that they refused to indict her. Watkins was sent to jail until she found sureties for her good behavior, yet was unable to do so "by reason of her deep poverty & want of Friends." In July, the justices of the Superior Court ordered her freed once her fees had been paid. But she could not accomplish even that. In August, she and another young woman who had been held in Boston petitioned the jailer, asking him "to provide master or masters to carry us out of this country into Virginia, our friends, relations, and kindred, slighting us to extremity." Calef later noted that she had been indentured to a Virginia master.[60]

Much, then, had changed in a year. A maidservant had accused her dame of being a witch (as Mary Warren had accused Elizabeth Proctor thirteen months before), but unlike Warren, Watkins was not believed. She had then confessed to being a witch herself (as Sarah Churchwell had done almost exactly a year earlier), but again was not believed. Yet one part of the story remained the same. Like Churchwell, Mercy Lewis, Susannah Sheldon, and Mercy Short, Mary Watkins was a refugee from the Maine frontier.

Daughter of Thomas and Mary Watkins, who had lived on the Kennebec River, Mary was (after about 1672) the stepdaughter of Thomas Stevens, who owned an Indian trading post north of Casco Bay. Her stepfather sold Bartholomew Gedney his property at North Yarmouth, the settlement that became one of the flashpoints of conflict in the early stages of the Second Indian War. Thomas Stevens himself was one of the hostages taken by the Wabanakis in retaliation for Captain Benjamin Blackman's seizure of twenty Indian captives in late August 1688.[61]

No record suggests that Mary Watkins was ever afflicted, as were her Salem Village counterparts, but another young Maine refugee was. Margaret Rule, the oldest daughter of John Rule, a mariner based in Saco until the mid- to late 1680s, began to suffer fits in Boston in the fall of 1693. Her neighbor and pastor, Cotton Mather, described her torments as resembling Mercy Short's "in almost all the circumstances of it, indeed the Afflictions were so much alike, that the relation I have given of the one, would almost serve as the full History of the other." Margaret too described the devil as *"a short and Black Man,"* suffered from pinches and pinpricks that left her black and blue, and contorted her body into strange shapes. And she accused a neighbor woman of bewitching her, but Mather persuaded the family to seek relief for her through prayer rather than prosecution. After weeks of prayer and fasting, Mather recorded, the evil spirits finally left her, saying, *"Go, and the Devil go with you, we can do no more."* After that, Margaret was "extream *weak and faint,"* but she slowly recovered. Hers was the last recorded affliction of a young frontier refugee in the early 1690s.[62]

· · ·

When the Wabanakis surveyed their group of sixteen captives in August 1688, they chose the seventy-year-old Thomas Stevens as their messenger to Sylvanus Davis at Falmouth because, as they informed the old man, he could "neither doe us good nor hurte." Tell Davis, they directed Stevens, that they would observe a truce until they heard from Boston, and that they wanted "all [their] Indeans or none." Then they added, "if ever it were a war again, it would not be as it was formerly."[63]

As this book has shown, the next four years proved the Wabanaki leaders to be remarkable prophets. No other war fought on North American soil has ever had such extraordinary consequences.

Conclusion

NEW WITCH-LAND

WHAT REALLY HAPPENED at Salem in 1692? Why were so many people charged with witchcraft? And why were so many of the defendants convicted and hanged? Such questions still haunt Americans at the beginning of the twenty-first century. Numerous responses to those inquiries have been proposed over the years, yet this book has shown that too many of the answers have failed to take into account the specific late-seventeenth-century context in which the witchcraft crisis occurred. In particular, historians have not fully recognized how two quite distinct phenomena combined to help create the crisis, and how examining the chain of events within a chronological framework can reveal the key patterns.

The foundation of the witchcraft crisis lay in Puritan New Englanders' singular worldview, one they had inherited from the first settlers of Massachusetts Bay more than sixty years earlier. That worldview taught them that they were a chosen people, charged with bringing God's message to a heathen land previously ruled by the devil. And in that adopted homeland God spoke to them repeatedly through his providences—that is, through the small and large events of their daily lives. Remarkable signs in the sky (comets, the aurora borealis), natural catastrophes (hurricanes, droughts), smallpox epidemics, the sudden deaths of children or spouses, unexpected good fortune: all carried messages from God to his people, if only they could interpret the meanings properly. New England's Puritans, even in the third generation, believed themselves to be surrounded by an invisible world of spirits as well as by a natural world of palpable objects. Both worlds communicated God's messages, because both operated under his direction. Satan, whom they understood to be (as Samuel Willard put it in a sermon in late May 1692) "the power of the air," leader of the "evil angels," played a major role in the invisible world. Yet because the devil was one of God's creatures even though he had revolted against divine authority, Puritans knew that Satan could do no more than God allowed. To believe otherwise would be to deny God's omnipotence.[1]

Then in the last quarter of the seventeenth century, two successive, devastating wars on the northeastern frontier, King Philip's War and King William's War—or the First and Second Indian Wars—together wreaked havoc with what had been prosperous settlements along the coast northeast of Massachusetts. The continued and seemingly unstoppable successes of the Indians and their French allies called into question New Englanders' ability to sustain the northern outposts that contributed significantly to the prosperity of their economy through the production of fish and timber. That their Wabanaki enemies were Catholic (or at least aligned with French Catholics) made matters worse, suggesting that the settlers' own Protestantism might not be destined for the triumph they had long assumed to be inevitable.

The First Indian War, though extremely costly, ended with a victory in southern New England in late summer 1676 and with a standoff in the northeast in spring 1678. When hostilities began again "to the eastward" a decade later, the precarious nature of the earlier truce became evident to all. Nevertheless, the colonists at first anticipated renewed success in the second war. Yet those expectations were not met. New Englanders instead suffered repeated, serious losses of men and women, houses, livestock, and shipping. In the aftermath of each devastating defeat, they attributed their failures not to mistakes by their military and political leaders but rather to God's providence. He had, they concluded, visited these afflictions upon them as chastisements for their many sins of omission and commission. They had developed similar interpretations of the causes of earlier setbacks, but the consequences of those beliefs never extended far beyond the walls of their meetinghouses, primarily affecting their religious attitudes. This time, however, something was different.

In early 1692, several children and teenage girls began having fits of a sort previously recorded elsewhere in old and New England. The wartime context could well have influenced the onset of those fits—that the afflicted first accused an Indian of tormenting them certainly suggests as much—but more important than such plausible, if not wholly provable, origins was the long-term impact of the young women's charges in the context of Puritan New Englanders' belief system. Since Puritans insisted that the devil could do nothing without God's permission, they logically decided that God bore the ultimate responsibility for the witches' malefic activities. As the Reverend Deodat Lawson instructed his former parishioners in Salem Village on March 24, 1691/2, "The LORD doth terrible things amongst us, by lengthening the Chain of the Roaring Lyon, in an Extraordinary manner; so that the Devil is come down in great wrath." God, who was "Righteous & Holy," would not afflict them "without a Cause, and that Cause is always Just." What was the Lord saying to them? they needed to ask themselves, for "these malicious operations of Satan, are the sorest afflictions [that] can befal a person or people."[2]

So too had God brought about their losses in the war, especially through providential actions during the 1690 campaigns against targets in New France. As will be recalled from chapter 3, in November 1690 Governor Simon Bradstreet attributed the failure of Sir William Phips's Quebec expedition to "the awfull Frowne of God." The contrary winds that halted the ships' progress at the mouth of the St. Lawrence, Bradstreet declared, showed "the providence of God, appearing against us." Additional "particular providences" to the same effect included "the loss of so many of our ffriends sent out in the Expedition, in and at their return by the contagion of the small Pox, Fevers and other killing distempers," amounting perhaps to two hundred men. Likewise, when Fitz-John Winthrop reflected on the disasters that had befallen his attempt to lead colonial militia against Montreal that same year, he concluded that the "Devine hand that governes the world, and pointes out the sorrowes and succes of all mankinde" had caused the plan to collapse. To God's "good pleasure in this matter, as in all things," he told the governor and council of Connecticut, "wee must submit, remembring that not one hayre of our heades fall to the ground without Gods appointments."[3]

The Lord, in short, was simultaneously punishing New England in two different ways—through the Second Indian War on the northeastern frontier and through the operations of witchcraft in Essex County. As the evidence presented in this book has demonstrated, the assaults from the visible and invisible worlds became closely entwined in New Englanders' minds. Those connections permeated the witchcraft examinations and trials, as revealed by repeated spectral sightings of the "black man," whom the afflicted described as resembling an Indian; and in the threats that the witches and the devil— just as the Wabanakis had—would "tear to pieces" or "knock in the head" those who opposed them. The links evident in legal proceedings are underscored by events elsewhere as well: the attack by apparitions on Gloucester in midsummer; Joseph Ring's repeated encounters with the spectral demonic militia; Mary Toothaker's pact with the "tawny" devil, who protected her for a time from his Wabanaki minions; Mercy Short's visions of meetings attended by both Indian sachems and witches; and Cotton Mather's later history of the war, which repeatedly described the Wabanakis as "devilish."

Joshua Scottow's "Narrative of the Planting of the Massachusetts

Colony," written shortly after the end of the witchcraft crisis, also tied the two themes inextricably together. Scottow, a longtime resident of Black Point who had earlier referred to several Wabanaki sachems as "Satan's Emissaries," presented the Wabanakis' attacks and those of the witches as related phenomena, both instigated by God. "These wicked Cannibals," he explained to his readers, are "Gods Sword, and have been so for many years together." But the "Cruel Cannibals, Scalping and Fleaing of our Bodies, burning us as Sacrifices," only killed their material selves, he observed, while "the Devourer out of the Bottomless Pit," the "Do-evil," threatened their very souls. God, he asserted, "calls us, now being Alarmed by these Spirits," to assess our spiritual estates. Pointing out that those "upon whom this Great Wrath is fallen . . . are chiefly the members of our Churches, or their Hearers and Dependants," and furthermore that the witches observed diabolic sacraments, he predicted that "*New England* will be called, new Witch-land.". Had the settlers not misbehaved, Satan would never have gained such an advantage over them, and they would never have experienced so many accusations, convictions, executions, and even "some Accused among our Rulers in Commonwealth and Churches." The combined assaults, Scottow contended, should rouse New Englanders from "our Læthal Lethargy" and return their churches to "*the good Old Way we have walked in.*"⁴

Accordingly, had the Second Indian War on the northeastern frontier somehow been avoided, the Essex County witchcraft crisis of 1692 would not have occurred. This is not to say that the war "caused" the witchcraft crisis, but rather that the conflict created the conditions that allowed the crisis to develop as rapidly and extensively as it did. In its early stages (that is, prior to mid-April 1692), the episode that originated in Salem Village resembled several other witchcraft incidents in seventeenth-century New England. Although the afflictions of Abigail Williams and Betty Parris were unusual, they were by no means unique, nor were adults' initial reactions to those afflictions unprecedented. But the girls' fits occurred in a supercharged atmosphere marked by ongoing conflict within Salem Village itself and, even more important, by the broader conflict on New England's northeastern borders. The afflictions that began in the Salem Village parsonage, after all, did not stop there, as did the fits in the home of Sergeant Daniel Wescott in Stamford, Connecticut, in April 1692, or as had the earlier afflictions in the Groton parsonage of Samuel Willard in 1671. Instead, the sufferings soon spread to other households, especially to those inhabited by youthful refugees from the frontier wars (Mercy Lewis, Susannah Sheldon, Sarah Churchwell) and by others with close ties to the frontier (Mary Walcott). All the afflicted joined in accusing others of bewitching them.

Under normal circumstances, New England's magistrates displayed a notable skepticism when confronting witchcraft charges. The judges believed in the existence of witches, but understood that providing legally acceptable proof of guilt in specific cases could be extremely difficult. In 1692, though, circumstances were not normal. For the reasons explored above and throughout this book, Bay Colony magistrates had good reason to find a witch conspiracy plausible in 1692. *It must always be remembered that the judges of the Court of Oyer and Terminer were the very men who led the colony both politically and militarily.*

William Stoughton, the chief judge, had unaccountably failed to effect a key hostage exchange at Casco in the fall of 1688, thus bungling possibly the last chance to avert the bloodshed that followed.

John Hathorne and Jonathan Corwin had most likely caused the devastating losses of Fort Loyal and Falmouth, and so all of Maine north of Wells, by recommending the withdrawal of Captain Simon Willard's militiamen on May 15, 1690, without provision for replacements. All councilors at the time (among them a near majority of the 1692 judges) were also implicated in that decision, with its catastrophic consequences.

Samuel Sewall and Stoughton (again) had committed Massachusetts' resources to the failed expedition against Montreal.

On that campaign, Fitz-John Winthrop, brother of Judge Waitstill Winthrop, had led men from New York and Connecticut into an unmitigated disaster north of Albany. (Indeed, Jacob Leisler, then in control of New York, adopted precisely that view when he ordered Winthrop's arrest after the expedition collapsed.)

Sir William Phips had, it was true, taken Port Royal, but that success was more than offset by the fiasco at Quebec and its terrible aftermath of a raging smallpox epidemic and seemingly endless indebtedness.

The colony's leading merchants—among them Sewall and Bartholomew Gedney, and presumably Peter Sergeant and John Richards as well—had promoted and encouraged the catastrophic attempt on Quebec, perhaps as much for anticipated profits from plunder as for the colony's welfare.

Gedney and Nathaniel Saltonstall both held senior positions in the Essex County militia, and Winthrop served as the major general of the colony's militia and was ultimately responsible for all its operations.

If the devil was operating in their world with impunity—if God for his own inscrutable reasons had "lengthened the chain" that usually limited Satan's active malevolence against mankind, to adopt Lawson's memorable phrase—then the Massachusetts leaders' lack of success in combating the Indians could be explained without reference to their own failings. If God had providentially caused the wartime disasters and he had also unleashed the devil on Massachusetts, then they bore no responsibility for the current state of affairs.

Thus first the Essex justices and then all the members of the court proved receptive to charges they would otherwise have most likely dismissed. In traditional witchcraft cases, neighbors alleged difficult-to-prove malefic activities by a vengeful witch at some point in the past. Judges, mindful of the rules of English law requiring two witnesses to a capital crime, had rarely convicted—and even more rarely agreed to execute—people accused solely of such offenses. But the Essex County cases appeared to be dramatically different. The initial accusations came from young girls, then later from teenagers and older women, whose terrible sufferings seemed obvious to all who beheld them. (For that reason, the 1692 indictments most often focused on the tortures endured by the afflicted during suspects' examinations, because many witnesses could attest to the severity of the fits and the painful nature of the sufferings thereby inflicted. Indeed, later members of the grand jury had themselves probably witnessed the torments of the complainants during examinations.)

By their own lights, the magistrates—first John Hathorne and Jonathan Corwin, then the other judges of the Court of Oyer and Terminer—did the best they could to properly assess the evidence against the accused and to apply the advice given in such English treatises as Michael Dalton's *The Countrey Justice* and Richard Bernard's *Guide to Grand-Jury Men*. Although bystanders from mid-January on pitied the afflicted children and unhesitatingly accepted the reality of their torments, not until such older accusers as Betty Hubbard, Ann Carr Putnam, and Sarah Vibber joined the group of complainants did crucial legal steps proceed. But the judges had too much personally at stake in the outcome. They quickly became invested in believing in the reputed witches' guilt, in large part because they needed to believe that they themselves were *not* guilty of causing New England's current woes. Simon Bradstreet alluded to such an interpretation in his November 1690 letter. The governor informed the colony's London agents that upon reading the dismal narrative he was enclosing of the Quebec debacle, "some may charge as matter of blame upon these or those Instruments Imployed in the conduct of that Affayre." Bradstreet, though, declined to do so, placing the responsibility instead (as was already indicated) on "the providence of God, appearing against us."[5]

Even before mid-April, most of the people of Salem Village and environs found the sufferings of the afflicted completely credible. When the accusations moved from the confines of the Parris, Putnam, and Griggs households to various makeshift courtrooms, the examining magistrates—Hathorne and Corwin, joined occasionally by Sewall, Gedney, Thomas Danforth, and others—too did not question the truth of the charges they were hearing. Not only did they, like all their contemporaries, believe in the existence of witches, witchcraft, and the devil, they also, like seventeenth-century judges in general, commonly dealt only with defendants who had committed the offenses with which they were charged. And so, assuming the guilt of those they questioned, they sought to elicit the expected confessions that played a ritual role in most New England legal proceedings. With the exception of Tituba and the little girl Dorcas Good, they failed miserably until they encountered Abigail Hobbs.

Then the young teenager, a Maine refugee, made the crucial connection explicit. After Abigail proclaimed in the Salem Village meetinghouse at her April 19 examination that the devil had recruited her in Maine four years earlier—just prior to the resumption of hostilities—Essex County residents first fully perceived the challenge they faced in the visible and invisible worlds combined. Not only were their menfolk being drawn off to the frontier to fight an elusive and often victorious enemy, witches in their midst had allied themselves spectrally with the Wabanakis. The younger Ann Putnam—mouthing opinions that could only have come from Mercy Lewis—revealed that George Burroughs, former pastor of the Village and longtime Falmouth resident, had admitted bewitching the soldiers during Andros's winter expedition of 1688–1689, the very campaign that, in its failure to engage the enemy, had set the pattern for future blunders throughout the war.

Other afflicted accusers, especially those with ties to the frontier, then started to identify as witches men like John Alden and John Floyd, whose actions during the war suggested that they had joined Burroughs in an alliance with malevolent spirits. And given the logic that lay behind such charges, it was not surprising that the accusers also identified councilors and wealthy merchants as among the demonic conspirators. Even though most such names were never publicly recorded, several contemporary accounts reported the allegations. Far from being inexplicable, accusations of the colony's leaders and their spouses—as Sir William Phips seems to have understood altogether too well—were possibly the most obvious of all. Residents of the northeastern frontier believed their region's leaders had betrayed them, and they readily conflated visible traitors with invisible attackers. Indeed, Mercy Short and Samuel Wardwell did just that when they described spectral meetings attended by both Indians and witches. Although neither named the witches they saw at those meetings, by identifying the Wabanaki attendees as sachems, they implied that the witch-representatives had equivalent stature in colonial society. Wabanaki leaders would certainly have negotiated only with men of their own rank, not with the stereotypical elderly female practitioners of the malefic arts.

As the nature of the conspiracy against New England described by the afflicted accusers became clear, ordinary Essex folk started to tell each other stories about those among them whom they had long believed to be witches, and about people whose recent activities—perhaps fortune-telling (like Samuel Wardwell), experimenting with countermagic (like Martha Emerson), or drunken mutterings (like Thomas Farrar Sr.)—had aroused their suspicions. The large number of people identified as witches in 1692, in short, provides historians today with an oral snapshot of prevailing gossip.

Imagine a camera pointed at Essex County in 1692 that captured not visual images but rather aural ones. The crisis revealed the gossip about witchcraft that spread through the towns and villages of Essex County over the period from mid-April through mid-September 1692. Some of that gossip would have existed at any time, and some was generated by the crisis. But it is preserved today only through a special lens, one provided by the willingness of Massachusetts judges to entertain in court (and thus to record for posterity) the charges about which the common folk were talking. As explained in this book, the accusations emanating from elsewhere in the county—from Beverly, Salisbury, Salem Town, Andover, and so forth—made their way to Salem Village, where they were repeated and confirmed by the core group of afflicted children and teenagers.

The charges were validated too by those who followed Abigail Hobbs in choosing to confess to being witches. Because confessors, having admitted an alliance with the devil, were not allowed to swear in court to the truth of their statements, the significance of their role in leading to convictions and executions has been overlooked by historians relying solely on written records. But, as such contemporaries as Cotton Mather, Deodat Lawson, and Thomas Brattle revealed, confessors' oral, unsworn testimony played a major role at most of the trials. After all, the English legal authorities consulted by the judges insisted that although the best proof of guilt in witchcraft prosecutions was a confession by the guilty party, the next-best proof was a confession from another witch, naming the suspect as a fellow supporter of the devil.

Although it is impossible to know exactly what such early confessors as Deliverance Hobbs, Mary Warren, Margaret Jacobs, and Sarah Churchwell said during the trials, their initial statements, augmented by the later, more detailed revelations elicited by the judges in repeated interviews in the Salem prison, offer at least an approximation of what must have been their official testimony. And in Andover in August and September many confessors—

notably Mary Lacey Jr., Richard Carrier, the Post-Bridges daughters, and Samuel Wardwell—participated actively in the examinations of those whom they had named as witches, urging them to confess as well. By then, as other scholars have pointed out, it had become clear to the accused that confessors were not being tried. Accordingly, self-interest, deference to authority or age, and physical or psychological coercion combined to cause many Andover residents to confess a guilt that they were later to deny. But their subsequent retractions could not retroactively alter the confirming impact of their confessions at the time they were initially given.

Before the magistrates achieved much success in extracting confessions from examinees, the witches' specters had already started to confess freely to the afflicted female Villagers. After the apparition of George Burroughs told Ann Putnam Jr. on April 20 that he had killed his first two wives, fifteen other specters obligingly offered confessions to the children and young women who were serving as conduits between the visible and invisible worlds. Some of those confessions consisted of identifying themselves as witches or admitting having recruited additional malefic practitioners, while others detailed murders going back to the 1680s. Significantly, almost all such confessions were offered between late April and early June, or before the justices encountered the willing Andover confessors after mid-July. At a time when the justices could not extract confessions, in short, the afflicted filled in as their surrogates. Once the justices achieved success, the specters ceased to speak to the afflicted and instead the witches spoke "in bodily form" during their examinations. The timing thus underscored the complementary relationship between the magistrates in the visible world and their young female counterparts in the invisible one.[6]

In other ways as well the accusers took on "official" duties in the invisible world. They solved crimes, disclosing who had committed murders both recently and in years past. They spied on the enemy, warning their fellow settlers of the militant witch conspiracy by reporting the musters of the spectral militias and by describing the nature of the meetings the conspirators attended. (If only the vulnerable outposts of Salmon Falls and Falmouth had received similar timely warnings of Wabanaki assaults!) By their adamant refusal to join the witches and their revelations about the conspiracy, they were defending New England against some of the most powerful enemies the region had ever faced. In fact, one might contend that the youthful female "magistrates" were defending New England far more effectively than had their male counterparts in the visible world during the previous few years.

That young women, especially servants such as Betty Hubbard and Mercy Lewis, would dare to assume those "public duties" was extraordinarily audacious, but nevertheless it accorded with the role they played throughout the crisis. From at least late February on, the afflicted served as intermediaries with the spirits in the invisible world, at the same time as they worked to establish their distance from the devil and his minions. Their repeated torments and the conversations in which they constantly said "no" to the requests that they sign Satan's book constituted the proof that, although they communicated with the malevolent spirits in the invisible world, they were not a part of it. Yet they remained potentially vulnerable to the charge that they had become *too* close to Satan, as was indicated, for example, in the Nurse family's attempts to implicate Abigail Williams in devilish doings because she conversed too easily with him. Over and over again the afflicted had to deny involvement with the witches in order to maintain their own credibility. By the late summer such critics as Robert Pike had begun to suggest that the accusers might themselves be complicit in the attack on New England: this reveals how fine a line they had been walking from the very beginning.

In the end, the fact that the afflicted girls and a few older women (especially Ann Carr Putnam and Sarah Vibber) had provided so much of the courtroom testimony caused the rapid collapse of support for the prosecutions. What had initially seemed the most compelling evidence—the torments the children and young women endured in the sight of many witnesses, and their testimony as to the identification of their spectral torturers—disintegrated once too many observers began to believe that Satan could assume the shape of an innocent person. The identifications then became the utterly untrustworthy "devil's testimony," and although few as yet charged them with dissembling (that would come later), Thomas Brattle called them decisively "these blind, nonsensical girls."[7] The trials' eventual critics focused on the young female accusers, ignoring all the maleficium witnesses and the older confessors who had also testified against those who had been convicted and hanged. The critics understood at some level that the most effective way to attack the trials was to attack the core group of accusers. When they and their charges had been successfully discredited, support for the prosecutions melted away.

The strange reversal that had placed women on top was then righted, and young women were relegated once again to what contemporaries saw as their proper roles: servers, not served; followers, not leaders; governed, not governors; the silent, not the speakers. Those momentarily powerful became once more the powerless. And only one of them ever went back to Maine.

Interpreting the Behavior of the "Afflicted Girls" and Assessing Responsibility for the Crisis

Although this book has asked many new questions about the Essex County witchcraft crisis, until now I have deliberately not addressed an issue that has preoccupied many scholars and others intrigued by the 1692 crisis: How should the behavior of the so-called "afflicted girls" be interpreted in modern terms? Were they faking? Had they ingested some sort of psychotropic material that made them hallucinate? Were they hysterical? If so, what led to that hysteria? I chose this course of action (or, perhaps, non-action) because I wanted to focus on narrating the crisis as it was understood in the late seventeenth century, not as we might understand it today. I often tell my students that one cannot answer historical questions one has not asked, but even so, in the case of Salem witchcraft, responses to such inquiries must, in the end, be considered.

The group commonly referred to as the "afflicted girls" actually comprised three distinct sets of people: first, five little girls, three from Salem Village and later two from Andover, age thirteen and under; second, older young people (including one male) living in both towns, in their late teens and early twenties, some of them servants; and, finally, married women in their thirties, most notably Sarah Vibber and Ann Carr Putnam. Although these accusers often acted as a group, they also need to be examined individually. Some (for example, Abigail Williams) were active early in the crisis, but then seem to have withdrawn from involvement; some (Susannah Sheldon and Elizabeth Booth) chimed in later; some (for instance, Betty Hubbard and Mary Walcott) persisted in offering accusations and testimony for many months. (See appendix 3 for these patterns.)

The attention scholars have paid to that core group of afflicted Villagers has largely obscured the significant role played by confessors. With the exception of Tituba and the partial exception of Mary Warren, historians have missed the centrality of confessions during the crisis. That of Abigail Hobbs created the link to the Maine frontier; that of her stepmother, Deliverance Hobbs, provided the template for later similar revelations; and the torrent of confessors from Andover and elsewhere convinced Cotton Mather (and surely many others), if he or they still needed convincing, that the afflicted were telling the truth about their spectral visions. Certain people (Warren, Churchwell, both Hobbs women, and many Andover residents) were both afflicted and confessors, as the two groups in effect merged into one in the latter stages of the crisis. Moreover, such confessors as Mary Post and Samuel Wardwell actively encouraged others to join them in admitting guilt.

Recall that English legal experts pronounced confessions the best evidence of complicity with the devil; that confessions uniformly appeared to confirm the afflicted accusers' descriptions of diabolic sacraments; and that Mather in *Wonders of the Invisible World* declared that if so many confessions were false, "all the Rules of Understanding Humane Affayrs are at an end." Indeed, Thomas Brattle in his October critique of the trials observed that "many of our neighbours" continued to insist that the confessions were truthful. Thus in attributing responsibility for the crisis, if that is one's goal, the confessors cannot be overlooked. (See appendix 4 for the confessors.)

An inquiry focusing specifically on the afflicted people must be split into two parts: the role played in initial accusations and that in convictions. Here the ages of the accusers mattered because of legal questions about the validity of sworn statements by witnesses under fourteen years of age. This narrative has shown that in several instances charges brought by children had to be supported by statements from older sufferers before authorities moved to arrest and question the suspects. *The children and teenagers offered initial accusations, but without support from other teenagers and adults the charges would not have led to trials and convictions.* When the trials began, age (and general credibility) then meant more than at earlier stages of the proceedings.

Thus, John Indian, an afflicted slave of unknown age, played an important role at several examinations, but never appeared before a grand or petty jury. A tormented teenager with lurid visions, Susannah Sheldon, rarely testified, whereas another offering stories that fit only the standard patterns, Betty Hubbard, was repeatedly called on to speak in court. Even more significant, the legal proceedings relied heavily on several adult witnesses: Ann Carr Putnam (whose descriptions of her March afflictions seem to have been critical in establishing the credibility of the accusations), Sarah Vibber (who frequently offered sworn testimony), and the adult male Putnams and Samuel Parris, who under oath repeatedly described the sufferings of the afflicted Villagers.

There still remains an assessment of those I have termed herein the core group of accusers. Seventeenth-century observers declared them, and others like them in previous decades, to be possessed, obsessed, or bewitched; in the eighteenth century, as Paul Boyer and Stephen Nissenbaum pointed out in *Salem Possessed,* religious fervor and the conversion experience seemed a more likely explanation; and in the nineteenth and twentieth centuries, "hysteria" (for the earlier era, a phenomenon centered in women's sexual organs) appeared an appropriate diagnosis. Recently, people seem more attracted to biological or medical explanations—hence the persistent search for some sort of "natural" or chemical cause of the afflictions, a search I believe to be misdirected. Even if the afflicted had ingested a hallucinogen, that would explain nothing of significance about the *content* of their visions. And there is always the possibility of fraud, as Bernard Rosenthal has forcefully argued in *Salem Story.*

Where, in the end, do I stand on such issues? The first afflictions of the little children, I have no doubt, were genuine (that is, not deliberately or rationally faked). What caused the girls' fits is unknown and probably unknowable, but such behaviors had been previously recorded and similarly handled at other times in the preceding century, and earlier, too, they had spread to other youngsters in the same or nearby households. Many subsequent afflictions also—especially those experienced by frontier refugees—were at least arguably genuine. Certainly with respect to Mercy Lewis, Susannah Sheldon, Sarah Churchwell, Mercy Short, and perhaps others as well, the phenomenon known today as post-traumatic stress disorder comes to mind as a plausible explanation for their behavior.

Then there are the physical manifestations (bleeding, pins, teeth marks) to consider. On the origins of those, I am an agnostic. Did witnesses like Deodat Lawson *really* see teeth marks on the bodies of the afflicted, or were they merely too suggestible? Surely the reports of bleeding and pins stuck in flesh can be believed, but what caused such phenomena? If the afflicted injured themselves, did they necessarily do so with conscious intent? Since I have no claims to psychological expertise, I cannot answer that question definitively, nor will I offer even a speculative response. But, as Rosenthal has contended, Susannah Sheldon in all likelihood could not have tied her own hands so tightly they could not be easily released. And the actions of *some* of the afflicted for *some* of the time (most obviously Sarah Vibber, and possibly Mary Walcott) do indeed seem contrived. Prearranged collusion is probably the only explanation for the reported unanimity of the afflicted in separately reporting seeing the ghosts of George Burroughs's first two wives during his trial.

Whatever their mental state at the beginning of the crisis, it is plausible to hypothesize that as the months went on some of the afflicted accusers, reveling in the exercise of unprecedented power, began to augment and enhance their stories. That retrospectively they told tales of being afflicted by non-Village witches in statements *not* supported by the sworn testimony of adult relatives who had observed and taken notes on their earlier behavior suggests that such enhancements were in fact occurring. None of them, however, ever admitted fraud, in contrast to some falsely "afflicted" predecessors in England.

The little girls, then, initiated the crisis, but it would not have persisted without the participation of the older teenagers and (especially) the afflicted and confessing adults, whose age and maturity lent weight to the children's accusations. And ultimately, whatever the reasons for the behavior of afflicted and confessors alike, the governor, council, and judges of Massachusetts must shoulder a great deal of the blame for allowing the crisis to reach the heights that it did. As *In the Devil's Snare* has argued, they attempted to shift the responsibility for their own inadequate defense of the frontier to the demons of the invisible world, and as a result they presided over the deaths of many innocent people.

Epilogue

The Second Indian War dragged on until 1699. A peace agreement negotiated by Sir William Phips in August 1693 lasted only a year. Major attacks by
the Wabanakis and the French on Oyster River (1694), Pemaquid (1696), and
Andover and Haverhill (1697) followed before the war ended. A European
treaty (the Peace of Ryswick), proclaimed in Boston in December 1697,
halted most but not all of the fighting. A local truce was negotiated once
again in Maine.[1]

Sir William Phips, beset by critics on all sides for his actions as governor,
was recalled to England and left Massachusetts in mid-November 1694. He
died in London in February 1694/5, shortly after his arrival and before the
Lords of Trade and Plantations could consider either the complaints against
him or his defense. In 1701, his widow married Peter Sergeant, formerly one
of the judges of the Court of Oyer and Terminer.[2]

Samuel Parris was forced to leave Salem Village in the summer of 1697 by
a campaign led by the Nurse family and other relatives of the executed. He
moved first to Stow, then to five other Massachusetts communities, alternately preaching, teaching school, farming, and running retail establishments.
Properties owned by a well-to-do second wife (his first wife, Elizabeth, died
in 1696) helped to support his growing family. He died in Sudbury in February 1719/20.[3]

Thomas and Ann Carr Putnam died within two weeks of each other in
1699. His intestate estate was small and heavily encumbered by debt,
although he left enough for his surviving children to inherit small legacies.[4]

Elizabeth Booth married Israel Shaw in Salem on December 26, 1695. They had at least two children. Her younger sister *Alice*, another afflicted accuser, married Ebenezer Marsh in Salem on November 25, 1700.[5]

Sarah Churchwell married Edward Andrews, a weaver, on August 11, 1709, in Berwick, Maine, after they had been fined for premarital fornication. She survived him and was still alive in 1731.[6]

Rose Foster died in Andover on February 25, 1692/3.[7]

Abigail Hobbs married Andrew Senter (or Center) of Ipswich on June 18, 1709; he came from a family with links to the Maine–New Hampshire frontier. They later lived in Wenham and had at least two sons, Andrew and Thomas. Her widowed stepmother *Deliverance* was probably living with the Senters when she died in Wenham in 1715.[8]

Betty Hubbard moved to Gloucester, probably to live with one of the three married children of William Griggs who had remained in that town when the doctor relocated to Salem Village. In late 1711 she married John Bennett in Gloucester; they eventually had four children. He died in February 1724/5, but her death date is unknown.[9]

Mary Lacey Jr. married her cousin Zerubbabel Kemp on January 27, 1703/4. They lived in his home town of Groton, Massachusetts, and may have had as many as seven children.[10]

Mercy Lewis went to Greenland (an outlying area of Portsmouth, N.H.) to live near her aunt, Mary Lewis Skilling Lewis, who before 1685 had married Jotham Lewis of Greenland (probably a second cousin). In 1695, Mercy bore a bastard child at the home of Abraham Lewis, Jotham's brother. Charles Allen, who testified when Mercy was prosecuted, and whom she married before 1701, probably fathered her child. They later lived in Boston.[11]

Betty Parris married Benjamin Barron in Sudbury in 1710. They had five children; he died in 1754, she in 1760.[12]

Ann Putnam Jr. died unmarried in May 1715. When she joined the Salem Village church in August 1706, she asked forgiveness and "to be humbled before God for that sad and humbling providence" in 1692 that "made [her] an instrument for the accusing of several persons of a grievous crime, whereby their lives were taken away." She now believed them to be innocent, she declared, "and that it was a great delusion of Satan that deceived me in that sad time." She had, though, done it "ignorantly," without "anger, malice, or ill-will to any person," and she particularly "desire[d] to lie in the dust" for her accusation of Rebecca Nurse and her two sisters, which caused "so sad a calamity to them and their families."[13]

Susannah Sheldon went to Providence, R.I., to live with John Sheldon, who was probably a cousin of her father's. On May 8, 1694, as a "person of Evill fame," she was ordered to appear before the Providence town council later that month, at which time she was almost certainly warned out of town. She probably died unmarried before 1697 and was most likely the "distracted" afflicted girl whose experimentation with a venus glass was described by John Hale.[14]

Mercy Short joined Boston's Second Church. Cotton Mather married her to Joseph Marshall on July 29, 1694, but in May 1698 excommunicated her for adultery with an unnamed man. She died before 1708; her husband subsequently remarried.[15]

Martha Sprague alias Tyler married Richard Friend in Andover on June 5, 1701. What happened to her after that is unknown.[16]

Mary Walcott married Isaac Farrar in Salem on April 29, 1696. They first settled in Woburn, his home town, then moved to Ashford, Connecticut, in 1713. They had six children born between 1699 and 1717.[17]

Mary Warren and *Abigail Williams* could not be traced. Although several young women of those names and approximately the right ages are recorded in New England in the late seventeenth century, all can be excluded from consideration because of known details of their lives. Perhaps these two died unmarried.

Samuel Sewall publicly apologized for his role on the Court of Oyer and Terminer on a fast day observed on January 14, 1696/7 to acknowledge "the Anger of God" against Massachusetts for the witchcraft trials and other offenses. In a statement read in church by his pastor, Samuel Willard, he asked "pardon" of both God and men and "Desire[d] to take the Blame and

Shame of it." He was apparently the only judge who ever changed his mind about the trials. He died in 1729.[18]

Thomas Fiske and eleven other petty jurors who had heard cases in the Court of Oyer and Terminer publicly admitted, probably also on the January 1696/7 fast day, "that we ourselves were not capable to understand, nor able to withstand the mysterious delusions of the Powers of Darkness, and Prince of the Air" in 1692. Acknowledging that they now "justly fear[ed]" they had an "insufficient" basis for conviction, they asked forgiveness and expressed "to all in general (and to the surviving Sufferers in especial) our deep sense of, and sorrow for our Errors, in acting on such Evidence to the condemning of any person."[19]

John Hale, who once had insisted with Stoughton that specters could not represent innocent parties, changed his mind (reported Robert Calef) after his wife appeared spectrally to Mary Herrick in November 1692. Before he died in 1697, he wrote *A Modest Enquiry into the Nature of Witchcraft . . .*, which was published in 1702. The book detailed his conclusion that the Salem prosecutions had been based on "unsafe principles" and that "following such traditions of our fathers, maxims of the Common Law, and Presidents [precedents] and Principles" had been an error. "Such was the darkness of that day, the tortures and lamentations of the afflicted, and the power of former presidents, that we walked in the clouds, and could not see our way," Hale memorably wrote.[20]

Deodat Lawson returned to England in 1696. In 1704, he published new editions of his 1692 sermon and his *Brief and True Narrative*. By 1714, he was enduring deep financial distress, and in 1727 he was described as "unhappy."[21]

Cotton Mather went on to become the most celebrated clergyman in Massachusetts Bay, famed for his sermons and prolific writings. Late in life he was involved in another major controversy when he supported the efficacy of smallpox inoculations over the objections of prominent Boston physicians; his position was vindicated in the epidemic of 1722. He died in 1728, outliving his celebrated father, *Increase*, by only five years.[22]

Nicholas Noyes died from a hemorrhage, thus fulfilling Sarah Good's curse that he would have blood to drink (or so Thomas Hutchinson learned from Salem residents in the mid eighteenth century).[23]

George Burroughs's reputation as a witch spread even to Wabanakia. Captain John Hill of Saco reported in 1693 that an Indian told him "that the *French* Ministers were better than the English, for before the *French* came among them there were a great many Witches among the *Indians*, but now there were none, and there were much Witches among the *English* Ministers, as *Burroughs*, who was Hang'd for it."[24]

Appendix I

Cases Heard by the Court of Oyer and Terminer in 1692

NAME	DATE OF FIRST INCIDENT	DATE OF COMPLAINT OR WARRANT	EXAMINATION	NO. OF AFFLICTED ACCUSERS[1]	NO. OF MALEFICIUM ACCUSERS[2]	NO. OF CONFESSING ACCUSERS[3]	GRAND JURY	TRIAL	OUTCOME
Sarah Good	Feb. 25	Feb. 29	Mar. 1, 5	8	6	6	June 28	June 28, 29	Hanged July 19
Elizabeth Proctor	Mar. 6	Apr. 4, 8	Apr. 11	10	1	3	June 30	Aug. 5	Guilty, Reprieve
Martha Corey	before Mar. 14	Mar. 19	Mar. 21	8	0	2	Aug. 4(?)	Sept. 8, 10	Hanged Sept. 22
Rebecca Nurse	Mar. 13	Mar. 23	Mar. 24	11	5	4[4]	June 3	June 29	Hanged July 19
John Proctor	Apr. 4	Apr. 11	Apr. 11	12	0	3	June 30	Aug. 5	Hanged Aug. 19
Giles Corey	?	Apr. 18	Apr. 19	11	1	3	Sept. 9	No Plea	Pressed Sept. 19
Bridget Bishop	?	Apr. 18	Apr. 19	7	11	5[5]	June 2	June 2	Hanged June 10

1. Includes all afflicted accusers, not just those who testified formally.
2. Includes maleficium witnesses before both grand and petty juries.
3. Includes all confessors naming the defendant.
4. Includes three posthumous identifications.
5. Includes two posthumous identifications.

NAME	DATE OF FIRST INCIDENT	DATE OF COMPLAINT OR WARRANT	EXAMINATION	NO. OF AFFLICTED ACCUSERS[1]	NO. OF MALEFICIUM ACCUSERS[2]	NO. OF CONFESSING ACCUSERS[3]	GRAND JURY	TRIAL	OUTCOME
Abigail Hobbs[†]	Apr. 13	Apr. 18	Apr. 19, 20; May 12; June 1, 29	6	0	0	Sept. 10	Sept. 17(?)	Guilty, Reprieve
Sarah Wilds	Apr. 17	Apr. 21	Apr. 22	4	9	3[6]	June 30	July 2	Hanged July 19
Mary Easty	?	Apr. 21	Apr. 22, May 23	8	4	0	Aug. 4	Sept. 9	Hanged Sept. 22
George Burroughs	Apr. 20	Apr. 30	May 9	8	10	12[7]	Aug. 3	Aug. 5	Hanged Aug. 19
George Jacobs Sr.	Apr. 20	May 10	May 10, 11	9	0	1[8]	Aug. 4	Aug. 4(?)	Hanged Aug. 19
John Willard	Apr. 23	May 10	May 18	8	23[9]	1	June 3	Aug. 5(?)	Hanged Aug. 19
Sarah Buckley	Apr. 23	May 14	May 18	5	6	0	Sept. 14, 15	Jan. 4, 1693*	Acquit
Mary Witheridge	Apr. 26	May 14	May 18	6	0	0	Sept. 15	Jan. 4, 1693*	Acquit
Dorcas Hoar[10]	"late Apr."	Apr. 30	May 2	8	11[11]	0	July 2	Sept. 6	Guilty, Reprieve
Susannah Martin	"late Apr."	Apr. 30	May 2	8	13	0	June 29	June 29	Hanged July 19
Rebecca Jacobs[†]	"early May"	May 14	May 18	5	0	0	Sept. 10	Jan. 4, 1693*	Acquit
Mary Bradbury	"early May"	May 26	July 2	4	4	3	Sept. 8, 9	Sept. 10	Guilty, Reprieve, Escape
Alice Parker	May 12	May 12	May 12	8	5	2	Sept. 7	Sept. 10(?)	Hanged Sept. 22
Ann Pudeator	May 12	May 12	May 12, July 2	8	3	1	Sept. 7	Sept. 10	Hanged Sept. 22

---

* Tried in new Superior Court of Judicature, not Court of Oyer and Terminer

† Confessor

---

1. Includes all afflicted accusers, not just those who testified formally.
2. Includes maleficium witnesses before both grand and petty juries.
3. Includes all confessors naming the defendant.
6. Includes one posthumous identification.
7. Includes five posthumous identifications (including one involving "several others").
8. Retracted before trial.
9. Includes 12 members of coroner's jury on death of Daniel Wilkins.
10. Confessed the day before execution.
11. Includes four witnesses to fortune-telling.

NAME	DATE OF FIRST INCIDENT	DATE OF COMPLAINT OR WARRANT	EXAMINATION	NO. OF AFFLICTED ACCUSERS[1]	NO. OF MALEFICIUM ACCUSERS[2]	NO. OF CONFESSING ACCUSERS[3]	GRAND JURY	TRIAL	OUTCOME
Martha Carrier	?	May 28	May 31	8	5	11[12]	July 1	Aug. 3	Hanged Aug. 19
Elizabeth Howe	?	May 28	May 31	8	13	5	June 30	June 30	Hanged July 19
Wilmot Reed	?	May 26, 28	May 31	6	3	0	Sept. 14	Sept. 14	Hanged Sept. 22
Ann Foster†	?	?	July 15, 16, 18, 21	3	0	6	Sept. 13	Sept. 17	Guilty, Reprieve, Died in Jail
Mary Lacey Sr.†	?	July 19	July 21, 22, 23; Aug. 3	3	0	6	Sept. 14	Sept. 17	Guilty, Reprieve
Margaret Scott	July 25(?)	?	Aug. 5	3	8	1	Sept. 15	Sept. 15(?)	Hanged Sept. 22
Abigail Faulkner Sr.†	c. Aug. 1	?	Aug. 11, 30	7	0	14	Sept. 17	Sept. 17	Guilty, Reprieve
Rebecca Eames†	?	?	Aug. 19, 31	1	0	2	Sept. 17(?)	Sept. 17(?)	Guilty, Reprieve
Samuel Wardwell[13]	Aug. 15	?	Sept. 1	3	5[14]	3	Sept. 14(?)	Sept. 14(?)	Hanged Sept. 22
Mary Parker	Aug. 31(?)	?	Sept. 2	6	0	5	Sept. 16(?)	Sept. 16(?)	Hanged Sept. 22

* Tried in new Superior Court of Judicature, not Court of Oyer and Terminer
† Confessor

1. Includes all afflicted accusers, not just those who testified formally.
2. Includes maleficium witnesses before both grand and petty juries.
3. Includes all confessors naming the defendant.
12. Includes three posthumous identifications.
13. Retracted confession at grand-jury hearing.
14. Includes four witnesses to fortune-telling.

Appendix II

*Participants in the Salem Witchcraft Crisis
with Ties to the Northern Frontier*

AFFLICTED ACCUSERS AND CONFESSORS

Sarah Churchwell
Abigail Hobbs
Deliverance Hobbs†
Mercy Lewis
Mary Swayne Marshall*
Margaret Rule
Susannah Sheldon
Mercy Short
Mary Walcott*
Mary Watkins

ACCUSED

John Alden
Mary Barker*
Sarah Hood Bassett*

* Close relative of person with frontier ties
† Probable link to frontier

Mary Bradbury*
Rev. George Burroughs
Sarah Towne Cloyce*
Mary Bassett DeRich*
Elizabeth Dicer
Philip English
Mary English*
Captain John Floyd
Nicholas Frost
Thomas Hardy
William Hobbs†
Ann Jacobs Moodey‡
Mary Osgood*
Lady Mary Spencer Phips
Elizabeth Bassett Proctor*
Ann Greenslade Pudeator
Margaret Thacher
Hezekiah Usher Jr.*
Samuel Wardwell
Samuel Willard*

JUDGES, JURORS, CLERGYMEN, AND OFFICIALS

Jonathan Corwin
Thomas Danforth
Thomas Fiske
Bartholomew Gedney
John Hathorne
Rev. Joshua Moodey
Sir William Phips
Major Robert Pike
John Ruck*
Nathaniel Saltonstall
Samuel Sewall
William Stoughton
Waitstill Winthrop

* Close relative of person with frontier ties
† Probable link to frontier
‡ Possibly accused

Appendix III

The Afflicted Accusers of Salem Village and Andover

NAME[1] (AGE)	DATE OF FIRST AFFLICTION[2]	NUMBER OF LEGAL COMPLAINTS[3]	NUMBER OF CASES WITH FORMAL TESTIMONY[4]	DATE OF LAST TESTIMONY[5]
Abigail Williams (11 or 12)	mid-Jan. 1691/2	41	7	June 3, 1692[6]
Betty Parris (9)	mid-Jan. 1691/2	3	0	N/A
Ann Putnam Jr. (12)	Feb. 25, 1691/2	53	28[7]	May 1693
Betty Hubbard (17)*	Feb. 27, 1691/2	40	32	Jan. 7, 1692/3
Mercy Lewis (19)*	Mar. 14, 1691/2	54	12[8]	Jan. 12, 1692/3
Ann Putnam Sr. (30)	Mar. 18, 1691/2	5	3	June 3, 1692[9]
Mary Walcott (17)	Mar. 19, 1691/2	69	28[10]	May 1693
Sarah Vibber (36)	Mar. 20, 1691/2[11]	16	15[12]	Jan. 4, 1692/3
Mary Warren[13] (20)*	before Mar. 25, 1692	40	16	Jan. 10, 1692/3
John Indian (?)†	Apr. 11, 1692	10	0	N/A
Susannah Sheldon (18)	Apr. 24, 1692	24	3[14]	Aug. 19, 1692[15]

* Servant
† Slave

---

1. Includes only afflicted accusers named in legal complaints, active in legal proceedings, or listed on indictments. Note that some complaints do not name all the accusers but instead identify a few and then employ such words as "etc." or "et al." (This reduces the numbers in column 3.)
2. The first *recorded* date; in some cases, afflictions began earlier.
3. Assumes that confessors who admitted afflicting the accuser had been named by that accuser, even if no other record survives.
4. The only depositions enumerated are those endorsed by the clerk or grand-jury foreman as sworn, but assumes that witnesses listed in indictments testified, even if no depositions survive.
5. Since some records have been lost, in some instances final testimony could have occurred later.
6. May also have testified orally at late June trials and possibly at trials of George Jacobs Sr. and George Burroughs in early August.
7. Possibly testified in two other cases with unlabeled formal depositions.
8. Possibly testified in three other cases with unlabeled formal depositions.
9. Probably orally repeated or confirmed this grand-jury testimony at trials of Rebecca Nurse (29 June) and Martha Corey (8[?] September).
10. Possibly testified in one other case with an unlabeled formal deposition.
11. As recorded by Deodat Lawson in his *Brief and True Narrative*.

NAME[1] (AGE)	DATE OF FIRST AFFLICTION[2]	NUMBER OF LEGAL COMPLAINTS[3]	NUMBER OF CASES WITH FORMAL TESTIMONY[4]	DATE OF LAST TESTIMONY[5]
Elizabeth Booth [1] (18)	May 18, 1692	15	5	Jan. 7, 1692/3
John DeRich (16)	Aug. 3, 1692[16]	12	3	Sept. 9, 1692
Sarah Phelps (12)	Aug. 9, 1692	4	3	Jan. 6, 1692/3
Rose Foster (13)	Aug. 20, 1692	15	5	Jan. 5, 1692/3
Martha Sprague (16)	Aug. 23, 1692	17	15	May 1693
Abigail Martin (19)	Aug. 28, 1692	7	2	May 1693
Alice Booth (14)	Sept. 5, 1692	5	1	Jan. 7, 1692/3
Elizabeth Booth [2][17](?)	Sept. 5, 1692	4	0	N/A

* Servant
† Slave

---

12. Possibly testified in one other case with an unlabeled formal deposition.

13. Also a confessor, but frequently testified as an afflicted accuser. See appendix 4 for information on her confessions. The numbers in the two lists do not overlap; she accused a total of 53 people.

14. Includes testimony against Martha Carrier as recorded by Cotton Mather in *Wonders of the Invisible World;* not in surviving court documents. Possibly testified in two other cases.

15. Date of Carrier trial (see n. 14, above).

16. Claimed repeated afflictions after late May.

17. Sister-in-law of Elizabeth Booth [1].

Appendix IV

Confessors Who Named Other Witches in 1692

CONFESSOR (AGE)	DATE(S) OF CONFESSION(S)	NUMBER OF OTHER WITCHES NAMED[1]
Tituba (?)[†]	Mar. 1, 1692	2
Dorcas Good (4 or 5)	Mar. 26, 1692[2]	1
Abigail Hobbs[3] (14)	Apr. 19, 20; May 12; June 1; June 29	7
Mary Warren[4] (20)*	Apr. 20, 21; May 12, 13; June 1	13
Deliverance Hobbs (?)	Apr. 22; May 3; June 1	10
Sarah Churchwell[5] (25)*	May 9; June 1; Sept. 5	6[6]
Margaret Jacobs (17)	May 11, 12, 13	4[7]
Ann Foster (72)	July 15, 16, 18, 21	5
Mary Lacey Sr. (40)	July 21, 22, 23; Aug. 3	10
Mary Lacey Jr. (18)	July 21, 22; Aug. 3, 11, 27	10
Richard Carrier (18)	July 22; Aug. 3, 4, 11	19
Andrew Carrier (16)	July 22	3
Martha Emerson (24)	July 23	2
Mary Bridges Sr. (48)	July 30	1
Mary Toothaker (47)	July 30	8
Betty Johnson (22)	Aug. 10, 11, 13	12
Sarah Carrier (7)	Aug. 11	4
Thomas Carrier Jr. (10)	Aug. 11	2
Mary Post (28)	Aug. 13, 25	12
Rebecca Eames (51)	Aug. 19, 31	3
Hannah Post (26)*	Aug. 25, 27	8
Sarah Bridges (17)	Aug. 25	4

* Servant
† Slave

---

1. Enumerates only those accused persons known to have been arrested and charged with witchcraft.
2. As recorded by Deodat Lawson; not in surviving court documents.
3. Also testified before grand jury 7 September.
4. See also appendix 3.
5. Also testified before grand juries on 4 August and 6 September.
6. Includes John Willard (see SWP 3:836).
7. Includes John Willard (see SWP 3:836).

CONFESSOR (AGE)	DATE(S) OF CONFESSION(S)	NUMBER OF OTHER WITCHES NAMED
Mary Bridges Jr. (13)	Aug. 25	4
Susannah Post (31)	Aug. 25	7
Mary Barker (13)	Aug. 29	4
William Barker Sr. (46)	Aug. 29[8]	5
Mary Marston (27)	Aug. 29	2
Elizabeth Johnson Sr. (51)	Aug. 30	10
William Barker Jr. (14)	Sept. 1, 2	6
Samuel Wardwell (49)	Sept. 1	2[9]
Sarah Hawkes (21)	Sept. 1	6
Mercy Wardwell (18)	Sept. 1, 2	5
Sarah Wardwell (41)	Sept. 1	3
Mary Taylor (40)	Sept. 5	1
Mary Osgood (55)	Sept. 8	5
Deliverance Dane (37)	Sept. 8 (c.)	1
Six children[10]	Sept. 16	2

8. Includes an undated confession a few days after 29 August.

9. Assumes "Mary" Lilly is Jane, and "Hannah" Taylor is Mary.

10. Dorothy and Abigail Faulkner Jr., Martha and Johanna Tyler, Sarah Wilson, Joseph Draper. Assumes undated confession by Martha Tyler, Sarah Wilson, "and several others" naming George Burroughs after his execution is offered by this group on 16 September.

Notes

AAS: American Antiquarian Society

AAS Procs: Proceedings of the American Antiquarian Society

BPL: Boston Public Library

Burr, *Narratives:* George Lincoln Burr, ed., *Narratives of the Witchcraft Cases, 1648–1706* (New York, 1914)

Calef, *MWIW,* in *WDNE:* Robert Calef, *More Wonders of the Invisible World* (1700), in *WDNE*

CO: Colonial Office Papers, Public Record Office, London

CSM Pubs: Publications of the Colonial Society of Massachusetts

CW: Colonial Williamsburg Foundation, Williamsburg, Virginia

DHSM: James Phinney Baxter, ed., *Documentary History of the State of Maine,* in *Collections of the Maine Historical Society,* 2d ser., vols. 4 (1889), 5 (1897), 6 (1900), 9 (1907)

EC Ct Recs: George F. Dow, ed., *Records and Files of the Quarterly Courts of Essex County Massachusetts,* 9 vols. (Salem, Mass., 1911–1975)

EC Ct Recs/WPA, ser. 2: Essex County Court Records, WPA typescripts, series 2, PEM

EIHC: Essex Institute Historical Collections

f: folio

fol.: folder

GDMNH: Sybil Noyes, Charles Thornton Libby, and Walter Goodwin Davis, *Genealogical Dictionary of Maine and New Hampshire* (1928–1933; reprint, Baltimore, Md., 1996)

HCTHS: Historical Collections of the Topsfield Historical Society

HL: Huntington Library, San Marino, California

JA, MSA: Judicial Archives, Massachusetts State Archives, Boston

LCMD: Library of Congress Manuscript Division

Lincoln, *Narratives:* Charles H. Lincoln, ed., *Narratives of the Indian Wars, 1675–1699* (New York, 1913)

MA: Massachusetts Archives series, Massachusetts State Archives, Boston

Mather, _DL_, in Lincoln, _Narratives:_ Cotton Mather, _Decennium Luctuosum: An History of Remarkable Occurrences in the Long War, which New-England hath had with the Indian Salvages . . ._ (1699), in Lincoln, _Narratives_

Mather, _WIW_, in _WDNE:_ Cotton Mather, _Wonders of the Invisible World_ (1693), in _WDNE_

MeHS: Maine Historical Society, Portland

MGHR: Maine Genealogical and Historical Register

MHS: Massachusetts Historical Society, Boston

MHS Colls: Collections of the Massachusetts Historical Society

MHS Procs: Proceedings of the Massachusetts Historical Society

MSA: Massachusetts State Archives, Boston

NEHGR: New England Historical and Genealogical Register

NEHGS: New England Historic Genealogical Society, Boston

NEQ: New England Quarterly

PEM: James Duncan Phillips Library, Peabody Essex Museum, Salem

Sibley's Harvard Graduates: John Langdon Sibley, _Biographical Sketches of Graduates of Harvard University, in Cambridge, Massachusetts_ (Cambridge, Mass., 1873)

SVR: Vital Records of Salem, Massachusetts, 5 vols. (Salem, Mass., 1916–1925)

SWP: Paul Boyer and Stephen Nissenbaum, eds., _The Salem Witchcraft Papers: Verbatim Transcripts of the Legal Documents of the Salem Witchcraft Outbreak of 1692,_ 3 vols. (New York, 1977)

SWP/SJC/PEM: Essex County Court Archives, Salem Witchcraft Papers, Supreme Judicial Court, deposit PEM

WDNE: Samuel G. Drake, ed., _The Witchcraft Delusion in New England,_ 3 vols. (Roxbury, Mass., 1866)

WMQ: William and Mary Quarterly

Wyllys Papers (Brown): Wyllys Papers, Annmary Brown Memorial, Brown University, Providence

Wyllys Papers (CSL): Wyllys Papers, Connecticut State Library, Hartford

I have retained original spelling in all quotations, but have silently expanded common abbreviations, lowered superscript letters and numbers, and replaced the thorn with the modern English letters th.

INTRODUCTION

1. As in this paragraph, all dates in this book are given in the Old Style (O.S.) or Julian calendar in use in England and its colonies in the 1690s. Under the Julian calendar, not replaced in the British domains with the New Style (Gregorian) calendar until 1752, the new year began on 25 March. Thus all dates between 1 January and 24 March in a Julian year were commonly written as both years: 1691/2. By

the late seventeenth century, the O.S. calendar was about ten days out of synchronization with the sun. Secondary works covering this period sometimes convert O.S. dates to N.S. by adding ten days, which has subsequently led to confusion about when certain events in the crisis occurred.

2. Exact figures on the number of people accused in the Salem witchcraft crisis are difficult to derive both because the documentary record is incomplete and because certain errors have crept into scholarship over the years. A few authors total all those people ever publicly named, even if formal complaints were never filed. Some use the number of people identified in the table of contents of *SWP*, but seven of those were accusers rather than accused. Moreover, one (John Lee) was not involved in the crisis but was included because of an archivist's mistake; one (Jerson Toothaker) is a phantom created by a WPA transcriber's misreading of a label on a document; two girls (Hannah and Joanna Tyler) were erroneously collapsed into one person; one, Rachel Hatfield Clinton, is listed twice, under both her surnames; and the records of one man (Daniel Eames) were completely missed by the 1930s researchers who compiled the data published in *SWP*. The figures in the text, therefore, are my own. Those against whom formal legal steps were taken are easier to identify than those who were merely mentioned by an accuser, and so I have employed the former figure as a benchmark.

3. The persistent ergot-poisoning hypothesis was first advanced in Linnda R. Caporeal, "Ergotism: The Satan Loose in Salem?" *Science* 192 (2 April 1976): 21–26; it was subsequently refuted in Nicholas P. Spanos and Jack Gottlieb, "Ergotism and the Salem Village Witch Trials," ibid., 194 (24 Dec. 1976): 1390–94, although Mary K. Matossian tried to resurrect it in *Poisons of the Past: Molds, Epidemics, and History* (New Haven, 1989), 113–22. Laurie Winn Carlson, in *A Fever in Salem* (Chicago, 1999), contends that both people and beasts in Salem Village in 1692 were afflicted with encephalitis. However, Prof. Maurice White of the Cornell University College of Veterinary Medicine, an expert on the diseases of livestock, concluded after surveying Ms. Carlson's evidence that "there is no realistic single explanation for the signs in the animals and people consistent with our present scientific knowledge of human and veterinary medicine" (personal communication, 16 April 2000). Major flaws in hypotheses involving disease, food poisoning, or drug-induced hallucinations are that even if correct they cannot explain the content of the girls' visions, and that they cannot explain contemporary observations that the girls appeared healthy whenever the specters were not tormenting them (that is, most of the time).

4. Chadwick Hansen, *Witchcraft at Salem* (New York, 1969) argues for the reality of witchcraft in Salem Village in 1692. Bernard Rosenthal, in *Salem Story: Reading the Witch Trials of 1692* (Cambridge, U.K., 1993), concludes that the girls were faking. For treatments of them as probable hysterics, see Marion L. Starkey, *The Devil in Massachusetts: A Modern Enquiry into the Salem Witch Trials* (New York, 1949), and Frances Hill, *A Delusion of Satan: The Full Story of the Salem Witch*

Trials (New York, 1995); and as delinquents, Peter Hoffer, *The Devil's Disciples: Makers of the Salem Witchcraft Trials* (Baltimore, 1996).

5. For Boyer and Nissenbaum's denial of the importance of the afflicted girls, see *Salem Possessed: The Social Origins of Witchcraft* (Cambridge, Mass., 1974), 35, n. 26: "we think it a mistake to treat the girls themselves as decisive shapers of the witchcraft outbreak as it evolved"; their thesis in general privileges men's concerns over women's. But cf. John P. Demos, "Underlying Themes in the Witchcraft of Seventeenth-Century New England," *American Historical Review* 75 (1970): 1311–26, for a woman-centered analysis of colonial cases. On England, see Clive Holmes, "Women: Witches and Witnesses," *Past & Present*, no. 140 (1993): 45–78; and Diane Purkiss, *The Witch in History: Early Modern and Twentieth-Century Representations* (New York, 1996), part 2.

6. A recent synthesis that conceptualizes a study of Salem witchcraft as a study of trials is Bryan Le Beau, *The Story of the Salem Witch Trials* (Upper Saddle River, N.J., 1998); two of those with a broader perspective are Larry Gragg, *The Salem Witch Crisis* (New York, 1992); and Boyer and Nissenbaum, *Salem Possessed*. *In the Devil's Snare* is a successor volume to my *Founding Mothers & Fathers: Gendered Power and the Forming of American Society* (New York, 1996), which examined the theme of gender and politics in New England and the Chesapeake before approximately 1675.

7. For Salem Village, see Boyer and Nissenbaum, *Salem Possessed;* for legal practice, Peter Hoffer, *The Salem Witchcraft Trials* (Lawrence, Kansas, 1997), and David T. Konig, *Law and Society in Puritan Massachusetts: Essex County, 1629–1692* (Chapel Hill, N.C., 1979); for women, Carol F. Karlsen, *The Devil in the Shape of a Woman: Witchcraft in Colonial New England* (New York, 1987). I found news of the Second Indian War in the overwhelming majority of the letters (business or personal) written in New England between 1688 and 1692. Cedric Cowing places the witchcraft crisis in still another context, that of English regional migration patterns, by contending that both accusers and accused in Salem Village came largely from families with origins in the northwest of England, whereas the town leaders and judges had familial roots in the English southeast. See Cowing, *The Saving Remnant: Religion and the Settling of New England* (Urbana, Ill., 1995), 77–108.

8. See Karlsen, *Devil in the Shape of a Woman*, chapter 7, esp. 226–28; and James E. Kences, "Some Unexplored Relationships of Essex County Witchcraft to the Indian Wars of 1675 and 1689," *EIHC* 120, no. 3 (1984): 179–212. More recently, John McWilliams, "Indian John and the Northern Tawnies," *NEQ* 69 (1996): 580–605, has addressed additional facets of the relationship. I largely concur with Kences and McWilliams, although in article-length studies they were barely able to scratch the surface of the subject, and both made a number of factual errors corrected herein. Typical of the brief treatments of the war in books on the witchcraft crisis are Hoffer, *Devil's Disciples*, 55–56; and Hill, *Delusion of Satan*, 38–41. Richard Godbeer, *The Devil's Dominion: Magic and Religion in Early New*

England (New York, 1992), 184–86, 189–93, 199–201, devotes more pages to the subject than most. And see Emerson W. Baker and John G. Reid, *The New England Knight: Sir William Phips, 1651–1695* (Toronto, 1998), chapter 7, for a discussion of the links between Maine and the trials particularly relevant to the career of Massachusetts' governor.

9. Other scholars, by contrast, have done so. Rosenthal, *Salem Story,* contends throughout that the accusers were liars and frauds, based on his assessment that they must have acted with rational forethought; Hoffer, *Devil's Disciples,* cites modern child-sexual-abuse cases and studies of female juvenile delinquency; and Hill, *Delusion of Satan,* is unabashedly presentist in her concerns, referring both to Joseph McCarthy's 1950s crusade against Communists in the federal government and to recent allegations of Satanic sexual abuse of children.

10. See David D. Hall, *Worlds of Wonder, Days of Judgment: Popular Religious Belief in Early New England* (New York, 1989), passim, esp. chapter 2; Jon Butler, "Magic, Astrology, and the Early American Religious Heritage, 1600–1760," *American Historical Review* 84 (1979): 317–46; and Godbeer, *Devil's Dominion,* for surveys of the New Englanders' worldview.

11. See Norton, *Founding Mothers & Fathers,* chapter 5 and passim, and Mary Beth Norton, "Gender and Defamation in Seventeenth-Century Maryland," *WMQ,* 3d ser., 44 (1987): 3–39, for extended discussions of the role of gossip in the seventeenth-century colonies. A study of gossip in the context of 1692 is Jesse Souweine, "Word of Mouth: How Gossip Informed the Salem Witchcraft Accusations" (unpub. honors thesis, American Studies, Cornell University, 1996).

12. Thus Le Beau, *Story of Salem Witch Trials,* organizes his narrative almost exclusively around the dates of examinations and trials; Rosenthal, *Salem Story,* uses execution dates. Other attempts to create chronologies (although constructed differently from mine) are Richard Gildrie, "Visions of Evil: Popular Culture, Puritanism, and the Massachusetts Witchcraft Crisis of 1692," *Journal of American Culture* 8 (1985): 17–33; and McWilliams, "Indian John," *NEQ* 69 (1996): 580–605.

13. Thus, for example, Karlsen, *Devil in the Shape of a Woman,* dedicates two full chapters to exploring the economic and demographic patterns common to women accused of witchcraft, while devoting only a few pages to a comparable examination of accusers (226–31). Of the accused men, only three—John Proctor, George Burroughs, and Giles Corey—usually receive more than a passing mention. The same failure to pay much attention to accused men characterizes scholarship on European witchcraft as well; see, e.g., Deborah Willis, *Malevolent Nurture: Witch-Hunting and Maternal Power in Early Modern England* (Ithaca, N.Y., 1995); Robin Briggs, *Witches & Neighbors: The Social and Cultural Context of European Witchcraft* (New York, 1996); and Brian P. Levack, *The Witch-Hunt in Early Modern Europe* (New York, 1987).

14. For instance, Hill, *Delusion of Satan,* 192–93; Boyer and Nissenbaum, *Salem Possessed,* 33, 190; and Hoffer, *Devil's Disciples,* 58, 100, barely mention the Andover confessors. Only Chadwick Hansen, in "Andover Witchcraft and the

Causes of the Salem Witchcraft Trials," in *The Occult in America: New Historical Perspectives,* ed. Howard Kerr and Charles L. Crow (Urbana, Ill., 1983), 38–57, has focused on that town and its residents.

15. Those who advance a "disease" hypothesis, although I believe them mistaken, at least understand that the Salem episode requires special explanation (see n. 3, above). Richard Weisman, in *Witchcraft, Magic, and Religion in 17th Century Massachusetts* (Amherst, Mass., 1984), poses this question (see esp. chapter 9), but he offers no definitive answer.

16. Thus John P. Demos, *Entertaining Satan: Witchcraft and the Culture of Early New England* (New York, 1982), examines all New England witchcraft cases other than Salem, whereas books such as Hoffer, *Devil's Disciples,* or Hill, *Delusion of Satan,* look only at Essex County in 1692. (Few prosecutions for witchcraft occurred outside of New England or the Puritan settlements on Long Island, and few have written about such cases.) Karlsen, *Devil in the Shape of a Woman,* combines analyses of Salem cases with others, but focuses on similarities rather than differences. Hoffer, *Devil's Disciples,* xv, remarks on Salem's uniqueness, but refers only to differences in size and chronology from other episodes.

17. These patterns are clearly described in both Demos, *Entertaining Satan,* chapter 3, and Karlsen, *Devil in the Shape of a Woman,* chapter 2, although the two authors differ in their interpretations of similar data. The same patterns characterized most witchcraft accusations in Europe; see Briggs, *Witches & Neighbors,* passim.

18. See Demos, *Entertaining Satan,* 351–55 and 509–13, on the Hartford cases. Demos counts eleven charged with witchcraft but declares that more people were accused. However, David D. Hall, who has published the surviving Hartford records in his *Witch-Hunting in Seventeenth-Century New England,* 2d ed. (Boston, 1999), 147–63, 355–58, identifies only eight people charged at Hartford.

19. See Christina Larner, *Enemies of God: The Witch-Hunt in Scotland* (Baltimore, 1981), passim, esp. chapter 5, on the Scottish trials. Alan Macfarlane, *Witchcraft in Tudor and Stuart England* (London, 1970), examines cases in Essex County, England, including the witch-hunt led by Matthew Hopkins, the so-called Witch-Finder General, in 1644–1645. The only major witchcraft episode in the English-speaking world later than Salem was a 1697 outbreak in Paisley, Scotland.

20. Cf. the list of accused witches in cases other than Salem in Demos, *Entertaining Satan,* 402–409, with that of the Salem accused in Weisman, *Witchcraft, Magic, and Religion,* 209–16. Fewer than 20 of the more than 140 accused lived outside of Essex County.

21. See the tables in Demos, *Entertaining Satan,* 154; and Karlsen, *Devil in the Shape of a Woman,* 184–85, for age and sex breakdowns of accusers. As Karlsen points out, ibid., 183, even if one includes those at Salem in the total, only about 10 percent of New England witchcraft accusers were afflicted by specters.

22. The accusations of members of this last group have mystified most scholars of Salem, who have cited them as a sign of the accusers' irrational overreaching. The argument in this book is quite different. I contend, as shall be seen, that the afflicted had good reason for such accusations.

23. On such patterns, see Karlsen, *Devil in the Shape of a Woman,* 48–51; Demos, *Entertaining Satan,* 402–409; and Weisman, *Witchcraft, Magic, and Religion,* 191–203. See also Clive Holmes, "Popular Culture? Witches, Magistrates, and Divines in Early Modern England," in Steven L. Kaplan, ed., *Understanding Popular Culture: Europe from the Middle Ages to the Nineteenth Century* (Berlin, 1984), 85–111.

24. See Norton, *Founding Mothers & Fathers,* 120–23, for the more common reaction to young women's legal complaints. Also Mary Beth Norton, " 'Either Married or Too Bee Married': Women's Legal Inequality in Early America," in Carla Pestana and Sharon Salinger, eds., *Inequality in Early America* (Hanover, N.H., 1999), 34–36.

25. Jane Kamensky, *Governing the Tongue: The Politics of Speech in Early New England* (New York, 1997), 171, and chapter 6, passim.

26. The standard pattern of continued suspicion is exposed in many of the cases described by both Karlsen, *Devil in the Shape of a Woman,* and Demos, *Entertaining Satan.* Many of the records of the compensation committees have been published in *SWP* 3: 975–1046.

27. *York Deeds* 12, pt. 2:273; 18:262; 17:37; 12, pt. 1:67; 16:145. (All preceding numbers are the original folios, not pages. *York Deeds* does not consistently supply the latter.) James Ross was the cousin of the accuser Mercy Lewis. These depositions were solicited by potential purchasers of Maine lands, who needed to clear title to the properties they planned to buy. Volumes 12 through 18 contain many other similar depositions.

28. See Kences, "Some Unexplored Relationships," *EIHC* 120: 180–87, on the military service of Essex County men in both wars.

29. See chapter 2, pp. 56–57.

30. Personal communications. Bremer has pointed out to me that an early spiritual diary kept by Waitstill's grandfather, the elder John Winthrop, has also disappeared and is believed by the editors to have been destroyed by the same nineteenth-century descendant, who was very concerned about maintaining the family's good name.

31. Some authors of books on Salem, most notably the witch-descendants Enders A. Robinson and Persis McMillen, have argued that the accusations themselves represented a conspiracy of some Essex County families against other Essex County families. See Robinson, *The Devil Discovered: Salem Witchcraft 1692* (New York, 1991) and *Salem Witchcraft and Hawthorne's House of the Seven Gables* (Bowie, Md., 1992); and McMillen, *Currents of Malice: Mary Towne Esty and Her Family in Salem Witchcraft* (Portsmouth, N.H., 1990).

32. Bernard Rosenthal, who is re-editing the trial records, has properly warned me against assuming that the documents known at this time constitute the full surviving record. After all, he, I, and others working with him have recently unearthed previously unknown materials that are cited herein and which will be included in the forthcoming volumes.

CHAPTER ONE   UNDER AN EVIL HAND

1. Mather, *DL*, in Lincoln, *Narratives*, 230 (see 230–31 passim); Floyd to Massachusetts Governor and Council, 27 January 1691/2, *DHSM* 5:314. See also *DHSM* 5:326–27; and the detailed description of the attack and its aftermath in Charles E. Banks, *History of York, Maine* (1931; reprint, Baltimore, 1967) 1: 287–300.

2. George Burroughs et al. to Massachusetts Governor and Council, 27 January 1691/2, *DHSM* 5:316. Although four other men also signed the letter, its religious tone suggests strongly that Burroughs himself wrote it.

3. Samuel Parris, "Meditations for Peace," 18 November 1694, in Paul Boyer and Stephen Nissenbaum, eds., *Salem-Village Witchcraft* (1972; reprint, Boston, 1993), 297.

4. Paul Boyer and Stephen Nissenbaum, *Salem Possessed: The Social Origins of Witchcraft* (Cambridge, Mass., 1974), 37–39; Richard Gildrie, *Salem, Massachusetts, 1626–1683: A Covenant Community* (Charlottesville, Va., 1975), 116–17 and passim.

5. Documents in Boyer and Nissenbaum, eds., *Salem-Village Witchcraft*, 229–34, 237–39, record the process of separation. See also Boyer and Nissenbaum, *Salem Possessed*, 40–43.

6. Quotation: Examination of William Barker Sr., 29 August 1692, *SWP* 1:66. On the problems of successive ministers: Boyer and Nissenbaum, *Salem Possessed*, 45–79 passim. On Bayley, see Boyer and Nissenbaum, eds., *Salem-Village Witchcraft*, 240–55.

7. Quotation: Boyer and Nissenbaum, *Salem Possessed*, 51 (see, in general, 48–53).

8. See Larry Gragg, *A Quest for Security: The Life of Samuel Parris, 1653–1720* (Westport, Conn., 1990), 1–54.

9. Ibid., 42–43, 60–68; James F. Cooper and Kenneth P. Minkema, eds., *The Sermon Notebook of Samuel Parris, 1689–1694* (Boston, 1993), 2–3, 18–19. According to James F. Cooper (personal communication, 26 October 2000), ministers could not baptize infants until they had been ordained, and so no Village clergyman prior to Parris could offer congregants the sacrament of baptism. The church records from 1689 through 1691 are published in Boyer and Nissenbaum, eds., *Salem-Village Witchcraft*, 268–77; for the baptism decision, see 271. Late in 1691 the church had 62 members and the Village approximately 215 adult residents, as estimated by Boyer and Nissenbaum.

10. Cooper and Minkema, eds., *Sermon Notebook,* 184–85. The notebook comprises some of Parris's sacrament-day sermons.

11. Despite enormous effort by many people, including Larry Gragg (personal communication), myself, and my research assistants, it has proved impossible to identify Abigail Williams or her precise relationship to Samuel Parris. She was most likely related to him through his wife, Elizabeth Eldridge, whom he met and married in Boston, because most of his own relatives lived in England. Her age is given as eleven or twelve in various sources. On his daughter, see Marilynne K. Roach, " 'That Child, Betty Parris': Elizabeth (Parris) Barron and the People in Her Life," *EIHC* 124 (1988): 1–27.

12. Many authors have placed the onset of the girls' fits in February, yet the evidence for mid-January is clear. The initial complaints against the first three accused witches, dated February 29, 1691/2, allude to "Sundry" afflictions "within this two moneths" (*SWP* 1:358); and on Wednesday, March 2, Tituba referred to "Six weeks & a little more fryday night" [January 15] as shortly "before Abigail was Ill" (*SWP* 3:753). I posit that Abigail's fits began first partly because she was older, and a leader; and partly because Tituba used the onset of Abigail's fits as her marker. Had Betty sickened first, the reference would more logically have been to her.

13. John Hale, *A Modest Enquiry into the Nature of Witchcraft . . .* (1702) in Burr, *Narratives,* 413. Another and often quoted early description of the girls' afflictions is in Calef, *MWIW,* in *WDNE* 3:4–5, but (unlike Hale) Robert Calef did not himself witness their behavior.

14. Hale, *Modest Enquiry,* in Burr, *Narratives,* 413; Salem church records, 27 March 1692, in Boyer and Nissenbaum, eds., *Salem-Village Witchcraft,* 278.

15. On Griggs, see Harriet S. Tapley, "Early Physicians of Danvers," *Historical Collections of the Danvers Historical Society* 4 (1916): 73–88; H. Minot Pitman, "Early Griggs Families of Massachusetts," *NEHGR* 123 (1969): 172; Anthony S. Patton, *A Doctor's Dilemma: William Griggs & The Salem Witch Trials* (Salem, Mass., 1998); and Anthony S. Patton, "The Witch Doctor," *Harvard Medical Alumni Bulletin* 72, no. 3 (Winter 1999): 34–39. (Thanks to Tony Patton for supplying me with copies of his writings on Griggs.) William Griggs's name does not appear on a December 1684 tax list for Salem Village but is on one drawn up in July 1689 (Boyer and Nissenbaum, eds., *Salem-Village Witchcraft,* 329, 354). That he was self-taught is suggested by the fact that he was termed "Goodman," not "Master," unlike most physicians of higher status; and that he might not have been able to write, although he surely could read. In 1674, for example, he signed a petition with a mark rather than a signature (*EC Ct Recs* 5:360–61). For his wife's and son's church memberships: Richard D. Pierce, ed., *The Records of the First Church of Boston, 1630–1868, CSM Pubs* 39 (1961), 1:58, 63–64.

16. Parris, "Meditations for Peace," 18 November 1694, in Boyer and Nissenbaum, eds., *Salem-Village Witchcraft,* 297; Cooper and Minkema, eds., *Sermon Notebook,* 188, 193.

17. Calef, *MWIW,* in *WDNE* 3:5; Hale, *Modest Enquiry,* in Burr, *Narratives,* 414. Although Hale's account does not make the chronology entirely clear, such private fasts would most logically have preceded public accusations. Another clergyman who undoubtedly participated was Nicholas Noyes of Salem Town.

18. Hale, *Modest Enquiry,* in Burr, *Narratives,* 413. The other roughly contemporary accounts are Calef, *MWIW,* in *WDNE,* 3:5–6; and Deodat Lawson, *A Brief and True Narrative of . . . Witchcraft, at Salem Village . . .* (1692), in Burr, *Narratives,* 162–63. For the statement that Tituba and John were enslaved and husband and wife, see *SWP* 1:208. Cf. Bernard Rosenthal, *Salem Story: Reading the Witch Trials of 1692* (New York, 1993), 26–27, on making the witchcake. An excellent discussion of traditional countermagic is Richard Godbeer, *The Devil's Dominion: Magic and Religion in Early New England* (New York, 1992), chapter 1.

19. Salem church records, 27 March 1692, in Boyer and Nissenbaum, eds., *Salem-Village Witchcraft,* 278–79.

20. Hale, *Modest Enquiry,* in Burr, *Narratives,* 414. Hale is the only contemporary narrator to describe the consultation and the initial interrogation of Tituba, which suggests that he participated in both.

21. The most extended treatment is Elaine Breslaw, *Tituba, Reluctant Witch of Salem: Devilish Indians and Puritan Fantasies* (New York, 1996), which argues that she was brought from the South American mainland to Barbados as a child and sold to Parris there. The only recent historian to contend that she was African (Yoruba, to be precise) is Peter Hoffer, *The Devil's Disciples: Makers of the Salem Witchcraft Trials* (Baltimore, 1996). Useful commentaries on Tituba are Chadwick Hansen, "The Metamorphosis of Tituba, or Why American Intellectuals Can't Tell an Indian Witch from a Negro," *NEQ* 47 (1974): 3–12; and Bernard Rosenthal, "Tituba's Story," *NEQ* 71 (1998): 190–203.

22. Thomas Hutchinson, *The History of Massachusetts from the First Settlement Thereof in 1628, until the Year 1750,* 3d ed. (Boston, 1795), 2:29. Hutchinson generally relied on John Hale for this part of his narrative, but Hale offered no information about Tituba's background. Indian allies of the English in South Carolina raided Spanish Catholic missions and settlements along the coast of modern Georgia and Florida, capturing and enslaving their Indian residents, then shipping them northward for sale. My thanks to Ann Plane for helpful conversations about "Spanish Indians" and to Alan Gallay for information on the Carolina Indian slave trade. My colleague Maria Cristina Garcia has pointed out to me that a mistress of Spanish origin would have been unlikely to engage in occult practices of any sort, but a well-to-do mestiza (more likely to have been found in such a marginal area as Florida or Georgia) might well have done so. Origins in "New Spain" could also mean that Breslaw's theory (n. 21, above) is correct. If Tituba was a Spanish Indian, the sort of witchcraft she would have been familiar with is described in Ruth Behar, "Sexual Witchcraft, Colonialism, and Women's Powers: Views from the Mexican Inquisition," in Asunción Lavrin, ed., *Sexuality and*

Marriage in Colonial Latin America (Lincoln, Neb., 1989), 178–206. (I owe this reference to Maria Lepowsky.)

23. See *SWP* 3:745, 756; 2:361, for the quoted descriptive phrases. By my tabulation of references in the documents, she is "Tituba Indian" or "the Indian" sixteen times and "Tituba" (or variant spellings) sixteen times. Children much younger than Betty and Abigail knew about the war. For example, in August 1691 Samuel Sewall noted in his diary that his son Joseph, then 3, said before going to bed one night, "News from Heaven, the French were come, and mention'd Canada." See M. Halsey Thomas, ed., *The Diary of Samuel Sewall 1674–1729* (New York, 1973), 1:281.

24. Hale, *Modest Enquiry,* in Burr, *Narratives,* 414. Betty Parris, the youngest afflicted girl, never testified in any court, although her name appeared on the first complaint. On the "age of credibility," see Holly Brewer, "Age of Reason? Children, Testimony, and Consent in Early America," in Christopher Tomlins and Bruce Mann, eds., *The Many Legalities of Early America* (Chapel Hill, N.C., 2001), 295–316. My thanks to Holly Brewer for allowing me to consult her then-unpublished paper, and for useful conversations on this point. In this context, it is important to note that neither Ann Putnam Jr.'s nor Abigail Williams's age was *ever* indicated on any of the many (surviving) depositions they offered during the 1692 legal proceedings, even though most depositions contained such information. The absence suggests a certain disquiet about the age of the little girls on the part of those before whom the statements were sworn, and perhaps even a desire to conceal the youth of these witnesses in the official records of the trials in order to avoid later questions about the legitimacy of the proceedings.

25. On Ann Putnam Jr. and her extended family: Boyer and Nissenbaum, *Salem Possessed,* 110–51 passim. Thomas Putnam's military service in Rhode Island is detailed in Harriet S. Tapley, *Chronicles of Danvers (Old Salem Village) Massachusetts, 1632–1923* (Danvers, Mass., 1923), 19–21.

26. See probate records of Isaac Griggs, 26 April 1690, Suffolk County Probate Files #1723, JA, MSA. Rachel Hubbard Griggs, b. c. 1628, was the daughter of the widow Elizabeth Hubbard or Hobart, who died in Boston in 1644. Rachel had two considerably older brothers, Richard and Benjamin. Nothing is known of Richard after 1644; Benjamin died on Long Island between 1675 and 1687. Either—more likely Benjamin—could have been Betty's grandfather. See Elizabeth Hobart, will, 29 December 1643, Suffolk Probate Files #30, JA, MSA. (Thanks to Elizabeth Bouvier for locating both these sets of records for me.) On Benjamin Hubbard, see box 2, fol. 4; and box 5, fol. 1A, Esther Forbes Papers, AAS.

27. Quotations: *SWP* 3:611–12. Ann Jr. named both Tituba and Osborne on 25 February, first identifying Good two days later. Betty Hubbard named Tituba on the 25th, Osborne on the 27th, and Good on the 28th. See *SWP* 3:756 (Tituba), 611–12 (Osborne); 2:372–73 (Good). It is unclear precisely when Abigail Williams first named Osborne and Good; her vague statement (made in May) is *SWP* 3:612.

Possibly Ann Jr. and Betty endured earlier fits, but no dates are specified in the surviving documents.

28. On Sarah Osborne: Carol F. Karlsen, *The Devil in the Shape of a Woman: Witchcraft in Colonial New England* (New York, 1987), 270–71; Enders A. Robinson, *The Devil Discovered: Salem Witchcraft 1692* (New York, 1991), 267. On Sarah Good: Karlsen, *Devil in the Shape of a Woman*, 110–12; and Boyer and Nissenbaum, eds., *Salem-Village Witchcraft*, 139–47.

29. For examples of the classic story, with or without Tituba: Boyer and Nissenbaum, *Salem Possessed*, 1–2; Marion L. Starkey, *The Devil in Massachusetts: A Modern Enquiry into the Salem Witch Trials* (New York, 1949), 34–38; Frances Hill, *A Delusion of Satan: The Full Story of the Salem Witch Trials* (New York, 1995), 13; Bryan Le Beau, *The Story of the Salem Witch Trials* (Upper Saddle River, N.J., 1998), 60. On Tituba's non-role, see Rosenthal, *Salem Story*, 13–14.

30. John Hale, *A Modest Enquiry into the Nature of Witchcraft* . . . (Boston, 1702), 132. The only contemporary evidence for group fortune-telling in 1692 refers to "two or three girls" in Andover employing "the sieve and scissors," not a larger group in Salem Village using the egg and glass (venus glass) method; see "Letter of Thomas Brattle, F.R.S., 1692," in Burr, *Narratives*, 181. Deodat Lawson—who was in the Village in mid- to late March and who in a sermon on 24 March speculated on possible reasons why Satan was attacking the Village— also did not mention any group fortune-telling by the afflicted girls. Instead, he primarily theorized about the contentious nature of Village life and about Villagers' use of countermagic. Presumably, had people at the time regarded the girls' experimentation with the occult as a precipitating factor in the crisis, Lawson would have made more than a very brief and unspecific reference to fortune-telling. See Lawson, "Christ's Fidelity . . . ," reprinted in Richard B. Trask, ed., *"The Devil hath been raised": A Documentary History of the Salem Village Witchcraft Outbreak of March 1692*, rev. ed. (Danvers, Mass., 1997), 98–100.

31. *SWP* 1:227.

32. The question still arises as to who she was. Although some have identified her as Abigail Williams, it is unlikely that she was one of the three Salem Village children or the almost-as-young Andover accusers. Little girls did not engage in fortune-telling about future husbands; older teenagers did. What later happened to some of the older afflicted eliminates them from consideration (because they are known to have married or to have lived beyond 1697), leaving only two possibilities: Mary Warren and Susannah Sheldon. For reasons given in the epilogue, I believe the young woman Hale mentions here was probably Sheldon.

33. *SWP* 3:745; 2:355; 3:748. Note that Samuel Parris was not a formal complainant.

34. For biographical information, see Robinson, *Devil Discovered*, 32–35, 71, 87–89. On Corwin's mills: box 1, fol. 8, Curwen Family Papers, PEM; on Hathorne's speculations, "Book of Eastern Claims," *MHGR* 7 (1893): 18. Corwin's sister's first husband was Hathorne's brother Eleazar, who died in 1680.

35. The original location: *SWP* 3:745; the meetinghouse: ibid., 2:357. One of the best discussions of the usual procedures followed by New England magistrates is Gail Sussman Marcus, "'Due Execution of the Generall Rules of Righteousnesse': Criminal Procedure in New Haven Town and Colony, 1638–1658," in David D. Hall et al., eds., *Saints & Revolutionaries: Essays on Early American History* (New York, 1984), 99–137. Clive Holmes suggested to me that clergymen might have proposed the public sessions.

36. Mary Beth Norton, *Founding Mothers & Fathers: Gendered Power and the Forming of American Society* (New York, 1996), chapter 7, discusses the patterns of guilt and conviction. As Carol Karlsen's summary tables demonstrate (*Devil in the Shape of a Woman*, 48, 51), of the forty-two witches tried in New England before 1692, fewer than half (twenty) were convicted, and just sixteen were executed.

37. This and the next paragraph are based on *SWP* 2:356–57, 372. See Thomas Barnes, ed., *The Book of the General Lawes and Libertyes Concerning the Inhabitants of the Massachusets* (San Marino, Calif., 1975), facsimile p. 5.

38. This and the next paragraph are based on *SWP* 2:610–11.

39. Calef, *MWIW*, in *WDNE* 3:6.

40. There are two records of Tituba's examination on March 1, Ezekiel Cheever's (on the same sheet of paper as his notes on the Good and Osborne examinations; see SWP/SJC/PEM 1:11–12), and another, by an unidentified scribe thought to be Joseph Putnam (Sergeant Thomas's half brother). They differ in detail but concur on main points. This paragraph and the next draw on both; see *SWP* 3:747–49 (Cheever), 750–53 (Putnam). The quoted depositions: *SWP* 3:756–57.

41. *SWP* 2:371, 370, form the basis for this paragraph and the next.

42. A summary, ibid., 3:746–47, lists all the examinations; an abstract of Tituba's confession and other evidence, prepared for Sarah Good's trial, reveals only one new piece of information: that a search of Tituba's body proved that Good had pinched her legs (*SWP* 2:362). Hale mentions one interrogation of Tituba in jail, and the surviving March 2 transcript fails to indicate the presence of anyone other than the magistrates and the accused (Hale, *Modest Enquiry*, in Burr, *Narratives*, 415).

43. *SWP* 3:753–55.

44. Ibid., 2:372.

45. Hale, *Modest Enquiry*, in Burr, *Narratives*, 415; *SWP* 2:352, 668. On Proctor and her grandmother, Ann Burt, see Karlsen, *Devil in the Shape of a Woman*, 142.

46. Richard Bernard, *A Guide to Grand-Jury Men* (London, 1627), 25 (see 11–28 passim); R.B. [Nathaniel Crouch], *The Kingdom of Darkness: Or the History of Dæmons, Specters, Witches, Apparitions . . .* (London, 1688), A2. For the statement that Bernard and Crouch (and other authorities) were consulted by the magistrates, see Hale, *Modest Enquiry*, in Burr, *Narratives*, 416.

47. John Darrell, *A True Narration of the Strange and Grevous Vexation by the Devil, of 7 Persons in Lancashire . . .* (n.p., 1600), 3; William Grainge, ed., *Dae-*

monologia: A Discourse on Witchcraft As It Was Acted in the Family of Mr. Edward Fairfax . . . (Harrowgate, Eng., 1882), 67; David D. Hall, ed., *Witch-Hunting in Seventeenth-Century New England,* 2d ed. (Boston, 1999), 149, 152. A recent study of an early incident involving fraud is James Sharpe, *The Bewitching of Anne Gunter: A Horrible and True Story of Deception, Witchcraft, Murder, and the King of England* (New York, 2000). See also James Sharpe, *Instruments of Darkness: Witches in England 1550–1750* (London, 1996); and Stuart Clark, *Thinking with Demons: The Idea of Witchcraft in Early Modern Europe* (Oxford, 1997).

48. Bernard, *Guide to Grand-Jury Men,* 2, 5. See also William Perkins, *A Discourse of the Damned Art of Witchcraft . . .* (Cambridge, 1608), 38–41. For a detailed discussion of such themes in Bernard and other contemporary authors, see Stuart Clark, "Protestant Demonology: Sin, Superstition, and Society (c. 1520–c. 1630)," in Bengt Ankarloo and Gustav Henningsen, eds., *Early Modern European Witchcraft: Centres and Peripheries* (Oxford, 1990), 45–81.

49. Bernard, *Guide to Grand-Jury Men,* 53–86 passim (quotations 60, 68, 73). On the distinctions among possession, obsession, and bewitchment, see David Harley, "Explaining Satan: Calvinist Psychology and the Diagnosis of Possession," *American Historical Review* 101 (1996): 310–12. For accounts of possession and exorcism on the European continent, see Lyndal Roper, *Oedipus & the Devil: Witchcraft, Sexuality and Religion in Early Modern Europe* (New York, 1994), chapter 8; and Christine Worobec, *Possessed: Women, Witches, and Demons in Imperial Russia* (DeKalb, Ill., 2001).

50. Bernard, *Guide to Grand-Jury Men,* 91–101 passim (quotations 92–93, 95). For an insightful contemporary explanation of why women were more likely than men to be seen as witches, see Roper, *Oedipus & the Devil,* chapter 10.

51. Bernard, *Guide to Grand-Jury Men,* 204–12 passim (quotations 204–205, 210–12, 207, 209).

52. Ibid., 207, 211, 208–10.

53. Large portions of both Increase Mather's *Remarkable Providences* (as the book is commonly known) and Cotton Mather's *Memorable Providences* are reprinted in Burr, *Narratives;* see the accounts of Knapp, 21–23; Stiles, 27–30; Tocutt boy, 136–41. Crouch included Increase Mather's tales in his 1688 *Kingdom of Darkness,* 2–33, so they received wide circulation on both sides of the Atlantic. John P. Demos has given detailed accounts of the case involving Stiles (a prosecution of his grandmother, Elizabeth Morse) and of Knapp's possession in *Entertaining Satan: Witchcraft and the Culture of Early New England* (New York, 1982); see 97–152. On the English debate, see Barbara J. Shapiro, *Probability and Certainty in Seventeenth-Century England: A Study of the Relationships between Natural Science, Religion, Law, and Literature* (Princeton, N.J., 1983), 212–21.

54. Burr, *Narratives,* 137–39; Hall, ed., *Witch-Hunting,* 208, 205 (see 197–212 passim for Willard's detailed account of Knapp's torments). Karlsen also discusses Knapp (*Devil in the Shape of a Woman,* 236–41).

55. Hall, ed., *Witch-Hunting,* 199, 211–12.

56. Mather, *WIW*, in *WDNE* 1:141. John Hale listed both *Memorable Providences* and the 1682 account of the trial presided over by Matthew Hale among the works the judges consulted in 1692; see *Modest Enquiry*, in Burr, *Narratives*, 416.

57. *A Tryal of Witches, at the Assizes Held at Bury St. Edmunds for the County of Suffolk; on the Tenth Day of March, 1664. Before Sir Matthew Hale Kt. . . .* (London, Eng., 1682), passim (quotations 2, 41, 16, 20, 23–24, 28–29). The date in the title was incorrect, as was the surname of one of the witches; given in the book and by Cotton Mather as Duny, it was actually Denny. See Gilbert Geis and Ivan Bunn, *A Trial of Witches: A Seventeenth-Century Witchcraft Prosecution* (London and New York, 1997), which reprints a facsimile copy of *Tryal* as an appendix.

58. *Tryal of Witches*, 12–14, 43.

59. Ibid., 46–47. Mather's summary is in *WIW*, in *WDNE* 1:142–51. He described the fits at some length, mentioned peculiar incidents involving toads and other creatures, quoted the doctor's testimony, and remarked that "Good Men have sometimes disputed" the validity of touch tests. He termed the father's statement "a small Reason" that only "attempted" to explain away the failed test. Mather's narrative makes clear that the maleficium stories told by neighbors, coupled with the fits of the afflicted, were more convincing to him than touch tests.

60. *Tryal of Witches*, 55–59.

61. Ibid., unpaginated introduction. On Hale, see Geis and Bunn, *Trial of Witches*, 22, 156–71 passim. Thomas Hutchinson in 1765 described New England's reverence for Hale as based on "his gravity and piety" as well as his knowledge of the law; see *History of Massachusetts* 2:27. In England, by contrast, Sir Matthew Hale's conduct of the Bury St. Edmunds trial aroused considerable negative comment, and his approach to the evidence was seen as aberrant. It is unclear whether New Englanders were aware of such criticisms; see Shapiro, *Probability and Certainty*, 206–208.

62. Hall, ed., *Witch-Hunting*, 266; Mather, *Memorable Providences*, in Burr, *Narratives*, 100.

63. Mather, *Memorable Providences*, in Burr, *Narratives*, 100–103, 105.

64. Ibid., 103–106. For Dudley as chief judge: Cotton Mather, *The Life of Sir William Phips*, ed. Mark Van Doren (New York, 1929), 138; for the date of execution, Thomas, ed., *Sewall Diary* 1:183. On other probable judges, see chapter 6, n. 7, below.

65. Mather, *Memorable Providences*, in Burr, *Narratives*, 123, 95–96 (quotations); for the naming of other witches, ibid., 107, 117. In 1765, Thomas Hutchinson wrote that the Goodwins' neighbors had informed him of the "great consternation" caused by the children's afflictions. He also commented that he personally knew one of the daughters (either Martha or her younger sister Mercy) as an adult; she "had the character of a very sober virtuous woman" and never admitted to having committed any "fraud." See Hutchinson, *History of Massachusetts* 2:25–26.

66. The trials' critic Robert Calef, for one, asserted in 1700 that *Memorable*

Providences had "conduced much to the kindling those Flames, that . . . threatned the devouring this Country" in 1692 (*MWIW,* in *WDNE* 3:154).

67. Thomas, ed., *Sewall Diary,* 1:287–88. Historians who have attributed elements of the witchcraft crisis in part to uncertainties over the new charter have not paid sufficient attention to the arrival of this definitive news in late January and early February. On the overthrow of Andros, see below, chapter 3.

68. William Perkins, *Discourse of Damned Art,* 200–203; John Gaule, *Select Cases of Conscience Touching Witches and Witchcrafts* (London, 1646), 80. Gaule also listed "unwarrantable" signs of witches that came from "Ignorance" or "superstition," among them identifications through countermagic; see 75–79. In 1692 the Connecticut magistrates confronting a witchcraft outbreak contemporaneous to the one in Essex County seem to have relied on Perkins's list; see their summary of it as printed in Hall, ed., *Witch-Hunting,* 351–53.

69. Gaule, *Select Cases,* 80–81; Perkins, *Discourse of Damned Art,* 203; Bernard, *Guide to Grand-Jury Men,* 228–40 passim (quotations 237–38).

70. *SWP* 2:363.

71. Bernard, *Guide to Grand-Jury Men,* 228, 239.

72. *DHSM* 5:326–27.

CHAPTER TWO   GOSPEL WOMEN

1. This and the next two paragraphs are based on *SWP* 1:260–61. For Putnam's post and Corey's church membership: Salem Village church records, in Paul Boyer and Stephen Nissenbaum, eds., *Salem-Village Witchcraft* (1972; reprint, Boston, 1993), 272–73. When disputes arose between church members, Puritans usually tried to resolve them without going to court. Biographical information on the Coreys from Enders A. Robinson, *The Devil Discovered: Salem Witchcraft 1692* (New York, 1991), 271.

2. *SWP* 3:752–53.

3. This paragraph and the next draw on *SWP* 1:261–62. Quotations in the fifth sentence come from the original document, SWP/SJC/PEM 1:39 (lines omitted in the published version of the conversation).

4. This paragraph is speculative, but Corey's is the only well-documented case in which the court records do not hint at the cause of the initial witchcraft accusation, with the exception of a brief comment during her examination that "Parker some time agoe thought this woman was a Witch" (*SWP* 1:253). For the other incident, see Mary Beth Norton, *Founding Mothers & Fathers: Gendered Power and the Forming of American Society* (New York, 1996), 91–94. Paul Boyer and Stephen Nissenbaum, *Salem Possessed: The Social Origins of Witchcraft* (Cambridge, Mass., 1973), 146–47, both discusses Corey's bastard son and argues—unconvincingly, I believe—that the complaint against Corey accorded with a Putnam family agenda.

5. *SWP* 2:595, 603. The conclusion that the identification took place within a

day is based on John Tarbell's statement in late March that the exchange quoted in the next paragraph occurred "be fore any was afflicted at thomas putnams beside his daughter" (*SWP* 2:603). If Tarbell spoke accurately, then Nurse's specter was positively identified before Mercy Lewis was afflicted on the afternoon of 14 March (see below).

6. *SWP* 2:603. On the Towne and Nurse families and the Topsfield boundaries, see Boyer and Nissenbaum, eds., *Salem-Village Witchcraft*, 148–54, 235–37. For the disputes: EC Ct Recs/WPA, ser. 2, 47:42/1–43/4; and Persis McMillen, *Currents of Malice: Mary Towne Esty and Her Family in Salem Witchcraft* (Portsmouth, N.H., 1990). Boyer and Nissenbaum, *Salem Possessed*, 147–50, make an elaborate psychological argument about Nurse serving as a surrogate for Thomas Putnam's stepmother, but given the history of enmity between the Putnam and Towne families, that seems unnecessary to explain the accusation.

7. This paragraph and the next are based on *SWP* 1:264–65.

8. Mather, *Memorable Providences*, in Burr, *Narratives*, 108. For the story of how one young captive was terrified by just such a threat of being roasted alive, see Mather, *DL*, in Lincoln, *Narratives*, 201. See also Alden T. Vaughan and Edward W. Clark, eds., *Puritans among the Indians: Accounts of Captivity and Redemption, 1676–1724* (Cambridge, Mass., 1981), 105.

9. The only detailed contemporary description of the attack, used as a basis for this paragraph and the next, is William Hubbard, *A Narrative of the Troubles with the Indians in New-England . . .* [part 2] *From Pascataqua to Pemmaquid* (Boston, 1677), 31–34 (quotation 32). For a map of Falmouth and Casco Bay, see pp. 126–127.

10. Thaddeus Clark to Elizabeth Harvey, 16 August 1676, in Samuel G. Drake, ed., *The Aboriginal Races of North America*, 15th ed., rev. by H. L. Williams (New York, 1880), 747n.

11. All biographical information on the extended family of Philip Lewis in the preceding paragraphs comes from *GDMNH*, passim. Precisely where Philip Lewis resided in Casco during the 1670s is not clear; the family lived "a considerable time" after 1663 on Hog Island, but he also owned land on the mainland. For his residence on the island and that quotation, see William Willis, *The History of Portland, from 1632 to 1864* (Portland, Me., 1865), 134.

12. *SWP* 1:265.

13. Ibid., 1:258, 263; 2:667, 597. For the first two weeks of Mercy's fits, only Ann Jr. identified her spectral tormentor as Martha Corey (ibid., 1:265).

14. Quotations: ibid., 1:265, 258. Earlier accounts of afflicted children in old or New England also mention the large number of spectators who came to observe them or to assist in caring for them. Other such references appear in the Salem records, too (e.g., ibid., 2:483, 674). On the demands of housework in seventeenth-century New England, see Laurel Thatcher Ulrich, *Good Wives: Image and Reality in the Lives of Women in Northern New England, 1650–1750* (New York, 1982), chapter 1; for daughters' contributions to housework later in the colonial era, see Mary

Beth Norton, *Liberty's Daughters: The Revolutionary Experience of American Women, 1750–1800* (Boston, 1980), 15–18, 23–26.

15. For evidence of Parris's note-taking, see the discussion on pp. 56–57. On household hierarchies, see Norton, *Founding Mothers & Fathers*, section 1.

16. *SWP* 2:604. Her fit, perhaps not coincidentally, occurred on the second anniversary of a Wabanaki raid on Salmon Falls (see chapter 3, pp. 102–103).

17. Many thanks to Jane Kamensky for allowing me to see and cite her unpublished paper, "The Devil's Book: The Material Culture of Witchcraft in Early New England," delivered at the January 1998 meeting of the American Historical Association. Abigail Williams and Betty Hubbard both later claimed to have seen Martha Corey's copy of Satan's book when her specter tortured them prior to March 18, but I strongly suspect that they retrospectively added a sighting of the book to the afflictions they suffered at the time. When they testified in early August, references to the book had become commonplace, which was not the case in mid-March. See *SWP* 1:258, 263.

18. *SWP* 1:247. Mercy's sister Priscilla married Henry Kenney Jr. in 1691. The complainant was probably his father, Henry Kenney Sr., rather than Mercy's brother-in-law.

19. Lawson, *A Brief and True Narrative of . . . Witchcraft, at Salem Village . . .* (1692), in Burr, *Narratives,* 147–48.

20. Ibid., 152–54.

21. *A Tryal of Witches, at the Assizes Held at Bury St. Edmonds for the County of Suffolk; on the Tenth Day of March, 1664. Before Sir Matthew Hale Kt. . . .* (London, 1682), 28–29; Mather, *Memorable Providences,* in Burr, *Narratives,* 108, 111–12; Thomas Hutchinson, *The History of Massachusetts from the First Settlement Thereof in 1628, until the Year 1750* (3d ed., Boston, 1795), 2:27.

22. For church attendees, see Lawson, *Brief and True Narrative,* in Burr, *Narratives,* 154. Joseph Pope was forty-one (*SWP* 2:683); women were usually a year or two younger than their husbands. John and Sarah Vibber's surname is today rendered as Vibert; he is believed to have come from Sark. Theirs was a second marriage for both, but her birth name and the name of her first husband are unknown. (Thanks to Ben Ray for forwarding information on the likely Vibert connection from the Salem witch trials descendants e-mail list on rootsweb.com.)

23. For biographical information on Nathaniel Ingersoll and Jonathan Walcott: Robinson, *Devil Discovered,* 72–74, 76; for John Walcott's military service in Maine: *DHSM* 5:109. For the Ingersolls' departure from Falmouth: *DHSM* 4:348–49; for their admission to residency in Salem on 11 January 1675/6, "Salem Town Records," *EIHC* 48 (1912): 21; and *GDMNH,* q.v. "Ingersoll, George." A petition complaining that George Ingersoll was an incompetent militia officer, dated 2 February 1675/6, is printed in *DHSM* 4:351–54.

24. Lawson, *Brief and True Narrative,* in Burr, *Narratives,* 154.

25. On Puritan practices and the Hutchinsonian challenge, see Norton, *Founding Mothers & Fathers,* 23, 370. In court, female witnesses and defendants

were called upon to speak, but in church women could seldom, if ever, voice their opinions.

26. *SWP* 2:604, 596.

27. Ibid., 1:263 (Hubbard); 1:258, 2:597, 667, 688 (Williams).

28. Lawson, *Brief and True Narrative*, in Burr, *Narratives*, 154. Parris and the senior male Putnams frequently submitted supporting depositions confirming dates of afflictions; see, e.g., *SWP* 1:164, 167; 2:598. Bernard Rosenthal, in *Salem Story: Reading the Witch Trials of 1692* (New York, 1993), speculates repeatedly about the possibility that adult witnesses at the trials were lying (chapter 3 and passim). But people took oaths very seriously at the time, because they believed that both their reputations and their immortal souls depended on their telling the truth. (See Norton, *Founding Mothers & Fathers*, 159–61, 208–10, 385–86.) More-over, in such a small community everyone knew everyone else's business, and out-right lies could readily have been exposed. Therefore, I think it highly unlikely that any seventeenth-century adult witnesses—especially clergymen—lied know-ingly and systematically under oath in the Salem trials. People told the truth as they saw it at the time. Later, admittedly, some of them reevaluated their earlier statements.

29. *SWP* 2:677–78. Parris's surrender of that page of his notes to the marshal at the time probably explains why 12 April is absent from Abigail's 31 May deposi-tions against the Proctors; Parris did not have that record in front of him when he later drafted those statements. He must have had other notes for 4 and 6 April, though, for those dates are included in the complaint against John Proctor.

30. *SWP* 2:389 (Abigail); 3:810 (Ann Jr.); 3:842 (June); 1:173 (July).

31. Lawson, *Brief and True Narrative*, in Burr, *Narratives*, 155; *SWP* 1:248. Law-son added yet another name to the list of the afflicted: "the ancient" Goody Goodale, mentioned for the only time in the crisis. She was Margaret, wife of Robert Goodale, whose stepson Jacob had been beaten to death by Giles Corey in 1675. See Robinson, *Devil Discovered*, 146. Because by the following Friday, Betty Parris was living in Boston at the home of Stephen Sewall (see below), she per-haps did not attend Martha Corey's examination.

32. This paragraph and the next are based on *SWP* 1:248–49, 259. Lawson, *Brief and True Narrative*, in Burr, *Narratives*, 156, records the observation of the "black man" but does not attribute it.

33. A keyword search on "black" or "blak" in *SWP* on the Witchcraft in Salem Village website produced hits in thirty-three different cases, some with multiple references to the phrase; the only person other than Tituba referring to clothing was William Barker Sr. (*SWP* 1:74). Two additional references are in the examina-tions of Ann Dolliver and Mary Ireson, not accessible through that index; see chapter 6, n. 31, below. Although English afflicted and confessors also occasionally termed the devil "a black man," that description did not predominate in their accounts, as it did in Salem. For example, the afflicted children in the Starkie case variously termed the devil a "very yll favored" hunchback, "a foule ugly man with

a white beard," "an urchin," "a beare with a fyer in his mouth," and "a white dove,"
in addition to "an ugly black man with shoulders higher than his head." See John
Darrell, *A True Narration of the Strange and Grevous Vexation by the Devil, of 7 Persons in Lancashire, and William Somers of Nottingham* (n.p., 1600), 11–12.

34. Quotations, in order: *DHSM* 4:455; David D. Hall, ed., *Witch-Hunting in Seventeenth-Century New England*, 2d ed. (Boston, 1999), 156; *SWP* 2:611; Mather, *WIW*, in *WDNE* 1:159. See also James Axtell, *The European and the Indian: Essays in the Ethnohistory of Colonial North America* (New York, 1981), 105 (thanks to James Axtell for this reference). The color designation would have been reinforced by the Algonquians' custom of blacking their faces for war or grieving; see Mary Rowlandson, *The Sovereignty and Goodness of God*, ed. Neal Salisbury (Boston, 1997), 101, 106; and Samuel Lee to Dr. Nehemiah Grew, c. June 1690, British Library Sloane Manuscripts #4062, f 235, transcript, LCMD. The *Oxford English Dictionary* defines "black" in one seventeenth-century usage as "having an extremely dark skin; . . . often, loosely, [applied] to non-European races, little darker than many Europeans."

35. John McWilliams, "Indian John and the Northern Tawnies," *NEQ* 69 (1996): 581 (see 581–85 passim). McWilliams does not link his "spectral Indian" to the "black man" of the examinations. On Indians as devil worshippers, see Elaine Breslaw, *Tituba, Reluctant Witch of Salem: Devilish Indians and Puritan Fantasies* (New York, 1996), 167–70; Richard Godbeer, *The Devil's Dominion: Magic and Religion in Early New England* (New York, 1992), 191–92; William S. Simmons, *Spirit of the New England Tribes: Indian History and Folklore, 1620–1984* (Hanover, N.H., 1986), 37–64 passim, esp. 37–38. Cotton Mather, in *DL*, in Lincoln, *Narratives*, often describes Indians as diabolical; see, e.g., 190, 208, 211, 212, 230, 238, 242. David S. Lovejoy, "Satanizing the American Indian," *NEQ* 67 (1994): 603–21, examines the general theme but dismisses any connection to Salem witchcraft. Alfred A. Cave, "Indian Shamans and English Witches in Seventeenth-Century New England," *EIHC* 128 (1992): 239–54, makes the link to Salem but focuses primarily on the nature of shamanic acts.

36. This paragraph and the next are based on *SWP* 1:250–53.

37. *SWP* 1:253; Lawson, *Brief and True Narrative*, in Burr, *Narratives*, 156, 163.

38. *SWP* 1:252–54; Lawson, *Brief and True Narrative*, in Burr, *Narratives*, 157.

39. *SWP* 2:604. The description of Nurse's specter as wearing a nightcap is crossed out in the deposition.

40. This paragraph and the next are based on ibid., 2:593–94. Elizabeth Porter was John Hathorne's sister; Daniel Andrew's wife Sarah was Israel Porter's sister. I date this visit on March 22 because during it Nurse told her visitors that she had been sick "allmost A weak" (probably six days), and at her examination on March 24 she said she had been confined to her house for eight or nine days. The visitors, as is clear from their comments, were also well aware of a major theme at Martha Corey's examination on March 21. Who asked the group to call on Goody

Nurse is not recorded. On Andrew and the Porters, see Boyer and Nissenbaum, *Salem Possessed,* 120–23.

41. Lawson, *Brief and True Narrative,* in Burr, *Narratives,* 157–58. Lawson's "sober and pious" description of Ann Carr Putnam is from the 1704 edition of *Brief and True Narrative,* as printed in Charles W. Upham, *Salem Witchcraft* (Boston, 1867), 2:531.

42. Complaints: *SWP* 2:351 (Good), 583 (Nurse); Walcott quotation: *SWP* 2:352.

43. This and the next four paragraphs are based on ibid., 2:584–87, and Lawson, *Brief and True Narrative,* in Burr, *Narratives,* 159. The interrogation revealed that Parris had been present at the Putnams' while Ann Sr. had fits, and that he had taken notes on what she said. Those notes could well have formed the basis for her deposition of 31 May 1692 (*SWP* 2:603–604).

44. Lawson, *Brief and True Narrative,* in Burr, *Narratives,* 159–60; Upham, *Salem Witchcraft,* 2:535. That the interrogation of Dorcas Good followed Rebecca Nurse's is evident from Lawson's reporting. He left the meetinghouse in the middle of Nurse's examination to prepare his sermon for later that day and had to rely on others for information about the questioning of Dorcas.

45. Lawson, *Brief and True Narrative,* in Burr, *Narratives,* 159; *SWP* 1:259–60.

46. *SWP* 2:683, 670, 665.

47. Lawson, *Brief and True Narrative,* in Burr, *Narratives,* 159–60; *SWP* 1:219, 216, 215. Sending an afflicted child away, usually to relatives, was common practice in England. For detailed discussions of Rachel Clinton, see John P. Demos, *Entertaining Satan: Witchcraft and the Culture of Early New England* (New York, 1982), chapter 1; and Carol F. Karlsen, *The Devil in the Shape of a Woman* (New York, 1987), 108–10.

48. Lawson, "Christ's Fidelity . . . ," reprinted in its entirety in Richard B. Trask, ed., *"The Devil hath been raised": A Documentary History of the Salem Village Witchcraft Outbreak of March 1692,* rev. ed. (Danvers, Mass., 1997), 66–67. (The sermon is on pp. 66–105 of that volume.)

49. Ibid., 67–68.

50. Ibid., 73, 75–77.

51. Ibid., 78–80.

52. Ibid., 80, 87, 91–92, 95–97.

53. Ibid., 98, 100.

54. This and the next paragraph draw on ibid., 94, 101–102, 104–106. An account showing a payment to Lawson amid other expenditures "for the Eastward" has been preserved among the papers of the colony's treasurer, John Usher, in box 1, f 147, Jeffries Family Papers, MHS.

55. Lawson, *Brief and True Narrative,* in Burr, *Narratives,* 161. Lawson, who probably left Salem Village late on March 26, misdated the incident as April 3. Robert Calef later claimed that the wind, not Sarah Cloyce, had closed the door

"forcibly"; see *MWIW,* in *WDNE* 3:14. Nothing else in the extant record suggests a reason for the accusation of Cloyce, but this incident had a striking impact on people in the meetinghouse that day; both Abigail Williams and another afflicted girl, Jemima Rea, later referred to it. For Williams, see below; for Rea, see *SWP* 2:606.

56. This and the next paragraph are based on James F. Cooper and Kenneth P. Minkema, eds., *The Sermon Notebook of Samuel Parris, 1689–1694* (Boston, 1993), 194–98.

57. This paragraph and the next are drawn from Lawson, *Brief and True Narrative,* in Burr, *Narratives,* 160–61. See also *SWP* 2:659. The witches' gathering first described here (and later presented in much the same way by many other afflicted and confessing people in 1692) differed greatly from those common in Europe. Cf., e.g., Eva Pócs, *Between the Living and the Dead* (Budapest, 1999), chapter 5, "The Alternative World of the Witches' Sabbat"; and Michael Bailey, "The Medieval Concept of the Witches' Sabbath," *Exemplaria* 8 (1996): 413–39.

58. *SWP* 2:669, 660. Bittford did not date his vision precisely; Gould saw the specters on April 7. On April 6, he had also seen Giles and Martha Corey at his bedside, and on another occasion Giles was accompanied by John Proctor in his spectral visiting (ibid., 1:244).

59. Ibid., 2:667, 670, 666, 665, 677. Parris noted (ibid., 678) that Walcott had not seen either of the Proctors' specters till the evening of April 11, but since the March 28 incident involved a "jest" rather than an actual sighting, the speaker at her great-uncle's house could have been she.

60. Biographical information on both Proctors from Boyer and Nissenbaum, *Salem Possessed,* 200–202; and Robinson, *Devil Discovered,* 281–83.

61. *SWP* 2:683–84. Mary Warren's background remains a mystery, for she has proved impossible to trace definitively, despite sustained effort by me and my research assistants.

62. Ibid., 3:796–97, 800.

63. Bernard Rosenthal and Elizabeth Reis contributed to the development of this analysis. Possibly Joseph Pope too objected to the proceedings and so prevented his afflicted wife Bathshua's name from appearing on any legal complaint. On husbands and fathers as legal gatekeepers for their wives and daughters in the seventeenth century, see Mary Beth Norton, " 'Either Married or to Bee Married': Women's Legal Inequality in Early America," in Carla Pestana and Sharon Salinger, eds., *Inequality in Early America* (Boston, 1999), 29–36.

64. *SWP* 3:795, 798; Lawson, *Brief and True Narrative,* in Burr, *Narratives,* 162. This paragraph is admittedly speculative, but it accords with the scanty surviving evidence. On a Sabbath, Mary Warren put up a bill of thanks for something; Lawson states that an afflicted girl named "Mary W." was said by others to have signed the book after she was "a little better at ease"; and the last date in Lawson's narrative is April 3, although it includes material revealed at the April 11 examinations. Burr identifies the "Mary W." of the narrative as Mary Walcott, but no

other source suggests that Walcott ever broke ranks with the afflicted, whereas Warren clearly did, as will be evident in the discussion below.

65. *SWP* 2:657–68. Only John McWilliams has devoted much attention to the role of John Indian among the afflicted; see McWilliams, "Indian John and the Northern Tawnies," *NEQ* 69 (1996): 597–600.

66. Biographical information on Sarah Towne Cloyce from Robinson, *Devil Discovered,* 273–74; for Peter and Thomas Cloyce and Susanna Lewis, see *GDMNH* and chart 1, p. 50, above. As widow Bridges, Sarah and her five children were warned out of Topsfield in September 1682, thus revealing her poverty; see G. F. Dow, ed., "Topsfield Town Records," *HCTHS* 2(1896): 41.

67. *SWP* 1:259 (Lewis); 2:686 (Putnam).

68. M. Halsey Thomas, ed., *The Diary of Samuel Sewall 1674–1729* (New York, 1973), 1:289. Calef, in *MWIW,* in *WDNE* 3:14–15, commented that the proceedings were filled with "hideous clamors and Screechings."

69. This and the next paragraph are based on *SWP* 2:658–59. Abigail Williams's question to Goody Cloyce at the witch meeting was reported in Lawson, *Brief and True Narrative,* in Burr, *Narratives,* 161.

70. This and the next two paragraphs draw on *SWP* 2:659–61.

71. Ibid., 661–62.

72. Ibid., 677–78.

73. Ibid., 601–602. Parris recorded the Putnam baby's death on 15 April 1692, along with other deaths in Salem Village during his ministry, in the church records. I thank Richard Trask, Danvers town historian, for supplying me with a copy of the relevant manuscript pages from the Danvers Archival Center, Peabody Institute Library, Danvers. Parris's list of deaths has been fully reprinted in *NEHGR* 36 (1882): 187–89, but with most dates erroneously labeled as one year too late.

74. Mary Swayne Marshall, deposition, 10 September 1692, BPL (thanks to Ben Ray for a copy of this document). The news of the Salem Village examinations would most likely have traveled by ship to Stamford. I have dated the onset of Branch's fits by working backward from the first precise date given in the documents (afflictions on April 25 that later became the subject of indictments), using information on timing contained in Daniel Wescott's statement, cited n. 75, below. He described about thirteen days of fits, followed by some additional days before a suspect was specifically identified, or perhaps two and a half weeks. The emphasis on identifying specters through clothing suggests familiarity with that theme of Martha Corey's case. For the indictments (giving the date of April 25), see Wyllys Papers (Brown), W-39; Wyllys Papers (CSL), f 37. The latter and a variant of the former are printed in Hall, ed., *Witch-Hunting,* 345.

75. Sgt. Daniel Wescott, statement, Stamford, 27 May 1692, Wyllys Papers (Brown), W-19; printed with modernized spelling in Hall, ed., *Witch-Hunting,* 317–19.

76. Jonathan Selleck to Nathaniel Gold, 29 June 1692, Wyllys Papers (Brown),

W-22; partially printed in Hall, ed., *Witch-Hunting*, 331–32. The war's impact in the region was confined to some deaths of militiamen from disease on a failed 1690 expedition to Montreal and losses of houses, livestock, and crops in a raid by French vessels along the coast in mid-July 1690. Information on the Connecticut situation can be found in the correspondence of Fitz-John Winthrop, box 24, Winthrop Family Papers, MHS.

77. Thus John Demos discusses them in his *Entertaining Satan*, a book conceptualized as dealing with all New England cases other than those related to Salem.

78. Hale, *Modest Enquiry*, in Burr, *Narratives*, 400. On the Hartford cases, see Hall, ed., *Witch-Hunting*, 147–63, 355–58; and Demos, *Entertaining Satan*, 351–55, 509–13.

79. *SWP* 2:413, 415. Spelling in the final quotation corrected by the original, SWP/SJC/PEM 1:158. That Deliverance Hobbs was herein referred to as Abigail's "mother" has misled some historians into thinking that theirs was a blood relationship. It was not; Abigail's mother, her father's first wife, was named Avis. See chapter 4, below.

80. *SWP* 2:416. The April 18 complaint against her and others: ibid., 1:239.

81. This and the next three paragraphs are based on ibid., 2:405–409, with minor corrections from the original in Miscellaneous Manuscripts, MHS.

82. When Abigail Hobbs was indicted in September 1692 for making a covenant with Satan, she was accused of doing so in 1688 at Casco Bay. Consequently, the grand jury accepted the dating of four years earlier as the appropriate timing of her encounter with the devil. I have herein accepted the grand jury's determination (*SWP* 2:414–15), but her ambiguous confession also implied either 1686 or 1689 as possibilities.

CHAPTER THREE   PANNICK AT THE EASTWARD

1. The first quotation is from Thomas Danforth to —, 27 June 1689, *DHSM* 9:23; the second, from the captivity narrative of John Gyles, who heard the story of the Cocheco raid directly from some of the Indians involved: Alden T. Vaughan and Edward E. Clark, eds., *Puritans among the Indians: Accounts of Captivity and Redemption, 1676–1724* (Cambridge, Mass., 1981), 101. Samuel G. Drake supplied one of the most detailed published descriptions of the Cocheco raid and of Waldron's reputation in his notes to Thomas Church, *The History of Philip's War . . . Also, of the French and Indian Wars, at the Eastward*, ed. Samuel G. Drake (Exeter, N.H., 1839), 161n.–163n. For Waldron's early history, see George M. Bodge, *Soldiers in King Philip's War*, 3d ed. (Boston, 1906), 293–95. On the Pennacooks: Colin G. Calloway, "Wanalancet and Kancagamus: Indian Strategy and Leadership on the New Hampshire Frontier," *Historical New Hampshire* 43 (1988): 264–90. I owe the Gyles reference to Alice Nash.

2. The unsuccessful attempt to warn Waldron can be traced in *DHSM* 6:499 and 9:22.

3. Quotations from Vaughan and Clark, eds., *Puritans among the Indians*, 101. Other accounts of the raid, which shocked New Englanders, are "News from New England Concerning the Indians," n.d. [c. early July 1689], *DHSM* 5:2; A. H. Quint, ed., "Journal of the Rev. John Pike," *MHS Procs* 14 (1875–76): 124; and Mather, *DL*, in Lincoln, *Narratives*, 195–96.

4. Vaughan and Clark, eds., *Puritans among the Indians*, 183. Evan Haefeli and Kevin Sweeney attribute the 1704 Deerfield raid in part to the Pennacooks' continuing anger over Waldron's betrayal; see their "Revisiting *The Redeemed Captive*: New Perspectives on the 1704 Attack on Deerfield," in Colin G. Calloway, ed., *After King Philip's War: Presence and Persistence in Indian New England* (Hanover, N.H., 1997), 42. Thanks respectively to Alice Nash and Lisa Brooks for these references.

5. Recent works on King Philip's War include Russell Bourne, *The Red King's Rebellion: Racial Politics in New England, 1675–1678* (New York, 1990); James Drake, *King Philip's War: Civil War in New England, 1675–1676* (Amherst, Mass., 1999); and Jill Lepore, *The Name of War: King Philip's War and the Origins of American Identity* (New York, 1998). Bourne devotes one chapter to the northern phase of the war; Drake gives it two and a half pages; and Lepore barely mentions it. Yet, as Baker (n. 6, below) points out, the war had more devastating effects in the north than in the south. See also Richard Slotkin and James K. Folsom, eds., *So Dreadful a Judgment: Puritan Responses to King Philip's War, 1676–1677* (Middletown, Conn., 1978).

6. Emerson Woods Baker II, "Trouble to the Eastward: The Failure of Anglo-Indian Relations in Early Maine" (unpub. Ph.D. diss., College of William and Mary, 1986), chapter 6, is one of the best discussions of King Philip's War in the north; he addresses its origins, 184–88.

7. Descriptions of these communities written in 1660 and 1677, respectively, are Henry F. Waters, ed., "Maverick's Description of New England," *NEHGR* 39 (1885): 33–47; and William Hubbard, *A Narrative of the Troubles with the Indians in New-England . . .* [part 2] *From Pascataqua to Pemmaquid* (Boston, 1677), 1–4. Falmouth is now Portland.

8. Quotation: unnamed Boston merchant to London friend, 16 May 1690, CO 5/855, f 3. For Maine residents' conflicted attitudes toward the Bay Colony: Maine General Assembly, petition to King Charles II, n.d. [summer 1680], *DHSM* 4:394–96. See, on the fisheries: Daniel Vickers, *Farmers & Fishermen: Two Centuries of Work in Essex County, Massachusetts, 1630–1850* (Chapel Hill, N.C., 1994), chapter 3 passim, esp. 100; on timber: Charles F. Carroll, *The Timber Economy of Puritan New England* (Providence, R.I., 1973), chapter 6 passim, esp. 110; and on the struggle to control Maine: Mary Beth Norton, *Founding Mothers & Fathers: Gendered Power and the Forming of American Society* (New York, 1996), 308–12; and Carroll, *Timber Economy*, 115–19. For the New England economy as a whole: see

Bernard Bailyn, *The New England Merchants in the Seventeenth Century* (Cambridge, Mass., 1955). Population estimate from Baker, "Trouble to Eastward," 179.

9. My understanding of the Wabanakis derives largely from the excellent work of Emerson Baker, Alice Nash, and Jenny Pulsipher. See Nash's succinct description of Wabanaki social structure in her "The Abiding Frontier: Family, Gender, and Religion in Wabanaki History, 1600–1763" (unpub. Ph.D. diss., Columbia University, 1997), 17–18. I also thank Baker, Nash, and Pulsipher for generously sharing unpublished essays with me.

10. For a brief discussion of Acadia, see John Mack Faragher, " 'Without these compromises it would be impossible to exist in this country': Acadian 'Neutrality' in the Age of Empire, 1604–1755," paper delivered at the conference on Greater American Histories, HL, March 2001. My thanks to Johnny Faragher for sharing this unpublished essay with me. On Madockawando and Castine, see also Alvin Morrison, "Dawnland Directors' Decisions: 17th-Century Encounter Dynamics on the Wabanaki Frontier," in William Cowan, ed., *Papers of the Twenty-second Algonquian Conference* (Ottawa, Canada, 1991), passim, esp. 232–34, 238–39. I owe this reference to Maria Lepowsky.

11. This analysis of the origins of King Philip's War in the north largely concurs with Nash, "Abiding Frontier," 5–6. For the assessment of the 1678 Treaty of Casco, see Mather, *DL*, in Lincoln, *Narratives*, 184.

12. Ingersoll to Alger, 10 September 1675, *DHSM* 6:89–90. On the problems along the Kennebec, see Hubbard, *Narrative* [part 2], 13–15; on the death of Squando's child, ibid., 29.

13. Ingersoll to Alger, 10 September 1675, *DHSM* 6:89–90; Daniel Denison to [Governor Leverett?], n.d. [after 16 October 1675], ibid., 84; Gardner to Leverett, 22 September 1675, ibid., 91–93. Gardner's cautionary message served only to arouse "more then Ordinary Suspition" that he was himself "tradeing with the french & Indians" and encouraging "the barbarous natives now in Hostillity." The council ordered his arrest a few weeks later. (Massachusetts Council to Brian Pendleton et al., 16 October 1675, ibid., 96.) Bourne, *Red King's Rebellion*, 225, states that Gardner was subsequently tried for treason, but acquitted. On the raids that fall: Hubbard, *Narrative* [part 2], 16–26.

14. For the controversies surrounding the troops in Black Point, see Richard Foxwell, et al., petition to Mass. General Court, n.d. [c. 15 July 1676], *NEHGR* 43 (1889): 71. Many of the depositions in Suffolk Court Files #1526 and #1828, JA, MSA, criticize Scottow's use of the soldiers during the winter of 1675–1676.

15. Leverett to [Sir Joseph Williamson], 15 June 1676, CO 1/37, f 16. One of the captives "freely" brought into Cocheco was Elizabeth Wakely, captured when her parents and grandparents were killed outside Falmouth on 9 September 1675. See *York Deeds* 16:145.

16. The fullest description of the 1676 attack on Falmouth is Hubbard, *Narrative* [part 2], 30–34. Burroughs wrote to Black Point from the island to obtain help. His letter has not survived, but it was mentioned both in Brian Pendleton to

Massachusetts Governor and Council [hereafter MG&C], 13 August 1676, reprinted in William Willis, *The History of Portland, from 1632 to 1864* (Portland, 1865), 206n, and in a council order the next day (*DHSM* 6:116).

17. Quotations: Gardner et al. to MG&C, 21 [August] 1676, *DHSM* 6:118–19; John Laverdure, deposition, 23 August 1676, box 2/32, Collection 77, MeHS; Edward Rawson to [Daniel Denison?], 23 August 1676, *DHSM* 6:119. See also two other depositions in box 2/32, Collection 77, MeHS; and Edward Pateshall, deposition, 3 April 1677, CO 1/40, f 49, on how the kidnappings aroused Indian hostility. Estimates of the size of the group seized ranged as high as thirty. See also Hubbard, *Narrative* [part 2], 29–30, 35–44; and Faragher, " 'Without these compromises,' " 14–15. "The humble Address of the Saggamores of Kennibeck & Andross Coggan Rivers and Easterne Side of Cascoa Bay in New England," received 4 December 1684, CO 1/56, f 133, attributed their entry into the war primarily to the kidnappings. Some Wabanakis in mid-1677 also referred to the problems caused in the winter of 1675–1676 by their lack of guns and powder (*DHSM* 6:178).

18. Richard Waldron et al. to [MG&C], 10 September 1676, *NEHGR* 42 (1888): 287. On the treaty of July 1676, see Baker, "Trouble to Eastward," 194.

19. Waldron did not send "about 10 young men" and their families to Boston, deeming them "very necessary" and "safe" to employ in the war. Richard Waldron to MG&C, 6 September 1676, box 2/42, Collection 77, MeHS; Waldron et al. to same, 10 September 1676, *NEHGR* 42 (1888): 287–88; Hubbard, *Narrative* [part 2], 27–28. Hubbard's account, which is the standard version of the incident, varies in two ways from what can be pieced together from Waldron's correspondence cited in this footnote. First, Hubbard claimed that Waldron, Hathorne, and the other commanders "mutually agreed" to capture the Indians, whereas the correspondence makes clear that they acted in response to orders from Boston. Second, Hubbard stated that about half the Wabanakis were not sent south, whereas Waldron specifically refers to having obeyed "yor Pleasures . . . to have all sent down to determine their Case at Boston" (*NEHGR* 42 [1888]: 288). Both alterations of the historical record worked to reduce the responsibility of the Boston authorities for the unwarranted seizure of the peaceful group and at the same time tended to increase the culpability of local leaders for that reprehensible act. Yet Waldron's subordinates expressed disquiet about what they had been directed to do, anticipating violent retaliation.

20. Quotations: Nicholas Shapleigh and Thomas Daniel to MG&C, 6 September 1676, box 2/42, Collection 77, MeHS (this letter and that of Waldron of the same date to the same recipients, cited n. 19 above, are on opposite sides of the same sheet of paper); Pendleton to MG&C, n.d. [c. early November 1676], *DHSM* 6:141. See also Hubbard, *Narrative* [part 2], 46; and Hathorne's reports of his lack of progress in *DHSM* 6:123–24, 128–30. There are numerous firsthand accounts of the surrender of Black Point in Suffolk Court File #1828, JA, MSA. One of the few registers of names of Maine refugees entering an Essex County

town is the list of people from Casco (including George Ingersoll) admitted to residency in Salem in January 1675/6: "Salem Town Records," *EIHC* 48 (1912): 21. See also the council order of 4 December 1676 requesting information about the "many necessitous persons in the severall Townes brought in distresse by the Indian warr," *DHSM* 4:144.

21. Hubbard, *Narrative* [part 2], 64–71 (quotation 70); Baker, "Trouble to Eastward," 207–10. Waldron's orders and commission are printed in *DHSM* 6:153–55.

22. Deogenes et al. to "governor of Boston," 1 July 1677, *DHSM* 6:178.

23. Quotation: Waldron to —, 18 April 1677, ibid., 163. A report from the leader of the men at the Kennebec, 23 April 1677, is ibid., 164–65. See Baker, "Trouble to Eastward," 211–12, on the battles around Black Point.

24. Quotation: motion of "Eastern Deputies," 6 June 1677, *DHSM* 6:170. On Andros's intervention, see ibid., 185–86; Baker, "Trouble to Eastward," 212–13; Andros's instructions to Lt. Anthony Brockholst, 13 June 1677, CO 1/40, ff 239–40; and Sir Edmund Andros, "A Short Account of New Yorks Assistance to New England, 18 April 1678," CO 1/42, f 118. The council detailed its suspicions of Andros (and of possible French encouragement of the Indians) in a letter to English officials, 5 April 1676, *DHSM* 6:112. For more about fears of the French: ibid., 150; and Henry Jocelyn and Joshua Scottow to Governor Leverett, 15 September 1676, box 33/21, Collection S-888, MeHS.

25. James Axtell, ed., "The Vengeful Women of Marblehead: James Roules's Deposition of 1677," *WMQ*, 3d ser., 31 (1974): 647–52 (quotations 651–52).

26. Ibid., 652. Axtell does not suggest that frontier refugees might have participated in this incident, yet a number of Maine families (most notably that of the 1692 accuser, Sarah Churchwell) are known to have lived in Marblehead at the time. The involvement of such refugees would help to explain what might otherwise seem a disproportionate response to the taking of ships and men, especially because captured sailors were commonly released unharmed by the Indians (as Axtell notes).

27. William woum Wood et al. to Massachusetts leaders, 1 July 1677, *DHSM* 6:177–78.

28. See MG&C, meeting minutes, 10 July 1677, ibid., 186–88; Brockholst to MG&C, 17 July and 18 August 1677, ibid., 189–93; Manning's journal, 21 July 1677, ibid., 179–80; Joshua Scottow, "Narrative of the Voyage to Pemmaquid," 3–28 August 1677, transcript, Peter Force Papers, LCMD (which summarizes the provisions of the treaty). Bourne, *Red King's Rebellion*, briefly describes these events, 240–41.

29. The Rev. John Pike, a resident of Dover, summarized the Indians' grievances; Mather included his observations in *DL*, in Lincoln, *Narratives*, 186–87. This analysis agrees with that of Baker, "Trouble to Eastward," 225–26. Nash, "Abiding Frontier," 257–58, places greater emphasis on French influence on the Wabanakis. There is no modern, comprehensive history of King William's War in northern New England; but see Francis Parkman, *Count Frontenac and New*

France under Louis XIV (France and England in North America Part Fifth) (reprint, Boston, 1899), and Samuel Adams Drake, *The Border Wars of New England* (reprint, Williamstown, Mass., 1973).

30. The rumors: Joseph Storer to Jonathan Corwin, 17 March 1681/2, box 1, fol. 8, Curwen Family Papers, PEM; and three letters written in late February–early March 1683/4 and forwarded from Maine to London, in CO 1/54, ff 274, 276, 277. The early 1688 incidents are described in depositions printed in *DHSM* 6:325–28 (quotation 325), and 413–18; the Sacos' actions in Edward Tyng to Andros, 18 August 1688, ibid., 419. On 19 August, Boston was "full of the news of 5 English persons killed at Northfield": M. Halsey Thomas, ed., *The Diary of Samuel Sewall, 1674–1729* (New York, 1973), 1:175.

31. The quotations come from reports of the rumors that reached England: "This Account Josiah Parker of Groton Received the 17th of August of an Indian," CO 1/65, f 157; and "An Abstract of a Letter dated Boston New England 20th Aug: 1688," ibid., f 106. Andros's aide Francis Nicholson recorded encountering widespread "fears of the Indians" in the environs of Boston in late August (ibid., ff 147–50). But another report, ibid., f 159, described a visit to the Pennacooks' encampment revealing "noe preparacon for Warr."

32. Dudley, Stoughton, Usher, and Shrimpton to MG&C, n.d. [October 1688?], *DHSM* 6:376. See also Joseph Dudley's statement, 5 June 1689, *MHS Colls* 53 (1889): 506; and Andros to William Blathwayt, 19 October 1688, vol. 3, fol. 4, William Blathwayt Papers, CW. In January 1689/90, the councilors Thomas Hinckley, Wait Winthrop, and Bartholomew Gedney associated themselves with the decisions by defending them in a formal statement signed by Stoughton and Shrimpton as well (MA 35:191–92; another copy in Winthrop Papers, oversize box 4, MHS).

33. Edward Tyng to Andros, 1 October 1688, *DHSM* 6:435. Andros disclosed that 16 of the 20 were women and children; see "Answer of Sir Edmund Andros to his Instructions," n.d., received 1 July 1690, CO 5/855, f 243. Although Sylvanus Davis twice indicated that Hope Hood was among the captives (*DHSM* 5:144, 6:432), another contemporary source suggested otherwise (*DHSM* 6:422).

34. I have pieced together the story of these confusing events from four retrospective accounts and the relevant contemporary correspondence in September 1688 as printed in *DHSM* 6:420–34 passim. The summaries are Tyng to Andros, 1 October 1688, ibid., 435–37; "Declaration of Silvanus Davis," n.d. [after 15 October 1690], *DHSM* 5:142–43; Andros to William Blathwayt, 19 October 1688, vol. 3, fol. 4, Blathwayt Papers, CW; "Answer of Sir Edmund Andros to his Instructions," n.d., received 1 July 1690, CO 5/855, f 243. Quotations: *DHSM* 6:441, 444, 446. See Mather, *DL*, in Lincoln, *Narratives*, 190–92. For biographical information on Tyng, see Bodge, *Soldiers in King Philip's War*, 169–70.

35. See *DHSM* 5:143–44; *DHSM* 6:346–47, 376, 437; Andros to William Blathwayt, 19 October 1688, vol. 3, fol. 4, Blathwayt Papers, CW (also the source of the quotation).

36. Edward Randolph to Lords of Trade, 8 October 1688, CO 5/905, f 23; Andros to William Blathwayt, 19 October 1688, vol. 3, fol. 4, Blathwayt Papers, CW. Andros's letters to subordinates have not survived, but their shaken responses reveal what his tone must have been (*DHSM* 6:438–39). Several councilors later declared that Andros had threatened to charge them as "high Offenders" for their actions in his absence; see William Stoughton et al., Grievances against Governor Andros, 27 January 1689/90, MA 35:191–92.

37. Andros to William Blathwayt, 19 October 1688, vol. 3, fol. 4, Blathwayt Papers, CW. Two copies of his proclamation of 20 October are in CO 1/65, ff 331, 332. Andros sent special orders to Falmouth to free the remaining captive held there; see *DHSM* 5:144.

38. "Answer of Sir Edmund Andros to his Instructions," n.d., received 1 July 1690, CO 5/855, f 244; John West to Fitz-John Winthrop, 23 February 1688/9, *MHS Colls* 53 (1889): 496–97; William Stoughton et al., Grievances against Governor Andros, 27 January 1689/90, MA 35:191–92. The councilors compiled evidence to support their contention that Andros's raid on Pentagoet had instigated the conflict (*DHSM* 5:38; MA 35:259). See also the statement on Andros's winter campaign prepared by the colony's agents in England, 30 May 1690, HM 1654, HL, printed in *DHSM* 5:120–24.

39. "Declaration of Silvanus Davis," n.d. [after 15 October 1690], *DHSM* 5:144; "Brief Relation" (1689), in "Hutchinson Papers," *MHS Colls* 21 (1825): 100; William Stoughton et al., Grievances against Governor Andros, 27 January 1689/90, MA 35:191. See the materials in next two footnotes for some of the rumors that circulated about the governor.

40. Statement of Joseph Graves et al., 3 January 1688/9, *DHSM* 4:446–47; Statement of Thomas Browne, et al., 22 March 1688/9, ibid., 448; List of Evidence against Sir Edmund Andros, n.d., MA 35:257. See also *DHSM* 6:472; MA 35:256.

41. List of Evidence against Sir Edmund Andros, n.d., MA 35:260 (quotation); *DHSM* 9:31. Another deposition dated in December 1689 accused Andros of having sent food and rum to Castine at Pentagoet during the winter of 1688–1689 (*DHSM* 5:22).

42. On northern Indians and firearms, see Patrick M. Malone, *The Skulking Way of War: Technology and Tactics among the New England Indians* (Baltimore, 1991). Recall that Davis's move to deprive the Kennebecs of their weapons helped to precipitate the First Indian War in the north. See the discussion below for the Indians' comment that Andros had "starved" them during the winter of 1688–1689.

43. Quotation: "A Particular Account of the Late Revolution," in Charles M. Andrews, ed., *Narratives of the Insurrections, 1675–1690* (New York, 1915), 197. Boston residents knew in late December 1688 that an invasion fleet was en route from Holland to England (*MHS Colls* 48 [1882]: 487), but they did not learn the outcome for five more months (Andrews, ed., *Narratives*, 215–16). On what little they knew and when they knew it, see Richard Johnson, *Adjustment to Empire:*

The New England Colonies, 1675–1715 (New Brunswick, N.J., 1981), 84. On the uncertainty in all the colonies, see David Lovejoy, *The Glorious Revolution in America* (New York, 1972), 237–39.

44. Most discussions of the much-studied Glorious Revolution in New England do not devote any attention to this consequence of the New Englanders' actions. But see Parkman, *Count Frontenac and New France,* 234.

45. *DHSM* 6:476–78 (quotation 478). Men in Saco and Cape Porpoise (Kennebunk) did not wait until Andros's overthrow; they deserted a few days earlier, perhaps realizing that his regime would soon end (*DHSM* 6:470–71, 473–75). On the chaotic situation in Maine after 18 April 1689, see, e.g., *DHSM* 5:35–46 passim; *DHSM* 6:479–95 passim; and Edmund Andros, n.d., "An Account of the Forces raised in New England . . . ," in "Hutchinson Papers," *MHS Colls* 21 (1825): 85–87.

46. James Weems to —, 1 June 1689, *DHSM* 6:485; Samuel Wheelwright et al. to "the Superior Power . . . ," 25 April 1689, H. H. Edes Papers, MHS. For divisions in frontier villages over the presence of garrisons: *DHSM* 6:479–83.

47. Lovejoy, *Glorious Revolution in America,* places the Massachusetts events in a broader context; see also Johnson, *Adjustment to Empire.* For protests against the decision to hold elections in spring 1690, see "Mr. Bullivants Journall," *MHS Procs* 16 (1878): 107.

48. Bradstreet to [Portsmouth magistrates], [29 June 1689], *MHS Colls* 21 (1825): 91 (see also 89–90); *DHSM* 9:10–11, 15–16, 17–18, 26; Lt. [James] Weems, "A Short Account of the losse of Pemiquid ffort in New England August the 3d 1689," CO 5/855, ff 75–76 (quotation 76).

49. See, e.g., *DHSM* 9:2–7, 12–13, 24, 26–28; *DHSM* 5:1–2; MA 107:157a.

50. Sylvanus Davis et al. to MG&C, 15 July 1689, *DHSM* 9:14; Charles Frost et al. to same, 27 July 1689, ibid., 20–21; Robert Pike to same, 29 July 1689, ibid., 25. The abandonment of North Yarmouth is described in Davis et al. to Thomas Danforth, 28 August 1689, ibid., 40–42. CO 5/855 is filled with letters recording these disasters; see, e.g., ff 33, 46, 73, 79, 99.

51. Davis to MG&C, 11 September 1689, *DHSM* 9:48–49; Davis to the inhabitants of Maine, 17 September 1689, ibid., 60. Other reports and orders: ibid., 58, 61–62.

52. Davis to MG&C, 22 September 1689, *DHSM* 4:455; Church to same, 22 September 1689, ibid., 456–57. See Church's descriptions of the battle in ibid., 459–63; and Church, *History of Philip's War,* ed. Drake, 160–71.

53. Church, *History of Philip's War,* ed. Drake, 170.

54. Mather, *DL,* in Lincoln, *Narratives,* 203; Church to [MG&C], 7 October 1689, *DHSM* 4:472. The scouting parties and the one skirmish (at a garrison house in Blue Point) are described in *DHSM* 4:463–72 passim. The disbanding and disposition of troops over the winter of 1689–1690 can be followed in *DHSM* 9:64–77 passim; and *DHSM* 5:3–19 passim.

55. CO 5/855, f 136 is a printed copy of the proclamation, issued on 3 December 1689. See Governor John Leverett to Lord Privy Seal, 6 September 1675, CO 1/35,

f 108, and Robert Pike et al. to [MG&C], 19 October 1676, *DHSM* 6:137–39, for similar thinking during King Philip's War.

56. *DHSM* 9:60; "The State of New England under the Goverment of Sir Edmund Andros," n.d., received 27 May 1690, CO 5/855, f 267. Other people made the same allegation about Boston merchants trading with the Indians; see, e.g., "Col. Lidget's Memoriall touching Trade with the Indians &c," n.d., received February 1692/3, CO 5/857, f 143. Edward Randolph's detailed letters to the Lords of Trade and Plantations while he was held in Boston for nearly a year after April 1689 show not only that he was able to communicate regularly with London but also that he had excellent sources of information; see, e.g., CO 5/855, ff 51, 88, 95, 104, and passim. Randolph, among others, named "the Bostoners" he suspected: David Waterhouse and John Foster. See Randolph, "A short narrative . . . ," 29 May 1689, CO 5/855, ff 10–13 (another copy in CO 5/905, ff 69–75); and "Particular Account," in Andrews, ed., *Narratives,* 198 and n.

57. When a group of Maine residents petitioned the king in early 1690, they too declared that ships from Boston had sold "stores of Warr & amunition" to the Indians shortly after the "most unhappy insurrection or Rebellion" (Thomas Scottow et al. to the king, 25 January 1689/90, *DHSM* 5:32–34). A petition from residents of New Hampshire asserted the same, 15 May 1690, CO 5/855, f 253. Of course, some frontiersmen themselves were accused of the same offense; see, e.g., "Declaration against John Paine," 15 July 1687, box 1, f 39, Jeffries Family Papers, MHS.

58. Thomas, ed., *Sewall Diary,* 1:251–52; Bradstreet to Earl of Shrewsbury, 29 January 1689/90, CO 5/855, f 160. Another contemporary account is "Mr. Bullivants Journall," *MHS Procs* 16 (1878): 105.

59. Many documents pertaining to the Schenectady raid and its immediate aftermath, from French as well as English sources, are printed in E. B. O'Callaghan, ed., *The Documentary History of the State of New-York* (Albany, 1849), 1:283–312 (hereafter *DHSNY*). A detailed description of the attack, perhaps prepared for publication, is in the Livingston Family Papers, Gilder Lehrman Collection, Pierpont Morgan Library. By March 7, residents of Salem had learned of the potential threat to New England; see Charles Redford (Salem) to Sir Edmund Andros (London), 7 March 1690, CO 5/855, f 177.

60. William Vaughan and Richard Martyn to MG&C, 19 March 1689/90, *DHSM* 5:57–58 (see also same to same, 18 March, ibid., 51). The phrase describing the composition of the force is from Mather, *DL,* in Lincoln, *Narratives,* 206.

61. This account draws both on the magistrates' report of their examination of the prisoner, 19 March 1689/90, *DHSM* 5:55–56, and on the retrospective entry for 18 March 1689/90 in "Mr. Bullivants Journall," *NEHGR* 16 (1878): 105–106.

62. Bradstreet to "your Lordship," 20 March 1689/90, *DHSM* 5:184 (quotation); Bradstreet to Peter Schuyler et al., 25 March 1690, Livingston Papers. The developing plans for the Port Royal expedition can be traced in *DHSM* 5:26–63

passim. By 14 March, the council had made a firm commitment to support the expedition; news of Salmon Falls arrived in Boston five days later (see Thomas, ed., *Sewall Diary*, 1:254). Because Robert Livingston was one of the emissaries sent from Albany to ask for help from Massachusetts and Connecticut, the Livingston Papers contain a considerable amount of information on his efforts. See also *DHSM* 5:63–70; *DHSNY* 2:175–77.

63. Bradstreet to Peter Schuyler et al., 25 March 1690, Livingston Papers; Sewall to Robert Treat, 24 March 1689/90, *DHSM* 5:64; Winthrop to John Allyn [c. March 1690], *MHS Colls* 53 (1889): 507–508. See also *DHSM* 5:184.

64. Sewall noted the order to the Essex militia on 5 April and the trip to Manhattan from 21 April to 5 May (Thomas, ed., *Sewall Diary*, 1:256–58); council instructions to Hathorne and Corwin, 24 April 1690, *DHSM* 5:86–87. The planning for the Montreal expedition can be traced in *DHSM* 5:75–78, 93–94.

65. "Garrisons, Soldiers, &c, in the Province of Maine," 30 April 1690, *DHSM* 5:91–92; Recommendations to Maine Magistrates by Hathorne and Corwin, 1 May 1690, ibid., 92–93.

66. Some of those who talked to Hathorne and Corwin thought that the two men had been convinced of the need for the soldiers; see *DHSM* 5:99, 102. That the troops left on May 15 can be inferred from Robert Pike to [Governor Bradstreet?], 18 May 1690, *DHSM* 5:100. Sewall also noted in his diary that Willard left "the very day before the Attack" (Thomas, ed., *Sewall Diary*, 1:259). Willard had warned the council of the danger to Falmouth as early as mid-April (ibid., 1:256), but that warning, along with the ominous information about the original target of the Salmon Falls raiders, was ignored. Although the evidence is not entirely clear, it seems that Willard's men wanted to be relieved (see *DHSM* 5:95–96). The council, however, could have replaced them with other troops rather than simply withdrawing them and leaving Falmouth to be defended only by local militiamen.

67. "Declaration of Silvanus Davis," n.d. [after 15 October 1690], *DHSM* 5:145–46. Mather described the battle in detail in *DL,* in Lincoln, *Narratives,* 218–20. See also "Mr. Bullivants Journall," *MHS Procs* 16 (1878): 107–108.

68. Charles Frost et al. to [MG&C?], 22 May 1690, *DHSM* 5:105, with council order, ibid., 105–106 (see also 101–102, 115–17); "News from New England," n.d., ibid., 189; Benjamin Bullivant to [John Usher?], 10 July 1690, BL 242, William Blathwayt Papers, HL (also in part in CO 5/855, f 293). "News from New England" was endorsed by an English clerk "1691," but its contents show it was written shortly after the fall of Falmouth; the original is in CO 5/856, f 378. For the generally accepted figure of 200 people lost, see, e.g., "Extract of a Letter to Mr John Usher from Boston," 27 May 1690, CO 5/855, f 289.

69. Thomas, ed., *Sewall Diary*, 1:259, 251, 260; Bradstreet to Jacob Leisler, 30 May–24 June 1690, *DHSNY* 2:259–61. See *DHSM* 5:125–26, 135–37, on the Bay Colony's deployment of additional men on the frontier during the summer.

70. "Abstract of Letters from Mr. Dudley," 8 July [1690], CO 5/855, f 328; Mather, *DL*, in Lincoln, *Narratives*, 223–24. The fullest account of the battle and its context is *DHSM* 5:131–32.

71. "Abstract of Letters from Mr. Usher," 4 and 7 July 1690, CO 5/855, f 324 (printed in *DHSM* 5:131–32). For complaints, see, e.g., Nathaniel Saltonstall to [MG&C], 10 July 1690, MA 36:156; John Emerson to Wait Winthrop, 26 July 1690, *MHS Colls* 41 (1871): 437–38.

72. The General Court order for the draft, showing that at most 700 men had volunteered for service under Phips, is MA 81:98. Quotations: Thomas, ed., *Sewall Diary*, 1:262; Complaints of John Alden, July 1690, EC Ct Recs/WPA, ser. 2, 50: 5/1, 7/1, PEM. The relevant General Court orders about the guns are MA 81:90, 92; and 36:162a.

73. James Lloyd to [John Usher], 8 January 1690/1, CO 5/856, ff 355–56, summarizes both disasters. See also the extensive criticism of Phips's leadership in "News from New England [from] Severall Gentlemen & Merchants . . . ," ibid., ff 379–80. Many letters to and from Fitz-John Winthrop in box 24, Winthrop Papers, describe the failed Montreal campaign and his subsequent arrest. Some of these have been published in *MHS Colls* 48 (1882) passim (quotation, 309); see esp. Winthrop's journal, 312–18. And see also *DHSNY* 2:288–90.

74. The death of Hope Hood was one of the pieces of news reported in *Publick Occurrences Both Forreign and Domestick* on 25 September 1690; the columns of this first American newspaper, which was immediately suppressed by the government, were dominated by the war. A copy is in CO 5/855, ff 337–38. Church's account of his campaign is in Church, *History of Philip's War*, ed. Drake, 177–97; Mather's is in *DL*, in Lincoln, *Narratives*, 225–27. See also Pike to [MG&C], 27 September 1690, *DHSM* 5:138–40.

75. Quotations: Bradstreet to Massachusetts agents in London, 29 November 1690, *DHSM* 5:171. Alden's treaty is in ibid., 164–66. Ten English captives were exchanged for eight Wabanakis—presumably the sachems' families. On the colonists' difficulties that fall, see *DHSM* 5:156–58, and Mather, *DL*, in Lincoln, *Narratives*, 227.

76. Bradstreet to Massachusetts agents in London, 29 November 1690, *DHSM* 5:167–68, 171. See also the similar reflections of Mather, in *DL*, in Lincoln, *Narratives*, 214.

77. Quotations: William Brattle to [Francis Nicholson], 25 March 1691, vol. 4, fol. 1, Blathwayt Papers, CW; Benjamin Davis to same, 19 April 1691, vol. 4, fol. 4, ibid. The report from Portsmouth is Edward Sergentt to Ensign John Hill, 18 February 1690/91, John Hill Papers, NEHGS. For distrusting colonists, see letters of Bradstreet (to Henry Sloughter, 30 March 1691, *DHSM* 5:185–86; and to Francis Nicholson, 15 April 1691, vol. 15, fol. 1, Blathwayt Papers, CW).

78. The preliminaries to the negotiations are detailed in *DHSM* 5:188–89, 231–32, and a summary of the proceedings is ibid., 233–35. Quotations: [William Brattle], "An Account of the Treaty with the Indians . . . ," CO 5/856, f 525. That

Brattle authored the "Account" is evident in Brattle to Francis Nicholson, 6 May 1691, vol. 4, fol. 1, Blathwayt Papers, CW, the letter enclosing it. The militia leaders were William Vaughan and Charles Frost.

79. Pike to [MG&C], 14 June 1691, *DHSM* 5:246–47 (see also same to same, 19 June 1691, ibid., 254–55). In a rare error, Cotton Mather dated the attack June 9; cf. Mather, *DL,* in Lincoln, *Narratives,* 228.

80. The parley with the Wabanakis was reported in Francis Hooke to [MG&C], 14 June 1691, *DHSM* 5:244–45 (quotation 245).

81. William Vaughan and Richard Martyn to MG&C, 17 June 1691, ibid., 249–50; Francis Hooke to Robert Pike, 19 June 1691, ibid., 256. See also Hooke to [MG&C], 17 June 1691, Thomas Prince Papers, MHS.

82. Account of the Eastern Expedition, 7 August 1691, *DHSM* 5:280–81 (quotations 281); MG&C to —, 9 August 1691, ibid., 284. On the planning for and delays of the expedition, see ibid., 261–72 passim. Another sizable Indian party killed or captured about twenty people at Sandy Beach, N.H., approximately five miles from Portsmouth, in late September (ibid., 296–98).

83. Burroughs et al. to MG&C, 28 September 1691, ibid., 294; William Vaughan to Simon Bradstreet, 17 November 1691, ibid., 303. See also Burroughs et al. to MG&C, 21 July 1691, ibid., 274.

84. MG&C to other New England colonies, 30 October 1691, ibid., 300–301 (replies in ibid., 304–309); Mather, *DL,* in Lincoln, *Narratives,* 230. Rhode Island's governor John Easton sharply criticized Massachusetts and its leadership, expressing sympathy for the Wabanakis and accusing Bay Colony merchants of profiting from arms sales to the French and Indians (*DHSM* 5:305–306). James Graham to William Blathwayt, 30 December 1691, vol. 10, fol. 5, Blathwayt Papers, CW, reported the failure of recruiting in Connecticut.

CHAPTER FOUR   THE DREADFULL APPARITION OF A MINISTER

1. For the dates of Abigail Williams's complaints in mid-April, see *SWP* 1:258; 2:597, 667, 688. For the others: *SWP* 1:241–42 (Corey); 2:415–16 (Hobbs). The April 18 complaint: ibid., 1:239.

2. Bridget Bishop had been convicted of quarreling with her second husband, Thomas Oliver, and was also suspected of theft. Because *SWP* and early scholarship confused Bridget Bishop with another Goody Bishop (Sarah) who *did* live in Salem Village, Paul Boyer and Stephen Nissenbaum's *Salem Possessed: The Social Origins of Witchcraft* (Cambridge, Mass., 1974), and their edited documentary collection, *Salem-Village Witchcraft* (1972; reprint, Boston, 1993), erroneously conflate information about the two women, who were unrelated to each other. Cf. *Salem Possessed,* 192–93, and *Salem-Village Witchcraft,* 155–62, with Bernard Rosenthal, *Salem Story: Reading the Witch Trials of 1692* (New York, 1993), 71–75, which (relying on the meticulous scholarship of David L. Greene) explains and corrects earlier mistakes. Some scholars continue to confuse the two women, however.

3. Hale testified at Hoar's trial on 6 September 1692; quotation, *SWP* 2:399. For another reference to "the Time when there was so much talk of the Witchcraft in this Country," see John Noble, ed., "Some Documentary Fragments Touching the Witchcraft Episode of 1692," *CSM Pubs* 10 (1904–1906): 18. Abigail Hobbs, though a Topsfield resident, does not fall into the same "outsider" category as Bridget Bishop, because Mercy Lewis knew her in Maine.

4. Ann's accusation of Farrar on 8 May caused his arrest on 14 May (*SWP* 2:323, 487–88). For the earlier court case from October 1690: EC Ct Recs/WPA/ser. 2, 49:121/1–124/5 (quotations 122/2). Farrar was also related by marriage to Sarah Hood Bassett and Elizabeth Bassett Proctor, both accused witches. Biographical information from Enders A. Robinson, *The Devil Discovered: Salem Witchcraft, 1692* (New York, 1991), 289.

5. On patterns of accusation of male witches, see John P. Demos, *Entertaining Satan: Witchcraft and the Culture of Early New England* (New York, 1982), 36, 60–62. This and the next two paragraphs are based on *WDNE* 3:169–73. I posit that Corey was examined first because no references to the results of the other examinations appear in the transcript of his interrogation. The three other cases considered on April 19 were intertwined.

6. This paragraph and the next are based on *SWP* 3:793–94, 804.

7. There are two versions of Bishop's examination, one by Parris, the other by Cheever. This account follows Parris's primarily, but relies on Cheever's for three phrases (ibid., 1:83–86).

8. Ibid., 3:794–95.

9. This and the next paragraph are based on ibid., 795–99. In jail, the examiners confronted Mary Warren with Giles Corey, thus setting off one of her fits. Before she saw him, Mary accurately described his clothing, "as severall then in Company Can affirm," remarked an anonymous note-taker (see 796). Thus a test that had not worked with his wife provided seeming proof of his guilt. The April 21 examination of Mary Warren is dated; the other is not, but seems by its contents to have preceded the dated one.

10. Ibid., 2:409–10. That Abigail Hobbs knew Judah White "very well" suggests that the Hobbs and Ingersoll households were located near each other in Falmouth. See further speculations on this point later in this chapter. Joseph was the son of Lt. George Ingersoll and so was Mary Walcott's first cousin once removed. As a resident of another town, Abigail could well not have known many specifics of what had happened in Salem Village until she was jailed in the company of Mary Warren. That on April 20 she knew the name Sarah Osborne and details of the devil's sacrament, whereas on April 19 she evidently did not, certainly implies an intervening exchange of information.

11. Ibid., 2:406, 411. Abigail Hobbs was born in August 1677; because she did not identify a month or season for her encounter with the devil, it is not clear whether she placed the incident before or after her eleventh birthday. See Topsfield vital records, cited n. 13, below, for her birthdate.

12. Joseph Dow, *History of the Town of Hampton, New Hampshire* (Salem, Mass., 1893), 2:747–48, identifies William Hobbs of Topsfield as the oldest son of Morris Hobbs of Hampton, but *GDMNH* does not link him to that family. (William cannot be placed in any other known Hobbs or Hobson family of Maine, New Hampshire, or Essex County, however.) The April 1668 petition from Wells signed by both Hobbs and Cloyce is printed in *DHSM* 4:218–19. On his residence in Lynn in 1660, see George F. Dow, *History of Topsfield, Massachusetts* (Topsfield, Mass., 1940), 49–50.

13. Hobbs's name does not appear on a 1664 tax list, nor evidently anywhere else in town records before November 1668, except for the 1660 land purchase noted in Dow, *History of Topsfield*, 49–50. See George F. Dow, ed., "The Early Records of the Town of Topsfield, Massachusetts," *HCTHS* 2 (1896): 7, 10. Hobbs's assessment for the minister's rates in November 1681 was below the median level in town, though not at the very bottom (ibid., 37). For the births in the Hobbs family, see *Vital Records of Topsfield* (Topsfield, Mass., 1903), 55–56. His name does appear on a 1687 tax list, which indicates only that he had not sold his property; see *NEHGR* 35(1881): 34–35. For Hobbs's assessment for the minister's rates in November 1689, see EC Ct Recs/WPA, ser. 2, 50:80/2.

14. For evidence of rented property in Falmouth in the 1680s, perhaps even a house occupied by William Hobbs (although the tenant is unnamed), see *DHSM* 6:313. The landlord was Thomas Cloyce, Mercy Lewis's uncle by marriage and brother of Peter Cloyce.

15. See *GDMNH*, q.v. "Philbrick," for the possible relationship of Abigail Hobbs and Mercy Lewis.

16. *SWP* 1:165.

17. Ibid., 164. This account is from her deposition offered in early August, first at grand-jury proceedings and then at the trial of George Burroughs. Thomas Putnam and two other men at that time attested that they had been present on 20 April during her spectral encounter. If Thomas Putnam did not dispatch this exact document to the magistrates on April 21, he sent one very like it.

18. Mather, *WIW*, in *WDNE* 1:152; Increase Mather, *Cases of Conscience Concerning Evil Spirits Personating Men, Witchcrafts, . . .* (Boston, 1693), unpaginated afterword. Only Bernard Rosenthal and John McWilliams have also argued for Burroughs's centrality. Rosenthal interprets Burroughs's significance primarily in terms of the minister's probable religious heterodoxy; see *Salem Story*, chapter 7. McWilliams, while linking Burroughs's importance to the war, does not appear aware of the minister's extended residence in Falmouth. See McWilliams, "Indian John and the Northern Tawnies," *NEQ* 69 (1996): 592–97.

19. John McWilliams too identified a chronological turning point related to the frontier during the 1692 crisis, but he chose a different one: the Wabanaki attack on Wells in June, discussed in chapter 6, below. His argument, however, has two flaws: he misdates that attack, erroneously employing an N.S. date of June 20 rather than the accurate O.S. date, June 11/12; and regardless of which calendar is

used, no explosion of accusations followed that battle. By contrast, in April the effects were immediate, as observed in the text. See McWilliams, "Indian John," 584–85.

20. Mather, *DL*, in Lincoln, *Narratives*, 242.

21. *SWP* 1:171–72.

22. Basic biographical information about Burroughs in this and subsequent paragraphs is from *GDMNH; Sibley's Harvard Graduates* 2:323–34; and Robinson, *Devil Discovered*, 78–81, 90–91, 325–26. Thanks to David Greene for alerting me to Neil D. Thompson's identification of Burroughs's first wife, as reported in the January 2001 issue of *The American Genealogist*. Other men who attended Harvard with Burroughs, and who later had relatives involved in the Salem crisis, were Samuel Mather (1671), cousin of Cotton Mather; Peter Thacher (1671), step-brother-in-law of Jonathan Corwin; and Nathaniel Higginson (1670), son of the Reverend John Higginson of Salem Town. Cotton and Increase Mather, Corwin, and Higginson thus all could have had personal knowledge of Burroughs's Harvard years.

23. *DHSM* 6:97–99 (gunpowder); *DHSM* 4:351–54 (petition signed by Lewis, Cloyce, and eighteen other men; quotation 352); Leverett to Sir Joseph Williamson, 18 December 1675, CO 1/35, f 265; Samuel Symonds to same, 6 April 1676, CO 1/36, f 75.

24. Remonstrance of General Court, 13 September 1677, MA 10:63, MSA, as quoted in James E. Kences, "Some Unexplored Relationships of Essex County Witchcraft to the Indian Wars of 1675 and 1689," *EIHC* 120 (July 1984): 202. The fullest account of the Pike-Wheelwright dispute may be found in Roland Warren, *Loyal Dissenter: The Life and Times of Robert Pike* (Lanham, Md., 1992), 114–25. I here adopt an interpretation developed in Molly A. Warsh, "Memories of the Eastward: Reexamining the Salem Witchcraft Crisis of 1692 in the Context of King William's War" (unpub. honors thesis, History, Cornell University, 1999), 44. Ironically, in 1698 Robert Pike's granddaughter Elizabeth Stockman married John Wheelwright's grandson Jacob Bradbury; I am descended from that marriage.

25. Quotation: *SWP* 1:176. For Burroughs's negotiations with Salem Village, see Boyer and Nissenbaum, eds., *Salem-Village Witchcraft*, 173–74, 319. Bayley had lived on property given him by Village supporters; see ibid., 240, 254.

26. Quotations: *SWP* 1:162, 163; examination: ibid., 153. For the funeral debt, see Boyer and Nissenbaum, eds., *Salem-Village Witchcraft*, 177–78. Alexander Osborne (husband of Sarah) went to Salem Town to purchase the wine for Burroughs.

27. Boyer and Nissenbaum, eds., *Salem-Village Witchcraft*, 170–79, reprints documents covering both controversies; quotation, 171.

28. *DHSM* 4:389–93, 400–22 (reestablishment of government in Maine); *York Deeds* 12, pt. 1:170 (quotation and compensation to other landowners); William Willis, *The History of Portland, from 1632 to 1864* (Portland, Me., 1865), 200 (state-

ment from town records about taking Burroughs's land). One of those granted a house lot in Falmouth (although he never seems to have occupied it) was the Massachusetts magistrate Bartholomew Gedney. See the house lot list in ibid., 226–28; the original (or an early copy) is in Collection S-1357, misc. box 65/14, MeHS.

29. Willis, *History of Portland*, 245 (Burroughs's statement, from town records); *York Deeds* 4:77 (exchange with Skilling); ibid., 17:311, 316 (sale of the 100-plus acres of marsh). Philip Lewis's lot adjoined Lt. George Ingersoll's property: "Book of Eastern Claims," *MHGR* 5(1888): 156–57. George Sr.'s land lay near that of his sons, George and Joseph, and Joseph's son later attested that his father lived for "many years" on two acres of land in the town center of Falmouth "about a Quarter of a mile from the fort," until he was "driven therefrom by the Indin Enemy": *MHGR* 6 (1889): 279. Willis, *History of Portland*, 230–33, sites the original claims on Portland's street grid in 1865; most Portland street names have not changed since the mid nineteenth century.

30. Quotations: *DHSM* 6:362, 382; see also 218–19, 294, 302–303, 377–79, 481–83, and Willis, *History of Portland*, 258–64 passim, on the Lawrence-Davis dispute. And see p. 163 for more on Burroughs's reputed hostility to Lawrence and his family.

31. *Sibley's Harvard Graduates* 2:326 (1686 description); Scarborough Town Records, vol. 1:34–36, 38–39 (quotation 39), Collection 1229, MeHS; *DHSM* 6:346 (Burroughs petition about his Scarborough land, c. 1688); *York Deeds* 17:311 (sale of remaining land); *DHSM* 4:457 (Church on Burroughs). Another statement placing Burroughs in Falmouth in September 1689 is in *SWP* 1:161. Although Scarborough made plans to build a house for its minister, there is no record of one being constructed, so perhaps Burroughs failed to relocate for that reason.

32. *SWP* 1:165; ibid., 168, for Mercy's comment about living with Burroughs's family; and "Book of Eastern Claims," *MHGR* 5(1888): 156–57, for proof that her father was alive in April 1689. Why Burroughs would have killed Lawson's wife because "she was so unwilling to goe from the village" is, however, unclear. Some historians have speculated that Mercy lived with the minister when she was a little girl after the August 1676 destruction of Falmouth, and that he took her to Salem Village with him in 1680, leaving her there in 1683. Because her parents survived King Philip's War to return to Falmouth, though, they are highly unlikely to have left a useful older daughter behind in Essex County. Since in the passage cited above Mercy mentioned having been in Burroughs's "study," she also had to have lived with him somewhere other than in John Putnam Sr.'s house, where surely there would not have been sufficient space for such a room. Moreover, if Mercy had lived in Salem Village during the 1680s, it is unlikely that she would have been a servant in Beverly in early 1690 (see *SWP* 2:537).

33. *SWP* 1:166. On what is known of Mary Burroughs, see David L. Greene, "The Third Wife of the Rev. George Burroughs," *The American Genealogist* 56 (1980): 43–45.

34. Burroughs et al. to Massachusetts Governor and Council, 21 July 1691,

28 September 1691, 27 January 1691/2, *DHSM* 5:274, 294, 316–17. Among the other signatories were sons of the Rev. John Wheelwright, and men of the Littlefield and Cloyce families (Peter Cloyce's first wife, before he married Sarah Towne Bridges, was Hannah Littlefield).

35. Quotation: Memorial of Thomas Newman et al., 31 May 1749, as printed in George H. Moore, "Notes on the Bibliography of Witchcraft in Massachusetts," *AAS Procs*, new ser., 5 (1887–88): 270.

36. *SWP* 2:483, 1:172.

37. Ibid., 1:172. That in this statement Abigail and Mary distinguished between a "black" woman and "an Indian" does not conflict with my argument in chapter 2 that the word "black" was employed to designate both "Negro" and "Indian" skin colors in the seventeenth century. Precisely because the word "black" encompassed an Indian's skin tone, the girls had to describe both the "black [Negro] woman" and the "Indian" explicitly to explain the exact nature of their vision to Hutchinson and Putnam.

38. Ibid., 3:805–806.

39. Ibid. For the naming of Sarah Wilds by Deliverance Hobbs on Sunday, April 17, see ibid., 2:407. As was noted in chapter 2, Ann Putnam Jr. claimed in late June to have been afflicted by Goody Wilds's specter as early as the beginning of March, but that dating cannot be verified. Nor is Mary Walcott's claim of affliction by her in early April supported by independent evidence (see ibid., 3:810–11). Still, the existence of these two statements suggests that Sarah Wilds's name might have surfaced in Village gossip prior to mid-April.

40. Quotations: ibid., 1:49–50 (case of Nehemiah Abbott Jr.). The missing examinations are those of Mary English of Salem Town and Sarah and Edward Bishop of Salem Village. That the examinations occurred in the meetinghouse is evident from ibid., 2:420.

41. Ibid., 2:419–20, for the quotations in this and the following paragraph. Note, though, that by her own account (offered during the examination) Deliverance had come to church in Salem Village the previous Sunday, and she had probably attended her stepdaughter's public examination three days before. On either occasion she might have attracted attention to herself, thus making identification by the girls easy and the experiment either moot or obviously rigged. But if that were the case, the magistrates would have understood their test to be meaningless, and therefore it is unlikely they would have tried it.

42. On the locations of the Hobbs landholdings and that claimed by Putnam: Dow, ed., "Early Records of Topsfield," *HCTHS* 2 (1896): 10. If my hypothesis that Deliverance was born in Maine (most likely Falmouth) is correct, then Deliverance and Mercy could have known each other quite well.

43. This and the next two paragraphs draw from *SWP* 2:419–22. In contrast to his wife and daughter, when questioned on 22 April, William Hobbs insisted on his innocence (ibid., 2:425–28).

44. Ibid., 2:421, 1:164, 3:798 for these phrases. In late May, Ann Carr Putnam

employed the phrase to describe what Martha Corey had done to her on 18 March (ibid., 2:603), but March records do not confirm that she used it at that time. Ann Jr. thus seems to have introduced it into the Salem lexicon.

45. For two earlier examples of the unusual threat of tearing to pieces, see John Darrell, *A True Narration of the Strange and Grevous Vexation by the Devil, of 7 Persons in Lancashire, and William Somers of Nottingham* (n.p., 1600), 22 [incorrectly numbered 32]; and esp. Cotton Mather's narrative of the Tocutt boy, in *Memorable Providences* (1690), in Burr, *Narratives,* 138–40. The Tocutt boy, who employed the phrase four times in his narrative, was however also told "he should live deliciously, and have Ease, Comfort, and Money" (138). The quoted words of temptation in the text come from Samuel Willard's account of the agonies of Elizabeth Knapp in 1671, in David D. Hall, ed., *Witch-Hunting in Seventeenth-Century New England,* 2d ed. (Boston, 1999), 203, 207.

46. Mather, *DL,* in Lincoln, *Narratives,* 208. See also ibid., 209–10, 212–13, for other accounts of the "tearing to pieces" of Salmon Falls captives. By 19 May 1690—two months after the Salmon Falls raid—gossip originating with an escapee had already carried the story of Rogers's death to Portsmouth, N.H. See "The Report of Captain John Holmes . . . ," CO 5/855, f 331.

47. *SWP* 3:806, 810. The original court document, SWP/SJC/PEM 1:164, contains the examination records of Sarah Wilds and William Hobbs. It is badly torn; words in brackets are conjectural. Biographical information: Robinson, *Devil Discovered,* 294–95. John Wilds was deeply involved in the Topsfield/Salem Village land dispute. Mary Gould Reddington, John Herrick's mother-in-law, was also Sgt. Thomas Putnam's first cousin once removed. My discussion of Sarah Wilds, here and later in this book, rests in part on the analysis in Jesse Souweine, "Word of Mouth: How Gossip Informed the Salem Witchcraft Accusations" (unpub. honors thesis, American Studies, Cornell University, 1996), chapter 2. For the equally perfunctory 22 April examination of the slave Mary Black, see *SWP* 1:113–14.

48. *SWP* 1:49–50. How Ann Jr. could identify him is not clear. Biographical information about Abbott from Robinson, *Devil Discovered,* 300. He points out that Abbott was related by blood and marriage to the Reverend Francis Dane of Andover, several of whose close relatives were later accused of witchcraft. Peter Hoffer too concluded that Lewis was the leader of the accuser group; see *The Devil's Disciples: Makers of the Salem Witchcraft Trials* (Baltimore, Md., 1996), 98–99.

49. *SWP* 1:288–89. Mary, born in England about 1634, married Isaac Easty of Topsfield in 1655; they had seven children. The family was among those involved in the land dispute with the Putnams. See Robinson, *Devil Discovered,* 273.

50. Biographical information from Carol F. Karlsen, *The Devil in the Shape of a Woman: Witchcraft in Colonial New England* (New York, 1987), 106–107. The defamation of her mother in 1679 is recorded in *EC Ct Recs* 7:238. Oral history descending in the family, reported a century later by a Salem clergyman, described

the circumstances of her arrest but not what occasioned it. See *The Diary of William Bentley, D.D., Pastor of the East Church, Salem, Massachusetts* (Gloucester, Mass., 1962), 2:24. This vivid narrative, relied on heavily by Bryan F. Le Beau in his "Philip English and the Witchcraft Hysteria," *Historical Journal of Massachusetts* 15 (1987): 1–20, is unreliable on many details. For example, it claims that while Mary English was being detained in the Salem Town tavern (rather than the jail) her husband visited her frequently, and also that she "kept a journal of the examinations held below, which she constantly sent to Boston." Because of her high status she might have been held initially at Thomas Beadle's tavern, but that would have contravened the magistrates' explicit order that she be jailed (*SWP* 2:429). And since her husband fled shortly after she was arrested, he could not have visited her anywhere more than once or twice. Some of the examinations between 22 April and 12 May, when she was sent to prison in Boston (ibid., 2:474), were indeed conducted at Beadle's tavern, but to whom she would have addressed accounts of them and to what purpose are both unclear.

51. Quotations: *SWP* 1:97; Calef, *MWIW,* in *WDNE* 3:17–18. Recall that *SWP* erroneously intermingles documents in the cases of Sarah and Bridget Bishop. The report of the inquest on Christian Trask, 24 June 1690, EC Ct Recs/WPA, ser. 2, 50: 19/1, gives her death date as 3 June 1690. This Edward Bishop was not related to Bridget Bishop's third husband (who had the same name), though some have mistakenly identified him as Bridget's stepson. For biographical information: Robinson, *Devil Discovered,* 297–98.

52. This paragraph and the next draw on *SWP* 2:423. Her second confession, titled "The first Examination of Deliverance Hobbs in prison," is undated on that page, but the date is given in the summary prepared for the case against Sarah Good, ibid., 363, the source of the second quotation. (My identification of Stephen Sewall as the author of that quotation is based on the handwriting of the original summary document, SWP/SJC/PEM 1:13.) Abigail's second confession, too, revealed what she had learned from other prisoners. Inga Clendinnen identified a similar effect among confessed Mayan heretics held together in a Yucatán jail in 1562 in *Ambivalent Conquests: Maya and Spaniard in Yucatán, 1517–1570* (New York, 1987), chapters 6, 7, esp. 94–95.

53. On 11 April, Williams said the deacons at the 31 March sacrament were Cloyce and Good (*SWP* 2:658–59). The four earlier confessors were, of course, Tituba, Dorcas Good, Mary Warren, and Deliverance's stepdaughter, Abigail. In prison on 3 May, Deliverance reconfirmed the contents of the 22 April confession. She also described a recent "feast" attended by the specters of Wilds, Bishop, Good, and Osborne (ibid., 1:91–92). Deliverance's failure to name Sarah Cloyce might have been what saved the latter's life; she was the only one of the three Towne sisters who was not hanged.

54. This paragraph and the next are based on ibid., 1:320–21, 105–106. Sarah Buckley's daughter was Mary Witheridge. Susannah's charge that Bridget Bishop killed "john trasks wife" (Christian) confused her with Sarah Bishop, just as later

historians and the compilers of *SWP* did. Sheldon's statement, which she penned herself, is undated but covers 24–30 April 1692; she seems to have composed it shortly thereafter. It was separated into two parts at some point; that which is printed on 105–106 has no date, but picks up where the other leaves off. The docket on the original of that document (words not published in *SWP*), SWP/SJC/PEM 1:153, reveals the relationship of the two statements. That she was "pinshed" in the Town (rather than the Village) meetinghouse is evident from her account of the site of her postmeeting encounter with the specters, which lay between the Town and her family's house.

55. Ellner Barge, deposition, 17 July 1676, Suffolk Court File #1526, JA, MSA; Ralfe Allanson and Joseph Oliver, deposition, 18 July 1676, ibid. Scottow's reluctance to aid the Algers might also have stemmed from their prior acrimonious relationship, or so observers might have concluded. See documents in BPL detailing a 1671 dispute and subsequent lawsuit: ch. A 242 and ch. K 1.40 v. 2, 298; and in William S. Southgate Papers, box 114, collection 74, MeHS. Henry Brookens recalled the exchange with the refugees differently, declaring that the men had refused to go to Dunstan, citing fears for their families' safety if they left Black Point essentially undefended. (Brookens, deposition, 2 August 1676, Suffolk Court File #1526, JA, MSA)

56. Quotation: Henry Brookens, deposition, 2 August 1676, Suffolk Court File #1526, JA, MSA. William Hubbard, *A Narrative of the Troubles with the Indians in New-England . . .* [part 2] *From Pascataqua to Pemmaquid* (Boston, 1677), 25–26, gives an account of these events that avoids all mention of the contretemps about Joshua Scottow, an ally of the Bay Colony's government. On the Sheldon, Scadlock, and Alger families and their relationships, see the entries in *GDMNH*. Susannah is designated as "c. 18" in the Salem records, so she was born about 1674 in Black Point. Although *GDMNH* and other genealogies do not so list Susannah, she clearly was the daughter of William and Rebecca Scadlock Sheldon. The name "Susannah" did not appear elsewhere in the Sheldon family, but it was common among the Scadlocks; Rebecca Scadlock Sheldon had both a sister and a niece named Susannah. Subsequent Sheldon genealogists apparently concealed Susannah's relationship to the family, an enterprise facilitated by the fact she seems to have died unmarried and without children. Such genealogical suppression is not unique among notorious participants in the Salem trials; for example, John Willard, condemned and hanged as a witch in September, cannot be definitively linked to the large Willard family of Groton (Nashaway), Massachusetts, although he undoubtedly belonged to it.

57. Thomas Cousens, deposition, 16 January 1679/80, Suffolk Court File #1828, JA, MSA; John Libby, et al., statement, 15 July 1676, *DHSM* 6:115; Henry Williams, court testimony, 28 January 1679/80, Suffolk Court File #1828, JA, MSA. Still other versions of the contested tale are given in Andrew Alger Jr., court testimony, 28 January 1679/80, ibid; an anonymous deposition sworn before Brian Pendleton, 17[?] July 1676, Collection 77, box 2/27, MeHS; and Michael

Edgecombe, deposition, 20 July 1676, as printed in part in *NEHGR* 43 (1889): 71–72.

58. For examples of reports of such statements by the Black Point men, see the depositions of John Purrington, 16 January 1679/80, and Thomas Cousens, 16 January 1679/80, both in Suffolk Court File #1828, JA, MSA.

59. See *GDMNH,* q.v. "Alger, Arthur," for his place and date of death. Anne Scadlock Alger survived to remarry; she must have fled from Dunstan with the other women and children at the first sign of trouble on October 10 or 11. As the messenger who in late October 1675 carried to Scottow a request for assistance from Saco's magistrate Brian Pendleton and his son-in-law Seth Fletcher, and then had to return with Scottow's rejection, Sheldon also personally experienced another example of the captain's reluctance to assist settlers in danger. See Brian Pendleton and Seth Fletcher to Joshua Scottow (endorsed as carried by Sheldon), 29 October 1675, Miscellaneous Manuscripts Bound, MHS. Sheldon signed the anti-Scottow petition to the General Court, n.d. [c. 15 July 1676], printed in *NEHGR* 43 (1889): 71. But Sheldon too had failed to help some in need; for example, he told Henry Brookens, whom Richard Waldron sent to his household in 1675, that he "was not willing to entertaine us at his garison saying that my Children would eat his victualls out of the pot." (Henry Brookens, deposition, 2 August 1676, Suffolk Court File #1526, JA, MSA.)

60. The records of later Suffolk County cases have supplied much of the evidence for this discussion; see #1526 (1676) and #1828 (1679/80) in Suffolk Court Files, JA, MSA; the Maine records do not survive. (Thanks to Elizabeth Bouvier for locating the documents for me.) Quotations: Waldron to Scottow, 29 January 1677/8, and statement by Waldron, 15 September 1679, both in Suffolk Court File #1828. The outcome of the 1676 case is printed in *NEHGR* 43 (1889): 72; an additional compensatory land grant to Scottow after the war is recorded in *York Deeds* 6 (1889): 9–10.

61. The Sheldons returned to Black Point by late 1681; see the tax list compiled on 28 November 1681, Scarborough, Maine, Records 1:3, Coll. 1229, MeHS, which shows William as the owner of 100 acres of land, 12 acres of marsh, and some livestock. On their presence in Black Point before and after the First Indian War, see also depositions in *York Deeds* 14 (1906): 30, 39–40.

62. The Sheldons were residing in Salem Village by 30 November 1688, when their ten-year-old son Nathaniel died there. Godfrey is believed to have been one of the "stout young men" of the Village who marched north under the direction of John Walcott and Bartholomew Gedney in late May 1690 (*DHSM* 5:109). For his death and those of his brother and father, see "Rev. Samuel Parris's Record of Deaths at Salem Village during his Ministry," *NEHGR* 36 (1882): 188. The compiled "census" of the Village in *Salem-Village Witchcraft,* 391, erroneously designates Rebecca and Ephraim as husband and wife rather than mother and adult son, placing Susannah in another (phantom) household headed by "Widow Shel-

don." *GDMNH* reveals that William's age at his death was sixty-eight rather than the eighty recorded by Parris.

63. Philip English's business papers, in box 1, English-Touzel-Hathorne Papers, PEM, show, e.g., that he was part-owner of a ketch based in Kittery and that he frequently sent cargoes of fish to St. Kitts (see esp. folders 2, 3). English has attracted a great deal of attention from scholars. See, e.g., the article by Bryan Le Beau, cited n. 50, above; George F. Chever, "A Sketch of Philip English—A Merchant in Salem from about 1670 to about 1733–4," *EIHC* 1 (1859): 157–81; Henry W. Belknap, "Philip English, Commerce Builder," *AAS Procs*, new ser., 41 (1931): 17–24; David T. Konig, "A New Look at the Essex 'French': Ethnic Frictions and Community Tensions in Seventeenth-Century Essex County, Massachusetts," *EIHC* 110 (1974): 167–80; and Phyllis Whitman Hunter, *Purchasing Identity in the Atlantic World* (Ithaca, N.Y., 2001), chapter 2 (which focuses on English in the context of Salem). Bernard Bailyn places English in a still broader context in *The New England Merchants in the Seventeenth Century* (Cambridge, Mass., 1955), chapter 7, esp. 144–45.

64. James the Negro, deposition, 31 May 1690, EC Ct Recs/WPA, ser. 2, PEM, 49:58/2; Elizabeth Moody, deposition, 1 June 1690, ibid., 49:56/1; Robin Negro, deposition, 30 May 1690, ibid., 49:57/2. See also the report of the examination of Mousher, 31 May 1690, ibid., 49:58/1. (His name was spelled variously Major, Mousher, Mojer, and Mager alias Mayor.) See also Konig, "A New Look at the Essex 'French,' " *EIHC* 110 (1974): 178–80.

65. Order of General Court, 22 December 1691, broadside, CO 5/858, f 257. English was elected a Town selectman in early March 1691/2; that too would have called attention to him by placing him in a position to undermine the war effort.

66. The records of the cases are in EC Ct Recs/WPA, ser. 2; see *English v. Reed*, 49:137/1–139/3 (Beale's testimony is 139/3); and *English v. Cromwell*, 49:69/2–78/3 (English's inheritance claim is 69/2). Ibid., 49:52/1 is the inventory of Eleanor Hollingsworth's estate, designating English as administrator. See the Cromwell case (which English appealed) in Ipswich Court Records, 30 September 1690, Misc. Manuscripts Bound, MHS. Karlsen has argued that the same sort of aggressive litigiousness over inheritance helped to lead to witchcraft accusations of women (Karlsen, *Devil in the Shape of a Woman*, chapter 3 passim). On the norms of conduct, see Mary Beth Norton, *Founding Mothers & Fathers: Gendered Power and the Forming of American Society* (New York, 1996), chapter 4 passim.

67. *SWP* 1:317–19. "Admired" here meant "were surprised by."

68. Ibid., 1:151; Calef, *MWIW*, in *WDNE* 3:127. For initial accusations in late April, see *SWP* 2:397 (Hoar), 2:575–76 (Martin). The group was collectively accused of harming Ann Putnam Jr., Mary Walcott, Mercy Lewis, Abigail Williams, Betty Hubbard, and Susannah Sheldon. Calef's source for his statement seems to have been *A Further Account of the Tryals of the New-England Witches* . . . (London, 1693), 10. On English's flight and destination: Noble, ed.,

"Some Documentary Fragments," *CSM Pubs* 10 (1904–1906): 18–19. For Sarah Morrell: Robinson, *Devil Discovered*, 355.

69. *SWP* 2:558–59. Other evidence against Martin will be discussed in the context of her trial in June; see chapter 6, below. For more on Martin: Karlsen, *Devil in the Shape of a Woman*, 89–95.

70. This paragraph and the next two draw on *SWP* 2:550–52. Another nearly identical version of her examination is printed ibid., 553–55. The original documents are both in the hand of Samuel Parris (SWP/SJC/PEM 1:174, 175).

71. *SWP* 2:389, 400, 394.

72. Ibid., 390–91, for this paragraph and the next. At the end of the day on May 2, Martin, Hoar, Morrell, and Dustin were all sent to jail in Boston (ibid., 2:550). Sheldon's altered identification seems to have postponed a formal complaint against Goody Buckley for another two weeks; see below. No one appears to have remarked on the fact that Sheldon's testimony indicated that a specter could *lie* about its identity; the truthfulness of apparitions' reported statements was commonly taken for granted.

73. Hall, ed., *Witch-Hunting*, 342–43, 349 (Clawson); 322–25 (Disborough). For Disborough's background, see Karlsen, *Devil in the Shape of a Woman*, 139–40.

74. *SWP* 1:152. The need to consult people in Boston probably accounted for the ten-day interval between Ann Jr.'s initial accusation and the issuance of the warrant for Burroughs's arrest. Because that warrant was dispatched (evidently from Boston) on the very day the formal complaint was filed against Burroughs in Salem Village, the process seems to have been carefully coordinated.

75. Ibid., 1:152, 174, 170. That he was held at Beadle's: ibid., 1:176. Mary would have been eight years old when Burroughs left Salem Village in 1683.

76. Ibid., 1:166. Note that again a specter had lied; Burroughs's apparition told Ann Jr. not to believe the specters of his dead wives, but since they told opposite stories, either they or he was not telling the truth. No one (even later critics of the trials) seemed to notice.

77. Ibid., 1:176–77. As was indicated in chapter 3, Daniel King was one of the leaders of the August 1691 expedition against the Wabanakis, and he presumably knew Burroughs in Maine.

78. Ibid., 1:168–69. The deceased Rebecca Putnam Fuller Sheppard (Mrs. John) had been Sgt. Thomas Putnam's cousin; the subject of this exchange seems to have been a currently afflicted daughter of hers not otherwise mentioned in the records.

79. Ibid., 1:171, 174. The Walcott quotation has been corrected by consulting the original, in Salem, Mass., Witchcraft Papers, MHS.

80. *SWP* 1:167, 171, 169. Birth records (see *GDMNH*) list only one death of a Burroughs child in infancy, but *GDMNH* also notes the surprising absence of a son named for George's father, Nathaniel. That Susannah Sheldon referred to two deaths of children without contradiction discloses her knowledge of his life in Maine (the birth in question would have been to Sarah Ruck Hathorne Bur-

roughs in Falmouth). Mercy's account of being taken by Burroughs's apparition to a high mountain and offered "all the kingdoms of the earth" echoed Christ's temptation by the devil (Matthew 4:8–9) and again demonstrated her familiarity with the Bible. Perhaps George Burroughs himself had instructed her in Falmouth.

81. M. Halsey Thomas, ed., *The Diary of Samuel Sewall, 1674–1729* (New York, 1973), 1:85; and see chapter 3, above, on Stoughton at Casco. That the examination occurred in the Village rather than the Town is evident from Sarah Vibber's testimony (*SWP* 1:167) and from the fact that another examination was held in the Village that day (ibid., 277), but whether it took place in the meetinghouse or in Ingersoll's tavern is not recorded.

82. This and the next two paragraphs are based on *SWP* 1:153–54. The original document is in the MHS. Some scholars believe it is in Cotton Mather's handwriting; in that case, he might have prepared it while writing his account of George Burroughs in *Wonders of the Invisible World*. Rosenthal hypothesizes in *Salem Story*, 130–35, that Burroughs could have been a Baptist, and that a lack of religious orthodoxy could have contributed to his condemnation. The evidence against Burroughs will be discussed in greater detail in chapter 7, below.

83. Increase Mather, *Remarkable Providences Illustrative of the Earlier Days of American Colonisation*, intro. by George Offor (London, 1856), 155–75, passim (quotation, 156); see also 162.

84. Miscellaneous Manuscripts, MHS.

CHAPTER FIVE   MANY OFFENDERS IN CUSTODY

1. *SWP* 2:375–76, 596–97. Sheppard (a cousin of Sgt. Thomas Putnam) and Holton both died in September 1689; see "Rev. Samuel Parris's Record of Deaths at Salem Village during his Ministry," *NEHGR* 36 (1882): 188. (On this source, see chapter 2, n. 73.) Mary Walcott also named John Harwood as a victim of Goody Nurse, but his death is not recorded in *SVR*. And on 10 May Betty Hubbard saw the ghosts of two dead children who accused Sarah Bishop of killing them (*SWP* 1:111).

2. On May 8, e.g., Thomas Putnam and his cousin John Putnam Jr. complained against three women from Woburn (Ann Sears, the recently widowed Bethia Carter, and her daughter of the same name) for afflicting Putnam Jr., Lewis, and Walcott. That same day they registered a similar complaint against Sarah Dustin of Reading, adding the name of Abigail Williams to the list of victims. All four suspects were summoned to Salem Village for questioning on May 9, but the records of that day's examinations (other than the summary for Burroughs) have not survived. Little is known about any of these accused women, but Sarah Dustin was the unmarried adult daughter of Lydia Dustin. Bethia Carter Jr. successfully fled from the authorities and never seems to have been arrested. For biographical information on Sears and the Carters: Enders A.

Robinson, *The Devil Discovered: Salem Witchcraft 1692* (New York, 1991), 346–47. The sparse documentation on these cases is in *SWP* 1:205–206, 277; 3:729–30.

3. So the legal historian Peter Hoffer, in *The Devil's Disciples: Makers of the Salem Witchcraft Trials* (Baltimore, Md., 1996), does not mention John Floyd or Margaret Thacher and refers only briefly to John Alden, all considered later in this chapter. The feminist historian Frances Hill, in *A Delusion of Satan: The Full Story of the Salem Witch Trials* (New York, 1995), names all three, but only in passing (Floyd appears in a list of names in a footnote). Bryan Le Beau's *The Story of the Salem Witch Trials* (Upper Saddle River, N.J., 1998) devotes two pages to summarizing Alden's account of his examination (discussed below), but entirely omits Thacher and Floyd.

4. For classic examples of the argument that late, overreaching accusations ended the crisis, see Hill, *Delusion of Satan,* 195–96, and Richard Weisman, *Witchcraft, Magic, and Religion in 17th-Century Massachusetts* (Amherst, Mass., 1984), 146–47. See Rosenthal, *Salem Story: Reading the Witch Trials of 1692* (New York, 1993), 178–79, for the rejection of such an interpretation. Only Carol F. Karlsen, in *The Devil in the Shape of a Woman: Witchcraft in Colonial New England* (New York, 1987), 245–46, understands the potential significance of the Maine ties of Floyd and Alden. Although she mentions Thacher, she does not place her in the same category.

5. *SWP* 3:850–51; "Parris's Record of Deaths," *NEHGR* 36 (1882): 188. The tangled relationships of John Willard and the Wilkins clan, of great importance in his accusation and trial, are sorted out in David L. Greene, "Bray Wilkins of Salem Village, MA, and His Children," *The American Genealogist* 60 (1984): 1–18, 101–13 (see esp. 11, 15).

6. *SWP* 3:847. Peter Hoffer speculates, undoubtedly correctly, that Bray Wilkins was suffering from a stone in his urinary tract or possibly an inflamed prostate (Hoffer, *Devil's Disciples,* 70–71).

7. *SWP* 3:848, 846, 821, 837–38. Of the four victims named by Sheldon on May 9, only one—Judith Cooke, widow of Henry—has a recorded death date (September 1689); see *SVR* 5:176. The others were the first wife of William Shaw (Elizabeth) and Goodman (Hugh) Jones and his child.

8. *SWP* 3:819, 2:473.

9. Ibid., 2:483, 1:211; see also 2:475. Sarah's surname is more commonly rendered as "Churchill," but appears as Churchwell in the Maine records, so I have selected that spelling. Mercy's recurrent statement that Jacobs beat her spectrally with his sticks could well imply that he did the same to his own maidservant in reality. The servants Mercy and Sarah would surely have discussed how their respective masters treated them when they encountered each other in the Village.

10. Ibid., 2:484–85.

11. Quotations: Richard Waldron to MG&C, 25 September 1675, in *DHSM* 6:94. The only recorded birth to Eleanor Bonython, later the wife of Arthur

Churchwell, was a bastard child in September 1667; and her only known child is Sarah. No age is ever given for Sarah Churchwell in the Salem records. Accordingly, I am assuming that Sarah was born in 1667 (and thus was twenty-five at the time of the trials). See *GDMNH*, q.v. "Bonython," "Churchwell"; and Charles E. Banks, "The Bonython Family of Maine," *NEHGR* 38 (1884): 54–55. For the locations of these houses and mills on the Saco: G. T. Ridlon, *Saco Valley Settlements . . .* (Portland, Me., 1895), 21.

12. Waldron to [MG&C?], 25 September 1675, in *DHSM* 6:94–95. For the death of John Bonython: *NEHGR* 34 (1880): 99. He was later said to have been "Killed by the Indian Enemy"; possibly he died a lingering death from wounds suffered in the Saco attack or a later one (see "Book of Eastern Claims," *MGHR* 4 [1887]: 281). Winifred Bonython, Sarah Churchwell's aunt, was married to Robert Nichols (or Nicholson), whose sister Catherine was the wife of George Ingersoll Jr., cousin of Jonathan Walcott. See *GDMNH*, q.v. "Nichols" and "Ingersoll."

13. *SWP* 2:473–76. No site is given for the examination of George Jacobs Sr. on May 10, but his second examination the next day took place at Beadle's tavern; the records are on the same sheet of paper, both in Parris's handwriting (SWP/SJC/PEM 1:224).

14. *SWP* 2:484, 491. At Margaret Jacobs's examination and confession on May 11, Hubbard and Walcott were afflicted, according to later indictments in her case (ibid., 2:489, 3:905–906).

15. Ibid., 2:484, 476–77.

16. Rosenthal's argument about pins refers specifically to manifestations at the examination of Elizabeth Howe later in May; see *Salem Story*, 37–38, and also 17–18.

17. *SWP* 3:841, 849, for the afflictions of Hubbard and Lewis.

18. This paragraph and the next two are based on ibid., 2:410–12. Abigail's statement that her victims lived away from Ft. Loyal "toward Capt. Bracketts" suggests that she was judging directions from a spot located between the fort and Anthony Brackett's farm (situated on the mainland to the west of Cleeves' Neck), or approximately where the Ingersoll and Lewis families' properties lay. James Andrews's property lay still farther to the west on the mainland. See the map of seventeenth-century landholdings in the Casco region tipped into William Willis, *The History of Portland, from 1632 to 1864* (Portland, Me., 1865), unpaginated. See *GDMNH* on Robert Lawrence, who died at the fall of Ft. Loyal in May 1690; his wife, Mary, survived him, but *GDNMH* does not know of the existence of a daughter with that name. The magistrates also questioned Abigail about a statement she had made on 11 May about "Davis's Son of Cascoe" (who could have been a son of Sylvanus, or of Lawrence Davis, a Falmouth resident during the 1680s). That same 11 May, Abigail declared that Burroughs had brought her the devil's book to sign (*SWP* 1:154).

19. Thus Abigail Hobbs was evidently not familiar with the details of Bur-

roughs's malefic activity described in visions reported by the afflicted after she was jailed, although she did now identify him as a witch (which she did not do on April 19 or 20).

20. This and the next two paragraphs are based on *SWP* 3:799–802. The specters mentioned five deaths and several accidents; one death, referred to as having happened "lately," had indeed occurred just five days previously (Michael Chapliman, 7 May 1692 [*SVR* 5:145]). Westgate and a "lost" crew member, John Lapthorne, were from Marblehead, although their deaths are not listed in the town's published vital records.

21. *SWP* 3:701, for the May 12 warrant for the two women. *SWP* erroneously intermingles documents about Alice Parker of Salem and the widow Mary Parker of Andover; see Rosenthal, *Salem Story*, 167–71, on distinguishing the two women. Karlsen, *Devil in the Shape of a Woman*, 315 n. 122, speculates that Alice Parker might have been Giles Corey's daughter. Biographical information on Ann Greenslade (or Greenslit) Pudeator from the Salem witch-descendants e-mail discussion list on rootsweb.com (communication from Helen Graves, 26 July 2000, forwarded to me by Ben Ray). After she married Jacob, Ann was suspected of complicity in his first wife's death; see *EC Ct Recs* 8:59–60. See also Robinson, *Devil Discovered*, 186, 317. Testimony about both women's reputations as witches was offered at their September trials; see below, chapter 8.

22. This paragraph and the next are based on *SWP* 2:623–24. Ann Pudeator was arrested and almost certainly examined on May 12; see ibid., 3:701–702 (a reference at her later examination to a previous one). It has proved impossible to trace the death of Warren's mother or the illness of her sister, or even her father's name. I think it likely that Mary referred to a stepfather, and that her mother, perhaps even her sister, had a different surname.

23. *SWP* 2:474, 662, 3:953–54; trial of Robert Swan, 17 July 1691, *EC Ct Recs*, ser. 2/WPA, 51:70/1–74/3 passim (quotations 74/1). Osborne died on May 10.

24. This and the next two paragraphs draw from *SWP* 3:733–36. On Abigail Soames and the links between Quakers and some of those accused of witchcraft in 1692, see Christine Leigh Heyrman, "Specters of Subversion, Societies of Friends: Dissent and the Devil in Provincial Essex County, Massachusetts," in David D. Hall et al., eds., *Saints and Revolutionaries: Essays on Early American History* (New York, 1984), 38–74 passim, esp. 54–55. Robinson, *Devil Discovered*, 359–60, gives basic biographical information. Heyrman speculates that Soames's relationship to her Quaker mother and brother lay behind Warren's accusation, yet the peculiarities of Soames's personal circumstances (as an unmarried woman in her late thirties who ventured out in public only at night) could also have called attention to herself as a potential witch.

25. "Letter of Thomas Brattle, F.R.S., 1692," in Burr, *Narratives*, 171.

26. The warrant is printed in *SWP* 2:487; the magistrates also renewed their earlier order to arrest Bethia Carter Jr. The previously identified group comprised George Jacobs Jr. and his wife Rebecca; Sarah Buckley and her daughter Mary

Witheridge; and Elizabeth Colson, the granddaughter of Lydia Dustin. The additions were Elizabeth Hart and Thomas Farrar Sr., both of Lynn, and Daniel Andrew of Salem Village, the wealthy brother of Rebecca Jacobs. The fugitives were Colson, Andrew, and Jacobs Jr. The constables' reports on the arrests and escapes are in ibid., 2:381, 493–94; 1:237. Useful biographical information is available in Robinson, *Devil Discovered:* 288–89 (Hart), 336–41 (Jacobs and Andrew), 344 (Colson). Robinson points out that Hart was related by marriage to John Proctor and, more distantly, to the family of Samuel Wardwell, members of which were accused later. Heyrman (n. 24, above) identifies Quaker connections for Hart, Farrar, and the Proctors.

27. M. Halsey Thomas, ed., *The Diary of Samuel Sewall, 1674–1729* (New York, 1973), 1:291. Knowing that Phips was en route with the new charter, the colony had elected him earlier in the month to the council of the ad hoc government, with the highest vote total (ibid.). That the examinations of Witheridge and Rebecca Jacobs occurred on the 18th is evident in *SWP* 2:495, 3:858. Of this group, only Buckley's examination transcript still exists (ibid., 1:145).

28. Worthington C. Ford, ed., *Diary of Cotton Mather* (New York, 1957), 1:148. Cotton Mather baptized Phips on 23 March 1689/90, the same day he was admitted as a member of the Second Church. This step cleared the way for Phips to become a political and military leader of the colony. On Increase Mather in London, see Richard Johnson, *Adjustment to Empire: The New England Colonies, 1675–1715* (New Brunswick, N.J., 1981), chapters 3–4. Negative letters about the interim Massachusetts government received by the Lords of Trade and Plantations, 1689–1691, in CO 5/855, 856, passim, vividly show the difficulties Mather had to surmount to achieve his goals. Stephen Foster, *The Long Argument: English Puritanism and the Shaping of New England Culture, 1570–1700* (Chapel Hill, N.C., 1991), 253, points out that Mather carefully balanced the councilors between supporters and opponents of the Dominion of New England.

29. This paragraph and the next are based on Emerson W. Baker and John G. Reid, *The New England Knight: Sir William Phips, 1651–1695* (Toronto, 1998), chapters 1–6, passim. On William and Mary Phips's many links to Maine in the 1690s, see chapter 7, passim.

30. Phips to William Blathwayt, 12 October 1692, and Phips to Earl of Nottingham, 21 February 1692/3, in Burr, *Narratives*, 196, 199.

31. An account of the swearing-in ceremony is in "Diary of Lawrence Hammond," *MHS Procs,* 2d ser., 7 (1891–92): 161; members of the council are listed in CO 5/785, f 86. Depositions taken by Pike in Salisbury on May 11, 13, 16, and 20 are printed in *SWP* 2:558–69.

32. Council minutes, 27 May 1692, CO 5/785, f 90. Hathorne and Corwin were not present; they had returned to Salem to continue examining suspects and to prepare for the upcoming trials. Phips, though, did not formally name them (and others) as justices of the peace in Essex County until May 30 (a copy of the commission is in the oversize box, Saltonstall Papers, MHS). A brief report on the

first council meeting is in Thomas, ed., *Sewall Diary* 1:291–92. On Courts of Oyer and Terminer: Hoffer, *Devil's Disciples*, 135. See Thomas Newton to William Blathwayt, 8 April 1691, vol 8, fol. 2, and James Graham to same, 5 May 1691, vol. 10, fol. 5, William Blathwayt Papers, CW, on the trials of Jacob Leisler and his associates. Parris and Stephen Sewall must have been close friends in Boston in the 1680s, for only relatives usually served as hosts for afflicted children.

33. Phips to Blathwayt, 30 May 1692, vol. 5, fol. 1, Blathwayt Papers, CW; Phips to Nottingham, 29 May 1692, CO 5/751, f 7. Since Phips could not write, his secretary handled all his correspondence. See Baker and Reid, *New England Knight*, 20–21, on this point. The council's minutes were also forwarded to England, although when is unknown; the general wording of the commission for the Court of Oyer and Terminer, while revealing the court's existence, concealed its specific function.

34. *SWP* 3:849, 851, 846, 822; "Parris's Record of Deaths," *NEHGR* 36 (1882): 188.

35. *SWP* 3:820–21, for Herrick; those afflicted at Ingersoll's on May 17 were Walcott, Lewis, and Vibber (ibid., 841). This paragraph and the next two are based on ibid., 826–29. There are two versions of the notes on Willard's examination, both by Parris; this account relies on the second, which is somewhat fuller.

36. Ibid., 3:771–73. Both the warrant and the order to jail him (and Willard, Farrar, and Hart) in Boston are dated May 18. Richard Godbeer, *The Devil's Dominion: Magic and Religion in Early New England* (New York, 1992), 68, identifies Toothaker as the only doctor ever accused of being a witch in early New England. Philip White was Phips's half brother; see Baker and Reid, *New England Knight*, 143. Roger Toothaker died in the Boston jail on June 16 (*SWP* 3:773–74), so he was never tried. His wife and two of his daughters were later accused of witchcraft; see below. Toothaker could well have abandoned his wife and children in Billerica when he relocated to Beverly; see Henry A. Hazen, *History of Billerica, Massachusetts* (Boston, 1883), pt. 2, 150.

37. This paragraph and the next two are based on *SWP* 1:294–301 passim (quotations 294–97, 301). For brief references to the others having cleared Easty, see ibid., 296–97, 300, 304. See also ibid., 287–88, 290–91, for complaint, warrant, and indictments of Easty for bewitching Lewis and Walcott during her May 23 examination. Why Mercy Lewis behaved as she did toward Easty is unclear.

38. The complaints: ibid., 2:691, 655–56; 1:117, 183; results of the governor's order: ibid., 3:953; Calef: *MWIW,* in *WDNE* 3:20. James Kences usefully points out that this flurry of witchcraft activity occurred around the second anniversary of the fall of Ft. Loyal at Casco. See Kences, "Some Unexplored Relationships of Essex County Witchcraft to the Indian Wars of 1675 and 1689," *EIHC* 120, no. 3 (July 1984): 207.

39. *SWP* 2:692, 3:803–804 (Elizabeth Booth); 2:693 (Sheldon). Other complaints against Sarah Proctor: ibid., 2:688, 692, 694. Elizabeth Booth was the daughter of George and Alice Booth of Lynn, then Salem Village. Her father, a

joiner, died in 1682; her mother remarried Michael Shaflin, who died in 1686. In 1692 she was living with her mother and her younger sister Alice, who later was afflicted, as was her sister-in-law (the wife of her brother George Booth Jr.), also (confusingly) named Elizabeth. *SVR*, q.v. "Booth" and "Shaflin," passim.

40. Incidents on May 15: *SWP* 3:839, 851, 1:145; May 17: ibid., 3:838–39, 841; May 20: ibid., 1:295–98, 2:692–93. Afflictions at May 18 examinations: ibid., 1:145, 2:495, 3:826–29, 858.

41. Ibid., 2:673–74, 688–89.

42. Cary's account, originally published in *MWIW* in 1700, and undoubtedly written at Robert Calef's request before the manuscript was completed in 1697, is reprinted in *SWP* 1:207–10, on which this paragraph and the next three are based. Mistress Cary was one of those formally complained against on May 28, *after* the events described in the text.

43. Mather, "A Brand Pluck'd Out of the Burning," in Burr, *Narratives*, 259–60. Mather states that Mercy's encounter with Sarah Good occurred in the "Summer," but since he calls Good at the time only a "Suspected" witch, the meeting must have taken place before her conviction in late June. Mather, as shall be seen below, did not become directly involved with Short until some months later, and his description of the onset of her troubles was vague. For a reference to another wealthy friend supplying Mary English (and her husband) with "victuals & provisions" while they were jailed in Boston, see John Noble, ed., "Some Documentary Fragments Touching the Witchcraft Episode of 1692," *CSM Pubs* 10 (1904–1906): 19.

44. Newton: *SWP* 3:867; Short residence: Mather, "Brand," in Burr, *Narratives*, 261; Thacher residence: Thwing index to seventeenth-century Boston property holdings, MHS.

45. These points will be explored further in the discussion that follows. On the meaning of "mistress" and "dame," see Mary Beth Norton, *Founding Mothers & Fathers: Gendered Power and the Forming of American Society* (New York, 1996), 18–19.

46. Few documents pertaining to Mistress Thacher survive today. Searches of the relevant fragments turned up no explicit connection to Mercy Short.

47. Quotations: Mather, *DL*, in Lincoln, *Narratives*, 207–208. See *GDMNH*, q.v. "Short, Clement," on the fate of the members of the family. At least five of Mercy's captive siblings survived; they too ended up in Boston.

48. Mather, *DL*, in Lincoln, *Narratives*, 209, 213.

49. See *GDMNH*, q.v. "Webb, Henry," "Sheafe, Sampson." Margaret Thacher's property was inventoried by her sons-in-law Jonathan Corwin and Sampson Sheafe after her death in March 1693/4; see the probate records of her intestate estate, Suffolk County Probate Records #2126, JA, MSA. See Richard Simmons, "The Founding of the Third Church in Boston," *WMQ*, 3d ser., 26 (1969): 241–52; and Hamilton Andrews Hill, *History of the Old South Church (Third Church), Boston, 1669–1884* (Boston, 1890), 1–122 passim (120–25 for biographical

information on Thomas and Margaret Thacher). Molly A. Warsh, "Memories of the Eastward: Reexamining the Salem Witchcraft Crisis of 1692 in the Context of King William's War" (unpub. honors thesis, History, Cornell University, 1999), first alerted me to the importance of Boston's Third Church in the crisis. Thomas Thacher was a friend of Henry Webb's before marrying Webb's daughter Margaret, for Webb left a legacy to Thacher in his 1660 will; see Suffolk County Probate Records #246, JA, MSA, printed in large part in *NEHGR* 10 (1856): 177–80 (thanks to Elizabeth Bouvier for locating all Webb, Sheafe, and Thacher probate documents for me).

50. Quotations: Margaret Thacher to Elizabeth Corwin, 28 October 1686, box 1, fol. 13, Curwen Family Papers, PEM.

51. Mather, "Brand," in Burr, *Narratives,* 260–61.

52. Ibid., 261–63, 266–67.

53. Ibid., 282.

54. Ibid., 270, 274, 276. Mather might well have suspected Mistress Thacher of being a witch; at the very least, he seemed to have little respect for her. His biography of Thomas Thacher identified the clergyman's first wife, praising her as "every way worthy of the man to whom she became a *glory,*" but barely mentioned Thacher's second marriage to an unnamed Bostonian. See *Magnalia Christi Americana . . .* (Hartford, 1855), 1:490–91.

55. Mather, "Brand," in Burr, *Narratives,* 271; "Letter of Thomas Brattle, F.R.S., 1692," ibid., 178.

56. The formal complaints: *SWP* 1:117, 1:183; a summary list dated 28 May: ibid., 3:871–72. Mistress Bradbury's status protected her from arrest until 29 June (ibid., 3:956).

57. Involvement of Gedney and location: ibid., 1:52. Little or nothing is known about four of those accused on these days—Elizabeth Fosdick of Malden, Sarah Rice of Reading, Elizabeth Paine of Charlestown, and Arthur Abbott of Ipswich—but I am assuming that the three women fell into the "usual suspect" category. See ibid., 2:339–40, 3:719–20. Other suspects not discussed in the text included a Proctor son and the young daughter of Mary Toothaker (see below). For the arrest of Philip English: ibid., 1:315; afflictions at his examination: ibid., 1:315–16; his capture: Noble, ed., "Some Documentary Fragments," *CSM Pubs* 10 (1904–1906): 18–19.

58. Quotation: Mather, *WIW,* in *WDNE* 1:200. Mary Toothaker is discussed in chapter 7. Because of an error by a WPA transcriber, who read the last name of another suspect, Ireson, as Jerson, a strange first name of "Doktr toothekers wiffe," there has been considerable confusion about Mary's identity (see *SWP* 3:765).

59. Quotation: Sarah Loring Bailey, *Historical Sketches of Andover . . .* (Boston, 1880), 202. Biographical information from Karlsen, *Devil in the Shape of a Woman,* 98–101. On smallpox deaths in Andover: Philip J. Greven Jr., *Four Generations: Population, Land, and Family in Colonial Andover, Massachusetts* (Ithaca, N.Y.,

1970), 107, and *Vital Records of Andover, Massachusetts, to the End of the Year 1849* (Topsfield, Mass., 1912), 2:375–76. For testimony against Martha Carrier, see below, chapter 7.

60. This paragraph and the next draw on *SWP* 1:184–85.

61. This discussion is based on ibid., 3:713–14. The other three cured were Sheldon, Williams, and John Indian. For Wabanaki use of "knocking in the head," see, e.g., *DHSM* 5:142, 6:178, 9:22.

62. *SWP* 2:434–35 is the basis for this and the next paragraph. Biographical information from Robinson, *Devil Discovered,* 301.

63. Biographical information on Floyd from Mellen Chamberlain, *A Documentary History of Chelsea* (Boston, 1908), 1:174–75, 178–79; the mutiny, *DHSM* 6:473–75; his leave, *DHSM* 5:336; the complaint, *SWP* 1:183, 3:872. Mary Walcott's brother probably served under Floyd with other Salem Village men.

64. Quotation: Cotton Mather, *DL,* in Lincoln, *Narratives,* 224. See also chapter 3, above; and *DHSM* 5:113, 126.

65. Quotations: *DHSM* 5:141 (see also 140); Mather, *DL,* in Lincoln, *Narratives,* 224. The deaths of four Village men in battle in July 1690 are noted in "Rev. Samuel Parris's Record of Deaths at Salem Village during His Ministry," *NEHGR* 36 (1882): 188 (misdated as 1691 in this printed version, but given as 1690 in the original manuscript, Danvers Archival Center, Peabody Institute Library). Although the dead men are not specifically designated as having been in Floyd's company and three (not Sheldon) are said to have died "at Casko," Floyd's men were the only ones engaged in fighting that week, when nothing was happening at Casco. Mather rarely acknowledged any criticism of a commander during the war, thus suggesting the probable widespread circulation and harsh character of the censures of Floyd.

66. "Diary of Lawrence Hammond," *MHS Procs,* 2d ser., 7 (1891–92): 160.

67. Quotation: *SWP* 1:52. Alden's narrative, like Nathaniel Cary's, was originally published by Calef. It was written in the third person, but Calef explicitly identified Alden as the author; see *MWIW,* in *WDNE* 3:26. I posit that Ann Jr. was the accuser because of two details in Alden's account: the accuser did not know him by sight, and she was little (a man held her up to see him). Ann Jr., who often spoke for Mercy Lewis, was always more interested in Maine than was the other little girl, Abigail Williams. I have not been able to confirm the charge that Alden fathered métis offspring.

68. Little has been written about Alden. Warsh, "Memories of the Eastward," pieced together some biographical details, 23–24. For the Aldens' Saco sawmill, see "Book of Eastern Claims," *MHGR* 7 (1893): 150. An account that came to my attention too late to incorporate into this discussion is Louise Breen, *Transgressing the Bounds: Subversive Enterprises Among the Puritan Elite in Massachusetts, 1630–1692* (New York, 2001), 197–212.

69. Boyer and Nissenbaum, *Salem Possessed: The Social Origins of Witchcraft* (Cambridge, Mass., 1974), 188. Most books on Salem cite Alden as a largely inex-

plicable suspect and do no more than summarize parts of the brief narrative Calef published. The list of Alden's sixteen trips was compiled primarily from *DHSM* 5, 9, passim; and from MA 36, 37, 81, passim, MSA. The sample trips mentioned in this paragraph can be traced in *DHSM* 9:14, 40, 61, 5:6–9 (defense of Falmouth, 1689); MA 81:90 and chapter 3, n. 72 (guns, 1690); and MA 81:90, *DHSM* 5:159, MA 39:429, CO 5/856, f 528 (voyages to Port Royal). Sarah Churchwell might not have been in Maine in the 1680s, but she would surely have known him as a young girl in Saco because of the proximity of her grandfather's and his father-in-law's property, and she could well have been living in Marblehead at the time of the mob action in July 1690.

70. Quotations: Isaack Miller, Deposition, 21 December 1689, *DHSM* 5:22–23. For the treaty, see chapter 3; and see *DHSM* 5:321–23, his orders to redeem prisoners taken at York in January 1691/2.

71. Edward Randolph to Francis Nicholson, 29 July 1689, CO 5/855, f 70; *DHSM* 5:159; Instructions to Captain John Alden, 7 March 1690/1, MA 39:429. Warsh, "Memories of the Eastward," 34, first recognized the implications of Alden's instructions.

72. Gedney to [Isaac Addington?] and vice versa, 12 August 1691, MA 37:115; Benjamin Allen to Massachusetts Governor and Council, 12 August 1691, ibid., 120; Isaac Woodbury et al., to Governor and Council, 26 August 1691, ibid., 124. See also ibid., 118a, 119, 121, 123.

73. The capture was recounted in a number of documents, but the accounts do not concur on specifics. See MA 37:176, 178, for a letter from Castine, 18 October 1691, carried to Boston by Alden, and the draft response; also CO 5/856, f 691; CO 5/1308, ff 7, 9; and M. Halsey Thomas, ed., *The Diary of Samuel Sewall, 1674–1729* (New York, 1973), 1:282–83. For a brief discussion of the incident: Baker and Reid, *New England Knight*, 157–58.

74. This paragraph and the next two are based on Mark Emerson, statement, Boston, 26 October 1691, CO 5/1308, f 9; and Samuel Ravenscroft to [Francis Nicholson], 5 November 1691, ibid. That the Indians needed ammunition to kill waterfowl reconfirms the evidence cited in chapter 3 indicating that after two or three generations of European trade they had lost their familiarity with bows and arrows or other traditional methods (snares or nets) of catching ducks and geese. Emerson's matter-of-fact mention of cannibalism is also noteworthy.

75. John Mack Faragher discusses the continuing trade between Boston and Acadia after the 1650s in " 'Without These Compromises It Would Be Impossible to Exist in This Country': Acadian 'Neutrality' in the Age of Empire, 1604–1755," unpub. paper delivered at the "Greater American Histories" conference, Huntington Library, March 2001.

76. See *DHSM* 5:321–23, 372–74, 377–81; and Thomas, ed., *Sewall Diary* 1:289, on this trip.

77. *SWP* 3:871; Hutchinson to Isaac Addington, 19 May 1692, *DHSM* 5:341. Those who registered complaints against Alden for "a long time" before 28 May were Walcott, Lewis, Williams, Putnam Jr., and Sheldon. Others listed as afflicted by him in the official complaint on 31 May were Elizabeth Booth and Mary Warren (*SWP* 1:51).

78. *SWP* 1:53–54. Gedney and Alden were both among the private investors in the 1690 expedition against Port Royal; see the proposal they and others presented to the council in mid-January 1689/90, in *DHSM* 5:30–31.

79. Newton to Addington, 31 May 1692, *SWP* 3:867. Another witness to the May 31 examinations, the Rev. Henry Gibbs of Watertown, wrote in his diary that at Salem Village he had "observed remarkable and prodigious passages. . . . Wonders I saw, but how to judge and conclude, I am at a loss" (excerpted in Joseph B. Felt, *Annals of Salem* [Salem, Mass., 1827], 305).

80. Quotations: John Whiting, *Truth and Innocency Defended* (Boston, 1702), 140; "Touching Sir William Phips Proceedings," [c. 24 March] 1692/3, CO 5/857, f 155. Another less specific statement referred to the accusations of "some Priest, and others accounted eminent." See Thomas Maule, *Truth Held Forth and Maintained . . .* (n.p., 1695), 182.

81. *DHSM* 5:340–41.

CHAPTER SIX   ENDEAVORS OF THE JUDGES

1. *SWP* 2:612–13, 3:756–57; 1:297–98 (23 May statements); ibid., 1:258, 2:597, 667, 688 (Williams), 2:605 (Putnams), all on 31 May. The day before, Hathorne and Corwin collected depositions describing maleficium attributed to Bridget Bishop (e.g., ibid., 1:92–94). Since the first official meeting of the new council occurred on May 24, the "order" to the magistrates must have been informal.

2. Newton to Addington, 31 May 1692, *SWP* 3:867. The 31 May warrant for the transportation of Sarah Good, Rebecca Nurse, John Willard, John and Elizabeth Proctor, Susannah Martin, Bridget Bishop, and Alice Parker was signed by William Stoughton, chief judge (ibid., 868).

3. Ibid., 1:172–73. The others in the group that came to Mary Warren were Alice Parker, Ann Pudeator, Abigail Soames, and John Proctor—all people she had previously accused—and Goody Darling, whom she did not otherwise identify but who was probably Mercy Lewis's aunt Hannah Lewis Darling, who lived in Salem Town.

4. Ibid., 1:103, 211–12. Quotations corrected by the original June 1 document, SWP/SJC/PEM 1:262. A daughter of John Trask's had died in December 1687 (see *Vital Records of Beverly, Massachusetts, to the End of the Year 1849* [Topsfield, Mass., 1906], 2:580). This accusation could also have represented a further variant of the garbled charge that Bridget Bishop had killed Christian, John Trask's wife, in June 1689.

5. *SWP* 2:600–601. The others Nurse's specter confessed to killing were Benjamin Holton, Rebecca Sheppard, and John Fuller. For Fuller's death, see *SVR* 5:266; Holton and Sheppard both died in September 1689. Sarah Carr, Ann's sister, was married to Thomas Baker, a Boston blacksmith.

6. Stoughton and Sewall, orders to George Corwin (sheriff of Essex County), 30 May 1692, Karpeles Manuscript Collection, Santa Barbara, Calif. (with thanks to Bernard Rosenthal for a copy of this recently discovered document). The twelve trial jurors' names are known because of a retraction they later signed, which is printed in Calef, *MWIW*, in *WDNE*, 3:134–35. (Krissa Swain researched their biographies for me.) Stoughton issued another summons for forty trial jurors on 31 August; that could well mean that the first forty had all either served or been challenged (*SWP* 3:869–70). Whether Ruck continued as foreman of the grand jury is not clear, because later indictments did not indicate the foreman's name. But because the 31 August summons for more trial jurors did not ask for more grand jurors, the same men probably served on that body throughout the court's existence.

7. Council minutes, 27 May 1692, CO 5/785, f 90. Richard Weisman, *Witchcraft, Magic, and Religion in 17th-Century Massachusetts* (Amherst, Mass., 1984), 246 n. 66, points out that Stoughton, Gedney, and Richards had sat as judges at the witchcraft trial of Elizabeth Morse in 1681 (so too, probably, did Saltonstall). Stoughton, Gedney, and Wait Winthrop, all members of the council under Sir Edmund Andros, were probably among those who tried and convicted Goody Glover in 1688, when Joseph Dudley was chief judge.

8. Biographical information on Stoughton: Enders A. Robinson, *The Devil Discovered: Salem Witchcraft 1692* (New York, 1991), 22–25, 30–32; Peter Hoffer, *The Devil's Disciples: Makers of the Salem Witchcraft Trials* (Baltimore, 1996), 136–37; *Sibley's Harvard Graduates* 1:194–208.

9. Lawrence to Andros, undated petition, *DHSM* 6:377–79; see also ibid., 218–19, the warrant for Lawrence's arrest in the dispute with Davis, 4 September 1686.

10. Saltonstall: *Sibley's Harvard Graduates*, 2:1–8; Sewall: ibid., 345–64; Winthrop: Richard S. Dunn, *Puritans and Yankees: The Winthrop Dynasty of New England, 1630–1717* (Princeton, N.J., 1962), 191–267, passim (quotation 191).

11. On Richards and Sergeant, see Robinson, *Devil Discovered*, 42–43, 193; on Gedney, ibid., 91, 122, 193; *York Deeds* 16:223–25; and *DHSM* 4:398–400, 6:222–23.

12. The marital relationships are conveniently summarized in Robinson, *Devil Discovered*, 218–19; and see, e.g., M. Halsey Thomas, ed., *The Diary of Samuel Sewall, 1674–1729* (New York, 1973), 1:109, 116–17, 130, 146, 166, 253, 272, 282, and passim.

13. Phips to Earl of Nottingham, 21 February 1692/3, in Burr, *Narratives*, 199; Hale, *A Modest Enquiry into the Nature of Witchcraft . . .* (1702), in ibid., 415–16.

14. Weisman, *Witchcraft, Magic, and Religion*, 12–13, explores these legal issues. See also David T. Konig, *Law and Society in Puritan Massachusetts: Essex County,*

1629–1692 (Chapel Hill, N.C., 1979), 158–65; and George H. Moore, "Notes on the History of Witchcraft in Massachusetts; with Illustrative Documents," *AAS Procs,* new ser., 2 (1882–83): 162–70. On the 1692 Massachusetts witchcraft law, see chapter 8, below.

15. C. L'Estrange Ewen, ed. and comp., *Witch Hunting and Witch Trials . . .* (New York, 1929), 19–21, reprints this law (quotation, 20) and its English predecessors (13–19). "Benefit of clergy" was a general commutation of capital punishment available to men (not women) convicted of most first felony offenses.

16. Joseph Keble, *An Assistance to Justices of the Peace, for the Easier Performance of their Duty* (London, 1683), 218. Cf. Michael Dalton, *The Countrey Justice . . .* (London, 1655), 341–42. John Usher's bookstore in Boston stocked copies of Keble and Dalton in the mid-1680s; see bills of sale from 1683 and 1685 in box 4, ff 89, 91, Jeffries Family Papers, MHS. For an insightful treatment of how English writers addressed the problem of achieving legal proof of witchcraft, see Barbara J. Shapiro, *Probability and Certainty in Seventeenth-Century England: A Study of the Relationships between Natural Science, Religion, History, Law, and Literature* (Princeton, 1983), chapter 6.

17. Keble, *Assistance to Justices,* 218–19, and Dalton, *Countrey Justice,* 342–43, differ only in some punctuation and capitalization. Yet Keble, significantly, omitted Dalton's paragraph summarizing Bernard's admonition that sometimes "strange diseases" could result from "natural causes" rather than witchcraft. William Perkins similarly gauged the significance of a confession; see *A Discourse of the Damned Art of Witchcraft . . .* (Cambridge, 1608), 211–12.

18. *Sibley's Harvard Graduates* 2:13–36. Willard later filed extensive claims for Maine lands once owned by his wife's father; see "Book of Eastern Claims," *MGHR* 4 (1887): 109–10; 5 (1888): 37; 7 (1893): 20.

19. This and the next two paragraphs are based on Samuel Sewall, sermon notebook 1691–92, ff 126–29 (headed "Mr Willard. May 29. 92 PM"), Sewall Papers, MHS. Other sermons in this cycle by Willard, recorded by Sewall and another member of the congregation, are discussed later in this chapter.

20. This paragraph and the next three are based on Mather to Richards, 31 May 1692, in Kenneth Silverman, ed., *Selected Letters of Cotton Mather* (Baton Rouge, La., 1971), 35–40. The witchcraft episode Mather cited was one about which he eventually wrote at length in *WIW*—that of Mora, Sweden, in 1669–1670 (see *WIW,* in *WDNE* 1:211–17).

21. Mather also endorsed a swimming test (the folk belief that a witch, bound hand and foot and thrown into the water, would not sink), which Keble and Dalton did not. Nearly a century earlier, William Perkins, in *Discourse of Damned Art,* 208, had already rejected the swimming test. No Salem suspect in 1692 was "swum," but the accused Connecticut witches that year were more than once subjected to the ordeal; see David D. Hall, ed., *Witch-Hunting in Seventeenth-Century New England,* 2d ed. (Boston, 1999), 321, 326.

22. *SWP* 3:868–69 (oaths of office); ibid., 2:591–92 (summons for Nurse wit-

nesses); ibid., 2:681 (physical examination of Willard and Proctor). The summons for Willard witnesses is not extant, but several testified to the grand jury on June 3 (see *SWP* 3:839–41, 852). For a good general discussion of trial procedures in 1692, see Hoffer, *Devil's Disciples,* chapter 7, passim.

23. "Jury of Womens Return," *SWP* 1:106–108. Dr. Barton, born in England, moved to Salem in 1676; he died in Barbados in 1694 (Sidney Perley, *The History of Salem, Massachusetts* [Salem, Mass., 1928], 3:100).

24. This paragraph and the next are based on *SWP* 1:87–91 (quotation 87); Calef, *MWIW,* in *WDNE* 3:76. On the need for two witnesses, see Perkins, *Discourse of Damned Art,* 213–14. See *SWP* 1:89 for what appears to be a list of the grand-jury witnesses in this case. Ewen, ed., *Witch Hunting,* 77–93, reprints many examples of contemporary English witchcraft indictments.

25. This paragraph and the next two are based on Mather, *WIW,* in *WDNE* 1:163–66. Although Mather did not give the name of the afflicted girl who claimed to have been carried off, it was probably Susannah Sheldon, who at other times made similar charges. He also did not name her as the one who testified about the spectral encounter, but her deposition survives (and is the source of the last quotation in the first paragraph) (*SWP* 1:104). For the case against Bridget Bishop and a detailed discussion of the confusion that has been caused by the inclusion of some evidence against Sarah Bishop in the documents in Bridget Bishop's case in *SWP,* see Bernard Rosenthal, *Salem Story: Reading the Witch Trials of 1692* (New York, 1993), chapter 4. As in the quotation in this paragraph, Mather continually interspersed his personal opinions with his summaries of the cases he included in *WIW,* but where the original documents survive it is clear that he summarized them essentially accurately. Because he knew that his accounts of the trials would be read by people who had witnessed the proceedings, he would not have significantly falsified or misrepresented what happened in the courtroom, for fear of having the validity of his book rejected by its intended audience.

26. Quotations: *SWP* 1:101; Mather, *WIW,* in *WDNE* 1:173. For a deposition with an especially clear account of how someone like Bridget Bishop came to be seen as a witch, see *SWP* 1:97–99. See, generally, ibid., 1:92–95, 97, 104–105, for these depositions; Mather's summary of them is in *WIW,* in *WDNE* 1:167–73. Robert Calef revealed that Samuel Gray, one of the witnesses, later withdrew his accusations on his deathbed, insisting that they were "groundless" (*MWIW,* in *WDNE* 3:30).

27. Mather, *WIW,* in *WDNE* 1:174; "Letter of Thomas Brattle, F.R.S., 1692," in Burr, *Narratives,* 187–88.

28. Brattle's summary of the court's procedure is printed in "Brattle Letter" in Burr, *Narratives,* 174–75. All five cases Mather recounts in detail in *WIW* fit the same pattern (see *WDNE* 1:152–200). Lawson's comments on individual trials appear passim in the 1704 edition of his *Brief and True Narrative,* which Charles W. Upham printed in an appendix to volume 2 of his *Salem Witchcraft* (Boston, 1867).

29. *SWP* 2:588.

30. Ibid., 3:839 (Putnam statement); 3:830-34 (Willard indictments); 2:588-91 (Nurse indictments). The undated indictments against both were signed by John Ruck, suggesting they were issued during the first court session. Some but not all of the deaths listed by Ann Carr Putnam on 2 June 1692 can be located in *SVR*. In addition to the adults Lydia Wilkins (d. 27 January 1688/9) and Samuel Fuller (d. 1 January 1688/9), she attributed the deaths of Aaron Way's child (31 March 1689), Sarah Putnam (d. 17 December 1689), and two children of Ezekiel Cheever (15 February 1689/90) to Willard, with the assistance of Hobbs.

31. Childin: *SWP* 2:375, 599; Vibber: ibid., 2:684; Tookey: ibid., 3:759-62 passim (quotations 759, 761-62). His other accusers were Warren, Sheldon, and Walcott. For his service in Black Point in August 1677: George M. Bodge, *Soldiers in King Philip's War*, 3d ed. (Boston, 1906), 339. For more about Tookey, see *EC Ct Recs* 8:330-38. On 6 June, the magistrates questioned two more suspects, Mary Ireson of Lynn and Ann Dolliver of Gloucester and Salem Town. The records of their examinations, hitherto unknown, were recently discovered by Ben Ray in the BPL, interleaved in a copy of Upham's *Salem Witchcraft;* Ireson's is at p. 211, Dolliver's at p. 194. Both women were said to be accompanied by the "black man," and they were both probably jailed. For biographical information: Robinson, *Devil Discovered*, 332 (Dolliver), 349-50 (Ireson). For the May 24 accusation of Ireson, incorrectly identified, see *SWP* 3:765.

32. *SWP* 2:672-73, 1:263 (quotation 672). Elizabeth Booth appeared as a grand-jury witness on 30 June to describe these visions, so they were taken seriously by the authorities. Of the deaths she listed, some (e.g., Hugh Jones, Elizabeth Shaw) had also been the subject of accusations by others, but only two can be traced in *SVR:* Michael Shaflin (12 December 1686) and Robert Stone Jr. (16 June 1688).

33. Quotation: Calef, *MWIW,* in *WDNE* 3:30; Vibber: *SWP* 2:481. Vibber's language in this deposition suggests that Mary Walcott might also have been present at the hanging. The judges all attended a council meeting in Boston on June 10, and so it is unlikely they were in Salem for the execution (council minutes, 10 June 1692, CO 5/785, f 166).

34. Mather, *DL,* in Lincoln, *Narratives,* 238-39 (see, in general, 232-39).

35. *SWP* 2:598-99, 606, 370-71, 374. Thanks to Ben Ray for supplying biographical information on Jemima Rea.

36. Mather, *WIW,* in *WDNE* 1:208. Alice Parker was hanged on 22 September; see chapter 8.

37. *SWP* 3:802-803, undated testimony by Edward and Sarah Bishop and Mary Easty, with a related statement, 1 June 1692, by Mary English. Mistress English explicitly attested to hearing "the Same words" as the others, dating Warren's utterances at approximately one month earlier, or after her first confessions in late April but before her more detailed statement of May 12. Warren later accused both Goody Easty and Philip English.

38. "Return of Several Ministers . . . ," printed in Thomas Hutchinson, *The*

History of Massachusetts from the First Settlement Thereof in 1628, until the Year 1750,
3d ed. (Boston, 1795), 2:52; Council minutes, 13 June 1692, CO 5/785, f 90.

39. Worthington C. Ford, ed., *Diary of Cotton Mather* (New York, 1957), 1:151.
For Stoughton's position, and criticism of it from England, see Hutchinson, *History of Massachusetts* 2:28.

40. This paragraph and the next two are based on "Return of Several Ministers," in Hutchinson, *History of Massachusetts* 2:52–53.

41. Calef, *MWIW,* in *WDNE* 3:159. See also ibid., 156–57.

42. Quotation: Ford, ed., *Mather Diary,* 1:151. Even so, a 1 August 1692 statement by the Cambridge Association, a group of eight clergymen including Cotton Mather and Samuel Willard, essentially adopted Mather's 31 May formulation: the devil could represent an innocent person, but "such things are rare and extraordinary, especially when such matters come before civil judicature." See "Records of the Cambridge Association," *MHS Procs* 17 (1879–1880): 268.

43. Sewall sermon notebook 1691–1692, "Mr. Willard. June 12.92. PM," ff 139–41, Sewall Papers, MHS.

44. Edward Bromfield sermon notebook, v. 6 (15 June–7 August 1692), "Samuel Willard: 1 Pet 5:8," n.d. [19 June, probably p.m.], Bromfield Papers, MHS; transcription by Mark Peterson, typescript pp. 9–11. For an article on Willard's sermons in the summer of 1692 based on Bromfield's notes, see Stephen L. Robbins, "Samuel Willard and the Spectres of God's Wrathful Lion," *NEQ* 60 (1987): 596–603; and, on all the sermons Bromfield recorded, see Mark Peterson, " 'Ordinary' Preaching and the Interpretation of the Salem Witchcraft Crisis by the Boston Clergy," *EIHC* 129 (1993): 84–102.

45. David W. Voorhees, " 'Fanaticks' and 'Fifth Monarchists': The Milborne Family in the Seventeenth-Century Atlantic World," *New York Genealogical and Biographical Record* 129 (1998): 70–74. William's brother, Jacob, the son-in-law of Jacob Leisler of New York, was executed with Leisler in May 1691. If George Burroughs was indeed a Baptist, as Bernard Rosenthal has suggested (see *Salem Story,* chapter 7), that would have given Milborne another reason to come to his defense.

46. The petition has been printed in J. Wingate Thornton, comp., "Witchcraft Papers—1692," *NEGHR* 27 (1873): 55. See below, chapter 7, n. 28, for the speculation that the other petition he wrote might also have survived, albeit unrecognized.

47. Council minutes (as upper house of assembly), 25 June 1692, CO 5/785, f 168. Printed in part in George H. Moore, "Notes on the History of Witchcraft in Massachusetts, with Illustrative Documents," *AAS Procs,* new ser., 2 (1882–83): 171n.

48. The undated petition supporting her, *SWP* 2:592–93, must have circulated in early May because one of the signers was Daniel Andrew, who fled after being accused on May 15.

49. Indictments: ibid., 2:588–91; Kettle: ibid., 2:457; Hutchinson: ibid., 3:853.

50. Ibid., 2:537, 3:731, 1:79–80. For Hutchinson's relationship to the Nurses, see ibid., 2:592, and Paul Boyer and Stephen Nissenbaum, *Salem Possessed: The Social Origins of Witchcraft* (Cambridge, Mass., 1977), 57–58, 65, 70, and passim. Admittedly, the statement about Mercy Lewis is so badly torn that it might have supported rather than challenged her. But the most logical reading of the document (and its missing words) is as an attack, and it most logically would have originated as such. The key sentences read, with brackets representing the torn material and my conjectures for the lost contents: While she lived with us "we did then Judg that [in m]atter of consione of speaking the truth [—] and untruth she would stand stifly to [her lies]"; "I Knew her when [she lived with my sister and all] of my neighbours and I all wayes tooke her to [be a liar] as the above writen evidences hath decribed" (*SWP* 2:537).

51. Sarah Nurse statement: *SWP* 1:80; Samuel Nurse signature as witness: ibid., 3:731.

52. See Sewall's notation on an indictment, ibid., 2:588.

53. Some authors indicate that Nathaniel Saltonstall resigned from the court before its second session. I found no document recording the date of his resignation, although Thomas Brattle claimed that Saltonstall left the court at an unspecified time, being "very much dissatisfyed with the proceedings of it" ("Brattle Letter," in Burr, *Narratives,* 184). The court seems to have planned to try John Willard at this session, but for unknown reasons his trial was postponed to the third session; see *SWP* 3:835–36. Rosenthal discusses this set of trials in quite a different way in *Salem Story*, chapter 5.

54. "Titabes Confession . . . ," *SWP* 2:362–64; Sheldon: ibid., 2:374; Parris: ibid., 3:757; indictments: ibid., 2:365–67. That "Titabes Confession" was prepared for the trial is evident from its listing of the witnesses for each of the three indictments (see ibid., 2:364). Good's spectral attack on Vibber on May 2 was described in chapter 5, above. Sarah Osborne, it will be recalled, had died in jail six weeks earlier. Other indictments could have been issued, but the content of "Titabes Confession" suggests that the record of indictments in this case is complete.

55. Ibid., 2:373, 377 (see also 366); Calef, *MWIW,* in *WDNE* 3:33–34. Mercy Short ("Mrs Thatchers maid") did not appear to testify against Sarah Good, probably because her mistress, herself accused as a witch, refused to permit it. In addition to any personal motives, Mistress Thacher, like her second husband, could have been skeptical of witchcraft accusations (see his letter to church leaders, 27 February 1653/4, printed in *MHS Colls* 41 [1871]: 375–77). I concluded Vibber was probably responsible for the subterfuge with the knife because of the similar behavior with a pin reported by Sarah Nurse; see below.

56. This speculative reconstruction is based on the contents of "Titabes Confession . . . ," *SWP* 2:362–63. For the statements in the original confessions, see ibid., 3:798, 801 (Warren); 2:407–409, 1:172 (Abigail Hobbs); 2:423, 1:92 (Deliverance Hobbs); and 3:747–55 passim (Tituba). It will be recalled that Newton asked

for Tituba to be sent from Boston to Salem for the first session of the court; he surely renewed that request (or simply kept her in Salem in the interim) so he could use her testimony against Sarah Good.

57. Maleficium stories: ibid., 2:368–69, 375; recent manifestations: 2:370–71, 377; Good's 2 March statements (to Samuel Braybrook): 2:372. For a maleficium tale presented to the grand jury but not, apparently, at the trial, see ibid., 369; in it, the cause and effect seem tenuous, and possibly Newton jettisoned it for that reason.

58. Indictments: ibid., 2:555–56; grand-jury testimony: ibid., 571–72. Other indictments have possibly been lost. Also, the foreman of the grand jury may not have fully annotated the documents in this case.

59. Quotations: Mather, *WIW*, in *WDNE* 1:175; *SWP* 2:573–74. Parris also testified, buttressing part of the statement by the Putnams and Ingersoll. *SWP* 2:558–69, 571–73, 577–78 reprints the maleficium depositions, which are adequately summarized by Mather, *WIW*, in *WDNE* 1:177–86. Deodat Lawson attended Martin's trial; see the appendix to the 1704 edition of his *Brief and True Narrative*, in Upham, *Salem Witchcraft* 2:534.

60. *SWP* 2:564–66; Mather, *WIW*, in *WDNE* 1:186–87.

61. Mather, *WIW*, in *WDNE* 1:187. See the women's jury report, *SWP* 1:106–108.

62. *SWP* 2:606–607, 603. Possibly Nurse's trial preceded Martin's; the sequence is not recorded. But both occurred on June 29, and Newton probably dealt with the easier prosecution (Martin's) first. (Mather gives the date for Martin's, and Nurse's can be dated by her daughter Sarah's statement, *SWP* 1:80.)

63. Ibid., 2:595–99, 602–605 passim (quotations, in order: 599, 602, 597).

64. Ibid., 2:598, 601, 600. Confessions: ibid., 1:92, 2:423. Abigail Hobbs did not name Goody Nurse as a witch-meeting participant in her June 1 confession, but she did charge Nurse with choking her (ibid., 1:172).

65. Ibid., 2:592–94; 1:80–81.

66. Calef, *MWIW*, in *WDNE* 3:37. Calef states that the incident occurred at one of the late June trials, but does not specify which one.

67. Ibid., 3:34–37; see also *SWP* 2:607–608.

68. Quotation: Calef, *MWIW*, in *WDNE* 3:37; and see *SWP* 2:607–608, 588.

69. Quotation: Calef, *MWIW*, in *WDNE* 3:34. On earlier patterns of accusations, trials, and convictions, see Carol F. Karlsen, *The Devil in the Shape of a Woman: Witchcraft in Colonial New England* (New York, 1987), chapter 2; and John P. Demos, *Entertaining Satan: Witchcraft in the Culture of Early New England* (New York, 1982).

70. *SWP* 2:436–37.

71. Quotations: Mather, *WIW*, in *WDNE* 1:188–89 (see 188–94 passim); *SWP* 2:441. On the death of Hannah Perley: ibid., 2:437–39, 442–43, 447, 454; statements on Howe's behalf: ibid., 440–44; bewitched horses: ibid., 444–46, 450, 453–54; beer: Mather, *WIW*, in *WDNE* 1:191–92 (summarizing some evidence not contained in *SWP*).

72. *SWP* 3:810–12 (quotations 812).

73. Quotations: ibid., 807–808. For Reddington's story and its consequences: ibid., 810, 812–18. Ephraim Wilds, the Topsfield constable, informed the justices that he feared Deliverance Hobbs had named his mother as a witch in "revenge" for his having arrested Deliverance and her husband on April 21, but since Deliverance first accused Sarah on April 17, Ephraim's "serous thoughts maney tims sence" were misplaced (ibid., 809).

74. Ibid., 2:662–64, 678–80; 1:186–87; 2:392–93. Perhaps other indictments were issued but have not survived; it is impossible to tell.

75. Ibid., 3:956 (arrest of Bradbury), 1:127 (Ann Jr.'s statement), 1:123, 126, 128 (other afflictions at the examination). Walcott also saw a vision of Ann Jr.'s uncle John accusing Mary Bradbury (ibid., 1:128).

76. Ibid., 3:702, 705–707.

77. Ibid., 2:385 (complaint), 1:179 (examination). See also John Hale, *A Modest Enquiry into the Nature of Witchcraft*... (Boston, 1702), 80–81, for a longer description of the poppets and the experiments with them.

78. Jacob Melijn to Dr. Johannes Kerfbijl, 11 July 1692, Jacob Melijn Letterbook, AAS (in Dutch, translation by Evan Haefeli, in possession of the author). I am deeply grateful to Haefeli for sharing this important unpublished material with me.

79. Quotation: Calef, *MWIW*, in *WDNE* 3:34; warrant and execution: *SWP* 2:377–78.

80. M. Halsey Thomas, ed., *The Diary of Samuel Sewall, 1674–1729* (New York, 1973), 1:293; Cotton Mather, "A Discourse on the Wonders of the Invisible World," 4 August 1692, in Mather, *WIW*, in *WDNE* 1:129. The passage in the last sentence, taken from Mather's sermon delivered two weeks later, refers specifically to how "Private Persons" should regard the Salem accused and appears directly related to the fast at Alden's house.

81. *DHSM* 5:343–44.

CHAPTER SEVEN   BURROUGHS THEIR RINGLEADER

1. Mather, *DL*, in Lincoln, *Narratives*, 243–47, passim. See also Marshall W. S. Swan, "The Bedevilment of Cape Ann (1692)," *EIHC* 117 (1981): 160–65.

2. Sighting of Pudeator: *SWP* 3:707; Ballard's action: ibid., 3:971; date: ibid., 2:523 ("thanksgiving day [July 14] at night"); Lewis and Hubbard: *SWP* 2:515. The witch-finders could also have been Mary Walcott and Abigail Williams, because five years later "several Aggrieved Persons" from the Village complained that Samuel Parris had sent inquirers to those girls "to know who afflicted the people in their illnesses." See Paul Boyer and Stephen Nissenbaum, eds., *Salem-Village Witchcraft* (Boston, 1993), 266. See also Calef's account of Ballard's act and its consequences, in *MWIW*, in *WDNE* 3:51–52. Most authors have identified

the witch-finders as Ann Putnam Jr. and Mary Walcott, following the lead of Marion L. Starkey, *The Devil in Massachusetts: A Modern Enquiry into the Salem Witch Trials* (New York, 1949), 181–82. But Starkey cites no source for her identification, and I have found no document specifying the names of those who first named the tormentors of Elizabeth Ballard. Ann Jr. and Mary Walcott were in Andover twelve days later on July 26, when they identified the specter of Mary Bradbury as the afflicter of Timothy Swan (*SWP* 1:121, 125).

3. Foster's confession: *SWP* 2:342–43 (this document seems incomplete, probably lacking a first page). No record of a complaint against Foster survives, although on July 16 she referred to Timothy Swan and "the rest that complayned of her." Ballard's formal complaint against the Laceys, mother and daughter, is dated 19 July (ibid., 2:513). Andrew Foster, Ann's husband, an original settler of Andover, died in 1685. Elizabeth Ballard died in late July 1692.

4. John Hale, *A Modest Enquiry into the Nature of Witchcraft . . .* (1702), in Burr, *Narratives,* 418.

5. The Lacey confessions on 21 July are extensive and survive in several versions. The quotations in this paragraph and the next three come from *SWP* 2:514, 522–24; and Richard B. Trask, ed., *"The Devil hath been raised": A Documentary History of the Salem Village Witchcraft Outbreak of March 1692,* rev. ed. (Danvers, Mass., 1997), 157. See, in general, *SWP* 2:514, 520–29, 531–33.

6. *SWP* 2:524–25, 1:197.

7. This paragraph and the next are based on ibid., 2:526–30, 1:197–98. In addition to the names of witches and suspected witches, Richard Carrier knew about the reports of a spectral yellow bird. His statement constitutes the only evidence that Elizabeth Parris suffered afflictions.

8. Ibid., 2:689. "Tying neck and heels" involved tying a prisoner's hands and feet together behind his back, arching it into an extremely uncomfortable position.

9. Edward Bromfield sermon notebook, v. 6, notes on Willard's sermons for 26 July [i.e., June], 10 July, 17 July, 24 July 1692, MHS (Mark Peterson, transcript, pp. 17–20, 33–35, 44–47, 52–54); "Joshua Moodey," *Sibley's Harvard Graduates* 1:367–80. For the reputed accusation of Ann Jacobs Moodey, see Joshua Broadbent to Francis Nicholson, 21 June 1692, abstracted in J. W. Fortescue, ed., *Calendar of State Papers, Colonial Series, America and West Indies* (London, 1901), 13:653. Broadbent, who wrote from New York, included garbled information about the crisis, and it is unclear whether his information about an accusation of Ann Moodey was accurate, for it cannot be confirmed in another source.

10. *SWP* 2:689.

11. The council met eleven times between 13 June and 26 July. Attendance records exist for ten of those meetings. Phips and Sewall were present at all ten; Stoughton and Winthrop at nine; Sergeant and Richards at eight; Corwin and Gedney at two; and Hathorne at one. See council minutes, 13 June–26 July 1692, CO 5/785, ff 90–96 passim. Phips's biographers are the only other scholars who

have realized how long the governor was in Boston that summer, but they do not ascribe the same importance to his presence that I do; see Emerson W. Baker and John G. Reid, *The New England Knight: Sir William Phips, 1651–1695* (Toronto, 1998), 144–52.

12. See Phips to William Blathwayt, 21 July 1692, vol. 5, fol. 1, William Blathwayt Papers, CW; and the related letter, Isaac Addington to same, 16 July 1692, ibid., vol. 5, fol. 3. Addington promised that Phips would provide in his letter a full "Account of the present State of Affaires here," which suggests that he thought Phips was going to inform colonial officials about the witchcraft crisis at that time, but Phips did not do so.

13. Quotations: *SWP* 1:210; 30 July date: M. Halsey Thomas, ed., *The Diary of Samuel Sewall, 1674–1729* (New York, 1973), 1:293. On Benjamin Fletcher and the Salem fugitives in New York, see more below. See also, for reputed details of this escape, Enders A. Robinson, *The Devil Discovered: Salem Witchcraft 1692* (New York, 1991), 216.

14. Susanna Hathorne, Philip and Mary English's great-granddaughter (who, ironically, married a descendant of John Hathorne), told this story, with some additional unlikely details, to the Reverend William Bentley of Salem in May 1793. See *The Diary of William Bentley, D.D., Pastor of the East Church, Salem, Massachusetts* (Gloucester, Mass., 1962), 2:24–25; and a formal version of the story prepared later by Bentley and printed in *WDNE* 3:179–81 (quotations from this latter source). Philip English later said that he was jailed for about nine weeks in Boston (*SWP* 3:989), so since he was captured on May 30, that would date their flight to the first week of August. For the daughters, see John Noble, ed., "Some Documentary Fragments Touching the Witchcraft Episode of 1692," *CSM Pubs* 10 (1904–1906): 18–20. Among the unlikely details in the oral history is the claim that William Phips conspired in the Englishes' escape, giving them letters of introduction to Governor Fletcher. But Fletcher did not arrive from England to take up his post as governor until late August, long after the couple fled from Salem, and Fletcher and Phips had an acrimonious relationship, which is evident from their surviving correspondence. I tried unsuccessfully to locate letters from New York that would confirm the accounts that the fugitives associated with Fletcher there, but for a reference to the Englishes and Carys (and John Alden, whose escape is discussed in the next chapter) being in New York in October, see Jacob Melijn to Johannes Kerfbijl, 5 October 1692, Jacob Melijn Letterbook, AAS (in Dutch, trans. by Evan Haefeli).

15. Phips to William Blathwayt, 21 July 1692, vol. 5, fol. 1, Blathwayt Papers, CW; Phips to Winthrop, 25 July 1692, box 24, Winthrop Family Papers, MHS; Phips to Stoughton, 27 July 1692, *DHSM* 5:345–46; Phips to Checkley, 27 July 1692, MA 40:264, MSA. The council approved Checkley's appointment at its meeting on 26 July; see CO 5/785, f 96. The new prosecutor's sister-in-law was Lydia, daughter of Joshua Scottow, and his wife was a daughter of John Wheelwright, so he had close familial ties to the northern frontier.

16. Emerson: *SWP* 1:307–309; Bridges: ibid., 131–32. The other two accused witches in late July were Hannah Bromage (or Brumidge) and Mary Green, both of Haverhill. Little is known about either. See ibid., 143–44, 3:960–61 (Bromage): ibid., 2:379–80 (Green); and Trask, ed., *Devil hath been raised*, 158. Bromage offered a partial and tentative confession. The fullest biographical information about the two is in Enders A. Robinson, *Salem Witchcraft and Hawthorne's House of the Seven Gables* (Bowie, Md., 1992), 328–29. More is known about Mary Bridges (ibid., 301–303). Several of the daughters and a stepdaughter of Goody Bridges would also be accused and confess; see below.

17. This paragraph and the next two are based on *SWP* 3:767–69; see ibid., 1:193, for her son Allen's war wound. How Mary Toothaker knew the exact number of witches given by Goody Foster is not clear. The magistrates could have supplied it in an unrecorded leading question, or she could have learned of it through gossip.

18. Henry A. Hazen, *History of Billerica, Massachusetts* (Boston, 1883), 127; cf. map between 16 and 17. Some warning of this attack might have been given; see the notation, verso, on the 30 July summons for Billerica witnesses against Martha Carrier, in Salem, Mass., Witchcraft Papers, MHS (omitted from the published version, *SWP* 1:188–89). In August 1695, though, Mary Toothaker was killed and her young daughter captured in yet another attack. (See *Vital Records of Billerica, Massachusetts* [Boston, 1908], 400.)

19. Cotton Mather to John Cotton, 5 August 1692, in Kenneth Silverman, ed., *Selected Letters of Cotton Mather* (Baton Rouge, La., 1971), 40.

20. Easty indictments: *SWP* 1:290–91; Corey: ibid., 256–57. The WPA transcriber did not record the "billa vera" (true bill) notation on the Corey indictment for bewitching Lewis in the Salem, Mass., Witchcraft Papers, MHS, so it does not appear in *SWP*. Of course, other indictments might have been issued but not survived. See Bernard Rosenthal, *Salem Story: Reading the Witch Trials of 1692* (New York, 1993), chapter 6, for another discussion of this set of trials.

21. Mather, *WIW,* in *WDNE* 1:200, 195; *SWP* 1:191–92, 194–96.

22. Maleficium stories: *SWP* 1:189–90, 193–94, Allen Toothaker: ibid., 192–93; Mather's account: *WIW,* in *WDNE* 1:195, 199–200. For references to Martha Carrier in the confessions of the Foster-Laceys and Martha's sons, see *SWP* 2:342–44, 514, 522–24, 526–27, 529, 531–33.

23. Indictments: *SWP* 3:830–34 (those numbered 5 and 6 are missing); Ann Jr.: ibid., 3:850–51; Ann Sr.: ibid., 3:839; Parris et al.: ibid., 3:840–41 (see also 3:845); Vibber: ibid., 3:841. See the list of "Evidences against John Willard," ibid., 3:836, which includes Ann Sr., who probably testified orally.

24. Ibid., 3:842–49 passim (quotations 842–45).

25. Carrier: ibid., 2:529, 1:197; "Evidences against John Willard," ibid., 3:836. See also, on Jacobs having named Willard, Calef, *MWIW,* in *WDNE* 3:43.

26. Indictments: *SWP* 2:662–63, 678–80; Holton: ibid., 688–89; Booth: ibid.,

672–73, 689, 692. See also statements of the afflicted: ibid., 666–69, 670–73, 684–86, 688; statements by Parris, Putnam, et al.: ibid., 671, 675, 686–88.

27. Confessions: ibid., 1:92, 172, 197; 2:413, 423, 529; 3:799–800; DeRich: ibid., 2:482.

28. This paragraph and the next are based on ibid., 2:664, 681–82. "Pleading her belly" would commonly save a woman from execution until after she gave birth. Both petitions are undated, but the second is addressed to the "Court of Assistants now Sitting In Boston" and refers to the Proctors as "under suspition" of witchcraft, not as having been convicted. The Court of Assistants no longer existed after mid-May, but the new council would have been the equivalent body. The first assembly session under the new charter ran from June 8 to early July; the second session did not convene until September, so this petition predated the court's third session by at least a month. Accordingly, I think it possible that this was the second petition drafted in June by William Milborne, one of the two that resulted in his being fined on June 25 and the one he did not himself sign.

29. Indictments: ibid., 2:477–79; quoted testimony: ibid., 2:486, 481; reports of examination of his body: ibid., 2:480, 1:159; Jacobs's confession: Calef, *MWIW*, in *WDNE* 3:43.

30. This paragraph and the next are based on *SWP* 1:164–67 passim (Ann Jr. and supporters); 170 (Hubbard); 174 (Walcott); 167–68 (Vibber); 168–69 (Lewis); Elizar Keyser, deposition, grand jury, 3 August 1692, Pierpont Morgan Library (the printed version in *SWP* 1:177 omits the crucial words "told her that" contained in this copy).

31. Warren: *SWP* 1:173, corrected by the original, Salem, Mass., Witchcraft Papers, MHS (most significantly, the WPA transcriber wrote "Mis Cory," whereas the name is obviously "Cary"); indictments: *SWP* 1:154–58; Maine evidence: 1:161–62.

32. Quotations: Cotton Mather to John Cotton, 5 August 1692, in Silverman, ed., *Selected Letters*, 40; Mather, *WIW*, in *WDNE* 1:153; Deodat Lawson, appendix to the 1704 edition of *Brief and True Narrative*, printed in Charles W. Upham, *Salem Witchcraft* (Boston, 1867), 2:535. That Hale attended seems likely from his detailed knowledge of the trial; see below. Governor Phips was in Boston on 1 August and reached Pemaquid by 11 August. Even allowing several days for the stop he made at Casco Bay to bury the bones of the May 1690 dead and to carry off cannon from Fort Loyal, he could have attended Burroughs's trial on 5 August before departing for the eastward, since the prevailing winds made for easy sailing along the coast in that direction. A modern sloop can make the voyage from Boston to Pemaquid in just two long days; Phips could have reached Casco in a day or two, and then Pemaquid in another day. (Thanks to David M. Brown for this information.) It is hard to imagine that a man with Phips's investment in the trials and ties to Maine (indeed to Burroughs himself) could have resisted attending on 5 August. See Thomas Church, *The History of Philip's War . . . Also, of the*

French and Indian Wars, at the Eastward . . . , ed. Samuel D. Drake (Exeter, N.H., 1839), 209–12, for the timing of Phips's voyage.

33. Mather, *WIW,* in *WDNE* 1:153. The eight confessors who named Burroughs before his trial can be identified from the surviving documents in the case; seven extant depositions and two recorded oral testimonies refer to his strength. Thus it would appear that the extant documentary record in the case is complete, or nearly so. Mather referred to John Gaule, *Select Cases of Conscience Touching Witches and Witchcrafts* (London, 1646), which questioned many traditional means of identifying witches and which is discussed in chapter 1, above. He did not mention that a men's jury found no witch's mark on Burroughs's body, and thus that the clergyman had passed one of the tests Gaule accepted. (See *SWP* 1:159–60.)

34. Mather, *WIW,* in *WDNE* 1:153–55, in part summarizing statements by Ann Jr. (*SWP* 1:164), Lewis (ibid., 1:169), and Warren (ibid., 1:173). Mather failed to explain how the minister's teeth marks could be distinguished from those of others.

35. Mather, *WIW,* in *WDNE* 1:156–57. Which afflicted person had this experience in the courtroom cannot now be determined, but it was surely one of the four who had seen such visions already. All of them, of course, had direct (Lewis, Sheldon) or indirect (Putnam Jr., Walcott) ties to Burroughs in Maine.

36. Lawson, 1704 edition of *Brief and True Narrative*, in Upham, *Salem Witchcraft* 2:529.

37. Mather, *WIW,* in *WDNE* 1:157–58; Lawson, 1704 edition of *Brief and True Narrative*, in Upham, *Salem Witchcraft* 2:535–36. For relevant parts of the confessions, see *SWP* 1:172–73, 2:343, 491, 523, 528, 3:767. More details on Richard Carrier's naming of Burroughs have been published in Trask, ed., *Devil hath been raised*, 157, 159; and see, on Deliverance Hobbs's confession, SWP/SJC/PEM 1:31, a fragment not published in *SWP*.

38. Hale, *Modest Enquiry*, in Burr, *Narratives,* 421. Perhaps this confessor was Ann Foster, because Hale twice talked to her in the Salem prison, before and after Burroughs's trial (ibid., 418).

39. Mather, *WIW,* in *WDNE* 1:158–59; Increase Mather, *Cases of Conscience Concerning Evil Spirits Personating Men, Witchcrafts, . . .* (Boston, 1693), unpaginated afterword. But Robert Calef later claimed that Burroughs's strength had been evident to his acquaintances even in his youth (Calef, *MWIW,* in *WDNE* 2:9). The case of the Lancashire witches, which involved extensive confessions and which provided important precedents for Michael Dalton and thus for Joseph Keble in discussing the law of witchcraft, is recounted in G. B. Harrison, *The Trial of the Lancaster Witches . . .* (London, 1929), incorporating an edition of Thomas Potts, *The Wonderfull Discoverie of Witches in the Countie of Lancaster* (London, 1613).

40. *SWP* 1:160–62.

41. Ibid., 1:160–61. Mather, *WIW,* in *WDNE,* 1:159. Stephen Sewall also noted that two witnesses testified about his strength by "word of mouth"—Major

Browne, to holding out the gun; Thomas Evans, to carrying barrels from a canoe without help—but without written texts it is impossible to tell whether Browne or Evans had actually witnessed or merely heard about these feats (*SWP* 1:178). Greenslade's belated testimony was suspiciously and remarkably comprehensive, suggesting the possibility of his committing perjury in a desperate move to save his mother. He could have justified it to himself, perhaps, by the thought that Burroughs had already been executed and so could not be hurt by his testimony.

42. Original testimony: *SWP* 1:176, 162–63; Mather's summary: *WIW*, in *WDNE* 1:160–61. The strawberrying story is recorded only in *WIW*; it seems to have been offered orally by Sarah's brother, Thomas Ruck (see *SWP* 1:178).

43. Mather, *WIW*, in *WDNE* 1:161–62, 159. Cf. Gaule, *Select Cases*, 80–81.

44. This paragraph and the next are based on Mather, *WIW*, in *WDNE* 1:162–63. The section Burroughs most likely used challenged the common argument that because God had allowed Satan to torment Job, he also permitted witches to send Satan to afflict men. Even if God can do it, does that mean a witch can do the same? Ady inquired. "If God should permit it, where do we read that a Witch hath any such power or command over the Devil, or any such league or covenant with the Devil? or that God permits the Devil to be at the command of a Witch?" See Ady, *A Perfect Discovery of Witches . . .* (London, 1661), 119; and also a related legal argument on 172.

45. Residents of Wells to Mass. Governor and Council, 28 May 1692, *DHSM* 5:342–43; Hale, *Modest Enquiry*, in Burr, *Narratives*, 421. The council sent a new minister to Wells on 8 July (see CO 5/785, f 92), but Wells did not acquire its first formal church and a properly ordained minister until October 1701. See First Church of Wells, Maine, Records, 1701–1811, photostat, LCMD.

46. This paragraph and the next are based on Mather, "A Discourse on the Wonders of the Invisible World," 4 August 1692, in Mather, *WIW*, in *WDNE* 1:49–136 passim (quotations: 55, 57–58, 109, 94–95, 101–102, 106–107). For an example of the sort of criticism to which Mather was responding, see Robert Pike to Jonathan Corwin, 9 August 1692, in Upham, *Salem Witchcraft* 2:538–44 (discussed at length in chapter 8, below).

47. *SWP* 1:213–14, for Mary Clarke, who was complained against on 3 August by Robert and John Swan of Andover for afflicting Robert's son Timothy. Margaret Scott may have been accused as early as the first week of July, but she does not seem to have been arrested until after another complaint on 26 July; she was examined on 5 August. See ibid., 3:727; and Trask, ed., *Devil hath been raised*, 162. Mary Post must have confessed before 4 August , and she was eventually indicted for afflicting Timothy Swan in July (*SWP* 3:925–26), but other dates are unknown.

48. See, on Usher's treatment, "Letter of Thomas Brattle, F.R.S., 1692," in Burr, *Narratives*, 178. Hezekiah Usher's papers have not survived, but some of his brother's are contained today in the Jeffries Family Papers, MHS; see vol. 2, f 147, and vol. 4, ff 148, 149 for material pertinent to Hezekiah or his partnership with John. John Usher was involved in Maine and the fisheries (see ibid., vol. 15, ff 33,

34; and *DHSM* 6:271). He arrived in New Hampshire to take up his new post before 12 August 1692; his return to America from more than two years spent in London might possibly have triggered the accusation of his brother ("Diary of Lawrence Hammond," *MHS Procs,* 2d ser., 7 [1891–92]: 163). For his attempts to raise taxes from Maine for Andros: John Usher, "Account Rates in this Government Standing outt . . . [for 1687 and 1688]," William Blathwayt Papers, BL 238, HL. The quoted words are from "Reasons Humbly offered . . . by William Vaughan . . . against John Usher . . . ," May 1703, Rawlinson Papers C 128, f 1a, British Library, transcript, LCMD. Bridget Usher left her business affairs in the hands of Samuel Sewall; his published letterbook, *MHS Colls* 51 (1886): 78–79, 86, 97, 138 and n., and passim, includes material relevant to her estranged husband.

49. Sarah Carrier: *SWP* 1:201–202; Thomas Jr.: ibid., 1:203. Thomas's three victims were Sarah Phelps, Walcott, and Putnam Jr. Sarah Phelps, b. 1682, was the oldest child of Samuel Phelps, a weaver, and his wife, Sarah Chandler. Capt. Thomas Chandler, Sarah Phelps's grandfather, led the Andover militia in the Second Indian War; his sister, Hannah, became the third wife of the Reverend Francis Dane after the death of her first husband in 1681. Hannah Chandler Dane, Sarah's great-aunt, was accordingly the stepmother of Abigail Dane Faulkner and Elizabeth Dane Johnson, both later accused as witches. See Sarah Loring Bailey, *Historical Sketches of Andover . . .* (Boston, 1880), 84–85, 96–97, 118. One of the few studies of this late phase of the crisis is Chadwick Hansen, "Andover Witchcraft and the Causes of the Salem Witchcraft Trials," in Howard Kerr and Charles Crow, eds., *The Occult in America: New Historical Perspectives* (Urbana, Ill., 1983), 38–57. A useful study focusing largely on the contents of the Andover confessions is Richard P. Gildrie, "The Salem Witchcraft Trials as a Crisis of Popular Imagination," *EIHC* 128 (1992): 270–85.

50. *SWP* 2:503–505 passim. She named Richard Carrier and Mary Lacey Sr. Such confessions involving witches' sabbats both resembled and differed from their European counterparts. See the excellent discussion of confession patterns in Robert Rowland, " 'Fantasticall and Devilishe Persons': European Witch-Beliefs in Comparative Perspective," in Bengt Ankarloo and Gustav Henningsen, eds., *Early Modern European Witchcraft: Centres and Peripheries* (Oxford, 1990), 161–90.

51. *SWP* 1:327; "The Examination of Daniell Emes," 13 August 1692, Miscellaneous Manuscripts Bound, MHS. Post also listed Mary Toothaker, Martha Carrier, Ann Foster, and "Chandler," otherwise unknown, as participants in her "company." Eames has never before been identified as one of those who faced prosecution for witchcraft in 1692; I located the documents pertaining to his case in the MHS.

52. This and the next paragraph are based on "Brattle Letter," in Burr, *Narratives,* 177; Calef, *MWIW,* in *WDNE* 3:38–39. George L. Burr concluded, and I concur, that Brattle's account suggests that he most likely attended the execution. Stoughton and Sewall were not there; see Thomas, ed., *Sewall Diary* 1:294.

Mather seems to have told Sewall that Burroughs's speech on the gallows "did much move unthinking persons," leading to "their speaking hardly concerning his being executed." On 18 August, complaints were filed against Ruth Wilford and Mistress Frances Hutchins of Haverhill for afflicting Walcott, Putnam, and Swan, but few documents survive about either (*SWP* 2:459–61).

53. Calef, *MWIW,* in *WDNE* 3:43; *SWP* 1:178, 2:467.

54. *SWP* 1:149–50.

55. Rebecca Eames: ibid., 1:279–82. In a second confession on 31 August Rebecca named Abigail Faulkner and Mary Toothaker in addition to her son. The timing of the first afflictions of the three girls is difficult to determine, but see ibid., 2:546, suggesting the date 20 August. They were afflicted before 25 August, in any event, since a number of examinations and confessions on that day refer to their prior torments.

56. Enders A. Robinson, *Salem Witchcraft,* 302, 306–11, sorts out the tangled relationships described in this and the following paragraph. Rose's mother was Hannah Eames Foster, daughter of Rebecca and sister of Daniel. Mary Bridges was also related by marriage to Sarah Towne Cloyce; John Bridges, Mary Tyler Post's second husband, was the brother of Sarah's first husband, Edmund Bridges (ibid., 316–17).

57. Quotations: *SWP* 3:647, 1:134–35. For the examinations in general, see ibid., 3:643–44 (Hannah Post), 1:139–40 (Sarah Bridges), 1:134–35 (Mary Bridges Jr.), 3:647–48 (Susannah Post). One or more of the Post-Bridges confessors named as witches Abigail Faulkner, Martha Emerson, Mary Clarke, Frances Hutchins, Ruth Wilford, Rebecca and Daniel Eames, Ann Foster, and Martha Carrier, along with Sarah Parker (the daughter of Mary Parker, accused later), and some-one named "Church," probably Sarah Churchwell, who was also referred to thus by Ann Pudeator (ibid., 3:709).

58. The three were John Jackson Sr. and Jr., and John Howard, all of neighbor-ing Rowley. The Jacksons were the sisters' distant relatives by marriage, for John Sr. was the brother of the executed witch Elizabeth Jackson Howe, whose hus-band was Sarah Bridges's uncle (and thus the stepuncle of the other three). Howard's examination does not survive, but all three men were interrogated on 27 August. See ibid., 2:465–70, for the Jacksons. Those confronting the Jacksons were Walcott, Warren, Putnam Jr., Sprague, Foster, Lacey Jr., Richard Carrier, Sarah Bridges, and Hannah and Susannah Post.

59. Ibid., 1:63, 59–60, 2:545–46. Also accused, arrested, and questioned a few days later was William's sister-in-law, Abigail Barker (the wife of Ebenezer), but little documentation on her case has survived (see ibid., 1:57).

60. Ibid., 1:65–66, 68. See also John Hale, *Modest Enquiry,* in Burr, *Narratives,* 420, for Hale's comments on Barker's confession and its evident validity.

61. Quotations: *SWP* 1:68, 328; 2:500. See, in general, ibid., 2:499–502, 509–10, for the statements of Elizabeth Johnson and her son Stephen. If her daughter Abigail made a similar statement, it is no longer extant. Deliverance Dane, a

sister-in-law of Abigail Faulkner and Elizabeth Johnson, was also accused and arrested, but the Rev. Francis Dane, Abigail and Elizabeth's father, though accused, was never charged (ibid., 2:616).

62. Ibid., 2:501; ibid., 1:75–76 (for correct date, see ibid., 2:633); ibid., 3:783, 781 (for the Wardwell confessions, see ibid., 2:387–88, 3:781–82, 783–84, 791–92 passim). The confessors were Hannah Post, Mary Lacey Jr., and Sarah Bridges. Samuel Wardwell was initially from Exeter, New Hampshire, and his wife Sarah Hooper Hawkes came from Reading. Through her first marriage she was distantly related to John Proctor and Elizabeth Hart (accused and jailed in mid-May). See Robinson, *Salem Witchcraft*, 313–22.

63. *SWP* 2:631–32. The confessors participating in this examination were Mary Warren, Sarah Churchwell, Hannah Post, Sarah Bridges, Mary Lacey Jr., and Mercy Wardwell. Mary Parker's daughter Sarah and nieces Rebecca Aslet Johnson and Sarah Aslet Cole were accused later, along with Rebecca's daughter, also Rebecca. For information on these families: Robinson, *Salem Witchcraft*, 251–55. Note that *SWP* erroneously intermingles evidence in the unrelated cases of Alice and Mary Parker.

64. John Usher to Massachusetts Governor and Council, 5 September 1692, CO 5/857, f 6. See the council minutes, CO 5/785, f 96.

65. Mary Swayne Marshall's complaint against the three Reading women does not survive, but she was mentioned in all their examinations. For Frost, see *SWP* 2:345; *York Deeds* 7:21; and *GDMNH*, q.v. "Frost, Charles." For Dicer: *SWP* 2:651; Swan, "Bedevilment of Cape Ann," *EIHC* 117 (1981): 166–67; and *GDMNH*, q.v. "Dicer, William." See also *SWP* 2:641.

66. Prince's 5 September examination is published in Trask, ed., *Devil hath been raised*, 160. The two Reading women who did not confess were Jane Lilly (related by marriage to Elizabeth Proctor) and Mary Dustin Colson, whose mother, sister, and daughter had already been named as witches. For Lilly and Colson, see *SWP* 2:539–40; Taylor, ibid., 3:741–42. At the examinations of Lilly and Colson, Mary Warren, three Booths, Susannah Post, and Sarah Churchwell were all afflicted. At Taylor's, the afflicted were Mary Marshall, Hannah and Susannah Post, Mary Lacey Jr., and Mary Warren. Two of the three Booth women were named Elizabeth—a single woman and her sister-in-law; the third was Alice, also unmarried. See also the 7 September examination of the Andover widower Henry Salter, *SWP* 3:723–24, with a somewhat different list of afflicted. On the Reading residents, see Robinson, *Salem Witchcraft*, 332–35.

67. The Salem magistrates ordered the arrest of two Salem Town residents (Hannah Carroll and Sarah Cole) on 10 September (*SWP* 1:245); the detention of a Gloucester woman (Joan Penney) on 20 September (ibid., 2:641); and the seizure of another Sarah Cole (of Lynn, sister-in-law of the eponymous Salem woman) on 3 October (ibid., 1:226). Other than the final Andover cases to be discussed below, those and the three Gloucester women (Mary Rowe, Rebecca Dike,

and Esther Elwell) accused by Betty Hubbard and others in early November constitute the last formal complaints in 1692. For the three November cases, see ibid., 1:305–306; and Betty Hubbard, deposition, 8 November 1692, Miscellaneous Manuscripts Bound, MHS. Calef, in *MWIW,* in *WDNE* 3:53–54, gives a brief account of these late accusations.

68. *SWP* 3:971 (undated). The only extant examination record for this group is that of Mistress Osgood (ibid., 2:615–16). Some historians have placed the touch test in July, near the outset of the Andover phase of the crisis, but it involved women accused in September, and the date of Osgood's examination on 8 September (when coupled with other accounts) places the touch test on the day before.

69. Ibid., 3:777–78. Mary Tyler's first name is here erroneously given as "Martha," the name of one of her young daughters, who was also arrested about a week later and questioned in a group consisting largely of other children (ibid., 2:335). See Robinson, *Salem Witchcraft,* 306–308. For a contemporary account charging that in Andover prominent husbands persuaded their wives to confess, see "Brattle Letter," in Burr, *Narratives,* 180–81.

70. Calef, *MWIW,* in *WDNE* 3:52–53. Calef does not give the timing of these events, but they must have occurred some time around mid-September. Neither the name of the "worthy Gentleman" nor the details of the lawsuit he reputedly filed have ever been uncovered.

71. On Andover in the wars, see Bailey, *Historical Sketches of Andover,* 168–80. The town was attacked in the Second Indian War, but after 1692.

72. Quotations: Jeremy Belknap, ed., "Recantation of Confessors of Witchcraft," *MHS Colls* 13 (1815): 222; Petition of Andover Inhabitants, n.d. [c. January 1692/3], *SWP* 2:618. Another account of a conversation with the confessors described similar motivations but added as a consideration their knowledge that "all, without confession were suddainly put to Death." (Thomas Maule, *Truth Held Forth and Maintained . . .* [n.p., 1695], 189). See, on the importance of consensus, Mary Beth Norton, *Founding Mothers & Fathers: Gendered Power and the Forming of American Society* (New York, 1996), 200–201, 217–22, 235–36, 241–42. Even if towns were racked by conflict, they valued consensus and aimed to achieve it. But without local mechanisms for dispute resolution, Salem Village could not aspire to that goal. The only potentially helpful institution in the Village would have been the church, but, as has been seen, it instead contributed to the dissension. Elizabeth Reis examines the possible religious motivations for the Andover women's confessions; see Reis, *Damned Women: Sinners and Witches in Puritan New England* (Ithaca, N.Y., 1997), esp. chapter 4.

73. CO 5/924, ff 58–59.

CHAPTER EIGHT　　ALL SORTS OF OBJECTIONS

1. This paragraph and the next two are drawn from Pike to Corwin, 9 August 1692, as printed in Charles W. Upham, *Salem Witchcraft* (Boston, 1867), 2:538–40. Cf. Daniel G. Payne, "Defending against the Indefensible: Spectral Evidence at the Salem Witchcraft Trials," *EIHC* 129 (1993): 62–83, for a modern critique of the ways spectral evidence was used by the justices, in which the reasoning differs from Pike's.

2. This paragraph and the next two are based on Pike's undated essay, enclosed with his letter to Corwin of 9 August, and printed in Upham, *Salem Witchcraft*, 2:540–44.

3. Mather to Foster, 17 August 1692, in Kenneth Silverman, ed., *Selected Letters of Cotton Mather* (Baton Rouge, La., 1971), 41–43. Foster also apparently asked Mather for his opinion of possible changes in the way accused witches were treated, especially those with only spectral accusations against them; the minister responded with some specific ideas, such as transporting them out of the colony rather than convicting and hanging them.

4. *SWP* 1:140, 66.

5. Mather to Stoughton, 2 September 1692, in Silverman, ed., *Selected Letters*, 43–44. See Mather, *WIW*, in *WDNE* 1:5, for Stoughton's endorsement. Cf. Perry Miller, *The New England Mind: From Colony to Province* (Cambridge, Mass. 1953), chapter 13, for an interpretation of Mather's work on *Wonders* that differs considerably from mine.

6. Council minutes, 5 September 1692, CO 5/785, f 96; *SWP* 3:869–70. The only judges who attended the 5 September council meeting were Samuel Sewall and Peter Sergeant. Stoughton was probably already in Salem. On Fort William Henry, see Mather, *DL*, in Lincoln, *Narratives*, 240–41; and Thomas Church, *The History of Philip's War . . . Also, of the French and Indian Wars, at the Eastward . . .* , ed. Samuel G. Drake (Exeter, N.H., 1839), 210–14.

7. Bernard Rosenthal, *Salem Story: Reading the Witch Trials of 1692* (New York, 1993), chapter 8, considers these same trials.

8. See *SWP* 2:395–97, 402 for the testimony of the afflicted (Ann Jr., Hubbard, Walcott, Vibber) and the Putnams; and ibid., 393–94, 397–403, for the statements by the Beverly residents (quotations 401, 397). On Hale and Hoar's past relationship: Barbara Ritter Dailey, " 'Where Thieves Break Through and Steal': John Hale versus Dorcas Hoar, 1672–1692," *EIHC* 128 (1992): 255–69. Possibly significant is the fact that neither Susannah Sheldon nor Abigail Williams (though their torments on May 2 were described by the others) testified in this or any other case during the September court session—nor, for that matter, did either evidently appear in any prosecution after August, including the ones in January and May 1693. See appendix 3 for details.

9. *SWP* 1:260–65; 2:423, 529, 603–605; 3:793, 801.

10. Descriptions of Lewis: ibid., 1:294–95, 300–301 (quotation, 300); maleficium: ibid., 1:301–302; jailers' statements: ibid., 1:293–94; defense petition: ibid.,

1:302–303. Her sister, Sarah Towne Bridges Cloyce, joined in signing the petition, but she was never tried, being released from custody in January after the grand jury failed to indict her (see ibid., 1:221–23).

11. Indictments: ibid., 2:624–26; depositions by the afflicted (Vibber, Walcott, Hubbard, Putnam Jr., Warren): ibid., 2:626–28; maleficium: 2:626, 632–36 (the last three depositions are erroneously printed in the records of Mary Parker, but are about Alice Parker). Her specter, it was said, had also attacked Lewis and Churchwell; Abigail Hobbs confirmed some of these attacks.

12. Indictment: ibid., 3:704–705; testimony, 705–709 (quotations 708–710). Those who testified against her: Warren, Churchwell, Hubbard, Putnam Jr., Walcott, and Vibber.

13. See ibid., 1:115–16, 121, 123, 125–28, for indictments and grand-jury testimony. Other indictments have possibly been lost.

14. This paragraph and the next are based largely on ibid., 1:122–25 (quotations 124–25). I am descended from the marriage of Rebecca Wheelwright Maverick and William Bradbury in March 1671/2; they are my eighth great-grandparents. For the confessions naming Mary Bradbury, see ibid., 1:198, 2:514, 526–27, 529; 3:769.

15. Ibid., 1:121, 119–20, 116–17. Robert Pike's daughter Sarah's first husband had been a now-dead Bradbury son, so Pike and Bradbury were in-laws.

16. Ibid., 1:241–45. Some time after 12 September but almost certainly before 19 September Alice Booth and her sister-in-law swore that Giles and another fifty witches had participated in a devil's sacrament at the home of the widow Alice Booth Shaflin (see ibid., 1:245).

17. Ibid., 2:413–17 (Hobbs); 2:497 (Fox petition); 2:494–95 (Jacobs indictments). Jacobs was tried and acquitted on the sole indictment in early January (ibid., 3:904–905).

18. James F. Cooper and Kenneth P. Minkema, eds., *The Sermon Notebook of Samuel Parris, 1689–1694* (Boston, 1993), 199–206 passim.

19. Paul Boyer and Stephen Nissenbaum, eds., *Salem-Village Witchcraft* (1972; reprint, Boston, 1993), 280.

20. David Jeffries to [John Usher], 16 September 1692, Jeffries Family Papers, vol. 3, f 68, MHS. Mistress Bradbury herself escaped from jail later in the year, probably in December. See *SWP* 3:980–81. Some historians have said that Alden went home to Duxbury in the former Plymouth Colony, but he was in New York in early October; see Jacob Melijn to Johannes Kerfbijl, 5 October 1962, Jacob Melijn Letterbook, AAS (in Dutch, trans. by Evan Haefeli).

21. Testimony and indictments for Foster: *SWP* 2:341–42, 344, and MS Am. 52, BPL (not printed in *SWP*); testimony and indictments for Lacey: *SWP* 2:515–17; Wardwell recantation, testimony, and indictments: ibid., 3:784–86. Similarly, Sarah Churchwell declared that when she tried to recant, Nicholas Noyes would not believe her (ibid., 1:212).

22. Wardwell: Calef, *MWIW,* in *WDNE* 3:46; Mather, "A Brand Pluck'd out of

the Burning," in Burr, *Narratives*, 281–82. Although Calef did not acknowledge it, other testimony revealed that Wardwell had told fortunes. Several Andover witnesses described how Samuel both accurately predicted the future and knew past secrets (*SWP* 3:787–88). Mather said that a person executed for witchcraft at Salem described the presence of the French and Indians at the witch meetings in a confession; Samuel Wardwell was the only confessor executed, so if Mather was correct, it must have been he. Ann Foster died in prison in November; Mary Lacey Sr. was reprieved in the spring. Mary Jr. was tried on two indictments, covenanting with the devil and afflicting Timothy Swan, and acquitted on 13 January 1692/3. On these points, see ibid., 3:930–31, 992, 1001.

23. *SWP* 1:328–33. See also the Barker confessions: ibid., 1:59, 68–69. Goody Faulkner's young daughters confessed and, like Dorcas Good, named their mother as a witch, as did a number of other young people who testified before the grand jury in her case (ibid., 2:335).

24. Buckley: ibid., 1:145–50, 3:905–906; Witheridge: ibid., 3:857–58, 3:908–909. (Buckley was charged with afflicting Putnam Jr. and Walcott; Witheridge, with afflicting Hubbard and Vibber. Again, some indictments could be missing.) Parker: ibid., 2:633–34 (see also ibid., 1:75–76); she was indicted for bewitching Sarah Phelps and one Hannah Bigsby (of Andover, wife of Daniel), but the grand jury replied "ignoramus" to the request that she be indicted for harming Martha Sprague (see ibid., 2:629–31). Reed: ibid., 3:715–18 (she was indicted for bewitching Hubbard, but the grand jury declined to indict her for afflicting Elizabeth Booth; see ibid., 3:712). Scott: ibid., 3:727–28; Richard Trask, ed., *"The Devil hath been raised": A Documentary History of the Salem Village Witchcraft Outbreak of March 1692*, rev. ed. (Danvers, Mass., 1997), 161–64. Scott was indicted for bewitching two Rowley women in late July and early August.

25. M. Halsey Thomas, ed., *The Diary of Samuel Sewall, 1674–1729* (New York, 1973), 1:295. "Letter of Thomas Brattle, F.R.S., 1692," in Burr, *Narratives*, 185, gives the expected date of the next meeting of the court as the first Tuesday in November. David C. Brown, "The Case of Giles Corey," *EIHC* 121 (1985): 282–99, offers a detailed examination of this incident, unique in the annals of colonial legal practice. There was an alternative to the *peine forte et dure*. When Jacob Milborne, the Leisler rebel, refused to enter a plea before a Court of Oyer and Terminer in New York in 1691, the court simply entered a plea of guilty and hanged him. See Thomas Newton to William Blathwayt, 8 April 1691, vol. 8, fol. 2, William Blathwayt Papers, CW.

26. *SWP* 2:246. The man Corey killed was the stepson of Margaret Goodale, one of the people afflicted in the Village in March. See Sewall's comment on Putnam's letter, in Thomas, ed., *Sewall Diary* 1:295.

27. Calef, *MWIW*, in *WDNE* 3:45. Calef misdated Corey's death, placing it on Friday the 16th, but Sewall's diary entries for 19 and 20 September make it clear that Corey died on Monday, 19 September, as does Putnam's letter to Sewall, which states that Ann Jr.'s vision occurred on a Sunday night (*SWP* 2:246).

28. *SWP* 2:403–404. See also Thomas, ed., *Sewall Diary* 1:296. That Phips sailed on 16 September is evident from council minutes, CO 5/785, f 97; he informed the councilors he was leaving that day "to give orders for the disposal of the Forces, and Setling of the Garrisons" at Pemaquid.

29. Calef, *MWIW,* in *WDNE* 3:45, 46, 48.

30. Mather to Sewall, 20 September 1692, partly published in Silverman, ed., *Selected Letters,* 44–45, with the first and last quotations in this paragraph from the full version as printed in *NEHGR* 24 (1870): 107–108 (original in NEHGS); Thomas, ed., *Sewall Diary* 1:297.

31. For an excellent summary of these points, see Emerson W. Baker and John G. Reid, *The New England Knight: Sir William Phips, 1651–1695* (Toronto, 1998), 147–51. For Phips's return: Thomas, ed., *Sewall Diary* 1:297. See also John Whiting, *Truth and Innocency Defended . . .* (London, 1702), 140; Calef, *MWIW,* in *WDNE* 3:159; and *A Letter from New-England* (London, 1694), 6, in CO 5/858, f 125. In a letter printed in *Some Few Remarks upon a Scandalous Book . . .* (Boston, 1701), 47, Cotton Mather denounced as "a putrid slander" Calef's charge that Phips halted the trials because his wife had been accused but, significantly, he did *not* deny that Lady Mary had been named in the first place. Whiting claimed that Cotton Mather's mother was accused as well. The legal records are so incomplete that it is impossible to determine which defendant might have been freed by Lady Phips.

32. Brattle comment: "Brattle Letter," in Burr, *Narratives,* 185; Easty petition: *SWP* 1:303–304. Even if some of the testimony offered in these late trials has not survived, the evidentiary base for the convictions appears to have been much less than that compiled in the earlier prosecutions.

33. Jacob Melijn to Johannes Kerfbijl, 28 October 1692, Jacob Melijn Letter-book, AAS (in Dutch, trans. by Evan Haefeli). The *S.* and *B.* of Willard's title were "Salem" and "Boston"; Willard, of course, was *B.* He probably published it anonymously because Governor Phips issued an order before 12 October forbidding the printing of essays on either side, to avoid "needless disputes"; see Phips to William Blathwayt, 12 October 1692, in Burr, *Narratives,* 197. On the timing of the publications in the fall of 1692, see Mary Rhinelander McCarl, "Spreading the News of Satan's Malignity in Salem: Benjamin Harris, Printer and Publisher of the Witchcraft Narratives," *EIHC* 129 (1993): 54–58, an account which must be partially modified because of the date of Melijn's letter (McCarl argues that *Cases of Conscience* was published in early November and Willard's *Some Miscellany Observations* after that). Mather did deliver a sermon on 31 July addressing the question "what makes the diference between the devills in hell & the Angells of heaven"; see Mark Peterson, " 'Ordinary' Preaching and the Interpretation of the Salem Witchcraft Crisis by the Boston Clergy," *EIHC* 129 (1993): 93–94.

34. Samuel Sewall read the manuscript of Willard's preface to Mather's work on 11 October (Thomas, ed., *Sewall Diary* 1:298). McCarl notes that Increase Mather finished his book (except for the postscript) by 3 October, and that

Willard's dialogue circulated in manuscript before its publication; see "Spreading the News," *EIHC* 129 (1993): 54, 56.

35. All quotations in this paragraph except the last are from Mather, *Cases of Conscience concerning Evil Spirits Personating Men . . .* (Boston, 1693), 49, 59, 65. See also ibid., A2 (premises, from Willard's preface, which was also signed by thirteen other clerics); 38–41 (possible possession or obsession). For similar positions, see Willard, *Some Miscellany Observations . . .* ("Philadelphia, 1692"), 5–7 (confessions or testimony by two witnesses), 7–8 (possible possession of the afflicted), 10–12 (diabolical representations of the innocent). The last quotation is from ibid., 15 (see also Mather, *Cases of Conscience*, 62–65). And see David C. Brown, "The Salem Witchcraft Trials: Samuel Willard's *Some Miscellany Observations*," *EIHC* 122 (1986): 207–36.

36. This paragraph and the next are based on Mather, *Cases of Conscience*, 21, and unpaginated afterword (after p. 67). In letters to Johannes Kerfbijl, Jacob Melijn declared on 5 October that the Mathers' "opinions differ greatly from each other," and then a week later said that "the Mathers reconciled their pamphlets in press" (Melijn Letterbook, AAS, trans. by Evan Haefeli). But see n. 50, below, on the problem of dating the second letter.

37. This paragraph and the next are based generally on "Brattle Letter," in Burr, *Narratives*, 167–90 passim (quotations in this paragraph: 169, 178, 181); see 177–78, 180–81, 184 for the comments on named individuals. Brattle did not identify Willard by name, but he is unquestionably the person meant (no other church had three members on the court). Jacob Melijn thought that all the clergymen, including Increase Mather, erred by attributing "too much . . . to the devil and the 'witch' or sorcery"; see Melijn to Johannes Kerfbijl, 5 October 1692, Melijn Letterbook, AAS (trans. by Evan Haefeli).

38. "Brattle Letter," in Burr, *Narratives*, 187, 183. Brattle indicated that Stoughton still thought the woman Knapp accused to be a witch "to this day" (ibid., 183–84). Cotton Mather later claimed that he had volunteered to care for six of the afflicted in order to see if "*Prayer* with *Fasting* would not putt an End unto these heavy Trials," but that his offer had not been accepted (Worthington C. Ford, ed., *Diary of Cotton Mather* [New York, 1957], 1:152).

39. "Brattle Letter," in Burr, *Narratives*, 174, 179, 186–88; Phips to Blathwayt, 12 October 1692, in ibid., 196–97; Mather, *WIW*, in *WDNE* 1:27.

40. Quotation: Mather, *Cases of Conscience*, unpaginated afterword following p. 67. See n. 33, above, for Phips's order. In a letter dated 20 October that accompanied a copy of *Wonders*, Cotton explained why he did not reciprocally endorse his father's book and described the resulting criticism; see Silverman, ed., *Selected Letters*, 45–46; see also Ford, ed., *Mather Diary* 1:152–54. For the conclusion that Cotton sent a copy of the published version of *Wonders of the Invisible World* to London on the *Samuel and Henry*, which sailed from Boston on 14 October, see George H. Moore, "Notes on the Bibliography of Witchcraft in Massachusetts," *AAS Procs*, new ser., 5 (1887–88): 258; and McCarl, "Spreading the News," *EIHC*

129 (1993): 58. Cf. David Levin, "Did the Mathers Disagree about the Salem Witchcraft Trials?" *AAS Procs,* 95, pt. 1 (1985): 19–37, which contends that father and son essentially concurred.

41. Mather, *WIW,* in *WDNE* 1:1–25 passim (quotations, in order: 1, 3, 15–18, 25).

42. Ibid., 29, 34–35, for quotations. The summaries of Perkins, Gaule, and Bernard are on 37–46; the Bury St. Edmunds trial, 140–51; Mora, 212–17 passim (quotations, 212). An excellent brief account of the Mora trials is Bengt Ankarloo, "Sweden: The Mass Burnings (1668–1676)," in Bengt Ankarloo and Gustav Henningsen, eds., *Early Modern European Witchcraft: Centres and Peripheries* (Oxford, U.K., 1990), 285–317.

43. The trial summaries, all from *WIW,* in *WDNE* 1: Burroughs, 152–63; Bishop, 163–74; Martin, 175–87; Howe, 188–94; Carrier, 194–200. The Stoughton-Sewall endorsement: ibid., 211. *WIW* itself closed with a prolix, unremarkable discussion entitled "The Devil Discovered" (ibid., 217–46).

44. Samuel Sewall noted in his diary discussions with people with varying opinions on the subject: on 7 October, the Rev. Samuel Torrey of Weymouth advocated continuing the Court of Oyer and Terminer, after "regulating any thing that may have been amiss," whereas Thomas Danforth told him on 15 October that "there cannot be a procedure in Court except there be some better consent of Ministers and People" (Thomas, ed., *Sewall Diary* 1:297–98).

45. Most of the quotations in this paragraph and the next are from Phips to William Blathwayt, in Burr, *Narratives,* 196–98. The others come from the additional 12 October letters: Phips to Earl of Nottingham, CO 5/751, f 21; Phips to Blathwayt, vol. 5, fol. 1, William Blathwayt Papers, CW (two different letters in same location). The original of the letter printed by Burr is in CO 5/857, with a copy in CO 5/904. See also Isaac Addington to Blathwayt, 4 October 1692, in Sir Thomas Phillipps Collection, LCMD, for more information about Phips's activities in Maine. In his 21 February 1692/3 further report to London about the crisis, Phips continued to lie about his whereabouts in the summer of 1692; see Burr, *Narratives,* 199.

46. Abner C. Goodell Jr., "Letter from Sir William Phips and other Papers relating to Witchcraft, including Questions to Ministers and their Answers," *MHS Procs,* ser. 2, 1 (1884): 353–58 passim (quotations 355–58, translated from Latin).

47. John Miller, *New York Considered and Improved, 1695,* ed. Victor Hugo Paltsis (Cleveland, 1903), 123–25 passim (first quotation 124). I located this source thanks to a note in the George Lincoln Burr Papers, Misc. Witchcraft notes, box 38, Cornell University Archives, Kroch Library. A photocopy of the Latin original (now in the N.Y. Public Library) is in the Cornell witchcraft collection. My thanks to my colleague James J. John for translating much of the document and providing the wording of the second quotation.

48. *SWP* 3:877; Jeremy Belknap, ed., "Recantation of Confessors of Witchcraft," *MHS Colls,* 13 (1815): 223 (see 221–25 passim); for Brattle's presence at the

interviews, *SWP* 1:284. Sarah Churchwell and Hannah and Mary Post, though, did *not* recant when they spoke with Mather. Confessors like Goody Barker evidently apologized directly to those they had accused; see Abigail Faulkner, petition to Sir William Phips, 3 December 1692, in ibid., 1:333–34. Several recanters indicated they were threatened with Samuel Wardwell's fate (ibid., 3:971–72).

49. The ministers' statement is printed in David D. Hall, ed., *Witch-Hunting in Seventeenth-Century New England,* 2d ed. (Boston, 1999), 348. See the records of these cases, ibid., 315–54, passim. During the course of the summer four women from Fairfield had also been accused of witchcraft by Branch or others, but the grand jury indicted only one of the four, and she was quickly acquitted. The additional defendants were Mary and Hannah Harvey, Mary Staples, and Goody Miller (who was tried and acquitted). Little is known about these women, but see John M. Taylor, *The Witchcraft Delusion in Colonial Connecticut, 1647–1697* (New York, 1908), 140–41, 154, and 117–18 (on Hugh Crosia, a Fairfield man accused later in the fall, but also not indicted); and Hall, ed., *Witch-Hunting,* 345–47.

50. Council minutes, 14 and 22 October, CO 5/785, ff 97, 98; 25–26 October are on ff 98, 99. Four decades earlier, Pike had been removed from office and disfranchised by the colony for his adamant opposition to certain policies of the government (see *EC Ct Recs* 1:366–68). The only judge missing on 14 October was Wait Winthrop, who was out of town; on 22 October, the absentees were Winthrop and Sewall. Two Dutch sources claimed that the letters from New York were decisive; see Jacob Melijn to Johannes Kerfbijl, 12 October 1692, Melijn Letterbook; and Hugh Hastings, ed., *Ecclesiastical Records, State of New York* (Albany, 1901), 2:1046. Despite considerable brainstorming, Evan Haefeli and I have been unable to resolve definitively the chronological question raised by Melijn's letter being nominally dated *before* the Dutch clergy's letter could have been received in Boston. The most likely explanation, I believe, is that Melijn added the date to his letterbook some weeks after he actually wrote the rough draft of the missive recorded there, and that "12 October" was a retrospective, inaccurate guess on his part. Other letters in the book appear to carry correct dates.

51. Thomas, ed., *Sewall Diary* 1:299. The closeness of the assembly vote confirmed that the trials still had many supporters. For the bill proposing the fast day and the information that the council did not agree to it: George H. Moore, ed., "Notes on the History of Witchcraft in Massachusetts; with Illustrative Documents," *AAS Procs,* new ser., 2 (1882–83): 172–73. But the council did eventually call a fast for Thursday, 29 December 1692, in response to "War, Sickness, Earthquakes, and other Desolating Calamities," especially because God had permitted "Witchcrafts and Evil Angels to Rage amongst this his People." See council minutes, 20 December 1692, CO 5/785, f 105; and CO 5/857, f 97 (a broadside announcing the fast).

52. Mary Herrick, Declaration before Mr. Hale and Mr. Gerrish, 14 November 1692, in J. Wingate Thornton, comp., "Witchcraft Papers—1692," *NEHGR* 27 (1873): 55. Some historians contend that this accusation of his wife changed

John Hale from a supporter to a critic of the trials: see the epilogue for further details.

53. On the debates and the election of judges, see council minutes, CO 5/785, ff 175–81, 102–103; and Thomas, ed., *Sewall Diary* 1:301–302.

54. See Moore, ed., "Notes on History of Witchcraft," *AAS Procs*, new ser. 2 (1882–83): 168–70; Rosenthal, *Salem Story*, 195–201, 219–20; and David C. Brown, "The Forfeitures at Salem, 1692," *WMQ*, 3d ser., 50 (1993): 85–111. Phips later claimed that Stoughton had ordered such confiscations "without my knowledge or consent" (Phips to Earl of Nottingham, 21 February 1692/3, in Burr, *Narratives*, 201). The text of the law is published in *SWP* 3:885–86.

55. Hall, ed., *Witch-Hunting*, 350–51 (see also 353). The statement is dated 12 May 1693 but defends an action taken earlier, probably shortly after Disborough's conviction in late October. Hall, ibid., 344, 347, omits the names of the jurors, but a comparison of those listed in the manuscript account of the trials, W-39, Wyllys Papers (Brown), shows that Thomas Knowles had been replaced by Joseph Rowland. Box 24, Winthrop Family Papers, MHS, contains numerous letters from Alleyn to Wait Winthrop in this period, although no letter reporting the results of the Connecticut deliberations survives in the collection.

56. For this paragraph and the next, see council minutes, 16 December 1692, CO 5/785, f 185; *SWP* 3:887–901 (calls for jurors); Phips to Earl of Nottingham, 21 February 1692/3, in Burr, *Narratives*, 200 (original in Blathwayt Papers, vol. 5, fol. 1, CW). Because of missing records, it is impossible to determine how many indictments were returned "ignoramus" in January, but grand juries failed to indict Martha Emerson, Hannah Bromage, John Jackson Sr. and Jr., Jane Lilly, Henry Salter, and Rebecca Aslet Johnson Sr., along with the Englishes.

57. Quotations: *SWP* 3:883; Phips to Nottingham, 21 February 1692/3, in Burr, *Narratives*, 201. Case records of those convicted: Johnson: *SWP* 3:923–24 (see also 2:503–505); Post: ibid., 3:925–26; Wardwell: ibid., 3:919–20 (see also ibid., 791–92). The jury that convicted Johnson on the 11th was nearly identical to that which convicted Post on the 12th; and four men who served on the jury that found Wardwell guilty on the 10th also were members of the other two juries. For the January–February proceedings in general, see *SWP* 3:903–37.

58. Phips to Nottingham, 21 February 1692/3, in Burr, *Narratives*, 201; *A Further Account of the Tryals of the New-England Witches* (London, 1693), 10. For Stoughton's return to court on 25 April, see *SWP* 3:937. In late January there were seven convicted but not yet executed witches: Dorcas Hoar, Abigail Hobbs, Abigail Faulkner Sr., Elizabeth Proctor, Mary Lacey Sr., Rebecca Eames, and Mary Bradbury. Bradbury had by then escaped from jail (see *SWP* 3:980–81). One of the two women initially reprieved for pregnancy (Faulkner or Proctor) had probably delivered her baby and was now regarded as executable, while the other had not yet done so. That would leave the five for whom Stoughton issued a death warrant.

59. Alden: *SWP* 1:54–55, 3:938 (for his return by 22 December, see Thomas, ed.,

Sewall Diary 1:302); April-May acquittals: *SWP* 3:939–44; Tituba: ibid., 755. A key error in *SWP* (the substitution of "1692" for "1693" as the date of the grand-jury proceedings in Tituba's case) has misled many scholars, most notably Peter Hoffer, *The Devil's Disciples: Makers of the Salem Witch Trials* (Baltimore, Md., 1996), 154–55, and Rosenthal, *Salem Story*, 28–29. The latter corrected his error in "Tituba's Story," *NEQ* 71 (1998): 198–99. That Tituba was jailed for at least a year is evident from "the prison keepers acount reagarning the withcraft for Diet," c. May 1693, Miscellaneous Manuscripts Bound, MHS, which lists as one item "Tatabe Yndan a whole year." The line has been crossed out, probably representing the payment on Tituba's behalf (this account was presented to the court at Salem for reimbursement).

60. Watkins: *SWP* 3:938; Calef, *MWIW,* in *WDNE* 3:128–29; William Stoughton et al. to Caleb Ray, Boston jailer, 14 July 1693, Fogg Collection 420, vol. 18, MeHS (I owe this reference to Ben Ray); Walter Watkins, "Mary Watkins: A Discolored History of Witchcraft, Cleansed by Modern Research," *NEHGR* 44 (1890): 168–70. For Dustin's death date, see Enders A. Robinson, *The Devil Discovered: Salem Witchcraft 1692* (New York, 1991), 345.

61. *GDMNH,* q.v. "Watkins, Thomas," and "Book of Eastern Claims," *MGHR* 7 (1893): 194, on the Watkins and Stevens families. See also Emerson Woods Baker II, "Trouble to the Eastward: The Failure of Anglo-Indian Relations in Early Maine" (unpub. Ph.D. diss., College of William and Mary, 1986), 120, 164, on Stevens and Watkins.

62. *GDMNH,* q.v. "Rule, John," and "Book of Eastern Claims," *MGHR* 4 (1887): 282, for the family; Mather, "Another Brand Pluckt Out of the Burning," in Calef, *MWIW,* in *WDNE* 2:27, 29, 40 (quotations), and 21–47, passim.

63. See *DHSM* 6:421–22 for Stevens's description of his capture and what the Indians told him.

CONCLUSION   NEW WITCH-LAND

1. "Mr. Willard. May 29. 92. PM," f 127, Samuel Sewall sermon notebook, 1691–1692, Samuel Sewall Papers, MHS. Such beliefs are examined in detail in Richard Godbeer, *The Devil's Dominion: Magic and Religion in Early New England* (New York, 1992); David D. Hall, *Worlds of Wonder, Days of Judgment: Popular Religious Belief in Early New England* (New York, 1989); and Michael P. Winship, *Seers of God: Puritan Providentialism in the Restoration and Early Enlightenment* (Baltimore, Md., 1996).

2. Deodat Lawson, "Christ's Fidelity the only Shield against Satans Malignity," reprinted in Richard B. Trask, ed., *"The Devil hath been raised": A Documentary History of the Salem Village Witchcraft Outbreak of March 1692,* rev. ed. (Danvers, Mass., 1997), 91. Lawson's sermon was formally endorsed by a large group of Massachusetts clergymen, including Samuel Willard and Cotton Mather (ibid., 66). See

Joshua Scottow's list of the colonists' sins, in "A Narrative of the Planting of the Massachusetts Colony . . . ," *MHS Colls* 34(1858): 309. For the related argument that God was specifically punishing the afflicted for their misdeeds, see Thomas Maule, *Truth Held Forth and Maintained . . .* (n.p., 1695), 185–86.

3. Bradstreet (writing for the council) to Massachusetts agents in England, 29 November 1690, *DHSM* 5:167–68; Winthrop to Connecticut governor and council, 15 August 1690, *MHS Colls* 48 (1882): 312. Thomas Maule declared that God was penalizing New Englanders for their past "unrighteous dealings" with the Indians; see *Truth Held Forth,* 194–95.

4. Scottow, "Narrative of Planting," *MHS Colls* 34 (1858): 310–15, passim. The "Satan's Emissaries" reference is from Scottow to Increase Mather, 30 October 1683, MS Am 1502, 5:40, BPL.

5. Bradstreet to Massachusetts agents, 29 November 1690, *DHSM* 5:168.

6. Only a few brief spectral confessions were described as occurring after June 2. See, e.g., *SWP* 3:708. Some short confessions cannot be dated with certainty; see ibid., 1:127, 244. The related accusations leveled by ghosts against their reputed murderers (which continued for a longer time) placed the afflicted in the role of witness-messengers rather than surrogate magistrates.

7. "Letter of Thomas Brattle, F.R.S., 1692," in Burr, *Narratives,* 188.

EPILOGUE

1. For the failed 1693 peace agreement, see MA 30, pt. 2:338, 340, MSA. For the rest of the war, see Thomas Hutchinson, *The History of Massachusetts, from the First Settlement Thereof in 1628, until the Year 1750,* 3d ed. (Boston, 1795), 2:68–104. Ian K. Steele, *Warpaths: Invasions of North America* (New York, 1994), chapter 7, places the Maine war in a broad regional context.

2. See Emerson W. Baker and John G. Reid, *The New England Knight: Sir William Phips, 1651–1695* (Toronto, 1998), chapters 10–12.

3. Larry Gragg, *A Quest for Security: The Life of Samuel Parris, 1653–1720* (New York, 1990), chapters 8, 9.

4. Paul Boyer and Stephen Nissenbaum, *Salem Possessed: The Social Origins of Witchcraft* (Cambridge, Mass., 1974), 142–43.

5. See *SVR* 3:120. Enders A. Robinson incorrectly identifies Elizabeth's husband as Jonathan Pease in *The Devil Discovered: Salem Witchcraft 1692* (New York, 1991), 123. The Elizabeth Booth who married Pease in 1693 was from Connecticut; her parents were Simeon and Rebecca Booth, not George and Alice Booth (later Shaflin), first of Lynn, then Salem Village (information from familysearch.org and Booth family genealogies).

6. *GDMNH,* q.v. "Churchwell, Arthur," and "Andrews, Edward." See also Neal Allen, ed., *Province and Court Records of Maine* (Portland, Me., 1958), 4:374, 376; and *York Deeds* 10:99.

7. *Vital Records of Andover, Massachusetts, to the End of the Year 1849* (Topsfield, Mass., 1912), 2:441.

8. Information from *GDMNH* (q.v. "Senter"); *Vital Records of Wenham, Massachusetts, to the End of the Year 1849* (Salem, Mass., 1904), 16, 204; *Vital Records of Ipswich, Massachusetts, to the End of the Year 1849* (Salem, Mass., 1910), 2:90.

9. *Vital Records of Gloucester, Massachusetts, to the End of the Year 1849* (Salem, Mass., 1923), 1:88–90, 2:283 (q.v. "Hibbert, Elizabeth" and "Benet/Bennet/Bennett, John and Elizabeth").

10. Information from familysearch.org. Her husband was the son of a sister of Mary Foster Lacey.

11. *GDMNH*, q.v. "Lewis, Philip" (two different entries). Jotham and Abraham Lewis's father, Philip, who was in New Hampshire by 1663, was probably a cousin of Mercy's father, also named Philip. Sloppy genealogists sometimes confuse the two men and their families.

12. Marilynne K. Roach, " 'That child, Betty Parris': Elizabeth (Parris) Barron and the People in Her Life," *EIHC* 124 (1988): 1–27.

13. Statement printed in Charles W. Upham, *Salem Witchcraft* (Boston, 1867), 2:510. Her death date: ibid., 511.

14. *The Early Records of the Town of Providence* (Providence, R.I., 1896) 10:13–14. Bernard Rosenthal, *Salem Story: Reading the Witch Trials of 1692* (New York, 1993), discovered the reference in the Providence records; see 226 n. 2. Susannah's strange visions suggest that she was seriously disturbed and accordingly that she was the most likely of all the Village afflicted to be the "distracted" girl to whom Hale referred in his book. William Sheldon had a brother named John, but he seems to have lived in Billerica. However, the John Sheldon of Providence could well have been William's cousin.

15. The marriage record is in *Boston Births, Baptisms, Marriages, and Deaths, 1630–1699* (Boston, 1883), 218; for the excommunication, see Worthington C. Ford, ed., *The Diary of Cotton Mather* (New York, 1957) 1:261. See also *GDMNH*, q.v. "Short, Clement."

16. *Andover Vital Records* 2:327 (q.v. "Tiler").

17. Robinson, *Devil Discovered*, 249. Information also compiled from family search.org.

18. Quotations: M. Halsey Thomas, *The Diary of Samuel Sewall, 1674–1729* (New York, 1973) 1:361n, 367.

19. Calef, *MWIW,* in *WDNE* 3:134–35.

20. Quotations: Hale, *Modest Enquiry,* in Burr, *Narratives,* 425–27. On his change of heart: Calef, *MWIW,* in *WDNE* 3:48. As late as 20 September 1692 Cotton Mather still saw Hale as a supporter of the trials. See Mather to Stephen Sewall on that date, as published in *NEHGR* 20 (1870): 112 (original in NEHGS, MSS. c2007).

21. Burr, *Narratives,* 149–50; George H. Moore, "Notes on the Bibliography of Witchcraft in Massachusetts," *AAS Procs,* new ser., 5 (1887–88): 268–69.

22. See Kenneth Silverman, *The Life and Times of Cotton Mather* (New York, 1984), chapter 12.

23. Hutchinson, *History of Massachusetts*, 2:56.

24. Calef, *MWIW*, in *WDNE* 2: pt. 2, 75. Although Calef did not date the conversation, it occurred after April 1693, when Hill was named to command the post at Saco (see *GDMNH*), but probably before the end of the year, because Joshua Scottow included a reference to the story in his narrative of the history of New England, which is commonly dated in 1693. (However, it could have been written the following year, for it seems to contain a reference to the 1694 attack on Oyster River.) See Joshua Scottow, "A Narrative of the Planting of the Massachusetts Colony," *MHS Colls* 34 (1858): 317 (Burroughs), 310 (possible Oyster River reference). Hill knew Burroughs, who carried a letter to him dated 18 February 1690/1. See notation on the letter, John Hill Papers, NEHGS.

Acknowledgments

When I began researching the Salem witchcraft crisis, little did I realize that I would be joining the ranks of a large, dedicated group of researchers, some of them descendants of participants in the trials. Their published scholarship informs nearly every page of this book. The current exemplars of the tradition have welcomed me into the fold, offered me assistance and advice, and served as my guides to the many arcana of Salem research. My warmest thanks go to Bernard Rosenthal, author of *Salem Story* (1993) and editor in chief of the forthcoming new edition of the witchraft trial records, who—though knowing from the outset that we were likely to disagree on many topics—has shared freely his infinite store of knowledge of Salem witchcraft and who read a complete draft of this book, blue pen firmly in hand, helping me to avoid factual and other pitfalls.

I also thank Benjamin Ray, professor of religion at the University of Virginia, whose NEH-funded website, Witchcraft at Salem Village (http://etext.virginia.edu/salem/witchcraft), is a boon to all students and scholars because of the ready access it offers to maps, excerpted publications, and transcriptions and images of the original legal documents. Through Ben I met Dr. Anthony S. (Tony) Patton, current resident of the Rea house in Danvers, who on a memorable July morning guided me to the sites of the meetinghouse, Ingersoll's tavern, and the parsonage, and offered valuable insights into the way the witchcraft crisis still affects the town where it all began more than three centuries ago. Richard Trask, the Danvers town historian, answered a number of questions and supplied me with a copy of a crucial document.

I am especially grateful to my guides to the world of late seventeenth-century Maine and Wabanakia—Emerson W. (Tad) Baker, Alice Nash, and Jenny Pulsipher—and to Evan Haefeli, who generously shared with me his unpublished translations from the Dutch of the important 1692 letters of

Jacob Melijn. For additional assistance and suggestions, I thank Chris Bilodeau, Elizabeth Bouvier, John Brooke, James Cooper, Stephen Foster, Pembroke Herbert, James J. John, Richard Johnson, Susanah Shaw, Maurice (Pete) White, and Michael Winship.

Throughout my research the Olin and Kroch Libraries at Cornell University served as my firm home base. Indeed, one of the reasons why I ventured into this topic in the first place was the magnificent Cornell Witchcraft Collection, created primarily under the direction of George Lincoln Burr and housed in the Kroch Rare Book and Manuscript Library. There, thanks to the consistently helpful staff, I read most of the basic texts of the crisis in their original print versions without leaving home. The reference and interlibrary loan librarians at Olin handled a remarkable number of requests with aplomb. And everywhere I went in the older Olin holdings, it seemed, George Lincoln Burr, once a member of my department, had been there before me. Numerous times I opened nineteenth-century volumes to find his tiny penciled marginalia, correcting published errors and giving important cross-references. One of the documents cited herein (the October 1692 opinions—in Latin—on witchcraft of the Reverend John Miller, chaplain to the English troops in New York) I located thanks to a note in Burr's personal papers in the Cornell archives. Typically, the meticulous Burr not only learned of the existence of the document, but also acquired a photostat of it for the witchcraft collection. It has never been published in its entirety in the original or in translation, and to this day it has been unknown to other Salem researchers.

I also wish to acknowledge the importance of the work accomplished by two more now-dead Salem researchers: Esther Forbes and her assistant, Kit, in the early 1950s. From Carol Karlsen personally and from her book *The Devil in the Shape of a Woman* (1987), I learned that at the time of her death Ms. Forbes had been working on a novel on the witchcraft crisis that took the same approach I do in this book—that is, stressing the significance of the links between the Maine frontier and Salem witchcraft. One of my first research trips accordingly took me to consult the Forbes Papers at the American Antiquarian Society in Worcester. Although the rough historical notes there (often reports from Kit to Ms. Forbes) contain some errors, they also pointed me in many right directions and saved me hours of tedious labor.

Even though many of the materials pertinent to the crisis are available in print, my desire to seek out contemporaries' comments on the trials and the Indian wars in the years from 1675 to 1695 led me to a number of manuscript repositories. My warm thanks go to the staffs of the American Antiquarian Society, the Massachusetts Historical Society (especially Nick Graham), the

Maine Historical Society, the Library of Congress Manuscript Division, the Boston Public Library, the New England Historic Genealogical Society, the Peabody Essex Museum, the Gilder Lehrman Collection at the Pierpont Morgan Library, the New-York Historical Society, the British Library, and the Public Record Office in London. This book could not have been written without them.

It could also not have been written without the financial support offered by Cornell University (in the form of three different funds: the Dean's Humanities Research Fund, the Col. Return Jonathan Meigs III Fund, and the Mary Donlon Alger endowment) and by the two institutions at which I spent a sabbatical year writing the book. In fall 2000, the Starr Foundation Visiting Fellowship at Lady Margaret Hall, Oxford, provided me with a quiet office, friendly colleagues, and an atmosphere redolent with learning. My special thanks go to Clive Holmes, Frances Lannon, and the principal of LMH, Sir Brian Fall, and his wife, Delmar, for making my term of residence so enjoyable and productive. Then in spring 2001 I held a Mellon Post-Doctoral Fellowship at the Henry E. Huntington Library in San Marino, California. Superficially, one could not imagine an environment that contrasted more sharply with that of Oxford, but it proved to be just as conducive to writing and contemplation. The Huntington Library collections and the other long-term resident fellows (especially Cynthia Herrup, Margaret Hunt, Jennifer Price, and Maria Lepowsky) created a space where I could both work and have fun socializing—not to mention taking long walks to watch the magnificent gardens passing through two seasons. Thanks to my old friend Roy Ritchie, research director of the Huntington, his assistant Carolyn Powell, and the staff of reader services (especially Susi Krasnoo) for their assistance during my all-too-brief stay in their bailiwick.

Several times before I embarked on this project I offered an undergraduate research seminar at Cornell on the subject of witchcraft in early modern England and America. The findings of the enthusiastic students who enrolled in those courses informed me about Salem and other witchcraft episodes. One of those students, Jesse Souweine, went on to write her undergraduate honors thesis on the role of gossip in the 1692 trials; I learned much from it and have cited it herein. Even more important to my own work was the honors thesis written by Molly A. Warsh, who served as my first research assistant on this book and whose independent work on the ties between Salem and the Maine frontier pointed up several key links I might otherwise have missed. Molly also worked diligently for me in the Massachusetts State Archives, the New England Historic Genealogical Society, and the Massachusetts Historical Society. And throughout my year away my graduate student Krissa Swain served as my efficient Ithaca resident research assistant. She answered many key questions by electronic or regular mail.

I have given presentations on the witchcraft crisis to diverse audiences, whose reactions have helped me sharpen my arguments and clarify key points. My thanks go to those who listened and commented at the annual meetings of the American Historical Association and the Omohundro Institute of Early American History and Culture, the Cornell University Women's Studies colloquium, the University of Pennsylvania and the McNeil Center colloquium, the College of William and Mary, Oxford University (especially Robin Briggs), Cambridge University, the Women's Studies Seminar at the Institute of Historical Research of the University of London, Stanford University, the Bay Area and Los Angeles Early Americanist groups, the Huntington Library, and the Universities of California at Riverside and Santa Barbara.

Several friends read the entire draft manuscript, and their comments improved it considerably. Bernie Rosenthal's invaluable aid I have already acknowledged; the same thanks are due to Gloria Main, Rachel Weil, and Virginia Yans, who brought to their task their different but equally helpful perspectives. Clive Holmes, Jenny Pulsipher, and Tad Baker read parts of the manuscript, offering valuable advice. My editor, Jane Garrett, offered much wise counsel as I struggled to tell the familiar story of the 1692 witchcraft crisis in a new way.

Finally, two personal notes.

This book is dedicated to my female and Americanist colleagues in the Cornell History Department, and especially to I. V. (Itsie) Hull, who fits in the first category but not the second. When I joined the department in 1971, I was its first female member. My senior male colleagues in American history were somewhat bemused, but largely supportive, as I increasingly abandoned traditional approaches to Early American history and moved into the then-new and untested field of women's (and later gender) history. I choose this opportunity to acknowledge publicly the important role they have played in my development as a scholar. For five years, I remained the only woman in the department; later, for another decade, Itsie and I were the only two women. Now the department is one-third female, but the ties Itsie and I forged during those ten years and thereafter, working together in teaching, on departmental matters, and in college and university politics, have brought us close together. She has been a wonderful colleague, a close personal friend, and a staunch ally in all things.

Before starting this project I learned that I, like so many other Salem researchers, am a descendant of people involved in the witchcraft crisis, although that was not why I chose to work on it. Mistress Mary Bradbury, convicted as a witch but not hanged for reasons I have explained herein, was my ninth-great-grandmother; and Susannah North Martin, convicted and hanged, was my ninth-great-*step*-grandmother.

But my familial ties to this project are deeper than that. On both sides of my father's family, my roots go back to Salisbury, Massachusetts, in the mid seventeenth century. My ancestors must have heard George Burroughs preach from John Wheelwright's pulpit in the late 1670s, after he had fled Falmouth for the first time. Indeed, both Wheelwright and his chief antagonist, Robert Pike, are my ninth-great-grandfathers. (And because I am descended from Pike, I am also related collaterally by marriage to the Carr and Putnam families, since one of his daughters, my eighth-great-aunt, married a brother of Ann Carr Putnam.) Pendleton Fletcher, who knew Burroughs in Wells in the early 1690s, was my eighth-great-grandfather; *his* grandfather, Brian Pendleton, the Saco magistrate during the First Indian War, was well acquainted with John Bonython, the grandfather of Sarah Churchwell. One of my ancestors was carried into captivity by the Wabanakis after the York raid of January 1691/2; others took shelter at Black Point in 1676 and would have known William Sheldon and his little daughter Susannah. How many times have I wished that—through witchcraft or magic—I could summon up the ghosts of my own ancestors to ask their assistance in my research. But since I cannot do that, I have tried my best to tell their story as accurately as possible, even, perhaps, the way one of them might have told it.

Index

FOUNDING MOTHERS & FATHERS

Gendered Power and the Forming of American Society

In this pioneering study of the ways in which the first settlers defined the power, prerogatives, and responsibilities of the sexes, one of our most incisive historians opens a window onto the world of Colonial America. Drawing on a wealth of contemporary documents, Norton tells the story of the Pinion clan, whose two-generation record of theft, adultery, and infanticide may have made them our first dysfunctional family. She re-opens the case of Mistress Ann Hibbens, whose church ex-communicated her for arguing that God had told husbands to listen to their wives. And here is the enigma of Thomas, or Thomasine Hall, who lived comfortably as both a man and a woman in seventeenth-century Virginia. Wonderfully erudite and vastly readable, *Founding Mothers & Fathers* reveals both the philosophical assumptions and intimate domestic arrange-ments of our colonial ancestors in all their rigor, strangeness, and unruly passion.

"An important, imaginative book. Norton destroys our nostal-gic image of a 'golden age' of family life and re-creates a more complex past whose assumptions and anxieties are still with us." —Raleigh News and Observer

History/Women's Studies/0-679-74977-2